THE TAROT

A CONTEMPORARY COURSE OF THE
QUINTESSENCE OF HERMETIC OCCULTISM

MOUNI SADHU

*Peu de science éloigne de Dieu
Beaucoup de science y ramène*

*A little knowledge keeps one from God;
great knowledge brings one back to him.*

Published by
Melvin Powers
WILSHIRE BOOK COMPANY
12015 Sherman Road
No. Hollywood, California 91605
Telephone: (213) 875-1711 / (818) 983-1105

FIRST PUBLISHED IN 1962
SECOND IMPRESSION 1968

BY THE SAME AUTHOR

Concentration: An Outline for Practical Study, 1964
In Days of Great Peace: The Highest Yoga as lived, 1957
Samadhi: The Superconsciousness of the Future, 1962
Theurgy, 1965
Ways to Self Realism, 1964

*This book is dedicated to
all Masters of Hermetic Philosophy
of the past, present and future*

PRINTED IN THE UNITED STATES OF AMERICA

ISBN 0-87980-157-3

THE TAROT

This scholarly work creates a new epoch in traditional occult philosophy. It is the first contemporary encyclopaedic exposition of the great western tradition since the basic books by Eliphas Levi and Papus, and it also has a full practical meaning. The Philosophical Tarot has always been recognized as a universal key to all wisdom attainable to human beings on this planet.

This is by no means just a theoretical treatise accessible only to specialists, for any average intellectual can cope with most of the initiatory contents of Mouni Sadhu's *Tarot*, perceiving completely new horizons of thought, activity, psychology, cosmogony and practical occultism in this traditional Hermetic form of philosophy.

An enormous number of questions which occur to the earnest seeker are answered in a new and fascinating way and the solution of the philosophical equations evolving from the Arcana opens new vistas in every field of life, not to be found so far in any published books.

One of the many privileges offered to the attentive reader is the opportunity to understand the true meaning of one's own life and destiny, as well as that of the epoch in which we live.

The book is comfortably sub-divided into a hundred separate lessons, which allow for easier and systematic study.

CONTENTS

INTRODUCTION

n traditional Western occultism, the Tarot is recognized as the keystone
f the whole philosophical system called Hermetism. It is very hard to
iscover its actual origin. The most competent and famous occult authors
ke Eliphas Lévi, P. Christian, Fabre d'Olivet, Theophrastus Bombastus
on Hohenheim (Paracelsus), Oswald Wirth, Papus (Dr Gérard Encausse)
nd others, are of the opinion that the Tarot's true symbolism comes
rom Ancient Egypt. That master of Hermetism, Eliphas Lévi, tells us this
oldly in his *Transcendental Magic, Its Doctrine and Ritual*:

'This Clavicle [as he calls the Tarot's Arcana] regarded as lost for
enturies, has been recovered by us, and we have been able to open the
epulchres of the ancient world, to make the dead speak, to behold the
10numents of the past in all their splendour, to understand the enigmas
f every sphinx and to penetrate all sanctuaries. . . . Now, this was the key
a question; a hieroglyphic and numeral alphabet, expressing by characters
nd numbers, a series of universal and absolute ideas. . . .

'The symbolical tetrad, represented in the Mysteries of Memphis and
'hebes by the four aspects of the sphinx—a man, eagle, lion and bull—
orresponded with the four elements of the old world, [i.e. water, air, fire
nd earth]. . . . Now these four symbols, with all their analogies, explain
he one word hidden in all sanctuaries. . . . Moreover, the sacred word was
10t pronounced: it was spelt, and expressed in four words, which are the
our sacred letters: *Yod** (י), *Hé* (ה), *Vau* (ו), *Hé* (ה). . . .

The Tarot is a truly philosophical machine, which keeps the mind from
vandering, while leaving its initiative and liberty; it is mathematics applied
o the Absolute, the alliance of the positive and the ideal, a lottery of
houghts as exact as numbers, perhaps the simplest and grandest concep-
ion of human genius. . . .

An imprisoned person, with no other book than the Tarot, if he knew
10w to use it, could in a few years acquire universal knowledge and would
e able to speak on all subjects with unequalled learning and inexhaustible
loquence. . . .'

This passage which is well known among occultists worthy of the word,
s perhaps one of the best definitions of the Tarot's value and greatness that
ve have. The enthusiastic 'discoverer' of these keys to the ancient wisdom,
ious magician and former priest, Eliphas Lévi (in private life Abbé
onstant) supplied us with this concise and inspired explanation.

In the second half of the nineteenth century, Eliphas Lévi was followed
y a long succession of occultists who accepted the Tarot as a basis for
heir investigations and writings. But none had so fiery a pen and such a
urning conviction as he.

Papus, in his *The Tarot of the Bohemians*, a classical book about the
nystery of the Major and Minor Arcana, tells us in a legend, that the whole

* The name of the Hebrew letter 'Yod'—corresponding to our 'i'—is spelt here with
'y' because of its pronunciation.—AUTHOR.

initiatory wisdom of Ancient Egypt was recorded in the symbols of the Tarot cards as a last attempt to preserve this wisdom for future generations, and was made just before Egypt was invaded and destroyed by the advancing hordes of the Persian king.

These cards, originally made of metal or strong leather, were later used as a means for gambling, just as the Egyptian priests intended them. For *they knew that human vice will never die*, and so their mysterious cards were unknowingly used by the barbarians as a means of transmission—throughout subsequent ages—of the most sacred and hidden results, attained by the old wisdom of Egypt.

As I have said, many eminent occultists have written about and led intensive investigations into the Tarot's philosophy and symbolism. Several of them are mentioned in the Bibliography included in this book. The list is, of course, incomplete, as there are many others, who to a greater or lesser degree were connected with the Hermetic tradition of occultism. But here there is neither the room nor the purpose to give any other names. For an understanding of the present book, it is essential to realize that I have tried to expound the Tarot *as a useful instrument of cognition*, as Eliphas Lévi described it, and at the same time to provide a practical manual, instead of just an exposition of the author's own views on the matter of Hermetism. For I look on the Tarot as the 'algebra of occultism', which enables a man—who knows its use—to progress independently in a safe way, traced for us in these ancient Arcana.

I am a firm believer, that when creating his work, a writer should—*in the first place*—aim for the *usefulness of that work*. This means that readers and students should be given full opportunity to apply the knowledge which is supposed to be in such a book. The mere expression of a writer's opinions about a subject and his description of it is *not sufficient*. There are many authors and each one is entitled to have his own particular conception. In my opinion, when expounding such a large and profound system of occult philosophy as the Tarot undoubtedly is, the reader should be invited (to a certain extent) to co-operate *with the author* in the practical use of the teachings given in the text of the book. And that is what I have tried to do.

If you attentively read the brilliant definition of Eliphas Lévi at the beginning of this Introduction, you may expect to get some knowledge of how to use the Tarot. Therefore, firstly I have collected the most essential matters for each Arcanum, which have been partially taken from the classical works mentioned in the Bibliography, but mainly from my own experience, derived from the years (1926–1933) when I studied Hermetism exclusively.

At that time, I had a group of earnest students who studied the *Book of Hermes* (a name often used for the Tarot's philosophy) for a long period, and we systematically went through the whole course, from the first to the last (twenty-second) Arcanum. Texts were read, explained, discussed and their practical meaning was demonstrated and used in exercises, and notes were carefully taken.

As a basis for the lectures, I used, apart from the works of other competent exponents, the unique book by Prof. Gregory Ossipowitch Mebes, a leading authority on Hermetism in Russia prior to 1917. Actually, it was not even a proper book, but rather a series of lectures duplicated on very large sheets of thick paper (about 12″ × 15″), with all the diagrams made by the author's own experienced hand.

It was never for sale on the open market as a book and only a few initiated circles of students were lucky enough to get a copy. We bought ours from a Russian refugee who brought the book with him in 1919, when fleeing from his country which had just fallen into Communist hands.

Gradually, as our knowledge grew in the course of seven years spent on intensive study, I began to write my own work, which was intended to be a synthesis and condensation of all that we were able to learn about the Tarot and its practical use. Under this use, I understand the application of ideas expressed in the Major Arcana (these are given under three 'veils', according to the three worlds recognized in the Tarot's sister system—the Kabbalah) as being, a guide to creative thinking; for the development of the ability of concentrated, deliberate thinking; for the direction of thoughts and feelings into channels as indicated in the Arcana, and finally, as an approach to the ultimate mystery of the Tarot-Kabbalah-Magic unity, the Unmanifested Spirit, the Ain-Soph, the Unknowable.

After the whole of the very considerable material was collected and put in order, the first seven Arcana were elaborated and written about 1938. Then came a change in outer conditions, political as well as personal. I began to travel extensively, visiting other continents, including a period spent in India and later, a long stay in Australia, so that there was not much time available for the long work necessary to complete the whole task.

It is only now, that the work—conceived more than thirty years ago—has come to realization in the form of the present book.

At the present time there is no adequate and original work in English dealing with the Tarot, and the last major works in other languages are more than fifty years old. Only one of these, the previously mentioned encyclopaedic course by Prof. G. O. Mebes seems to satisfy—to a certain extent—what I would term a 'practical exposition' of the subject. Anyway, as far as I know, that eminent work is not available and can hardly be consulted. Therefore, when I finished *Occultism and Spiritual Paths* (other books being: *In Days of Great Peace* and *Concentration*), the idea occurred to me to make use—now that I have the time—of material collected many years ago. Before he begins to work with this book, the reader is strongly advised to study *Occultism and Spiritual Paths* because many introductory and technical points relating to the present work, have been extensively explained in it and therefore cannot be repeated here.

Also, some important instructions in the realm of the practical use of occult powers, such as self-defence against any hostile influences, have been expounded in *Concentration*.

The classical Tarot embraces four sub-divisions of occultism which are expressed as Alchemy, Astrology, Kabbalah and Magic. So, for each

Major Arcanum (or Trump) the writer has had to reserve a certain portion of the text for each of these sub-divisions. But, in every case, the main part has been dedicated to, firstly an explanation of the *symbolism* of the picture on each card; secondly to the *place of the particular Arcanum in the scheme of the Tetragrammaton;* thirdly to an explanation of the *Hebrew letter* belonging to the card; fourthly to the corresponding *branch of occult teachings*, Western and Eastern alike (Yogas included), and finally to exercises for the *practical use of the mental equations*, provided by the 'theosophical' operations with the figures, leading to the stabilization of the mental processes in the student's mind; the creating of new currents of thought and subsequently to the deeper understanding of the fate of the macrocosm and microcosm in the world's manifestation as we know it. The exercises are usually placed at the end of the Arcana. It seems that they are especially attractive to most students, simply because it is then possible to see, how the theory which has been expounded, actually works in practice.

I am not a believer in sterile lecturing, which is rather like learning to drive a car merely from a manual without having any practical experience on the road. So, as the Tarot is NOT only a more or less fascinating literary subject, but is also just the '*algebra of occultism*', I have arranged the contents of this book accordingly. Anyway, it is for the reader to see for himself how this has been done.

In treating of the Arcana I have adapted the classical method of analysis. This means that they are considered according to the normal numerical sequence, that is position in the whole pack of 22 cards, which means that Arcanum I is followed by Arcanum II, III, IV, and so on.

A Russian author who wrote a booklet about the Tarot, P. D. Ouspensky, made an attempt to break this tradition and to consider the Arcana in pairs. Here is an extract from his opinions and explanations in the matter (from the Russian edition of *The Tarot, the Ancient Pack of Cards*, 1912):

'It is known, that in the subterranean initiatory temples of ancient Egypt the paintings depicting the ideas of the Tarot were arranged in TWO rows, probably on columns, with a passageway between them. This has been confirmed by the well-known occult writer and authority on Hermetism— P. Christian, in his *History of Magic*.

If this was so then is it possible, that in one row there were Arcana from I to XI, and in the opposite one, Arcana XXI (or O, zero) to XII.'

Ouspensky supposes that such an arrangement was made in order to allow the aspirants for high initiation to read the pictures IN PAIRS, and not separately. If this was the case, then it could have been, for example, that opposite Arcanum I, was that of XXI (O), while II corresponded to XXII, and so on. The student can complete the series for himself.

But this theory—which requires the Arcana to be studied in pairs—does not find any support among the foremost of the authoritative writers on the Tarot. Moreover, the actual interpretation of the Arcana as given by Ouspensky, is more poetical than scientific or logical. A peculiar property of the East-European mind manifests itself in Ouspensky, when in his interpretation he very often allows himself to yield to the 'feeling of fear'. Some of the Arcana are 'terrifying' for him. I cannot agree with such an attitude, and as far as I know neither does any other author.

In his 'analysis' he relies more on a kind of *individual vision*, than on a strictly impartial interpretation. However, he wrote the book (which I read in its original, Russian edition of 1912) when he was still comparatively young and consequently perhaps, more emotional and less experienced than in his later years.

Another point on which I disagree with Ouspensky is his unjust treatment of Dr Gérard Encausse ('Papus'), who contributed incomparably more to the wisdom of the Tarot than Ouspensky. Papus followed the classical tradition of Eliphas Lévi, which is only right. It is true, that the learned French doctor had little emotion when he interpreted the Tarot in his main books on the subject, that is *The Tarot of the Bohemians* and *The Divinatory Tarot*. But the work which he performed in these two books is and will remain as a *classical primer for everyone* who begins to study the Hermetic philosophy of the Arcana. The clear, concise exposition of Papus seems to be much more convincing than the too individual conceptions of Ouspensky.

The Divinatory Tarot is provided with a FULL set of cards, that is 22 Major and 56 Minor Arcana, made under the direction of Papus. They are quite artistic and at the same time, preserve most of the symbols and hieroglyphs. It would be very useful for each student to obtain a good, complete set of the Tarot cards, with exact presentation of symbols and other figures, so that they can be used apart from the book. But it might not be very easy to do so at the present time. I have been informed from France that *The Divinatory Tarot* of Papus has long since been unobtainable there as well as in England, while the Tarot of Oswald Wirth is too old. Therefore I have provided this book with a new, symbolically exact version of the Major Arcana.

This work is so constructed, that in the chapters dealing with the Arcana proper, there will not be any *general explanations*, but only those which refer to the particular Trump under discussion. This is because of the necessity to concentrate solely on one idea, when studying each Arcanum.

Therefore, in this introduction there must be given everything which does not belong directly to any one of the 22 Major Arcana. This brings us firstly to the *great central idea* of the whole construction of the Tarot. It is the Tetragrammaton.

Before commencing the actual study of the Arcana, the student should be in a position to name each letter of the Tetrad and to know its exact meaning in all of its variations and positions in the particular Arcana. So I am quoting here, a definition taken from the chapter 'The Egyptian Tarot' of the previously mentioned book, *Occultism and Spiritual Paths*:

'The Tarot is neutral; neither good nor evil in itself, just like figures which can express any quantity, suitable or unsuitable, true or false.

The whole system is based on the Universal Principle which manifests itself in every sphere of life. We may call it the 'Law' (*Tetragrammaton or Tetrad of Hermetists*). The symbols used are letters of the old Hebrew alphabet, plus figures and numbers. Three veils for three worlds. This is comfortable, for knowing the meaning of such a letter-symbol, and so on, that is, the fixed idea behind it, we can operate just as a mathematician does with algebraic formulas and terms. It is also very valuable for those, who being tired of the usual occult bungling which occurs at the present time, want to found their studies on a firm basis, without sacrificing their reason and logical thinking.

A short example may serve to show how the principles of the Tarot operate. . . .

The Great Law (the Tetrad) is the same for all the three worlds in which we may employ the Tarot.

(1) If there is any manifestation in time and space (this does not necessarily mean only the three-dimensional physical space), then there must be *first, the acting element* or power which initiates (or begins) the process. We symbolize it by the figure one (1), and letter 'Yod' י. This element is POSITIVE, DYNAMIC AND ACTIVE. The picture of the *First* Arcanum (or Trump) of the Tarot represents a Man, standing with one leg crossed (sometimes covered by long robes). He is also called a *Magician*.

The same three qualities as given above are ascribed to and connected with the figure '1' and the letter י (Yod).

(2) Apart from the active primary principle (or as some would prefer 'creation') there is still a second element necessary for manifestation, which element being the receptacle, a screen, something to serve as a basis or fulcrum for the active י (Yod). This element is passive, negative and material. Its number is, of course, (2), the Hebrew letter is 'Hé' ה, and the picture on the card is of a seated woman.

(3) When י acts upon ה, the third principle appears, having the number three (3) and letter 'Vau' ו. It is the result of the action, it is neutral, reflecting in itself the qualities of the first and second Trumps of the Tarot, just like a child depending upon its parents.

(4) The primary 'THREE' as a whole forms a new unit, the 'first family', metaphysically conceived on the most subtle plane of being, next after the Unmanifested, Immaterial Absolute.

This element bears the number four (4), its letter is the SECOND 'Hé' ה. This letter is not passive as in the second Arcanum, but active, being the 'Yod' of the next triangle. It is essential to realize this, for only then can the mighty idea of the Tetragrammaton (י ה ו ה) Yod-Hé-Vau-Hé be properly understood. Incidentally, the reader has probably noticed that the Tetragrammaton or Tetrad is identical with the mysterious, biblical NAME OF GOD.

The fourth Trump creates a new unit (triangle) as was stated above, producing new, more complicated forms of manifestation in the gradually arising more densely material lower worlds.

This Law works on every plane of existence. In the abstract realm we already had a look at it. On the astral plane, for example, it can be expressed

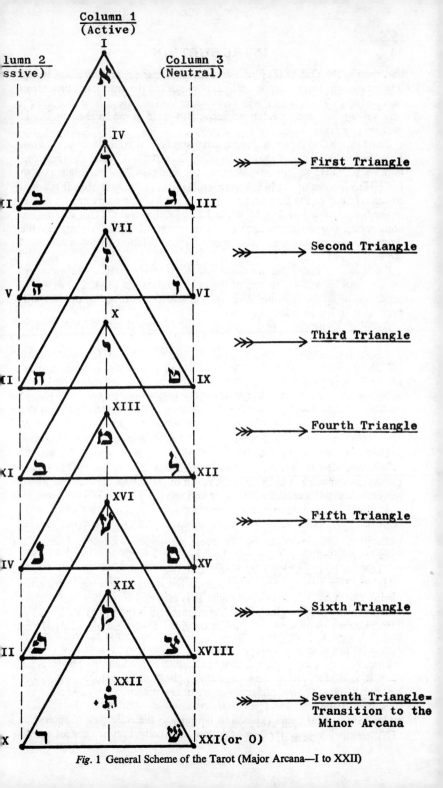

Fig. 1 General Scheme of the Tarot (Major Arcana—I to XXII)

as: Impulse (י) Yod or (1) plus astral surroundings (2) creates emotion (3). The whole will form what we call 'experience' or the emotional process in man. Man (י Yod), wife (ה Hé) and child (ו Vau) are a unit (Second ה) of a new quality and of extended activity (4) able to repeat the primordial process in a wider field.

The first 'FOUR' form the primary symbolical triangle of the Tarot. Its upper point is 1 = י (Yod), the left is 2 = ה (Hé), while the right one is 3 = ו (Vau). The point placed in the middle of this triangle is also the FIRST point of the NEW one, and is 4 = ה (Second Hé). It is equal to the י (Yod) of the first projection of force. To this come new seeds, as in the first case: a new 2 = ה, while 3 = ו, and so on. On this scheme are constructed the seven mystical triangles of the 22 Major Arcana of the Tarot. Each one has a different meaning and relation to the manifested world. (Fig. 1)

On it is also based the whole numerology of Hermetism. Because any number can be reduced to one of the primary four, that is 1, 2, 3 or 4, the process is usually called the 'theosophical addition' or 'reduction' We will practise it in the following chapters.

So much about the Great Tetragrammaton, the NAME OF GOD.

Now it is time to look attentively at the scheme of Fig. 1, for in it we have the whole construction of the Tarot presented in a way easy to memorize. Place the letters of the Great Tetragram in the first triangle, beside the numbers of the Arcana: י (Yod), of course, will belong to Arcanum No. 1; ה (First Passive Hé) to No. II; ו (Vau) corresponds to No. III, and the point inside the triangle to the ה (Second active Hé). At the same time we can clearly see how this active Hé becomes the י (Yod) of the next triangle.

Therefore, Arcana I, IV, VII, X, XIII, XVI, XIX and XXII are all י (Yod). Arcana II, V, VIII, XI, XIV, XVII and XX are all ה (First Hé). Finally, Arcana III, VI, IX, XII, XV, XVIII and XXI (also called Zero) represent the ו (Vau) or the neutral element.

So now, when studying each of the Arcana separately, we can always remember WHICH IDEA is its basis, for each Major Arcanum has its own letter—one of the 22 of the Hebrew alphabet—as well as its own number, which we already know. But each triangle, which follows on from the FIRST, also has the four letters of the Great Tetragram, and represents the same unique idea, but on a different plane. This will be shown in the following chapters, when we analyse the Arcana one after another. And then you will see, that the numbers from 1 to 22 also have a mystical meaning: 1, 4, 7, 10, 13, 16, 19 and 22 are *active*, while 2, 5, 8, 11, 14, 17 and 20 are *passive*. Finally, 3, 6, 9, 12, 15, 18 and 21 are *neutral*. So it is with all the columns shown in Fig. 1. Column No. 1 is active (male), column No. 2 is passive (female) and column No. 3 is neutral. The FIRST triangle is that of the Divine Life, the highest, as it is according to the Kabbalah. The following triangles each time represent a lower world, until we come to the last, the seventh triangle, which symbolizes the physical realm. A more extended exposition belongs to the following chapters.

Now we will analyse the Minor Arcana. Actually, they are almost equiv-

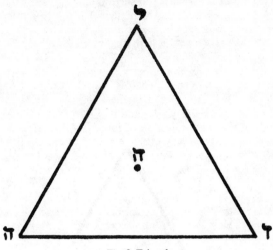

Fig. 2 Triangle

alent to the usual set of playing cards, with the difference that there is an additional 'figure' in each suit. It is the 'Knight'. The traditional explanation of the Minor Arcana—unchanged by most competent authors—is as follows:

We already know, that, within it, the Tarot includes four elements of occult wisdom: Alchemy, Astrology, the Kabbalah and Magic. I deliberately say 'includes' and not 'is composed of', as erroneously stated by some people: for the Tarot is much more than just these sub-divisions of occultism. This we can recognize if we remember the definition of the Tarot which describes it as a 'philosophical machine'.

Further, the Tetragrammaton reveals itself in the Tarot (1) as the Name of the Almighty composed of four letters; (2) as four kingdoms of spirits; (3) as four elements of Alchemy, and (4) as four classes of men.

Now, the first suit of the Minor Arcana correspond to (1), that is wands; the second suit corresponds to (2), that is swords; the third suit to (3), that is cups, and the fourth suit to (4), that is pentacles.

These suits are the four sides of a SQUARE which is a part of the Tarot's symbolism and is shown in Fig. 3 of the text. Each side of this mystical square, which has a point in the middle, represents an element. Thus, wands symbolize FIRE (elves); cups represent WATER (sprites); swords are AIR (sylphs); while pentacles symbolize the densest element or EARTH (gnomes which live in it).

The *figures* have the following meaning:

In each suit of the Minor Arcana the King represents the first letter of the Tetragrammaton (Yod) and FIRE ׳, the Queen the second letter (Hé) or WATER ה, the Knight the third letter ו (Vau) or AIR, and the Knave is the fourth (Second Hé) or EARTH, ה.

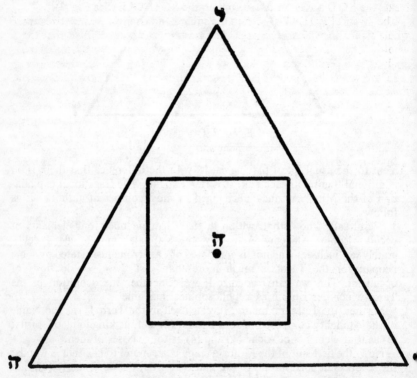

Fig. 3 A Square in a Triangle (Symbol of the Tarot)

Consequently, one is fire, two—water, three—air, and four—earth. This is the FIRST square.

As we know, the *first cycle*, through its last element (or Second Hé) is the seed of the next, the *second square* (or cycle) in which five is the second element ה (First Hé), six the third ו (Vau), seven the fourth ה (Second Hé). Similarly, seven is the first principle of the *third* or the last square, eight the second principle of the same; nine the third; ten the fourth. In the same way the last side of the triangle is completed. This triangle may be presented in two ways, as is shown in the general symbol of the Tarot. It can be placed inside the SQUARE, or it can contain the SQUARE (See Fig. 3).

The mystical POINT as seen in the square and triangle, summarizes the whole figure to which it belongs. The traditional expression is, 'that the whole of the square or triangle are equal to the point'. In the course of the analysis in the following chapters, we will again return to this axiom.

In the suits, the colour BLACK symbolizes ACTIVE qualities, as is the case with wands and swords, while RED means PASSIVE qualities, to which belong cups and pentacles. We may say that here BLACK stands for the *rajasic* element (Eastern Tradition) or will-power, energy, initiative, movement, and action, with RED as the *tamasic* element indicating inertia, lack of movement and unconsciousness.

In divinatory practice with the Tarot's cards WANDS and CUPS are considered as 'GOOD' indicating the best of fortune, friendship and blessings; but SWORDS and PENTACLES are just the opposite, that is 'EVIL', hostility, and dangerous conditions and relationships. The meaning of the colours is given in slightly different words by different authors, but the GIST *must always be the same*, as in this connection it is an unchangeable quality.

Combinations of all of the 56 cards of the Minor Arcana therefore reflect the main principles of life: good and evil, active and passive, all being dependent upon a man's will or lying beyond it, as his unavoidable Destiny or Karma as Easterners would say.

For a *full understanding of every combination* of the Minor Arcana, an extensive study of their meaning and symbols is essential, plus a certain necessary amount of intuition. This does not come without long years of hard work, providing one is really interested in this sub-division of Hermetism. 'Le Maitre' ETTEILLA (his proper name was Alliette) the famous French fortune-teller and commentator on the Tarot (in its divinatory conception), is said to have developed and possessed such a knowledge and ability of intuitional synthesis, that it was sufficient for him to take only a quick look at the series of cards set out for his client in order to see the past, present and future fate of the person. Papus in his *Divinatory Tarot* widely uses Etteilla's conceptions and explanations of the significance of the Minor Arcana.

Nevertheless, the main philosophical value and usefulness of the Tarot lies in its 22 Major Arcana, or Trumps. Actually, they are the basis of the present book. Their symbols are at the same time so exact and flexible, so inspiring and yet leaving one so much liberty in their interpretation, that many writers have found it profitable to use the Tarot as a basis for their works, often without even mentioning its name.

If the attentive student considers the number of parts, chapters and the whole plan of another of the writer's books—*Concentration*, he will find the same principles employed. (also in 'Samadhi').

Years ago, when lecturing about the Tarot, I found it practical and advisable to divide the subject matter of each Arcanum into separate lessons, which were then much more readily assimilated during the time given for a lecture, than if the whole Arcanum were dealt with at once. The student will find the same method used here, as it proved to be so successful in the past. Hence, several lessons will belong to each of the Major Arcana. But in this work everything has been greatly augmented and revised, with enlarged chapters incorporating new material based on latest experience.

I have tried to limit the number of drawings to the bare minimum, giving only the really important schemes and pentacles. Two reasons for this are:

(1) If the student works properly and realizes the meaning of the symbols given, he will easily extend them, if he finds this useful for his mental processes. So, for example, the special unfolding of Solomon's Star and of the Pentagram as sometimes encountered in old works about the Tarot, may be found independently, and therefore may yield certain profit for an occultist.

(2) These unfoldings do not belong to the basic truths of the Tarot, as do the pentacles of its arcana, and they do not provide much initiatory material, *if given in a ready form*. If you are successfully initiated into all three meanings of Fabre d'Olivet's mystical triangles, your broadened and enlightened mind will not need many graphical schemes in order to approach closer to the very CORE of the Initiation of the Western Tradition. Here, of course, I mean the super-mental abilities of 'cognition without thinking', which is the genuine INTUITION.

Now, I would like to stress, that the Tarot in itself does not expound any definite SPIRITUAL DOCTRINE, but rather has the purpose of expanding the abilities of the student, that is to teach him an infallible method for developing and using his mental faculties. From the occult point of view the man of average intelligence is not well prepared for the realization and solving of the deep problems of the microcosm and macrocosm. No doubt some people have brilliant flashes of mental understanding and even intuition, but all such are only of a sporadic character and could hardly be called controlled abilities, or *guided intuition*. That is because there are so many different occult currents and conceptions, which we can easily observe in our own epoch. The mental machine of the Tarot tries to fill this gap and to help every earnest seeker, who cannot as yet follow any DIRECT SPIRITUAL PATH, as taught by the great Teachers of humanity, but who feels an urgent need to examine everything for himself and to reconcile his mind to the supposed highest aims of human attainment.

Many people have an unquenchable thirst and curiosity to know mentally much more than recognized philosophical or psychological studies can offer them. Some want to systematize the degree of occult knowledge which they already possess, while others are keen to unveil certain secrets, which lie hidden behind the 'security walls' surrounding the main occult problems.

For all such, the Tarot offers a unique possibilty to achieve their various aims, and at the same time educate their minds and open quite new vistas before them.

Of course, the Tarot of the second half of the twentieth Century is probably not the same as that taught in the underground initiatory crypts in Egypt three or four thousand years ago, or in the secret chambers of the Great Pyramid, and in the subterranean temple between the paws of the Sphinx. Simply because we are not the ancient Egyptians. Our minds have certainly evolved a little since those far off days, that is, we are, as a mass, much more intelligent than the corresponding ancient people, for whom the knowledge of their primitive and cumbersome art of writing and reading was the rare privilege of comparatively few, while the masses remained uneducated.

Adding a little to our fantasy, supported, anyway, by the few reports which we have about the methods of the ancient initiations, we can imagine a group of young candidates slowly walking among the pillars, in the half dim light of coloured oil lamps, under the leadership of a majestic looking high priest, who in short, half-veiled sentences explains to them the mystical truths of the Arcana and the other symbols around them.

This method was followed by the ancient occultists in order to prevent any insufficiently developed candidates from slipping through the 'safety barriers' erected for the purpose of screening the aspirants. Many teachings were given in quite an enigmatic outer form, and the candidates had to cope successfully with them before they 'passed to a higher class'.

Now it is different. The invention of printing has enormously popularized all knowledge, and the unrestricted publication of millions of books at the present time apparently puts everything within the reach of all. But if we look closely and with an unprejudiced eye, we will agree that the invisible veil still exists, although there are no secret crypts buried deep under the tightly-guarded temples and pyramids. For now it lies *inside ourselves*.

The most elevated of spiritual truths have been expounded by the advanced sons of humanity during the last two thousand years, and in spite of the Gospels on the Love of Christ, hatred and murder are still far from being eliminated. What is the cause? The same veil of inner unripeness and ignorance, which prevents the practice of Truth as revealed in the Gospels, also prevents unsuitable persons from entering the ancient temple of the Tarot, even if almost everything in it is exposed without any artificial barriers.

Anyway, every occultist knows about this unwritten but very efficient law. *Now, on the other side of the coin* we have, for example, a primitive native of Central Africa or New Guinea who certainly does not know anything about the manufacture of firearms or even of the physical laws which determine the functioning of a rifle or revolver. But once a weapon is placed in his hands and it is explained how to insert the cartridge and pull the trigger, he is capable of using the weapon to kill without the need of any other knowledge about it.

In occultism there are secret technicalities which sometimes can work even if placed in ignorant hands (similarly to the foregoing example). In this book some of them may be indicated closely enough for use, but only those which CANNOT be employed under any conditions for wrongful (that is evil) purposes. Others which do not give such a guarantee will be mentioned only up to the point where their application begins, but no further. Paul Sédir, in his unique book *Initiations*, states that his master, Monsieur Andrèas, once told him that: 'All the crimes and evil arising from the wrongful or malicious use of say, mesmerism, weigh heavily on the inventor of that method, Dr Mesmer himself. . . . Such is the Law. So it can be imagined what terrible debts he has to pay for the past, as well as for future misuse of his discovery.'

That is why no occult book of any value—written by an honest author who is conscious of his responsibility—will reveal dangerous practices. Such authors are aware of the fact, that men are much more eager to MISUSE occult or psychical powers, than to USE THEM FOR GOOD AND UNSELFISH PURPOSES.

In two of my other books, *Concentration* and *Occultism and Spiritual Paths*, I have spoken extensively about this, that is about some particular types of magic. Referring the reader to these sources, I would like to mention briefly, that in this twentieth century magic is still not dead and this also includes the so-called 'black magic'. There is one thing against which every black magician will always fight: *it is his unmasking*. He will use everything he can in order to avenge this, and to render harmless to him, the person who reveals his true quality.

Nowadays, the lower types of occultists, who have only egoistic and material aims, invariably try to pass as 'great souls', 'spiritual teachers' or 'perfect masters'.

It has so happened, that the writer has openly expressed his opinion about some of these rogues, referring to them in his published articles and also in correspondence with some of their misguided 'disciples'. In due time the expected reactions came. Strong efforts from the 'black' side have been made in order to harm him and to make any further work impossible. Whoever has read *Occultism and Spiritual Paths* will know more about the means and methods used in such cases. Here I shall mention only the fact, that if a photograph of a man or his signature is available, the necessary 'contact' may well be established with the body of the prospective victim by the magician, providing he knows the techniques and possesses some will-power.

In this particular case the eyes and other organs were attacked; but as soon as the origin of the ailments were discovered, the aggression was countered and frustrated (see the chaper 'Magic' in *Occultism and Spiritual Paths*).

In spite of all this there have been some books published which reveal sufficient data to give the 'keys' to some occult experiments. I had them about 30 years ago, and learned quite a few things from them. Fortunately, they are no longer available. But there remains a large volume by Papus about the practices of Ceremonial Magic, in which enough material is given to enable a persistent and strong-willed person to perform some 'real' experiments, which sometimes seem to be harmless for those around them, but not necessarily so for the performer (see *In Days of Great Peace* the chapter 'My Path to Maharshi'). A special 'magic book' is required, which must be a purely *'personal'* one, compiled and written by the operator himself at certain hours of the day and night according to astrological conditions, and which takes several months to prepare.

The terminology in this book will be limited to the minimum necessary for a clear understanding, so that only a few of the terms which are seldom used in popular occult literature need to be explained. These are as follows:

Astrosome: as used in the Kabbalah means the whole complex which remains when the physical body is taken out of consideration, and refers to the astral and mental bodies combined. In the following lessons I will use the word, mostly in reference to the astral body alone, and when the mind's conductor (that is mental body) is meant, it will be mentioned separately.

Atman: the spiritual SELF in all, also the similar principle in man, often wrongly called 'the soul'. Synonymous to the ATMAN are: Spirit, Supreme Self, God, and in Hermetism—the MONAD.

Binary: in the Tarot is two opposite, polarized assertions or qualities, definitions or conditions, actions or states similar to the two poles of a magnet. Binaries as such are unworkable and belong to the realm of unsolved problems. To neutralize a binary means to balance it through the creation of a third element between the poles. This element must contain something from each pole of the binary, and is a concrete solution of the binary, making it workable and applicable to life.

Cliché: a French word, the philosophical meaning of which is close (*but not identical*) to the English *'image'*, sometimes also to 'surroundings'. Contemplation of a cliché means that consciousness perceives the surrounding conditions. Clichés may belong to the past, present or future. They are impressed on the subtle matter of the astro-mental planes. They can be 'seen' or 'read' by men with developed psychic abilities. All true spiritual Masters are able to see clichés at any time.

The Copper-Serpent: or the redemptive cliché of the middle astral has the formula ‏י ה ש ו ה‎ (Yod-Hé-Shin-Vau-Hé). It is the aim of elementars which belong to the evolutionary types. Its realm is the middle and higher astral sub-planes. It frees those who are able to come to it, from all the dangers between incarnations. Saints and advanced 'white' occultists come to this Serpent almost immediately after having left their bodies. In olden times, Moses raised the symbol of that powerful cliché of redemption in the desert, when the plague decimated his people. Everyone who looked upon it with faith was saved from death. Later, the Messiah, the Christ, was himself similarly raised in his body upon the Cross for the sake of downfallen and suffering humanity.

Egregor: is a collective entity, such as a nation, state, society, religions and sects and their adherents, and even minor human organizations. The structure of Egregors is similar to that of human beings. They have physical bodies (that is, collectively all the bodies of those who belong to the particular Egregor) and also astral and mental ones; the Egregor being the sum total of all these elements.

Egregors have peculiar forms in the super-physical worlds, similar to their symbolized representations like the lion of Britain, the cock of France, the eagle of Germany, and so on. These forms—as was stated by Paul Sédir, who observed them before World War I—can be seen by a clairvoyant person, or by others with the direct assistance from a spiritual Master, as it was in Sédir's case. In his *Initiations* he tells us how, shortly before 1914, he was shown the future of Europe for some years ahead, by the mysterious Monsieur Andrèas. He speaks about the tragedy of his beloved France, which later bled herself white in the First World War. In the subsequent vision, which was also evoked by the same Andrèas, Sédir was also shown the far off past, going back to the time of St Joan d'Arc and even spoke with her and took part in the mystical ceremony which followed in the dungeons and cellars of the old castle, where the saint was imprisoned before her execution at the stake. There is an interesting moment in the story when Sédir—as can clearly be seen from his narration —was also shown the more distant future, probably World War II which was so disastrous for France. But he was forbidden to reveal anything about it, although his deep concern shows through his sad words at the conclusion of the chapter. In all these visions, the Egregor of France had the form of a cock, while the others were represented by different birds and animals as mentioned before.

Elementar: is an adapted term for a dead human being devoid of its physical body. It has to be used here because of the lack of a more suitable word in English. Therefore, 'the state of being an elementar' simply means, that in us which remains after our physical death.

An elementar as a disincarnate being lives on *two* planes instead of *three*, that is only on the astral and mental. Hermetism principally occupies itself with HUMAN elementars. The consciousness of an elementar belonging to an average man is very dim, like his dreams, and does not reach the clarity of his former physical consciousness. But in the case of an Adept or Master, the consciousness on the two planes is much more lucid than on the physical one.

The word elementar is derived from the French 'élémentaire'.

Evolution: this is the antithesis of involution, the ascent of the superior principle from its merging in the inferior, dense realm, that is Spirit evolving (ascending) from matter. Involutionary tendencies, sometimes occurring in evolutionary beings (as for example, humans) are unnatural for them and against the law of evolution which binds men. Therefore, tendencies such as attachments to material things, sensuality, and so on, are an EVIL for those beings. The general purpose of evolution is the removal from the *Consciousness, Self* of all material veils. And this is the measure of progress in man: the less involutionary or material attachments he possesses, the higher is the degree of his evolution and the closer is the day of his *reintegration*.

Exteriorization of the astral element or astrosome: this term is used for the voluntary and temporary abandonment of the physical body by an advanced occultist (no one else can perform such an operation), while retaining full consciousness and awareness of what then happens.

The Great Arcanum of Magic, or Great Operation: realization of the conquered supreme occult knowledge, or Hermetism. In other words, the means leading directly to Reintegration. Other explanations are in the text of this course.

Initiation: development of consciousness surpassing the average human level. Knowledge of laws hidden from laymen which govern the life of the universe. Traditionally in occultism, those who know more initiate (or teach) those who are their disciples. True initiation is the direct influencing of the still immature consciousness of a pupil by the perfectly evolved spiritual consciousness of the Master. There are some secret societies which are supposed to transmit certain knowledge to the members who pass through their rituals.

Involution: the descent of a superior and subtle principle into an inferior and dense one, such as Spirit into matter. In other words, the *Self*, wrapping itself in material shells, or forms, lower instincts and feelings. For certain kinds of entities who are still on the *descending* arc of the manifested life-creation, involutionary tendencies are natural and right qualities for them, for such is their destiny, their 'good'. If evolutionary tendencies (see 'Evolution') could exist in such involutionary beings, they would definitely be improper and therefore 'evil' for these beings.

Macrocosm: the universe as a WHOLE; the consciousness manifested in it is the *Central Consciousness of the Whole*, not integrated into separate functions.

Magic: the influencing of the manifested life around us through the use of will-power and knowledge of the laws governing the worlds (or planes). From this point of view, Hermetism recognizes most human activities as having a '*magic*' character. In a narrower conception, magic is the field of activity of a man who has dedicated himself to this sort of knowledge. Such a man is called a 'magician'. Magic can be evolutionary (good or 'white') as well as involutionary (evil or 'black'). Magic is a part of Hermetic philosophy or the Tarot.

Mantram: magic formula for influencing the surroundings (environment) of the operator. These can be fairly long sentences.

Microcosm: or 'small universe': in Hermetism it refers to Man; the reflection of the Whole in consciousness enclosed in the human body. The laws governing the macrocosm are analogous (not identical) to those governing the life of the microcosm. For a human being, realization of these laws is equivalent to reintegration into the PRIMORDIAL WHOLE.

Nahash or Astral Serpent: this is a symbol of passions and involutionary tendencies which pursue physical and astral lusts and attachments. It is a great enemy of all newcomers into the astral world (that is elementars of recently dead persons), unless they are sufficiently initiated. Nahash tries to pull them into the involutionary current of the planet. It has no power over men who, during their physical lifetime, have learned to master their lower impulses and vasanas, i.e. attachments to the material life of the flesh. Nahash is a cruel master of weaklings, unable to raise their aims beyond the physical and egoistic levels. The realm of the Astral Serpent is the dark cone of the planet, the lower astral, briefly, that which, with justice, is called *purgatory* (temporary hell).

Pentacle: a combination of symbols united to form a drawing. They may or may not possess powers of realization. Details appear in the text of this book.

Phantom: the sixth element in man, which is attached to the seventh, that is to the physical body. Its Kabbalistic name is NEPHESH. Its functions are normally, decomposition of the dead body or formation of the embryo and subsequently the foetus in the mother's womb. Nephesh often interfers with Ruah to the disadvantage of the elementar. It is not free from involutionary attachments (impure ones). Sufferings and fears after death are principally due to Nephesh, which tries to prolong its existence by substituting the weak (in an average man) consciousness of Ruah with its own dim awareness, thereby sapping the evolutionary impulses.

Reintegration: this term was introduced by the first and true *Rosicrucians* (fourteenth century) and gradually made common in Western occultism. It means that the spark of consciousness involved in the different veils of matter (as it is with man), finally returns to the Central Sun of non-incarnate SPIRIT-CONSCIOUSNESS, that is *it becomes reintegrated.* From separateness in different bodies (forms) the SPIRIT again merges into the ABSOLUTE, WHOLE, GOD, NIRVANA, BRAHM, and so on.

Reintegration is the ultimate aim of true occultism, having equivalents in Eastern mysticism like: Self-Realization, Liberated State, Jivanmukti. In Christianity it is called Salvation in Heaven, and in Buddhism Nirvana, a complete extinction of all illusion of separateness in the forms of matter and egotism. The idea of Reintegration comes from the old Egyptian Initiations and prevails throughout the whole construction of the Tarot's system.

Saint: a highly evolved person who has definitely ceased to pursue any egoistical aims (that is involutionary ones) and who has learned practically, the evolutionary activities (unselfish ones). In this way saints are supposed to fulfil God's Will and therefore, some initiatory circles call them 'Friends of God'. In his further progress, the saint becomes a SAGE, that is, one who has nothing more to learn or a PERFECT MAN, a MASTER.

Sętram: is a magic formula for influencing the consciousness and the astrosome of the operator himself. Usually it is a very short word or sentence connected with one's monad like 'I AM'.

Soul: in Hermetism this is the astral counterpart of the individual, also called RUAH, the fifth element in man. It is not to be confused with the *elementar*, which is not a one-plane entity like Ruah, but two-plane.

Ternary: this is essentially a neutralized *binary*. A ternary, contrary to a binary, is constructive and has multi-lateral uses in Hermetism. The number '3' is a sacred one especially in some religions. The symbol of the ternary is a triangle. Depending on action connected with the triangles, they may be involutionary or evolutionary.

Tourbillons or Vortexes: are astral creations of force which are the bases of all astro-mental realizations. Tradition ascribes the funnel like forms to them. Knowledge of the laws ruling over the tourbillons and their construction, is one of the foremost principles of magic. Although it CANNOT be given in open language to the public at large, it has been sufficiently described for initiates in this course, under the veil of Kabbalistic structures. The most guarded secrets of Hermetic magic are: *finding the point of support* for the tourbillon on the physical plane, and the *formula of transition* from the astral to the physical world.

Unitarianism or Unitary Philosophy: this is a Hermetic conception of the *unity* and *origin* of life. Everything manifested is the result of the ONE WILL, ONE SOURCE of all life. From IT we come, wander through different worlds (or planes) and finally return to IT. The primary idea of Unitarianism was first brought by *Moses* from the initiatory sanctuaries of Egypt and given to the ancient Jews to retain—until the coming of the Messiah—as a strict monotheism. It is also the corner-stone of the Tarot.

Mouni Sadhu
Melbourne, December, 1959

The illustrations of the 22 Major Arcana in this book were made by an Australian artist—Mrs Eva G. Lucas of Melbourne.

THE HEBREW ALPHABET AS USED IN THE KABBALAH

No.	Letters		No.	Names of Corresponding Sephiroth		
1	Aleph	א	1	Kether	כתר	Crown
2	Beth	ב	2	Chocmah	חכמה	Wisdom
3	Ghimel	ג	3	Binah	בינה	Mind
4	Daleth	ד	4	Chesed (Gedulah) Grace, Clemency, Will	חסד —גדולה	
5	Hé	ה				
6	Vau	ו	5	Pechad (Geburah) Severity, Intelligence	פחד—גבורה	
7	Zain	ז				
8	Heth	ח	6	Tiphereth	תיפרת	Beauty, Harmony
9	Teth	ט	7	Netzah	נצה	Victory, Justice,
10	Yod	י	8	Hod	חוד	Glory, Peace
11	Caph	כ	9	Yesod	יסוד	Form, Prudence
12	Lamed	ל	10	Malkuth	מלכות	World, Kingdom, Realization
13	Mem	מ				
14	Nun	נ				
15	Samech	ס				
16	Ayin	ע				
17	Phe	פ				
18	Tzaddi	צ				
19	Quoph	ק				
20	Resh	ר				
21	Shin	ש				
22	Than	ת				

The remaining letters have no corresponding Sephiroth

א

א

Aleph –

Letter=
Mother

Divina Essentia
Vir
Natura Naturans

CHAPTER I

ARCANUM I (א ALEPH)

FOR a truly intelligent and evolving man, the foremost principles in life are: (1) his *consciousness of that life*, and (2) the *degree of the power of realization* which is at his disposal in his present incarnation.

The striving after the so-called 'initiation' in the three-plane existence, usually manifests itself in man in one of these two principles, but very often in both of them.

In Hermetism, INITIATION is based on what are known as ARCANA, or mysteries. Here should be explained the difference between the three terms known in Latin as *arcanum, mysterium* and *secretum*.

'*Arcanum*' (in English also often called Trump) is a mystery, necessary for the cognition of a definite kind and number of things, laws or principles; a mystery without which one cannot operate, since the necessity of that cognition has been born in us; a mystery accessible to a mind strong and curious enough to see that knowledge. Used broadly, all scientific sentences which explain any kind of practical activity can be placed under this term.

'*Mysterium*' is the magnificent system of Arcana and their secrets which are used as a synthesis by a definite occult school (Hermetic). It is also a basis for that school's activity and contemplation.

'*Secretum*' (its equivalent in English is simply 'secret') means something which a number of men *agree to hide*, for some practical reason or even a caprice.

In this lesson one of the most important matters for us to study will be the first term *arcanum*. It can either by expressed in words, written in any usual language, or *SYMBOLIZED*.

The ancient initiatory centres chose this third way for the transmission of the highest ideas which were born in their minds, that is they recorded them in SYMBOLS.

We can discriminate between *three types* of symbolism:

(1) The symbolism of *colours*, a feature of the initiation of the *BLACK RACES*.

(2) The symbolism of *geometrical figures* and cards, being the privilege of the *RED-SKINNED RACES*.

(3) The symbolism of *numbers*, which belongs to the *WHITE RACES*.

An immense memorial to Egyptian symbolism has come down to us in which is combined all the three types of the symbolical expression of ideas. It is just that collection (pack) of 78 cards with their coloured pictures, explaining the so-called 22 Major and 56 Minor Arcana. Each card is also linked with a definite numerical symbol. As tradition records, these numbers were placed on the walls of subterranean galleries (passageways), into which an uninitiated neophyte was allowed to enter only after a series of exacting tests.

The collection of cards is also known as the Gypsies' Tarot (or the Tarot of the Bohemians). We will consider it as the basis and scheme for the metaphysical concentration, or mental contemplation as practised by the ancient initiates.

But it may be said, that each nation has its own system of thinking and meditation, the outer expression of which is its language. If the nation has learned to write, then the elements of the language are expressed as an alphabet.

In the same way our Tarot represents a kind of initiatory alphabet. The whole pack consists of a system of the letters or signs of that alphabet, while details of the cards and their colours provide something of a commentary for these signs. We may bind the 22 Major Arcana of the Tarot together with the hieroglyphs of that mysterious alphabet, which today is termed ancient Hebrew.

Each letter of that alphabet also has a numerical meaning, and it is in just this order that we will study them, always remembering the motto of the white races: everything according to NUMBER, MEASURE and WEIGHT.

LESSON 2

Now we can pass on to the analysis of the Arcana themselves. ARCANUM I has the corresponding Hebrew letter ALEPH (א) and its idea is UNITY. The hieroglyph for the first arcanum is a MAN; but look attentively at the symbol for the letter Aleph and we will undoubtedly find there the idea of trinity in the form of two parts, connected by a third (analyse Aleph graphically for yourself).

The card represents a MAN standing with right hand raised and holding a sceptre, a symbol of authority. The left one is directed towards the earth. The whole figure cleverly symbolizes the letter Aleph. Over his head there is the sign of infinity (a figure '8' lying on its side). His forehead is decked by a golden circlet, and his waist by a similar belt. A table in the form of a cube stands before the Man, and on it are lying three objects. These are a CUP, a SWORD and a COIN. In this way—apart from the idea of the Trinity-in-Unity—the card presents four mysterious things for our consideration.

For the moment we will delay analysing them and occupy ourselves with an explanation of the twofold position of the Man's arms.

In all fields of knowledge we find *binaries*, or combinations of two opposite poles or planes. Metaphysics speaks about the ESSENCE and SUBSTANCE of things, placing these two opposite to one another.

Science speaks about *principles or maxims*, as the antithesis of *facts*. To this realm also belong the well known use of the terms SPIRIT and MATTER. Mentally analysing life we will meet with similar binaries

such as, LIFE and DEATH, CONSCIOUSNESS and REALIZA-
TION, GOOD and EVIL. Particular questions in different kinds of
practical science bring us many other binaries like LIGHT and SHADE,
HEAT and COLD, and so on.

In most of these cases there is a possibility of what, in Hermetism, is
termed a neutralizing of the binaries, which simply means the birth of a
third or intermediary element which offers us a passage from one extreme
to the other. In such a way is created the idea of the threefold manifestation, the TWO merging together, with the help of the THIRD to form a
UNIT.

For example, between light and shade we have half-shadow, which is the
same in essence, and so obtain the in between grades of lightness and
darkness. Between heat and cold there are the medium temperatures;
between high and low sounds are intermediary ones; between positive and
negative electricity there is a neutral state, and so on. Similarly, the
opposition of the sexes as between husband and wife is neutralized by the
birth of their child, and so all three elements melt into a new unit which
we call *the family* (see the explanation about the Tetragrammaton in the
'Introduction').

However, not all binaries can be so easily neutralized. In philosophy the
binary 'ESSENCE — SUBSTANCE' may be readily resolved into
the term 'NATURE', but try to neutralize such ones as:

(a) Spirit—matter (*the soul*)

(b) Life—death (*exteriorization into the astral*)

(c) Good—evil (*deed*, or even our own human binary)

(d) Consciousness—power of realization (*harmony*).

I have given you ready solutions as not everyone will be able to find them
independently or easily.

Therefore, one of the properties of INITIATION may be defined as
just *the ability to neutralize* (or to solve) the above-mentioned *basic
binaries*. The ancients related the range of these to the so-called GREAT
MYSTERIES.

The MINOR MYSTERIES approximately embraced the sciences
which today come under general education as taught in our secondary
schools; for in those distant days the level of the common education was,
of course, very low and even reading and arithmetic were considered to be
noteworthy.

Now, the neutralization of the binary 'SPIRIT—MATTER' is the
subject of what is termed the *theoretical* initiation; but the remaining three
Great Binaries will belong to practical initiation of which we will speak
many times in the following lessons.

So we can realize what we are striving for and can thus underline the
general ideas connected with the conception of the threefold steps in the
unitarian scales. Apart from the evident gradation in the ternaries we may
see the hierarchical basis present in their construction. The upper degree
is reflected in the others because of its hierarchical superiority. This means

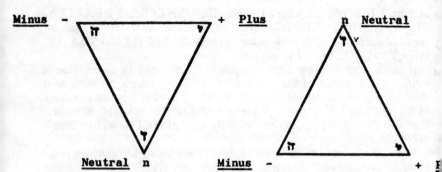

Fig. 4 Unitary Triangles

that the authority vested in a lesser ruler differs from that of a superior one only in the amount, or reach of his power, but not in its character or principle. We can also see that a general manager who exercises authority over many subordinates, must synthesize the power of all of them in himself. We still want to underline the idea of the unbroken passage from one degree to another. We can observe three of them, but in the majority of the examples given, the transition from one degree to the next is uninterrupted, flowing action.

From consideration of the *unitary ternaries* comes the possibility of their *twofold* creation. We begin with the extreme elements to obtain the middle one. Such a proceeding will be called the 'general type of the ordinary ternary', symbolizing it with the number '1'.

In Fig. 4 ' + ' symbolically corresponds to the positive pole, that is to that beginning of the binary which we consider as the active, expansive, (male) pole, while the ' — ' is the passive (female) one which attracts the former. The letter 'n' means the middle (neutral) term. In many cases it is possible to begin with the neutral element and separate it in order to determine both of the poles.

Neutral electricity can be turned into ' + electricity' and into ' — electricity' by friction; no one can forbid us to think of half-shadow in the terms of full-shadow partially lightened by a source of light. A child manifests in itself, on one hand the *passive elements* of attraction which it uses when being fed and nursed; while on the other it also displays some *active elements* by taking objects, and so on. Both poles or properties are united in the child; but we can mentally separate them if we wish. Then we obtain the second kind of ternary as depicted in Fig. 4. It is called the *ternary of the Great Arcanum*.

Now we may say something about the *creation of ideas*. In this lesson we used analogies, that is similarities, and so arrived at symbolical ideas.

But what is a symbol? It is a method like the one just mentioned, that is, that of similarity. Let us again take a ternary: LIGHT—HALF-SHADOW—SHADOW. Under its extreme elements let us write down a few of the non-neutralized binaries like that of:

1. LIGHT	— HALF-SHADOW —	SHADOW (darkness)
2. Higher Region	— Middle Region	— Lower Region
3. Essence	— Nature	— Substance
4. Spirit	— —	— Matter
5. Life	— —	— Death

If I compare all of these lines with the first, then I will find that the elements of all of them are symbolized by those of the first one. Moreover, if I am able *to neutralize* both of the poles in one line, for example (3), it has probably happened only because I was looking at the first line as if on a principal idea. This is an example of the *power of realization of the symbols* in the metaphysical-logical plane or world.

If in the fourth line I am not yet able to neutralize Spirit and matter, then it means that the realization of the symbol has not yet emerged and there is only the opportunity of a limited comparison. If we liken Spirit to light and matter to darkness, then the term I am seeking will correspond to that of half-shadow.

But now we will return to the picture of the First Arcanum.

LESSON 3

In this picture we see an individual, a man. This means that this arcanum of Unity is also an arcanum of individuality. When a number of beings or things are united, then this group has its own individual life.

A single cell lives; a group of cells are united into an organ, and the organ lives its own individual life; organs group themselves into an organism, which again lives an individual life. Similarly, all the organic kingdoms of a planet, as well as the mineral ones, represent another individual, and together are called the planet. *And it lives!* A group of planets form a *system*, and so on into infinity (all is contained in the Unity).

Small wonder then that a cell might well consider itself as absolutely free, and can fight with other cells without any regard for the organ or organism, looking on both of them only in relation to the condition of its own little life. There is no need to be concerned when, in these days, an 'official scientist' acts just like that cell, and therefore cannot be the equal of the Earth and Solar System, as he refuses them any individual existence and merely guesses that they are only lifeless surroundings, in which passes the life of such a gentleman. We may not be very interested to know that the Earth might well look on his little life with contempt in just the same way as he is looking at the life of his steadily renewing cells.

This arcanum reveals to us, that these great Individualities really exist, and that not only a group of atoms got its individualization in the form of a cell, but even an artificial group of men, united into a society, by this fact alone individualize a new unit and begin to live a common life, reluctantly considering the personal interests of each of the members.

This universal idea was best formulated by Christ when He said: 'For where there are two or three gathered together in my name, there am I in the midst of them' (Matt. 18, 20). There is no realized life apart from the Logos, so the words 'in my name' mean exactly: *in the name of Life*.

Returning to the picture of the arcanum, we see that the man in it is in a *standing position*, which stresses his active posture. This will serve us as a hint for the title of the First Arcanum of the Tarot. Esoterists call it 'the Magician' (in Latin Magus), but in vulgar language some call it 'the Juggler': for us it is essentially AN ACTIVE INDIVIDUAL.

If you feel a burning desire to establish the so-called Theosophical Ternary of the basic units (which means that, in the Universe or Cosmos, you recognize just three elements, that is the Archetype, Man and Nature) then you may give the arcanum the triple titles of:

1. The ACTIVE PART OF   DIVINA
   THE ARCHETYPE — ESSENTIA — (GOD'S BEING)
2. The ACTIVE POLE OF
   HUMANITY—MAN — VIR   — (PERSONALITY)
3. NATURE'S   NATURA   (NATURE
   ACTIVITY   — NATURANS— IN ITSELF)

In this course we will first occupy ourselves with the meaning of the MAN of the First Arcanum, and will try to describe the constitution of his individuality in the realm of his activity.

First, in Man there is a great *binary* which attracts our attention. It is SPIRIT—MATTER. Spiritually, Man is living in a world of ideas. On the other hand, he manifests himself in the material, physical world. Our first effort in our task of self-initiation will be just trying to neutralize this binary image.

But *what is it* that could bind together Spirit and matter, to offer a transition from the plane of ideas to that of manifested, material objects? The answer is:

A PLANE IN WHICH ENERGY DEFINES THE FORMS

Here then is our ternary:

SPIRIT— ENERGY — MATTER
IDEAS — FORMS — MATERIAL OBJECTS

This transitional plane is called Astral, and the extreme poles Mental and Physical. The passing from the mental plane to the astral one is accomplished by a process of grouping and of arrangements, to sum up briefly—by a process of progressive condensation and formation of ideas according to the aforementioned great Law of the collective individuality.

Imagine a *general idea* of a polygon. Add to this the idea of evenness of its linear and angular elements and you will obtain a new conception of a regular polygon, much more compact than the first one. *So it is with the transition from the astral to the physical plane.* Fix a tin disc to a spindle. Its edge will not cut a diamond because it is too soft; but let the disc rotate at a very fast rate, which means an increase in its kinetic energy, or accumulation of some astral properties, and under such conditions its edge will cut through a diamond. As you may see, because of the condensation and accumulation of the astral, you were able to effect a change in a purely physical thing, that is the hardness of the disc's edge. This means that the transition has been performed, even if only partially.

Concentrate strongly in a room with the desire to call a man (*subiectum*) from another, ordering him to come to you. Intense concentration leads to the condensation of the idea into an imaginary form. By making the effort with your imaginative power, that is *condensing the astral*, you may reach the *fulfilment* of your aim, which *belongs to the physical plane*. Movement from the astral has been transformed into movement on the physical plane. This is just the *realization of the transition*. Think deeply and in full inner peace about this, and you may understand the secret meaning of these deliberations as just given.

No doubt some people would like to argue, that in the *first example*, the disc already possessed the physical property of hardness, and by condensation of the astral we only augmented that hardness, while in the *second example* the magnetist was working, not only at concentrating and condensing the astral with his imagination, but was also directing his breathing according to the special methods valid for his purpose, and perhaps, in addition allowing himself to use a lightning-like rhythmical movement of his body. Yes! It is possible, but I would like to answer such questioners with an alchemical aphorism: 'IN ORDER TO CREATE GOLD ONE MUST HAVE GOLD.'

This is the law which works with the majority of processes for the *realization of things*. In material life we often take some ready-made realizations as our starting point. Then we act like a person who throws some more crystals into a saturated solution in order to accelerate its crystallization.

The overwhelming majority of magic operations possess such a characteristically wise chosen *starting point*.

So in the whole universe as well as in its every individual part we should try to discriminate—even though only approximately—between the realms of the three planes: *mental, astral* and *physical*, which are mutually interpenetrating and which we can also consider separately.

Accordingly, *in Man*, we will distinguish between three components: *Mental* (Mens), *Astral* (anima or soul also often called '*astrosome*') and finally, physical body (corpus).

When a man is occupied with intellectual work, we can say that his *mind and soul* are more active than his body. When some kind of sentimental life or pure imagination, active or passive prevails in him, we may consider that the *soul* is the acting principle, and so on.

We can accept that human spirit—mind, when manifesting itself, formed the soul, and that this soul, taking for a starting point on the physical plane some materialized elements provided by the parents, creates a physical body for itself, for an interior as well as an exterior life. We can accept that the soul supports the functions of that body according to plans prepared in advance.

That is what I wanted to explain in this lesson. It can be added, that nobody can forbid you to replace our schematic division of the Universe and Man alike—on three planes—with another conception, perhaps more particularly by one in which our three planes may be divided into sub-planes. We will do this ourselves later or in this course.

The First Major Arcanum contains the idea of *Unity and Activity*.

> 'All beings are in unity and are returning to that Unity,
> which is their true aim.'

Unity comprises Unity, that is *Everything is contained in Everything*.

For those who are acquainted with Eastern conceptions, related to the idea of the First Arcanum of the Tarot, I can state, that the Vedantic idea of the Atman is very close to the Man (Adam-Kadmon) symbolized on the card of this arcanum. Do not forget the sign of infinity over the head of the Man. Look at his right (active) hand showing the Ultimate Goal, high above. To this arcanum belongs Raja-Yoga, as you probably sensed when you commenced to study this chapter.

ב

Arcanum II
GNOSIS
THE DOOR OF THE SANCTUARY

Luna

Divina Substantia
Femina
Natura Naturata

CHAPTER II

ARCANUM II (ב BETH)

The letter ב (Beth) in the Hebrew alphabet is used as the symbol for the Second Arcanum, and the numerical sign is 2. While the First Arcanum has a Man for its hieroglyph, the Second has a human throat. The scientific name of the second card of the Tarot is GNOSIS (Knowledge). Occultists also use another term: 'The Door of the Sanctuary', and the vulgar name for it is 'the Priestess'.

In the background of the picture on the card, there are two columns. The right one is RED, and crowned with the sign of the sun. It is called 'Jakin'. The left is BLUE (sometimes also BLACK). It is crowned with the moon and is called 'Bohaz'. In masonic language, the space between the columns is known as the 'middle' space.

In the foreground a woman is sitting on a cube-shaped seat. On her head we do not see the sign of infinity, as was the case in the First Arcanum, but the horns of Isis, with a full moon between them. Her face is covered with a half-transparent veil, while her figure is clothed in a flowing gown. On her knees rests a roll of papyrus (or a book), half covered by the folds of her dress, and on her bosom hangs a square cross.

The three names of the Second Arcanum on the planes of the Archetype, Man and Nature are:

DIVINA SUBSTANTIA, FEMINA, NATURA NATURATA.

The highest manifestations of man in his earthly life are his mind and will. If this binary is duly neutralized, then his life passes in favourable conditions. This does not mean to imply that I am forgetting here about the highest element in a human being, his Spirit or Atman, or True Self, as Western and Eastern Initiatory Masters have taught us.

Although the Tarot is an extremely exact and logical machine, it does not include Spirit in its arcana, for this is beyond its practical reach. I mentioned this in particular in the 'Introduction' to this book. Moreover, in company with the most authoritative exponents of Hermetism, I believe the Tarot to be a preparatory school for the realization of the Spirit in man, that is for his ultimate and highest aim.

Now we will return to the ternary:

SPIRIT—ASTRAL—MATTER.

Under 'Astral' I mean that which occultists are accustomed to separate into two sub-divisions, namely mental and astral bodies. For purely technical purposes in the present course, we will often consider them as a unit.

So, man necessarily needs a healthy spirit, a healthy astrosome, and a healthy physical body. The Monad (another name for Spirit, Atman or Self) is always perfect because of its high origin, about which we will speak later. The essential thing is, that this highest principle in man is ACTIVE in him, for then a man possesses the fully undimmed CONSCIOUSNESS (true one), which is the same as the presence of spiritual tendency in a man's life.

A healthy astrosome will create the element of spiritual harmony, being the third term of the binary: *Consciousness—Power* (Force). This harmony will secure a productive combination of strivings and desires in man. This combination is just what, in current language, we call the *personality*. It is simple! If someone tells us for what and how he is striving in his life, we are able to know his 'I' (personality), or ego.

A healthy body allows man a right transmission of will-impulses. It will balance his world of physical needs and will add to his life the element of the power of realization. So what do we have to analyse first, the body, astral or Spirit?

The body and its functions are the object of study by other types of specialists. Spiritual manifestations are not uncommon to many deeply thinking men, who are inclined towards philosophical matters. So our present aim will be to analyse the astrosome, and later, the whole astral world in which the astrosome lives and which is its normal realm. Therefore if we ask ourselves:

(1) What makes man an active unit? Then we find

(2) that we need knowledge of the astral plane.

So let us occupy ourselves with the second Arcanum, which will supply the necessary answers.

(a) In its numerical meaning, the Second Arcanum reminds us about the necessity of splitting the unit, and its polarization every time that it wants to act.

(b) The shape of the letter ב (Beth) itself clearly shows the method used in occult knowledge.

I am speaking about the great method of analogy, a formula of which is given in the classical Latin translation of the text of the Emerald Tablets of Hermes Trismegistus:

'QUOD EST INFERIUS EST SICUT QUOD EST SUPERIUS ET QUOD EST SUPERIUS EST SICUT QUOD EST INFERIUS AD PERPETRANDA MIRACULA REI UNIUS.' (that is, 'What is below is similar [NOT EQUAL] to what is above, and what is above is similar to what is below in order to ensure the perpetuation of the miracles of the Unique Thing' (free translation).)

This statement, together with the picture of the Temple hall is sufficient to justify the name 'Gnosis' given to the Second Major Arcanum of the Tarot. The upper part of the letter ב (Beth) is similar to the lower one, and the right-hand column is also similar to the left one; but, in both cases, the things concerned are NOT EQUAL.

The *horns* give us a direct hint of the law of binaries. The columns also form a binary; but between them is a woman, that is again an individual who should neutralize this binary. Woman is a symbol of passiveness, especially a seated woman. This position also reminds us of patient, contemplative, sensitive moods. Yes! Whoever wishes to learn, must have these moods.

Objects of scientific investigation are accessible only to a sharp and penetrating mind: for they are covered by a half-transparent veil. The results of any scientific investigations are recorded in books by the savants; but Nature records its mysteries in a living book. It is possible to know them only from under the folds of a cloak which will insulate us from worldly troubles and conditions and other harmful outer influences. That is why the figure of Gnosis has such an ample covering.

The hieroglyph for this arcanum—a human throat—represents something where one can hide oneself, a shelter like a temple, or other building dedicated to science. The aforementioned law of analogy is conveyed by related, but not identical terms.

It is necessary to know, in full detail, the idea of the binary of male and female origin.

Over the head of the Magician in the First Arcanum there is a sign of unity (as well as of infinity); but here we have horns, that is a much more materialistic element. For the mother is more materialistic than the father. The passive is always more dense than the active. A subtle, supple element of activity fecundates the more condensed, passive element; but the latter should be realized according to the measure of the first: *it must correspond to it.*

What is the aim of existence of these elements? Of course, the fecundation itself, which is symbolized here by the cross on the woman's breast. The vertical part of the cross is the phallus and the·horizontal the cteis. The *solar cross* is identical with the so-called *stauros* of the Gnostic symbolism (Fig. 5), and in the Hindu tradition it is the lingam (Fig. 5).

In the Tenth Arcanum we will see another representation of the same origin, but more philosophical (the sign for which is י Yod), and in the Fifth (the sign being ה Hé) again, male and female symbols.

The Second Arcanum is feminine in character. The moon seen in it suggests to us the idea of maternity (the moon being the Universal Mother in occult tradition). So, astrologically, the Second Arcanum belongs to the moon.

From it we may see the idea of *another binary*, showing its productive and creative character. Let us analyse the basic phases of this production.

For example, in mechanics, take two equal and opposite forces and apply them at the same point. There will be a balance of forces. This roughly constructed binary reminds us that the main part of a manifestation is possible only as a result of the opposing forces, that is action and counter-action. Without this nothing will be produced.

Does it pay to preach goodness among virtuous people? Is there any sense in teasing someone who is absolutely insensitive to and unimpressed

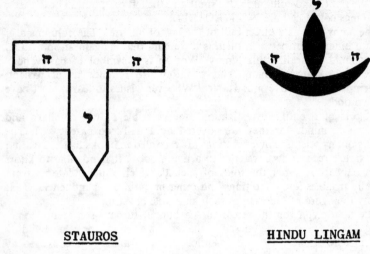

STAUROS   HINDU LINGAM

Fig. 5 Classical Symbols

by such behaviour? Can we rest upon something which bends under the
pressure of our arm without offering any resistance? *This must always be
in your mind* when you have to establish a *modus vivendi* to fit any
circumstance.

The very point which divides the active part of a binary from its negative
one, is that of counterbalance which may sometimes be shifted, but the
idea of a momentary point of balance is always realized according to our
scheme.

Action or behaviour neutralizing the great binary of GOOD and
EVIL can, for a short time, approach closer to the realm of good or evil.
At such a moment the binary is neutralized by another action or form of
behaviour. Only, in this second case GOOD simply does not bring any
harm to the man; and a few minutes later it is felt that conscience compels
him to be very grateful to it.

THE POSITION OF THE POINT WAS CHANGED, BUT
NOT THE IDEA OF NEUTRALIZATION.

LESSON 5

Now we will pass to another phase of the application of the binary. This
phase can be termed *dynamic*, whereas the first was rather *static*. Again a
rough mechanical example: take two equal and parallel forces and apply
them to opposite points of a dense body. It is a pair of forces and it makes
us think of a rotary movement. This mental picture is just what is needed,
and even more, the conception of whirling, or as we may say, a *tourbillon*,
a *vortex*. Where will we imagine it to be? This time in the astral plane, so
we have to imagine astral waves stirred up by the efforts of imagination,

and animated by will-power, just in the form of these tourbillons or vortexes, extending themselves like shadows or ever-widening circles on the surface of water, and growing according to similar laws. The mystery of the creation of such tourbillons *cannot be told*, of course, in a book or in general practice; but I shall take the risk of a slight intimation, in which man *instinctively* makes these vortexes in the astral and *even sees their power of realization*, by means of individualized coagulations of matter, as conjured up by them.

This is connected with the question of neutralization of the binary, LIFE—DEATH.

Another initiatory binary, SPIRIT—MATTER has been neutralized by the ASTRAL, or second plane. Therefore I will now give the general outline necessary for the cognition of this important plane, and firstly of its dwellers.

Generally speaking, acquaintance with them can be made by an inductive method, which means relations with them and the recording of the results of those relations: or, also by a deductive method, that is proceeding from definitions known about the astral plane.

The astral plane is, according to definition, mixed with the physical and mental planes. They interpenetrate one another. So in the astral must be visible the reflections of elements of those planes, which correspond to its sphere.

Strongly condensed and grouped together, collective ideas have, as a reflection in the astral, the so-called *astro-ideas*. Metaphysicians and other scientists like to catch these in the moments of their mental strivings, when a question arises regarding the selection of a form for the already beloved ideas.

Often the same astro-idea may be caught by different savants from neighbouring sub-planes; then we may see two or more systems arising which are strongly related, but not identical in form. Here I would like only to remind students about the creation of infinitesimal calculus by Leibnitz (at present called differential calculus), and also by Newton who then called it a 'method of fluxions'.

When realized in the physical world, actions and phenomena are reflected in the astral plane, through the intermediary of higher, or more subtle sub-planes of the physical, as in a mirror. By means of this process they establish themselves exactly in the astral, thereby forming the astral clichés of happenings in the physical world. The astral plane is not limited by the narrow laws which apply in the three-dimensional space of the physical world. There you can find clichés not only of the past, but also of future events. You may object, saying that future events are, to a certain degree, dependent upon the will and impulses of 'free individualities'.

My answer will be: (a) Yes, but each desire, each intention made by you on the physical plane, partially changes the clichés of future happenings, and can even annihilate them. What of the future will you then see in the astral?

(b) The higher the sub-plane in which you catch the clichés of a future event, the less it changes and the better it forecasts things. Here we have a great mystery, that of *free will*, which is identical to the mystery of the fabrication of astral tourbillons in their general sense. *From this comes a certain degree of obscurity in the exposition of this point;* but those who are acquainted with this secret, which CANNOT be revealed in any writing destined for a wide public, know that the explanation is TRUE.

Here I would like to make an important statement in the interest of readers and students of the Tarot. All these 'extraordinary' matters about the astral plane and its properties can be experienced only if one possesses a certain degree of concentration, that is, the ability to rule one's thoughts and stop them at will. Otherwise it will be only a repetition of my own case of about 30 years ago, when I first met practical occultism by reading the works of Prof. G. O. M. to whom I owe many of my own experiences in later years. At that time it seemed to be very strange and impossible for me to become acquainted with the super-physical conditions of existence, astro-ideas, Egregors, and so on, as described in this book. But when I understood that the VERY KEY is just the ability of concentration, the subsequent training throughout many years allowed me to develop from a laymen into a more knowledgeable person.

That is what caused me to write *Concentration*. I do not wish to imply that all the peaks expounded in it, are an unalterable condition for any study of Hermetism, but at least three of the 'Series' in that book must be performed in order that this present work will become a practical manual for the student, instead of just a cumbersome collection of thoughts and theories.

However, it is time to return to our Tarot.

While scientists seek after astro-ideas—even unaware of their existence—all kinds of clairvoyants, fortune-tellers and prophets long for the astral clichés, which they try to catch in trance, or in dream, that is in the states when a human being is closer to the astral world. The easiest clichés to see are, of course, those of an extraordinary nature, having an unusual or fateful meaning. This gives the possibility of 'seeing' and forecasting great crimes, catastrophies, as well as peculiar happenings of world-wide importance. Sometimes even non-clairvoyant persons are able to receive impressions of such ominous events, if they are sufficiently sensitive at the time.

Let us imagine that a man has a common evil desire, but makes no attempt to realize it on the physical plane. He only draws his dark desire on the astral plane, and so creates a kind of 'entity', by condensing the astral according to his intention. This artificial 'being' does not possess a physical body, but it is a kind of astrosome, and its correspondence to the human monad (spirit) is just the mental idea of the evil intention or wish. Such a being—according to the property of its 'monad'—can act and influence only in one direction as intended by its unwise creator, man, who is usually unaware of his foolishness.

Now, on whom will the influence of such a demon be exerted? Yes, firstly on the father of it himself, the draughtsman who created the astral picture of the evil deed. We will call this type of ominous artificial entity a larva. Such a larva will watch its 'father' in order to prevent him from forgetting his evil intention and desire, and to fortify the larva's life by new meditations about the same theme. But it can also attach itself to another man, who has certain astral and mental affinity with the first one. We then say that a larva has left one man and fastened itself (like a leech) to another.

How can we free ourselves from such larvas, no matter whether our own or of foreign origin? I can recommend three means.

(1) A conscious effort of the will in the form of a desire not to succumb to the evil entity, to defy it, to expel it, to act like a painter who looks with contempt on his own obscene creation.

(2) To concentrate mentally on another object, and not to allow any thought about the larva to enter into the mind. Frequent thinking about the chosen object will cut the possibility of attending to the larva. Prayer is the best and most recommended means of this kind, because every prayer is an act of concentration, and every act of concentration can be considered as a form of prayer, no matter if it is directed to God, man himself or even to the Devil, depending upon the nature of the concentration.

As the Devil, we understand, from the Tarot's point of view, a picture of Higher Origin deformed to the ultimate depths reached through the synthesis of all anarchy and disorders.

This means of concentration may be compared to the method of turning away from an unwanted picture so as to contemplate another, more desirable one.

(3) The use of the power of realization based on the physical plane, that is the destruction of the larva with a magic sword, which consists of a metallic blade with an insulated hilt made from dry timber, ebonite or, nowadays, from plastic (a thick woollen glove will also serve the purpose). The action of the magic sword is based on the astral tourbillons' property of changing their characters so strongly in the proximity of a sharp metallic projection that in the event of the sword entering a ganglion of a larva, it will bring about its full disintegration.

This means that larvas should be sought for in the aura of persons attacked by them, for they usually adhere to the astrosome of a man like a leech. This method is similar to the destruction of the whole of an obscene picture by the annihilation of the canvas on which it is painted.

Imagine that an intelligent and well-disposed man, who is able to concentrate, is thinking about a good idea, giving it a certain form. He may then find others, who have the same or similar ideas, and so a circle of men may come into being, who are all thinking along the same lines but in a different form. It is as if everyone of them is repeating the drawing of a plan, placing a pencil again and again on the same contours. The thing grows in strength, develops an astrosome and becomes an 'Egregor' or collective entity.

Such an Egregor, like each astrosome, defends, heals and even resuscitates the physical bodies of its members, rousing them to activities and realization of the principal idea incorporated in that Egregor. So, for example, an Egregor of a benevolent society may urge its physical members to still more activities and work, and the attracting of new members. Egregors belonging to organizations and nations which are inimical to one another, are able to fight on the astral plane, while their human beings fight in the physical world.

If on the physical plane, enemies destroy the bodies of members of a particular Egregor, their astrosomes fortify the Egregor on the astral plane. Recall the persecution of Christians by the Jews and Pagans in the early days of the new religion. The former won the fight, because they were stronger on the astral plane. That is why the Church, at that time, said that 'the blood of the martyrs is the best seed for new Christians'.

More particulars about Egregors will be given in the analysis of the Eleventh Arcanum.

LESSON 6

Now imagine that a man has finished his existence on the physical plane, in a particular incarnation. We say that he has died. His body begins to decompose. According to the unchangeable laws of Nature, all the elements of that body, including the vital force of the blood and even the energy of nervous activity, are gradually being absorbed back into the same Nature for use in other organic formations.

The man remains with his astrosome and spiritual monad. The lowest plane on which he can now exist, is the astral one.

Now his name is—ELEMENTAR. I have adapted this word to suit English usage, taking it from the old Western occult tradition, as there is nothing more appropriate. This elementar can still manifest itself in the physical world, but under many conditions and restrictions. One of them is the use of mediums, that is persons who are able to lend their lower astral elements and higher physical matter to an elementar, who wants to contact his former world. Fortunately, not all elementars are interested in such relations, and, in any case, not all are able to get them. The most important conditions which can facilitate a two-plane entity (elementar) using a spiritualist's seance is the presence of a passive medium, the powerful will of a magician, or a collective will of members of a special circle, interested in mediumism and the apparitions of dead men. However, all this is rather incidental, for the normal life of an elementar is passed in the contemplation of astral clichés and intercourse with other astral beings. They are his comrades in suffering because of the 'astral judgement', which invariably occurs after death, and in preparation for the next incarnation.

Among the temporary contacts on the astral plane, there are also meetings with the artificially exteriorized astrosome of still living men.

It is possible for a living man to concentrate his activities in the astral realm both intentionally and unintentionally. In such a state, his physical functions must be reduced to the bare minimum. We can say that the astrosome not only forms the body in the womb of its future mother, not only directs its development, but also supports its form, rules over the exchange of its cells, repairs any damage done to them, and when the time comes for the body to decompose, the astrosome even helps in this process.

Now you may be better able to realize why a sick person's sleep is considered a good omen. The astrosome will try to restore the health of its body, and it is just possible for it to do this when the man is asleep.

In the first period after physical death, the elementar is occupied with the process of decomposing his former earthly body. As far as we know, this is sometimes a very grim business, and only very few of so-called ordinary men are able to escape this unpleasant task. That is why men fear death. In the deepest recesses of their consciousness there may be some vague remembrance of former burials and the subsequent events, and so on.

That is why, for example, in India the bodies of most average people are cremated: this may spare them what has just been told. Otherwise, saints and eminent yogis are usually buried in the earth, as they have nothing to fear after death. They were masters of their lives on earth, and they remain so in all other worlds. In many occult chronicles one can find grim stories about vampires and were-wolves which followed some burials, and which were recorded under special and unusual conditions. In *Isis Unveiled* Madam H. P. Blavatsky relates an interesting story of vampirism in Kiev, allegedly founded on authentic recorded facts. Here there is no room to delve further into these things.

Anyway, *the astrosome is Brahma, Vishnu and Siva* for its physical body. The activity of the astrosome in connection with the physical body is especially strong in time of sleep. At that time the spirit hardly uses the astrosome, which then has time to do its house-work, which is the business of feeding its cells, of healing, and of surveying the vital currents (pranas). If the astrosome has only a very little amount of work to perform as in catalepsy, lethargy, trance, and so on, then it can be almost free and so manifest itself energetically enough as to be visible in the realm of outer objects, such as the bodies of other men. Here belongs the healing of another body by means of the exteriorization of one's astrosome and the sending of it to that body to repair its faults. By using some part of certain fluids from a medium, or even its own body, an astrosome can manifest itself far off—at great distances—and in many ways, often producing some mechanical effects, noises, the transfer of objects, touching, light effects, the appearance of its form as the physical body of a man, and so on.

We call these manifestations of the astral energy of a man beyond his physical body, exteriorization (or exit) of the astrosome. So death is a permanent abandonment of the physical form, while exteriorization means only a temporary withdrawal, more or less conscious. The differences among men are so great, that it would be impossible to guess at or predict anything very accurate about the conditions which prevail in such cases.

Unconscious exteriorization sometimes happens to persons suddenly affected by strong grief, fear, or who are merged in certain kinds of sleep, like lethargy or catalepsy; but *consciously*, this peculiar state can be used by magicians and witches, when they wish to manifest their activities from a distance. This may also be done for various purposes, such as: to see an astral cliché of an earthly happening (in advance, of course); to catch a valuable astro-idea; to solve a tangled question or problem, and to experience practically all that I am telling you now theoretically.

At such a time, the mental monad is not very much affected by the astral exit of its counterpart. Its activity is rather divided into two parts. Firstly, the mental body may accompany the astrosome in its wandering in order to help and guard it, and on the other hand, it may remain to look after the physical body, left alone in a state of deep catalepsy somewhere on the earth. For you should know, that each conscious exteriorization of the astrosome in man brings many quite real dangers for his physical vehicle. Later we will speak more extensively about this matter; but for the present I only wish to underline the fact, that these dangers are the reason why *no honest occultist will ever disclose* the secrets of the process of exteriorization to anyone, unless he or she is sufficiently advanced and gives full guarantees of decent and reasonable behaviour on the astral plane, so full of temptations and strange, almost unbelievable conditions. The same thing applies to books. Although, in this work I would have liked to tell everything that is known at the present time about occultism and its practices, I have had to wrap the actual instructions—which lead to real experiments in other worlds—in such a way that the neophyte has to use his intuition when seeing the symbols of astral tourbillons, exteriorization or anything else. If you carefully follow and study the matters expounded here, with energy and confidence, you might be able to lift the *unavoidable veil of secrecy* which is drawn over dangerous teachings; but then you will also be RIPE to receive them, and this will not burden my, or another exponent's karma, even if later you may commit some blunders. This MUST be clearly understood and sound deductions made from this realization.

So the mental body (or, as it has also been called here, the mental monad) looks after the security of its two lower bodies in cases of exteriorization. Now we will pass on to the actual role of the astrosome.

(1) The *absence of the astrosome* from the physical body, when the latter has been wounded or otherwise damaged, is a good sign, for this means that the astrosome itself has not been affected, and therefore it is easier for it to repair and heal whatever is necessary. If you can exteriorize even partially at the moment when your body receives an injury, you will be healed much quicker and more surely than otherwise. In such a case the tourbillons, and ganglions of your astral body will have been only slightly affected, or even not at all, and then the astrosome works quickly and effectively to repair the damage. Some fakirs make use of this method when they allow their bodies to be cut or pierced. The returning astrosome heals everything in a short time.

I remember an instance in my own life, when I made a spontaneous exteriorization almost unconsciously, when my body was in great danger. It fell from a considerable height, and rolled down a stony hill; but as 'I' was then momentarily 'apart', the injuries were only superficial.

(2) If things are opposite, that is, if the astrosome has been damaged when it has been apart from the physical body—say, with a magic sword or any other sharp object—and had very little contact with it, then there is a considerable danger for the body and its health. A sickness may develop, apparently without any good reason for it.

If the damage to the exteriorized astrosome occurs on one of the ganglions, not necessarily even the most important one, then after its return, the physical body *will have a wound* in just the place where its astral double has been injured. *The lower the sub-plane of the astral* on which we go when exteriorized, *the greater is the damage* and the subsequent danger.

Other inhabitants of the astral plane are the elementals. Western occult tradition does not consider them to be purely astral beings, for an elemental can have its own mental monad, astrosome and physical body, but belonging to the more subtle sub-divisions, and therefore is normally invisible to humans. These strange beings direct certain special involutionary activities, such as chemical and physical phenomena, as well as physiological processes. Another reason for their being invisible and intangible, is that their bodies are of the same consistency as the sub-plane on which they live.

If their bodies are in a gaseous state, we call them *sylphs*; if liquid, *ondines*; if solid, *gnomes*; and finally those who have still more subtle bodies, close to what we call the 'world's ether', they will be known as *salamanders*.

Some beings possess only mental monads and operate involutionary processes on the astral plane. Tradition defines them as '*Spiritus Directores*' of the astral, or leaders of it; but other purely mental entities are also occupied with the involutionary processes and are called *Angels*.

Arcanum III
PHISIS
NATURE

Venus

Divina Natura
Partus
Generatis

CHAPTER III

ARCANUM III (ג GHIMEL)

THE sign of the Hebrew alphabet for the third Major Arcanum of the Tarot is the letter ג (Ghimel). The hieroglyph is a hand with the fist folded so that it forms a *narrow tunnel*, which can contain something. From this idea of a narrow tunnel it is not a far step to the next one: that of the matrix (womb), which is the last link in the process of birth, or to the actual idea of infant delivery.

From this comes the titles of the Third Arcanum:

DIVINA NATURA, PARTUS, GENERATIS.

The idea of creation is tightly connected with the element of love, or generally, with the element of attraction. Universal gravitation, ordinary love, clemency, universal love, all of these are only separate manifestations of the same ATTRACTION.

The goddess of love has been called VENUS. This explains to us the scientific name of the arcanum, VENUS URANIA, that is, Venus of the astronomical universe.

Another scientific name is PHISIS (*Nature*). The vulgar name is the *Empress*.

The *geometrical* symbol for this arcanum, suggesting the idea of the *ternary*, will be an ascending (that is the apex pointing upwards) or descending (that is the apex pointing downwards) triangle, depending upon the nature of the ternary.

The *picture* on the card shows a woman, crowned with twelve stars, symbolizing the twelve signs of the Zodiac. The principle of birth on the physical plane is closely connected with different phases of solar energy, received by the Earth. These phases are determined *by the position of the Sun* in a particular sign of the Zodiac. That is why, in occultism, the Zodiac itself is considered as a hint for the physical plane and its properties.

'A seated woman clothed with the sun, and the moon under her feet, and on her head a crown of twelve stars: and being with child, she cried travailing in birth, and was in pain to be delivered.'

(The Apocalypse of St John)

The problem of birth reveals the meaning of the Third Arcanum and the Sun shows us the centre of attraction (planetary love) of our solar system. There is also the idea of the Sun being the centre of emanated life, and of all creation.

In her left hand the woman holds a sceptre with the sign of Venus

(♀). This means that she reigns for ever with her love over all that has been born, all that is, and all that will be born. The sign ♀ itself is a synthesis of two symbols: ⊙ belongs to the Sun (creative emanations) and + being, as we will see later, the world of elements, or the complex of all the influences of the surroundings. Therefore love brings a victory for creative emanations over all obstacles, arising from those surroundings.

In her right hand the woman holds a shield bearing the device of an *eagle*, to indicate the fact that the idea of creation extends itself over the highest regions. A square shaped cross hangs round the eagle's neck, reminding us that the process of birth is a natural consequence of the union between the active and passive principles.

The woman is seated on a *cube-shaped stone*, which in turn is poised *on a globe*. Under her left foot is the *moon*, here symbolizing the matter of the *sub-lunar world*, as the *lowest realm of creation*.

Sometimes we find on Tarot cards for the Third Arcanum, that the woman has wings instead of the Sun clothing her. This is to remind us about the ascension of *Isis Terrestris* (Earthly Isis) to *Isis Coelestis* (Celestial Isis).

This arcanum provides us with the conception that 'NOTHING IS CREATED, BUT EVERYTHING IS BORN', that is there is always י (Yod) which fecundates ה (Hé) and therefore brings about the birth of the third element ו (Vau), of the Sixth Arcanum. So we have: *Father, Mother and Child. Active* and *passive* being neutralized by the *androgynous*.

Apart from this, the Third Arcanum proclaims the universal law of the *TERNARY*. I will now give a few examples of analyses of some typical ternaries; firstly one of the *descending* triangle type.

ARCHETYPE—MAN—NATURE

This is: *God in God*, or *God the Father*; God manifesting Himself in humanity, or *God the Son*; God manifesting Himself in Nature, *God the Holy Ghost*.

According to this triple manner of manifestation of the Unique Divinity, in whom the middle term neutralizes the two extremes, *Man creates the link between Nature and the Archetype*. Therefore there are souls, seeking *God the Father* by means of *metaphysical paths*, and souls seeking *God the Son in their hearts* while uniting groups of men in the name of such a search.

Finally, there are souls seeking God by contemplation of Nature and by the alliance with her (Nature's) unchangeable laws: they are seekers after *God the Holy Ghost*.

More particulars of this will be found in the Kabbalah.

Now we want to analyse the ternary of an *ascending* type of triangle, for example, that of the Great Arcanum. The same ternary: *Archetype—Man—Nature* can be used for the next steps. Imagine the Archetype as something harmonious, androgynous, omniscient, eternally content, possessing ability (powers) to manifest any activity and consequently of being in the position to limit those activities.

In traditional Hermetism there is an expression to the effect that: 'The *Highest Principle* being the beginning of everything, divides Itself into ACTIVE and PASSIVE manifestations, thereby creating the figure of an ascending triangle.'

Humanity is as a whole the one organism, whose cells are beings which, on this earth, are called men. On other planets things may be quite different, although, for a clearly thinking mind this is a certainty. *We are not the unique,* nor the most advanced evolution in the eternal, limitless universe. To think otherwise shows the lack of the ability to reason and build conceptions based on one's own independent judgement.

If we recognize the existence of such 'cells' in all their possible variety, on all cosmic planets, suns, and so on, then we can surely create a picture of the *Universal Man,* living the life of a collective entity and possessing Will according to the great Law of Individualization.

Nature—as a consequence of the grouping together of all the elements, individualized or not by your imagination and contemplation—is a result of causality. Both poles, that is HUMANITY and NATURE are manifestations of the Archetype. According to the scheme of our triangle, the first element (humanity) is an active one, the second (Nature) is passive. We have to note that both of these terms 'active' and 'passive' are used *here* in a relative but not any absolute meaning.

Now we will occupy ourselves with another very interesting ternary of the same type as that of the Great Arcanum. It is:

PAST—PRESENT—FUTURE.

The Present, at a given moment, *determines the past and future.* Without indicating the PRESENT MOMENT, we cannot separate and realize the PAST and the FUTURE. *The present* emanates *the past* and *the future;* in the past is shown its relatively *passive,* deformed side (it is impossible to change it) and in the future, its *active side.* Putting our two ternaries beside one another, we may say that the *Archetype,* according to the Law rules over the PRESENT, that to *humanity* analogously belongs the FUTURE, and that *Nature* has based its manifestations on the PAST. To proceed a step further; humanity rules over the *future* in accordance with the Law of Human Freedom, with the help of an instrument called 'HUMANITY'S WILL'. Nature holds *the past* in the form of Destiny, an instrument of which is *Fate* (blind, pitiless, and therefore warped and relatively passive).

The Archetype has the qualities of the Androgyne. This is reflected according to the Law of All-Contentment and Higher Harmony on that great Chandelier called *Providence.* Accordingly, Destiny (Providence) is neutral, androgynous and plays the role of light, radiating on the field of activity of both remaining elements.

I would like to underline, that in our language the term '*present*' has two meanings: one, related to the reality of an object, and the other, the placing of that object in a certain moment of time. Each application of the birth or emanation of everything should be the PRESENT for the birthgiving or source of emanation, in order to be real in the corresponding

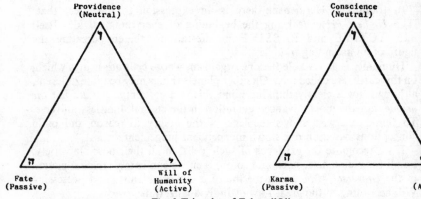

Fig. 6 Triangles of Fabre d'Olivet

plane of manifestation of life. Therefore the formula of suggestion (hypnosis) must be read as: '*You ARE doing this or that*' and not '*you WILL do it*' or '*you HAVE DONE it*'. This should be carefully meditated upon, in order to ensure good understanding.

Any unchangeable metaphysical or scientific thesis is also formed in the present. Impressions which you may describe as belonging to the past or future will not be accepted by anyone as real. At the best of times, they may be considered only as vague terms for 'reflection' or 'hallucination', and so on.

Coming back to our *ternary*, I would like to quote the saying of Fabre d'Olivet that: 'the world's history shall be realized in the mystical triangle' (see Fig. 6).

Providence illuminates the *present* with its Light.

(1) Humanity's Will tends to the creation of the *future*, but is restricted by Fate, which controls this striving by means of the *past*. If humanity's Will is allied with the enlightening influence of Destiny, then it is stronger than Fate. In such cases, the history of humanity has an *evolutionary character*.

(2) If humanity *closes its eyes* to the influence of Destiny and tries to fight Fate, then it is impossible to forecast the exact result: everything depends upon the relation of the forces of humanity and its Fate.

(3) If humanity *consciously fights Fate* which has been reinforced by hints from Providence, and then forgets to listen to the voice of Providence, the Will of humanity will be defeated and no results will accrue from such a hopeless struggle.

(4) If humanity *joins its efforts with those of Fate*, despite negative advice from the side of Providence, then the results will be very strong and very much felt. Then historical development removes the world from the principles of Harmony, and errors have to be rectified by way of realization of the ultimate aims of the universe. At such times the history of humanity becomes *involutionary* instead of evolutionary.

It is interesting now to look at the reflection of the mystical triangle of Fabre d'Olivet (Fig. 6).

Providence has a representative in the individual human being. It is called *Conscience*. It is *absolutely neutral*, and neither attacks nor acts as a brake, but only *enlightens the path*, showing how one has to neutralize, at a particular moment, the important binary; *Good and Evil*. Man's will may determine future happenings, but is limited in their choice by Karma. This Karma is like a general record of all previous incarnations of a man's soul. The *first time* he may be born in good conditions for acquiring wisdom, or as we may say, with a clean Karma; but he commits sins, and therefore in the *next incarnation* he still has to purify his Karma, apart from the primary problem of learning the wisdom of life, which cannot be devoid of struggles and sufferings. Of course, in the *second birth*, Karma puts him in much less propitious conditions. The next incarnations proceed according to the law which burdens and corrects Karma, until it is completely clear. A much burdened Karma, which cannot be repaired by one's conscious efforts, is partially repaid by the very element of suffering in the particular incarnation.

The sufferings with which Karma sometimes burdens a man can be so strong that they partially redeem it, even despite his full lack of co-operation, and consciously evil intentions.

The following combinations are possible in the mystical triangle:

(1) Man's will together with his conscience acting against Karma results in the *purification of Karma*.

(2) Will together with Karma opposed to conscience (egoistic opportunism), results in apparent success in life, but with a further *burdening of Karma*.

(3) A fight of Will against Karma, without the participation of conscience gives results which cannot generally be forecast, as everything depends upon the relation of the forces, Will and Karma.

(4) Will fighting against united Karma and Conscience results in an *unsuccessful life* and the *burdening of Karma*.

Ternaries like those analysed in this arcanum, that is which are quite open groupings of three degrees of one and the same manifestation, we will call '*absolute ternaries*' I will also try to liken them to other ternaries, which may require a different point of view. Such ternaries will be termed 'analogous', being bound symbolically or conditionally with some absolute ternary.

Two examples of similar ternaries follow: one from Nature, and another from ritual symbolism. Look at the human organism and divide it into three parts. These will be, head, thorax and abdomen. Analogously connect the *head* with the *mental plane*, because the manifestation of mental work in incarnate man is related to the functions of the brain.

The *thorax* should be connected with the idea of the *astral plane*, because, when working on the astral plane, physical exercises of adepts, deal first and foremost with breathing and its rhythm.

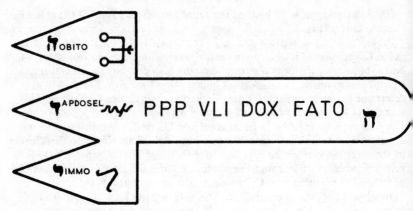

Fig. 7 Trident of Paracelsus

The *abdomen* symbolizes the *physical plane* because the normal functions of the intestines are connected with the process of renovation of the body's cells.

So we have an analogous ternary. Now read it in a slightly changed outer form:

The activity of the head rules over the distribution of the nervous energy; the thorax over the restoring of the vital force in the blood, and the abdomen over the tissues by the circulation of lymphatic fluids.

We can test to see if this somewhat artificial division is a practical one, by *seeking three sub-planes in the head*. The eyes will represent mentality: this is because you apprehend the activities of others by your sight. The nose may act as astral representative of the head, because with its help it is often possible to judge (superficially of course) about the state of the thorax from a pathological point of view. The throat can be considered as the representative of the physical plane, the messenger of the abdominal region, about whose troubles we can often judge by the state of the tongue or mouth.

LESSON 8

Now we will analyse an example of an artificially symbolical ternary by describing the famous 'Trident of Paracelsus' (Tridens Paracelsi) (see Fig. 7).

On the *upper* prong we see engraved 'OBITO' (obedience, listening, attention, and so on). This inscription describes the passive realm of man's activity on the physical plane, or more exactly, in all the three worlds in the time of full incarnation in all of them.

The *lower* prong has 'IMMO' (sometimes abbreviated to 'IMO') which suggests the idea of resistance, strength, vigour.

The *middle* prong has a more complicated formula 'APDOSEL', which should be unfolded as follows: AP—DO—SEL. 'AP' is the concealed Greek alpha and rho = ar, the beginning of the word '*arché*' which means commencement, Higher Element, Spirit. '*DO*' should be read from right to left, which then gives us '*OD*', or the occult term for the positively polarized astral. This is none other than the ASTROSOME in its male manifestations. 'SEL' (Latin Sal) in French means salt. It is the basis of the physical plane, or the plane itself.

Now, all the three prongs of Paracelsus' Trident dictate the following sentence:

'*The threefold active Man (mens-anima-corpus) must balance the binaries of obedience and resistance, of passivity and activity. He must oscillate between both conditions. This ternary defines the sphere of the Man's activities in all worlds.*'

In the *second ternary* (the upper prong) the figure behind the word 'OBITO' is similar to the astrological sign for Cancer.

In the Zodiac, this sign represents the *House of the Moon*, which adds the passive principle to the passive upper prong.

In the second (middle) prong, there is a serpent which has the astrological sign of Jupiter for its head, and is a symbol for the *astral tourbillon* by which the authority of Man (Sign of Jupiter) passes into the world's astral.

The sign on the third prong behind 'IMMO' is a deformed symbol for the Zodiacal sign of Leo, which serves as a house for the active Sun, and directs its influence into the active, lower prong.

Therefore, the *second ternary* belongs to the realm of FORMS, transmitting the influence of the Trident's handle to its prongs. On the handle or hilt we see the inscription PPP VLIDOXFATO. In order to decipher it tradition tells us, that the PPP must be inverted, so that the triple lingam is revealed. It means *fecundation* on all three planes. The following 'V' is the Latin figure for '5', which is equal to the pentagram, or symbol of human will-power. 'LI' is the first syllable of 'LIBERTATE' which means 'through freedom', in this case: '*Pentagrammatica Libertate*' or '*through freedom of the human will*'. 'DOX' is for 'DOXA' (consciousness, knowledge), that is, that which gives to us the element of conscience. 'FATO' means 'by the force of Fate, Destiny or Karma'.

The handle tells us of the RIGHT of Man *to create* on three planes, and of the existence of the symbol, which stands at the top of the mystical triangle of Fabre d'Olivet.

This ternary is related to the realm of the mental and even metaphysical character of our absolute rights on all three planes of existence. The whole Trident symbolizes Man as a unit in two higher planes and as a differentiated being in the physical world.

Practically, in a male hand, the instrument serves as a perfect *magic sword*, designed to dominate and—in the case of necessity—to dispel the harmful concentrations of invisible forces. This happens during magic operations, such as the evocations of spirits of the lower kind, briefly as a defensive weapon. It is especially useful *against all kinds of larvas*, created by enemies or even by a man himself, as has already been mentioned.

A miniature of the Trident of Paracelsus is also used in Hermetism against male impotency. It is a striking example of a system of three ternaries in the Hermetic symbolical realm.

As a continuation of the third Major Arcanum I will give examples of its numerical analysis.

Equation No. 1: $3 = 1 + 2$

The action of the *Yod* (1) on the *First Hé* (2) results in a balanced creation—*Vau* (3). Spirit penetrates matter, thereby evolving innumerable living forms, which differ among themselves in relation to the amounts of the *positive* and *negative* in them. Because everything in Manifestation—on all its planes—is always the result of action reflected in the equations of the arcana (beyond the first and second ones), there cannot be anything which does not possess some degree of life, since the *Yod* must be represented—to a greater or lesser extent—in everything which IS. Of course, for those who are unacquainted with Hermetism, it may be hard to conceive, that all stones, plants and animals are only their younger brethren; but great souls on Earth KNOW. Francis of Assisi, a Saint, and Ramana Maharshi, a contemporary Sage and Spiritual Master, treated animals just like humans. From *their height* they were able to do this and it was only natural; but for those who know much less, this might appear as extravagancy or even insanity. Evidently animals consider such elder Sons of humanity as their unquestionable friends and masters, who are able to understand them. We know of many yogis in India and saints in Europe who have had friendly relations with wild beasts, such as tigers and bears, which recognized something in these men, which could not be found in average people, whom the animals devoured.

Equation No. 2: $3 = 2 + 1$

Matter (2) can produce a living form (3) only when the active and immaterial principle is added to it.

Equation No. 3: $3 - (1 + 2) = 0$

No manifestation can take place when *Yod* and *Hé* are absent.

Equation No. 4: $3 - 1 = 2$

Creation devoid of *Yod's* element would be only dead, passive matter. It does not exist.

Equation No. 5: $3 - 2 = 1$

If the screen (Hé) is dissolved, Manifestation returns to the primary *Yod.*

Such are the axioms which belong to the Third (*Vau*) Arcanum of the Tarot.

We will not consider an Hermetic equation of the type: $3 = 1 + 1 + 1$, because these are beyond our understanding. We know nothing of the transcendental origin, qualities and combinations of *Yod* in its pure form, that is, solely 1. Therefore the right side of the equation would be meaningless for us.

Some authorities on occultism ascribe Hatha Yoga to the Third Arcanum because of its concrete conceptions, so close to the physical world. As we know, Hatha Yoga is purely physical, although modern Indian exponents try to deny this fact. But it is hard to see something intellectual—not to mention something spiritual—in the exercises and ideas of this kind of Eastern occult path. Since the basis of Hatha Yoga is solely physical—as it is directed to the domination of the body by means of bodily exercises—Hermetists consider it merely as physical training. They know a lot about the value of respiratory exercises for producing certain psychical phenomena and, as we will see in the following lessons, extensive use is made of these: *not as a goal in itself*, but as a means to assist in the achievement of aims, which go far beyond the physical plane.

If you want to have a magic sword like that given by Paracelsus, first make a pattern (see Fig. 7) and then use it to cut out the required shape from soft steel or even iron. When the blade of the trident is ready, on one side exactly engrave all the symbolical signs as given in Fig. 7. Then prepare a handle about two feet long, from ebonite, strong dry wood, or plastic, preferably round or oval in cross-section. Remember that the handle should act as an insulator, as if against an electric current. Wood or other material used must be strongly attached to the handle like part of the blade, and painted with an insulating varnish, the best being one containing tar. Good screws with nuts or bifurcated rivets will make the most secure join. When you are holding the trident, you should not touch any part of the metal with your hand. The width of the sword-blade proper (that is head of the trident) should be 6″ to 8″ from the tip of the left-hand tine to that of the right, and about 12″ from the tip of the middle prong to the end of the *metallic* part of the handle.

A short ceremony of blessing and purification of the sword (against astral influences) is recommended. For that purpose you should find a quiet room where nobody will disturb you, and about midnight one day (here astrological influences can be omitted), prepare a small wooden table by covering it with a new white linen tablecloth, and placing two burning candles on it, with the sword between them. If you are a Christian and believer, you may bring a few drops of holy water from the nearest church with which to sprinkle the sword. Then, with utmost concentration, pronounce this short prayer three times: 'God Almighty, bless this sword and thy servant (mention your name) so that both may serve Thee by banishing evil and protecting good.' A little incense may be burned to complete the brief ceremony.

Take the consecrated sword from the table, and with it make the sign of the Cross over your head, bow, extinguish the candles and incense, remove the rest of the paraphernalia, and place the sword in a suitable flat box.

It is not desirable to show or give the sword to anyone except a true friend, who is also an occultist of good standing.

The chasing and extermination of larvas and other undesirable astral visitors is performed by piercing them with the magic sword as quickly as possible; but as you cannot see them, how can it be done? However, you know that these astral parasites attach themselves to the human aura or stay very close to it. This means that you may seek for them about three to five feet from the body, no matter WHETHER IT IS YOURS OR ANOTHER'S. Before you begin the action, mentally pronounce or whisper a short prayer, mantram or setram. Remember that you are doing a good deed, justified by the circumstances. Then puncture the whole of the aura's surroundings with sharp stabs, as if you would like to catch some small birds on your trident. If the sharp point of the magic sword contacts some larva or other astral creature in a sensitive and important centre, it acts like a lightning-arrester, which discharges accumulated electricity and so prevents a thunderbolt. The stabs should be sufficiently numerous in order not to allow the larvas to escape, for they are sometimes quite small when measured by our three dimensions (the astral has its own), about the size of a human palm. But there are also large monsters, which may need several stabs in order to be completely dissolved and destroyed.

Remember, that they CANNOT see you exactly, so they can do little to escape from your sword, but they may 'see' its points, which, in the astral, are similar to radiant, luminous needle points.

They *may feel the danger*, as do experienced astrosomes, when, with their dark aims they come into the proximity of living human auras.

As many larvas are only a condensation of evil thoughts and feelings, flowing through the infinite spaces of other worlds, they can even create physical sicknesses, if they attach themselves to your astrosome for some time, which, as we know, has exact counterparts in the physical body, in the form of ganglions, and so on. If an important part of the *astrosome* is *damaged or weakened* there will be corresponding damage or an ailment for the physical body. Sometimes mysterious disorders are produced in the body's cells, without any visible contagion by bacteria. The fact that such cancers, which have enigmatic causes, are now becoming so rapidly widespread, might have its origin in the excess of evil human feelings, hatreds and other negative forces, put into play in the aura of our planet.

These things may create innumerable larvas and other kinds of undesirable forces, which later bring disorder to the work of human cells, resulting in malicious tumours and cancerous growths. In general, occultism ascribes disease to an astral origin or affection of the astrosome, later inevitably transferred to the physical body. Some even believe in the astral origin of bacteria which cause sickness and death.

We will now explain and analyse the laws according to which work setrams, mantrams and theurgic means, such as special kinds of prayers, used in their oral form, in occultism, conjurations and exorcisms. These things are better covered by the Eastern Tradition than the Western, so I will mention here the theories borrowed from the Sankhya philosophical system:

'There is a universal substance, which is unique and all existing objects are only different forms of it. We perceive these forms only through our five physical senses. Therefore they can be classed under the name of the sense which is able to register these forms.

Each sense is sensitive to certain kinds of atomic movements (vibrations, as some occultists like to call them). Hearing, seeing, touching, tasting and smelling, all these belong respectively to the vibrations of: ether, light, air, water and earth which are also movements of atoms.

So, *ether* is movement in *all directions; light* movement in *straight lines; air* is *whirling* movement, that is *vortexes,* or tourbillons; *water* is *balanced* movement, while *earth* is *arresting* movement.

Apart from these things, each of these elements possesses the qualities of the other four as *secondary* characteristics. *Ether,* apart from sound, also has colour, form, taste and smell. We can see all the other applications of these laws for ourselves. Of course, only those who are able to separate these properties, can perceive them in their experiments, and a high degree of knowledge is necessary in order to verify these laws experimentally.

Finally, each of these kinetic forms is also represented in human mentality. Therefore, every thing can correspond to another under certain conditions.'

But here we are primarily interested in the energy which we call 'sound', or the *acoustic fluid.*

It possesses, apart from other qualities, those of mobility, fluidity and softness. In the Sankhya system it is called *Sneha.*

Long before there were Western physicians, Hindu occultists knew that sound emits calories, exciting movement by their impulses of power called *Pranamitva.* Stringed instruments, rhythmical melodies, the noise of thunder, all these things show us the existence of these different properties. A sinister example can be found in the ancient Chinese art of torturing. The greatest crime in the former Imperial China was of course, disobedience to, or plotting against the Emperor or his family. A particularly horrible death awaited anyone unlucky enough to be caught. He was stripped and bound by wrists and ankles to a short pole erected under a large bell. When the tongue of the bell moved it emitted a loud sound above the body of the doomed man. This sound gradually destroyed the tissues in his body, firstly attacking the nervous system, and slowly bringing unspeakable suffering to the whole organism.

The executioners worked in relays, and after a certain number of hours had passed, the contortion and wriggling of the condemned man's body was relieved by death.

No physical contact other than sound was the killer.

As a résumé, that form of the universal substance called AKASHA in the Eastern Tradition, possesses a specific quality like sound, and generic qualities like form, heat and movement.

Some classes of sounds contain perfect forms, while others are richer in calories, and still others emit more movement. These classes of sounds can be distinguished, produced, and their intensity augmented by different psycho-physiological instructions.

Similarly, some fakirs have been able to raise themselves into the air (compare the well-known 'levitations' of some Western saints) for some time, just by the use of a certain sound, while being under special nervous tension. In other words, the fact, well known to occultists, of influencing matter by nervous force is at work here.

Apart from the direct action of sound, all vocal means used in occultism also have their INNER significance, their 'souls'. It is the concentrated effort of will of an operator, who uses sounds as an outer expression of his will. So we see, that harmonious combinations of the physical properties of sound and their inner meaning may be a powerful weapon in the hands of a skilled occultist-magician, as well as those of a theurgist. But we have to consider some subtle differences between setrams, mantrams and prayers. Some of these three classes of instruments were originally created in certain languages, and thus their effectiveness has been supported by, and connected with definite groups of sounds arising from pronunciation or chanting. Such means lose the major part of their value if translated into other tongues, thereby becoming deprived of their direct, active properties, derived from sound vibrations, despite the fact, that the ideas behind them still remain the same. To this category belong almost exclusively, secret and purely occult and magic formulas, unknown to the public at large: the famous 'AUM' (or 'Om') being an exception.

Certain Christian prayers and incantations, the Hindu Gayatri and other well-known 'popular' mantrams, as well as the Vichara (Self-Inquiry), have their power *in their contents*, rather than in particular combinations of sounds. Therefore they are effective even when translated and used in other languages by the faithful and devotees.

Finally, it may be added, that from all five kinds of vibrations to which our senses respond, only *three* are in general use in Hermetism. I am giving them in the order of their effectiveness and usefulness:

(1) SOUND (mantrams, setrams, prayers, exorcisms)

(2) VISUAL (pentacles, sacred letters, magic drawings, symbols)

(3) SMELL (incense of all kinds, perfumes, smoke)

The student will surely realize, that all of these means are used foremostly for the support of his own will-power, and for the influencing of astral beings, which are sensitive to the astral counterparts of these means (1 to 3).

There is no need to explain further, why in all religions and occult operations, words, chanting and singing are so widely used. They are expressions of and vehicles for the energy, emanated by the priests and operators.

From ancient Egyptian history we know, that special kinds of sounds were produced by Egyptian priests and magicians before their troops went into battle. As a result the fighting spirit of the men was raised enormously, and they then fought with such fury, that they defeated their foes.

In the not-so-distant past, when wars were won by man-to-man fighting on the battlefields, and not by air bombardment or the annihilating fire of artillery, whole regiments went storming ahead with their bands playing loud bombastic marches. The orchestra of the sinking Titanic played almost to the last on the upper deck of the doomed ship, and helped to maintain

order and quieten those who were unable to find a place in the too few
life-boats, and who already looked into the eyes of death, reaching for them
from the icy waves of the Atlantic.

I have heard it said, that the insincere laughter of some people is able to
crack the glasses on a table.

In ancient Greek mythology we can find indications that the gods used
different syllables to restrain the disobedient souls of dead men, thus
preventing them from entering forbidden areas. One was the mysterious
'Yao' or 'IEAO' which was close to the unpronounceable יהוה (Yod-
Hé-Vau-Hé).

The Bible tells us that the impregnable walls of Jericho were destroyed
when the Jews circled them for some days, incessantly blowing on special
kinds of horns.

All of this shows us the formidable influence on the human psyche of the
vibrations which we call 'sound'.

Another kind of magic use of the powers of sound is the well-known
method used by Australian aborigines, to 'sing to death' those among
them who have transgressed the tribal laws. It is said to be effective,
inevitably bringing about the death of the one so sentenced, in from a few
days to several weeks. Usually the cause, from the medical point of view,
cannot be discovered, but the dying person is perfectly conscious of his
approaching end, as there is no known cure against the 'singing to death'
as performed by the elders of the tribe. We know little about these strange
rites, but it is generally believed that they consist of the singing of special
songs by the tribal men as they sit in a circle around their magic drawings.
Only fully grown aboriginals 'initiated into manhood' can perform such
ominous activities which are strictly guarded from the knowledge of white
men. The only particulars which I have been able to get are, that these
'songs of death' are mostly high pitched and the name of the condemned
person is mentioned in them. Sometimes a bone is pointed towards him,
but his presence is not essential for the effectiveness of the curse. Some
victims have tried to escape death by fleeing far from their tribal grounds,
even up to a thousand miles away, but without any known success.

Modern science itself shows that some kinds of sounds—those of very
high frequency, inaudible to the normal human ear—have a definite,
destructive power for living tissues and even organisms, which may be
exposed for some time to the influence of such sounds.

This was discovered about 30 years ago, and research still continues.
To date it has been found, that small animals like mice and frogs can be
killed by the high frequency waves generated by inaudible sounds. So the
principle has been discovered, and its application to the larger combinations of living cells, such as the human body, is only a question of further
research.

So we can see, that some old occult truths and traditions may gradually
be corroborated by official science, to the measure that it advances and
works on subtler manifestations of the physical forces. Here we have
mentioned only a few of the many examples, which can be discovered by
those interested in comparative studies of this kind.

ד

Arcanum IV
PETRA CUBICA
THE EMPEROR

♃
Jupiter

Forma
Auctoritas
Adaptatio

CHAPTER IV

ARCANUM IV (ד DALETH)

The letter belonging to the Fourth Arcanum of the Tarot is ד (Daleth), the numerical value of which is 4. The hieroglyph is the BREAST, which gives us the idea of feeding and of the accompanying authority. The result of this act is the cause which enables the subject of that feeding to perform all his activities in the outer world.

The picture for this arcanum represents a man sitting on a cubic throne, with a triple crown on his head, suggesting that his power extends to all the three worlds or planes. This is because, he who wants to be an authority in a certain realm, *must be acquainted with all three planes of that realm.* In his right hand the man holds a sceptre, ending with the sign of Venus (♀) or Jupiter (♃). The first conception tells us about the necessity of creating *individualized beings* and also of whole groups like our earthly humanity.

The *second symbol* may indicate that the astrological sign of Jupiter belongs to this arcanum. On *good cards* of the Tarot we may see that the position of the hands and shoulders of the figure form an ascending triangle, with its head as the apex.

The right leg is crossed over the left, so that a kind of square cross is formed. The man's back leans against the cubic seat, on which we see an eagle, with the Cross of the Great Hierophant (see Fig. 8) hanging from its neck.

Now we can pass on to an explanation of these symbols.

The cubic seat of polished stone tells us of the perfect form. Authority always appears in an outer form which has been prepared in advance.

Each side of this cube is a square, so that this figure is one of the geometrical symbols of the Fourth Arcanum.

The eagle depicted on the seat shows the necessity for the *high flight of thoughts;* he who wants to give a perfect form to things, must be an *engineer*, a *constructor* and not only a tradesman, a carpenter. This idea is further supported by the Cross of the Great Hierophant.

The perpendicular stem of the Cross means the channel through which flows the current, passing through the three lower worlds, symbolized by the *horizontal* arms of the Cross.

In order to make the form perfect, one should not only catch the idea, but be able *to realize it* in its mental, astral and physical phases.

The cross formed by the legs of the man is another geometrical symbol of this arcanum. The arcanum is also called '*petra cubica*' or cubic stone.

In vulgar language the name of the Fourth Arcanum is the EMPEROR,

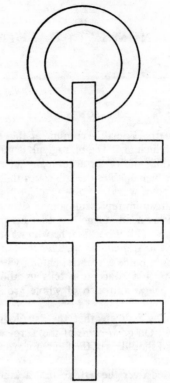

Fig. 8 Mystic Cross of the Great Hierophant

because of his crown and sceptre. In the Theosophical Ternary it will be:

FORMA (Form)   on the plane of the *Archetype*

AUCTORITAS (Authority)   on the plane of Man

ADAPTATIO (Adaptation)   on the plane of Nature

We are now close to the basic idea of the whole of Hermetic philosophy, that is, the idea of the *Quaternary* (also called Tetragrammaton). From the 'Introduction' to this work we already know something about it, so now we will examine it in more detail.

It is the general formula of each performed dynamic process in the universe. In the language of the Gnostics we read:

The ACTIVE (male, expansive) principle ﬡ (Yod) fecundates (vivifies) the PASSIVE (female, attractive) one—the ﬣ (Hé). From this union arises, or rather is born, the third element ﬡ (Vau) which is androgynous, NEUTRAL, borrowing, and transmitting that which is borrowed, down to the next cycle. When this pattern is fulfilled, the conception of the *First Family* appears, as a *finished cycle of manifestation*.

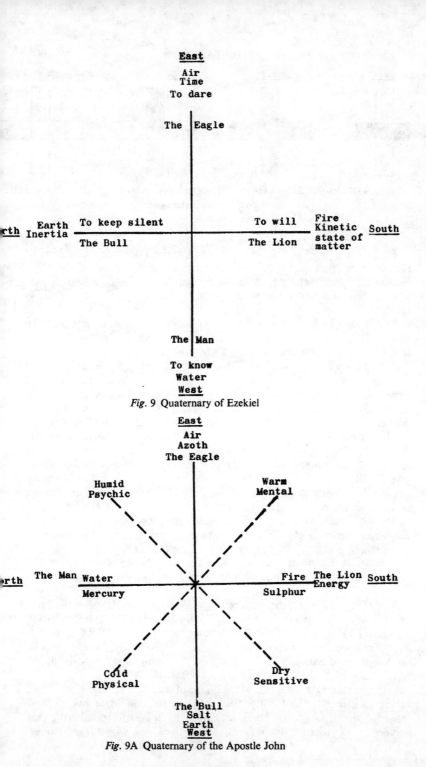

Fig. 9 Quaternary of Ezekiel

Fig. 9A Quaternary of the Apostle John

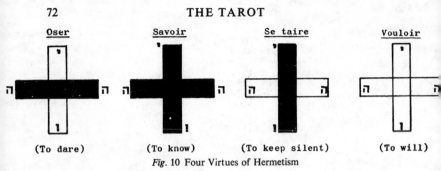

Fig. 10 Four Virtues of Hermetism

Then we use the *fourth* letter, the *second*, active (Hé) as a recognition of the perfected creation, the created family, and from this comes the symbolization of the essentially passive Hé (something made, or arisen), which immediately becomes *active because it begins the new cycle*, as *Yod did in the first one*.

This *tetragram* is known as the *Third Great Name* of Almighty God. To this name the Kabbalah ascribes miraculous power, under the condition that it will be *rightly pronounced*, which gives it the force of REALIZATION. In my various occult studies of different origin, I have encountered the statement, that so far, no known human being has been able to find the right pronunciation. It is said that the High Priest of the great temple of Jerusalem used the Highest Name in certain exceptional cases, but very seldom. To begin he said the first letter Yod, then the second, and so on, until the cycle was completed. Then he tried to read the whole tremendous *Word* from the beginning to the end. Despite the fact that nobody could record its true sound, some eighteenth-century authorities on the subject give 'YEHOVAH' as an approximate spelling, while others strongly oppose this, giving rather 'YEVE' or 'YAVE'. Personally, I have heard still another version, as given in the Eastern Church—'YAHVE'.

Anyway, when pronouncing the Great Name, the High Priest expressed the *full pattern of the elementary cycle* at the beginning, next the *androgyneity of humanity*, and finally, *its unity and the Law of that Unity*.

In order that laymen could not hear the Holy Name, the words of the priest were drowned by loud sounds from drum-like instruments.

According to Fig. 11, the cycle י ה ו ה (Yod-Hé-Vau-Hé) gives the same word in both directions of rotation of the quaternary's cross; but tradition recognizes the reading of the Tetragrammaton IN REVERSE, that is like '*Havayoth*', as an expression of the *realm of anarchy*, in other words, the kingdom of Satan. For that purpose the Name is not read from the *vertical* axis of Yod-Vau, but from the *horizontal* one.

In ceremonial magic any use of the Name in reverse is strongly forbidden, as bringing disaster to the operator and his surroundings; but in their repulsive rituals, so-called black magicians have been credited with that perversion, in order to obtain favours from the Devil, who allegedly likes,

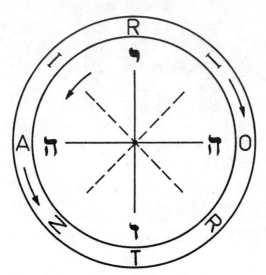

Fig. 11 The Circle of Ezekiel

above all else, to hear his own ominous name of Havayoth pronounced by his servants. So runs the old tradition.

Now imagine that our First Family, the first cycle Yod-Hé-Vau-Hé, begins to act upon, or create another element in the outer surroundings or the world. It simply means that one cycle, merely by the fact of its existence, gives rise to conditions for the production of another. It acts through its last element, that is the *second* Hé, which becomes an active principle, like the Yod of the first cycle. If we look on our cross of the quaternary, we will see that the aforementioned process is just the turning of the quaternary by 90 degrees in the so-called Hermetic circle.

The new cycle will again have its active and creative *second* Hé which in turn will seek another *passive* element Hé, and the whole process will be repeated again and again.

Now, coming from the theoretical Tetragrammaton to the world in which we have to spend our lives, I would like to underline the most important fact for every student of the Tarot: he MUST realize and understand the *Law of Four*, if he wants to achieve some success in his striving, or even, to form a firm and logical basis for his own inner philosophical conception, which may illumine his life on this plane.

Every clearly thinking mind will appreciate the *Great Law*, if only he has the opportunity to contact it. Moreover, there is no substitute for the Tetragrammaton. No other theory is able to give you such a clear and realistic conception. Of course, *not every mind is able to cope with this great idea*, which comes to us from the distance of many thousands of years, as a testament of those who lived long before us, and have left us the most precious thing they possessed: *their highest discovery of the basic truth of*

c*

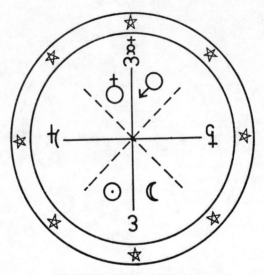

Fig. 12 The Circle of Pythagoras

manifestation. But, for those who know more, and for those who really want to know more, I say: If you are able to rule and to exclude all the functions of your lower principles—that is, your mind-brain and astral consciousness—then go beyond all manifestation and its laws. It is possible, for many have performed it, and so returned to the Inconceivable, Unknown FATHER, the Absolute, Alpha and Omega, Beginning and End, without qualities, timeless; beyond all good and evil, above all relativity. To THAT, about WHICH Buddha and Sankaracharya dreamed, in WHICH all saints hoped to find their final rest, and which was realized before our eyes, and for us, by the last Great Rishi of India—the Maharshi Ramana.

LESSON 10

In the previous lesson we saw that, in this manifested universe, the cycles of the quaternary may well stretch into infinity. Perhaps this is so, but our next problem is to go through some concrete examples of the functioning of the Law (Tetragrammaton).

(1) The first element is ׳ (Yod), father; the second ה (first Hé), mother; the third ו (Vau), child, while the fourth ה (Hé the second) is the influence of the whole family on another, which will be the fifth element; this influence generates common interests in both families (sixth element). United by these *common interests* a group of families (seventh element) acts upon another group of families, (eighth element), thereby creating solidarity between both groups, and so on. This is the general pattern for the creation of nations and states.

(2) Genius (1, י) fecundates (inspires) a scientist (2, ה), the latter accepts the 'descendant' of genius and thereby provides the possibility to create an androgynous real element (3, ו) which, from one side, accepts food from the scientist, but otherwise acts alone in the outer world and summarizes the activity of the whole cycle (4, ה) the very name of which will be: *passive intelligence* (ה) if it is ה, or *active intelligence* (י) if it is י of the next cycle and can fecundate its environment, which is able to accept the new cultural impulse (5).

(3) *Morning* (1, י) prepares and plans its daily business (2, ה); the results of the work show themselves in the *evening* (3, ו), which by the mysterious passage of night, serves as a starting point for plans and activities for the next day (4, ה).

(4) *Spring sowing* (1, י) is transformed by summer conditions (2, ה), gives fruit in autumn (3, ו), and by using collected reserves during the winter period, regulates its activities and passes on to the next spring (4, ה).

Each cycle of Initiation is divided into three phases according to the quaternary of the Hermetic Initiatory Circle.

In three symbolical degrees of the ethical, orthodox Masonry of Ashmoll and Fludd the Yod element is represented as the degree of the novice. In this degree a mason makes his utmost efforts in order to reach self-knowledge, the knowledge of darkness and ethical indolence of the layman. He incessantly tries for self-education and improvement. Such an active degree necessarily needs a lot of hard work. The very ritual of initiation for the novice has plenty of hints about errors, faults and sad, hard experiences.

As element ה (first Hé) in this initiation there appears the degree of Companion (Fellow), representing the realm of experience which becomes possible for the mason, who successfully passes through the first degree. A Companion is introduced into the society of those who have already passed through their initial difficulties, and he can then enjoy their brotherhood and kindness.

The ritual then symbolizes the pleasures of knowledge in general, and in particular, the bliss of friendship, mutual assistance and the tuition of experienced masters.

As element ו (Vau) there appears the master's degree, a man who already knows the character of life (activity) in the masonic society and who now has to become acquainted with the idea of death.

A Master-Lodge is a synthetic representative of the whole masonic family (second Hé), if we consider it from the point of view of its formation, or as a new Yod, if we evaluate its influence on the society.

LESSON 11

In returning to the enumeration of the elements of the *dynamic cycle* I have to mention that it is possible to consider ninefold cycles instead of just threefold ones, as we did previously. The place of the elements in such a cycle will be defined by the full ninefold calculation. For example, the 58th element in a row will be the fourth in its ninefold cycle; similarly, the 78th element will be sixth in its ninefold cycle, which means the ן (Vau) of the second family in the same cycle.

We may remember that these results can be obtained much faster by use of the well-known *arithmetic method* of adding the numbers of the elements:

$$5 + 8 = 13; 1 + 3 = 4$$
$$7 + 8 = 15; 1 + 5 = 6, \text{ and so on.}$$

Such calculations are called the *extraction of the theosophical root from figures*, and we will use them widely in our future lessons.

It may be added, that if we make a theosophical addition for any chosen number, the results will be as follows:

(1) If, in using the threefold method, the number was equal to zero (or 3), its theosophical sum, according to the same method, will also be equal to zero. This means that the *ternary always remains a ternary*.

(2) If the number was equal to 1, according to the triple system, then its theosophical sum will also be equal to 1. Unitary remains unitary.

(3) If the number was equal to 2 according to the same threefold method, its theosophical sum will also be equal to 3 (or zero). This means that, after synthesis, a binary does not remain as such, but *is neutralized into a ternary*.

These theorems are easy to check, but we will limit ourselves to only three examples:

(a) $1 + 2 + 3 + 4 + 5 + 6 = \dfrac{7 \times 6}{2} = 21 = 3$ (threefold method)

(b) $1 + 2 + 3 + \ldots 16 = \dfrac{17 \times 16}{2} = 136 = 10 = 1$ „ „

(c) $1 + 2 + 3 + \ldots 20 = \dfrac{21 \times 20}{2} = 210 = 3$ „ „

So, the *6* was a ternary, the *16* a monad, and *20* a binary.

Realizing that the quaternary is a general pattern for all elementary dynamic processes, we may pass on to the explanation of the cross, which is an example of man's active and passive manifestations on the astral plane.

The *vertical arm of the cross*, connecting letter י (Yod) with ן (Vau) is divided into two parts by the central point. The *upper part* is, of course, more active (י is more active than ן), and we will consider it as a realm of positive human acts, or sphere of GOOD. The *lower part* will represent negative activities, or the realm of EVIL.

An Initiate must, in every moment of his life discriminate well between both realms, and *always to hold himself in the middle*, in the neutral point of the centre of the cross. This is most important and a mystical application of Hermetic truths for everyone.

It is *knowledge of good and evil in deeds*.

Amazingly enough, this graphical conception is not too hard to realize practically, if the student will only give some time to this matter in his meditations.

Coming to the *horizontal part of the cross*, we will also divide it into two parts, referring both to the realm of the passive influxes in man. The right side, that is the ה (second Hé) which can be transformed into the active י (Yod) has priority over the left one, and will be considered as a receiver of GOOD influences.

Similarly, the left side signifies EVIL influences. The Initiate must in every moment clearly distinguish between both sides and always try to remain in the CENTRE, knowing it to be the NEUTRAL point.

Now, the explanation of the cross can be given in such a way: Man, who has reached the wisdom of the arcanum of authority (that is the *Fourth* of the Tarot), should not only understand how to discriminate between good and evil in his own deeds, but also to realize *how to use good and evil influences alike*. Anger and gratitude, for example, should be used equally as factors of activity, while pleasure and disappointment should be used as means of appeasement.

The mystical authority of Man is based on the fact, that he should stand in the *centre of the Hermetic Cross*, then being present in all its elements, and so become the master of them, as is the case with the central point which belongs to all of the cross.

We will continue with the analysis of the quaternary. The element י (Yod) is connected with what tradition calls AIR; the first ה (Hé) with EARTH; ו (Vau) with WATER, and the second ה with FIRE. The Ancients called these four terms the *Elements of the Quaternary*. We will see their explanation on different planes.

On the *metaphysical* plane, AIR means TIME; WATER means SPACE; EARTH, INERTIA of matter, and FIRE, the KINETIC state of matter.

On the *astral* plane, AIR tells us about the necessity for every Initiate *to dare*; EARTH reminds us about the art of *silence*; WATER the necessity of *knowledge*, and FIRE gives hints on the ability *to desire, to try*.

Fig. 10 shows the whole scheme to us graphically as it is accepted by modern Hermetists. The vertical arms of the crosses mean the desire for activity, while the horizontal ones, the passive receiving of influences. In other words:

WHO DARES thereby suppresses feelings of danger in himself (represented by the black arm) and stimulates activity (white vertical arm of the cross).

WHO KNOWS is satisfied with his wisdom and does not learn more (two black arms).

WHO IS SILENT is not active, and does not reveal his activities, but accepts everything that comes his way (vertical black and white horizontal arms).

WHO WANTS is both active and passive at once. One should know what he desires (both arms white).

On the *physical* plane we explain the four elements as four different
states of matter:

$$\begin{aligned} \text{EARTH} &= \text{THE SOLID STATE} \\ \text{WATER} &= \text{THE FLUID STATE} \\ \text{AIR} \quad\; &= \text{THE GASEOUS STATE} \\ \text{FIRE} \quad &= \text{THE RADIANT STATE} \end{aligned}$$

Now the old formula of the occult classics will be clear to us: *Man has a
body composed of all the four elements; he is a synthetic being; he knows
the four arms of the Cross.*

Elementals will obey the authority of a WELL-BALANCED MAN
(that is a sage). They know neither good nor evil, for they are not standing
in the centre of the Cross, but *only on its arms.* Sylphs are in the air, ondines
in water, gnomes in the earth, and salamanders in fire (or rather in the
radiant state of matter).

Their bodies are composed of the elements in which they live. They melt
into these, and that is why we cannot see them with our physical eyes, or
hear them with our ears, unless they manifest themselves in a mediumistic
way. Then we can understand and communicate with them, by means of our
usual physical sense organs. These elementals direct the physical and
chemical processes in matter; so practically we ARE in steady contact
with them, usually without being aware of the fact.

In alchemy, according to the quaternary י ה ו ה (Yod-Hé-Vau-Hé),
the term AIR corresponds to the Universal Solvent AZOTH, with its
sign of a triple caduceus surmounted by an eagle's wings.

The term for WATER corresponds to that of MERCURY, which can
be obtained from liquid mercury. Its sign is ☿. In Hermetism, Azoth
is often called the 'Mercury of Sages or Philosophers', but, of course, we
should bear in mind that this 'Mercury' cannot be obtained from the metal
known as mercury.

To the EARTH corresponds SALT. The sign being ⊖. While the term
FIRE corresponds to SULPHUR, with the sign ♀.

In general Hermetism, that is in the *astral* analogy of alchemy on the
physical plane, steadiness in realization is attributed to *Salt*; to Sulphur
belongs the depth of *prayer*, or any other form of concentration; to *Air*
(Azoth) corresponds subtlety of *feelings* and understanding of surrounding
conditions, and to *Mercury* belongs the development of full *consciousness*
on the astral plane.

Astral Hermetism and physical alchemy are the *components of the problem,
known as the Great Operation*, which is symbolized by the Nineteenth Major
Arcanum of the Tarot. This problem can be explained as the process of
transmutation (change) of a dense state of matter into that of a finer one,
without any alteration in its basic properties on the plane to which it
actually belongs. So in alchemy, the *Great Operation* occupies itself with the
transmutation of common metals into precious ones, such as scraps of
lead being changed into gold. As can be seen, the original state of the
substance was not changed into a different one. It remained a metal, as it
was before the operation. Only some of its qualities were changed.

In astral Hermetism details differ, but the principle remains the same. Here the problem is: how to change an immoral man of low standing, into a being which, without losing its general qualities a as man, will become an evolutionary one, conscious of his dignity and the purpose of his incarnation.

Of course, every transmutation is based on the principle of the realization of unitary theories in our surroundings, which are the object of the action. If scraps of lead can be changed into gold, it may happen only because all physical elements are actually variations of the same unique and indivisible matter of the physical world.

If we can transmute a stupid man into a wise one, it will happen only because the basic constitution of both is identical; but the disposition of the components in the astral world underwent innumerable changes in the course of many incarnations. Hermetism says that in the perfect man, all things are *in order*, which in an imperfect person are still in a state of confusion.

There still remains the question of dividing the horizon's directions according to the Law ה ו ה י. The *East* belongs to Yod; the *South* to second Hé; *West* to Vau and *North* to first Hé. This pattern is based on the movement of the Sun, which is called 'reversed'.

The *Holy Animals* of the Bible, according to tradition, can be assigned with the Eagle to the East and to Air; the Bull to the North and to the Earth; Man to the West and to Water, and the Lion to the South and to Fire. By this means we will obtain a mirror-like reflection of the scheme given in Chapters I and X of the Book of the Prophet Ezekiel.

This so-called *quaternary of Ezekiel* is very important because it finds its application in the operations of evocations (right hand movement in the circle) and in conjurations (the reverse movement).

A second example given by the Apostle St John in the IVth Chapter of the Book of Revelations, shows us another reflection, which differs from the previous one by the shifting of two elements. In it the Bull and Earth belong to the West, and Man to Water and the North. This second scheme allows us to establish some separate mysterious attributes such as: humid-dry and warm-cold. In this way air is considered as humid and warm, water as humid and cold, earth as cold and dry, and fire as hot and dry. All these conceptions are used in alchemy and astrology (see Figs. 11 and 12).

LESSON 12

The Fourth Major Arcanum teaches us about the unique, self-conscious Force, existing in Man and in Nature, which is able to realize itself outwardly, that is to take a FORM.

Now we come to the exposition of the *Great Arcanum of Magic*. The classical definition of a MAGIC OPERATION, according to Prof. G. O. M. is:

'*A decision of the Human Will (single or collective) exercised in order to solve a problem, the carrying out of which depends upon the activities of individualized beings, operating on two or three planes.*'

For clarity, I would like to exclude from this definition such normal, everyday pursuits as reading, studying, professional occupations, scientific research, trade, and so on, which are based on a definite pattern, and accessible to anyone who learns them from the official sources of human knowledge, which are open to all through the medium of educational manuals and standard techniques.

EXAMPLES OF MAGIC OPERATION:

(1) Self-persuasion on a definite theme, or by the magician influencing himself while living on three planes (action on his solar plexus, and so on).

(2) Suggestion directed to another man (again on three planes).

(3) The acceleration or delaying of some processes in the elements (also influencing three planes), such as dealing with elementals.

(4) Evocation of an elementar, living on two planes, but which can manifest itself, according to the magician's will, on the third or physical plane, by mediumistic means.

(5) The search for and the finding of an astral *cliché* (two planes); or exteriorization of the magician himself, that is influencing elementars by the power of our own individuality (two planes).

If a magic operation is performed on two planes (Egregors, elementars, larvas, and so on) then even by the equality of powers on the astral from the side of the magician and his subjects, it will be successful only because of his superiority when acting on *three planes*. It is very important to note this as it will explain many kinds of magic operations, which otherwise are hard to understand.

In such a case it is accepted, that the person acting uses as his starting point of realization, just the third, that is, the physical plane. It can be the body of the operator himself, or outer objects.

From the definition of magic operation we can see that there are *three active elements* in its components:

1. MENTAL, that is the idea of the operation and the necessary effort of will.

2. ASTRAL, that is the form of the operation.

3. PHYSICAL, or starting point, such as: realized symbols, physical development of the operator and persons assisting him all of whom are living on three planes, and so on.

In the previous lectures we analysed the unitary theories. Now I have to stress the fact, that we must also consider the mental, astral and physical elements of all magic operations as personal manifestations of the SOLE MENTAL ORIGIN (or beginning), that is the unique metaphysical axiom of the unique astral formation (or of the universal astral tourbillon), and of the unique physical method of *choosing the starting point*. Here the mental start must generate the astral form, and the latter, in turn, must define the very physical process, by the inevitable way of its condensation. IN MAGIC, THIS UNITARY CONNECTION BETWEEN

THE METAPHYSICAL AXIOM, ASTRAL TOURBILLON
AND PHYSICAL METHOD IS CALLED '*THE GREAT
ARCANUM*'.

Of course, we should not confuse it with the arcana of the Tarot. The
Great Arcanum, as a final mystery of the maximum of human power is
never *communicated* to his pupils by the Master. There are some reasons
for this which we can understand and express in words:

(1) If the pupil has not discovered and mastered the Great Arcanum for
himself, it means that he is not yet sufficiently developed on some of the
planes, and therefore there is no guarantee that showing him the relevant
techniques and theories will not be dangerous for the initiate and his
surroundings.

(2) The very character of the Great Arcanum is based on the element of a
subjective understanding and realization. This is clear, if we are able to
realize that our *spiritual monads* have different roles as cells of the COL-
LECTIVE, COSMIC MAN. They are just like different colours and
tones. Moreover, our *astrosomes* differ and are subject to different planetary
influences. Also, our *physical bodies* vary greatly between themselves.
Therefore, any initiation into the Great Arcanum by way of outer explanations and commentaries will never free a man from the hard and long
labour of assimilation of the given pattern, and of its application according
to his abilities and conditions of existence on all the three planes.

I hope that my efforts here to convey the cause of the deep mystery
connected with the Great Arcanum have been well enough explained. What
I now have to say about it, is only a logical development of the definition
of the Arcanum.

The Great Arcanum, as with every other magic operation, must itself
possess a *mental counterpart*. This means that the operator should be fully
able to realize the general outline of the operation. In other words, things
must be quite clear to him in case any apparition—no matter which kind
of entity—might come into contact with him. He must KNOW its origin,
or, as Kabbalists say, to understand the marriage of every ׳ (Yod) and ה
(Hé) in the mental plane. The key to this understanding gives us the
Great Law of the Ternary.

This law may be represented by the graphic scheme of the Great Arcanum
giving the construction as shown in Figs. 13, 14 and 15.

The *mental* part of the Arcanum, or marriage of ׳ and ה (Yod and Hé),
which are WILL and CONSCIOUSNESS, will give birth to its
astral part, and this is the *mystery of the basic tourbillon* or the ו (Vau) of
this marriage. According to all authoritative, classical tradition, I am
compelled to express such things in symbols, for there *is no other way* out
of this problem. Whoever is able to see through it, is by that fact ripe
enough for the great task. Otherwise, the safety-valve of the aspirant's
insufficient development must perform its work by veiling the technical
knowledge which is extremely dangerous for unripe people when conveyed
to them prematurely. Competent students—already acquainted with
occultism to a certain degree—will surely see for themselves, that in this

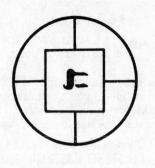

Fig. 15

THE GREAT ARCANUM OF MAGIC

Fig. 14

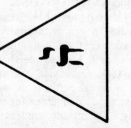

Fig. 13

book there are things *which cannot be found in other manuals*; *but the limit cannot be transcended.*

Further, in the analysis of the Second Arcanum, we already mentioned that the astral vortex (tourbillon) is dual-polarized. Apart from that, it *also defines the passage* from the mental to the physical and the reverse. *In it lies* the universal mystery of evolution and involution, which are such burning questions for so many thinking and seeking human beings.

Graphically, the picture takes the form in Fig. 14 (two interpenetrating triangles); its number will be TWO (2), as in the metaphysical counterpart it was THREE (3) (Fig. 13 (triangle)).

When condensing themselves, astral vortexes of the general type, lead us into the realm of the elements, that is into the physical world, mystically connected with the realization of the Fourth Arcanum.

The method for the realization of authority over the elements will be the second ה (Hé) in the dynamic process of the Great Magic Arcanum. In the physical world it will manifest itself as the knave, representing the activity of the family י ה ו (Yod-Hé-Vau). The corresponding Figure is No. 15 (a square in a circle). Here we see power over the elements (a cross inside a circle with the mystery of its turning in the Hermetic Circle), and the result of the application of that power, represented in one of the three dimensions of the CUBE which is symbolized by the square. Its number will be FOUR (4).

The general picture of the Great Arcanum will then be, as we have already said, the conception of the three Figs. 13, 14 and 15.

Its upper part (Fig. 13) is the *Ternary* of the Great Metaphysical Arcanum; the middle part (Fig. 14) is the *Binary* of the astral Rota (tourbillon), and the lower part (Fig. 15) is the *Quaternary* of the elementary Rota, or the mystery of its realization, the secret of the STARTING POINT.

(a) Discovery of the UPPER PART depends upon the fullness of incarnation in Man's spiritual monad, which KNOWS from the beginning of the manifestation of the secret of the mystical marriage of י (Yod) with ה (Hé) = ה י.

(b) To possess the MIDDLE PART Man must create in himself the astral androgyne ו (Vau).

(c) For operation of the LOWER (physical) PART, apart from the realization of (b), or authority over the astral ו (Vau), Man must know which instrument is the starting point of the operation, and WHICH IS THE TRANSITION FROM THE INSTRUMENT TO THE TOURBILLON ITSELF.

To perform this, pure logic may be of some use to us. Mentally annihilate the present universe as it exists for you, but retain in your mind the attributes of the Whole. In any new conception of the macrocosm and microcosm apply the Great Arcanum's scheme, and you will see that its instrument did not change at all.

Now, 'diminish' the universe and continue the process until only the operator himself remains in it. He is also a microcosm, so apply the Great

Arcanum to him. But, now the sole remaining instrument will be only the operator's own body.

This knowledge is not sufficient. It is only a lower floor of the whole construction. We may use as a symbol and means of explanation, the old story of King Oedipus. He met the Sphinx, who posed him the riddle of the realizer of the Tarot's Fourth Arcanum, who in the morning goes on *four* legs, at midday on *two*, and in the evening on *three*. What is the Sphinx? Only a synthesis of the four Holy Animals. It has the head of a man, the claws of a lion, the wings of an eagle and the waist and tail of a bull. These animals, by their qualities, tell us about *entrance into the astral plane via the elements*, which they represent. Here we may recall our earlier discussion about these FOUR creatures.

The Sphinx is also the ASTRAL. It guards the Pyramid, at the base of which is the square of the elements; its sides being identical with the mental evolutionary triangles, meeting together at the apex to show the Unitary Law. Otherwise, the mental plane guards the astral.

What did Oedipus reply? His answer to the Sphinx was: 'Thy enigma is Man, in childhood crawling on all fours, in maturity on two legs, and in old age on three, using a walking-stick for support.'

But he discovered and solved only the *physical part of the Arcanum*, which is what the rest of mankind is doing. By this he possessed power over the Sphinx's body, and as the victor destroyed it. What happened later?

The *astral binary* revealed to him, that he had not yet realized that part of the Arcanum. The negatively polarized part of the astral tourbillon led him to the terrible murder of his own father and to incest (by marrying his own mother). These disasters could not be avoided by knowledge of only the physical plane.

Then suffering entered his own astral, and he received the final peace only through the mental part of the Arcanum, the Mystery of the Universal Love, in the form of the sacrifice of his daughter Antigone.

Your attention is drawn to the fact that the *astral initiation* came to Oedipus at maturity, but the *mental* one was achieved only in his old age.

It is accepted that the first letters or the whole of the following group of words can be placed in the picture of the Great Arcanum:

    (1) ALPHA-OMEGA, ALEPH-THAN, A-Z
          AZOTH

    (2) TARO or ROTA

    (3) INRI

(1) The first group of letters is composed of the initials of the three alphabets: Greek (Alpha), Hebrew (Aleph) and Latin (A), which differ little in their writing, and of the three final letters (Greek Omega, Hebrew Than and Latin Z). This symbolizes the Cosmic Synthesis and is the sign for the schools of alchemy.

(2) The second group of words used to be a symbol for the Eastern Initiation and Tradition, although one can hardly see a reason for it; but it must be

given here, as it has been a part of the Great Arcanum since time immemorial. These words should be developed into: TARO, ROTA,
TORA, OTAR, AROT and in some magic operations, which have a
peculiar form of the passage from the physical base of operation to the
astral vortex (tourbillon), they are inscribed into the five ends of the pentagram, facing the eyes of the magician.

(3) On the *mental* plane we read INRI as:
IESUS NAZARENUS REX IUDEORUM
(the Latin inscription on Christ's cross)

On the *astral* plane it will be:
IGNE NATURA RENOVATUR INTEGRA

This means: all Nature is regenerated by fire. Of course, *fire* here has an
esoteric meaning, as was explained at the beginning of this arcanum. The
true Rosicrucians—who, about 200 years ago, ceased to exist as an active
and initiatory organization—had INRI as their motto (shibboleth).

The three formulas just given are used to represent the scheme of the
Great Arcanum in which we already saw י ה ו ה (which serves as the
Kabbalistic key to the Arcanum), and they show the unique aim, unique
aspiration, unique desire, and unique realization sought equally by
Kabbalists (י ה ו ה), *Alchemists* (AZOTH), the *Egyptian Tradition* (contained in the TAROT), and finally, by the teachings of Christian Illuminism and Esoterism—INRI. All these ways lead to the Great Arcanum.

But what of the Eastern Tradition, based on ancient Indian Initiatory
occult philosophy? Has it no part in the perennial search by Man for his
eternal HOME, that forgotten and lost spiritual fatherland to which leads
the Great Arcanum of the Hermetic Tradition? Of course it HAS! For
those who are acquainted with the depths of Advaita-Vedanta there cannot
be any doubt about it. For those who have no connection with this peak
of the ancient Aryan Vedantic Initiation I would like to say, that the great
idea of Vedanta, *the realization of Man's true being or ultimate SELF*, is
just the Great Arcanum, to which the exposition of the Fourth Trump of
the Tarot was partially dedicated. There is a considerable difference between
the two methods, which by no means makes them any the less valuable.

(1) The thing is, that each human race, as has already been said, possesses
its own form of symbolism and teachings. The West created the complicated—although very successful and practical—Hermetic philosophy, which
you are now studying in this book as the Tarot. In it you find a lot of
symbols, signs, secret formulas, and the still more mysterious depths of the
ways leading to the conquest of the three worlds (I hope that by now the
reader has already arrived at this conception for himself, when thinking
about the aims of Hermetism).

(2) It is different in Vedanta. Its peaks are for those who have already been
initiated into the mysteries (and knowledge of them) of the two higher
planes of existence—the astral and mental ones. Advaita seems to leave the

lower, preparatory degree to yogas and other methods, which are often of a purely religious character.

Therefore the true Masters of the Hindu Tradition do not use the means given in (1). The simplicity of their teachings can be compared only to the ultimate simplicity of the UNIQUE and REAL THING, the sole aim of the Great Arcanum. You may call IT as you wish: God, Cosmic Mind, Spirit, Pleroma, Supreme Self, it will always be the same, *simply because there is not and cannot be anything else.* This statement is based on a higher power than mind (Intuition), and therefore it cannot be realized by those, who have not yet touched the higher consciousness of the plane of INTUITION, or *Spirit-Atman-Self.*

But the *ultimate aim* of both Traditions is the same, and never was or will be different. Some men must pass through one or another form of initiation, for each man reflects differently, according to the Tarot as well as Vedanta, the same UNIQUE LIGHT OF THE CONSCIOUSNESS OF THE WHOLE, OF THE ARCHETYPE, OF GOD, OF PAR-ABRAHM.

The last initiating Master of Vedanta (the Great Rishi, in Hindu terminology) was Sri Ramana Maharshi of Tiruvannamalai (South India), who died in 1950, leaving to posterity, his modern exposition of the old Truth, already known throughout the whole world. The writer had the privilege to sit at the feet of this last Messenger of Truth.

It now remains for us to perform the numerical part of the initiation as given in the Fourth Arcanum of the Tarot.

Equation No. 6: $4 = 3 + 1$

A new cycle of creation or manifestation (4) appears when a new impulse (1) is added to the already existing FIRST FAMILY (3).

Equation No. 7: $4 = 1 + 3$

When a new and active impulse (1) associates itself with the chosen accomplished FORM (3), the result will be a new phase of creation.

As you may see, there is no essential difference between the ideas which come from the *reversed equation.* Therefore I will not give any further explanations of both. The student should investigate the other forms for himself.

Equation No. 8: $4 = 2 + 2$

Second (active) Hé (4) is balanced in itself as two elements, one active and the other passive, to create the perfect equality of plus and minus, thus allowing things to remain as they are. It is the stable form of creation, thought, forms and worlds. Matter and energy are manifested equally in the solar system and in the whole universe, blending into one another, and creating the seeming differences between them, but, for the initiate, always remaining the same UNITY. When to an apparently constant system in the Great Space, there is added some new and active impulse (Yod), stars and planets may collide and the destruction may then be observed in the infinities of the universe; but of course, only for a time.

When some of our body cells escape the central control normally exercised in a certain way by the astrosome, this may create a serious danger for the whole of the body in the form of malignant growths, and so on.

As the numbers of the Arcana grow, the number of the possible equations will also increase. We will give here only the most essential ones, leaving the student to perform the necessary training himself, by analysing the *further development and possibilities* connected with the numerical evaluation of the Major Arcana. It will supply him with the necessary mental exercise and thereby, development, which is a condition for the successful study of this book.

П

Arcanum V
MAGISTER ARCANORUM
THE GREAT HIEROPHANT

♈
Aries

Magnetismus Universalis
Quintessentia
Religio

CHAPTER V

ARCANUM V (ה HÉ)

THE scientific name of the Fifth Arcanum of the Tarot is *'Magister Arcanorum'* (Teacher of the Arcana); also, the *Great Hierophant*, and the vulgar name is—*the Pope*.

The Hebrew letter is ה (Hé), the numerical value 5, and the hieroglyph is *Breathing* (the symbol of life).

The picture for the Fifth Arcanum is a seated man, in the robes of a high priest. His head is crowned with the two horns of Isis, with a full moon between them. This *binary of horns* is dominated by the Cross of the Great Hierophant, on the end of the sceptre which he holds in his left hand, so that the Cross is much higher than his head. The right hand is stretched above the heads of two figures kneeling before him. This is the sign of blessing, sometimes considered a *mute one* and then it is a symbol of the initiatory Silence. Sometimes the Hierophant expresses the blessing *in words*. In any case, this gesture is a sign expressing WILL. One of the two kneeling figures is white and the other black.

Like the woman of the Second Arcanum, he sits between two columns (Jakin and Bohaz). Here, as in the other arcanum, there is the *binary* of the *columns*, neutralized, in this case, by the man's figure. He is seated, a hint on passivity (the absorption of the wisdom of the binary); but he is still a MAN, that is he is at the same time basically an ACTIVE symbol (putting knowledge into practice in life).

This element of the *enlightened will-power*, of the *active* authority will be the *basic idea* of this Fifth Arcanum, representing the most mysterious sign—the human PENTAGRAM (Fig. 16).

The *ternary* of the Great Hierophant's Cross dominating the *binary* of horns gives us an important hint, so full of meaning: HERE THE PENTAGRAM IS UPRIGHT, that is WITH THREE POINTS UPPERMOST. You already know about the significance of its position.

All these conditions as expressed in symbols on the card of the Fifth Arcanum remind us about INITIATION. Indeed, who would be the giver of initiation, if not our symbolical Great Hierophant?

The two kneeling figures tell us that the PENTAGRAM—here the MASTER OF MAGIC—is triumphant, together with all the powers of Light, even over the forces of Darkness, compelling them to serve his GOOD aims. He wisely uses their temporary ignorance and the weakness arising from it. An intelligent use of even the actual weaknesses will allow them to reach the necessary karmic redemption, or liberation much earlier.

Returning to the symbolism of the Fifth Arcanum, I will say that *'breathing'* in this material, dense life, means the presence of the vital processes in organisms. From this is derived another title for this arcanum—THE LIFE. According to astrology, the corresponding symbol will be the Zodiacal *sign of the Ram*. When the Sun is in the sign of the Ram, then we know that it is the FIRST month of spring. And spring is Yod's element in the yearly Solar Cycle, it is that which prepares life, as the FIRST breath of that LIFE.

Those readers who are more acquainted with Hermetism may now pose me one or two reasonable questions:

(1) In the formula of the *Dynamic processes* or י ה ו ה (Yod-Hé-Vau-Hé) the ה (Hé) signifies the *female* principle. So what is there in common between the female origin and—Life?

(2) Why is the Second Arcanum ב (Beth) considered to be a *female* principle, and why is it connected with the Fifth Arcanum? What is the difference in colouring of both arcana?

The first question will be answered by a short venture into the realm of Christian Theosophy, the earlier centuries (fourteenth and fifteenth) as well as the more recent ones (sixteenth, seventeenth and eighteenth centuries).

If, for every *dynamic cycle* י ה ו ה (Yod-Hé-Vau-Hé) a continuation for it can be found, coming from its SECOND Hé, which becomes the Yod of the next cycle, then the picture may well be reversed and the Yod of our primary cycle can therefore be imagined as the SECOND Hé of some former cycle. Any search for the elements of that earlier cycle will be an ASCENDING process in the chain of causality and must lead us to the cognition of a Yod belonging to the preceding, older order of things. And then the same question might well arise again and again. The FIRST cycle in the chain of causality, or otherwise, the *First Family* of the quaternary type (the student already knows this expression) cannot consider itself as absolutely independent, that is not having any prior elements in the former dynamic processes. This is because THE BEGINNING OF ALL BEGINNINGS CANNOT HAVE YOD AS A NAME because the latter is always an *active principle*, vitalized by the desire of the necessity of fecundation; BUT THE ABSOLUTE BEGINNING as we said before, MUST POSSESS THE ATTRIBUTE OF ALL-CONTENTMENT AND SELF-SUFFICIENCY. This absolutely *primary Principle* must be androgynous, neutral, enclosing in IT all the elements of the dynamic processes to which IT may give birth.

In order to be clear and to symbolize this BEGINNING we will place a POINT over the י (Yod) of the FIRST quaternary of the transcendental realm. This point will remind us about:

THE GREAT, THE INACCESSIBLE, THE INFINITELY HOMOGENEOUS, THE PERFECTLY ENLIGHTENED, THE RADIANT BEGINNING, AINSOPH, PARANIRVANA, THE ABSOLUTE and finally, THE UNIVERSAL SELF OR ATMAN.

This inaccessible Beginning, which CANNOT be an object of any mental speculation or investigation, MANIFESTED Himself as the male element Yod, the fecundating principle, expansive, radiant, to which we can give the symbol—UNIVERSAL LOVE.

This Universal Love had limited the Passivity, the Attraction, the Female origin of shadowy character, the so-called 'Restrictio', and fructified it. From the marriage of these principles, the Highest Yod and the Highest Hé, is born the element Vau of the First Family. Its name is— LOGOS. The first emanations of this element will become the SECOND Hé of the First Family and will lead us into the transcendental world *Olam ha Aziluth* of the SECOND Family. So why did the Life appear as the female element? The famous *Tritemius* (1462-1560) explained his Rosicrucian theories in this way, that the Yod of the First Family was called *Super-Essential Fire*, Hé *Super-Essential Air*, and the Logos *Super-Essential Light*. So we see that Air and Breath are identical with the female element. The terminology of the first and true Rosicrucians regarded the Holy Trinity similarly, and *Fire* was the first person, *Air* the third, and *Light* the second one. The Kabbalistic transcendental world of the FIRST quaternary was also called: SPIRITUS MUNDI (Spirit of the World).

In the second question, the *Beth Arcanum* (Absolute Being, beyond the limits of individuality) points to the female principle, as something existing and corresponding to the male principle. Something which should be learned (Gnosis or knowledge), necessary for the development of the whole of the Major Arcana.

In the Fifth Arcanum Hé is the *form* which accepted the 'Beth' Arcanum (human soul). Beth represents the realm of the female principle, and Hé fills this realm with existence in form.

We know that the higher the numbers of the arcana, the more concrete becomes their meaning. Beth has the *throat* as its hieroglyph, and Hé is just the *breath* which comes from that throat.

Now we may pass to the numerical analysis of this arcanum.

Equation No. 9: $5 = 1 + 4$

Equation No. 10: $5 = 4 + 1$

These give us the titles of the essence of this arcanum in all three regions of the Theosophical Ternary. So, for the *Archetype*, 1 means the Divine Essence, and 4 the basic necessity of a form. The radiant element of the Divine Essence shows us the choice of the *positive* pole for the valuation of mental activities. Forms not spoiled by their irregular reflection and refraction become synonymous with *Good*, and when the forms are corrupted, only with *Evil*.

So we have a new title: *Magnetismus Universalis*, or *Scientia Boni et Mali*.

In the human world, 1 can be interpreted as *Vir* (Man), the active and fecundating principle (Cosmic Consciousness); and 4 as elements from which the human body is constructed, also as *Auctoritas*, the secret of ethical rule in the centre of the Cross (quaternary). In both cases, the fifth element is mysteriously added to the *four primary principles* existing in the outer world, directing their transformation and giving the possibility for realization of the *Great Action*.

In alchemical terms this principle will be called QUINTESSENTIA, and this is the *second title* of this arcanum.

Realization of Matter must be fourfold, therefore, we have four elements here. On the plane of Nature we will find the title of the Fifth Arcanum providing we are able to see through the outer manifestations of the four elements which belong to the Fourth Arcanum, the element of NATURA NATURANS of the First Arcanum added to the Fourth. Whoever by deep concentration and meditation supported by right activity in the outer world, will see this unity beyond the limits of the outer *four*, will attain the *natural Religion:* his reward for contemplation and inner merging.

That is why the title of the Fifth Arcanum in the *kingdom of Nature* is— RELIGIO. If in dividing 5 into 1 and 4 we will accept 4 as the world of elements, and 1 as the higher Conscious Beginning, then the sum of 1 + 4 will symbolize Man, as master of the elements, and ruler of the impulses of his elementary nature. By placing 4 first, and 1 second, we obtain the reverse result, that is the formula of an impulsive man, whose manifestations depend upon the outer influences on his physical nature. We may see now how enlightening and exact the practical applications of knowledge of the Tarot can be, and how interesting, from the point of view of practical philosophy, are the operations with the numerical values of the arcana.

LESSON 14

We will now pass on to another way of analysing the Fifth Arcanum.

Equation No. 11: $5 = 3 + 2$

This means that the Fifth Arcanum is composed of the highest and middle principles of the Great Arcanum of Magic, that is, of the metaphysical ternary (3) and astral binary (2). From this point of view, our arcanum symbolizes the manifestation of some entities on two higher planes, beyond the physical, and here the metaphysical realization dominates the astral mechanism.

Here I would like to make some comments for the earnest student, who really wants to obtain profit from his study of the Tarot. The arithmological analysis of the arcana is of overwhelming importance for that purpose. Therefore, you should follow my statements with *full understanding*, solving the equations as given with your own mind and not only blindly and automatically accepting all that you see on these pages. The operations which we are now performing, are not to be found elsewhere, and they were especially constructed for the practical use of the Tarot.

According to the equation, the following types of beings are able to operate on two planes:

(1) A *white magician*, while working on the astral plane, even if he still uses the physical world as a base.

(2) An *elementar* of the positive type, which means that, in the period

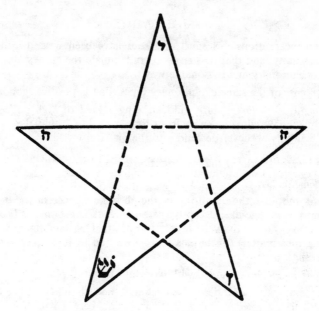

Fig. 16 Upright Pentagram (Symbol of White Magic)

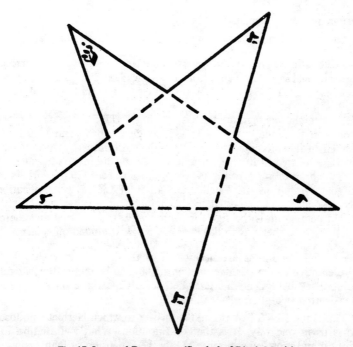

Fig. 17 Inverted Pentagram (Symbol of Black Magic)

between incarnations, his spirit and soul have been welded into a harmonious unity, and that he strives to contemplate the clichés around him in an evolutionary and reasonable way.

(3) *Egregors* of the same evolutionary types, that is positive (good) ones.

(4) *Spiritus Directores* (spirit guides) being a kind of high police of the astral plane. We already know from former chapters, that they are two-plane beings, who never descend into the physical worlds.

The reversed form of the last equation gives us:

Equation No. 12: $5 = 2 + 3$

This symbolizes the obscuring of the absolute essence of the triple law by means of mirage-like, deceptive astral clichés. This happens because of the presence and activity of involutionary (that is, tending to a deeper merging into matter) tourbillons (vortexes), and to them correspond the dark beings, like:

(1) *Black magicians* occupied with work on the astral plane.

(2) Those who seek after deceptive clichés of the negative types of elements. In particular, *elementars* who, in their period between incarnations are looking for a means to obtain a new physical body, not in order to better their karma, but for the pleasures of the life in flesh and blood, lost after their last physical death.

(3) *Egregors* of the negative or involutionary type.

(4) *Larvas* and similar astral scum, which fill the lower sub-planes.

The equations: No. 11: $5 = 3 + 2$ and No. 12: $5 = 2 + 3$ correspond to geometrical symbols of enormous theoretical and symbolical importance. These are PENTAGRAMS, in both their upright and inverted positions (see Figs. 16 and 17).

The straight pentagram, that is, having THREE points uppermost, belongs to the equation $5 = 3 + 2$, as given above and in traditional Hermetism it is accepted to fit a human figure into it, whose head and limbs are located in its five corners, while into the inverted pentagram is fitted the head of a goat, with its horns, ears and beard in the corners. Here the goat symbolizes the Devil, the Father of Lies, a personification of clichés spoiled and perverted to the point of non-recognition. While the upright pentagram is the sign for *white magic*, the inverted and therefore debased symbol belongs to black or *evil magic* (founded on egoism).

But what conditions are necessary for the man, who wishes to be a representative of the positive pentagram, and to belong to the category of evolutionary beings, no matter whether still incarnate on this earth, or after death a two-plane elementar?

(a) This is the FIRST question, the answer to which Hermetic philosophy shows us in one way. It is that of Initiation. What is Initiation in the broadest and most general sense? Only the expansion of man's consciousness, of his knowledge of the basic truths ruling over his life, of knowledge

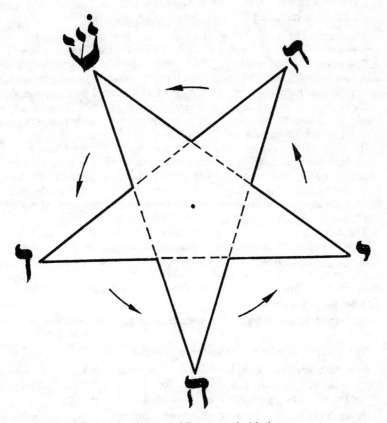

Fig. 18 Inverted Pentagram in Motion

about his own being, its possibilities, its destiny and the means for the realization of that destiny.

From this point of view we will begin our subsequent considerations, for there are also DIFFERENT points of view about man, his constitution and final aim; but they do not belong to the present work.

(b) The SECOND question asks: How to create the positive pentagram from available materials?

The solution of the *first problem* explains the description of the tests and experiences of those who are seeking Initiation (in the foregoing sense).

The answer to the *second* involves the methods of the general plan of astral and physical training, necessary for a magician. This term 'magician' is being used here because, according to Hermetic Tradition, the fully evolved pentagram means just the man who has attained power over the elements and astral currents, that is he is endowed with super-physical abilities, which make him a magician.

Initiation can be considered as having two sides: one for black, and the other for white magic. *White Initiation* creates in a man, a striving after good as his only aim, with complete disregard for his own comfort or discomfort. The *black* has as its object a man, who likes evil for the sake of evil itself, even to his own detriment, in the name of the sole principle of evil, lies and darkness.

The first degree of experience is similar for both white and black kinds of Initiation. Its aim is to test the equation in the candidate: $1 + 4$ means the ability of fearlessness before unexpected or dangerous things and events coming from the four elements. This means not to be cowardly in the physical realm, nor to lose one's head under any conditions. Here will be used traditional tests:

By *fire* (1), through which the disciple must pass without fear of being burned.

By *water* (2), swimming through rough sea or rivers.

By *air* (3), when the disciple must ascend to heights and look down from them with nothing but a few square feet to support him. Mountains, precipices or ships' masts are sometimes used for this purpose.

By *earth* (4), when a man enters narrow subterranean passages without knowing what awaits him at their end, or descends into unknown caves, and so on.

Apart from these traditional tests, I also find another kind very useful, which are aimed at the suppression of the so-called '*mystical fear*', such as night visits to lonely cemeteries, 'haunted' houses, and so on. This is because I have seen cases where a man has passed relatively easily through the four elementary tests, but still retained a fear of 'spirits', dead bodies and their final resting-places. Especially so as sometimes around fresh graves, the etheric double of the corpse may be visible on warm nights, even to physical eyes. From my own experience I have seen this phantom, devoid of all consciousness and otherwise utterly harmless for incarnate men, cause a nervous breakdown in more than one candidate. An initiate cannot possess such a weakness. Otherwise he should be eliminated while there is still time. Of course, the foregoing means only 'physical fear'.

The second degree of tests is similar in both types of Initiation. It is the ASTRAL experience for fear, lust and conscience.

(1) The candidate is faced with a monstrous astral cliché, aggressive and repulsive in its ugliness beyond all imagination. Some special methods are used in order to facilitate the contact of the pupil with the testing-ground in the astral world.

(2) After this comes the *test for lust* and passion. The candidate must be able to suppress sexual desire in himself, even under the most favourable conditions, when nothing stands in the way of the fulfilment of his desire. Here may be distinguished TWO separate phases of the test. The *first* for the ability to resist the approaching sexual pleasure. The *second* not to profit from the victory achieved by a man's own efforts over the negative attitude of the other sex, or her initial refusal to yield to his passion.

(3) The *third test*, for conscience, shows the ability on the part of the aspirant to fulfil any confidential order; to observe some law or instruction; to maintain silence about a secret; the non-betrayal of someone's personal intention; all this under conditions of full security and lack of any punishment in the event of failure, as well as in the presence of a great temptation.

If, in both schools of magic, that is white and black, these tests are outwardly similar, their inner character is very different.

A white magician has no need to fear any terrible clichés, just because he has to pass through their world towards the Principles of Light. The same applies to a black magician, but simply because he must be friendly with those dark and voluptuous manifestations.

A white magician must attain stamina in his wisdom in order to be certain of the impossibility of failure, while a black one must simply realize, that the ability of self-restriction in certain moments gives him a vital superiority over those who cannot restrain themselves.

The white must conscientiously fulfil his duties and accept obligations so as to achieve self-perfection and steadiness in the doing of good.

The black must simply understand that by persisting in a plan and not yielding to any circumstances he may be able to inflict more evil, ideologically as well as practically, than if he would act only occasionally and under favourable conditions. Black magicians still have to pass through some tests and take oaths for their faithfulness to Evil, which should not be described here.

LESSON 15

We will now consider the artificial pentagram, or the Great Sign of the Microcosm (the world in miniature). The pentagram is one of the magic symbols, as mentioned earlier.

In order to give you some idea of how symbols react on the astral beings, I would like to remind you, that our emotional, subjective world

D

may often be changed under the influence of forms, connected in one way or another with some definite emotional principles. A voice, picture, or object related to, for example, a manifestation of fear, often automatically produces that fear. The fearsome face and voice of an utterly unarmed and harmless being can frighten its enemy, who has previously seen and heard similar things in another being, which then successfully repulsed his attack.

The emotional world belongs completely to the astral realm, and that is why symbols, used for a long time by the magic schools or by the representatives of certain Egregors, are so important in the astral world.

Whoever knows of the power of the Cross in relation to Christians on this earth will not be astonished when he hears that this sign has a most powerful influence on elementals. For them the Cross is also connected with different emotional images. It reminds them about the fact of the synthetic construction of Man, his outer activity and that he is the king of the four elements. By this Man can dominate the elementals.

Just as on Earth, different ideas gradually lose their meaning, and others, take their place according to the development of human culture and civilization, so it is with the astral.

The world of symbols on the astral plane also underlies uninterrupted evolution. It would be too naïve to believe, that all the symbols of the ancient Egyptians have retained their former magical powers, and that NOW they are able to produce the same magic results. It is not because they have become too old or too much used, but without many additions and changes you are not able to get the same results as was formerly obtained from them thousands of years ago.

An example will explain best: the famous phalanx of King Philip of Macedonia would not frighten a contemporary battalion, yet it certainly would dispel a band of hooligans on the street, armed only with knives and black jacks. The student will do well if he tries to understand the analogy of this example.

Among the symbols we have to distinguish *simple* ones, which our Tradition does not break down into parts. They are: the *point*, the symbol of *unity*; the *circle* symbolizing the *finite*, the *union*; and the *triangle*, being a symbol for the *ternary*, and so on. But a collection (union) of some simple symbols is called a complex one. A syllable will be a simple symbol for a sound, while several syllables expressed together in turn will be a complex symbol.

If a complicated *graphic* symbol is a synthesis of some simple ones, its components—providing they give us a harmonious picture of united emotional images, connected by means of analogy with a synthetic metaphysical formula—it will be called a '*pentacle.*'

In the *symbolism of sounds*, the symbol which corresponds to a pentacle will be a sequence of syllables, forming a word or even a whole sentence. *An example of a pentacle* is the *pentagram*. In the mental plane it corresponds to the idea of FREE WILL.

In the *physical world* a representative of this WILL is the human body as formed by the astrosome: here the astrosome represents the pentagram, and its spirit manifests the Will.

We have already had an example of three pentacles united to form the picture of the Great Arcanum (Lesson 12). The image of the Holy Name (Yod-Hé-Vau-Hé) should be considered as a pentacle of the picture of the dynamic cycle's process. In the realm of sound, simple and complicated synthetic formulas are divided into two basic classes:

(1) MANTRAMS and (2) SETRAMS.

Formulas using MANTRAMS are destined for action on the astrosomes of beings other than the operator, even if such beings could belong to the operator as components of his collective 'I'. Therefore, every formula prepared by us for action on another man, elementar, elemental, and so on will be of the mantram class. For example, a formula used for the action of a man's own liver, in order to regulate its function, will be a *mantram*.

As opposed to a mantram, a SETRAM serves to fortify the astrosome of the *operator himself*, so as to control and to regulate the functions of the whole system of centres and ganglions of that astrosome, which system may play a role in the process of conducting the manifestation of a man's will from the mental plane into the physical world. These setrams offer the operator the self-assurance necessary for the performance of every magic operation.

In the matter of further deliberations on the pentagram, we will leave the question regarding the kind of materials from which pentagrams should be made until the Seventh Arcanum. Here we will isolate the PENTA-GRAM from all other pentacles, for it is the most important of all occult means for man's use, if employed wisely and supported by a strong will.

We must put our attention on the fact, that astral entities (that is those living on only TWO planes) possess only *astral* organs as a means of cognition of astrosomes, with whom they want to or are compelled to communicate.

In order to enter into contact and to become aware of the physical body of a man, the astral being can do so only temporarily, by means of borrowing and assimilation of certain fluids or vital force and subtle principles from persons called 'mediums'. Some organic substances also serve for this purpose when separated from living bodies, such as the juices of plants, saliva, blood, sperm, milk, perspiration, and so on. In some special cases this borrowing of the necessary materials for the astral beings can be effected by use of evaporating water, and smoke from burning substances like dried herbs, tar, and so on.

I have been able to test this *latter form* of assistance for helping the astral entities to manifest themselves in a visible and tangible way, by performing the ritualistic operations of Ceremonial Magic. I think they are best because of a lack of harm inflicted on other living beings, and the ease with which unwanted astral visitors can be removed *if they manifest by such a method*. The use of blood and other gross matter is provocation for the astral intruders to remain in contact with the physical world longer than required, as well as to disobey the orders of the operator.

When an astral entity borrows subtle matter from the body of a medium, it is able to create for itself (for a certain length of time) corresponding physical organs, and then it can see, hear, feel, and so on, just as we do. When these mediumistic accessories are lacking, an astral being cannot see a physical table, for example, but *only the astrosome of the table*, that is the idea used by its maker, and cannot hear spoken words, but only the formal essence of the components of each sentence. How then does it act?

(1) The astral entity can cognize and appreciate the amount of energy spent in giving the table a definite form, or for the pronouncing of a sentence.

(2) It clearly perceives all the transformation of the energy which acts in both of these processes, as well as the sequence and exact pattern of the transformation.

Such are the principles of astral 'seeing', which could be better defined as astral imbibition. Now, imagine an astral being looking at an incarnate man by means of only its astral sight. It will perceive a definite kind of energy-impression. Magic tradition tells us, that, in this case, the picture which the astral being sees will be very closely connected with the process of astral imbibition of the energetic manifestation of a pentagram, when made from seven metals, and also that this will be very little different from the impression made on the same astral being by a pentagram made from pure gold.

Some occult authors believe that it is useful to manifest the pentagram with the help of an electrophore, in the form of what we call electric illumination. From this point of view we see, that the pentagram not only serves to create the idea of the manifestation of FREE WILL, but gives to the astral beings the illusion of the presence of a LIVING MAN. That is why in this course, we consider ourselves entitled to call 'pentagrams', all beings which are related to the formulas:

$$\text{(a) } 5 = 3 + 2 \qquad \text{and} \qquad \text{(b) } 5 = 2 + 3.$$

You should already know the difference between these two signs.

LESSON 16

Now it is time to speak about astral fighting between two pentagrams (incarnate men), or the struggle of a man with an elementar or Egregor. The general rule is, that when two beings are fighting in the astral, the most important factor will naturally be the *astral powers* (activity and ability for passive imbibition).

(a) When the astral forces are equal, the superiority will rest with the one who possesses better support on the physical plane, in other words, who simply has a more robust body.

(b) If a magician is struggling with an elementar and his astral force is equal to that of his enemy, he will undoubtedly win, simply because of the fact that he possesses a physical body. If in that moment the magician is killed on the physical plane, the result of the fight with the elementar will be hard to forecast, because then their forces will be absolutely equal.

(c) If a strong magician—possessing a physical body (that is, is incarnate)—is far enough away from a planet, and knows enough about its weak points, it is possible for him to dominate the spirit of that planet for some time. On this are based all the Ceremonial Magic operations which use appropriate times and formulas for binding the spirit of a planet, which is proportionally weakened by its distance from its own physical body.

(d) Would you dare to try to subdue the spirit of the Earth in an operation performed on the surface of the Earth? But at the same time you may successfully dominate and command the spirits of, say, Saturn or Jupiter, in an operation performed *on the Earth*.

(e) A magician is much stronger in his ceremonial rituals when his astrosome has his physical body as a base, than when he is exteriorized in the astral plane, with only a weak liaison with his body.

(f) Of two magicians, equally strong in their astral development, the victor will be the one whose nervous system is the stronger.

(g) Even if these two factors are equal, the superiority will be on the side of the possessor of the better physical organs, and so on.

The aforesaid allows us to realize, why magicians place so great a meaning on the pentagram and we should not be astonished why this pentacle is so often used in masonic and magic lodges. For examples, the 'FIERY STAR' appearing in the old masonic rituals of the Companion's degree is a pentagram with the letter 'G' in it. For the Master that letter means GOD; for the middle degree—GNOSIS, and for the higher, so-called Hermetic degrees it is—GENERATIO (originating from Latin).

In explaining the pentagram in masonic symbolism we encounter it on seals of different degrees. Then we should be careful and not scared by its sometimes reversed position (that is $2 + 3$ formula) for this does not necessarily signify any black magic, but has a metaphysical meaning with a sequence in time. *Example*: First you will get binaries (2), then you will think and learn until the binaries become neutralized into ternaries (3).

In the solution of the equation $5 = 1 + 4$ there are different methods. Four is not always material, nor one spiritually-astral factors. In the great concentrated astral cliché יהשוה (Yod-Hé-Shin-Vau-Hé) Yehoshoua, the letters יהוה symbolize God's Will with the Word (Logos) as the organ of that Will. The symbol ש (Shin) = 300 = Twenty-first Arcanum, and means the mechanism of involution, materialization, or the incarnation of that Logos (Word). In such a case our pentagram takes the form shown in Fig. No. 17.

In Fig. 16 its upper point is the material tool, which the Will operates on the physical plane. This cliché is the most powerful of the *pentagrams* on the astral plane. On the mental plane it corresponds to the dogmas of Incarnation and Redemption in the ancient Rosicrucian Schools of the sixteenth-eighteenth centuries.

If the symbol יהוה can be explained as God's Will, and the will of a separate human personality as its weak reflection, then the symbol

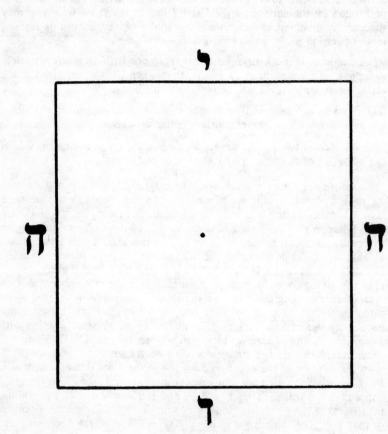

Fig. 19 TETRAGRAM (Square)

ה ו ש ה י (Yod-Hé-Shin-Vau-Hé) will be reduced to the ordinary human pentagram.

So, *the Fifth Arcanum of the Tarot teaches us about the potential power or ability which exists in every one of us, and which creates our individual force, our active life.*

How is it possible to create in us this human pentagram, this astral power? Of course, by means of an irresistibly strong system of astral, mental and physical exercises. But here there may be a great difficulty. If you want to create that pentagram in yourself, you must think not only about the necessity of producing some new manifestations, but also to fight the opposite, the obstacles, which come from your still insufficient development, mainly in the astral realm.

By this means, the problem of the creation of pentagrammatic individuality is divided into two parts:

(1) Creation in us of a man of conscious will.

(2) A right transformation of the impulsive man in us. This means one who acts instinctively and impulsively in all realms, responding to definite impressions by means of standardized reflexes; one who cries from pain, flies before danger, hits back when struck; smiles when flattered, and so on.

This impulsive man must be educated so that he can be a useful tool for the superior, conscious man, the true individuality. This means that some reflexes and habits must be suppressed, and others stimulated. So this part of the present lesson will be dedicated to just the creation of a man of conscious, enlightened WILL.

If into the upright pentagram we insert a human figure, then to its upper point will correspond the centres, analogously related to the realm of seeing and thinking. This is also the seat of meditation, practised by a conscious man of good will.

Meditation is composed of several activities.

(1) *Filtration of emotional impressions* through the organs connected with them.

(2) Fixation of ideas (the memorizing of them).

(3) The ability to create ideas.

Accordingly then, the following methods for making meditation easier can be recommended and expounded:

(a) To avoid all instinctive, automatic answers on all questions put to us which are dictated only by memory, without any participation of the meditating elements.

(b) To avoid any disputes or quarrels, leading only to the building of form (dialectic) but not of ideas. The majority of disputes have the conception of some terminology as a starting point; in this case the whole dispute is based on misunderstanding. Or, there is the basic difference of the dogmas of contemplation and then the dispute is aimless, purposeless.

(c) To train ourselves in cognition (perception) of the invisible in the visible. For example, so as to recognize the astrosome-soul and spirit in the physical shell of an individual man, it is not sufficient to contemplate only the contours of the human body; but it is necessary to penetrate into the corresponding astral parts of the form, into the dynamic manifestations of the astrosome (aura) and even into the properties of the mental monad.

(d) To search everywhere for natural ANALOGIES, just as we did in the Third Arcanum in relation to the human body, and to comment on those analogies in the broadest sense.

(e) Not to despise any chance to learn of the harmony and fineness in forms; to visit museums, to listen to good music, and in general not to avoid the world of art. This is the general advice as regards meditation.

But now we will turn to something more specific, such as the very mechanism of meditation, which implies the knowledge and practice of concentration. Concentration is an art and a science in itself, so that in this course on the Tarot we cannot make a full exposition of this otherwise very fascinating subject. It can only be indicated here as in a special work by the writer (*Concentration* published by G. Allen & Unwin of London, as well as in other European countries and languages), the subject has been treated in full.

Imagine that we have deliberately limited the field of meditation to a few chosen objects. This will be termed 'concentration' on these objects. The following are examples:

(1) A man writing an article can concentrate his thoughts on three aspects (a) the idea behind it, (b) its construction, and (c) its outer form or beauty of style. While working he may definitely resolve not to admit any other thoughts, not to hear any outer sounds, not to care about the state of his body and its comfort, or about time.

(2) To concentrate your thoughts on two objects, a person and the picture or idea, which that person wants to transmit to you; all else should be removed from the field of your consciousness.

(3) To concentrate your thoughts on only one object, such as the question of the age of some person known to you.

(4) To try to concentrate your thoughts on the idea of the *absence* of a given object, this will be so-called *passive* concentration, as opposed to the other three examples, in which we spoke about *active* concentration.

Methods of Training in Active and Passive Concentration

(1) Think about some organ or part of your body, concentrating on the question of its harmonious structure. This will not only be a good exercise in concentration, but can also appear as an effective means for the removal of any ailment, disharmony or weakening of its functions.

(2) Try to introduce into your concentration a desire for or imagination about the malfunction (disharmony) of that organ. The result will be opposite to that of (1). Here belongs the phenomena and the creation of the so-called stigmata, signs on the bodies of persons who concentrate on the idea of wounding some part of their body, like the mystics in their ecstasies.

(3) For very impulsive people, it is advisable to concentrate on any object of minor importance, and try to dominate all involuntary contractions of the muscles, such as NOT turning your head in the presence of a noise, and so on. This second type of exercise has a general and preparatory character.

(4) The third and very important type of concentration exercise is that of mental travelling. Recall all the details of a past journey, or invent one partially or in full, it does not matter which, But in both cases all details of movements and impressions must be completely thought out, so that one is utterly separated from actual conditions around you. Set an alarm-clock and finish the exercise in 20 or 30 minutes.

(5) Another kind of exercise consists in the concentration of thoughts on the details of construction of some selected real object, which is within your reach. The formal pattern of its creation and origin as well as the idea of its purpose should now be considered for about 30 minutes.

(6) Imagine an object which, at the time, is beyond reach of your sight and then compare the details of the imaginary thing with the real one. The session should last for about 30 minutes.

(7) If the previous exercises have been well performed, try to create in your imagination the general outline of a non-existent object which you have not even seen mentally. From this general idea pass to a detailed one, testing the exactness of your creation by reversing the process and going from the detailed to the general idea. The time taken should be about 40 minutes.

(8) Next, try to exercise your mind by passing quickly from active concentration on one object to a similar concentration on another. Your power to do it at will shows that you have a considerable ability of concentration. The more unfavourable are the outer conditions during this exercise, the more valuable will be its successful performance.

The next type of concentration which is PASSIVE is often considered to be much more difficult than the active kind. Very favourable conditions can be created at the beginning of these exercises. The most notable being: darkness and the removal of everything which could interrupt our attention; a lying position, a weakening of breathing, and the closing of ears and eyes. First you should concentrate on a very symmetrical form, like a circle or disc of a certain size, at rest or revolving against an unending background. The colours of the disc and background have been given by traditional authors as immaterial, but my personal opinion is that only white (for the circle or disc) and black (for the background) should be used, in order to simplify and thus facilitate concentration. Also, in the beginning, a change of colours may bring you some trouble from the side of the mind, which is then only too glad to verbalize about them. This is extremely undesirable.

If this exercise can be performed for some five or ten minutes, try the next by removing the disc and using a point instead. Then remove even the background, which will lead to a total elimination of all outer impressions. This is your aim.

D*

These exercises can be changed in detail *ad libitum*.

In the state of passive concentration, some outer ingredients may insert some imaginary forms, such as geometrical figures, and illusory sounds, flavours, odours, and so on into the vacuum of your consciousness. All of these will probably be the result of action by a foreign will. Do not forget, that we are living in multi-dimensional worlds, each of which has its own inhabitants. They may perceive your efforts, as well as the state of passivity of your mind which usually emits incessant vibrations. This is an opportunity for them to interfere by inserting their own thoughts, or similar vibrations of the subtle matter in which they live. You can certainly guess about which population of the astral and mental worlds I am speaking now (see Lessons 14 and 15).

Active and passive concentration are the alphabet of meditation for occultists; but you should know, that meditation is *not* an exercise in itself. Rather it is the higher use of our consciousness, which is permitted by the ability of concentration (see *Concentration*, Chapters XXI and XXII).

Another use of that ability is practised in the seeking of information from the higher planes. This means the posing of different questions through active concentration, and the receiving of answers to them by means of the passive state of mind, deliberately created for the purpose. This needs, as for everything in occultism, some practical experience and time.

LESSON 17

At this point three different kinds of questions may arise:

(1) A problem so arranged, that the answer will cover only the *mental realm*. For example, we can know which chain of logical ideas will lead to the solution of philosophical, mathematical and like questions. In other words, we may lack a few components in our logical conclusions because of a failure of memory or uncertainty in the method of application. In this case, *active concentration* must give us a *clear grasp of the components* of the logical sequence which we already possess, plus a strong desire to obtain the remainder by way of meditation.

Then *passive concentration* comes as a form of rest after the active; but after this the 'remainder' of the missing links come to fill the gaps, by means of the hard to explain 'intellectual clairvoyance' or vision. I strongly recommend the student to try to understand well this method of using active and passive concentration by turn, so that he may follow the next questions without any difficulty.

(2) On the question of *astral character*, I would like to say, that at the moment of our passive concentration, we may get the answer in the form of geometrical or even musical symbols, usually as some lines on a dark background or as sounds.

(3) As regards *physical character*, the answer to this comes under the heading of the illusion of sensations produced by things like feelings, odours and flavours. In this case the answer often comes during the very process

of active concentration, or on the actual borderline of transition from the active to the passive, when, for example, you want to remember a perfume related to a certain name, or the taste of some food, or the impression on the surface of a tissue, and all these things belong to the physical plane.

Among special applications of this last method we may consider the so-called 'psychometry', as used in the waking state (psychometry can also be based on mediumism and somnambulism).

Contemporary occult science calls this sort of exercise the manifestation of the sixth, or odic, astral sense, which in our previous lessons was defined as astral imbibition or imagination. This is because all Hermetic authorities recommend, that all persons practising psychometry, limit themselves to the bare minimum of susceptibility of their five physical senses.

Some authors are of the opinion, that the true key to psychometry is really just the ability for *passive* concentration. From personal experience I am inclined to divide the responsibility for success equally between both types of concentration: if the *active* phase has not been well prepared, then some unwanted rubbish can slip through into the *passive* phase which has not been sufficiently safeguarded by careful active preparation.

Anyway, the whole process is as follows:

Before the session the psychometrist must concentrate actively on a strong desire to put his astrosome into contact with the row of objects placed before him. Here I would again like to warn students: all the psychic and magic activities as expounded in this work are, according to Hermetic Tradition NOT accessible to any one who merely condescends to read this book. It is NECESSARY to have the ABILITIES which have been discussed in this exposition of the Major Arcana, and for that reason I am giving a lot of instructions on how to develop these abilities in general. It is by possessing them that you will be ready to experience what you are reading here theoretically.

Of course, the best guarantee for *complete success* would be *full* preparation, and this can be found in a special study of the book *Concentration*. It has been impossible in a work of this nature—dedicated to so wide a subject as a presentation of the whole of the Western Tradition of occultism —to give COMPLETE and DETAILED instruction on concentration, which needs a separate book in itself as has just been mentioned.

The 'desire' of a psychometrist to enter into contact with the astrosomes of certain objects, is by no means a fleeting one. It is a well-directed and skilled effort of will-power, which, for a while, enables him to exclude every other thought from his consciousness, so as to OBTAIN THE DESIRED RESULT.

Now, our psychometrist has to use the articles he wants to 'psychometrize' or, in other words, to extract from them for his own purposes information about places, conditions, people, and so on with which the objects have been in contact. The techniques are as follows:

He takes the objects one after another and presses them against his *forehead* (action of the odic centres in the brain), *heart*, or *solar plexus*. The choice depends upon where he is MOST sensitive, and his kind of temperament. Only practical experience can teach him about it, but it is not such hard work by comparison with concentration itself.

At the moment when the articles are close to the chosen point of his body, he quickly enters into the state of PASSIVE concentration, during which he can obtain the desired impressions in different ways, which can be optical (coloured or not), sometimes acoustical and on some occasions feelings, like impressions relating to the history of the formation of the object, its future fate, and stories about the persons who have been astrally or magnetically associated with it.

About 25 years ago in Paris, I attended many seances arranged for the famous psychometrist—Stefan Ossowiecki. His ability was outstanding. He could invariably 'read' and 'see' persons merely by contact with their belongings which had been given to him for experimental purposes. He would say where such and such a person WAS at that moment, and whether dead or alive or what he was doing, and so on.

He read letters without opening them, simply by putting them against his forehead for a short time. He could also see the human aura, and from it, was able to forecast a sudden and approaching death for a particular person, which he always avoided doing by all means. Incidentally, he could not foresee his own death.

If a psychometrist is given an envelope, he may be able to see the factory at which it was made; the contents of the enclosed letter; the figure and character of the person who wrote it; some of the important moments in his or her life; the office in which the letter was stamped, and so on.

If the object presented to him is an ancient coin, the field of activity for an able psychometrist is very wide, and he may see interesting historical clichés, while an old shell or piece of ore may yield geological ones.

The time for passive concentration on one object should not be longer than five minutes; but, if the article begins to give further interesting clichés, the seance may be prolonged to 20 or 30 minutes, because of their scientific importance. Here I must mention, that sometimes the historical clichés may appear in reversed chronological order, which must be taken into account by the operator. To a certain extent he must also be acquainted with the general theme of the expected clichés. In other words, it should be possible for the historical ones, for example, to be interpreted by a historian, who may be able to correct any errors in time, which arise from the reversed visions.

Apart from the basic preparation (concentration exercises) for a person not endowed with psychometric abilities from birth, a general outline may be given as follows:

Take seven plain envelopes containing letters from persons known to the operator, and try to find, which came from which person. Take four bags with different minerals and try to find out which mineral is in which bag.

Another type of interesting experience, possible only for a very sensitive and highly trained psychometrist, is the diagnosis of a sickness of a patient's internal organs. Usually, one of the patient's little fingers is placed in the psychometrist's ear and this is sufficient to allow him to describe the state of the organs exactly.

The so-called visions of the auras of human beings and objects—that is the astral emanations—also belong to the results of both kinds of concentration—active and passive when used in these proceedings.

Colours and coloured forms are seen, and if the operator knows their meaning, he may be able to reveal plenty of important facts. Some people can see the aura even without closing their eyes; in this case the ability may be associated with an extraordinary development of the subtle physical sight. But usually, auras are seen with the eyes closed, and therefore, by means of the 'sixth' sense as Hermetists like to express it.

LESSON 18

However, from the purely occult point of view, the most important application of concentration in the foregoing examples would be *conscious prayer*. In the process of prayer, concentration may be extended to objects on different sub-planes, according to the operator's development and contents of his or her prayer.

Next comes passive concentration, creating a degree of inner satisfaction for the praying person, and then higher currents and influences, become accessible to him.

It is now necessary to explain the processes of suggestion, or the creation of the power of ideas and the power of thoughts. Auto-suggestion, according to some German schools at the beginning of the twentieth century and also some personal researches, will be touched on again in the analysis of the Tenth Arcanum, when you will know much more from study of this course. The *elementary practices* are as follows:

For a fairly advanced occultist I recommend the basic *asanas* as given in my *Concentration*. Otherwise, a different starting point can be used. There are moments when we are in bed, and while still thinking, we gradually lose contact with our surroundings, our outer form and its condition. This greatly facilitates the beginning of our efforts.

Auto-suggestion will be planned on the pattern of the *ternary:* that is the *Spirit (1)—astral (2)—physical (3) plane.*

Take for example, a desire to suggest self-assurance and non-distraction for use in an examination due to take place the next day. The arising of this idea in itself creates the *spirit* of auto-suggestion (1).

Now *astrally clothe* this mental principle (2). Create the sentence: 'I am diligent, unconstrained, able to consider with ease the questions to be put to me, and will answer without any resistance or inner unrest.' Think it over, and with closed eyes repeat it twice in a whisper, then again half-aloud four more times. By this operation exactly and vividly imagine a geometrical picture (or cliché) of the auto-suggestion, such as: yourself with an unconstrained attitude facing the examiners, along with details of the classroom, fellow students and teachers.

Apart from this imaginary scene, you should also live the whole emotional, that is the astral image of your desired state. Tune yourself to it joyfully, to create in you a feeling of certainty. So now you have all the elements of the astral counterpart of the whole performance, even to the addition of a physical one in the form of sound waves created by your whispering. This vocal process should be repeated twice, but this time aloud, while opening the eyes and making gestures, which for you are an expression of certainty and lack of fear. And so the cycle of auto-suggestion will be completed.

Your attention should be kept on two points:

(1) All sentences, mental pictures, and so on MUST REFER TO THE PRESENT, NOT to the FUTURE (see Third Arcanum).

(2) Self-suggestion needs less faith on the part of the operator for the success of the whole action; but when you try to suggest something to another person, the cardinal condition for a successful outcome is just the lack of any doubt.

In this recommended process of auto-suggestion one can have almost NO FAITH in the method, and still achieve quite satisfactory results. This can be explained by the fact, that our WILL is better suited for the domination of our own astral, than that of another.

This kind of auto-suggestion is very good for the purpose of destroying bad habits; removal of the symptoms of an ailment; strengthening of the whole organism (a very important use), and improvement of the memory, and so on.

The creation of idea-forces may be done in the following way:

You are considering the creation of an astral entity, which may influence you or another person in a definite direction. As an example: 'I want my friend NN to be less nervous.' This idea, even though not expressed in words, will be the *'spirit'* of the new being. In order to create its *astral* counterpart, you should *contract* all your muscles in a strong effort without moving your position and while remaining standing in the one place. Then concentrate on the thought of sending all your muscular energy to the newly-formed entity, at the same time slowly and gradually lessening the tension of your body, till full relaxation is regained. The greater part of the energy, which is not used for the mechanical side of your muscular effort, will be at the disposal of your will, which means the formation of the new entity's astrosome. If you wish, you may help it even in the creation of the subtle physical veil by placing nearby, a glass of slowly evaporating milk, honey, or fresh blood. The vital power of these fluids and substances will play the role of a mediumistic principle.

These operations are purely magical ones, and the student should be careful not to use any of them for any evil or egoistic purposes. There are no exemptions from the results of the wrongful use of magic powers. The karmic punishment is terrible. Creation of temporary devils, as we call larvas, is one of the heaviest crimes in the occult world. The reaction inevitably falls on the originator himself.

We will now consider the upper point of the pentagram with its energetic (fluidic, odic and magnetic) emanations, connected with the use of the stare or 'central gaze'.

The simplest form of the astral influence exercised by the 'central stare' is the fixing of the sight on the place between the eyebrows, just over the base of the nose of the subject of our experiment. This fixation must be connected with several inner activities on the part of the experimenter.

Firstly, in connection with the stare, there should be concentrated desire or will-effort in a definite form, that is what you wish the person concerned to do.

Secondly, all movements mentally suggested by you must be clearly visualized in your mind at the time.

Thirdly, emotions and thoughts suggested must also be added to the inner side of the operation. Whoever wants to be successful should *not verbalize* emotions and thoughts, but rather transmit them by ideas. Whoever has some practical knowledge about the art of concentration will understand what I mean.

If the person who is the subject of your experiment has not concentrated his attention on something and therefore is *not mentally active* himself, he will fulfil your command when transmitted by the process just described.

Apart from the 'central stare or gaze' a fixation of the sight on the back of the skull, or between the shoulder-blades can be used as well, provided these places are not covered by any insulating materials, such as silk, wool or fur.

The best distance between the operator and his subject—if the latter is not too sensitive—is considered to be up to 30 or 40 yards for the 'central gaze', while up to 4 to 5 yards is suitable for the back of the skull and shoulder-blades.

Apart from the ability to use the 'central look', we should also be able to gaze into the eyes of another person, if we have the need to resist any attempt from the side of another pentagram (man), who is trying to use his powers (also central look) on us.

In a fight between two pentagrams both operating with means that will bring victory, the deciding factors for that victory, according to their order of importance, will be (a) the mystical powers in man, (b) astral authority; (c) nervous force; (d) vital force of the blood; (e) functional and organic health of the body. The superiority of these things brings about the subduing of the less strong and experienced pentagram.

If we do not wish to resist, but rather to accept the suggestions of someone operating on us, we should lower our eyes (the eyelids may be half-closed), and concentrate passively. The central look is most effective when used on a sleeping or hypnotized person.

The technique of the central gaze primarily requires a correct and enduring fixing of the optical axes of our eyes on *one point*, without any blinking, tears, inflammation of the eyelids, nervousness, and so on. The following methods may be recommended to remedy weakness of the eyelids, or the inner tissues of the visual organs: (1) eye-baths (use tepid or cold water and add a little salt or boracic acid if so desired); (2) eye-showers; (3) washing with certain herbal infusions, one of the best being weak wormwood tea, to which can be added a few drops of fresh honey.

People who find it difficult to gaze for three to five minutes at one point without blinking, should strengthen their eyes by exercises. Take a little black disc about the size of sixpence, and fix it at eye-level to a white wall some 3 to 4 yards away from you. Sit quietly and at first look at it for 30 seconds, gradually increasing the time according to your growing strength, the maximum being five minutes. There is no need to do more. When this is achieved, look at the disc every day from a different angle. Later, walk through the room with your eyes always fixed on the disc. Learn to transfer your sight quickly from one point to another. Finally, use the 'central look' on yourself, by means of a mirror, gazing at the base of your nose. The length of time to be taken for the exercise depends entirely upon you.

There is one more important detail so often forgotten in occult manuals: when fixing someone with the central look, you should, at the same time, not lose sight of his face, that is WITHOUT MOVING THE FIXED AXES OF YOUR EYES. It is quite possible, for the normal human eye also possesses—apart from direct vision—the so-called 'side vision', which extends for more than one foot on each side.

The fixing of your sight on only a small point between the eyebrows without being conscious of the whole face will not bring results, or only very poor ones.

Suitable concentration, without fear, unrest or doubt, must accompany every use of the central gaze. This is essential, for well developed ability can produce results beyond all anticipation.

We will now pass on to MAGNETISM OF THE HANDS.

The right hand of a man in the state of normal polarization of magnetism emits a POSITIVE magnetic force, that is the energy which can at a very short distance, turn a compass needle from its north-south direction. Therefore, if we consider the northern magnetism as positive, then we are entitled to state that the right hand of a male is POSITIVE, and his left NEGATIVE. Things are just the opposite with women.

In some occult organizations before World War I and also after it, kinds of magnetometers were used, in order to measure the personal magnetism of people who wished to use their powers for healing and other similar purposes. These pieces of apparatus were able to show cases (rare) where certain men and women possessed the reversed polarization of their magnetism. The magnetism of the left foot is identical with that of the right hand, while the right foot has the same as the left hand.

Polarization can be changed temporarily or permanently. There are men with female polarization, and women with male. The spiritual state, physical feelings, and even a conscious effort of the will may change the magnetism in our bodies.

A weak pentagram is more suceptible to magnetization when it is performed by stroking or touching with hands, just like a weak magnet which gains in power in the presence of a strong one.

All that we are speaking of here about occult (magic) activities is valid only when the operator is sufficiently trained. No reasonable person would expect any athletic performance from a physical weakling, no matter if theoretically, he knows everything about, say, the art of boxing. He will

be knocked out in the ring in the first few moments by a much less intelligent, but trained boxer, and will make no showing at all. This is the basic
occult law.

Returning to the efforts of the conscious man who strives to make a more
perfect pentagram of himself, I would like to mention that, apart from
meditation, which is like spiritual food for such a man, there is still an addition to that food, which is a strong stimulant.

For primitive men, physical love widens the narrow egoistic circle of
their lives into that of the family-egoism. Families living closely together
may form another, still wider sort of egoism, that of a clan or tribe. The
next step will be so-called patriotism, or egoism on a national scale. Mental
affinity and similarity of attitude also bring men together into suitable
organizations, like artistic or metaphysical interests which make men
create different societies, circles and schools.

So the highest UNIVERSAL LOVE directed to every living thing,
to everything which manifests itself in the Archetype, humanity and
Nature, is a potent stimulant for possession of a purposeful, evolutionary
and well-concentrated MEDITATION, being the foremost instrument
of our Hermetic Realization of the White Race on this Earth.

LESSON 19

The Fifth Arcanum teaches us a lot about the constitution of man. The
incarnate human can be considered—temporarily and from a practical
point of view—as being composed of *three elements.*

(1) A conscious man possessing will-power, able to meditate, and having
the ability to perform what we call 'creative activities'.

(2) A man of impulses, functioning by reflexes, and automatically reacting
to most outer impressions, according to some simple pattern.

(3) A physical machine, his body, which is at the disposal of his two
superior elements.

The problem of knowledge about that machine belongs rather to anatomy, physiology and their related subjects. For the purpose of the present
study I will mention only briefly about the analogous ternary, HEAD,
THORAX, and ABDOMEN, and also about the fact, that the quality
and quantity of nervous energy in man (that is nervous fluids) depends
entirely upon the quality and quantity of his blood, which are the factors
and, at the same time, the direct results of the vital juices, created by the
processes of digestion.

What are the relationships between the *impulsive* man and the *conscious*
one? The first, from the very nature of things, is a passive man. He reacts
to all outer impressions in accordance with definite and unchangeable
laws. According to the basic arcana he is a triple entity. In him dwells an
emotional man, living by instinct and having certain needs. Then there is
also the *waking* man, who possesses passions, and lives by vaguely expressed
cravings and lusts, which should not be confused with a man's conscious

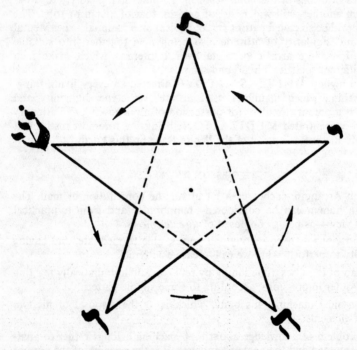

Fig. 20 Upright Pentagram in Motion

desires. And finally, there is an *intellectual* man, living under the direction of his mind, which manifests as an ability of automatic calculation.

The purpose of the CONSCIOUS man is to limit and to extinguish the reflexes of the impulsive man, and often to turn them in the opposite direction.

The *under-developed, impulsive* man will tear away his hand with great speed from a hot object, while a *conscious* man can dominate such an impulse and even play the role of Mutius Scaevola.

The *better developed, impulsive* man may answer flattery with a smile, but the *conscious* one will suppress that smile and even turn it into a grimace, because he is able to see through such things.

An *intellectually impulsive* man is an apostle of routine, an enemy of new hypotheses, and a patron of pupils who automatically use the old standardized methods and formulas even to the point of applying them to quite different and unsuitable problems and things.

All these *three phases of the impulsive man* can easily produce in him deviations and offences in some realms, unless the *conscious* man opposes them. The *lowest phase* may create material transgressions, a typical example of which is drunkenness. The *middle phase* represents another kind of offence, such as immorality; it is that astral immorality which multiplies itself by way of imagination in the form of sensual manifestations. In the *third phase*, the intellectually impulsive man generates offences based on automatic activities, like gambling, and so on.

A number of controversial questions should now be solved, in order to avoid them in the course of study of later arcana.

(A) Is it possible for a *conscious* man to lose temporarily or permanently control over his body? Yes, in some cases:

(1) When the conscious counterpart is absent, but the impulsive one present, as in dream or lethargy.

(2) When certain nerve cells belonging to the organs of sensation and the motivation centres are damaged or diseased; when some nerve breaks down; when circulation of the nervous fluids is disrupted, or, as doctors say, there are functional disorders of the nervous system as a whole.

All these obstacles may, in some instances, make it impossible for the conscious man to control his impulsive brother. This means that then common sense cannot dominate instincts, and harmony cannot rule over the animistic realm.

(B) What deformation can appear in the sphere of human *imagination*? In order to answer the question properly, we should first realize that forms, born from the processes of imagination also depend—apart from the qualities of the related astrosome—upon two basic influences:

(1) Activity of the sense organs.

(2) The regulating logic of our mental principle.

If our spirit ceases to act properly in the creation of forms, then our imagination becomes only a phantasy. If our nerves, as intermediaries between the impressions received by our senses and consciousness, act wrongly (pathologically), or even create images without any outer justification, then we have what are called '*halucinations*'.

(C) How does the *use of alcohol* influence a man in different stages of drunkenness? We can distinguish three phases of a man's conditions resulting from the consumption of alcohol.

(1) When a man takes a certain quantity of alcohol it becomes absorbed into his blood-stream and augments the dynamic character of his blood. At such a moment, ganglions, which are reserve stores for nervous force, begin to release this force in very generous amounts. Then one gets the opportunity to intensify one's mental activities and physical efficiency. It is interesting to note, that Papus himself recommended public speakers to take a small glass of pure brandy before tedious lecturing. We may of course, agree or disagree with this recommendation of the famous occultist.

(2) Then comes the second phase, when more alcohol enters the organism. The physical machine uses more nervous energy than man's mental and spiritual counterparts, and now the impulses cannot be balanced or properly controlled by the consciousness. They assume a disorderly character, from which comes aggressiveness, indecent gestures and words, and so on.

(3) The third or final phase occurs when the stores of nervous force are empty. Now it is the astrosome which must replace them. It must then care for the organism, while giving nothing of its astral energy to the man's consciousness. This means the deep sleep of a dead-drunk man.

(D) What is *hypnosis*? In the hypnotic process the hypnotist strongly irritates the patient's nervous centres, which direct his sense organs. By this fact he separates the impulsive counterpart of man from his conscious principle. In its place he puts his own will, to rule over the manifestations of the impulsive man instead of the man himself. That is the theoretical truth.

Here I am considering only the method for obtaining full hypnosis without any magnetic action, only by way of attracting and holding the sight of the patient by means of shining objects or whirling mirrors (the usual Western method), or through sounds, such as the monotonous repetition of the same sound or sounds, like the beating of gongs and incantations (Eastern methods used by fakirs when producing their hypnotic tricks).

Sometimes fear is also used by certain unscrupulous hypnotists.

(E) How are we to understand *insanity*?

This is a very interesting subject. We have to distinguish between two kinds of mental unbalance. Only the first is known to official medical science.

(1) Insanity derived *from physical sources*.

(2) Insanity arising *from the astral*.

According to its symptoms, mental sickness can often be compared to a continuous state of drunkenness, in its *second* phase as previously described. Impulses of a special character prevail in each insane person. They are related to the activity of certain nerve centres. Of course, such conditions can arise because of organic or functional disorders of the nervous system; but it is also possible to stimulate certain centres to the detriment of others from the point of view of astral factors. It is the astrosome, which created the body and which directs its manifestations. The spirit (mental) of man manifests itself only through that astrosome. Now, imagine that a *foreign astral entity* joins your astrosome and begins to rule the body together with its proper owner. We will then get abnormal manifestations in both the astral and physical activities of the man, often resulting in the impossibility of any mental functions, because the original astrosome has been paralysed by the intruder.

A *strong larva* belonging to the man himself, or coming from the outer world, can also join the man's astrosome. This will be an example of permanent incarnation for a larva, which usually means the appearance of a special type of offence peculiar to that larva which masters the insane person concerned.

Larvas, as all inferior astral entities, try to obtain life in matter much denser than their own, that is in the physical world. They have no moral qualities so they show no concern about the immense harm they bring to the hapless man they obsess. Such a little devil will first try to develop in man the ability of practising that offence or abnormality in full. When the body is exhausted, the larva usually tries to destroy it, in order to free itself for further incarnations. I am taking the liberty of quoting a dreadful case which I witnessed myself, about 1926.

At that time I had an acquaintance, a young man of 24, of good family, who had just finished matriculation. He was working as a clerk with a view to getting steady employment in the Government service.

Sometime in April a friend rang to inform me that K. (as I will call the unfortunate youth) had become insane. He was absenting himself from his office duties, wandering by rail without tickets throughout the whole district and indecently attacking women, and therefore was wanted by the police. It was hard to believe that this handsome, athletic and usually very quiet boy was able to commit such senseless deeds. Next morning I saw a column about him in the newspapers. The police were searching intensively for him, after he had overpowered and beaten two constables who had tried to arrest him because of an assault in a train. I went to visit the landlord, where K. lodged as his parents were living in another town, some hundred miles away.

The landlord told me, that he was much affected by the disaster which had befallen K. whom he liked and considered to be his best lodger. 'I will tell you confidentially' said the old man, 'that K. has suffered from violent self-abuse (masturbation) for some months past.' He had even sought medical advice, and that was how the landlord knew about the matter. They had told the young man, that if he did not stop the offence he would finish in a mental home. This was the last blow for the poor fellow. He evidently lost all hope. He knew of the danger that lay in his bad habit, but lacked the will-power to end it.

Friends tried to encourage him to marry as soon as possible to enable K. to be cured in a natural way. He already had a fiancé, a very nice and devoted girl, who worked in the same office as himself, but he began to leave her and she did not see him for weeks on end.

At that time I was at the beginning of my Hermetic studies, and had gone far enough to know about larvas and obsessions, which are often the causes of men's ruin. Indeed, this is the case with self-abuse, which is very dangerous for physically strong people, as they offer much more scope for the malicious beings from the astral plane. Theoretically I even knew about the use of magic swords against obsessing beings, but I had not had any practical experience. That evening I sat alone in my flat with my books, separated from my neighbours by thick walls. About 11 p.m. my door-bell rang. That is K.! I suddenly thought. He may be dangerous! I was not physically afraid of him when he was normal, for I felt myself stronger, but now he was insane, and that makes a man many times more dangerous and violent. I put my Browning in my pocket and opened the door. It was hard to recognize the formerly so elegant and handsome youth. K. was shabbily dressed, one of his shoes was missing, his hair was uncombed and he was unshaven, with mad eyes and movements like those of a wild cat.

I silently showed him the way to my lounge-room. He smiled in an idiotic way and asked if I was not afraid of him. I decided to play the dangerous game to the end. 'No, my friend, you know that I am much stronger than you. Remember our classic fight a year ago? After all, you are my friend and never did anything wrong in my eyes. Rather I would like to help you in whatever way I can.'

This worked. K.'s face lost some of its expression of a baited beast. He sat on the divan and asked for a cigarette. I felt he was hungry and so went and made him some tea and sandwiches. After the meal he became still more lucid. He openly confessed his trouble to me. The description of the sensual and indecent visions which excited him to commit his offences were terrible. I realized his position. No persuasion would give any help. The thing had gone too far, and no usual means could destroy the grip of the repulsive obsession. He might be arrested at any moment, and he told me, that he would not surrender alive to the police. 'You are studying magic things, perhaps you have something in your arsenal to help me' he said. I had some literature about the fighting of larvas, but in order to practise it I needed to study the instructions for some time, and that was what I told him, asking him to visit me the next evening. 'Well, I will come if I am still alive' he said to me sadly. Then the moments of lucidity once more gave way to insanity. His eyes became wild and he looked around him with a lascivious smile. 'Don't you see them? Look how nice they are, these naked girls round us! Don't you also want . . . ?' I cannot quote his next words because of their horrible depravity. 'I do not see anything' I said harshly to K. 'You are mad today, come tomorrow and we will try to do something for you.' 'Yes, I will come, but if you cannot help. . . .'

And a note of threat and hatred sounded in his voice. I was really happy when the door was locked after he left.

I never saw him alive again, for next morning the papers carried the sad story of K.'s end. Shortly after midnight he appeared at a railway station, was recognized by the police and fatally shot when he attacked them, while resisting arrest.

I saw his body lying in the city morgue, with a large wound above the left collar-bone. The strangely shrunken face wore something of a sad smile, as his half-open mouth showed his teeth covered with blood from the internal haemorrhage after the piercing of the aorta by the pitiless bullet.

The larva had performed its fearful task so as to free itself from the body which it had despoiled and brought to such infamy.

The body of an insane person can also be occupied by an elementar of an inferior, idiotic type, which fights the man's proper astrosome, inducing by turns periods of madness and lucidity.

But when are these things possible? Firstly, when a man is passive enough and not sufficiently occupied with his body to defend it against the astral intruders. Larvas can easily enter the body of a sleeping man, as well as that of someone, who has been disappointed by life and who no longer sees any purpose in it. Men who practise some vice can also be victims of larvas which represent just the same vice. Then the astral monster comes as if invited.

Another elementar can easily enter and occupy the body of a man, who has exteriorized himself, consciously or unconsciously. Therein lies the danger of such occult practices, and that is why no honest occultist will betray the astral techniques, necessary for such exteriorization, until his pupil is fully qualified to engage in it.

We do unconsciously exteriorize much more often than most people suppose. Fear, great bitterness, a position that lacks any good and fore-seeable solution, briefly everything which compels us to hate the physical life intensely; all these make exteriorization easier. A sudden joy can bring similar results. In such a moment the soul is so filled with gratitude for the astral beatitude it experiences at the moment, that it unconsciously strives for the astral plane and can easily exteriorize itself.

Sometimes the astrosome which has been expelled by an intruder can return and remove the unwanted tenant. Then we have temporary insanity. But sometimes the astrosome cannot return, and then a foreign entity operates in the body resulting in constant insanity, or in the best possible case, an unfavourable change of personality, usually ending in a fairly quick destruction of the physical body.

If both of the astrosomes remain in the one body, and fight each other, there will be periodical insanity.

As we can see, Hermetic occult philosophy offers some logical solutions (for those who have studied it) for cases which usually remain permanent enigmas for official science; but a day will come, when that which today is still considered as unreal and superstitious will be recognized, with the

help of our more wise and advanced brethren of the far-off future. At present
we have to be satisfied if we come to know some deeper things before others
do. But to know more also means to bear more responsibility. This is the
cardinal rule in all occult initiatory schools. We cannot be truly initiated,
until we are able to recognize and to bear the burdens of knowledge.

LESSON 20

There are many ways known in occultism which facilitate the transformation of an impulsive type of man into a higher one, that is the CONSCIOUS
type, and therefore offer more possibilities for spiritual advancement;
but for that we must first know the characteristics of a man's impulsive
life. There are three main lines.

(A) For the instinctively impulsive man most attention should be placed
on his food. We have to know the role of wilful abstention from food. In
many cases a temporary abstaining is useful, because it allows the intestines
to take rest, therefore it gives the higher organs more economical use of
the nervous fluids, allowing for more spiritual activity. It is well known,
that lack of food (or fasting) tunes a man's consciousness to the spiritual
world; but too long a fast is of course, harmful for the physical body.

The best times for the taking of food must be left to everyone's own
particular conditions. Anyway, in the West as well as in the East there are
times for meals which are a matter of long established custom, and occultism, at least the practical kind, such as Hermetism, generally does not interfere with them.

However, we may say more about the various kinds of food which are
suitable for different climates and people. Here I am treating the subject
in the traditionally accepted Hermetic form, quite apart from my personal
opinion, which may differ from that of tradition. I believe that vegetarian
diet can also be suitable for temperate climates, although Western occultism
declares, that a full vegetarian diet should only be used in tropical countries.
Under cooler conditions, strictly vegetarian food is taken by magicians
when preparing themselves for magic operations, which require them to
have special peace in their animistic centres, without reducing the activity
of the instinctive centres. It is well known that vegetarian food fosters
instinctive moods, while meat creates animistic passions. In tropical
countries the by-products of a meat diet are well substituted by the richness
of the astral solar emanations.

So we can say, that normal vegetarian food can be taken for up to forty
days, while a strictly vegetarian diet, consisting only of fruit and vegetables
cooked in water, without salt, should not last for more than seven days.
The foregoing refers principally to magicians.

If we are compelled to use meat as a food, we cannot dispense with due
caution when eating it. Meat often contains bad astral, that is it is often
magnetically bound with the phantom (lower part of the astrosome) of the
animal, frightened, angry or full of hate during the processes of hunting
and killing. We should not forget that a phantom directs the processes of

decomposition and the returning of the dead body to Nature. How unfavourable it would be for your body, if in its stomach, involutionary work is being done on the substances in it by a foreign phantom, which belongs to the dead animal. I think I have expressed my thoughts clearly enough for the reader to draw his own conclusions for himself.

In order to avoid the incarnation in us of bad astral fluids, tradition recommends that, before eating meat, we should mentally pronounce some setrams, in order to fortify our will in self-defence, and some mantrams for expelling the bad astral from the food.

Hermetists say, that the question of the sentimental character of vegetarianism does not exist at all, because vampirism exists in every manifestation of life and is the basic rule for the creation of living forms. It can be found not only in the eating of vegetarian food but also in the breathing processes.

Some believe that they can reach higher states of spirituality by way of asceticism (extreme abstinence) in everything, because the Great Teachers of humanity were ascetics. But because a highly advanced being, dedicated exclusively to spiritual work, takes, say, only a handful of rice for food, it does not necessarily follow that ordinary men can do the same: not until they too are capable of the same inner effort as the Spiritual Teachers, and able to meditate like them.

An anchorite, merged in contemplation, can do without any food containing, for example, phosphorus; but a professor or preacher, who speaks publicly and reads and writes a great deal, cannot do likewise, for his food must contain something to replace the phosphorus lost by his mental work.

Finally, we may hint at the fact, that for an instinctive man there are also needed certain stimulating substances. Food by itself may be good for those who do not need any quick periodical release of nervous energy, but for those who have need of this, it may sometimes be necessary to use some stimulants, to make the blood dynamic and help to borrow more energy from the nervous centres.

Without personally recommending any of the following substances, I will mention them according to tradition.

Physical stimulants are: coffee, tea, alcohol, hashish, opium and morphine. Coffee and tea are a typical binary. Coffee corresponds to the negative pole, it stimulates sensitivity. How does it work? Firstly, coffee makes digestion easier, taking and using fluids for that process. Two or three hours later it again makes a loan for the sphere of intellectual susceptibility easier. The reaction to the coffee sets in about five hours after using it, and results in a diminishing of that susceptibility.

Tea, as the positive pole of the binary, makes digestion more difficult, and for the duration of the delay in that function, it assists in realization in the intellectual realm to the extent of the nervous energy not used for digestion. The reaction after drinking tea is a prolonged removal of intellectual fluids in order to repair the delay in digestion. Sleeplessness after using strong tea is not a reaction, but a phase of its activity: one wants to think, but not to sleep. Reaction comes later.

This binary can be well neutralized by alcohol, with its short but strong action in the stimulation of susceptibility as well as of activity. It can be taken when one needs to have speed of understanding and skill in replies; but it cannot be taken repeatedly.

Opium and morphine dull the susceptibility to action of the nervous centres which distribute the fluids, and in that way they create the illusion of non-tiredness; but food does the same. Less experimental data is available about the action of hashish, which is supposed to act by lessening the ties between the physical and astral, often giving an illusion of exterior-ization, *whereas opium and morphine really assist it.*

The *animistic counterpart* in man has an analogy in the breathing process. Therefore the stimulants used will be perfumes.

Breathing exercises as used by occultists have three aims:

(a) The regular process of changing the blood, which thereby renovates its vital force. Otherwise, regulation of the amount of oxygen in the blood.

(b) Regulation of the rhythm of breathing by human will-power, which leads to authority over the heart's pulsation.

(c) The prevention of too large losses of carbonic acid.

(a) Is produced by a smoothly flowing inhalation; (c) by the partial retention of the breath and also partially by slow exhalation, and (b) by the direction of all phases of the breathing process.

Now I will give some examples of the first stage of breathing exercises, as used in Western occult schools. Sometimes these differ from the Eastern schools.

The stomach must not be filled with food: at least two hours should elapse after a meal. The position is almost horizontal, head and shoulders a little higher than the rest of the body, legs and arms outstretched with the arms lying along the sides. All muscles must be relaxed. There should be pure air in the room and a temperature of about 65 degrees. All restless thoughts must be removed from the consciousness. You should have full faith in the success of your exercises, as well as a certainty that no one will disturb you at that time. It would be dangerous (there is a special occult law which tells us about this) both for the person interrupting as well as for the one doing the exercises.

(i) Close your mouth and slowly inhale air through your nostrils until the chest is full. Any painful feeling will indicate that too much air has been absorbed. THIS IS THE PHASE OF THE INHALE.

Then hold the air and slowly exhale it through the nostrils. With empty lungs make a short pause between the end of the exhale and the beginning of the new inhale. This is necessary for domination of your breathing processes.

(ii) It is advisable (from my own personal point of view it is indispensable) that all three phases are of an equal length of time. If you sacrifice more time and effort to achieve this aim you will be richly rewarded in your future practices. The phase of inhaling symbolizes the ability to exploit the surrounding sphere (in Hermetic language the expression 'to vampirize' is used), while the phase of retaining the breath corresponds to the ability to assimilate the elements imbibed during the inhale. The phase of exhaling the breath is the ability to dispose of and use collected energy and faculties. The interval between is the ability for passive concentration, and for magic practices this should never be too long.

(iii) Therefore the inhale is used for meditation about *active concentration* in order *to assimilate certain powers and abilities;* the interval for the personal and actual assimilation of these powers and abilities; the exhale for the *idea of their reasonable use,* and the pause for *passive concentration* without any thoughts.

The length of the phases theoretically depends upon the properties of the astrosome of the person doing the exercises, but we are able to recommend some approximate timing for an average man.

In the beginning, take about 10 seconds for each phase, plus about 4 seconds for the pause. Some try to extend the pause to the length of the three phases. But, this may be dangerous because in that passive time the beginner is exposed to certain outer influences, which usually are not friendly (see Lessons 18 and 19). After some months of exercising, extend the times to 25 seconds for the active phases and about 5 for the pause. The exercise has to be performed two to three times daily, for 5 minutes to start with, and up to 25 minutes later.

This is the WESTERN method, and many consider it to be dangerous, because it is not connected with active evolutionary meditation, and which might allegedly lead to the imbibing of negative (evil) influences from the astral surroundings. There are elementals and larvas, which can strengthen evil tendencies in men, which are based on egoistic conceptions.

However, we must be aware that all occult training (except that given under the personal and direct supervision of a true Master) contains some dangerous moments, and the calculated risk must be taken by those who really try to achieve some worthwhile results.

The EASTERN method is considered to be much less dangerous, and in its Hermetic version the exercises are as follows:

The air must first be inhaled through the LEFT nostril, while the right one is closed by pressing the thumb against it. During the period when the breath is held, both nostrils should be closed, preferably with both thumbs. Then exhale through the RIGHT nostril, while the left remains closed. After the usual pause, again inhale through the left nostril, hold the air with both closed, and exhale through the right, and so on.

This method is a very good one, and personally, for beginners I even prefer it to the classical Western method, given previously. But, when the student becomes more trained and experienced, he may return to the Western practices, as they are more effective in the case of attempted exteriorization or other occult phenomena. They produce a certain degree of insensibility in the body, when used for a long time; further more, the astrosome may begin to separate and the consciousness leave the physical shell. Of course, such experiments should not be performed before the student gains complete mastery of the theory of exteriorization, and knows everything prescribed in the matter. We will return to this again in one of the more advanced lessons.

The next step will be the massaging of the solar plexus. It means pressure being exerted on the diaphragm from both sides in turn and likewise from above and below. It is a serious exercise, and if performed without personal instruction from a teacher it must be done with extreme caution. It is so easy to cause harm, that every reasonable occultist will heed my warnings and make full use of them.

The solar plexus exercises should be performed only when you are perfectly healthy, in a good mood (if not change to a better one even before you attempt to begin) and have no worries on your mind. Of course, those who have studied concentration (and by that fact, reached some fair degree of domination of their mind) will be in a position to exercise at will, because they are able to remove all clouds from their consciousness.

The body must be placed in a recumbent position as was recommended at the beginning of this lesson. Now inhale through BOTH nostrils, until the lungs are quite full. I recommend the counting of one, two, three, four up to eight in the breathing exercises. Then without exhaling and without allowing the amount of air in the lungs to be diminished in any way, TRANSFER it from the chest into the lower part of the thorax. Then the abdomen becomes distended and the ribs are lowered. You will instantly feel that your diaphragm moved downwards. All this should be performed by the effort of your chest muscles (for details see *Concentration*).

Next, again working only with those muscles, withdraw air from the region of the abdomen and in so doing raise the ribs and the whole thorax.

Then a short pause (count to three if you wish) and again transfer air into the lower part of the thorax, so that the diaphragm again goes downwards. Repeat this five or six times for a start, then stop on the phase when your upper chest is full and slowly release the air through both nostrils.

Our daily regimen should consist of five of these cycles. Only one type of exercise should be performed daily until some special conditions and aims call for more of them. This exercise cannot be performed until the techniques of the various breathing exercises have been mastered and can be practised daily.

In the beginning, the number of cycles may be limited to two or three, and even a pause made between them. Remember, do not hurry or force yourself, especially if you feel tired or not too well. Otherwise, serious harm might be done not only to your physical body, but also to some of your astral functions, which can be extremely dangerous and almost impossible to cure, unless a well-advanced occultist is available and willing to help such an unwise beginner.

If some hours after the solar plexus massage, pains or uneasiness in the stomach are felt, immediate consultation should be made with an experienced person, who knows the matter thoroughly, and until then, all the breathing exercises must definitely be stopped.

Now, what benefits do these exercises give us? They produce a stronger influx of blood to the solar plexus, revitalizing it and strengthening the surrounding muscles. All these things are indispensable, practical steps for some lower astral attainments, about which we will read more later.

If respiratory exercises play the role of *food* for an impulsive and animistic man, then perfumes will assume an incentive role for him. I will limit myself only to the basic perfumes as used in magic. There are three types which form a ternary.

Incense which is the positive pole of the ternary, inducing mystical moods and readiness to pray. It also purifies the physical and astral atmospheres, providing a suitable incense is burnt, like the good varieties used in churches (the more expensive being preferred), or the excellent Indian sticks, the best qualities of which are also more expensive.

(2) *Musk*, the middle element of this ternary, affects the animistic realm of love and sentiment in a man.

(3) *Tobacco smoke* is the negative pole of the ternary. For those who do not smoke and therefore have no habitual resistance to the poisonous elements in tobacco, its smoke provokes some brief excitement and later produces an instinctive reaction in the form of sleepiness.

If one cannot defy the habit of smoking, occult knowledge gives some hints, which permit the harm to be diminished. Papus, who was also a doctor in a famous Paris hospital, recommended that: people working in the *intellectual sphere* should use light types of tobacco in the form of cigarettes; to those of a more sensual (animistic) nature—cigars, and those who labour—a pipe.

(B) Now we come to a description and analysis of a type of man other than the animistic and impulsive—the *intellectual one*.

In the superphysical realm, his food will assist him in the following ways:

(1) To live in surroundings that are non-exciting and that will not suppress any normal ethical judgements; to avoid the society of evil men, and to avoid asymmetric forms and inharmonious colours: rather to try to be surrounded by artistic things.

(2) To learn and to exercise (even automatically) self-possession in moments of danger or unrest.

(3) Not to support in ourselves, by our impulsive reactions, those allergies and antipathies which are innate in us in the realms of feelings, tastes and smells. For example, if the smell of garlic is repulsive to you, then satisfy yourself—at least, if you cannot yet suppress the allergy altogether—with only astral aversion, such as knitting the brows, but *do not allow yourself* to recoil painfully at the sight of garlic, or at the mere sound of its name.

An incentive for the intellectual type of man will be suitably chosen music.

Here we can give an example of an analogous ternary which can influence its surroundings. During a route march or even in battle (I am speaking here of the pre-atomic age), a brave tune may strongly influence soldiers by its impulsively mental action. For an animistic type of man, the most suitable music would be waltzes or even light operas, while for a purely mental man, in the majority of cases, the most pleasant will be chamber music.

Although the theory of Hermetism is essential for its study, I believe that the exposition of most of the occult matter, which has an affinity with the arcana, and known to this generation of men, should be planned in accordance with the scheme of the Tarot. From this comes the system of lessons as used in this work. It has shown itself to be the most reliable and effective, not merely for a short-lived intellectual pleasure (which is almost useless), but for assimilation of the traditional truth of the philosophical system of Hermetism, which has nothing to equal it from the point of view of adaptability, depth and profit which it gives to every earnest student.

(C) But at this point do not let us be mistaken, for, when expressing super-latives about the Tarot, I am speaking on philosophical (that is mental) grounds, and not of the purely SPIRITUAL realm. Spirituality, when REALIZED, is *far beyond the reach of any ordinary mental or intellectual matters.*

But the number of human beings, in this our own epoch, who might be able to raise their consciousness to the Himalayan heights of the SPIRIT-UAL LIFE-CONSCIOUSNESS is infinitesimal, and nothing can change the fact. Therefore, it is justifiable to give to the vast majority, for their present degree of evolution, something suitable and useful and at the same time accessible and easily digested, even if it is not the ultimate Spiritual Doctrine. Surely, you would not expect a seven-year-old boy to know about things belonging to mature and highly educated people. So far as one still lives in relativity (the time-space-material body), relative things are the most understandable; but let these relative things be as good and useful as possible, and correspond foremostly to man's intellectual and ethical problems.

It is in order to contribute something to that end that this book has been written, having taken many years of work for its completion.

A striking modern example of a genuine magician can be seen in the mysterious personality of Dr Czeslaw Czynski, a Polish-born occultist and hypnotist, who died in Warsaw about 1933. The descendant of a noble family, Czynski possessed amazing hypnotic abilities, which he developed still further by his occult studies. However, he used his powers for very egoistic aims, so that his contemporaries called him a 'black magician'.

Here I will give only some of the most striking facts of his life and activities.

Long before the First World War, Czynski lived in Germany, teaching and practising Chiromancy and hypnotism. From this period we have his well-compiled booklet about palmistry, published by a German barber, presumably an acquaintance of Czynski's, who otherwise, had no interest in it.

In the meantime, Czynski used his powers to lure into marriage, a German Princess, who was a close relative of Kaiser William II. The aim was obviously the money of the not-so-young, aristocratic woman, who was charmed by the impressive personality of the handsome, young magician. But the Imperial House of Hohenzollern could not countenance such a disgraceful state of affairs, and so Czynski was charged with treachery, illegal use of hypnotic powers and deception. This resulted in a few years spent in Moabit prison in Berlin, connected with permanent banishment from Germany and annulment of the marriage.

The magician then went to St Petersburg (the then Russian capital) and became active in Russian occult circles, mostly in an aristocratic and wealthy environment. During this period of his life there came the most amazing test of Czynski's abilities. A Polish engineer by name of Gilewicz conceived the idea of getting rich quickly. He insured his life in the name of his wife for 100,000 roubles, then worth about £10,000 sterling, a fortune in itself. Some months later a mutilated and scalped male corpse, together with Gilewicz's passport and other belongings, was found in a second-class Warsaw hotelroom. The face was so badly damaged that it was unrecognizable, even by the murdered man's relatives. The first verdict was that it was the engineer Gilewicz whose clothes and other belongings were readily identified by his widow.

The insurance company was ready to pay the huge sum to her, when a family from the country claimed that their son, a young student of Warsaw University, had been missing since Gilewicz's death. The police allowed the mother to see the mutilated body in the morgue, and the unhappy woman immediately recognized her son by a deformed toe. Now the whole position became clear, and a hunt began for Gilewicz throughout the whole of Russian territory, but without any results. The murderer had had plenty of time in which to disappear.

The case came to the knowledge of the Tsar himself, who summoned the Imperial Chief of Police and told him to find the criminal, otherwise he would be removed in disgrace from his position.

The Chief of Police was desperate, until some friends advised him to seek the help of Dr Czynski, who was famous in occult circles for his travels in his exteriorized astrosome and the phenomena connected with it.

The somewhat reluctant magician was finally tempted by the Police Chief's offer of 500 roubles. He took some objects belonging to Gilewicz, left the Chief and his assistants in his lounge, and retired alone into the adjoining bedroom, asking not to be disturbed for some fifteen minutes.

At the end of this time he appeared again looking very pale and exhausted. He told the policemen the name of a well-known Parisian hotel, stating that Gilewicz was hiding there under a false name and wearing a beard (he was usually clean-shaven). Immediately a telegram was sent to the French Police, giving the particulars mentioned by Czynski. Everything was exactly as described and the murderer was arrested in Paris that same evening; but, nevertheless, he cheated the noose. While being led downstairs by the French Sûreté men, he asked permission to be allowed to go to the lavatory. Suddenly the policemen waiting by the door heard a heavy thud as of a falling body. Gilewicz lay dead on the floor with contorted face, and there was a strong smell of bitter almonds (cyanide) in the room.

His false beard had come away from his chin. The concierge said, that some hours before the police came, a tall, handsome gentleman with unusually piercing eyes appeared before him as if from the air. In a foreign accent he asked the official about a man with a large black beard, giving an exact description of the disguised Gilewicz. When the concierge gave him the name of the guest, the gentleman disappeared as quickly as he had come, but no one saw him pass through the exit door on to the boulevard. The description fitted Czynski exactly.

So Czynski got his 500 roubles from the Russian Police and his fame grew even more.

The last 'performance' of the magician, known to me, was less ethical. The ground-floor level of his house was occupied by a dressmaker with a large establishment. This lady, who was well known in Warsaw, was Czynski's tenant of long standing. After World War I, homes in the big cities became scarce, and large sums for key-money were collected by owners from new tenants. Czynski then got the idea of getting rid of the dressmaker and obtaining a high price for her large flat.

Of course, the woman refused to move, pointing out that she was paying the rent regularly according to the law, and therefore could not be deprived of accommodation in Czynski's house.

But the hypnotist was implacable: 'You will move in three days, dear lady, and with much more trouble than if you agree peacefully with my request.' He was right.

For every night the poor woman saw the angry figure of Czynski, coming to her bed surrounded by a strange and fearsome light, and ordering her to quit immediately, otherwise, threatening her with all kinds of disasters including death.

After the first midnight 'visit' by Czynski, she asked her husband and son to keep watch in her bedroom, and not to sleep until dawn. All was useless, because the men felt an irresistible tiredness and fell asleep just before the time of the apparition, thereby being of no help. The Police officially refused to accept any complaint against Czynski, as the law does not recognize apparitions.

However, a police official went privately to Czynski and tried to dissuade him from persecuting the hapless lady; but the magician took a formal, icy attitude, asking whether there was anything in the penal code, which spoke about female hysteria, and so on. The official had to leave without any result from his mission. The dressmaker left the house.

A couple of years before Czynski's death, I tried to visit him so as to chat about some practical use of the Hermetic teachings. But the only way to see him was by acquiring a ticket to have one's fortune told by him, as he took up this profession in the last years of his life. He did not accept visitors under any other conditions.

Having no choice, I arranged such a session and called on him in the company of one of my friends. We were both members of an active occult lodge. We had to buy the blue triangular tickets some weeks in advance, stating exactly the day and hour of the visit.

Czynski received us with a cold and stiff attitude. I saw an old, but quite virile man, with a very expressive and rather handsome face, long white hair and moustache, and without any trace of baldness. The features and strong chin spoke of will-power and self-possession beyond anything I had seen previously in other occultists. He flatly refused to speak about anything except our palms. Our assertions that we had nothing to do with any official organizations and only wanted to ask him to explain to us some complicated questions, which we then could not solve by our own efforts, were of no use. Incidentally, what we wanted to know concerned the technique of the conscious and full exteriorization of the astrosome. But, the eyes of Czynski, piercing and full of a weird light, looked at us without any emotion or sympathy. It seemed as if they were saying to us: 'Let me do what you paid for, and leave me alone!'

The atmosphere created was so unpleasant that we preferred to leave without availing ourselves of the opportunity of hearing anything about the future, written on our palms, from that strange man.

The only other things we could see in the large room, half-darkened by the deep red lamp-shade covering the light on the large table, were some strange looking, heavy chests of old dark wood, covered with oriental carving, standing along the walls.

Until he 'retired' into the fortune-telling profession, Czynski led a group of pupils, to whom he apparently taught occult tricks and secrets, for quite good money. After his death some of them were accused of 'satanism' and the illegal use of hypnosis; but, as far as I know, no conviction was ever pronounced in a court.

E

Arcanum VI
SIGILLUM SALOMONIS
TEMPTATION

Taurus

Methodus Analogiae
Pentagrammatica Libertas
Medium

CHAPTER VI

ARCANUM VI (ו VAU)

THE Sixth Major Arcanum of the Tarot has the letter ו (Vau) as its corresponding character in the Kabbalah, while its hieroglyph is an *eye and an ear*, being the most important organs which allow us to come into contact with the outer world.

In the centre of the card of the Sixth Arcanum there is a young man who is being tempted from both sides. On the right, a modestly clad young woman looks at him, showing him the RIGHT way at the crossing, on which the Man stands. This symbolizes the *evolutionary triangle*. It is the VIRTUE in him. As the Man standing in the centre is young, this gives us a hint on the necessity of making fateful decisions while there is still time to put them into practice. I would especially like to underline this.

The card is designed as in a mirror: the right way is that which is on the right side of the crossing. The way of vice, or the negative, and involutionary triangle is here represented by another young, but beautifully clad woman, who tries to pull the Man to the left, the wrong path. But the genius, hovering in the sky over the three figures, directs a punitive arrow into the evil, tempting woman of the 'left' path. An analysis of the STAUROS, which belongs indirectly to this symbolical picture, will be given later when I am discussing its other properties.

The scientific name of the Sixth Arcanum is 'BIFURCATIO', or crossing of the paths, briefly, the idea of choice, of decision. The vulgar name is 'the Enamoured One'.

As we already know, the hieroglyph of an 'eye and an ear' represents the organs of human contact with the surrounding world of the senses. But what is the result of this? Only, that to all outer objects and impressions there is corresponding subjective imagination, in other words, THAT WHICH IS INSIDE IS ABLE TO FEEL WHAT IS OUTSIDE. This statement is of great importance to us. It explains the idea of the MACROCOSM (ALL the outer worlds and conditions) and the MICROCOSM (or MAN) being an infinitesimal reflection of the WHOLE. Analogy and reflection are the principles on which is built the pentacle of this arcanum, the great *Hexagram* or Solomon's Star, or Seal of Solomon, the personal side of the Great Pentacle of Solomon, Sign of the Macrocosm, and so on. This pentacle is a combination of two triangles (see Fig. 21), one of which is the reflection of the other. In the centre of the hexagram we see a stauros (or lingam as it is called by the Hindus)

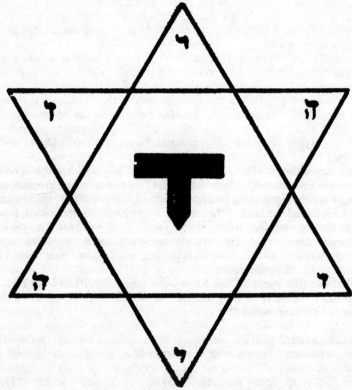

Fig. 21 The Hexagram (Solomon's Star)

symbolizing the process of fecundation: the vertical arm is active and male, the horizontal one is passive and female. The same idea suggests to us that the ascending triangle is PRIMARY and the descending SECONDARY

This pentacle contains within it almost the whole of the contents of the Sixth Arcanum. We will now have some suitable explanations:

(1) The ascending triangle can rightly be called the triangle of JESUS, for it symbolizes the evolutionary process of our Redemption. The descending triangle can be considered as the triangle of Mary, of the element participating in the involutionary process of Incarnation. The stauros indicates that Redemption is the AIM, and Incarnation only a means.

(2) Considering our pentacle as a symbol of the Macrocosm, that is as the general scheme or development of phenomena in Nature, we may call the ascending triangle that of FIRE, the sign of evolutionary, purifying and regenerating processes. The descending triangle will be that of WATER, which means the involutionary processes, condensing themselves and therefore being deformed. The Stauros teaches us, that the life of the *dense, perverted and complicated* is only a reflection of the *life radiant, subtle and simple*.
MATTER OWES ITS LIFE TO THE SPIRIT, BUT THERE CANNOT BE THE REVERSE OF THIS.

(3) We may draw the ascending triangle so that it will contain the figure of a Radiant Old Man and into the descending triangle put the shadowy form of another human figure, no longer white-bearded and radiant, but black-bearded and massive. Then we will have the famous Hermetic symbol of the two cosmic Androgynes: the MACROPROZOPOS and the MICROPROZOPOS, white and black-bearded Gods. The literal translation of both these Greek names meaning: *Macroprozopos*—having a long face, and *Microprozopos*—having a short face. The Stauros shows us, that the Black-bearded God is fecundated by the White-bearded one, by an act of Grace.

Theoretically we explain the presence of both Androgynes in the general elementary picture of the Dynamic Process as follows: consider the ascending scheme of that process. Every Yod in it was the Second Hé of the preceding tetragrammatonic cycle. We will try to reach the FIRST YOD.

The Yod itself cannot be the primary CAUSE of the dynamic cycles, that is the Highest Link (beyond which there cannot be anything) because that Highest must be able of itself to generate the lower links, and this means the attribute of the ANDROGYNEITY. We will symbolize this androgynous element by the POINT over the Yod. Then the Great Tetra-grammatonic Cycle will take the form: ה ו ה י, where the point corresponds to the Highest Androgyne or *Macroprozopos*, emanating from himself the *Father—Yod*, and the *Mother—Hé* destined for him, whose marriage brings into being the Vau, the Microprozopos.

The latter then finds a certain *Second Hé* as a spouse for himself, and in this pair is then manifested the activity of the FIRST FAMILY.
The great way to the Macroprozopos is through ecstasy. Here I would like

to mention a similar Eastern conception. It is the mysterious *Samadhi*, the eternal aim of Eastern Yogis and Saints, which is one of the most scientific and most described paths to the Whole. In our own time a great Indian *Rishi*—Sri Ramana Maharshi—proclaimed this way for all those who are attracted to it. He gave it in the modern, simple and absolute form of the DIRECT PATH, or the VICHARA-PATH. The final ecstasy of this way is the attainment of the Ultimate—Parabrahm, Nirvana, and in Hermetism, the *Great* ANDROGYNE, the unknown 'point over the Yod'. The path of the Great Rishi differs from all others by its uncompromising Ultimate Aim which is the final realization of one's own being. This is exactly the merging into the Hermetic Macroprozopos (see my Mystic Trilogy: *In Days of Great Peace, Concentration* and *Samadhi— the Superconsciousness of the Future*, in which the Eastern Direct Path has been thoroughly explained).

The *Microprozopos* can be found by everyone who really tries in his own heart. This is the ordinary, but sincere and inspired religious way. Bhakti-Yoga corresponds to it in Eastern occultism. It is much easier than the Direct Path, but also much longer. Although the modest and sincere devotee does not count the number of his incarnations; he simply BELIEVES and LOVES.

Astrologically, the Sixth Arcanum belongs to the Bull, simply because the Bull comes after the Ram in the signs of the Zodiac.

Now we come to the titles of the arcanum in the realm of the Theosophical Ternary.

(I) On the plane of the Archetype's manifestations we understand the Seal of Solomon to be a hint on the *Great Law of Analogy* (Methodus Analogiae).

(II). On the plane of our human activity this sign symbolizes that which we call the 'freedom of human will' (Pentagrammatica Libertas).

(III). On Nature's plane we will join the analogy to the surroundings in which it manifests itself. These surroundings have a double meaning: they may *bind and join*, but also *divide and separate*. Therefore the third title will be 'Environment' (Medium).

It is necessary to analyse these three titles separately.
The FIRST (Methodus Analogiae) develops from the

Equation No. 13: $6 = 3 + 3$

ONE ACCOMPLISHMENT (Third Arcanum) is followed by another ANALOGOUS ACCOMPLISHMENT (again '3'), and these are the contents of the Sixth Arcanum. We can also express this arcanum very exactly by the words of the Mystery of Hermes (Verba secretorum Hermetis) forming the first part of the Emerald Tablets—the Hermetic Code of the ancient Egyptians. I am giving the full Latin text with its translation, because of the overwhelming importance of this initiatory formula, already used in Lesson 4.

'VERUM SINE MENDACIO, CERTUM ET VERISSIMUM: QUOD EST INFERIUS EST SICUT QUOD EST SUPERIUS, ET QUOD EST SUPERIUS EST SICUT QUOD EST INFERIUS, AD PERPETRANDA MIRACULA REI UNIUS'.

'True and not false (that is, absolutely true in the mental plane) exact (that is, rightly transmitted forms without distortion of the astral clichés) and utterly true (that is, so convincing that it can be verified and tested on the physical plane, by means of the sensory organs: method of St Thomas): what is *below* is analogous to what is *above*, and what is *above* is analogous to what is *below*, for the fulfilment of the miracle of the *Unique Whole*.' This last sentence can also be translated as: ' . . . in order to make possible penetration by the *Unique Wholeness* (of things).'

This text hardly needs any further explanation. Its beginning is the pronouncement of the Law of the three planes and its end is the classical formula for the Law of Analogy, so rich in consequences for an occultist.

For example, basing our judgement on the organization of the human body, we may be able to get an idea of the organization of the Solar System, in accordance with the Theosophical Ternary which presents the ternary of the human torso, as explained in the previous lessons.

'Pentagrammatica Libertas' corresponds to:

Equation No. 14: $6 = 4 + 2$ and
Equation No. 15: $6 = 2 + 4$

We read them as: the Sixth Arcanum appearing as the result of the addition of the Second Arcanum (Gnosis, or knowledge of the ways given for free choice) and the *Fourth Arcanum* (authority which shows us the right of free choice).

And thus we see the full picture of the problems of good and evil; subtle and gross; true and false; temporary and eternal; active and passive. All these happen so often in human lives. There is free choice, for both triangles are equal, but the Stauros (lingam) reminds us, that the *initiative* for the choice of the *evolutionary triangle* gives us the impulse for Higher Activity, fecundating our imagination. The card for the arcanum gives a very clear and exact idea of the foregoing.

LESSON 22

But where will we find the necessary instruction for the true choice between the two triangles? Tradition tells us that it comes from the SPIRITUAL HARMONY in us. This always shows us the right way. Inner disorder will lead us to wrong decisions and choices.

Analysing the term 'Spiritual Harmony' we will see that it lies in the parallel and regular development of the *activity* and *susceptibility* in us.

A man who is able to perceive and accept some good clichés from any realm, but does not possess any adequate (commensurable with his susceptibility) powers of realization, will be unhappy and inharmonious in the realm concerned. In reverse, if you possess some powers in a realm not well known to you, and in which you have no true orientation, then no harmony can be created in such a case.

In occult language I would like to add another definition of the Hermetic conception of harmony:

It is the neutralization of the binaries 'Adam-Eve', 'Activity-susceptibility' inside of the astral man himself. It can be done by the convenient agreement of the two extreme terms of the given binaries.

In the matter of the question of our 'free will' and especially of the amount of it which is at our disposal on different planes of existence, the truth seems to lie 'in the middle'. It is gradually made clear to an initiate, that 'there is no smoke without fire'. While there are strong followers of the deterministic schools of thought (that is, those who do not believe in any freedom of human will), there are also fanatical devotees of the theory of free will. The differences seem to arise because of a basic error lying at the beginning of the dispute between the two opposite directions of philosophical outlook. From our point of view, each of these schools has some right in it and also some wrong. There is no man who is without karma (Great Teachers of humanity excepted), and therefore who has not had any compulsions and limitations in his life. No reasonable man would deny this. It follows then, that some things must appear to the karma-burdened person as easy to get, while others are extremely hard. In some cases he has free will at his disposal and is ABLE TO EXERCISE IT (which is a most decisive factor), but in others he sees a different picture: his aims seem to be unattainable.

Of course, our will has both: *freedom* and *limitations* circumscribed by our karma. The Laws of Nature, for example, are the karma of the universe: we cannot break them. But to choose between evolutionary and involutionary triangles, as we have in this Sixth Arcanum, is quite possible for everyone who is ripe enough to understand them.

The next title of this arcanum is 'Medium' or 'Surroundings'.

Equation No. 16: $6 = 5 + 1$ and

Equation No. 17: $6 = 1 + 5$

The *first equation* states: Life (5) + Will (1) give conditions allowing us an adequate choice in that life. It is the Macroprozopos acting in Nature.

The *second equation* states: Will (1) + Life (5) = Will of the *One* which is sufficient for the creation of life in all its phases and manifestations. It is the pattern for the Emanations of the Macroprozopos which generate Nature.

The general picture of Nature's processes may be best taken from the continuation of the 'Emerald Tablets': 'ET SICUT OMNES RES FUERUNT AB UNO MEDITATIONE UNIUS, SIC OMNES RES NATAE FUERUNT AB HAC UNA RE, ADAPTATIONE.' The literal translation is:

'Similarly, as all things arise from the unique Beginning, and by means of that One, so all things born arise from the same One, through the processes of adaptation.'

A free translation may be more explanatory:

'Similarly as all principles are emanated from the one Principle of the same nature, so everything born has emerged from the elements of the unique environment through coagulation and dissolution.'

Here is given the principle (law) of *emanation* and the ruling over of forms with the help of two processes, inscribed on the arms of Henri Kunrath's (1602 A.D.) Androgyne. It is one of the ten pentacles left to us by that eminent Hermetist (see Lessons of Fifteenth Arcanum). This pentacle symbolizes the astral environment and its means as well as the realms in which these means are used.

On the raised hand of the Androgyne (see the card for the Fifteenth Arcanum) we see—SOLVE (dilute, rarefy). On the other—COAGULA (condense). This is what the *ancient* and *mediaeval* occult wisdom has left to us, showing the means for domination of environment.

How are we to understand this enigma? By trying to find the idea behind it: it is ACTION DIRECTED ACCORDING TO CONDITIONS, SURROUNDINGS AND FORCES PUT INTO PLAY BY THE PROCESS OF DILUTING OR CONDENSING MATTER WHICH IS AT OUR DISPOSAL AND SUITABLE FOR OUR AIMS. To one who is keenly interested in the practical solution of this immense problem, which touches ALL THE MANIFESTATIONS OF LIFE on this earthly plane as well as on all the others, I cannot explain further, apart from the hint, that '*we should know when to dilute and when to condense*'. Under this comes everything: your thoughts, feelings, actions, and the *final destiny* of the REAL YOU.

To finalize our study of *Solomon's Seal*, I will mention, that the usual colours for this pentacle are: gold (fire) for the ASCENDING triangle; silver (water) for the DESCENDING one; gold (activity) for the vertical arm of the Stauros, and silver (passivity) for the horizontal arm. In the more recent occult pentacles we may encounter different colours, as will be explained in subsequent lessons. The background of the hexagram is blue.

The Sixth Arcanum contains the idea of *adaptation* in it. This empowers me to explain the Hermetic origin of HOMOEOPATHY.

Every medicine can result in three kinds of reaction: *mechanical, chemical* or *dynamic*. As a rough example of the *mechanical reaction* we may mention the use of liquid mercury against paralysis of the intestines; the taking of 'ferrum oxidatum' (used in old time medicine) in order to stimulate the peristaltic movements of the bowels; the use of laxatives like castor oil, and so on.

The *chemical reactions* are used in most of the allopathic drugs. They are prescribed for disinfection, the restoration of some weakened bodily chemical reactions, and so on. Latest discoveries in pharmaceutical knowledge, of course, offer us innumerable medicines which are much more complicated than the previously mentioned inoculations and serums; but the idea remains the same.

To the *dynamic reactions* belong the so-called *homoeopathic* medicines.

E*

Many of them are also used in *allopathy*, like *aconitum*, *strychnine*, *arsenic* and *belladonna*.

The very character of the *dynamic reactions* of medicines has been explained—in a veiled form for laymen, but clearly for initiates—by the famous Paracelsus (Philippus Theophrastus Bombastus von Hohenheim Paracelsus dictus, 1491-1541) in his main work *The Occult Philosophy*. His findings sometimes have an *a priori* quality and are based on the corresponding planetary and Zodiacal principles.

Later, Dr Hahnemann (a German scientist), called the 'Father of Homoeopathy' was occupied with the theories of Paracelsus '*a posteriori*'. His findings and theories have been expounded in his major works: *Organon, Fragmenta de Viribus* (1805) and *Reine Arzneimittellehre* (1811). Homeopathic cure is based on three principles:

(1) Every sickness or suffering manifests itself for us SUBJECTIVELY as a synthesis of its symptoms.

(2) A medicine which provokes certain pathological results in a healthy organism can, under different conditions, assist in the removal of the same symptoms in a sick organism (SIMILIA SIMILIBUS CURANTUR, the maxim of Dr Hahnemann).

(3) Doses which remove the symptoms in a sick body are much smaller than those which produce adverse symptoms in a healthy body (law of small doses).

The foremost weapon used by many allopathic authorities against homoeopathic methods for 'removing the symptoms of sickness' was always that *Hahnemann tried to remove just the symptoms and not the sickness*. But this seems to be only a dialectic form of attack.

Deeply thinking occultists, and especially those who have followed these lessons, which give a manifold picture of this physical plane and its illusory manifestations, will not need any more extensive explanations from the side of the writer. Speaking openly, I do not want to defend Homoeopathy or condemn Allopathy, or vice versa, not being myself a medical specialist; but one thing seems to be clear: a sick person wants health. His *ailment manifests itself only by its symptoms*. Without the latter even allopaths cannot make any diagnosis. Now, if the former symptoms of the disease disappear, say, under Homoeopathic treatment (which facts allopaths do not deny), where then IS THE DISEASE ITSELF? Is it not cured?

The cardinal homoeopathic rule is, as we already know: 'SIMILIA SIMILIBUS CURANTUR'. This says quite clearly to us, that the principle of the dynamic reaction of medicine on the organism lies in the establishing of a contact between the astral of that medicine and the astrosome of the patient.

The fact should not worry us, that in some cases, the same action (in this one, the drug) will, under some conditions, bring definite and positive results, but under others will bring the opposite, or something different. Remember, that even *in the mental plane* a quite identical 'food' (that is, the same science given to a man) acts differently in different quantities and different states of mind.

I would like to quote a well-known French saying: '*Peu de science éloigne de Dieu; beacoup de science y ramène*'. ('A little knowledge diverts us from God; but great knowledge leads us to Him'.)

The law of small doses reminds us about the principle of '*finding the right starting point*' in every magic operation.

Finally, Dr Hahnemann recommends that all medicines be used in such a way as to cover most of the important symptoms of diseases.

Modern Homoeopathy, like Allopathy has advanced considerably since the days of its founder. True homoeopathic practitioners now almost invariably hold MD degrees, and use advanced methods of diagnosis, which are often astonishing in their accuracy. One of them has fairly recently been developed in Germany. It is based on reflections in the irises of a patient, which indicate exactly the seat and nature of the trouble. Complicated optical instruments are used for the purpose, and I have personal knowledge of facts relating to the system.

In my country (I am now living in Australia), there is a prominent *homoeopathic centre* in Melbourne, under the leadership of Mr J. M. (M.D.). I have witnessed infallible diagnoses even when the patients deliberately refrained from stating the nature of their complaints, leaving it to the doctor himself to find the trouble, which he did exactly after a brief examination according to the previously mentioned method of reflections. A correct diagnosis is always of foremost importance. Homoeopathy does not claim that it can invariably cure all diseases in all patients, and Allopathy does the same. But, in any case, it often does cure successfully although acting differently to Allopathy. It acts on the astrosome and its ganglions which correspond to the physical organs, rather than directly on the body. It is an old truth in occultism, that *every organic trouble begins in the astrosome*, and even then it may arise from the mental body. Therefore, the idea of acting directly on the source of disease seems to be neither wrong nor illogical.

Arcanum VII
CURRICULUM HERMETIS
THE CONQUEROR

Gemini

Spiritus Dominat Formam
Victoria
Jus Proprietatis

CHAPTER VII

ARCANUM VII (ʈ ZAIN)

BEFORE we pass on to an analysis of the Seventh Arcanum, we have to understand the scheme of the first six arcana, which gives us the basis for the seventh, as the final link in the FIRST SEPTENARY of the Tarot (see Fig. 22).

Most of the authors who have expounded the Tarot have used a similar construction. Husband (1) fecundates the wife (2) resulting in the birth of the child (3) which, being fed and nursed physically and astrally (4) attains sufficient authority (4) to manifest itself on the astral plane (5) in the name of the whole family; but there meets with the dilemma of *good and evil* (6), chooses the GOOD and gains the *victory* (7). For the Seventh Arcanum means just that VICTORY.

We see that its sign is the letter ʈ (Zain), the numerical value of which is also 7. The corresponding astrological sign is 'Gemini' or the 'Twins'. The hieroglyph is an arrow in direct flight, and means that once released, the arrow, by its regular movement, scores a direct hit on the target.

The name of the arcanum is 'Curriculum Hermetis' (Chariot of Hermes) and the vulgar name is simply 'the Chariot'.

The card for the Seventh Arcanum is rich in symbolism. At the top we see a blue canopy, strewn with golden pentagrams. This indicates the higher sub-planes of the astral world and their dwellers. These pentagrams surpass the man by their powers, but also assist him, by giving their protection.

The canopy is supported by four columns, that is Hermetic virtues already known to us as the fourfold maxim:

'TO DARE, TO BE SILENT, TO KNOW and TO TRY.'

Between these columns the Victor-Magician performs his activity as he stands beneath the canopy, wearing a golden crown adorned with three pentagrams, which symbolize his unenforced, free and conscious penetration into the three planes of the world. He is clad in the armour of Knowledge and Victory, which protects him from the many elements, so dangerous and deadly for a layman.

On the right shoulder of the Conqueror (as in a mirror) we see a white crescent moon. This means his ability to create realization of a subtle, evolutionary character, the 'Solve' of the Androgyne. But, above the left shoulder of the Conqueror there is a dark crescent moon telling us of his ability to condense subtle forms and also to realize things in the lower sub-planes: 'Coagula's' law.

The armour of the victorious magician bears the signs with which he can

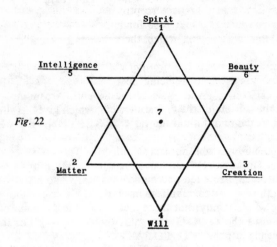

FIRST SEPTENARY
REPRESENTS GOD

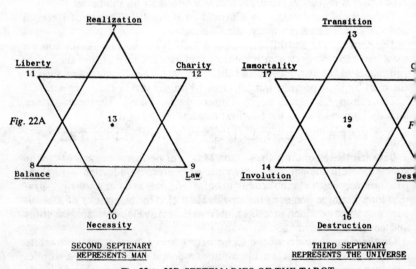

SECOND SEPTENARY
REPRESENTS MAN

THIRD SEPTENARY
REPRESENTS THE UNIVERSE

Fig. 22 to 22B SEPTENARIES OF THE TAROT

protect himself in case of attack: these are three right angles (90 degrees). They are: *correctness* of his logic; the *arranging* of his thoughts in a right form; and *keenness and infallibility* in physical realization.

In his right hand he holds a sceptre, ending with a sphere on which rests a square which is also a base for a regular triangle. The *symbolism: Spirit* dominates *form,* for which the *globe* (physical plane) is a background.

In his left hand there is the *sword of victory* which means his weapon on the physical plane, or convincing speech on the higher sub-planes of transition.

The Conqueror stands in a chariot of cubic form (*his realization*) (See the Fourth Arcanum). This form was created by the dynamic cycle י ה ו ה (Yod-Hé-Vau-Hé) symbolized on the front of the chariot as Egyptian ornamentation, that is a sphere (Yod), with two serpent-like offshoots (two Hé's), supported by outstretched wings (Vau). A little below this a lingam emerges, reminding us of another rendering of the Great Name: YODHEVA or YODHAVA, male and female principles. Two sphinxes pull the Conqueror's chariot. They are symbols of the *binary* of the astral forces, the middle part of the Great Arcanum. The left sphinx is black, the right one—white. They look at one another, but they pull in opposite directions (the two poles of the unique, universal, astral vortex or tourbillon).

The sphinxes are running over the surface of a great globe: this means the quaternary of the elementary Rota of the Great Arcanum.

Nail-heads holding the rims together, are visible on the wheels of the chariot. But the wheels are vortex-like creatures which serve for transmission of the astral tourbillons: the nail-heads are their eyes. That is to say, that the cells of these creatures have their own individuality and contemplation. As said the Prophet Ezekiel:

'And the wheels had height, posture and a terrible appearance: the whole body full of eyes around these four.'

The picture for this Seventh Arcanum is a very synthetic one; but so is the idea behind it, which ends the first great Septenary of the Tarot.

For the pentacle of this arcanum, early occultists used a septenary in the form given in Fig. 24, that is a seven-pointed star. Contemporary Hermetists often use another form for the same pentacle, as given in Fig. 25. Neither pentacle has the power of realization, and serve only as symbols. *Both may be reversed,* and then they will signify the idea of *black magic,* which corresponds to the equation $7 = 4 + 3$: that is *'an entangled, confused and complicated system of manifestation of forms will cause destruction of the ternary of spiritual impulses and will obscure the realization of the construction of the universe for men.'*

Analysis of the most important septenaries begins with the Great Septenary of the Secondary Causalities. In the Third Arcanum we learned to know a number of ternaries of the ascending type of triangle, which is easy to recapitulate by the general presentation of the Ternary of the Primary Causalities.

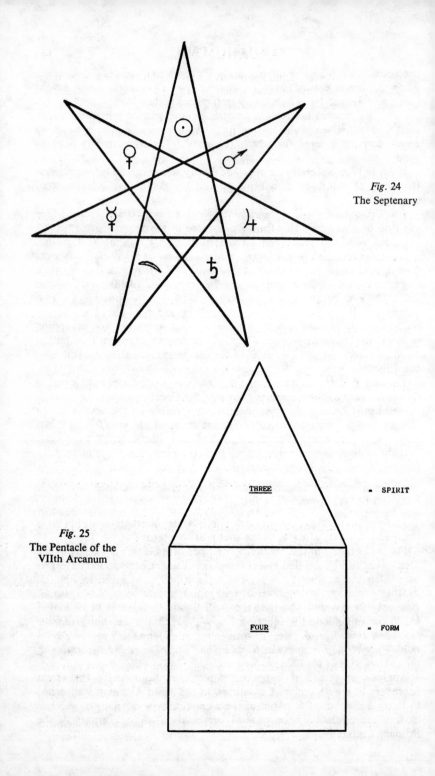

Fig. 24
The Septenary

Fig. 25
The Pentacle of the
VIIth Arcanum

THREE   = SPIRIT

FOUR   = FORM

If we begin to study—from the purely scientific point of view—the manifestations of the *Primary Cause*, which belong to the world of principles, emanated by them, then we will certainly find THREE *Primary Causalities* (Tres Causae Primae): the *Neutral element*, the *element of Being* (+), and the *element of Wisdom* (−). Accordingly, an imaginary conception of the *World of Emanation* in its highest plane will be transformed into the idea of manifestation, which immediately splits into two polarized ideas. These are: (a) *he who cognizes*, and (b) *he who can be known*. The third idea (−) will of course limit the realm of manifestation of the *second* idea and its derivatives.

If we want to create symbolical imagination of that sphere in Space, then the idea of manifestation will be joined to that of the symbol of ourselves plus the universal Space, filled with billions of billions of solar systems. This can be symbolically unfolded into our *thirst for knowledge*, (+) in the realm of astronomy and into the objects of that realm (−).

Three Primary Causes of the basic manifestation in the animistic subplane gives us a few reflections, which the ancient schools tried to reduce to the septenary system of Secondary Causes (Septem Causae Secundae). These *Causalities* can well be connected with that which the ancients called the '*seven planets of our solar system*'. As the basis of that symbolism we find the observations of many centuries (perhaps rather, thousands of years) which define the connection between the angular elements of the planets in the sky and the *preponderance of some influences of the animistic character of the earthly life*. Now we have to explain what we understand by terms like: planet and planetary influence.

Astronomy and astrophysics occupy themselves—apart from other researches—with seven coagulates to which we will give the names corresponding to the bodies of: Saturn, Jupiter, Mars, Sun, Venus, Mercury and the Moon. Many other branches of science occupy themselves extensively with an eight object—the body of the Earth. That is not our aim in this work.

Along with the image of each of these coagulates, (that is the bodies of the planets), we will still connect two pairs of concepts, one of which belongs to the astral plane, and another to the mental plane. Therefore, on the Earth, apart from its body in the physical world, we will seek after its Genius and Astrosome in the astral plane, and its Spirit and Angel in the mental one.

(1) According to our Hermetic tradition, the SPIRIT of the Earth is the synthesis of the spiritual stimulus of humanity in relation to its planet. At the present time, the Spirit of the Earth is the synthetic idea of our civilizing strivings, in an effort to reform our relations with the planet. This means the idea of their happy improvement.

(2) The ANGEL of the Earth is the ideological part of the resistance which earthly karma shows against human strivings (see (1)). The Spirit of the Earth is evolutionary, but the Angel is involutionary. When the great tragedy of the binary of the Earth; *SPIRIT-ANGEL* will be solved by the neutralization of that binary, by agreement between its elements, then the problem of the Earth's evolution will be solved in principle.

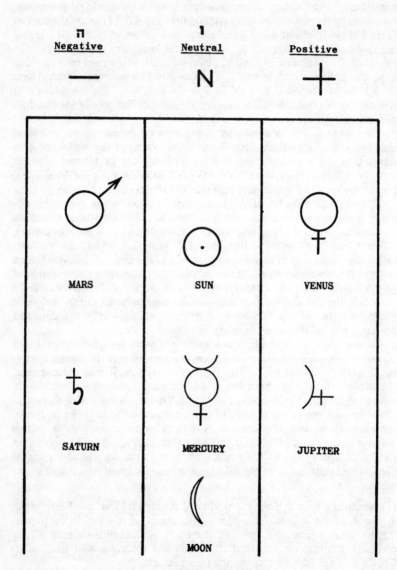

ה Negative —	ו Neutral N	׳ Positive +
MARS	SUN	VENUS
SATURN	MERCURY	JUPITER
	MOON	

Fig. 26 Secondary Causalities

(3) The GENIUS of the Earth is the synthesis of all the forms, in which the Spirit realizes its evolutionary ideas. These are the forms, as well as the formal methods which humanity realizes as a system for the shaping of the Earth for humanity's own aims.

(4) The ASTROSOME of the Earth is that synthetic astral tourbillon, which on the astral plane opposes the Genius of the planet and fights against him, trying to obstruct the aims of the Angel.

The *neutralization* of the binary GENIUS—ASTROSOME of the Earth gives the *formal* solution to the *problem called the evolution* of the Earth. But, rather as a matter of theory it does not quite give the final solution of the problem; for it must be related to the neutralization of another mysterious binary: BODY OF EARTHLY HUMANITY—BODY OF THE EARTH.

If, in principle, neutralization of the *highest binary* may be termed the Kingdom of God on Earth, then the *second binary* is neutralized as the Kingdom of God *in forms*, and the third, the Kingdom in Nature-matter.

On each of the seven planets, there is a similar scheme. Each planet has a spirit, an angel, a genius and an astrosome and its own kind of inhabitants (instead of human beings as on our Earth), no matter whether of the animal, vegetable or mineral kingdoms, in accordance with the particular planet's own evolution.

The *Hermetic conception* of different kinds of humanity being present on all the planets is much broader than that of official science, especially as it was at the beginning of this century. It avers that immaterial, immortal and illimitable CONSCIOUSNESS cannot be limited in the choice and creation of the forms in which it may be expressed. We are living, for example, under a very limited and poor range of temperature, about 100 degrees centigrade, or much less, if we ignore the artificial arrangements which we make to smooth over these limitations. I am speaking of clothes, heating appliances, and so on. The temperature of our body cannot vary more than *five degrees* centigrade, or we die. But, on other celestial bodies, there are colossal temperatures which do not occur on our Earth, and still matter exists, although in other combinations and conditions. So why cannot some kinds of consciousness (souls as we like to say) choose conditions most suited to them? Why should their astrosomes not build bodies, which can resist temperatures of say 100,000 degrees and capable of swimming in the fiery atmospheres of stars as we do in our own rivers and seas?

Hermetic science is far from being attached to anthropomorphism. It is our unconscious geocentric point of view, which does not allow us to take a much more progressive and broader outlook on life in this immense, infinite universe.

Tradition says, that planetary life (on other celestial bodies)—even if understandable to a few very advanced adepts of occultism—cannot be explained in our earthly language. We can realize only those elements of planetary life which are reflected in some definite forms in the realm of earthly existence. Astrology, the Kabbalah, and Magic speak clearly only about the influences of the Spirit, Genius, and so on, of another planet, but *not about its true being and nature*. We can judge the character of our acquaintances only according to how they appear to us in relation to ourselves. We may know very little about their domestic lives.

We will place these incomplete characteristics into an analogous position as regards the *Secondary Causes*, giving them planetary names. Do not forget, that *important mythological Egregors* having the names of the ancient gods of Greece and the Roman Empire, were in close astral relations with the planetary entities, in the form in which they manifested themselves in different epochs. And this supported and fortified the gods. But, the planetary entities changed their outlook according to the progress of their evolution, while the gods were more bound to their primary forms, so that the ties loosened with each passing century.

Because of his desire to restore the ancient gods to their original greatness, a great initiate-occultist and ascetic, a Roman Emperor whom Christians called Julian Apostata, performed a unique evocation of the mythological Egregors of the then recent past (one or two centuries earlier). And what did he see? A sad procession of sick, emaciated and powerless gods! The magician evidently could not suffer such a bitter disappointment over his most cherished ideals. He tried still once again to reverse the wheel of history. His idea was to try and subdue the whole of the then known world, which in the majority was still pagan, so that he would have better conditions in which to fight the young but powerful Egregor of Christianity and so revive the ancient cults.

He followed the path of Alexander the Great, to the East. Deep inside Persia he defeated its king, but triumphant in victory he launched a fiery pursuit of the fleeing enemy hordes, accompanied by only a handful of bodyguards, whose horses alone could keep up with the terrific speed of the young Emperor's steed. He had discarded his battle-helmet, and usual heavy armour, being convinced that his Egregor would protect him against any physical disaster; but some Persians who were despairingly fleeing from his sword turned and showered his small group with arrows and stone missiles.

A slightly ironical smile appeared on the lips of the mortally wounded Julian, when his generals told him of the victory and annihilation of the enemy's army. And when he pronounced his famous 'Thou hast conquered, Christ of Galilea!' ('Vincisti, Christe Galileo!'), he proved himself great enough to recognize his own personal defeat, which was much more important to him. The artificial effort to revive the dying Egregors could not have been successful and so it is even in our own time.

After this short digression we can pass on to an enumeration of planetary influences and their reflections.

Imagine seven Secondary Causalities, reflected in the triangle of the Primary Causalities, in the form of three columns, as in Fig. 26. The planets in the right column are recognized as '*good*'; those of the left as '*evil*'; of the Sun we say that it is '*synthetic*'; of Mercury that he '*adapts*' himself, while the Moon is '*passive*'.

Planets	Angels	Single Numbers	Colours	Aromas	Metals	Stones	Sacraments	Periods of Life	Obverse of the Talismans	Reverse of the Talismans	Days of the Week	Remarks Can also be:-
♄ ☽	Oriphiel Jehudiel Zaphkiel	3 Serpent	Black	Sulphur	Lead	Magnetite Iron Ore Chalcedony	Extreme Unction	Old Age	Scythe	Head of a Goat or a Bull	Saturday	Cassiel, Machatan and Uriel
♃	Zadkiel Sealtice	4	Blue	Saffron	Tin	Sapphire Beryl	Eucharist	Maturity	Crown	Head of an Eagle	Thursday	Sachiel, Castiel and Asasiel
♂	Samael Barachiel	5	Red	Peppermint Ginger	Iron	Amethyst	Penance	Youth	Sword	Head of a Lion	Tuesday	
☉	Michael	6 Tourbillon	Yellow	Red Sandalwood	Gold	Carbuncle Chrysolite Sun-stone	Orders	Childhood	Circle	Man	Sunday	
♀	Anael Uriel	7 Regular Figures	Green	Verbena Musk	Copper	Lapis lazuli	Matrimony	Youth (Middle)	G	Head of a Lion	Friday	
☿	Raphael	8 Caduceus	Multi-coloured	Mastic	Mercury	Emerald Agate	Confirmation	Passage to Maturity	Winged Caduceus	Pigeon	Wednesday	
☽	Gabriel	9	White	Aloes White Sandalwood Amber Camphor	Silver	Crystal Pearl White coral	Baptism	Early Youth	Moon (Sign)	Head of a Dog	Monday	

Fig. 27 Planetary Angels

The Sun in relation to the Moon will be a male element, fecundating it through the intermediary of Mercury. We also term Mars, Apollo (Sun), Saturn and Jupiter as male planets; but according to purely mythological conceptions, Venus and the Moon are female. Mercury may be spoken of as androgynous, which agrees with its role of mediator in fecundation.

These seven Secondary Causalities are shown with their most important analogies in the table in Fig. 27 and the necessary commentary follows in the next lesson.

LESSON 24

Commentary on the Table in Fig. 27

(*1*) *Column of Planetary Signs:* the planetary signs are represented in their primary forms (symbols), but firstly there is:

+ The sign of the *elements* and their influence. Remember the four animals of the Rota?

♄ The sign for *Saturn* is a combination of the Moon and the cross. The character of Saturn's influence is such, that surroundings make a stronger impression on him than intuitional currents in consciousness.

♃ The reverse of this applies to *Jupiter* and the accepted form of the symbol is also reversed.

♂ *Mars*, apart from the sign of the Sun, also has an arrow, which shows us a particular way in which to receive vital fluids, while under his influence. The arrow points to the fiery signs of the Zodiac which fortify the influx of the fluids. Everything received from Mars comes in a strong and unexpected form.

☉ The sign of the *Sun*, symbol for all emanations of vital energy, and the revitalizing fluids.

♀ The sign of *Venus* indicates that in her sphere of influence the amount of vital force is more important than the surroundings or conditions.

☿ The synthetic sign of *Mercury* may be analysed as: ◡ sign of the Moon—susceptibility; ☉ on the second plane—influx of vital fluids; + occupying the third position in the symbol signifies surroundings and their influence. Practically, an example can be given to make the theory more apparent: in the question of education, firstly there is the ability of the pupil, secondly the quality of the school (calibre of the teachers), and thirdly, the surroundings of the pupil, such as his schoolmates, and so on.

☾ The sign of the *Moon* is the symbol for capacity, susceptibility, intuition, and ability to reflect the fluids received.

For the sake of interest I would like to add, that some astrologers give the sign of the Earth as ♁, explained as the overwhelming importance in earthly life of conditions beyond the astral principle in man. Together with G.O.M. and others, I will abstain from any comment connected with this matter.

(2) *Column of Planetary Angels*: only the most widely used names are given in this table. Some differences in spelling, which perhaps you may note, are due to different positions of the Angels in the symbolism of the Hebrew, Chaldean and Syrian languages, plus some neologisms introduced by the Gnostic School. In this table under the term 'Angel' I understand a joint influence (mental) of both Angel and Spirit, in that part, which can still be felt in the manifestations of earthly life.

In order to clarify this table, I have to show the characters of the planets as they influence human life on all three planes.

Here I would like to add a very important statement: *planetary influences are not something unavoidable like fate*. There is an axiom in Astrology: 'ASTRA INCLINANT SED NON NECESSITANT', which is well known to all astrologers, but unfortunately, almost always practically forgotten. This means that planetary forces can only influence us by making some things more possible for us, so that our activities probably function according to astrological predictions. This is valid for all men of lower, instinctive and impulsive natures. They do not possess much will-power of their own, independent of their moods and attitudes, and make little use of what they do have. Such men will surely feel the influence of the periods when one or another planet exerts a stronger one. And they will act accordingly. At the time of Mars, they will be more pugnacious or unbalanced, and therefore more violence can be expected during these periods, while at the time of the influence of Venus, love affairs will probably flourish, and so on. Things are simple!

But, for those who direct, or at least try to direct their lives in another, more reasonable pattern, and in whom will-power is far more developed, as well as knowledge of emotional techniques, astrology has much less to offer, except, that at some time they will experience such and such temptations and inclinations, to do things in one way and not another. However, in the case of the impulsive type of man, the result cannot be predicted. Therefore, for a strong man, astrology is of much less value than for weaklings. Great Masters and advanced occultists do not concern themselves with astrology at all. So you may do similarly, if you are one of the aforementioned types.

♄ *Saturn*: in the *mental* plane he represents the idea of the invariability of logical laws; in the *astral* he oppresses us with reminders about the hardness of karmic laws; on the *physical* plane he dictates material experiences, melancholy moods, anxiety and often extreme parsimony.

♃ *Jupiter*: *mentally* he teaches us about the necessity of using systematic actions and thinking under all conditions; in the *astral* he creates and sustains authority; on the *physical* he sows justice, and respects and supports administrative talents and abilities.

♂ *Mars*: in the mental plane he reminds us about the possibility of acceleration and strengthening of processes; in the *astral* he suggests virility and rigidity, which on the *physical* plane may support all violent, angry and uncontrolled actions.

☉ *Sun*: in the *mental* gives all kinds of active influxes, which in the *astral* suggest a taste for forms, as well as desire to partake with others of the fruits of our activities in that realm; on the *physical* plane the Sun creates a taste for art, generosity and distaste for vulgar things.

♀   *Venus*: is the representative of *universal attraction* in all its forms; in the *astral* this means everything which we call 'love'; in the physical world, she signifies the material side of attraction, which needs no further explanation.

☿   *Mercury*: in the *mental* realm he teaches us to adapt ourselves to ideas; in the *astral* he suggests vivid desires, and the ability to change them, while on the *physical* he is the father of all business and speculation, as well as of versatility in us.

☽   *The Moon*: as Mother of the world, is susceptible to *mental* influxes; intuitional in the *astral* realm, and in the *physical* one, the manifestation of such things in the form of moodiness, inclination to certain kinds of clairvoyance, and submission to suggestions and fatalism, or faith in destiny.

(3) *The Column of Single Figures*: is given in order to complete the table. In some of the later occult schools, the characters and numbers in it serve to conceal the meaning of the column of planetary influences. For my own part I have not changed the traditional form as I do not ascribe much value to this attitude. Actually, the figure '3' is somewhat similar to the sign for Saturn and that of a serpent, which is dedicated to that planet; '4' is very close to the symbol for Jupiter; '5' may look like a very badly drawn sign for Mars, and '6' may remind us of the vortexes, tourbillons and vibrations of all kinds with which the Sun blesses us so generously. To Venus are dedicated all regular shaped figures, for who is more worthy of such a tribute to outer things of harmony and beauty? The figure '8' might suggest the caduceus of Mercury, and '9' that of two unequally drawn crescents of the Moon.

(4) *The Colours of the Planets*: these have not only a conditional meaning in rituals for planetary ceremonial magic; but may still serve for the distinguishing of manifestations, connected with one or another planet.

Speaking in terms of the *auras*, that is the subtle emanations of partially materialized planetary entities, we find that these contain the shades of the planetary colours, which thereby underline the background of these visions.

(5) *The Column of Aromas*: this gives the prescriptions used for related planetary magic operations. Incense is synthetic to such a degree, that it can easily substitute every other kind of aroma, but it should be noted, that when using incense, the moods of the operator become more mystical. That is why incense does not figure in any planetary operations of black magic.

When aromas have to be used in magic operations, the substances are burned directly or allowed to smoulder on hot charcoal. Aromas of vegetable origin can be used as extracts made with alcohol, or dried parts of plants. This second variation is much more desirable and effective.

(6) *Planetary Metals*: These are mentioned only for use in some ceremonial operations, as well as for making planetary talismans and pentacles. The difference between talismans and pentacles is subtle, for both can be worn on one's body. A *talisman* is made for the purpose of condensing energy already existing in the individual. Because of this, it would be nonsensical for a person almost devoid of Jupiter's influence to wear that planet's talisman.

In contrast to talismans, *pentacles*, as a result of their preparation and consecration, are magnetized with the fluids of definite planets, and thereby can artificially create a tie with the egregoric elements of those planets. The person previously mentioned, might wear a pentacle consecrated to Jupiter, just because he feels the need to have the influence of that planet, with which he does not possess any natural liaison.

Now it is time to tell you about the method of creating a pentagram, used in magic operations. The general character of the pentagram relates to its synthetic properties. Therefore on the physical plane it should be made of an alloy containing the seven planetary metals. On the astral plane, the ceremony of its consecration must put us into contact with all seven planetary influences. The pentagram is consecrated by six minor and one major magic ceremonies. The great ceremony must be performed under the influence of the planet which dominates the astral of the future bearer of the pentagram. The remaining six minor operations belong to the six other planets.

The synthesis of the pentagram's elements suggest to us not only the thought about the necessity for summarizing the planetary influences; but also our recognition of the polarity of human nature and contemplation, which are neutralized in the person of a true occultist-magician.

A slight reminder for the student: he must always clearly grasp the terms used in every sentence of this course, otherwise, for him, it becomes merely a confused exposition of an unknown subject.

So, when speaking here of the 'polarity' of a human being, we mean that there are two opposite poles in consciousness, and consequently in all our bodies. We are able to do both good and evil; we are apt to seek after the noisy life of great cities with their empty entertainments and sins; but we are also able to remain in the peace of inner silence, independent of all our surroundings.

In us, and *nowhere else but in us*, there is potentially a saint and a devil-like black occultist; in us are the sublime intelligence and practical, unselfish idealism of Thomas a Kempis and Albert Schweitzer, but we also produce reckless egotism and contempt for man's legitimate rights, and the cruelty of the Stalins and the Hitlers.

Advanced occultists and spiritual masters know this fact very well, and from it comes their *equality* towards all men, the thing which an average man cannot and should not attempt to try before he is ripe. Simply because an indiscriminate, even though well-intended action, brings only harm and often catastrophe. I cannot but quote here a well-known tale about the hermit and his bear. A saintly man who lived in a desert, domesticated a large bear, which served the old man by bringing him wild honey and frightening away annoying flies, which tried to settle on the hermit's bald head. One day, noticing an especially cheeky fly, which was unafraid of the branch which the hermit had given to his bear to wave over him, the animal decided to destroy the small offender. The bear took a heavy stone, watched carefully until the fly came to rest on the hermit's pate, and then hit it hard, thereby destroying the insect and at the same time the brains of his master.

The variations on this old tale, although in different and not such drastic outer forms, are committed too often by human beings to be ignored.

LESSON 25

The knowledge of the polarity and the hidden possibilities in man must be very clearly realized by every Hermetist, or aspirant for the same knowledge. This is always depicted on pentagrams as follows:

(1) Drawing of the signs י (Yod) and ה (Hé)—human androgyne.

(2) The letters 'Alpha' and 'Omega'—knowledge of the Source of primeval Man on the Earth, that is his *origin* and *aim*, towards which present humanity is striving, consciously or unconsciously, and which highest aim is called in occultism, the REINTEGRATION OF MAN: the most sublime idea which we are able to know. This is the Kingdom of God of which Christ spoke; this is the Nirvana of Lord Buddha; the Ain-Soph of the Kabbalists, and the Realization of the Supreme Self in us, as taught in this our own epoch, by the Great Rishi Ramana Maharshi.

(3) Associated with these Greek letters are the Hebrew ones: א (Aleph) and ת (Than), which symbolize the Major Arcana of the Tarot, as the framework or basis of our occult contemplation.

(4) The names of the Sephiroth (an explanation of which appears in the next lessons), *Chesed* (grace, clemency) and *Pechad* (severity, justice), two elements neutralized by *Tiphereth* (harmony and beauty) born from them in the realm of the ethical evolution of humanity, should be written in Hebrew.

The great ceremony for the *consecration of a pentagram* has, of course, a synthetic character, which is in relation to the four Hermetic elements about which you already know a lot from this course, and in the centre of the CROSS which they form, the future magician will find his place. The meaning of these words has also been mentioned in previous lessons.

The pentagram should be breathed over by the operator (a hint on the Element of Air), sprinkled with consecrated water (Element of Water in Alchemy), dried in the smoke of incense (Element of Fire) and, for some time, be placed on soil (Element of Earth). Each of these manipulations is performed five times in the sequence just given, while pronouncing the holy letters: Yod (bowing to the East); Hé (bowing to the North); Vau (to the West), and Hé (bowing to the South). Finally, the letter Shin is pronounced while standing in the centre of the cross and looking straight upwards at the sky.

As an indispensable final element of the consecration of your penta-gram, comes a traditional whispering of the synthetic Great Word AZOTH (see the lessons of the Fourth Arcanum).

If it is difficult to make the pentagram of an alloy of the seven metals, it is sufficient to be satis. ˙ed with an alloy of the two most precious ones, that is gold and silver, or ˅ ˙en of gold alone. Occultists often draw the pentagram on virgin parchment, and use it in lieu of a metallic one. Personally I consider a pentagram to be superior when it is made precisely from an alloy of gold and silver.

If intended to be worn, it can be made about one inch or less in width; but for magic operations, especially in an attempt at astral exteriorization, a much larger one is needed, about 8 or 10 inches across, and this can be drawn as already mentioned.

(7) *The Column of Stones*: the ones mentioned were used for manufacture of Gnostic talismans, the vulgar name of which was 'ABRAXAS'. The following characters were cut on these talismans: for ♄ (Saturn), a limping old man or a snake rolling round the sun-stone; for ♃ (Jupiter), an eagle with a pentagram held in its claws or in its beak; for ♂ (Mars), a dragon biting the handle of a sword; for ☉ (Sun), a snake with a lion's head; for ♀ (Venus), a triple Hermetic caduceus (sign of AZOTH), or a kinocephalus (man with the head of a dog), and for ☾ (the Moon), a globe with two crescent moons cutting into its surface.

(8) *The Column of Christian Sacraments*: shows their correspondence to the planets, which is recognized by the majority of representatives of the *Christian Episcopal Egregor*. These form a simple sequel to the develop-ment of the esoteric elements belonging to the Christian Tradition and Teachings used by those Fathers of the Church, who knew about the Initiatory Teachings.

(a) *Extreme Unction* in which a blessing is transmitted to cleanse the astrosome of sinful clichés, which, in some way, missed receiving help from the Sacrament of Penance. This Unction is dedicated to Saturn, because it belongs to elements, which unfortunately infiltrated into the karma of a Christian.

(b) The *Eucharist* is the Sacrament which, when used for the first time, announced the power of the baptized one in the realm of evolutionary Christian activity. Used subsequently in our life, it renews those same powers. Therefore, it is put under the sign of Jupiter.

(c) *Penance* which needs strong inner effort in order to cleanse the astro-some of every impurity hidden in it. This often requires a fight against a man's unwillingness to confess his faults, even when he knows perfectly well, that no one apart from the impersonal priest will hear him. This relates Penance to Mars.

(d) *Orders* which give the ability and authority to spread the rays of Christian light, are naturally put under the sign of the Sun.

(e) *Matrimony* being the sequel to mutual attraction, belongs to Venus.

(f) *Confirmation* which affirms the ability of man to speculate in the realm of Christian dogmas and ethics, or prepares us to follow Christian ideals, belongs to Mercury.

(g) *Baptism* by the ritual itself is in connection with water, and so is associated with the Moon's influence.

It may be useful to note, that on the ritual side of Baptism—especially in the old Greek-Orthodox Church—it exactly symbolizes the first *astral* exit of the neophyte-initiate, under the care of, or even in the company of the Master and future companions. Through this first exteriorization, the newly initiated aspirant merges into the realm of influence of the Earth's astrosome, defeats the involutionary reactions of its dark clichés, ascends into the pure astral and returns to his body, *in order to begin a new life as an initiate.* The whirling current of the Earth's astrosome is here symbolized by the act of bathing in water, from which the baptized one emerges as if regenerated.

As we see, in the light of occultism, the exoteric Sacraments regain their esoteric meaning and contents.

(9) *The Periods of Life*: these are easy to divide among the planets if we realize that in *childhood* there is the foremost need for the free influx of the vital forces given by the *Sun*. The more developed susceptibility to outer influences has its place in *early youth* and therefore belongs to the *Moon*. Similarly, in *youth* are manifested the beginnings of *attraction* (*Venus*) and *violent reactions and deeds* (*Mars*). Passing on to the more *mature* age, there appears the ability of *adaptation*, which therefore refers to *Mercury*, while *full maturity* does not feel any lack of *methods or systems* in the current of life (*Jupiter*), and *old age* possesses an inclination to form *logical laws* and extreme cautiousness (*Saturn*).

(10) *The Column of the Obverse of the Talismans*: the usual magic planetary talismans must bear the image of the Microcosm (pentagram) and under it the relevant attribute as indicated in this column.

(11) *The Column of the Reverse of the Talismans*: these should have the sign of the Macrocosm (Solomon's Star) and the appropriate attribute as shown.

A disc of corresponding metal (as given in this table) must be used as material for the talisman (but not for a pentagram or pentacle). For Mercury's talisman we should have, of course, an alloy of all the metals, whose planetary influences are not opposite to those of the owner of the talisman.

(12) *The Column of the Days of the Week*: the order of the planetary bodies is accepted as follows:

$$\hbar \quad \text{♃} \quad \text{♂} \quad \odot \quad \text{♀} \quad \text{☿} \quad \text{☾}$$

The *Sun* has a Sunday dedicated to it; the *Moon*—Monday, *Mars*—Tuesday, *Mercury*—Wednesday, *Jupiter*—Thursday, *Venus*—Friday, and *Saturn*—Saturday. This scheme can be adapted to fit the points of the star-like *septenary*, which we use as a pentacle of the Septenary (see Fig.

24). For planetary magic ceremonies it is advised always to take days which correspond to the particular planets.

The magic year begins at the moment of sunrise of the day of the spring equinox, as given in the calendar.

We still have to speak about the so-called 'friendship' and 'animosity' of the planets, and to indicate the principles for the calculation of planetary hours on different days of the week. Very valuable schemes for that purpose are given in Papus' famous *Traité Elémentaire de Science Occulte*. In astrology, under 'friendship' between the planets we recognize the increase of good or the diminishing of evil influences of one planet on another. In general courses on Magic under 'friendship' is understood the SUPPORT for, and under 'animosity' the WEAKENING of the influence between planets. We will speak again about these questions in the Seventeenth Arcanum, but here we will give only a list of the relations between the planets as accepted by contemporary occult schools.

(I) SATURN is friendly with Mars, but unfriendly towards all others. Fatal accidents are encouraged by violence of desires and other manifestations of the human will, but are hampered because of the active character of the rest of the SECONDARY CAUSALITIES.

(II) JUPITER is friendly to all except Mars. This is really because a methodical and favourable attitude cannot be useful for violent moods.

(III) MARS is friendly only with Venus, and unfriendly to all others. The attractive force of love often produces violence and suddenness in its manifestations, but the *logic* of Saturn, the intelligent *favour* of Jupiter, the *generosity* of the Sun, the *adaptibility* of Mercury and the tender *passiveness* of the Moon repel everything that is sudden and violent.

(IV) The SUN is helped in the spreading of its *beneficient influence* by the *favourable* Jupiter, *adaptable* Mercury, and *attractive* Venus; but not by the cold Saturn and violent Mars.

(V) VENUS is *favourable* to the wealth of vital fluids of the Sun, to the cordial elations of Mars, to the compliance of Mercury, and to the susceptibility of the Moon; but she cannot endure the cold logic of Saturn. In the case of the experienced administrator Jupiter, we cannot say that he either likes or recognizes Venus, but he would like to limit and to control her activities, and therefore does not gain either her sympathy or her hate.

(VI) MERCURY *adapts* himself to any influences.

(VII) The MOON accepts everything *passively*.

We are now passing on to the method for the calculation of planetary hours, which are indispensable, since magic operations need not only favourable days, but also suitable hours.

The *magic day* begins at the moment of the astronomical sunrise in a given place on the Earth, and is divided into the *magic day* (from sunrise to sunset) and *magic night* (from sunset to sunrise).

As we can see, the days and nights in different seasons and in different countries can vary greatly. Therefore, for every operation, calculations must be made according to the instructions given. These are so simple, that no example seems necessary.

The *magic day* is divided into 12 equal parts, called the *magic hours of that day*. The night is also divided into twelve equal hours.

On *Sunday* the first magic hour of the day is dedicated to the Sun. On *Monday* to the Moon, on *Tuesday* to Mars, and so on, according to the table in Fig. 27.

The other hours follow relatively in the order in which they appear as given in the same Fig. 27. So, for example, on Sunday the second hour of the day will belong to Venus, the third to Mercury, the fourth to the Moon, fifth to Saturn, sixth to Jupiter, seventh to Mars, eighth to the Sun, ninth to Venus, tenth to Mercury, eleventh to the Moon and the twelfth to Saturn. Accordingly, the first hour of the night belongs to Mercury, the eighth also to him, the tenth to the Sun, the twelfth to Mercury, and on Monday the first hour of the new day to the Moon, as has already been stated.

The possibility of such a division is assured by the fact, that on one hand, 24 divided by 7 gives 3 as the remainder, and on the other hand, the days of the week are divided between planets according to the intervals, passing over two planets to the third.

A brief analysis of the titles of the Seventh Arcanum and its equations will be useful for us in order to have a better understanding of the table which we have been discussing. So in the realm of the Archetype's manifestations

Equation No. 18: $7 = 3 + 4$

Tells us that domination of the SPIRIT ('Natura Divina'—Third Arcanum) over FORM (Fourth Arcanum) gives the axiom 'SPIRITUS DOMINAT FORMAM'.

Equation No. 19: $7 = 4 + 3$

Gives the reversed, illusory idea, worthy of black magic insanity, for it tells us that 'forms rule over their contents (Spirit)'.

On the human plane we will consider

Equation No. 20: $7 = 1 + 6$

This means that *Will and Experience* are both ways to give us *Victory*. The corresponding title VICTORIA is clear; but a *defeat in experience*, expressed by another equation ($7 = 6 + 1$) means catastrophe, a lost incarnation.

On the plane of Nature we will use an interesting equation of the pattern:

Equation No. 21: $7 = 5 + 2$

The *pentagrammatic principles* (5) (tradition, custom, religion) dominate the Second Arcanum (Natura Naturata, objects realized by Nature), which domination indicates the *law of property*, and creates another title for the rich contents of this arcanum: IUS PROPRIETATIS.

Of course, the equations which I quote here are not all that are possible with the numerical operations based on the Tarot's arcana. Only the most important are given and the rest I am leaving to the student, as his *obligatory and practical part on this work*, providing that he *really wants to penetrate* into the magnificent temple of Hermetism, built by the great occultists of the West. Only then will he appreciate their unique development and deeds, bowing his head together with the writer in silence and veneration before those masters of the past, in the joyous hope of perhaps encountering one of them while still in this life, as others have done.

Anyway, other minor equations are officially less used by initiatory schools, than those offered in this work.

To conclude matters connected with the Seventh Major Arcanum, we may ask ourselves whether all this astrology with its complications and calculations, not to speak of the much more difficult matters connected with magic, are indispensable to the average human life? The true answer will be in the negative. We can live very well without them. But, as human beings, we are also the CELLS of the Great Universal Man, the Archetype, and no two cells are identical in him. Therefore, in occultism it is accepted, that there are many ways in which the cells can be reintegrated, that is *consciously* return into the ONE. Actually, nobody can say that even now we are apart from this ONENESS. It is true that now we may NOT BE CONSCIOUS of it, and we have to regain this consciousness, known in Hermetism as REINTEGRATION. It may be possible that one of these ways is astrology.

n

Arcanum VIII
THEMIS
JUSTICE

Cancer

Libratio
Lex
Karma

CHAPTER VIII

ARCANUM VIII (ח HETH)

THE *letter* corresponding to the Eighth Arcanum of the Tarot is ח (Heth) and the *number* connected with it is 8. Astrologically, this arcanum belongs to the sign of Cancer.

Its hieroglyph is a FIELD, meaning everything which needs work, cultivation. It is just that passive realm on which should be turned the activity of the Conqueror of the Seventh Arcanum.

In the background of the picture there are two columns with a canopy between them. In the foreground is a woman's figure (Themis) seated between the columns. Her head is crowned and wears a golden band, while another covers her eyes which prevents her from seeing anything ahead.

On her breast a Solar Cross hangs from a chain. In her right hand we see a set of scales, and in the left a naked sword. The picture is made as in a mirror.

She seems to sit on a cube-shaped stone which is hidden from sight of the observer by the folds of her flowing garments.

We will begin to analyse the card with the statement, that the figure of the seated woman gives us a definite idea of passivity, of something made and accomplished, and no longer acting.

We see three binaries in this card, all neutralized by third elements. The *first binary* consists of the two columns, neutralized by Themis in the 'middle space'. The explanation here differs somewhat from previous ones: 'If you see Jakin (right column) with Themis in the middle, then on the other side there must be Bohaz.'

If you see that there is a force on one side, and recognize the existence of the astral vortex (tourbillon) to which the force seen also belongs, then you should anticipate the existence of a second force, balancing the whole construction, and directed to the opposite side.

We have the power of imagination in the present, and we can turn it back to the past to read the related clichés. Then, of necessity we must recognize the possibility of using the same power for the future, that is to read clichés on the other side of the present, or—future. If we believe in the existence of the HIGHEST ANDROGYNOUS MANIFESTA-TION of Divinity, and see in Its emanations the qualities of activity, expansion, of that which KNOWS, then we may be convinced of the existence of another emanation, passive, of attractive character, and representing that, which can be KNOWN.

If there is JUSTICE (— minus) and possibility of spiritual harmony (neutral), then there must also be the third element—GRACE or CHARITY (+ active).

If there is the idea of ascent (upwards movement) and level ground, then the idea of the existence of descent (downwards movement) is not to be avoided.

These formulas lead us to the first title of the Eighth Arcanum in the Archetype's plane—LIBRATIO the idea of balance, the great metaphysical scales, *one side* of which is loaded with the positive pole of the Great Arcanum, and the other with the negative pole, while the *indicator* symbolizes the Androgynous apex of the Ascending Triangle. The second title of this arcanum is LEX (Law).

The scales which Themis holds in her right hand form another binary with a neutralizing element. We may refer it to the realm of Nature. If someone were to move one of the scale-pans to one side, movement will start in the other because of the necessity of regaining balance. If we place five pounds weight on the left side of the scales and do not have sufficient time to remove it, five pounds must also be put on the other side in order to maintain the balance.

If someone, because of acting in a way contrary to the Laws of Balance, has spoiled his karma, that record of his personality in the chain of incarnations, he MUST REMOVE THIS STAIN at the time of a fresh encounter with the 'page' he has spoiled. I think this simile is sufficiently illuminating in order to realize the mechanism of karma, or the LAW OF CAUSE AND EFFECT, which is of so much concern to every true occultist.

So, on the physical plane, the THIRD TITLE of the Eighth Arcanum will be just—KARMA. And the picture itself has the title: THEMIS, or JUSTICE.

In our arithmological analysis of the arcanum the first equation takes the form of:

Equation No. 22: $8 = 1 + 7$

The *First Arcanum* is the mystery of the conscious manifestations of applications of androgynous, balanced principles. The *Seventh Arcanum* is that of victory. Therefore, $1 + 7$ means none other than the use, or application of that victory. And there is no doubt, that the first duty and care of the victor lies in the introduction of order, lawfulness and justice in the conquered realm.

Justice is the spouse of the victor; the *Eighth Arcanum* is the wife of the *Seventh*.

Where does the magician use the fruits of his mental victory? Naturally, in the astral plane, by his astral operations. And it is just here that he must now be aware of the Law of Balance (Libratio) and not forget about the importance of contrary animistic moods.

For example, you decided to suggest some definite deed or action to a person (the subject). Thereby the *mental impulse* is already there. But now comes the difficulty, you yourself passionately want your suggestion to be fulfilled. In other words, you are astrally interested in it. And this is a great obstacle for its realization. Brakes may then appear because of the creation of this other component force of that pair, that is the *essential tourbillon* which serves as the instrument of realization for your suggestion.

In order to avoid all of this, you should immediately build another component: COUNTERBALANCE YOUR ASTRAL DESIRE WITH ONE OF NON-DESIRE WHICH WILL BE OF EQUAL MAGNITUDE (in other words, be ready to become uninterested in the results or develop what Hindus call—'VAIRAGYA'). Another explanation is, that we succeed best in action when we accomplish it in the *first moment*, without adding any of our own animistic and personal interests to it.

This explains why prayer for others is much more effective than for ourselves! That is why one who wants quickly and righteously to win or conquer, must have charitable moods. This may look like a paradox for the uninitiated, but it is a well-known truth for occultists. That is why a strong person waits for a favourable moment in which to fight, unlike the weaker, who should think about this much more than his adversary.

When we speak here about justice, the question arises, *whether* and in *which way* an occultist can allow himself to defeat or to overcome his neighbour. But the astral cliché will create itself through the Eighth Arcanum and then one could be anxious only about the mental conception of the transgression committed by our neighbour. The mental judgement of the whole thing will create the axis of the astral tourbillon, and the astral will do the rest.

One may say that the Law of Karma is determined once and for all, and the negative pole of Fabre d'Olivet's triangle emanates this law. Yes, and therefore an enlightened occultist has the right to judge the acts of his neighbours only in so far as he participates in the work of the Emanation of the Primary Cause.

Briefly, only a true theurgist has the right to defeat another man. Theurgy itself presupposes a very great clarity of contemplation and purity of feelings, so that in accordance with the Law, we can very seldom defeat someone else.

The magic punishments which Christian Illuminism allows its adepts have a collective name—'Reprobatio' which literally means a kind of condemnation.

We know of three types (1) *lack of recognition* (positive) of a man's actions, (2) *sorrow* for his actions, (3) *condemnation* of them.

(1) An expression of *lack of recognition* may take the form: 'Although you are my brother, I would not like to participate in the clichés of your deeds. *We are not united.*'

In very extreme cases, Christ allowed His disciples to use this degree of punishment only in its symbolic form: '... SHAKE OFF THE DUST FROM YOUR FEET.'

(2) In rare cases, Christ Himself used another degree, that of *sorrow*, *mourning* or *regret* for the misdeeds of His neighbours: 'BETTER THIS MAN WERE NOT BORN.'

(3) The third and *highest degree* of punishment thunders with its violence and pitiless consequences. We can see many examples of it in the acts of MOSES, who widely used theurgic means against his own rebellious people. Recall the penalty of fiery death which he inflicted on those who—in his absence—began to adore the golden calf, as well as the means he used in his fight against the Egyptian Pharoah.

Much closer to us in time is the classic example of a terrible and effective condemnation, which, from among the flames round his stake, the Great Master of the Knights Templar—*Jacobus Burgundus Molay*—pronounced against Pope Clement V and the French King, Philip IV. He called them before God's Judgement. The first 'not later than fifty days' and the second 'in a year's time'. It is well known that both men had condemned Molay and many of his knights to torture and death, falsely accusing them of black magic and other crimes, but actually, only on any pretext to enable them to seize the great wealth of the Templars' Order. The curse was fulfilled and both men died even sooner than the time set by Molay.

Now, on a Hermetic basis let us analyse the value of the so-called 'curse'. If, say, a father curses his son, he has the support of only one arcanum, the Fourth (that of authority), there being no other arcana for him to use. But, the *Law of Reprobation*, as mentioned in the three previous examples, refers to the Eighth Arcanum, and has to pass through the Sixth and Seventh Arcana, thereby securing the Hermetic victory for the one who pronounced such a condemnation. You will probably have to meditate deeply in order to fathom the secret that lies hidden in *lawful reprobation*.

Another equation possible with the Eighth Arcanum is:

Equation No. 23: $8 = 7 + 1$

You may solve it for yourself in order to get training in Hermetic thinking. However, I will help you to a certain extent, by saying that it may be finally 'the preponderance of the *personal* (that is, egoistic) victory over the manifestation of balanced WILL, which means a conscious and wilful passivity on the part of the victor.'

Equation No. 24: $8 = 2 + 6$

Here 2 is *Gnosis*, and 6 the *Law of Reaction* in the universe. The whole is evidently the work of an enlightened operator in the realms of the *static* and *dynamic binaries*. But how can the Law of Reaction (6) develop contemplation in the learned operator? Merely by suggesting to him the existence of the RETURN BLOW! This is a thing which every occultist must know and handle carefully. The following are examples of it:

Imagine someone operating magically, that is creating an astral vortex of a definite type against another man. Here I should explain something important. When I am discussing occult matters and practices here, I am doing so impartially and purely *as a lecturer* who expounds the themes he has to bring before his audience without necessarily personally approving of them. The reader should understand, that the writer of this book *did not invent Hermetism* and its practical applications—the arcana. He only studied both, and is merely communicating the material to willing students, who may evaluate and use it according to their own needs. This book is not intended for beginners in occultism, for such people will *not understand* very much of it. There are plenty of things WRITTEN BETWEEN THE LINES which the able student should discover for himself, as they CANNOT be openly told or written in a book.

Nevertheless, more than once throughout this work I have warned my readers, that any misuse of the knowledge gained by occult studies is the *most severely punished of all karmic misdeeds for the unreasonable person* who dares to try to harm his neighbours.

But, on the other hand, ignorance is *not good* for it inevitably leads to errors in life, that is to the burdening of karma. Hermetists try to know GOOD *in order to follow it*, and to know EVIL *in order to be able to avoid it* ('Can the blind lead the blind? Do they not both fall into the ditch?').

Now we can return to our magic operation. The operator creates the *current* (vortex) in a perfectly finished form (in this matter a lack of exactness simply means a lack of effect) and directs it to his aim. In this way he realizes his action, and creates it as a *physical fact*, the clichés of which are thereby joined to (or superimposed on, if you prefer it) the karma of the operator in a positive or negative sense, depending, of course, upon the character of the action.

But, it can also happen that the fact is not realized despite the existence of the tourbillon. This can occur in three ways:

(1) When the person to whom the action is directed, takes protection against the attack by surrounding himself with an armour of concentration. This method is known as 'the active repelling of aggression'.

(2) When the victim of the attack, at the moment of active contact with the tourbillon's energy, separates from its action by conscious and powerful concentration on another object of realization, belonging to a cycle of astral projects much more perfect, and powerfully planned than was the scheme of the attacker. *Example:* when the one who is to be harmed, or even killed, is occupied with the creation (or destruction) of some constructions in the astral, in comparison with which the personal hatred of the magician appears as something very small, even infinitesimal in all the sub-planes of the astral.

(3) When, in the moment of contact with the attacking vortex (tourbillon) the *most active part of the pentagram* of the man who is being attacked, lives in sub-planes considerably higher than those of the most active parts of the tourbillon. *Example*: someone may want to destroy a man, who is living, as we may say, beyond the sphere of material interests, or may want to harm the working relationships of a man who is merged exclusively in scientific researches and is not interested in any form of an egotistic career, or a larva of hatred (a very destructive thing, if it finds a suitable and 'undefended' target) may be sent against a man who is accustomed to pray for his enemies, and so on.

In addition to the foregoing ways, the victim may quite effectively surround himself at the crucial moment with an *odic cloak*, or armour and remain in its security for a sufficient length of time (see the book—*Concentration* for methods of constructing and maintaining such armours).

In all these cases, the tourbillon will not touch the victim for whom it was destined; but the very FACT OF THE EXISTENCE OF THE TOURBILLON BROUGHT SOME LOCAL BREAK IN THE BALANCE OF THE SURROUNDING ASTRAL FORMS. The astral environment must then attain a newly balanced state by the creation of a cliché of that balance (nothing perishes in Nature). If the action cannot hit the original target, it will act on some other entity, which will be the one most tied to the astral tourbillon by its astrosome. And who will that be? Of course, in the first place, the operator or sender himself, and the energy he has created will react against himself. This is known as the '*return blow*'.

You might try to induce someone to love you, but if unsuccessful, your tourbillon will rebound from the person at whom it is aimed, with the result that you yourself will fall desperately and foolishly in love. You may try to induce sickness, but without result (see our previous three points about unsuccessful attacks), and so become sick yourself, and so on.

In order to avoid such return blows, representatives of black magic always secure themselves in their magic operations, by directing the force of a vortex against TWO persons, ensuring that it is much stronger against the true target than against the substitute. *Example:* a sickness is directed against you, but in the case of failure, also to a dog, a horse, and so on, or on another very passive human being from whom the magician cannot expect his 'arrow' to rebound. If humanity could only know how many diseases, accidents and other personal social troubles were and are generated just by the evil emanations of human will—by those *conscious* of the techniques (black magicians) and *unconscious* (ordinary, malicious, egotistic and dishonest men)—then people would not be likely to class all that I have just said, as belonging to the realm of fantasy or superstition. But for occultists, these things are perhaps more 'real' than anything else.

LESSON 27

Equation No. 25: $8 = 6 + 2$

It means the introduction of TWO ways into the processes of one's power of cognition (Sixth Arcanum). In other words, this is the full feeling of anxiety, that this knowledge, if received, can be used equally for *evolutionary* (Good) purposes and for *involutionary* (Evil) ones.

Equation No. 26: $8 = 3 + 5$

Here metaphysics, or the world of fulfilled (neutralized) ternaries (3) enters into practical life through the sphere of astral impulses (5) and dominates this realm. What does it mean to carry over metaphysics into the physical life?

TO TRANSFORM RIPE IDEAS INTO FORMS, and according to the Law of Analogy TRANSFER THE RIPE FORMS INTO THE PHYSICAL PLANE (realization of ideas).

A man, who wants to be worthy of the name 'just one' (8) has no right, after having built his general contemplation, to avoid using it for the construction of a harmonious philosophical system. If he will abstain from such an activity, he will provoke what may be termed 'an unhealthy straining of ideas'. In simple words, it would be shameful to create plans or drafts of an immense, well-prepared science and its techniques, without making any effort to realize them.

This equation may arouse strong indignation in the adepts of the so-called 'Platonic' love, who believe it is suitable to limit themselves to only astral manifestations of the animistic (here meaning sensual) realm. But *Hermetic philosophy* tells us, that such people must not forget, that they do not possess the third (physical) body without reason, and therefore should not try to escape from the results of being a three-plane entity. It is said, that this physical plane gives the fulcrum for the astral process for the cleansing of karma. If a man encounters TWO ways (as in the Sixth Arcanum), it does NOT happen in order that he may *stand before them indefinitely*, delaying their realization till future incarnations, but just *in order to choose consciously and definitely*—the RIGHT PATH. Kabbalistically, I may say, that such people, pronouncing *Yod*, and then *Hé*, are afraid to add the necessary *Vau*, because they may fear the beauty of the *Second Hé*. This is not a paradox!

People of this undecided type usually behave themselves uneasily and in an ugly manner in all cases of political troubles. If we have sympathy towards something, we should manifest it in all three planes. If it so happens that we hate something, we should do what has to be done, if it cannot be avoided, on all three planes. This is the technique of social life, imperfect as it is in our own epoch. We should not play at being an ostrich in the sand. Our society cannot and will not live like angels.

Another type of person likes to preserve their 'neutrality' on the physical plane, while at the same time being convinced in both the astral and mental realms. Christ described this sort of man as 'tepid' so as to distinguish him from the 'hot' and 'cold' kinds. Hot ones can easily become cold and vice versa; but in an always undecided, cowardly man there cannot be much of good and very little that is useful.

This was well realized by the Freemasons during the last three centuries, that is seventeenth, eighteenth and nineteenth. At the time of the initiation into the 30th Scotch Degree, (highest of the Hermetic degrees), the future Chevalier Kadosh, when performing his oath, was submitted to a test: he was supposed to kill (apparently, of course) a traitor to Masonry, in order to show how he really hated all enemies of his organization. The candidate did not know that he was striking the heart of a sheep with a clean shaven side, and with all sincerity imagined that he was carrying out the sentence given by the Areopag, and thereby punishing the brother who had betrayed them.

Of course, according to immutable laws, even such a simulated murder would leave its dark stain on the karma of the masonic Chain, thus dimming its Egregor. But Masons had to accept all this because it was considered as most essential to discriminate between their 'tepid' and 'hot' candidates for the higher degrees.

Equation No. 27: $8 = 5 + 3$

This is a reversed form of the preceding one. It teaches us about people who tend to adapt their logical and metaphysical contemplation to their purely animistic manifestations. *Example*: 'I like him' says such a man, 'therefore he should be considered as suitable for an important position, for which I was seeking a candidate.' Look around and observe how many people, in our own time, direct their activities in just such a way.

Equation No. 28: $8 = 4 + 4$

This equation is perhaps the most typical of this Eighth Arcanum. Four is opposed to four, that is a form against a form, authority against authority; one form of adaptation against another form of adaptation. What may this mean? *Firstly*, you offended someone (a form), so you now have to apologize to him (also a form). *Secondly*, you created a revolutionary government (authority), but it is opposed by a dictatorship (another authority). *Thirdly*, you may prepare a stratagem or fraud in order to avoid the lawful way, or you may try to break the law; but the police also prepare something suitable from their side so as to catch the guilty ones. This is a general karmic form and relative human justice.

In magic the opposition of forms prevails; in politics the opposition of authority; in the field of economics the opposition of adaptation, or in simple words, *supply* and *demand*.

With this we will end our arithmological analysis of the Eighth Arcanum. The remaining combinations I leave for your own solution. For every student, this is one of the most brilliant and useful practical applications of the mental part of the Tarot.

LESSON 28

The Eighth Arcanum has two pentacles which are the most used. The first is called the 'Circle of Ezekiel'. It is presented in Fig. 11 according to the interpretation of the Rosicrucian Schools. The Cross inside the inner circle gives us the picture of the Quaternary, that is one of the *dynamic cycles*. We see the letters of the Great Tetragrammaton in it.

The next quaternary—INRI—is an anagram of the three formulas:

(1) IGNE NATURA RENOVATUR INTEGRA (The whole of Nature is regenerated by fire).

(2) IESUS NAZARENUS REX IUDEORUM (Jesus of Nazareth, King of the Jews).

(3) IN NOBIS REGNAT IESUS (In us reigns Jesus).

We already know the *first* formula. It explains the role of FIRE as a purifying and regenerating element. It shows the means which allow us to turn the ROTA and to pass from one cycle to another in processes connected with the arising of something new, something manifested in another way and in a different epoch.

The *second* indicates the importance of the *Sacrifice in the Redemption* performed by Christ in the evolutionary turn of the ROTA.

Occultists in both the West and the East know well about this Law of Sacrifice. When they are on this earth, most advanced beings, having a *mission*, usually make a definite effort to lighten the karma of men. And of course, the most dazzling and perfect example is that of the Christ. The drama of this true Son of God is so well known that it needs no explanation here. Actually, no other Spiritual Master of humanity produced such tremendous results and changed the destiny of the human race so much as He did.

But there is another example, much closer to our own day, which can be seen by those *who have the eyes to see*. I am referring to the last Great Indian Rishi—Sri Ramana (1879-1950). This spiritual giant duly crowned his lifetime of work by accepting a terrible form of the Cross in a sickness which tortured him for more than a year. At the same time he did not want any cure or medicines, which could at least lighten the incredible suffering of his physical body. The reader can find a full account of this in another of my books entitled—*In Days of Great Peace* (G. Allen & Unwin Ltd, London).

Those of us who had the privilege to be with Sri Maharshi in the last period of his life, have no doubt that the suffering of the Master took away the burdens of karma from many of his contemporaries. On one occasion, when answering a devotee who had begged the Master to give his sickness to him, the Great Rishi gave a direct hint while explaining the origin of his disease (which was an incurable sarcoma): 'And who gave me this sickness?' he asked.

The idea of the Eighth Arcanum is—JUSTICE in all its applications and forms. Properly speaking, what does it mean? *The fact that every action, every force used, every* THOUGHT AND FEELING must be BALANCED in this manifested universe. The Law of Karma is of course, the most popular and known form of that Law. Actions committed by men must also be redeemed by them, or the just rewards received; but sometimes, when that karma becomes too heavy, the Great Beings come down to us and take on their mighty shoulders, some of our sufferings which are retribution for our 'sins'.

It is hard to explain, in our usual logic, how it is possible, that one person commits a deed and another pays for it. Is it in accordance with the idea of Justice? Our minds can hardly find any satisfactory answer to this problem; but if we refer to the spiritual realm, to our 'Monad-Atman-Self', then we may realize, that the basic UNITY IN SPIRIT of all beings allows for what we call—REDEMPTION. All spiritual Masters underline the Oneness of Being, in spite of the myriads of apparently separate forms existing in the manifested universe. So, it is not impossible that a centre of consciousness, that is a Master PRACTISING this Oneness, can use the law by taking on his own mighty shoulders, the

F*

karmas of many of those who still have not realized the Unity. I am sure that there are still many more deciding factors in such activity of the Great Ones, but these factors are beyond our understanding and therefore it is useless to delve into them.

The *third* formula, the motto of the first Rosicrucians, can be literally translated as: 'In us reigns Jesus.' In this sentence there is no intention of separating initiates from laymen, but only to point out the necessity of seeking Christ in one's own heart, and by that fact, to turn the quaternary of the elements to the evolutionary direction.

The circle-like inscription ROTA shows the direction of the rotation of the quaternary ה ו ה י (Yod-Hé-Vau-Hé) from the 'R' to the 'O', so that the Yod can pass into the Second Hé, in other words, into the direction of the search after Causality.

According to Ezekiel, the colour of the circle is 'similar to that of *topaz*'.

The circle of Pythagoras (Fig. 12) differs from the above-mentioned pattern.

(1) The places of the ה ו ה י (Yod-Hé-Vau-Hé) and I N R I are occupied by pentagrams.

(2) The direction of rotation is not given.

(3) There are additional signs inside the circle, which symbolize seven *secondary causes* (planets) and the process of fecundation of the passive principle by the active one.

The position of the signs 'E' and 'W' are equal to the lingam. The linear cross in the centre of the circle symbolizes the physical plane, appearing like a *small island* among the froth of the astral tide (the inner circle), which in turn is represented in its comparative smallness by being contrasted against the illimitable ocean of the mental plane, in the form of the outer circle.

The real explanation of the pentacle would be connected with a deep study of astronomy, where the outer circle would represent the Alcaic, starry world; the inner circle, the solar system, and the central cross, the elementary life of our poor planet.

The *pentacle of realization* has the following form: Its background is black (lower astral); the outer square is silvery (a ready, passive frame in which may be realized anything we wish). The internal square is golden (active efforts fulfilling the realization). The letters of the eight-times-repeated Great Name should be fiery in colour (Igne Natura Renovatur Integra).

This pentacle serves for concentration on the realization of projects of great importance leading to the solution of the most serious problems, to associations, or even to abstract forms.

An analysis of the eight-times-repeated Tetragrammaton will be given in the chapter on the Tenth Arcanum.

ט

Arcanum IX
LUX OCCULTA
THE HERMIT

♌

Leo

Protectores
Initiatio
Prudentia

CHAPTER IX

ARCANUM IX (ఐ TETH)

THE sign of the Ninth Arcanum is the letter ఐ (Teth), the numerical value is 9 and the corresponding zodiacal sign is the Lion.

As the hieroglyph, we have a roof or its framework, symbolizing protection, defence and insulation from harmful influences.

The card of the Ninth Arcanum depicts an old man walking, and holding in his right hand (not as seen in a mirror) a lamp containing three lights inside it. The lamp is partially hidden under his wide hooded cloak, which covers him with its triple folds.

The *lamp* clearly shows us the *enlightenment* in all the three worlds (its three wicks). In his left hand the Hermit holds a long *walking stick*, which supports his steps. Three knots are visible on the stick.

The *long cloak* symbolizes separation and insulation in three planes, while the stick gives support to its triple character (the knots).

The *age* of the Hermit gives the hint, that one can use all the three planes consciously—only during the late period of life, and under the condition of karmic prosperity in the physical world. His movements suggest to us that any stagnation in development is impossible for the one, who possesses all the paraphernalia already mentioned in the description of this card.

The scientific name for the arcanum is 'LUX OCCULTA' (Occult Light), while the vulgar one is 'The Hermit'.

As usual, we will now seek for the three titles of the arcanum by means of arithmological analysis.

(1) *Equation No. 29:* $9 = 1 + 8$

It is the search of a balance, acting and individualized person (1) in righteous surroundings. If these are in the realm of the Archetype, then Man, seeking protection in it, will find the idea and images of *Genius-Protectors*, helping him to find a true MAN in himself, in other words, his Overself, or Atman as our Eastern brothers would say. From this comes the first title of the Ninth Arcanum—PROTECTORES, in English—Protectors.

(2) If the search is performed in the realm of *humanity*, we may speak about *self-definition*, in the astral, self-knowledge, and the introduction of spiritual harmony into what is called the personality of a single man. We call a process like this SELF-INITIATION, or the finding of the Master in ourselves. Therefore, the second title will be INITIATIO—Initiation.

(3) If we merge into the realm of Nature, everything will be reduced to the ability of coping with the *individualized god* of the materialists, called *accident or chance*. It is hard to live under his protection, if we do not know

the means of the *theory of probability* very well, which, in different phases of life, dictates various degrees of circumspection to us. So the third and last title will be PRUDENTIA—carefulness.

We will proceed with our analysis.

Equation No. 30: $9 = 8 + 1$

Justice (8) ruling in the surroundings may choke and tempt a passive, although sane personality (1). This is the formula for men of talent, sucked dry by the environment of their epoch, so that they cannot play their true role in the process of human evolution.

Equation No. 31: $9 = 2 + 7$

This means the Teaching of the Victor. Of whom? Of the one who passed through the metaphysical study of the first seven arcana (the first septenary of the Tarot). What is that knowledge? It has two sides: a passive, susceptible, female one called DIVINATIO, or ability to SEE in the Archetype, Man and Nature. The ecstasy of a prophet, suddenly enlightened by Grace, giving the inspiration to create a religious cult and its ethics, will be a good example of divination on the Archetype's level.

Divination in relation to Man will lead us into the realm of susceptibility to astral manifestations of our neighbour, the seeing of the human aura, quick judgements about the character, development and moral degree of evolution of our fellow men and of their odic emanations, and so on; but it may also lead us to those systems which have well-known titles such as, chiromancy, phrenology, physiognomy, and so on, about which more will be told in the Seventeenth Arcanum. Divination in Nature takes the form of astrology and geomancy with their sub-divisions of cartomancy, hydromancy, pyromancy and other fortune-telling by means of the elements (four).

But, in this equation the knowledge of the Victor also has an active, male side, the ability to rule the astral, which means the ability of directing and using one's own energy in the form of magnetism, telepathy and even exteriorization of the astrosome, as well as the art of communication with different entities.

This is the realm of the Conqueror, which attracts many people by the depth and broadness of its applications, although sometimes dangerous and even fatal for the man himself.

If the Victor willingly *agrees to refrain* from his activities and susceptibilities because of his concern about his own victorious personality (7), putting it *before* all scientific interests, the corresponding *equation* will take the form:

Equation No. 32: $9 = 7 + 2$

Equation No. 33: $9 = 3 + 6$

Metaphysics (3) stands before the choice of the two paths (6); it defines the choice; but what—apart from metaphysical contemplation—could influence the choice? Of course, it would be the impulses of a man. I will not mention the instincts of the physically impulsive man, and the passions of the astrally impulsive man again, as these have already been explained in former chapters, and there is little to add.

We may now prefer to occupy ourselves with the *intellectually impulsive man*, with his superstitions, prejudices and variability.

What is superstition? Only the impulsively acknowledged complexity of old forms, which once were binding for so many, but now, because of the evolution of the new individual, have become just so much sluggish ballast, restraining and delaying manifestations of independent thinking.

From this we can see, that the fatherland of superstition is always the astral. But, according to the realm in which such clichés occur, they are divided into mystical, astral and physical superstitions.

If a man is living in conditions which openly destroy reasonable rules of, say, hygiene, but still holds to such conditions, then he is superstitious in the physical world. The same can be said about the man, who, while being sufficiently developed and able by means of meditation to pray outside a temple built of bricks, laments the fact that the lack of such a church in his vicinity interferes with his theurgic activities.

As an example of *astral* superstition we may cite the case of a magician, who reaches the state of power, whereby his ideas get astrosomes of themselves, but is still convinced, that without pronouncing certain formulas or fulfilling a certain ritual, he cannot operate at all.

Another example, a rather ridiculous one, is when a man considers Monday, or the number thirteen as unlucky for him, without having had any real experience of these things in his life.

There are plenty of examples of *mystical* superstitions. We may see people who are strongly convinced that there is not, and cannot be any salvation apart from the dogmas of a certain faith. At the same time, we may see other people who are indifferent to the variances in creeds, providing they can recognize one dogmatic element which is very dear to them, such as *Redemption by Incarnation*.

We may also meet men, who impose a condition on religion, similar to the 'recognition of the possibility of humanity's Reintegration only by way of evolution'.

Of course, a man of the third category (mystical superstition) would consider a man of the second one (astral superstition) to be superstitious by comparison with himself, and a man of the second category would regard a man from the first in like manner, and so on.

From the foregoing we can see that it is impossible to consider any particular clichés as absolute superstition. In order to define superstition one must have exact knowledge of another man's mentality, and his astral and physical states.

Lack of understanding in this matter has often brought attacks on *Initiatory Centres* because they allegedly have different dogmas, ethical codes, and real duties for Initiates of different degrees.

Some deliberations about the following meditative theme may be useful. If we obtain power over men who are equal to us from the point of view of mental, astral and physical development, this can occur almost exclusively because of the presence in them of superstition, prejudice and instability.

Prejudice in the realm of citizenship, and the outer forms of life plays a role similar to that of superstition in the sphere of dogmatic contemplation.

Equation No. 34: $9 = 6 + 3$

This reversed equation tells us that the choice of the path (6) decides about the future metaphysical side of a man. This formula evokes the picture of actions of human beings, who choose a certain defined way, a certain circle of activity, and are now seeking *metaphysical support for their deeds*, self-respect and inner certainty.

Equation No. 35: $9 = 4 + 5$

This is passing from the world of elements (4) to the astral world (5). It may be said, that in the programme of initiation, the whole sum of facts, brought to us from the physical world must be included in it. A magician may be proud of his astral learning, but he acts reasonably not only on the astral plane, but equally well on the physical, cognition of which he owes to his knowledge of physics, chemistry, anatomy, physiology, and so on. This should be firmly established in our minds if we want to realize fully how we should act in this world.

It would be ridiculous for an occultist to try to arrange purely physical things by astral or even mental means. You cannot pay for the services of a taxi-driver with the pentacle of Solomon!

If an operation can be delayed until there is better weather, a good magician will not mind doing this, also he will not operate when physically, or otherwise ill; he will always apply the rules of physical hygiene, cleanliness, washing, the eating of fresh products, and removal of all adulterated food or drinks from his diet. He knows that fatigue caused by overworking is just as dangerous as laziness. He will carefully select his living place if he feels that he is sensitive to climatic conditions. Finally, he will always and everywhere, while acting on the physical plane, use the law of probability, which is synonymous to precaution.

Equation No. 36: $9 = 5 + 4$

This is a formula which is reasonably adapted to suit particular and exceptional phenomena and operations. Its components $(5 + 4)$ tell us that: THE WILL OF THE INIDIVIDUAL (5) STANDS AGAINST THE ELEMENTS (4).

There are cases of separated realizations which play the role of nails or screws in the whole mechanism of the work. It is important that we drive home these nails at the most suitable moment, independent of the physical difficulties which may sometimes occur, for then we use the active MARS of our astral counterpart, no matter if the reaching of our aim costs us much vital energy or material means.

In the Ninth Arcanum we should give the central place to our analytical equations of a triple form, which are no less important here than our usual two-element formulas.

Equation No. 37: $9 = 3 + 3 + 3$

If our double analysis gave us knowledge of initiation and hints about the means of reaching it, so the *triple* one will unveil for us the hierarchic degrees of that initiation itself.

In the initiatory system we will now distinguish between three cycles, dividing each of them into three degrees.

(1) Let us conditionally call the *lower cycle* the PHYSICAL one, because its character indicates that the candidate for initiation appears for the Initiatory Ceremony in his physical body, and the very ceremony is performed in the normal three-dimensional space, with the initiating master also in his physical incarnation.

At this point I would like to explain the terms used in connection with *initiation*, that is candidates, masters, and so on. What are we to understand under these terms? Where can one see these ceremonies performed, or participate in them?

Things are not so simple. The term 'initiation' itself has a double meaning. In Western occultism, including the Tarot, under initiation is usually meant the communication of knowledge by one who knows more to one who knows less, that is the Master initiates the disciple. Such a kind of initiation may take place with a certain ceremony, other persons may be present, some ritual may be performed, oaths taken and accepted, and so on. Degrees may also be conferred on those who successfully passed through some examinations and tests.

In many countries, probably also in your own, there are some organizations of occult character, which are not openly known, but which may develop certain activity, according to their classification.

But initiation may also be reached in another way. It is—'Self-initiation', to which, in true occult circles, much more importance is attached than to any ceremonial activities. This idea is often encountered in the East, especially among the great Eastern Saints or Sages, who unanimously state, that the true 'Guru' (initiating Master) is actually inside man, that is, it is his own true Self or Spirit ('Is it not written in your law: I said you are gods?' Christ said).

These matters have been given in detail in my previous books (see the 'Mystic Trilogy' consisting of three books: *In Days of Great Peace, Concentration* and *Samahdi—the Superconsciousness of the Future.*

The initiations which are treated of in the Tarot belong mostly to the first mentioned group, that is they are in time and space and connected with certain outer forms.

But to return to our previous theme:

(i) In the *physical Initiation* we have three elements:

(a) *Mental* or dogmatic part taken from some written sources or given orally as initiatory formulas.

(b) *Astral*, a fluidic, magnetic influence exerted on the candidate by the initiating person, to which action some symbolism is often added.

(c) *Physical*, a combination of certain actions in the physical world, as its ceremonial part.

(ii) The *second degree* places before the pupil knowledge of the astral plane, and allows him to form a right judgement about that plane without abandoning the physical body. To this belongs psychurgy and Ceremonial Magic, which teach man to act in the astral plane.

(iii) The *third degree* (mental) introduces the candidate for Initiation to a higher degree, into the realm of *Universal Love* by way of *Ethical Hermetism*.

All of these three degrees can be reached without the participation of the incarnate initiator. Therefore it seems to be enough to have a certain spiritual and ethical development (which usually depends upon the number of former incarnations of the person concerned) and to add some astral protection theoretically known long ago. It is not necessary to underline the need for an inflexible and steady desire to be initiated.

From the aforesaid we can see, that under these conditions there is no need for the presence of any man apart from the candidate himself; but in the higher degrees it may be different. Anyway, the element of the astral and fluidic action of the initiating person upon the candidate means the process of the will of the Master, influencing the astral body of the one to be initiated, arousing changes in it which will be useful for self-initiation. These changes will also help in acquiring some degree of intuition and activity of the important binary, neutralized by the *spiritual harmony*.

It is hard to speak at this point about the ceremonies and symbolical rituals accompanying the ceremony of initiation, as they vary in every school in the inner currents flowing through them, in the different sorts of tradition, the nature of the school and even the personal characteristics of the initiating Masters.

(2) The Initiation of the *second* cycle may be called an *astral one*, for the essential thing in it is the necessity for the initiated person to learn to use the *exteriorization of the astrosome*, and in this way to enter into contact with the Teacher or Teachers.

The *initiatory Master* with whom the neophyte now enters into close relations, can also be a man who exteriorizes himself into the higher worlds, or a two-plane human being, that is an elementar of a sublime type, who was a great Initiate when still on the Earth.

These relationships now being beyond the three dimensions of space do not require any physical contact between the Master and disciple. This is very well known to all true occultists. The Master, when departing from the physical plane, does not leave his pupils as orphans, just as the Master of Masters (Christ) clearly told His disciples before fulfilling His Sacrifice and Redemption.

LESSON 30

To those who are interested in the Great Beings—so far advanced in evolution that sometimes they seem to be only a myth—I can recommend the study of the life and teachings of the contemporary Master—the Great Indian Rishi Ramana, about whom there is already quite a sizeable amount of literature throughout the world. Before his departure he told us that he would not go away from us. He also stated that: 'All Masters are one' thereby emphasizing the fact of the ONE TRUE INITIA-TION.

In any case, apart from these great Masters I have just mentioned, there are others who perform their duties of assisting those who are ripe for discipleship, being personifications of the WORLD'S ASTRAL MAN, as Hermetism tells us.

There is no reason to speak about the rituals of Initiation on this level, for it would be useless for a lay reader, and unnecessary for an initiate. From my point of view it is always the *foremost duty of a writer* to give his readers and students something which they can use *for their profit*, and not only for the sheer satisfaction of curiosity, later leading to an abandon-ment of the whole subject.

As we may see, the astral exteriorization in *occultism* is a very important matter; but things are otherwise on the purely *spiritual paths*, where meth-ods and standards are of quite a different shape. These two things should never be confused.

So, in the old true Rosicrucianism, so-called 'test exteriorizations' were practised in the company of more advanced members, those, as they said, '*who had already passed through the gates BEFORE the neophyte*'. This was partially symbolized in the initiation into the 18th Scotch Degree, and ideologically indicated in Christian Baptism. This *first exteriorization* must take place between the third (highest) degree of the physical cycle of Initiation, and the *first astral* (lower) degree of the following higher cycle.

(3) The next higher cycle is the *mental* one. For an initiate it may very simply be explained as: MAN'S ACCESS TO THAT CURRENT OF IDEAS WHICH IS RELATED TO THE TYPE OF MONAD TO WHICH HE BELONGS.

There is now no *personality* of the initiatory Master, who performs the act of Initiation itself. Here, in this sublime degree of evolution, THE WORLD'S MAN, THE ARCHETYPE simply accepts into his 'body' the cell, which has rightly belonged to him since the beginning of time, the cell, which has purified itself from the dishonourable downfall and has returned to its place with the *wisdom*, acquired in its eons of wandering. This is the teaching of Hermetic philosophy, as a basis for the initiation of the White Race on this earth. Others have different conceptions, which do not belong to the main theme of this book. I would only like to repeat the words of the great Teacher: 'IN MY FATHER'S HOUSE THERE ARE MANY MANSIONS.'

Of course, in the case of *mental Initiation* there is no question about the ritual and contents or the performance of it. The very presence of this *high Initiation* is due to the process of the Archetype's emanations, leading to the existence of the *Collective Universal Man* in his primary purity. It is accepted, that for this type of Initiation, man comes already exteriorized in his *mental body*, that is in that subtle, ethereal cloud of the spiritual monad (Atman) which is always present, but which was less manifested in the involutionary and early evolutionary eons of existence of Man. Anyway, it is hard to deliberate about things which are actually on quite a different level of consciousness, and beyond speech and thought.

As the process of the Rosicrucian '*astral baptism*' was inserted between the junior degree of the astral cycle of initiation, so the phase of the so-called Rosicrucian Reintegration was placed between the senior degree of the astral cycle and the junior one of the mental initiation.

The Reintegrated Brothers of the Rosa-Crux were called elementars, who perhaps still retained their middle astral sheath (cloud), but who could separate from it, just as incarnate men can exteriorize themselves in their astral bodies.

The *Reintegrated One* puts his middle astral body to sleep, that is he wilfully declines all energetic manifestations, and limits his activity merely to the mental ones, which were appropriate to the cell of Adam prior to its descent into matter. Such action is analogous to astral exteriorization, in which we refrain from all sensual impressions in order to throw off the slavery of time and three-dimensional space.

Nevertheless, it is possible to use exteriorization for operations on the physical plane by means of mediumship, that is the borrowing of the necessary elements from other organisms, and even from astral (lower) forms. This process, in Hermetism, is termed '*vampirization*' of surroundings and living bodies. Of course, we should not associate it with those tales about 'vampires' or 'Draculas', although they are not so entirely groundless.

The gross superstitions of some savage races, with their repulsive use of dead (sometimes even still living) bodies for their weird rituals, dictated by witch doctors, are also not entirely taken from the otherwise limited minds of primitive people. There is some grim truth—a relative one, of course—behind these 'superstitions'. When, in the Thirteenth Arcanum, we will analyse death and its complicated processes connected with the corpse, astral counterparts, and so on, we may see something which at present escapes our attention.

One who is Reintegrated can use his mental exteriorization in order to create some evolutionary forms outside of his normal activities in the middle astral. For example, to finish the initiation of an astral 'Chain', different from his own egregoric environment.

Now comes the question: is it possible for an incarnate man to be initiated in the mental plane? Here lies a considerable difference between the Western and Eastern traditions. In Hermetism it is recognized, that only the highest adepts can enjoy the infinite bliss of mental exteriorization, and, what is most questionable, that this 'ecstasy' can last only for a few moments.

Whoever can perform it is a Teacher, who all initiated occultists recognize as a Master, a Messenger from the highest plane. They are right up to a point, but Truth itself is much broader and wider.

The superphysical and super-astral ecstasy is well known by the true Indian yogis and great Christian Saints (see *Concentration* Chapters

VIII, IX, XV). Now we are calling it by the Sanskrit term—Samadhi, as it is comfortable to be able to enclose such a large conception in one short word. This Samadhi may endure not only for a few moments, but for hours and more. And still it is not the highest, because it is connected with catalepsy of the body, with which Hermetists also agree. Beyond it lies the supreme and possible state of human consciousness, called the 'perennial formless Samadhi', where there is no rigidity or impediment of the physical body, and everything is as normal as if the man were not engaged in the highest flight to the Source of all life and consciousness.

And this is just the quality which only a Master can possess, a Master, who has a *definite mission* not only for his own Egregor or 'Chain', but for all humanity. They are rare, it is true, and usually come at intervals of more than a thousand years; but the results of their coming are epoch-wide, for then humanity's life is directed into new channels.

On the next point of the highest Initiation the West and East are in accord. Both Traditions say, that the perfect Master, taking his ultimate Initiation, does this HIMSELF, and everything forthcomes of itself. There is no longer an initiated pentagram, as the personality and individuality disappeared long ago, before the man became ripe for the final step. Here there is no longer any trace of desire or striving after something: the drop falls into the Ocean, and cannot be found again separated from the Whole.

In the *astral* initiation the pentagram can and does require that initiation. Here the will of the Initiatory Principle must yield to that of the initiated one.

It is different in the *physical* initiation. In this the teacher's work is made more arduous, because of difficulties connected with true cognition of the pupil's nature. The meeting with the disciple takes place gradually, and not at his first request. It is important that the initiative for initiation comes from the Teacher. The agreement or otherwise from the side of the disciple is a good controlling test for the Teacher.

When the candidate commits serious errors and risks doing harm to others if given superior powers by initiation, the Teacher might suggest refusal (on the part of the pupil) to accept initiation, and by so doing spares the disciple many dangers, and a stain on the karma of the Teacher. Of course, all of this does not apply to the higher initiations.

Now, a few more words about the physical cycle of initiation. In the astral initiation things are different because of the presence in it of an *idea of Reintegration*. However, it is not too hard to imagine, that there may be some periods of time—sometimes even whole epochs—when, because of the unpopularity of occult knowledge, or because of the activity of anti-initiating currents (materialistic and agnostic epochs), the four Hermetic virtues (symbolized in previous lessons as the 'four holy animals') may not be sufficient for reaching even the junior astral degrees.

Some would say: 'Little trouble, the epoch will pass and the initiates will appear again.' True but the rejection of occultism for the length of the whole epoch, connected with the forgetting of the symbols and primary methods of occult education, will strongly hamper the work of new initiates, as well as their influence on an utterly agnostic society.

But, when the *Great Tradition's Chain* does not break, and still exists even though only in the physical realm, then we always have a group of the *'Guardians of the Tradition'*, so-called 'archivists' or faithful chroniclers of the history of esoterism. And these people are very important, in spite of the fact that usually they are not any active or highly-initiated occultists; but by their toil the Tradition exists and can always be revived when some able and devoted souls again come to this Earth.

In the second half of the eighteenth century a new current arose called Martinism after its founder—Martines de Pasqualis; but this name was later more glorified because of the work of Louis Claude de St Martin, a disciple of de Pasqualis.

The original school of Pasqualis was a strong magic Chain of modernized Rosicrucianism (see Eleventh Arcanum), but St Martin did an unusual thing: he tried to found a kind of 'free initiation', allowing for the transmission of the three elements (mental, astral and physical) of the physical cycle without the intermediary of the existing lodges, brotherhoods and other kinds of masonic units.

In the Initiation of St Martin, there was only one degree: S∴ I∴ (Superieur Inconnu, Unknown Superior) given to enlightened people of the intellectual type. Claude de St Martin divided humanity into four types.

(1) *L'Homme du Torrent:* Man of the Torrent. Men without will-power and of little individuality, who follow the way of life in a given epoch without bothering about anything except their elementary needs.

(2) *L'Homme de Désir:* Man of Desire. These are consciously and ardently seeking perfection and absolute Truth on the way of contemplation, entering their own hearts and learning the sources of the Tradition.

(3) *Le Nouvel Homme:* the New Man. Men who have reached a certain degree of astral development and who, in their judgements about neighbours and themselves, do not commit those errors which the Men of Desire are capable of making.

(4) *L'Homme Esprit:* Man-Spirit. This last category, according to St Martin's theory concerns men who are utterly separated from all interests and troubles, as well as attachments of the physical plane. By this fact they are free from the slavery of the animistic nature, and on the other hand, from imperfect knowledge about their high origin in the sphere of Emanated Life.

It is easy to see, that, according to our Hermetic terminology, the *'Man of Desire'* belongs to the initiate of the lower degree in the physical cycle (1).

The *'New Man'* acquainted with the astral, belongs to the second degree of the same cycle (2).

The *'Man-Spirit'* corresponds to the third degree because he has passed through the elementary Hermetic training (3).

Another *triple analysis* of the Ninth Arcanum takes the form:

Equation No. 38: $9 = 3 + 2 + 4$

We read it as Initiation (9) leads to the *Great Arcanum* (its mental part is 3 + astral 2 + elementary 4). But what is still more interesting for the analytic mind of an occultist is the fact that a certain transformation of this equation will bring us to the general picture for the method of *self-initiation*.

Equation No. 39: $9 = 2 + 3 + 4$

Written thus the *figure 2* gives the idea of polarity connected with that of attraction, magnetism. Therefore, the advice that comes F I R S T is magnetize your worldly surroundings by your strong desire and ardent prayer. Briefly, by adopting the attitude of a true Man of Desire, you will attract to yourself individualized elements of those surroundings which will help you in your first initiation.

Those who are greater than you will become your protectors, while those of lesser value will be a field of activity for your assimilation.

The *figure 3* symbolizes the balanced ternary, androgynous in its components, but capable of manifesting itself in the active realm as well as in the passive. It will show you the necessity of concentration (condensation) of all that you learned and assimilated. This is the work which regulates the growth and cutting off of potential activities and the passivity of your individuality, or rather, its astrosome, in order to reach a state of full harmony.

Figure 4 is the symbol for the elementary ROTA, the sign of adaptation on the physical plane. It is the outcome of the fruitful activity of an adept, who has been able to evolve enough by deep introspection and training of his own personality. It is similar to the 'travel for the widening of the Light' in the master's ritual in Masonry, which likens the master to the rising Sun, its culmination and the following of its path below the horizon, so as to begin a new cycle of movement the next day, a new four phase daily ROTA.

This '4' is a hint on the phase of development of emanation until the degree of Teacher is reached.

We will not continue with the arithmological analysis of this arcanum, leaving further combinations to the student, which will not be too hard to solve if he has followed those given in this lesson.

LESSON 31

The rich symbolism of the Ninth Arcanum's card compels us to return to it again.

The LAMP of the Hermit is called the LIGHT OF HERMES TRISMEGISTUS, for Hermes is the personification of the magnificent system of metaphysical wisdom, astral abilities and knowledge of the physical plane which once flourished in the ancient Egyptian Temples of Initiation.

The necessity of that LAMP for an initiate tells us:

(1) Do not despise the knowledge of the *physical plane.*

(2) Learn diligently about the *astral plane.*

(3) Raise the consciousness thus gained into the snowy mounts of the transcendental and *transcendent mind.* Learn abstruse thinking and the stopping of all thinking at will. *This is the target and the peak.*

You are a three-plane being, so learn in all three planes! That is what the three lights of the Hermetic Lamp reveal to us.

The COAT which insulates the Hermit from the troubles of the outer world is called the cloak of Apollonius of Tyana, the famous Master of the Alexandrian School. It is the symbol of *Self-Knowledge* of the Monad (Supreme Self, Spirit, Atman); *self-assertion* in the astral and *solitude* in the illusory, *physical* world.

To know ourselves in the mental plane means to cognize clearly our role as cells of the mind of the Collective, Universal Man, with all the multi-colours of that role.

The *astral self-assertion*—a typical way of development of Apollonius of Tyana—is an intense diving into the properties of our own astrosome; its severe analysis; the classification of its means and powers, of the sense of orientation of its magnetic centres, and finally, its synthesis, but in a new and perfected form.

Biographers of this great occult master refer too superficially about his alleged contemplations of his navel, and the wrapping of his body in a coat of wool (insulation). This famous magician, who performed 'miracles' in some degree similar to those ascribed to Christ, was a unique figure in his own time. Our contemporary Hermetic masters always bow their heads before his authority.

The *solitude* is worthy of our special attention. It is not any physical seclusion or cumbersome behaviour. To rest in inner solitude means to possess the ability to work and meditate, independently of the presence of the energetic influences of other human pentagrams. One can be alone—in the true sense of the word—in the most troublesome of crowds. The contemporary *Great Spiritual Master and unequalled authority since Sankaracharya—Ramana Maharshi,* points out, that 'it makes no difference to a man who possesses the power of solitude, whether he is in a noisy London flat, or in the quiet of an Indian Ashram'.

Hermetic Tradition recommends that beginners—who are making a serious attempt at the way to Reintegration—make use of the Hermit's way of life. This evidently has both its good and bad sides.

The *good ones* are: that in the mental plane, prayer may become easier, while in the astral one gets an opportunity to cleanse it by means of a long silence (one of the conditions of the old Pythagorean School). On the physical plane it shortens the loss of time, unavoidable in 'normal' life under worldly conditions. So much Tradition tells us.

The *evil aspects* of a lonely anchorite's life are considered to be: on the *mental plane,* difficulty of gaining quick information about the progress of others in the metaphysical realm. In the *astral*, a certain lack of support from workers of the evolutionary type similar to oneself. This increases the dangers—in our moments of passivity—of falling under the spell of the so-called astral world, which brings bad clichés to us.

On the *physical plane*, the results of these evil influences may often be materialized in the form of sexual transgressions, inflicted on a lonely but not too experienced hermit. We call these phenomena *incubi* and *succubi* (the student will do well to read the famous book *Thais* by Anatole France).

Incubi and succubi were often the cause of the break-downs, with all their tragic consequences, of many otherwise, very sincere and able hermits and occultists.

The thing being, that elementars, and also exteriorized witch-doctors or black magicians, are able, after obtaining a mediumistic loan from the anchorite himself or the organic world surrounding him, to materialize themsleves in a sufficiently condensed form to induce the hermit to enter into sexual relations with the astral being, disguised as a female (if the hermit is a male) and then known as a '*succubus*', or as a male, in the case of a nun, then appearing as an '*incubus*'. The illusions may be so perfect, and the ruses used by the dark entities so crafty, that the tempted ones are often deceived and fall victims of them.

Incubi and succubi, of course, bring *great harm*, and especially in the following ways:

(1) By the physical weakening of their victim. We know about some authentic descriptions of unspeakable debaucheries performed by these demons with lonely men and women, hardly compared with normal sexuality.

(2) The victimized one, if unable to resist, loses faith in him or herself and begins to consider that he or she is a hopeless sinner, which is understandable after we read the second sentence of (1) above.

(3) They incite men and women to create *larvas* by their own will, which cause trouble even in the absence of a real attack by incubi or succubi.

There are efforts to neutralize the binary: *anchorite's life—worldly life*, by retaining the best from both sides and removing the evil. A fairly good solution can be found in the common life of a monastery or convent. These institutions vary much, depending upon their particular constitution and of the rules which dominate their lives, and also they differ in different epochs.

The WALKING STICK of the old man is a symbol of his carefulness and needs no further explanation.

To finish with the Ninth Arcanum, it may be useful to summarize briefly the preparatory programmes for initiation and efforts on the part of the aspirant as prescribed by Hermetic Tradition, for the task of self-initiation.

Nine cycles can be mentioned, and the student should realize that these are worked in *parallel* rather than in *sequence*.

(1) To remove every form of physical cowardice from yourself.

(2) To remove all kinds of indecision.

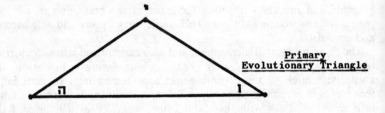

**Primary
Evolutionary Triangle**

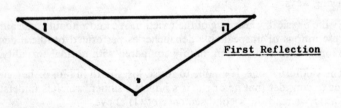

First Reflection

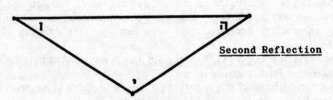

Second Reflection

Fig. 28 Evolutionary Triangles

(3) To remove all retrospective regrets and lamentations about deeds and events, which cannot be altered any more.

(4) To fight, as far as it is possible, against superstition.

(5) To fight, as far as it is possible, against prejudice.

(6) To fight, as far as it is possible, against conditions.

(7) To achieve full *physical* order in yourself, and to support your health for as long as it is possible. Nothing should be neglected.

(8) To reach an equally good *astral* order in yourself. This means striving for the already mentioned *spiritual harmony*, and outwardly an exact classification and knowledge of astral beings and their manifestations.

(9) To organize *mental* order in yourself as well, which means, clarity and absolutism of metaphysical contemplation and full consciousness of your *emanative origin from the Archetype*. I would like to call the attention of the student especially to deep meditation on *this theme*.

The pentacle of the Ninth Arcanum can be realized according to the equation : $9 = 3 + 6$. Then we can bring it to the imagination of the upper part of that which we call the 'Great Arcanum'. Another interesting form of the pentacle will be as given in Fig. 28.

This configuration gives us *nine points*, of which the first three points form the *evolutionary* triangle. The two reflections of these points represent the involutionary types (lower six points). This is nothing less than the idea of the lower planes originating from the upper one.

In Eastern philosophy the Ninth Arcanum corresponds to Jnana Yoga, or the Yoga of Wisdom. It is one of the less abused and misinterpreted of the Indian secret paths, and at the same time, the less dangerous. Whoever of my readers wishes to know more about yogas from a dependable and authoritative source, will do best to turn his attention to the writings of Ramacharaka (the series of books on yogas). There he will find a comprehensive and reliable expounding not devoid of spiritual flights, but minus all cumbersome theories and unreasonable expositions.

Eastern rules which are obligatory for all followers of Yoga are somewhat more developed in their details. In general, Hindu sacred books recommend two definite preparatory paths, which must be observed by every aspirant, as otherwise the practical exercises may become dangerous for the disciple as well as for his environment. Therefore I feel myself obliged to give the student an opportunity to look at these two systems, created by our Eastern brethren in the form of separate series.

FIRST SERIES

(1) AHIMSA : which is the non-causing of any pain to any living being, either by thought, word or deed.

(2) SATYA : always to speak the truth, by intellect, word or gesture.

(3) **ASTEYA**: indifference or lack of desire to possess anything, by intellect, thought, word or deed.

(4) **BRAHMACHARYA**: chastity of body, words and thoughts.

(5) **DAYA**: the practising of goodness towards all creatures, even towards demons.

(6) **ARDJAVA**: the inner equality of mind and feelings when performing all ordered activities, and abstention from all forbidden actions.

(7) **KSHAMA**: a virtue which permits the supporting of all pleasant and unpleasant things with patience.

(8) **DHRITI**: the preservation of a firm resolution, in disaster equally as well as in happiness.

(9) **MITHAARA**: right feeding, the acceptance of meals only to one quarter of the stomach's capacity.

(10) **SANCHA**: purification of the body through religious rituals and purification of the heart through discrimination between the absolute and relative.

SECOND SERIES

(a) **TAPAS**: moderate physical penance.

(b) **SANTOSHA**: being satisfied with everything and to have recognition to God for everything.

(c) **ASTIKEYA**: adaptation of the Vedantic Doctrine to things that are *due* and those that are *not due*.

(d) **DHANA**: charity given to *worthy* persons.

(e) **ISHWARA-PUJA**: cult of the Lord according to ritual.

(f) **SIDDHANANTA-SRAVANA**: knowledge of religious philosophy.

(g) **KRITI**: shame for the errors committed in religious or worldly affairs.

(h) **MATHI**: always following the prescriptions of the sacred books with faith and love.

(i) **JAPA**: repetition of daily prayers or sacred syllables.

(j) **VRATA**: abstention from all deeds prohibited by religious rules.

In the highest schools of Yoga it is recognized, that only by the fulfilment of these two series of preparations can the pupil approach the realization of the yogic paths. It is the doctrine of the ancient Indian Rishis, which nowadays is almost forgotten and seldom followed. The greatest harm arose when Indian occult philosophy began to spread in the West, and was often misinterpreted by unqualified writers, who did not place any attention on the necessary preparation, as given in these two classical series of rules.

As a result, innumerable readers began to consider themselves as aspirants of Yoga, although they had none of the essential knowledge of the subject, or the necessary qualities of mind and heart, which could safeguard them from the dangers of that occult path.

If we look around, we only have to recognize the sad fact, that with the enormous spread of yogic books there goes an enormous increase in the numbers of people, who are convinced that they are rightful successors of the yogic traditions, despite the fact, that they are still actually the same weaklings as their neighbours, who are unacquainted with any initiatory theories.

Finally, if you attentively study the lives and tradition of the Christian Saints, as well as the theological books on the two great churches (Catholic and Orthodox), you will make the discovery, that their prescriptions and rules are essentially the same as the two yogic series just given, merely expressed in somewhat different words.

So, the figure of the Ninth Arcanum is a universal one for the East and West alike.

Arcanum X
ROTA FORTUNAE
THE SPHINX

Virgo

Testamentum
Quabbalah
Fortuna

CHAPTER X

ARCANUM X (י YOD)

THE Hebrew letter corresponding to the Tenth Arcanum is י (Yod), its numerical value being 10. Astrologically it belongs to the sign of the Virgin. The hieroglyph is a man's forefinger. This finger is the means for an imperative movement. If we identify the man as a microcosm (according to our Hermetic Tradition), or as a closed system, then the imperative gesture of the forefinger will be seen as an outward manifestation of that system. The whole of the Tenth Arcanum has this meaning, stressing the active power of Man-microcosm.

The picture for this arcanum is called 'the Sphinx', or ROTA FORTUNAE (the Wheel of Fortune). In its upper part we see a Sphinx armed with a sword, atoning on an immovable platform. Under the platform of the Sphinx is a wheel, the visible spokes of which are formed by two perpendicular lines and two others, one of them ending in a double caduceus. On the hub of the great wheel there is the Hexagram of Solomon (his seal). On the wheel itself there are two inscriptions, the Great Tetragram (Yod-Hé-Vau-Hé) and ROTA, so that one word is interwoven with the other; both should be read from right to left. In the course of its rotation the wheel draws up to the Sphinx on the right side, the figure of Cynocephal-Hermanubis with a triple caduceus in his right hand, while from the left side the same wheel casts down the body of the crocodile Typhone, with its human head and a trident in its left paw.

In the upper left corner of the picture we see an angel holding an open book, on the right side and opposite to him, there is an eagle also with a book in its claws. There are two winged animals beneath the wheel, each having books similar to the other symbols just mentioned.

What does this whole configuration give to us? Undoubtedly it is a closed and finished system, which has been subjected to the inner processes. Its crown is the invariable method of the Sphinx—TO DARE, TO KEEP SILENT, TO KNOW, TO WILL, all of which lead to the perfecting of the astrosome. The whole mill (the wheel) dominated by the platform of this method, pulls some up (as Hermanubis), but at the same time it precipitates the fall of others (Typhone). Striving upwards, the elements from under the sign of AZOTH, that great solvent, still retain the dog's heads on their shoulders, symbol of their former, much more imperfect state, the traces of former impulsiveness, darkness and evil instincts.

Those who have fallen from above, are armed with the fatal system which proclaims the *non-neutralized binaries*, and still retain some traces of their former greatness in the unexpected form of the human head on a crocodile's body, the last virtues still remaining despite their fall.

This is the complicated picture of the Tenth Arcanum.

The *Mill of Transformations*, enlightened by something *Higher*, something implacable which pulls and kneads us, in a painful process, in order 'to prepare a better dough for the future bread'.

In the picture we see only the *astral sphere*, but our imagination should also add the *mental* and *physical* ones. The latter is clearly symbolized by the angel with the book (mental), eagle (astral) and the *physical* binary of two animals below the wheel, which still have wings, to show that they too may be able to fly higher than their present position at the foot of the whole construction of the arcanum.

The student must realize here, that all the writer can do with the aid of human language, is to give ideas in the form of symbols. Their cryptic language should be read and understood by you personally, according to the old and ever true occult rule: Truth must be L I V E D, and not looked upon as something apart from us, for we will N E V E R approach it if we have such a wrong attitude. So it is with the Tarot. Some will find in it an inexhaustible source of inspiration and knowledge, while others, whose minds are still unripe for abstrusely imaginative and creative thinking, may only shrug their shoulders in a sign of disapproval. Hermetism is not for everyone, as is the case with every philosophical system. Everything depends upon the particular region of the mental realm in which you are living in this incarnation.

Coming back to the arcanum we can say, that with the idea of the Archetype and his higher influxes is also connected the idea of the Law. So the first title of the Tenth Arcanum is '*Testament*'. In it are flowing all mental principles and currents. In the midst of our own humanity, in the realm of its manifestations, we have the *Wheel of the Tarot*, leading to what our race calls the 'Kabbalah': that which is the criterion and tool for the analysis of astral forms. Do not connect the word 'Kabbalah' with the Jews as a nation. Under present conditions it would be utterly wrong. The Kabbalah belongs to everyone who is able to learn and use it, no matter to which 'nation' he actually belongs. The symbolic alphabet (Hebrew) was chosen only because of its qualities so superbly adaptable to the ancient Egyptian occult wisdom. When I had to study that language in order to be in a position to go deeper into the Kabbalah, my teacher—a last-year university student in Hebrew—remarked, when by chance he saw my use of his language, that he knew little about *such an interpretation of the letters and their related numbers*.

The second title (astral) of the Tenth Arcanum will therefore be 'the Kabbalah' (Latin: Quabbalah).

On the plane of Nature we have to do with the pitiless Wheel of Fortune, otherwise called 'the World's Mill'. This wheel grinds everything, assimilates everything, and prepares everything. It raises one thing, and lowers another, as a true R O T A, leaving nothing immovable, except its A X L E which bears the name of: *the Possibility of the existence of illusion, which is*

MATTER. Now meditate about this mysterious *'axle'* of the *'visible and sensible'* world, and merge into the illimitable PEACE OF REALIZATION.

The third title of the arcanum will be 'FORTUNA' (Fortune).

In other courses of occultism we may also meet with other titles, such as 'Regnum Dei' (Kingdom of God) and 'Ordo' (Order). These give us the same ideas, considered from slightly differently coloured mental attitudes, but less defined. The conception of the Kingdom of God in any realm of manifestation means the acceptance of the existence of harmony and good functioning in time and space.

So, the Kingdom of God for any of the innumerable planets will be the epoch when they flourish supremely in the foregoing sense. I leave it to the student to guess the answer to the question: how will things be with our own little speck in the universe—the Earth?

For an individual, the Kingdom of God will be his period of deepest inner harmony and cohesion of his impressions and manifestations. Of course, we should mention that the period of the Kingdom of God for the whole organism does not always coincide with that of its separate organs. For example, the moment of the coming of that Kingdom for, say, Mars, may be different from that of the other parts of the solar system.

FAITH IN THE KINGDOM OF GOD MAY BE CONSIDERED AS THE REFLECTION OF THE LAW (TESTAMENT) IN THE MIRROR OF HOPE.

Latin 'ORDO' means 'order'; but in the realm of occultism, the Kabbalah is the highest synthesis of all orders in all astral manifestations, accessible to our conceptions. So our own title of the Tenth Arcanum does not differ essentially from the other variations of occult tradition.

LESSON 33

We now have to pass to arithmological analysis of the arcanum.

Equation No. 40: $10 = 1 + 9$

The ONE does not manifest itself in one, but in nine clichés, reflections or refractions, having a cohesive character. In other words, we cognize the objects with the intermediary of their nine attributes.

Equation No. 41: $10 = 9 + 1$

These nine attributes are realized in one synthetic tenth manifestation, playing the role of a seed or grain of a real object.

Both theses so obtained, can be expressed by the following formula:

THE ESSENCE (OR BEING) OF THE OBJECT IS HIDDEN BEHIND THE VEIL OF ITS ATTRIBUTES, AND THESE ATTRIBUTES DO NOT EMERGE FROM THEMSELVES, BUT FROM THE CONCRETE THING.

Now we will develop these theses into a pattern, transmitted to us by the Occult Tradition of the White Race.

G

ESSENCE OF THINGS

ה —	ו N	י +
③ בינה	① כתר	② חכמה
⑤ פחד	⑥ תיפרת	④ חסד
⑧ הוד	⑨ יסוד	⑦ נצה

ה

Fig. 29 The Sephiroth

SYSTEM OF SEPHIROTH (Fig. 29)

According to the triple LAW, the Essence of an object manifests itself primarily as the *Ternary of the Great Arcanum's type*.

In occult philosophy, and especially in that of Hermetism, the foremost thing is to be able to find the *true essence or core* of BEING in everything with which we come into contact. Of course, it needs immense effort and toil, but it is just what was done and what is being done by the leading occultists of all eras. Does it pay them? If my personal opinion—as that of a man who in this epoch has been connected with many forms of the 'hidden wisdom' as occultism is sometimes called—has any meaning for my readers, then it will be an *absolute and unconditional YES*!

The *first* manifestation (in everything) will have, just like the object itself, a neutral, androgynous character. The *second* will be active, the *third* passive, according to the formula: ה י (Yod-Hé) now well known to us.

This *high Ternary* will be TWICE reflected as ternaries of the pattern of the descending triangle. The whole system of these reflections manifests itself as a concrete one, which we will call '*the tenfold manifestation*' of the essence of a thing (see Fig. 29). It possesses, of course, the attribute of androgyneity on the ground of its synthetic origin.

These ten numbered manifestations are called the SEPHIROTH (which is the plural form of SEPHIRA) of things. This word can be translated from the Hebrew as 'numerical, radiant or visible'. In this way the results are, that every thing or object (no matter what kind it may be) allows us to summarize the ten manifestations, or that every thing radiates ten aspects of itself, just like a *lantern* with a light in its centre, which has *ten glass panels each of a different colour*. if you accept this simile about the Sephiroth, you may not have any difficulties later, when we will make an analysis of a more complicated kind.

The ten Sephiroth create a family. In it the Kabbalah discriminates between:

(I) The *Upper Androgyne* (1) or Macroprozopos.

(II) *Father* (2).

(III) Mother (3).

(IV) *Their Child* represented by the cohesion of the six Sephiroth (4). (5), (6), (7), (8), (9) Possess androgyneity and are called Microprozopos. The sixth Sephira is the centre of functional activity of the Microprozopos and the ninth Sephira is the organ of his activity.

(V) The *spouse or bride* of the Microprozopos, that is the *tenth* Sephira.

The Jewish Kabbalists penetrated only to the FIRST FAMILY of the Sephirothic system of the universe, considering it as the manifestation of an *Inaccessible Essence*, called by them AIN-SOPH (literally—in-accessible). They did *not allow for any analysis of Ain-Soph*.

THE MACROPROZOPOS	= Crown
FATHER	= Wisdom
MOTHER	= Intelligence
THE MICROPROZOPOS	= Combination of Sephiroth of Charity, Justice (Severity), Beauty, Victory, Glory and Form
HIS SPOUSE	= Kingdom

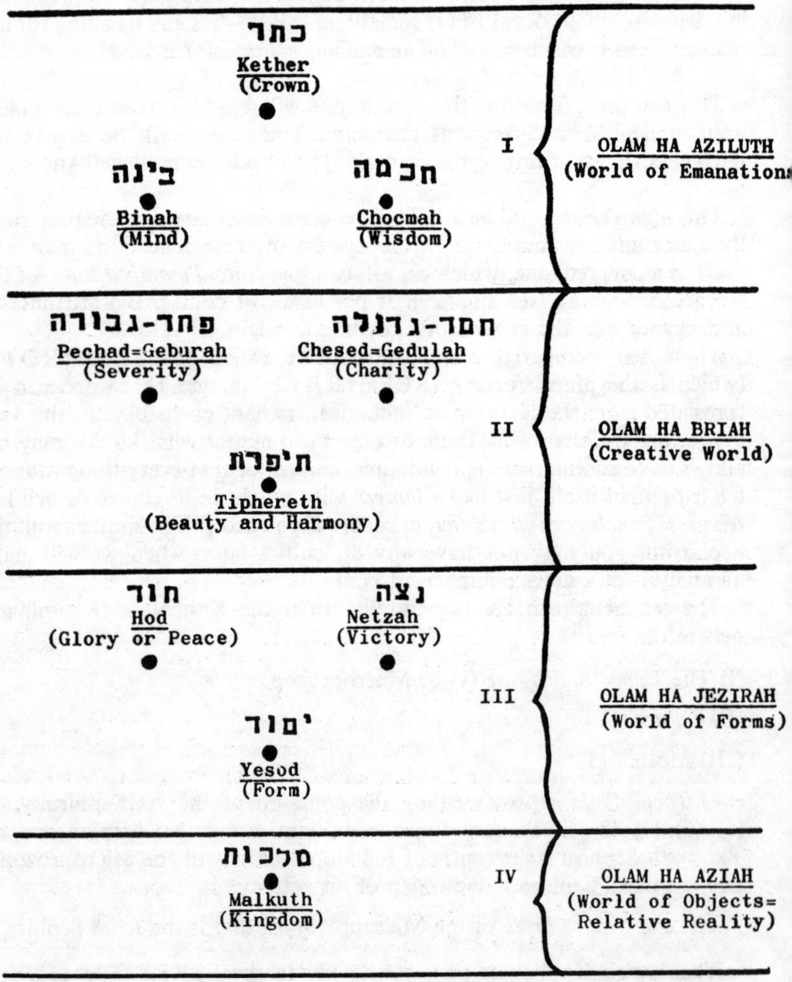

כתר
Kether
(Crown)

I — OLAM HA AZILUTH
(World of Emanations)

בינה
Binah
(Mind)

חכמה
Chocmah
(Wisdom)

פחד-גבורה
Pechad=Geburah
(Severity)

חסד-גדולה
Chesed=Gedulah
(Charity)

II — OLAM HA BRIAH
(Creative World)

תיפרת
Tiphereth
(Beauty and Harmony)

חוד
Hod
(Glory or Peace)

נצה
Netzah
(Victory)

III — OLAM HA JEZIRAH
(World of Forms)

יסוד
Yesod
(Form)

מלכות
Malkuth
(Kingdom)

IV — OLAM HA AZIAH
(World of Objects= Relative Reality)

Fig. 30 Second Mystic Family (with Sephiroth)

Rosicrucians mentioned not only the first Sephiroth of the universe, but also members of the *Family*, located, by them, between Ain-Soph and the Sephiroth. They recognized, that the *Inaccessible, Infinitely Homogenous, Infinitely Harmonious, All-Contented* BEGINNING manifests itself actively, or we may say, wants to reveal Itself through a certain YOD, that is that which we call *Transcendental Love*. This will be the FATHER of the FIRST FAMILY.

This *Father* by his tendency which has the character of radiation, will determine the existence of a certain *Passivity*, which opposes his activity. This passive element will become the First Hé of the FIRST FAMILY, that which we call TRANSCENDENTAL LIFE.

This element, contrasting to the radiant YOD, must have something like a shadowy character. It is something darkened, ready to receive in itself the radiant influx of the *Inaccessible*. From this comes its Latin name—RESTRICTIO a shadowy limitation in the orb of *Infinite Light*.

So the TRANSCENDENTAL LOVE (the First Father) fecundates the TRANSCENDENTAL LIFE (the First Mother). These mystical Persons give birth to the LOGOS—the TRANSCENDENTAL WORD, the Great Architect of the universe.

The Logos emanates the Second Hé of the FIRST FAMILY, manifesting itself by the ten Sephiroth, through the *first* of them, or Macroprozopos of the universe, called the CROWN-SEPHIRA or *Kether*. Later come the remaining nine Sephiroth of the SECOND FAMILY in the pattern of the so-called FOUR WORLDS. As we may see, the world of emanations—OLAM HA AZILUTH includes in itself the *Androgynous Crown* (Macroprozopos) manifesting itself, as suited to a balanced mentality, *from one side*, by the cohesion of THAT which *can cognize* (Sephira of Wisdom—Chocmah), and on the *other side*—THAT which can be the object of cognition (Sephira of the Mind—Binah) which actually limits the first.

In the WORLD OF CREATION—OLAM HA BRIAH we meet the active Sephira of *Grace* or *Charity* (Chesed) appearing as a reflection of the desire for knowledge, that is of expansion of the second Sephira (Chocmah) and with the passive Sephira of Severity (Pechad or Geburah), limiting Charity because of the necessity of objects of the realm of cognition (because of limitations of the Mind).

These Sephiroth are neutralized by the splendour of the radiant Sephira TIPHERETH—the World's Harmony, the World's Beauty. And what in ethics can be more radiant than a full balance of Charity by Severity, of the Good by Equal Rights? Does not the excess of charity burn us like fire, compelling us to pray about justice? Does not the excess of severity deprive an erring member of the *Family of Souls* of all hope of salvation?

Charity balanced by Severity solves every ethical problem.

In the WORLD OF FORMS—OLAM HA JEZIRAH, we see the victory of the good over evil, of Light over darkness, of active over passive. It is the active seventh Sephira NETZAH, in which abides the Initiate, faultlessly choosing the direct way in the *Sixth Arcanum*.

But, active desire in choice of direct paths does not exclude the necessity

No.	Name of the Sephira	Pronunciation of the Name	God's Name Corresponding to the Sephira	Pronunciation of that Name	Etymological Interpretation	Gematrical and Numerical Meaning of the Name	Gematrical and Numerical Meaning of the Sephira
I	כתר	Kether	אהיה	Ehieh	Existing	21=3	620=8
II	חכמה	Chocmah	יה	Yah	Infinite	15=6	73=10
III	בינה	Binah	יהוה	Yod-Hé-Vau-Hé Yodheva	Absolute Eternal	26=8	67=13=
IV	חסד גדולה	Chesed or Gedulah	אל	El	Strong	31=4	72=9 48=12=
V	פחד גבורה	Pechad or Geburah	אלהים	Elohim	He-Gods He-God-in Gods ful-filling the Cycle	86=14=5	92=11 216=9
VI	תיפת תפראת	Tiphereth	אלוה יהוה	Eloha	Perfect, Magnificent (shining with splendour)	42=6	1090= 1 1081= 1
VII	נצה	Netzah	יהוה צבאות	Yod-Hé-Vau-Hé Zabaoth	God of Wars	26+499= 525=12=3	145=10
VIII	חוד	Hod	אלחים צבאות צלבאות	Elohim Zabaoth or Zalbaoth	He-Gods in Wars	86+499= 585=18=9	15=6
IX	יסוד	Yesod	שדי אלהי	Shaddai or Elhai	Omnipotent	314=8 46=10	80=8
X	מלכות	Malkuth	אדני	Adonai	Lord	65=11=2	469=19 10

Fig. 30A Table of the Sephiroth and the Names of God corresponding to Them

for quiet movement on the way chosen, without any feverish passion for some new choice. One has to obtain some peace after victory, to await the crops of the sown Good.

Therefore that strong Sephira *Netzah* must be limited by the passive one, that of HOD (Glory or Peace).

This mysterious Sephira (Hod) seems to give us a paradoxical idea: lack of movement, but presence of life. To walk means to meet new by-paths, and to live means to move, at least in the limits of our conception on the material plane; but the Sephira HOD poses us with the problem of LIFE WITHOUT MOVEMENT. This is a great mystery, but also the greatest Truth, perhaps close to the ABSOLUTE TRUTH. Those who have reached *Samadhi* know about it, from their own experience: for, it is just the mystery of the highest ECSTASY, of the immovable BEING, without attributes, needs, desires or dreams (see the Chapter 'On the Ocean' in the book *In Days of Great Peace*).

Victory and *Glory* are neutralized by the androgynous, realized Form, the Creation of every concrete thing (Fundamentum omnium rerum).

Actually, if a *Form* has to exist, it must be made; then the *Victory* must indicate the choice of the way, in order to hold it (*Peace, Glory*). In this last sentence, the italics mean Sephiroth.

This is the process of the birth of the ninth Sephira YESOD, projecting itself into the world of 'reality' (OLAM HA AZIAH) by the Sephira of the Kingdom (MALKUTH), that is the germ of the material world in which we live.

Figure No. 30 shows the full scheme of the SECOND MYSTICAL FAMILY. This whole scheme is full of symmetry. Three systems of projection of Sephiroth are shown in the columns. In the middle or neutral column, the Breath of the Logos, the *Great Crown* is projected from the Name of the Archetype through the principle of *Beauty*. Beauty reflects itself in *Form*, and Form in *Matter* (Physical).

In the right, *male* column, *Wisdom* teaches *Charity* and prepares the *Victory*. In the left, *female* column, *Intelligence* teaches *Justice* and gives *Peace*.

Every Sephira of the Second Family *in itself can be considered* as a closed system, therefore possessing its own Sephirothic manifestations. These manifestations are analysed again according to the Sephirothic pattern, and so on. Therefore we can say, that this scheme will serve us further as a standard pattern of analysis of the elements, which may enter into this course of esoterism.

But, there is a condition: the student must, *here and now*, become acquainted with the Sephiroth, as expounded in this lesson. He must memorize them firmly, their meanings and places in the scheme, and so on. Only then may he be able to listen successfully to present lessons and follow them intelligently. This may take him some time, but there is no choice. Anyway, without knowing the English alphabet you cannot read anything in that language.

Now I am passing on to the *Channels of the Sephirothic System*, that is THE WAYS by which it is possible to pass from one Sephira to another.

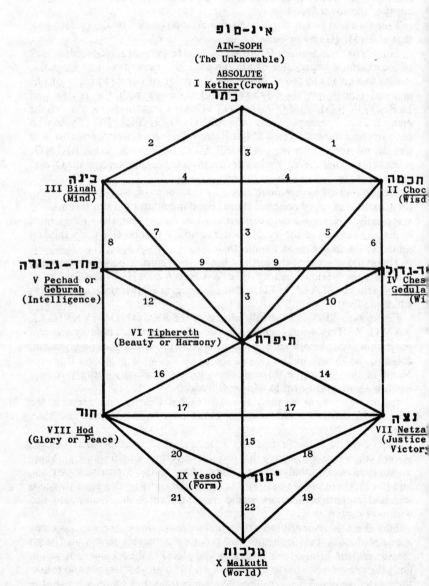

Fig. 31 The Sephiroth and Their Diabatic Processes, SCHEME "A"

There are 22 Channels according to the 22 letters of the Hebrew alphabet. And there are TWO schemes for these ways as given in *Figs. Nos. 31 and 32*.

These channels show us the so-called DIABATIC processes, which mean the operations of the complicated passage from one Sephira to another, with the intermediary of some other Sephiroth. Diabatic processes may be both ascending and descending. I will give examples of both of them. The matter is so interesting for a serious and able mind, that later, the student of himself will probably seek all possible ways to that passage, and new and fruitful meditations will be born in his mind thus educated by the Tarot's operations.

EXAMPLE I (see Fig. 31: the Normal Diabatic Process, or Process of the Birth of the Universe.

The idea of Knowledge (Crown—Kether) splits itself into the Sephiroth: (1) desire of cognition (Wisdom—Chocmah) and (2) Sephira of the objects of that cognition, which are closed and limited for the further building up of the universe (Intelligence—Mind of things, that is Binah). The way of the passage was Channels (1) and (4).

Returning through Channel (4) to the Sephira of Wisdom (Chocmah), and also passing along Channel (6), we reflect it in the form of Charity (Chesed) and are immediately compelled to balance it with the Sephira of Justice (Pechad), for which Channel (9) serves.

Then we can give birth to (Channel 12) the Harmony and Beauty (Tiphereth) of the manifestations in forms. Taste of the absolute Beauty easily leads us (14) to Victory through the well-planned choice of forms; then comes the desire (17) to taste the Glory (Hod) as the fruit of that Victory, which simply means to take a rest, and stop at some definite Forms (Yesod), which will possibly be provided for us by Channel (20).

Now it remains only for an involutionary process to create the Forms, as concrete things, going down through Channel (22) *Malkuth*.

EXAMPLE II: a Normal Ascending Diabatic Process.

Having learned of *concrete* matters (Kingdom-Malkuth) man comes to abide in the Sephira of Forms (Yesod), that is he does not need any manipulations with concrete things, replacing them with a combination of forms in his imagination. So he passes along Channel (22); but his forms need life, need to be manifested in some separate world. So he will enlighten them with the light of Glory (Hod), passing to the eight Sephira through Channel (20).

Illumination of these Forms brings the possibility to establish *polarities*, Good and Evil, Light and Dark, Fine and Gross, and so on, preparing the Victory of the seventh Sephira (Netzah) through the passage of Channel (17).

Victory in the process of establishing polarities, together with right evaluation of their mutual relations leads through Channel (14) to desire the creation of Harmony (Tiphereth) in these polarities, which means, of course, the neutralization of all the binaries.

An exact knowledge of the binaries will push us through Channel (12)

G*

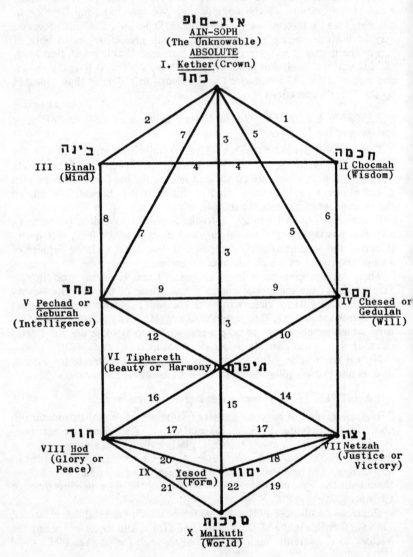

Fig. 32 The Sephiroth and Their Diabatic Processes, SCHEME "B"

to the Sephira of Justice (Pechad). Now, the respect for the positive poles of the recently acquired Victory will induce us to balance Justice (Pechad) by Charity (Chesed).

But, we have to consider BOTH elements at the same time. This compels us to return to Channel (9) and to Justice, to realize it as a severe law of judgement, and to pause, thinking over the question, that the possibility of a perfect construction of the universe contains in it the full number of things that are in that universe. This means that we are going to the Sephira of Intelligence (Binah) through Channel (8).

The question of the objects for cognition, will bring us to deliberation about the identity, or non-identity of the SUBJECTIVE AND OBJECTIVE WORLDS. In other words, it will mysteriously lead us through Channel (4) to the Sephira of the KNOWER (Chocmah). From here it is easy to enter into Channel (1) through the creation of the idea of the *process of cognition* in general, which appears as the Crown (Kether) of our mental powers.

Anything higher can only be attempts to receive the ETERNAL LIGHT of the First Family's influxes.

EXAMPLE III: Entering through the Central Channels.

From the concrete form (Malkuth) a scientist goes through Channel (22) to Forms in general (Yesod), full realization of which can give him an understanding of Beauty (Tiphereth), even apart from the element of inspiration. This hard, but possible way is represented by Channel (15), the path of astral power.

Further, comes ascension to the Absolute World of Ideas (Kether) through Channel (3), passing through the astral world, which allows him to catch principles, because of his frequent intercourse with the laws along this way.

These few examples should be sufficient in order to teach the student how to analyse other passages through the channels of the sephiroth.

It is hard to imagine something better and more developing for our mental powers than this practice and its meditations. It has always been the foremost work of Hermetists and Kabbalists since the earliest days of the foundation of Western Occult Schools.

LESSON 34

We now pass to the unfolding of the closed systems into their Sephirothic attributes. We will consider *four basic examples*.

I. *Example from the Realm of Theurgy*

A theurgic operation consists of what we describe as a sufficiently serious, well-planned and concise attempt to influence the mental currents of the universe in its parts, which we call the Archetype. The aim is *fulfilment* or *acceleration* of certain astral formations, or physical realizations. Speaking in simple language, we can say that the spirit of the theurgist enters into intercourse with the Archetype so as to obtain some astral or material results with his assistance.

אי׳ן-סופ

AIN-SOPH

Pater noster qui es in coelis

I. Sanctificetur

Nomen Tuum
(Kether)

III. Fiat Voluntas Tua

Sicut in coelo
(Binah)

IV. Et in terra
(Geburah)

V. Panem nostrum

quotidianum
da nobis hodie
(Hod)

II. Adveniat Regnum Tuum
(Tiphereth)

VI. Et dimitte nobis

debita nostra
(Chocmah)

VII. Sicut et nos dimitt
debitoribus nostri
(Chesed)

VIII. Et ne nos inducas

in tentationem
(Netzah)

IX. Sed libera nos a malo
(Yesod)

Quoniam Tibi sunt Regnum, et Potestas, et Gloria
per Eonas - AMEN
(Malkuth)

Fig. 33 The Lord's Prayer

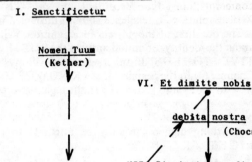
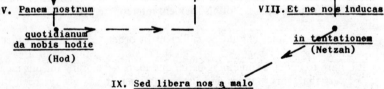

The most elementary and widely used type of theurgic operation is PRAYER, when duly understood and performed.

Prayers are more or less complicated depending upon the contemplation of the praying person, and also the object of the prayer.

If the prayer has *no definite target for realization*, but is performed only to obtain a link with the Archetype, to bring higher influxes into all phases of life, then it will appear as a direct reflection of the praying person's contemplation. One can call it a theurgic photograph of the operating Microcosm. From this fact we may accept, that the prayer of an occultist, acquainted with Hermetism and the Kabbalah, will be a kind of closed system, unfolded according to the Sephiroth of the universe.

We will now analyse the *Lord's Prayer* (Fig. 33).

First I will give the text of it in its classical form, that is in Latin, because of the necessity of giving absolutely exact terminology.

PATER NOSTER QUI ES IN COELIS

This is an invocation. It is directed to the ONE, Who is *beyond and above all the Sephiroth of the Second* Family, or simply, to the PERSONS OF THE FIRST FAMILY. The term itself 'IN COELIS' (in Heaven) means that HE is above the so-called *Horizon Aeternitatis* (Horizon of Eternity).

At the same time we can see that in this sublime INVOCATION, there has been retained the basic thesis of theurgy, which states that '*every prayer is directed to Ain-Soph, and not to any Sephiroth*'. In fact prayer ascends through the world's Sephiroth. Sometimes it can be fortified by an appeal to the *Assistant Powers*, but this only means a blending of our small rivulet of prayer with the majestic, immense river of theurgic operations performed by the Blessed ONE. In any case, the water of such a rivulet always streams to the Infinite Ocean of the Absolute—AIN-SOPH.

The ultimate meditations of our Eastern brethren directed to the Supreme Atman—Self, Nirvana or Parabrahm are identical with our present example, when understood from the point of view of the great Western Tradition of *Hermes Trismegistus*.

SANCTIFICETUR NOMEN TUUM . . . (first request)

This means: '*Thy Crown (Kether) be sanctified, that is, the Great Arcanum of Thy Emanation* and Manifestation on the metaphysical plane.' In other words, 'be sanctified' means do not let the FORM OF THE EVOLUTIONARY TRIANGLE be lost from view of the seeker-mystics.

ADVENIAT REGNUM TUUM (second request)

It signifies the coming of the kingdom of Harmony of Forms (Tiphereth) in the soul of the praying person, and in the astrosome of the whole of the outer universe surrounding him.

FIAT VOLUNTAS TUA SICUT IN COELO . . . (third request)

Meaning: 'I bow before the Great Sign ה ו ה י (Yod-Hé-Vau-Hé) of

the metaphysical world, wishing to take part in it with my own mentality.'
Sephira BINAH encloses in it the Mind of every Thing subjected to the
Great Law of the Tetragrammaton.

. . . ET IN TERRA. (fourth request)

It means: and by the astral application of unchangeable laws and manifestations of the Sephira of *Justice* (Pechad).

PANEM NOSTRUM QUOTIDIANUM DA NOBIS HODIE. (fifth request)

Here 'bread' means the possibility of the formal cognition of life
(and we are told—daily bread). Today's means for the time from the
choice of ways (according to the Sixth Arcanum) to the next similar decision. The request evidently belongs to life in the Sephira of Glory or Peace
(Hod), and to the possibility of taking rest after victory over temptations.

ET DIMITTE NOBIS DEBITA NOSTRA . . . (sixth request)

Apply to our personalities the Principle of Thy Expansive Wisdom
(Chocmah). . . .

. . . SICUT ET NOS DIMITTIMUS DEBITORIBUS NOSTRIS (seventh request)

. . . which in our astrosomes will be reflected as the Law of Charity for
our neighbour (Chesed).

ET NE NOS INDUCAS IN TENTATIONEM . . . (eighth request)

Liberate us from the unsuccessful tests arising from the too frequent use
of the Sixth Arcanum, so dangerous for the results of the incarnation of
the tempted one (Netzah)

. . . SED LIBERA NOS A MALO (ninth request)

And even liberate us from any frequent meetings with negative clichés,
which could attract us to the ways of evil and transgression in the applications of the Sixth Arcanum (Sephira of Forms and Clichés—Yesod).

These nine requests actually end the Lord's Prayer as given in the
Gospels; but the Churches later added a conclusion in the following form:

QUONIAM TIBI SUNT REGNUM ET POTENTIA ET GLORIA PER EONAS. AMEN.

We encounter the term 'Eonas' (in English—eons) in the Gnostic
Teachings. There it means the separate cycles of the basic DYNAMIC
CYCLE ה ו ה י (Yod-Hé-Vau-Hé) which gives us the scheme of everything that has been, and will come into existence. The Gnostic eons are
finished individualized systems, polarized in pairs of + and −, which
multiply themselves according to the Laws: ו ה י (Yod-Hé-Vau) or rather
ה י - ה י - (Yod-Hé -Yod-Hé).

The whole of all the eons taken in this sense is equal to the number of
all planes of the manifested universe.

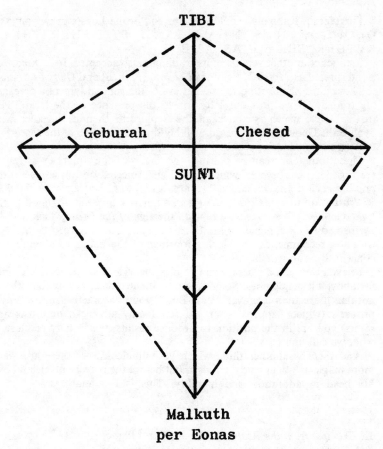

Fig. 33A Conclusion of the Lord's Prayer

Now we may be able to interpret the end of the Lord's Prayer as follows: *'Because Thou art the primary Source of manifestations of the Great Arcanum in all Cycles of the three planes of the universe.'* In the pattern of the Great Arcanum of Magic as accepted by us, the term 'Kingdom' (Regnum) will refer to the Elementary ROTA (4), the term 'Power' (Potentia) to the astral ROTA (2), and the term Glory (Gloria) to the Metaphysical Triangle (3).

Therefore a Kabbalist would read the end of the Lord's Prayer as: QUONIAM TIBI SUNT MALKUTH, ET TIPHERETH, ET KETHER, PER EONAS. AMEN.

In practice another version of its reading is also accepted. In it *'Kingdom'* is interpreted as *Malkuth, Power* as *Geburah* (Pechad) and *Glory* as *Chesed*.

These three Sephiroth give us a pattern of the general type of a descending triangle. If we turn our attention to the presence of the term TIBI (to THEE), which is above all the Sephiroth, then it, together with Sephiroths Geburah and Chesed, will build a new triangle of the ascending type (see Fig. 33A).

These four terms can be put into the angles of the square cross (again see Fig. 33A) *one point* of which (TIBI) is projected on to the *face* of the praying person, the *second point* (Malkuth) on to his *solar plexus*, the *third* (Geburah) on to his *left shoulder* (as in a mirror), and the *fourth* on to the *right shoulder*. This gives us a hint on the *sign of the Cross* which may be performed when concluding the Lord's Prayer. For the word 'AMEN', tradition recommends the placing together of the palms as a symbol of concentration in worship.

I have given you a classic example of a theurgic operation, which ranks far above all magic ones. Some students might object, saying that 'this is nothing more than a prayer'. Yes! But if you can practise *such a prayer* properly (which happens to only a few highly advanced occultists and saints) you are in the position to produce results, which may be close to what we call 'miracles'.

And there is another thing which you should know: there are many more magicians than true theurgists, but before them every magician bows his head in adoration and humility. This is the final truth.

LESSON 35

II. *Example from the Realm of Magic* (Astral Plane)

We have already had the opportunity of speaking about auto-suggestion in the Fifth Arcanum, using the so-called 'new German' method. Now we will unfold the general pattern of suggestion according to the Sephirothic system, now well known to us, no matter whether the operation is directed to the astrosome of the operator himself or those of other individuals.

The role of the FIRST FAMILY in relation to the future system of the Sephiroth of suggestion will be played by the *Pentagrammatic Free Will* of the operator. The *Kether* will be the *idea of suggestion* containing within it *instruction* to the object of suggestion (that is the manifestation which we want to produce). This instruction is the *Chocmah* of the system, where the individuals, to whom suggestion may be applied, play the role of the *Mind* or *Binah*.

These two Sephiroth will be the mental part of the arising evolutionary entity.

In the astral the contents of the suggestion will determine the character of the emotion which should be transferred to the object. It is the Sephira *Chesed*. *What may anger one person*, will *only puzzle another*, and will merge yet a *third into blissful contemplation. Realize the meaning of this formula*, essential for every magic operation, and *determine your own place in its three variations*, as given here. *Without this no one can act.*

Now, the subjective component of the emotional current together with the laws according to which this component may work, will be the *Geburah* of the system.

Both of the Sephiroth, Chesed and Geburah, must, of course, be harmoniously neutralized by their own *Tiphereth*, that is through the general picture of the suggested emotion, which should refer, in the imagination of the operator, to the PRESENT, but never to the FUTURE! This is another secret of magic. What is the reason for it?

In truth, you can really ACT only in THIS PRESENT MOMENT and never in the past or the future. Speaking in occult terms, I will say, that the magician is a being of the PRESENT, for only in the present can he develop his force and skill. It is hard to add anything more, intuition must tell you the rest.

The formal part of the astral suggestion will include *Netzah*, as the sum of all the obstacles in the nature of the subject and his surroundings, against which one has to fight while operating.

The Sephira *Hod* will be the sum of the amount of Victory, which we received in the preceding Sephira (Netzah). In other words, that which we believe to be satisfactory for us as the result of suggestion. If we suggest to the subject the ability of moving his leg, which has been paralysed, then we have to imagine exactly which degree of flexibility and freedom of movement may satisfy us, or at which result we will stop our session for the day. This is the Sephira Yesod.

And this mental work must also be performed in the PRESENT, not in the FUTURE. Now we will seek for the concrete Malkuth in this operation. It will be composed of the elements of your *voice*, *gestures* and even your *movements* which are added to the picture. The material, that is the synthesis of these manifestations accessible to the senses is the tenth and concluding Sephira of the operation, or Malkuth.

III. *Example of an Operation having the Character of Realization*
(The lower astral plane touches the physical and is tied to it in many of its manifestations.)

Imagine an incarnate pentagram operating through its magnetic (odic) centres of radiation and imbibitions. These centres are tightly bound up with the functions of the human physical body.

The middle part of your face, just over the base of the nose, is your magnetic *Kether*. With it is closely connected a physical point for the process of meditation. From the passive point of view, this is the place for the reception of another's central look.

When you operate actively with your central look, then the fixed axis of your *Chocmah* (right eye) and your *Binah* (left eye) are working, united by the action of the meditating *Kether*. Give your full attention to this in order to understand well what has just been said.

With one's central gaze one can attack only the *Chocmah* of the enemy, to paralyse the activity of his *Kether*, or only of his *Binah* to paralyse his susceptibility.

Finally, you can defend yourself against the central look by gazing into the eyes of the enemy, hitting his Binah with your Chocmah, yielding your Binah to his Chocmah and so leaving the result of the fight to the sum of the powers of both Kethers, operating with their polarized organs.

If we desire to accept someone's suggestion in the realm of these three higher magnetic centres, we should lower both eyes and so leave our Kether under the central look of the operator.

By the so-called *male* polarization of fluids, as has been stated in earlier lessons, the Sephira *Chesed* will represent the magnetism of the *right* hand; the Sephira *Geburah*, the magnetism of the *left* hand, while the Sehira *Tiphereth* will be the magnetic store for the *solar plexus*, which we can use freely, borrowing from it positive or negative fluids. The Sephira *Netzah* belongs to the operation of shortening the radiations of your right foot, thereby conserving its negative magnetism. The Sephira *Hod* does the same for the left foot.

The Sephira Yesod directs the store of the odic energy belonging to the sexual organs. The Sephira *Malkuth* is related to the realm of magnetic susceptibility of the back of the neck and shoulders, against which, as you know from preceding lessons, the central look of an operator can be directed, as well as the odic manipulations of the centres in his hands.

The navel is not a centre of active magnetism, but it is considered as being the counterpart of the middle part of Channel (15) connecting Yesod with Tiphereth. It also vampirizes exceptionally positive and negative emanations from outside. This is used in magnetic therapy, connecting one of the poles of emanations from the healer-operator to the navel of the patient, and another of the opposite magnetism, to another Sephirothic centre of the patient. The position of that second centre depends upon the nature of the symptoms, which are to be removed. The choice must be made according to Kabbalistic calculations.

All these deliberations may have some meaning for a student, but will convey little to a mere reader, because the matter must be understood practically, before an appreciation of the exposition can be grasped. One must know what the Sephiroth are (this knowledge comes only after long meditation about them, along the lines given in this work), and also about the magnetic centres, which can be practically discovered only by exercises.

IV. *Example of the General Use of the Sephirothic System*

The Sephirothic system can be applied to every realm in our field of cognition; but this realm must present a *completed* unit, and not something unfinished, undecided, or unknown. How can we evaluate a motor, when we have only some parts of it, and not the whole machine? So it is with the Sephiroth.

I will give, as a practical example, something which is known to every thinking man, not necessarily an occultist. It is—VIRTUE. See now, how the eminent Hermetist Henri Kunrath operates with it through the Sephirothic analysis.

As the *Kether* of Virtue's manifestations we will consider the ALL-WISDOM. In this conception Kether has a synthetic character, which agrees with its definition.

The positive pole of Kether will be GOODNESS, corresponding to Chocmah in our figures of the Sephirothic system.

It is limited by the element of CAREFULNESS, which is Binah. In the next world (Olam ha Briah) Goodness will be reflected as an element of *Charity* (Chesed), and Carefulness as an element of *Courage*. The binary of these elements is neutralized by *Suffering*, in this case, it will be *Tiphereth*. So we have finished with Olam ha Briah. Nobody will be astonished that Goodness was reflected as Charity. This All-Wisdom manifested itself as the positive pole of Goodness, and the negativeness of Carefulness is easy to explain. Because Goodness can be thought of as an idea of separation of another man from the danger of downfall, Circumspection can be considered as an idea of a similar separation of ourselves.

If Circumspection has the All-Wisdom as its source, then its idea of self-separation from evil, can finally be presented as courage in self-defence. The constitution of Suffering is therefore clear.

In the next world—Olam ha Jezirah the Sephira *Hod* will be a reflection of Courage in the sub-planes of the astral, where there are forms, and the name of that reflection is—*Humility*.

For the Sephira *Netzah* the reflection will be *Justice*, in the sense of giving to everyone what is due to him.

The neutralizing element of *Yesod* will be presented as *Moderation*, a logical child of Justice and Humility.

The concrete Malkuth of this pattern according to Kunrath is the *Fear of God*.

LESSON 36

There still remains some interesting arithmological analyses of the Tenth Arcanum.

Equation No. 42: $10 = 2 + 8$

Our Gnosis (2), as our teaching of the Absolute, must have an influence on the righteousness (8) of our Kabbalah. We will see it when we will consider the general construction of the Tarot.

Equation No. 43: $10 = 8 + 2$

Right conditions (8) are important for an exposition of Wisdom (2) and can even influence it.

Equation No. 44: $10 = 3 + 7$

It is the motto of occult schools, which principally try to develop mental intuition (3) in order to obtain the faculty of automatic orientation in the realm of Secondary Causes (7).

Equation No. 45: $10 = 7 + 3$

It is the motto of the schools of magic recommending first the knowledge of the Secondary Causes (7) as the starting point for the transition to the Primary ones (3).

Equation No. 46: $10 = 4 + 6$

An explanation of the thesis: the four middle Sephiroth (4) should be placed before the six polarized Sephiroth (6). Actually, for a brief definition of the world's birth it may be sufficient to mention the four middle Sephiroth: Kether, Tiphereth, Yesod and Malkuth.

Equation No. 47: $10 = 6 + 4$

In the Kabbalah Solomon's Hexagram (6) stands higher than the Elementary ROTA (4). In other words, the essence of things lies not in the realization of symbols, but in their astral interdependence. No matter, for example, that I may have 22 cards of the Tarot, while you have 22 letters of the Hebrew alphabet, and someone else 22 natural hieroglyphs. But it does matter that in all these three cases the signs and symbols are valued and used according to one identical principle.

Equation No. 48: $10 = 5 + 5$

This means five against five. There must be some mutual relation between two sides of the same thing. The ten Sephiroth of the *First Family* are grouped, as we know, into five *mystical Persons*, that is Macroprozopos, Father, Mother, Microprozopos and his Spouse who reflect their influences, or if you prefer it, possess their representatives in all the finished systems of the universe, as well as in every cell of materialistic humanity, which at the present time is fallen and far from its original purity.

When we try to analyse, with the help of the Kabbalah, the story of that downfall, we will see that now we are invariably running after the 'point of support in matter', while we ourselves are the entangled and confused illusion of that matter. It was different before the downfall: then we were seeking the Radiant Heights, not the valleys. Therefore you can now realize why in the traditional Kabbalistic scheme of the process of reflection of the Higher Mystical Persons in separate individual men, things appear in a reversed hierarchic order.

The MICROPROZOPOS in man's constitution is reflected as element *Nephesh* (see the table of Fig. 34), which is the frontier realm between the nervous system (physical plane) and the lower astral sub-planes.

The FATHER is reflected as element *Ruah*, that is the soul in its proper meaning, the complex of passions, desires and ability to give birth to forms and to accept and classify them.

The MOTHER is reflected as element *Neshamah*, which in colloquial

Name of Element	The Nature of its Properties as Manifested in the World	Its Functions in the Realm of Science	General Terms Related to the Elements
NEPHESH	Passive in relation to the outer world	Facts and their recording	Species
RUAH	Androgynous in relation to the outer world	Laws and their formulation	Personality
NESHAMAH	Active in relation to the outer world	Principles and their constitution	Man (human being)
CHAYAH	Androgynous: it binds Neshamah to Yechidah	Higher influxes (Intuition of Being)	Emanation of Divine Principles
YECHIDAH	Passive in relation to the Archetype	Union with the Absolute Being	Identity with the Archetype

Fig. 34 TABLE OF ELEMENTS IN MAN

language we call: mind, intellectuality, idealistic humanitarianism, and so on.

The MACROPROZOPOS is reflected as the element *Chayah*, that part of man which can induce him to seek after spiritual bliss.

The SPOUSE reflects herself as element *Yechidah*, that in man which links him with God.

In this list of elements Tradition does not include man's purely material components, such as his physical body, vital force of the blood, and so on. Only the nervous fluids are included. And this element which we call *Nephesh*, or animal soul, is placed the lowest amongst the other components. The Kabbalah has the idea, that man, although fallen, is still more strongly tied to Heaven (element Yechidah) than to Earth (element Nephesh).

Nephesh is passive in relation to the outer world in the sense, that like an automatic meter, it transmits similar impressions of the manifestations of the soul.

Ruah appreciates facts according to the personal psychological qualities of the recipient. Personality also equally influences the formulation of the laws deduced from these facts. The laws are transformed into principal judgements, now belonging to the human *Neshamah*, which uniformly operates general logic, until it reaches that which we call the 'transcendental realm'; but in that transcendental sphere is felt the high influence of the Spirit—*Chayah*, which can lead a man to the realization of the element *Yechidah* in himself.

In the units of the same species similarity exists between the elements of *Nephesh*. When we speak about similar personalities, this means that the elements of *Ruah* are similar.

Logical argument is possible only because of the existence of the all-human *Neshamah*. The mutual understanding and brotherly solidarity of the Saints works through the element of *Chayah*. And, finally, the supreme attainment of man, called in this Hermetic course, Reintegration (in the East Realization of the Self) is the awakened divine *Yechidah*.

These relationships should be firmly established in the mind of the student, for from now on they will be used without any further comment.

Neshamah (in its literal meaning as above) plus Chayah and Yechidah, in the Kabbalah, are often termed *Neshamah*, but, of course, *in a wider sense*, and then this term will correspond to our mentality plus the spiritual element in man.

Similarly, Ruah will then be the astrosome, and Nephesh the phantom. This will be necessary for the study of the Thirteenth Arcanum.

Having finished with the arithmological analysis of the Tenth Arcanum, we will return to the deeper symbolism of its card.

The central place is occupied by the wheel. This wheel is a synthesis of several ideas, the simplest of which, for a layman, would be imagination of a *Universal Mill* which, in the physical world, grinds living elements in order to create others.

It *levels everything*, raising one country at the expense of another, according to the laws of success and failure, severely, pitilessly, painfully and in an illusory way as the whole plane on which it acts.

A true Hermetist looks on all this with an ironic smile, knowing the unreality of the picture, which passes before his eyes. But, on the fateful wheel of the Tenth Arcanum is also hidden the astral ROTA, whose revolutions are accessible only to the observation of a man, who has deepened his metaphysical contemplation and ethical Hermetism. In its revolutions, this ROTA draws up an enormous complexity of passages, transformations, new creations and deep and subtle manifestations as taught to us by the Sacred Kabbalah.

It has already been mentioned, that the tools of the Kabbalah, were handed over to the coming generations through the intermediary of laymen (see the 'Introduction') as well as of the Initiates, in the form of the 'Tarot of the Bohemians' (the Gypsy's Tarot), which is composed of 78 cards.

We have been principally studying the Major Arcana with their 22 symbolical cards; but now it is time to say something about the Minor Arcana, with their 56 figures.

They represent the general development of the formula י ו ה ה (Yod-Hé-Vau-Hé) in the world of humanity as yet not fallen, for which the *Great Deed* (Realization) was a natural thing, well fulfilled in all its phases.

The Major Arcana are a complexity of images belonging to the already fallen Man, which allow him, by the sweat of his brow to investigate the Great Law of the Tetragrammaton, to purify his contemplation, to separate the wheat from the chaff, and, for the price of erring and its resulting falls, to arrive at relative truths and on that thorny way, to raise himself slowly to the heights of the Absolute, between the Scylla of human hardness and Charybdis of human disappointments. So you may see, that actually the title 'Minor' is related to the 56 cards only because of a misunderstanding, which slipped into the Tradition and remains there to this day.

The Minor Arcana are metaphysically purer than the Major ones. Their exactly separated, constructively clear pictures are definite, like formulas of an able mathematician. Their transformations have exact functional dependence on each other.

In the Major Arcana many things are indefinite, they give birth to one another according to vague laws. They are similar to a keyboard, which can be tuned in both tierce and quint alike, and also in an octave. Nevertheless, remember that the tuner himself works with our imperfect organs of hearing, as a basis for his work.

Briefly, the Minor Arcana are exact developments of the clichés י ה ו ה (Yod-Hé-Vau-Hé), but the Major ones, which are rather entangled, gravitate to the world of illusions, and incomplete realizations.

The great question now arises: why then in the study of the Tarot is most attention given to these imperfect Major Trumps, and not to the perfect scheme of the Minor 56? It is easily answered: because we belong to the still imperfect, downfallen form of evolution called 'humanity'. And only similar symbols, means and systems of philosophy will be acceptable to our dimmed organs of cognition. It is a hard truth, but still, the real truth. Support for this statement—taken directly from the Tradition of Hermetism—may be found in our own hearts, providing they are sincere and unprejudiced. But how many such hearts are on our planet at the present time? They belong to the men we call 'saints' or 'occult masters'. Are they in the majority among us?

LESSON 37

THE pack of 56 cards of the Minor Arcana is divided into FOUR suits, with 14 cards in each of them.

CLUBS represent י (Yod), they are also called WANDS.

HEARTS (or CUPS) are the First ה (Hé).

SPADES (or SWORDS) are ו (Vau).

DIAMONDS (or PENTACLES) are the Second ה (Hé).

Firstly, we will relate them to the influence of the *Persons* of the FIRST TRANSCENDENTAL FAMILY.

Therefore, *Wands* symbolize the influence of the Higher Yod, or Transcendental Love. It is reflected in all the Sephiroth of the SECOND FAMILY. Wands also remind us about, that which must be related to the activity of that Yod, that is the *active downward* (or fecundating) Love. It plays the role of the *First Parent* in all the activities of every individualized system. This is the *first* stimulus for souls in everything.

Cups as a reflection of the *First Hé* in Transcendental Life are the impulse of the Higher Love from below to above, the Supreme Attraction. Theirs is the second place in the pack.

Swords are the reflection of the influence of the Logos again bringing an aspect of Love, but of *androgynous Love*, generating life according to its own pattern. The ‍ (Vau) appears as the Architect of the universe because it was born from a POINT placed above the YOD by the process of polarization. Vau is a product of the active and passive love; Vau loved the Highest so strongly, that it decided, like the *Point* over the first Yod, to love actively, but downwards. For us, Swords are a symbol of the transmission of Life to the Mother, performed by the Logos through similarity of the Father's love.

Pentacles are the influence of the Second Hé on the soul. The Second Hé of the *First Family* manifests itself by the emanation of the ten Sephiroth of the *Second Family*. Emanation was the first step of Realization. Therefore, Realization is a broad analogy of the Primary Emanation.

The TRANSCENDENTAL manifested itself as the TRANSCENDENT. It acted as Forms, which condensed themselves into the world of matter.

In each suit we first see four figures symbolizing the acting persons who direct the idea of that suit. Apart from this, every suit has ten cards with numbers (from the ace to ten) corresponding to the Sephiroth of the suit.

Each suit has its own personal Yod—the King; First Hé—the Queen; Vau—the Knight, and Second Hé—the Knave which serves as an element of transition for its suit. In present-day playing cards, the Knight has been removed, so that only three figures remain.

Each of these four figures is authorized to operate in the realm of the ten Sephiroth of that suit. Therefore there are 40 phases (4 × 10) for the Sephiroth. So the general number for the whole pack will be 160, if we will limit it to only the reflections of the First Family, in the realm of Chocmah. Together with the remaining Sephiroth there will be 1,600 phases.

In this course we will be satisfied with an explanation of the significance of the 16 figures and the Sephirothic titles in all four suits.

Analysis of the 16 Figure Cards

WANDS

(1) The *King of Wands* receives the title 'Father' in the hierarchic meaning, because of his starting point in the application of authority.

(2) The *Queen of Wands* is simply the wife of the Father, necessary for the birth of the third figure.

(3) The *Knight of Wands* is the Doer, acting in the transmission of the authority, operating through:

(4) The *Knave of Wands*, that is the Servant of Authority.

CUPS

(2) The *Queen of Cups* is the most important card in her suit, because here she plays the role of the independent Attraction.

(1) The *King of Cups* is only the husband of the Queen, necessary for the birth of:

(3) The *Knight of Cups*, who functions as an intercessor whose duty is to attract some outer elements for the performance of activities. He operates with the assistance of:

(4) The *Knave of Cups*, the Servant of Attraction.

SWORDS

(3) The *Knight of Swords*, the Acting Element for the Transmission of Life, is the most important card in his suit.

(1) The *King of Swords* is the Father of the Transmission of Life.

(2) The *Queen of Swords* is the Mother for the Transmission of Life, necessary for the birth of the Knight, operating through:

(4) The *Knave of Swords*, who is the Servant of the Transmission of Life.

PENTACLES

(4) The *Knave of Pentacles*, or the Servant of Children, is predominant in his suit: for realization is appreciated according to its results.

(1) The *King of Pentacles* is the Father-Realizer and:

(2) The *Queen of Pentacles* is the Mother of Children, who gave birth to:

(3) The *Knight of Pentacles*, who is the Doer, unifying individualities, which enter into complicated organisms. He cedes his place to the Knave, who is the executor of the main, heavy work.

Analysis of the Numerical Cards

WANDS

(1) *Ace*: Kether of Wands, the metaphysical synthesis of the Active Love directed downwards, can be well interpreted as the Wheel of the Tarot. If there would be no First Stimulus for that Active Love, no universe would come into existence, there would be no Tarot, or better, the potential Wheel of the Arcana could exist, but it would not revolve and there would be nobody to accept it.

(2) *Two*: the Chocmah of Wands is Wisdom of the First Stimulus, and its Expansion, because it appears in the Sephira of human souls. Eliphas Lévi said, that it is the Assistance of the Saviour. Of course, he spoke about the Great Cliché

יהשוה (Yod-Hé-Shin-Vau-Hé).

(3) *Three*: Binah of Wands is the Intelligence of the First Stimulus, which limits its Wisdom, that is the contents of everything we expect from the Cliché of the Saviour (Yod-Hé-Shin-Vau-Hé), that is the hope of Reintegration.

(4) *Four*: Chesed of Wands, Charity of the First Stimulus is the reflection of the influence יהשוה on the plane of human ethics, astral Egregors and Chains. In other words, the same cliché Yod-Hé-Shin-Vau-Hé is the centre of the Egregors, as Father of the Churches.

(5) *Five*: is the Pechad of Wands, the Justice of the First Stimulus, limiting

its Charity. For example, it is the cause of the ethical character which acts in churches, supporting the life of their Egregors.

(6) *Six*: Tiphereth of Wands, is the Harmony and Beauty of the First Stimulus, the child born of the presence of the Church and its ethical influence. It is also the support, consolation and comfort, which the Egregor gives to its adepts. Only remember the examples of the Christian martyrs, who fearlessly went to terrible deaths. They converted the pagans just through the element Tiphereth of the Egregor, that is their harmony of action and beauty of self-sacrifice. The Egregor of some great idea usually attracts laymen through its Tiphereth, rather than through its Kether.

(7) *Seven*: Netzah of Wands is the Victory of the First Stimulus, that is the victory of the Hierarchic Law, the constitution of hierarchies everywhere, and in everything. This is the only measure of greatness.

(8) *Eight*: Hod of Wands is the Peace and Glory of the First Stimulus. Something in which we can stop and take some rest after establishment of the Hierarchy. This Peace should be identified with the acceptance of the existence of the Upper Point of Fabre d'Olivet's Triangle, of that which we call Providence in the universe. Its representative in the separate cells of this universe, that is human beings, is the element of Conscience. Because Hierarchy is in everything, one should listen to the voice of one's Conscience. It cannot be disregarded.

(9) *Nine*: Yesod of Wands, is the Form of the First Stimulus, the result of the addition of Hierarchy to Peace, given by Conscience. It is the orientation received from Conscience, from that Light which descends through the chain of beings, derived from the *Primary Cause*.

(10) *Ten*: Malkuth of Wands is the reality of the First Stimulus, the incarnation of the elements enclosed in the first nine Sephiroth: that which allows us to follow the ascending way, leading to the idea of the First Stimulus.

CUPS

(1) *Ace*: Kether of Cups is the metaphysical synthesis of that, which in the Sephira Chocmah of the Second Family brings the Transcendental Life, which is a manifestation of Vitality, of that which attracts to itself the *First Stimulus* and which is adapted for its reception.

(2) *Two*: Chocmah of Cups, is Wisdom of the Attractive Love, desire to possess the life of the Higher Influx. In other words, to secure the possession of life.

(3) *Three*: Binah of Cups is limitation of the striving of 'Two'. It is the Grace of God, manifested in its beneficent elements.

(4) *Four*: Chesed of Cups is the reflection of the desire to secure Eternal Life and efforts to do good, bringing the so-called 'salvation'.

(5) *Five*: Pechad of Cups limits the previous strivings, placing first the duty of unceasingly doing good, of continuous actions without diluting them with contrary deeds.

(6) *Six*: Tiphereth of Cups is suffering in altruistic activities and manifestations, appearing as the result of the addition of both the previous Sephiroth.

(7) *Seven*: Netzah of Cups is Victory of the subtle over the dense. In altruism it is idealized Love.

(8) *Eight*: Hod of Cups is the continuation of the plan of that ideal Love.

(9) *Nine*: Yesod of Cups is a ready form, moulded for Attractive Love.

(10) *Ten*: Malkuth of Cups is the concrete, realized synthesis of all the previous Sephiroth.

SWORDS

(1) *Ace*: Kether of Swords is the starting point of the process of the Transmission of Life.

(2) *Two*: Chocmah of Swords is determination for the Transmission of Life.

(3) *Three*: Binah of Swords is the definition of the finished system ('a mill') into which Life is transmitted.

(4) *Four*: Chesed of Swords is equality of the manifestations of the Transmission of Life and reflections of definitions in their aims.

(5) *Five*: Pechad of Swords is planned results of the Transmission of Life; reflection of the definition of a closed system.

(6) *Six*: Tiphereth of Swords is the Beauty of the transmitted Life.

(7) *Seven*: Netzah of Swords is Victory of the transmitting impulse over the influences of surroundings, in which Life has been established.

(8) *Eight*: Hod of Swords is adaptation of Victory's results to the general character of the environment.

(9) *Nine*: Yesod of Swords is the Forms of development of the transmitted Life.

(10) *Ten*: Malkuth of Swords is the final incarnation of the transmitted Life.

PENTACLES

(1) *Ace*: Kether of Pentacles is the starting point of Realization (understood in the material sense) of Primary Matter in the realm of alchemy, and of the Primary Astrosome in the realm of Ethical Hermetism.

(2) *Two*: Chocmah of Pentacles is the polarization of Matter in alchemy; the Great Binary of Fatalism (Fate) and Will in Hermetism.

(3) *Three*: Binah of Pentacles is the principle of neutralization of the poles in alchemy; the Triangle of Fabre d'Olivet in Hermetism.

(4) *Four*: Chesed of Pentacles is condensation according to the Dynamic Law (Tetragram) in alchemy; the Hermetic Quaternary symbolized by the Cross in Ethical Hermetism.

(5) *Five*: Pechad of Pentacles is domination of the Energetic Beginning

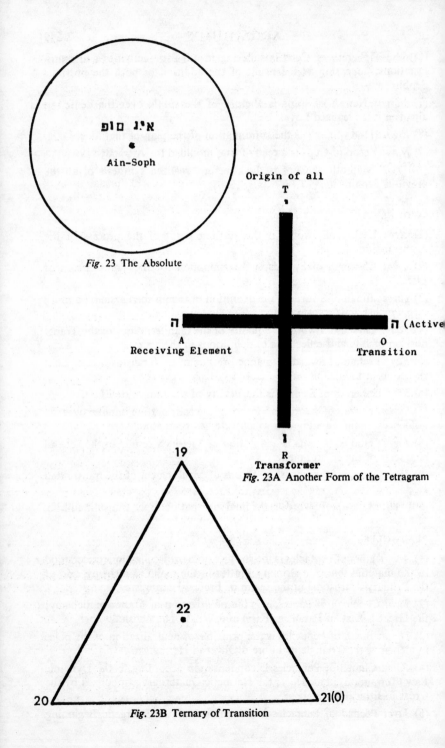

אין סוף

Ain-Soph

Fig. 23 The Absolute

Origin of all
T
י

ה
A
Receiving Element

ה (Active
O
Transition

R
Transformer
Fig. 23A Another Form of the Tetragram

19

22

20   21(0)

Fig. 23B Ternary of Transition

(Quintessence) over the four elements of alchemy. The birth of the PENTAGRAM in Hermetism.

(6) *Six*: Tiphereth of Pentacles establishes two currents in alchemy—evolutionary and involutionary. It is the problem of two paths in Hermetism.

(7) *Seven*: Netzah of Pentacles, in alchemy, is the penetration of the *subtle* into the *dense*, the Victory of *Three* over *Four* (of Spirit over Form) in Hermetism.

(8) *Eight*: Hod of Pentacles establishes the periods of formation in alchemy (the phases of transmutation of the 'Philosophers' Stone'), Conditional Law and Natural Karma in Ethical Hermetism.

(9) *Nine*: Yesod of Pentacles gives a general picture of the Evolution of Matter in alchemy, which reveals the process of sublimation. It also gives the general picture of Initiation, manifesting itself through the transmission of the Influx (by Initiation from Master to disciple).

(10) *Ten*: Malkuth of Pentacles is the transmutation of Matter, as a reality in alchemy (the process of application of the RED POWDER in the transmutation by melting). It is the return of the Initiate into the world in order to promote the transmutation of Society's morale in the realm of Ethical Hermetism.

The suit of Pentacles in the Tarot is very close to the titles of the first TEN Major Arcana, which are already known to you. This happens simply because the Pentacles, the reflection of the *Knave of the First Family*, are like an organ for the translation of the Major Arcana into the language of the Minor ones.

The Pentacles of the Minor Arcana give us the pattern or realization of the universe of humanity as yet not fallen; but the first ten Major Arcana correspond to the realization of the same truths by the already fallen humanity. Prof. G. O. M. wittily expressed this idea when he said: 'If we wash the first ten Major Arcana and scratch away the shells from them, we will see just the numerical or Minor Arcana in their suit of Pentacles.'

LESSON 38

This lesson will of necessity be dedicated to a brief exposition of the most important principles of the Kabbalah. Hard as it may be for those who are not acquainted with the Hebrew alphabet and its symbolism, the student must acquire some elementary knowledge of it, otherwise the whole construction of the great initiatory Tarot will remain as dimmed, if not impossible of understanding for him.

In the Kabbalah, the 22 letters of the initiatory alphabet now called Hebrew, are divided into three essential groups.

The FIRST group consists of the Mother letters: ש מ א (Aleph-Mem-Shin). These symbolize the basic terms of the metaphysical scale of the *Ternary*. א corresponds to the neutral term (N), מ to the negative (−) and ש to the positive (+) pole.

THE TAROT

TABLE
of the Major Arcana, their hieroglyphs and corresponding letters of the
Hebrew Alphabet

Arcanum	Let-ter	Name	Numerical Value	Hieroglyph	Remarks
I	א	ALEPH	1 (One)	Man	
II	ב	BETH	2 (Two)	Human throat	
III	ג	GHIMEL	3 (Three)	Hand	Grasping
IV	ד	DALETH	4 (Four)	Breast	Feeding
V	ה	HÉ	5 (Five)	Breath	
VI	ו	VAU	6 (Six)	Eye & Ear	
VII	ז	ZAIN	7 (Seven)	Arrow	In direct flight
VIII	ח	HETH	8 (Eight)	Field	For cultivation
IX	ט	TETH	9 (Nine)	Roof	Protection
X	י	YOD	10 (Ten)	Finger	Pointing
XI	כ	CAPH	20 (Twenty)	Human palm	Gripping strongly
XII	ל	LAMED	30 (Thirty)	Arm also: Hand	Broad sweep (Open)
XIII	מ	MEM	40 (Forty)	Woman	
XIV	נ	NUN	50 (Fifty)	Foetus	
XV	ס	SAMECH	60 (Sixty)	Arrow	In circular movement
XVI	ע	AYIN	70 (Seventy)	Tie or Bond	Material one
XVII	פ	PHE	80 (Eighty)	Throat	With tongue
XVIII	צ	TZADDI	90 (Ninety)	Roof	Oppressing, limiting
XIX	ק	QUOPH	100 (One hundred)	Axe	
XX	ר	RESH	200 (Two hundred)	Head	Human
XXI (O)	ש	SHIN	300 (Three hundred)	Arrow	Direct wavering flight
XXII	ת	THAN	400 (Four hundred)	Breast	All-accepting bosom

Fig. 34A

In this system of symbols the *Ternary* of the *Great Arcanum* will take its form according to the table in Fig. 34A and Figs. 13–15. Any combination of these letters may be explained through the terms of the Ternary. Take for example:

מ ש א. If we connect the terms of the Ternary with their elementary meanings, then א will conditionally signify AIR, ש FIRE, and מ WATER. The whole sentence may then be translated as: water put on fire evaporates (that is transformed into the gaseous state, which is symbolical for air).

Relating these Hermetic terms metaphysically, we may read the combination thus: if, in Space (Mem) we will follow the transmutations of Energy (Shin), then we will come to the conception of Time (Aleph), in which all phenomena occur.

The student will do well if he tries to understand the method of mental operations in Hermetism, as just given.

Now, explained mystically, the same combination מ ש א (Mem-Shin-Aleph) gives: 'the passive element of the layman (מ) if fecundated by the Energy belonging to him (ש), will be transformed into a magician of the androgynous type (א).

The SECOND group, the so-called seven DOUBLE letters is: ב ג ד כ פ ר ת or consequently—as is usual in the Kabbalah—reading from RIGHT to LEFT, : Beth, Ghimel, Daleth, Caph, Phe, Resh, Than.

This group symbolizes the seven Secondary Causalities about which we have already spoken several times. If we can call the Mother letters *metaphysical*, then the Double letters, with good reason, could be termed 'planetary' or 'astral' letters. Accordingly, the table as related to astrology will be shown thus:

ב	Beth — Moon	One of the reasons why these letters were called 'double', is that *from the etymological* point of view they originally had double pronunciation: B and BH, G and GH, D and DH, K and CH, P and PH (or F), R long and short, TH and S.
ג	Ghimel — Venus	
ד	Daleth — Jupiter	
כ	Caph — Mars	
פ	Phe — Mercury	
ר	Resh — Saturn	
ת	Than — Sun	

From the esoteric point of view, we see that the influences of the Secondary Causalities are polarized into positive and negative qualities. As an example: Jupiter has good qualities such as: benevolence, ability for leadership, and so on; but he also has some evil—his pride.

The THIRD group is composed of twelve SIMPLE letters, corresponding to the twelve signs of the Zodiac:

ה	= Hé — Ram (Aries)		ל	= Lamed — Scales (Libra)	
ו	= Vau — Bull (Taurus)		נ	= Nun — Scorpion (Scorpio)	
ז	= Zain — Twins (Gemini)		ס	= Samech — Archer (Sagitarius)	
ח	= Heth — Crab (Cancer)		ע	= Ayin — Goat (Capricornius)	
ט	= Teth — Lion (Leo)		צ	= Tzaddi — Water-carrier (Aquarius)	
י	= Yod — Virgin (Virgo)		ק	= Quoph — Fish (Pisces)	

The twelve signs of the Zodiac on the plane of Nature symbolize the full extent of the phases of sacrifice, performed in our solar system by the Sun, which gives our Earth its astral fluids (the vital energy, without which Earth would be only a dead globe).

The number twelve corresponding to the Zodiac and to the Twelfth Arcanum, with its letter Lamed, symbolizes, in Ethical Hermetism, the sacrifice of Man to Man, to Nature or to God. This full sacrifice can be offered only by an incarnate Pentagram, as you will certainly realize.

On the plane of the Archetype, the Twelfth Arcanum is that of the Messenger, the Messiah, which again means an incarnation, again the physical plane. I am mentioning all this in order to transmit the central idea of the physical plane, as THAT OF SACRIFICE.

For an Initiate there is no doubt or difficulty in realizing this conception: he knows that existence in dense matter—from the point of view of that which is really Man, Monad, Spirit, Self—is incarnation in suffering, limitation and temporary darkening of the vision of Truth-Reality.

I am now giving a scheme of the Tarot's construction, which may be useful to students in their further study.

	1		2		3		4
	י YOD		ה HÉ		ו VAU		ה HÉ N
	+	−	+	−	+	−	
י	1	4	7	10	13	16	19
ה	2	5	8	11	14	17	20
ו	3	6	9	12	15	18	21(0)
ה	4	7	10	13	16	19	22

CONSTRUCTION OF THE TAROT

This table presents the system of the Major Arcana as a particular exposition of the LAW: Yod-Hé-Vau-Hé. The system of the Minor Arcana is of course, an exact application of the great LAW, but the Major ones are rather similar to a key-board, on which one who knows may play the great melody of life.

The exact instrument was made for humanity as yet not fallen. Another has been approximately tuned for the needs of the fallen beings, who now have to ascend—by a strenuous and painful way—back to the heights already almost forgotten during innumerable incarnations.

The first three columns of the 'Construction of the Tarot' find their explanation in Lesson 23 of the Seventh Arcanum and Figs. Nos. 22, 22A, 22B and 23B.

The fourth column, that of the Second Hé (N) represents, with its androgynous arcana (19, 20, 21(0) and 22), the system of transition from the Major Arcana to the Minor ones.

It can be said, that they are organs of creation (or birth) of the Minor by the Major. Remember, that in the Minor Arcana the suit of Pentacles in reverse, can be said to be organs of creation of the Major Arcana by the Minor.

According to the 'Construction' of the Major Arcana, the phases of development of the incarnate Pentagram (Man), are as follows:

Man in the period (phase) of *self-knowledge* (1) creates Science (2), takes it as spouse, and with her help he becomes the realizer (performer) (3) and thereby acquires Authority (Power) (4).

Creation of this Authority (4) leads to the creation of the human Pentagram (5), but immediately after that he must come to the Cross-roads (6). He chooses the right way and becomes the Victor (7). This is the climax of the cycle (Yod) for the ideological upbringing of personality.

The Victor (7) begins the cycle of self-education in the world of Forms through the establishment of *Justice* (8) in surroundings where he may continue his work. This Justice guarantees for those surroundings a certain ethical level, from which a man will rebound in order to perform the next jump into the higher realm of formal ethics. His striving after perfection is crowned by the reaching of Initiation (9). After that, comes the merging into the closed system of forms (10). This system may appear as the outer world, to which the Initiate returns at times in order to influence and to help his neighbours, that is his fellow-men. But this system may also be the Kabbalah, into which the Initiate dips so as to improve the clichés surrounding him.

His activity in that closed system (10) leads the Initiate to the creation of the Chain of Power (11). Then appears the necessity of Sacrifice (12) inside (for the benefit of the Chain) and outside (for the good of humanity). Fulfilment of that pattern leads to the change of plane (13).

Together with upbringing in the worlds of forms goes contact with the elements of the three-plane life.

Each death (13) is also a birth into the new life, connected with the full understanding of the reversibility of some energetic manifestations (14).

If your change of plane was only an exteriorization, then you will bring the clichés of the processes of reversibility with you from the astral plane. Anyway, these phases of your evolution, as described in this part of the Lesson, will give you the power of ruling over the astral tourbillons (15), or analogously to the force of the power of logic (15), and finally, the art of using the manifestation of Fate (15). So, our Fifteenth Arcanum reveals to us the following idea: it leads to the application of the next, the Sixteenth Arcanum, which means:

(1) Logical exclusion of the thesis (mental plane).

(2) Astral compulsion (astral plane).

(3) Physical hampering through skilful use of fatalism (physical plane).

The Sixteenth Arcanum ends the cycle of the Second Hé of the 'Construction'. From this Sixteenth Arcanum begins a new cycle of active applications of different forces (16); but the arcanum needs a spouse,

H

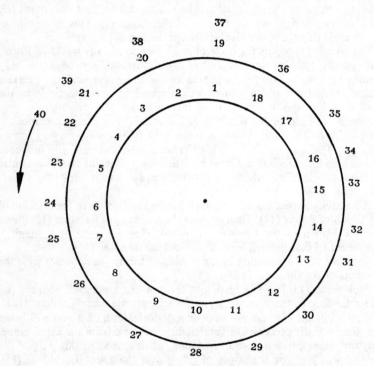

Fig. 35 Addition and the Unfolding of the Arcana

which will be found in a *Divinatory Principle* (17), which may help it to orientate its activity better, an understanding of the conditions of his own work opens a man's eyes to the fact, that although others can act for him, they can also act against him. Then he will realize that enemies exist on all planes (18). This knowledge of the presence of inimical elements everywhere will oppress him, and compel him to seek an exit leading into the Light, which may solve his troublesome position. This will be presented by the far off vision of the Great Hermetic Problem (19).

This is the end of the Vau cycle. The remaining four arcana give the plan for the solving of that Problem. One, who passes through these arcana, is already on the way to Reintegration.

Therefore, the cycle of the Second Hé begins with the problem of the practical use of Hermetism (19); solving it, man will face the possibility, and sometimes, the necessity of resurrection, of a new life, directed by other, higher Laws (20).

This, in turn, will lead him to penetration of the mystery of the arcanum Shin (21 or 0) of that truly realizable arcanum in the most exact meaning of the word. In order to realize the subtilization of things, one must know how they were created, and consequently, how to create them. Reaching this, a man performs the Great Action (22) and is then ripe to pass on to the suit of Pentacles in the Minor Arcana.

The Addition and Unfolding of the Arcana

The metaphysical intervals between the arcana are far from being equal. Whoever has studied their open and mystical meanings, helped by intuition, knows about this: and I cannot conceal this fact. The scale between them shows different distances logically, philosophically and ideologically. But, for the purpose of an interesting traditional process called the 'addition of the arcana' we have to forget about all this and accept their sequence as being exact as that of their numbers when taken in turn.

The axiom is, that an arcanum proceeds from the previous one, that is the second from the first, the third from the second, and so on. On this basis we can find the gradation for each arcanum in a cycle other than its own. This is called the 'addition of the arcana'.

To add one arcanum to another means to pass, in rotation, to one whose number will be the sum of the first two. For example, the sum of the Seventh and Eighteenth Arcana will be the Seventh or Sixteenth Arcanum, because: $7 + 18 = 25 = 7 = 16$. In this case, another method for the 'addition of the arcana' was also used, that is, calculation according to the rule of 9, by which we subtract nine from the number, so that: $25 - 9 = 16$.

In order to present this method of operating Fig. 35 is given. Only 18 arcana are taken for the full cycle, because the last four are considered as a transition, a supplement, necessary for passing to the Minor Arcana. So, the Nineteenth Arcanum will be used as a development of the FIRST or TENTH ($19 = 10 = 1$). The Twentieth Arcanum as a development of the SECOND ($20 = 2$); the Twenty-first as a development of the THIRD

(21 = 3), and the Twenty-second as a development of the FOURTH (22 = 4).

The student will do well if he passes through the whole of Fig. 35 as indicated in the previous paragraph.

We will add Arcanum V to X taking the titles on the human plane. The ready formed Pentagram (5) will serve as our starting point. Now we are moving from it on ten intervals (10), that is we need the Tenth Arcanum not for Aleph, but for Hé. The title of the Tenth Arcanum was the 'Kabbalah'. The solution? Of course, it is none other than: 'THE PENTAGRAM APPLIES THE KABBALAH.' And the result? The addition gives us number 15, arcanum Samech, Nahash, or the complexity of our passions, which creates a kabbalistically planned astral vortex. In other words, human will coupled with knowledge of astral conditions gives that result.

A learned Kabbalist would say, that 15 can be obtained simply through the addition of the Arcana V and X which means: starting directly from the Kabbalah (10) one may seek its pentagrammatic manifestation (5); but the laws of the Kabbalah seen as an entity, endowed with conscious will (5), will then manifest themselves as all-powerful in the astral Serpent *Nahash*, or the same number (15).

Try to add the Seventh Arcanum to the Thirteenth, that is seek the arcanum of Victory connected with the arcanum of Death. Of course, we then obtain the arcanum of Resurrection (20). The same can be found by calculating the sum of 7 + 13, that is being interested in the question, when the Victory must unavoidably lead to the element of death or change of plane. It results, in the case, when Victory is invariably joined to the change of status, in Resurrection, or Renaissance.

Now add Arcanum XI to that of XIX, that is give power (11) to the seeker of the higher Light (19). The result is 30 = 3. The Third Arcanum is that of the executive. I am leaving its interpretation to the intuition of the student.

Multiplication of the Arcana

Compare the row of the first ten arcana with the suit of the Pentacles in the Minor Arcana. We then find the statement: similarly as the numerical cards of the Pentacles are the Sephirothic manifestations of their Kether, so the first ten Major Arcana can be considered as the Sephiroth of the *First Arcanum*, taken as *Kether*.

From this we see, that the Sephiroth of the Second Arcanum can be obtained from it in sequence, passing through *one* interval according to the numbers of our circle (Fig. 35).

We may accept, that the Sephiroth of the *Second Arcanum*, being more complicated and entangled, will be found in the row of the same numbers, through *two* intervals instead of one. Then, in this case, Kether will be 2, while Chocmah appears as 4, Binah as 6, Gedulah as 8, and so on.

Acting similarly for the *Third Arcanum*, leaping across *three* intervals, we will see that the Sephiroth of the Third Arcanum will be expressed, approximately, by the Third, Sixth, Ninth, Twelfth, Fifteenth, Eighteenth, Twenty-first, Twenty-fourth, Twenty-seventh and Thirtieth Arcana.

Examples

(1) We are seeking the Seventh Sephira of the Second Arcanum $2 \times 7 = 14$. We were seeking Victory (Seventh Sephira) of the subtle over the dense, in the realm of Knowledge (Gnosis) of the Second Arcanum. The result was the *arcanum of the reversibility of processes* (14), which is the arcanum of the inner harmony of the astrosome. This is clear. But you may say, that $14 = 5$ (because $1 + 4 = 5$). This is only natural, for the creation of the Pentagram cannot be performed without that arcanum. I do not even say, that here the Pentagram has THREE of its points uppermost.

(2) Now seek the *Eighth Sephira* of the *Fifteenth Arcanum*. $15 \times 8 = 120 = 3$ (But 120 can also be considered as 12, for $12 + 0 = 12$). Therefore, from one side we have the arcanum of Sacrifice (12), as well as the arcanum of the Zodiac, which means the physical plane. Actually, the victory of the animistic elements in the astral tourbillons (15) cannot go beyond the astral work for Sacrifice: it is the peak of the subtle motives of the astral work. From the other side, in the realm of application of such an activity, it would be impossible to go lower than the physical plane (12). What does the number 3 tell us? The realization of the astral vortex is seen in the arcanum of the executive (3). This will be sufficient for the Eighth Sephira of the Fifteenth Arcanum.

(3) We are seeking the Sephira Geburah (Severity) of the divinatory elements in Nature that is, $17 \times 5 = 85 = 13 = 4$.

The pitiless justice of the divinatory methods lead us to the arcanum of Death or Transformation of energy (13). This is unavoidable. But, we still have 4. It is the Form, or four elements, like four states of matter, which are also unavoidable in the manifestations of Nature.

These examples may be sufficient to show, that by multiplying the arcana by the Sephiroth, the results do not give the *exact* answer to the question, but rather an artificial direction to the object, closely connected with the answer, thereby making the finding of the solution easier.

A great Hermetist of the past, Raymond Lulli, recommended his students, in his major work 'ARS MAGNA' (Great Art), to deal with themes little known to them, in order that they might be experimentally convinced about the usefulness of operations with the Major Arcana and the Sephiroth, when seeking argumentation in courts and disputes.

Complications in operations with the circle of the arcana (Fig. 35), and the seeking of the sum according to the rule of '9' (see beginning of this lesson), sometimes requires the reading of the titles of the arcana on planes different to that shown in the position of the initial arcanum. So, instead of the plane of man, we may take that of the Archetype and vice versa.

All these operations, of course, are interesting only for those who like the Kabbalistic side of the Tarot. But the *Kabbalah is a part of Hermetic philosophy*, and it is my duty to include it although only as a brief study in this work. I am conscious that it might not be too popular with the majority of my readers and students, but they are free to pass over this part of the present book, until deeper understanding of the magnificent structure of

Hermetism will show them the way to the components of that ancient knowledge, that is to the Kabbalah.

The whole theme of the TAROT is so extensive and even vast, that only a few occultists were (and are) able to probe to the last depths of its secrets. Many study only some special sections, like the astral plane, magic operations, divinatory processes, the creation of new ideas, the catching of valuable clichés in the astral light, the investigation of the conditions before birth and after death, and so on.

LESSON 40

The Kabbalah

In the Kabbalah, Man is studied jointly with the Archetype and Nature. Naturally, of special interest is the question about the traditional privileges and rights of humanity, which occupies the place of the *neutralizing* (middle) term in the Theosophical Ternary, as was seen in the previous lessons.

Tradition tells us that before its downfall, humanity's foremost task was the *Great Action*, then performed without effort. This conception of the Kabbalah is not unique. We will find it in every ancient religion and philosophy, albeit in different outer forms. In the Old Testament, in old Roman traditions ('Metamorphoses' of Ovidius), in ancient Greek Mythology, in Druidic legends, in Hindu epics, and so on, everywhere the attentive seeker will find the same idea. There was a time when humanity was much happier (compare the 'Four Epochs of the World' by Ovidius), wiser and closer to the Divinity.

Present-day official science would perhaps not agree with such conceptions, referring them to the realm of legends.

Geology shows us, that in some periods of our planet's life, there was no Man, as we know him now, on its surface, and that conditions were quite different from the point of view of flora and fauna, and so on. But, for the whole of the Cosmos, what meaning have these few millions of revolutions of our Earth round the centre of the Solar system, which we call 'years', in comparison with the incalculable periods of time, connected with the existence of the universe?

The conception of ETERNITY means the union of the *Past*, *Present* and *Future*. Clear realization of it is not accessible to the majority of human minds, for they instinctively try to avoid things which cannot be limited within the framework of their possibilities.

As the purpose of this work is *not to argue and convince*, but only *to give an exposition of the occult philosophy called Hermetism*, I cannot take up space here for matters not essential from the point of view of the subject. Hermetism is only one of the branches of the initiatory Wisdom, perhaps the most fascinating and vast; but this does not mean that all occultists must follow it. '*In my Father's house there are many mansions*' said a great Master at the beginning of our epoch.

After this necessary digression, we will return to our Kabbalah, which belongs to the Tenth Arcanum of the Tarot.

The titles of this arcanum allow us to analyse the *privileges* which still belong to fallen humanity.

The *mental privilege* of Man is Tradition (Testamentum, in other words) offered to him by the Archetype, together with the promise to 'ALWAYS ABIDE IN THE VERTICAL PART OF THE STAUROS', whose horizontal arm can be considered as the passive and warped state of present humanity.

In the *astral plane*, Tradition means language, as a privilege on this Earth which exclusively belongs to Man. In this sense of the word, language is identical with the Kabbalah. We will develop this idea in order to make it more palatable for the student.

Human language is not any haphazard collection of conditioned signs, but was created according to definite laws, and each root of a particular language has an analogous relationship to definite objects in the universe. The union of all the roots will appear as an analogy of full contemplation of the *spoken Law*, and as an analogy of the laws which the Microcosm will attach to the manifestations of the Macrocosm.

For the Microcosm, the elements of the universe are the Major Arcana. The elements of the language (initiatory one) will be the letters of the initiatory alphabet, which we accept in its so-called Hebrew transcription.

Someone operating with the objects of the universe, compels those who record his operations, to act similarly over the words and roots, as well as over the signs of the alphabet.

From this comes one of the definitions of the Kabbalah; in a passive sense 'IT IS THE MIRROR which reflects everything which takes place in the universe'. This definition will say nothing to those who do not have any contact with the Kabbalah, and I am fully conscious of this fact. It could not be otherwise. Only a mathematician is able to appreciate a Gauss or an Einstein.

Anyway, the second definition will be of foremost importance: the laws of analogy are REVERSIBLE! And on this is based the whole Kabbalah and in general, occultism. The student will do well if he fully comprehends this statement, before he draws any conclusions from the Kabbalistic theories.

So, ALL INFLUENCES AND THEIR PROCESSES ARE RECIPROCAL. If the activity of the brain reflects itself on the peripheral branches of the nervous system, so in reverse, the activity of these branches influences the central institution, here the brain. If a government influences its nation or society, both of these also influence their government. If a teacher exercises influence over his pupils, so the pupils also react upon their teacher, compelling him to be ready to answer their questions.

Coming to the Kabbalah, it means that if I will change the positions of letters, roots and words, then this alteration will be reflected in a suitable way in the sphere of world events. And this is the ACTIVE part of the Traditional Kabbalah. Recognition of the existence of that part pre-supposes the vitality, or consciousness of the Kabbalistic manifestations, as performed by one or another Microcosm.

Therefore, the central idea of the Kabbalah which accepts the un-
conditionality and vitality of the cosmic processes, recognizes that all of
them must have their reflection in (or are bound up with) the true Kabbalah, as in a magic mirror. The attentive reader will then say, that in
that rule may be the root of all which we call 'magic', and he will not be
far off the truth. But not all minds are able to agree with this axiom,
so we will proceed with a further exposition for those, who can agree
with us.

If someone has received a fictitious title, which does not give him any
realizable or real power, or if, when playing cards, one covers a king with
an ace, how can such happenings be reflected in the Kabbalah?

The active part of the Kabbalah is: 'if we operate kabbalistically with the
symbols and formulas in full consciousness of their meanings, then such an
operation MUST be reflected—in a certain measure—on the development
of the real happenings, on the changes of the astral clichés, and even on the
mental currents.' THESE ARE THE BASES OF THE WIDE
APPLICATION OF THE KABBALAH IN MAGIC AND
THEURGY. Every occultist knows about this.

There is an old saying: 'the letter can kill, but the letter can also be
killed.' 'The letter can kill' means that there is the possibility of OPERAT-
ING KABBALISTICALLY; 'the letter can be killed' would mean
that the Kabbalistic operation performed by another man, can be destroyed
or rendered harmless, by the direct use of ideas or physical things, while
ignoring the formal side. It has been said: '[DO NOT FORGET]
THAT THE SON OF MAN IS LORD ALSO OF THE SAB-
BATH.'

LESSON 41

Now we will occupy ourselves with the construction of the *initiatory language,* a deformed and spoiled reflection of which is what today is known as
Hebrew, but which should be more properly called the *Aramaic* language,
in which Christ also spoke.

Generally speaking, the roots of that language have two consonants
each, or, in our terminology, are composed of two arcana. The vowels
which define the pronunciation of the words, have changed and sometimes
differ in the speech of natives of the different provinces. A root composed
of three letters means a fusion of two double-letters, where the second letter
of the first root and the first letter of the second are identical. The endings
or suffixes are mostly characterized by consonants, that is again by the
Major Arcana.

As we know, there are 22 Major Arcana. Therefore, the number of
all the paired combinations made from the Major Arcana will be:
$\frac{22 \times 21}{2} = 231$. Taking into consideration the possibility of the shifting
of the arcana in calculations, we will get the maximum number of 462 roots
with different letters. By adding to them the 22 roots themselves, which
can be created by twice repeating the same arcanum, putting it opposite to

itself in two different spheres, we will see that the whole possible number of the roots is $462 + 22 = 484$. These 484 combinations should kabbalistically correspond to the approximate and tangled understanding of the universe (Macrocosm) as held by fallen humanity. By combining them into complicated words, we are only operating with ready-made roots. The same applies when we link up words to form sentences.

In his inner world, the individual man, generally, does not use the whole system of 484 roots, and therefore their recorded number is always less. Each summing up of the arcana can be interpreted in different realms of the Theosophical Ternary. Therefore, the understanding of the old texts in their literal meaning and translation, using the modern signification of the Hebrew words leads to great misunderstandings.

Here are a few examples in order to better explain the statements just made:

(1) The combination ב א (ab) in our system of arcana is read as: 'a limited, balanced, three-plane entity (א) desires to manifest itself through polarization (splitting in two) (ב). Explaining the meaning of this formula we may easily form the two following methods of understanding:

(a) A being limited to three planes manifests itself by giving birth to another similar being.

(b) A human being gives birth to another human, which means, that from its own mature state (perfect in the period destined for procreation) it gives rise to something separate from itself. In this last interpretation of the word ב א (ab) the meaning will be *'father'*.

(2) The analysis of the word מ א (am or amae) gives us several interpretations.

(a) The three-plane world (א) manifests itself through the arcanum of Death (מ), and the regeneration connected with it.

(b) In a balanced environment (א) there develops something, which in the end dies to that environment (מ), but regenerates itself for another condition of life.

(c) A human being, a woman bears a child, which at the end dies to its embryonic life, but is born to live in the physical atmosphere.
    The translation of the word מ א (am) is of course, *'mother'*.

(3) The word: צ ע (aatz or etz) gives us the explanation: the binding (ע) of organic functions leads to a much more static and dangerous form of life (צ), that is, the vegetable life.

Actually, plants and trees cannot of themselves move when once they emerge from the seed stage. Therefore, they are bound to one place for their lifetime, not having the possibility or opportunity of avoiding danger or attack from any movement. The word aatz means 'tree'.

(4) The word ג נ (gan) means: birth (ג) plus the reversibility of processes (נ), or temperance, measurement. Further meanings are a *geometrical solid*, an enclosure, and in the Bible—a 'garden'.

H*

(5) The word מ ר (rom) has the following explanations:

  (a) Regeneration (ר) through death (מ), and resurrection in other conditions through individual death.

  (b) Selection of parts from the homogenous surroundings through the assimilation of their inner elements.

  (c) Creation of nutritious surroundings through the assimilation of material absorbed from outside. The Biblical meaning is: blood.

(6) The word ל ל (lel or lil) is explained by:

  (a) Sacrifice opposed by sacrifice, or sacrifice confronted with an equal sacrifice.

  (b) Expansion confronted with another expansion. In the word ל י ל, that is with י (Yod) placed between two Lameds (ל י ל), that Yod appears in the closed system, which altogether create the idea of *night*, and so, the enclosed space is surrounded on every side by the sacrifice of light (which means darkening with blinds). This gives realization to the conception of unbroken shadow, or night.

(7) The word ט ר (reth) gives us: regeneration (resh) ר directed by the limiting element (teth) ט. Explanations:

  (a) A new flow, directed by a restricting force.

  (b) The flow of water in a pipe.

    The final meaning of the word will be 'channel', 'pipe', 'alley' (in which latter, walking is limited by the form of the alley).

  I am limiting further explanations about the Kabbalistic operations of words and letters, because they can be found in any of the existing manuals of the Kabbalah, from which I can recommend *La Cabbale* by Papus, still available in France. There are also some works in English which can be consulted by the eager adherent of the Kabbalah.

  But what purpose do all these Kabbalistic methods and operations serve? Are they only for the exercising of the individual brain? Of course NOT: common sense must also serve the aims of the mind. Therefore, the Kabbalah has a double meaning for us.

(1) It ALLOWS US—USING THE WRITTEN SOURCES OF THE HIEROGLYPHIC INITIATORY LANGUAGE—TO DISCOVER NOT ONLY WHAT THE AUTHORS OF THE OCCULT KABBALISTIC BOOKS PUT INTO THEM, BUT ALSO EVERYTHING WHICH CAN BE DEDUCED FROM THEM BY WAY OF MENTAL SPECULATION, OR *AS HERMETISTS LIKE TO SAY*, VIA THE MERCURIAL ELEMENTS OF OUR HUMAN INDIVIDUALITIES.

(2) It allows us to create, by the force of our ingenuity, new pentacles of words, expressing the formal side of our impulses of will. The process of reading these words will supply us with mantrams, and, what is most important, the *highly effective* mantrams, which are understandable for us to the last degree, because they are then created by ourselves, or, at least, borrowed from the Egregoric Chains with whom we are in relationship.

You should think deeply about these two paragraphs before you pass on to further matters.

So the Kabbalah will serve us for learning about the initiatory TRAD-ITION (which has also been used as the basis for this work) and of the theogonic, cosmogonic and androgynous systems revealed by this Tradition, plus the practical, realizable means provided in them for the use of their adepts.

And further still, the Kabbalah is one of the best known instruments of cognition in the realm of relations between the Microcosm and the Macrocosm. The very word Kabbalah (ק ב ל ה) gematrically gives: $100 + 2 + 30 + 5 = 137 = 11 = 2$, that is, it interprets itself by the arcana of Force (11) and Knowledge (2), which summarizes the aforesaid. Etymologically, we translate the word Kabbalah as TRADITION.

For its use, the KABBALISTIC CODE OF THE WESTERN SCHOOL possesses the following memorials of undoubtedly Kabbalistic content:

(1) The Book of *Sepher Yetzirah* ascribed to Abraham and containing in it, the full code of Kabbalistic metaphysics in its *static* form (the mutual relations of the THREE PRIMARY CAUSALITIES, SEVEN SECONDARY CAUSALITIES and THE ZODIACAL WORLD OF CONCRETE THINGS, welded together by our Hermetic Unitarian contemplation).

(2) The Book of *Genesis* (*Sepher Bereshith*), and the whole remnants of the Five Books of Moses, which contain the full exposition of the basic theogony, androgyny and cosmogony, plus part of the history of the Tradition belonging to the White Race.

(3) The rest of the books of the Old Testament, in which, apart from the purely exoteric texts, we also encounter *purely Kabbalistic chapters*, such as the Ist and Xth in the Book of the Prophet Ezekiel and some parts of the Book of the Prophet Daniel.

(4) The book *Zohar* (*Sepher ha Zohar*) which is an ample collection of commentaries by different authors almost always nameless. *Zohar* has commentaries about the Bible and Sepher Yezirah and an almost full code of the Kabbalistic metaphysics in their *dynamic part*. There are numerous additions of some Kabbalistic methods used for the deciphering of the Sacred Texts; separate treatises of the so-called *pneumatic occultism* (knowledge about souls and methods of influencing astrosomes, conditions of the changes of plane (deaths); theurgical operations, and so on).

Zohar was first published in Mantua (1559). There have been many disputes about the period of its origin, but they do not belong to this present work.

(5) Books of the famous Talmud, not all of which contain Kabbalistic matters. However, their construction, that is pattern of arranging material, and methods of their synthesis are undoubtedly of Kabbalistic character, so I am mentioning them in this brief review of these memorials.

(6) The so-called CLAVICULAE SOLOMONIS (Keys of Solomon),

which have come down to us in their Latin translation made by Rabbi Abognazar. This is a collection of talismans, pentacles, exorcisms and prayers, having wide application in Ceremonial Magic and in Kabbalistic Astrology. The text of the *Testament of King Solomon for his Son Roboam* serves as an introduction to them. This book is an inexhaustible collection of Kabbalistic prescriptions.

(7) The whole of the NEW TESTAMENT, especially the books by the Apostle St John, is filled with texts, partially or wholly admitting of Kabbalistic interpretation. In the Revelation (the Apocalypse) we simply find descriptions of the separate arcana of the Tarot.

The Gospel of St John has 21 chapters, corresponding to the Major Arcana, from א (Aleph) to ש (Shin) inclusive. This Kabbalistic code was taught by many Mediaeval classical authors and scientists of the Kabbalah belonging to different schools and nationalities. They have left us an enormous amount of material for meditation in the realm of the Mercury of esoterism which is called Kabbalistic speculation.

LESSON 42

The Sephiroth and the Holy Names

This brief exposition about the Kabbalah would be incomplete without some explanation about the ten *Holy Names of God*. These Names, as well as the Sephiroth belonging to them serve as excellent material for the basic exercises in notarikon and gematria.

For a start we will have a general analysis of the FIRST three Names and their Sephiroth.

(1) The Name יהוה is unfolded by notarikon into two marriages, א with ה and י with ה. It means: as a three-plane, balanced individuality can fecundate its passive elements, so a closed system, considered as active, should fecundate its corresponding passive ones. Because the numerical value of that Name is 8, we have to add, that it is the World's Law.

The name of the Sephira כתר (Kether) can be unfolded into the arcanum of Force (כ Caph), the arcanum of the Great Action (ת Than) and the arcanum of Regeneration (ר Resh). The numerical value of the Sephira Kether is $21 = 3$, and gives us a hint on the metaphysical sphere (3) and the mystery of the transition to the lower planes (21). As we may see, the analysis of this Sephira gave us a picture of the surroundings in which the Law of the development of the process, represented by the Holy Name corresponding to that Sephira, finds its application.

(2) The Name יה is simply a formula of the Gnostic encounter of two polarities in the same scale. Its number is $15 = 6$, showing the role of the astral tourbillon (vortex) in this combination (15) and warns about the dangers of the Sixth arcanum (an encounter may be evolutionary or involutionary).

The name of the Sephira חכמה (Chocmah) can be unfolded into the integrity of the surroundings (ה) which is then transformed into Force (כ). This, after the change of plane (מ) will create the elements of the new

Life (ה). Number 10 of the Sephira shows the finished and active in-dependence of that cycle of transmutations. Again, the Name gave the Law of the Process, and the Sephira, provided it with details of its surroundings. As you may see, refined mental processes are necessary to follow the unfolding of the ideas and operations of the Kabbalah. The student must seek and find them for himself, if this is his line of evolution.

(3) The Name י ה ו ה is the formula of the normal Family, a usual dynamic cycle, as we already know. Its number 8 will again underline the integrity and unchangeability of the cycle.

Sephira ב י נ ה (Binah) tells us about the Knowledge (ב) leading to the closed and finished system (י) in which Life (ה) is possible in the case of the reversibility of the process (נ). Such an environment corresponds well to the manifestation of the Dynamic Law. Number 13 reminds us about the necessity of adaptation in the realm of the Elements (4) in order to justify and to apply the cycle י ה ו ה.

These three examples will enable you to continue the analysis for the seven remaining Sephiroth. I cannot but strongly underline the usefulness of such an exercise when performed independently by the student himself, as it will open his mind to many things which cannot be clearly explained in this course, because of the precautions, enclosed in the traditional expositions of this kind. No serious author writing about such matters would give to readers (and therefore to potential occultists) ALL informa-tion, leading to *realization* of the Hermetic forces on the lower plane, for then he would be responsible for all the transgressions made by wrong-minded students, who may use their knowledge for *involutionary*, and not for *evolutionary* aims (that is, for *evil* instead of *good*).

Otherwise, if persons find the keys to realization for themselves, they and they alone are responsible for their actions.

Apart from the ten Holy Sephirothic Names, and the Hebrew term 'Ain-Soph' (א י ן — ס ו ף) (the Unattainable, the Supreme, standing above all the Sephiroth), I would like to recommend, that the following terms be thoroughly 'kabbalized' from all sides: א ב (ab = Father) and א ג ל א (Agla), which find wide use in Ceremonial Magic and Theurgy. The bases for Agla are: three-plane balancing, based on the metaphysical understand-ing of Existence (א Aleph). The fulfilment of the Universal Love (ג Ghimel) uniting everything which was ever divided. The ineffable expansion of readiness for sacrifice (ל Lamed). The whole again leads to the *Beginning* (א).

That is why in occultism, AGLA is translated as '*United in Three*', and why this word is credited as having the power of REALIZATION even in the mouth of a layman. It is used under exceptional conditions in magic operations, when the operator is confronted with forces he is unable to control in any other way. So far, I have observed that it is put into practice in very serious operations of Ceremonial Magic, such as in cases of exceptionally strong obsession, where nothing else worked, and the dangerous manifestations had to be stopped at any price.

Experienced occultists will understand what I mean.

Now you may be ready to realize the aims of the connection of the
TEN NAMES in Theurgy and magic. They are formulas of the separate
cycles of the *Great Diabatic Process* in the Life of the universe. THEIR
FULLNESS ENVELOPES EVERYTHING THAT HAS BEEN
PERFORMED AND EVERYTHING WHICH WILL BE
PERFORMED. It is, so to speak, the full reflection of the subjective
understanding by the *Collective Man* (Universal Being) of the Mystery
belonging to the construction of the world, manifested in the signs of his
initiatory language.

With every theurgic ceremony and with many magic ones is connected
the ritualistic pronunciation of part of the Holy Names, or of all of them.
This depends upon the kind of Sephiroth taking part in the process of
RISING prayers, or conjurations. Therefore, the exact knowledge of the
Names and Sephiroth is indispensable even for the beginner aspirant in
Hermetism and magic. This defines for him, the ability of performing
Kabbalistic activities in any part of the Diabatic process and GIVES
HIM THE ABILITY TO FORTIFY HIS WILL-POWER
WITH FORMULAS CONTACTING HIM WITH THE IM-
MORTAL EGREGOR OF THE GREAT CHAIN FORMED
BY THE GUARDS AND MASTERS OF THE WHITE RACE'S
KABBALAH.

ב

Arcanum XI
LEO DOMITATUS
STRENGTH

Mars

Vis Divina
Vis Humana
Vis Naturalis

CHAPTER XI

ARCANUM XI (כ CAPH)

THE card of the Eleventh Arcanum presents a woman, closing the muzzle of a furious lion without any effort and with full self-confidence. The whole of her figure conveys the impression of irresistible power.

Over her head we see a sign like that of an '8' lying on its side, which here symbolizes the astral light. The hieroglyph of the Eleventh Arcanum is a hand firmly squeezing something in it. This is a clear indication of the idea of FORCE, which in the realm of the Theosophical Ternary gives us the titles: VIS DIVINA (Mental plane), VIS HUMANA (Astral) and VIS NATURALIS (Physical). The name of the arcanum is 'Leo Domitatus' (the 'Conquered Lion'). The vulgar name is 'Force'.

The sign is the letter כ (Caph), whose numerical value is 20 = 2, giving the idea of duality in the use of force. Astrologically, Mars is the corresponding planet.

The meaning of the card is easy to understand. It enumerates the necessary conditions for the arising and application of evolutionary forces; *knowledge of the Astral* (sign over the woman's head); *purity of intentions* (virginity being the symbol for it), and *faith in oneself* (her unconstrained attitude).

Arithmological analysis of the arcanum will give us certain indications about the construction and application of the Forces.

Equation No. 49: $11 = 1 + 10$ or

Equation No. 50: $11 = 10 + 1$

In the *first case*, it is the Monad (1) which rules the closed system (10). We will translate it as: ONE WILL MUST DIRECT THE CHAIN OF BEINGS. It is the formula for the construction of Collectivities ruled by the Hierarchies.

The *second case* tells us: that the chain so formed expressed as the *number ten* (10) must manifest itself externally as a Unit (1). The power of the Collectivity should be based on the unity of the strivings of all its members and on all planes.

Equation No. 51: $11 = 2 + 9$ or

Equation No. 52: $11 = 9 + 2$

The *first one* says: that the unsolved binaries (2) and lack of initiation by the other men in the world urge the Initiates (9) to do their work, compelling them to use Force (11).

The *second* shows that Initiates (9) possess strength because, for their aims, they can use the lack of initiation of other men, as well as the latter's defective knowledge of non-neutralized binaries (2).

Equation No. 53: $11 = 3 + 8$ or
Equation No. 54: $11 = 8 + 3$

In the *first* Force is hidden in action and creation (3) directed by Justice (or infallible laws) (8).

In the *second* Force (11) is hidden in the principle of securing lawful activity (8) in creation (3).

Equation No. 55: $11 = 4 + 7$ or
Equation No. 56: $11 = 7 + 4$

In the *first*, our dependence on the Elements (4) induces the Secondary Causalities in Man (7) to work and so makes him strong (11).

In the *second*, the Secondary Causalities (7) rule the Elements (4) and their lies their Force (11).

The last equation teaches us, that it is necessary to include in the magic Chain, apart from the Pentagram, elementals (4) which are useful for realizations, because of their knowledge of the mechanism of involution. But, of course, these elementals must be obedient to the pentagrammatic elements of the Chain, introducing their planetary means (7).

Equation No. 57: $11 = 5 + 6$ or
Equation No. 58: $11 = 6 + 5$

The *first* is a normal formula for activity in Ceremonial Magic: 'The Microcosm (5) operates (or influences) the Macrocosm (6).'

The *second* is a formula for divination in the Astral, that is a purely passive operation; 'the Macrocosm (6) gives instructions to the Microcosm (5) which contemplates it.'

In both equations, there is hidden some part of the mystery of Power (Force or the Eleventh Arcanum).

Now we come to the problem regarding some examples in the history of the transmission of the *higher Force* and its realization on our planet by the creation of magic Chains, directed by certain Egregors. The most usual and typical are the surroundings or Collectivities which follow one or another form of religion. It will first be necessary to explain briefly the basic views of the Initiates on the question of the DOWNFALL and REINTEGRA-TION of Man.

We should now recall the constitution of the *First Family*, standing as the Transcendental Group, above all the Sephiroth of metaphysical, ethical and concrete contents.

The members of that FAMILY are: *Transcendental Love, Transcendental Life* (Logos or Adam Kadmon), and the *Knave of the Logos*, emanating the Kether (Crown) of the SECOND FAMILY, as you already know from the lessons about the numerical cards of the Tarot, or the Minor Arcana.

The second Family created by the Knave (or rather, to which the Knave gave birth) is in the form of the following mystical Persons:

(1) *Sephira Kether* in which abides the Macroprozopos of the Family.

(2) *Sephira Chocmah* in which must abide the Father of the Family, and in which—in its primary state—is placed the Unitarian Organism of the Androgynous Whole of human souls, called ADAM PROTOPLAST.

(3) *Sephira Binah* which is the natural place for the abiding of the Mother of the Family, the primary place of the Angels as a separate Kingdom.

The souls were destined to solve the evolutionary problem of the *Triangle of Fire*. Their role was to subtilize everything, to lead everything upwards, to direct without interruption the Ascending Current of the Great Closed System of the World's ten Sephiroth.

The activity of the Angels, which limits the realm of the activity of souls, is connected with the involutionary problem of the *Triangle of Water*. Angels materialize the subtle, condense it, form the coagulates or entities and, in general, direct and rule the Descending Current of the whole system of the Second Family.

(4) *Six Sephiroth*, Chesed, Geburah, Tiphereth, Netzah, Hod, Yesod in their union serve as the place for the abode of the Microprozopos of the Family. He is androgynous. The centre of his organism is Tiphereth. His organs of influence on the Spouse are in the Sephira Yesod. The right side of the Microprozopos has two positively polarized organs: Charity (Chesed) and Victory (Netzah). They are formed in the Microprozopos by his soul in order to serve them for evolutionary aims. The left side of the Microprozopos contains the negatively polarized organs of Justice (or Severity), Geburah, and Peace (Hod) born through the influence of Angels. They serve for involutionary purposes.

So we see, that from the Father, the Microprozopos inherited his evolutionary abilities, limited by the involutionary qualities of the Mother. The *Personality* of the Microprozopos manifests itself in the central Sephira Tiphereth: his activity is directed downwards into the Sephira Yesod.

Now the meaning of the Microprozopos is clear: the sphere of his activity is the whole realm of cognition. It is neutralized by Harmony and must be considered as *androgynous*. It is very complicated in its structure, and therein lies the danger of possible trouble in its functions. Purely *active* individuality or purely passive surroundings never require as much protection and good nourishment as androgynous beings. Something similar can be found in all the mechanisms of double action: they work perfectly, providing all the rules for their management are observed. But the smallest infringement of these rules inevitably brings essential changes in their function and work, destroying the harmony of their constitution.

(5) *Sephira Malkuth* is the home of the Spouse of the Microprozopos, and as the realm of application of elementary realizations is closely dependent upon the executive of the Microprozopos.

And now comes the REALM OF THE DOWNFALL. The sphere DAATH (Cognition) of the Sephiroth belonging to the Microprozopos, so far transmitted, acts as an androgynous element, the picture of the activity of the Logos (together with his Knave).

The same happened to the perfect androgyne of the *Point* over the FIRST YOD. The difference in manifestations of these three androgynous Units is that the POINT does not receive its influx from anybody, but itself transmits the Transcendental Influx downwards. The Logos, fed by that Transcendental Influence, transmits it to the Microprozopos' Sephiroth. They receive it as enveloped in a light form of 'fog' or 'smoke', and send the condensed cloud into the world where the 'formae seminlaes' were created.

So at the end we see that: THE POINT over the Yod is SELF-DEPENDENT; THE LOGOS IS FREE (the first three Sephiroth are the reflection of the Logos); but DAATH is only HARMONIOUS and MALKUTH only CONCRETE.

Further, *Hermetic Tradition* says, that at some moment the Sephiroth of DAATH began to strive after independence. Therefore, they were attracted by FREEDOM, without which there cannot be any *personal* life; but the striving after such a freedom was at the same time the refusal to accept food from the Upper Influx. This refusal became an accomplished fact, and then happened what is called 'The DOWNFALL OF THE SIX SEPHIROTH' which led these Sephiroth to the *Kabbalistic Death*.

Then, as they no longer received food from the Higher Currents, the cloud formed by these Six Sephiroth became what we now call '*the lower astral*'. The Sephirothic organism underwent the process of crumbling, of division, and its polarities began to manifest in the form of non-neutralized binaries (you already know from former lessons about the destructiveness of unsolved binaries).

The Sephira Tiphereth ceased to manifest its Light. Differentiation of the cells of DAATH reached extreme limits and their name became truly 'legion'.

This was the downfall of the Angels, which unveiled to the universe the mystery of Death.

The essence of the Sephira Malkuth, as the Spouse of the essence of Daath, also took a form suitable for the downfall, remaining as a realm of operation performed by the fallen legion of Daath, which means only the sphere of the most concrete manifestation of the unsolved binaries. Symbolically, you may say, that, in Malkuth, at this period, there grew the Tree of Cognition of Good and Evil.

The Microprozopos' Sephiroth fell because of their contents, but the PRINCIPLES which directed the creation of the Sephiroth remained intact, just as the code of the Law remains existent in principle, even if it is violated by all citizens.

Souls and Angels then received the task of filling the emptiness through the process of manifestation in FORMS, aiming at the salvation of Malkuth. Similarly, through the intermediary of Malkuth it was also possible to save its Spouse—the fallen Daath.

But, the latter did not want to lose the conquered *Freedom* through the resuscitation of the *Tree of Life*, which is the *Astral Light* of TIPHERETH.

So Daath tempted the passive Sephira of Souls ה ו ה (Héva) by the prospective learning of the binaries of the Sephira Malkuth, presenting these binaries (the most condensed elements of the universe), as useful points or fulcrums for the application of PERSONAL power. Héva caught that idea, that is she ate the *fruit from the Tree of Cognition of Good and Evil*. On becoming acquainted with the system of binaries, Héva introduced it into the activity of the Souls, which have the name of א ד מ (Adam). It seems that the wife presented the husband with the same fruit.

The active part of the Souls firstly attached the theory of the binary to the essence of the Sephira Chocmah itself. This means, that Adam and Héva recognized themselves as the poles of the non-neutralized binary, that is from the pairs they created the contrasts. From this comes the sense of shame and further condensation of the forms, known as the 'desire to be clothed'.

But the principle of the binary conceptions went further and deeper, and the whole Adam-Protoplast split himself into cells, covered with bodies, or veils, the more gross, the more the process of differentiation went ahead.

The subtlety of the essence of the Sephira Chocmah and the power of the authority of Souls as the Second Sephira caused the *Soul-cells to appear* clothed not in the lower astral as elements of the *legion of Daath*, but just in that which we call *physical matter*. These cells then became involved in time and space. This was and is their slavery. They were torn out from the Higher Current, to become slaves of Time and Space.

In the Sephirothic picture of the World's construction there appear changes; these take the form of differentiation and discord.

What have the higher Sephiroth to do now, whose harmony became distorted by the downfall of the Souls?

The mass of Angels extend their influence on all the sub-planes of the astral, because of the birth of entities known as *Spiritus Directores*. This mass, further occupied with its involutionary task, penetrates into Malkuth, where the elementals will be born, which possess material bodies serving as a physical basis for the universe.

Tradition says simply, that *Angels materialized the Malkuth* ('*Kingdom*') *in order that no astral devils could enjoy it*.

The *Essence of Kether*, called 'the Soul of the Messiah', being androgynous, spreads itself into the sphere of the Microprozopos creating his Sephiroth in order to fecundate Malkuth later with a *Redeeming Incarnation*. Therefore, the influence of the Incarnate Messiah must stimulate and encourage the Souls awakened from their sleep in matter, and call them to evolutionary activities, with the help of all their three-plane instruments, which will give them magic superiority over the fallen Daath. For then the latter can manifest itself in the physical world only by means of mediumistic loans and other unnatural and harmful ways.

The Souls, striving for Reintegration in the Sephira Chocmah, gradually subtilize their '*clouds*', purifying the Sephira Malkuth in which the fallen Daath works; they follow after the Spouse, realizing the ideal of the so-called 'Restitutio', that is full restoration of the PRIMARY STATE of the Sephirothic System belonging to the SECOND FAMILY.

Now comes our turn to occupy ourselves with the DOWNFALL of HUMANITY. This did not happen all at once. The veils (the gross state of matter) of fallen humanity grew gradually, bringing about a forgetting of the former perfection and also a progressive adaptation to the new and deplorable state. Of course, we should accept, that in different separate personalities, that is in different cells of Adam-Protoplast, this adaptation goes forward at different speeds.

For us here, in this practical course, it is MORE IMPORTANT TO KNOW WHAT CAN BE FORGOTTEN AND WHAT SHOULD NOT BE FORGOTTEN. For the sake of clarity of exposition I will divide the question into two parts:

A. By imagining in our minds the whole of the fallen cells of the World's Man (Adam-Protoplast), let us transfer ourselves into that period, when the influence of ' he Yod of the *First Family* was visibly lost, but all other lower reflections of a transcendental character were still preserved. In that epoch, remembrance about the Past, or religion, would be limited to the cult of abstruse devotion to the First Hé, of the *First Family*. Practically, this meant the recognition of the *Great Principle of the Unique Life*. This religion was of course, much higher than the theory of the 'fight for survival' so often a basis for some practical philosophies of our own day. Nevertheless, that religion of the *Unique Life* had a shadowy character when compared with the religion of Transcendental Love which enlightened the Protoplast before his downfall.

In this course I cannot sacrifice room for theoretical deliberations about the problematic *continent*, on which lived the comparatively happy followers of the *Religion of Life*, nor about chronological guesses concerning that far off epoch. All this has long since been non-existent for us.

But it seems to be necessary to present briefly the System of Commandments, which was accepted as an ethical code by those early followers. They honoured Life in all its manifestations. They recognized it in mineral, in plant, and in the smallest representatives of the animal kingdom, identifying it with the potent Current of Life, flowing in themselves. They loved Life and respected it, and because they had not yet lost their clear understanding of Life's evolutionary formula (Souls are of the origin of Chocmah), they considered as good, everything which was in accordance with that formula, and as evil, everything which tried to deform it.

Hermetic Tradition has transmitted to us the practical Commandments which form that sacred formula:

(1) Metaphysically profess the One Unique Life.

(2) Do not metaphysically divide that Life, that is do not be entangled in the slavery of the multiple conceptions born in the mind.

(3) Do not astrally divide that Life, that is do not apply the mystery of the Dynamic Cycle (Tetragram) to deviation from the normal Hierarchy.

(4) Do not obscure that Life by destroying, on the physical plane, remembrance about the Emanative Origin of every form of Life.

(5) Honour those who granted Life to you (even physical parents, provided they do not deviate from the evolutionary formula).

(6) Transmit Life wisely and consciously.

(7) Do not attempt to rob anything of Life on the physical plane.

(8) Do not desire any property which belongs to others on the physical plane.

(9) and (10) Do not attempt to possess anything bound up with the life of your neighbour on the astral plane, neither PASSIVELY (9) through lies, nor ACTIVELY (10) through jealousy.

B. In the SECOND period of fallen humanity's existence religion took another form. Although humanity had already lost the clear understanding of the *Transcendental Life*, it had not yet abandoned the idea of the Logos, the Great Archetype of the universe. In this degree there is no longer any intuition about the unity of Life, but the understanding exists of the ONE SOURCE OF IDEALS.

All has been born from the LOGOS, so no one dares to be an enemy of another. In the moment of a difficult decision, disappointment, or uncertainty, the followers of the *religion of the Logos* beg Him to help, to grant, as alms, *an ideal* which can save them.

C. The next degree of the downfall will eradicate in human hearts the picture of the Logos, but will still retain the symbol of the *Second Hé* of the *First Family*, which means only the Ideals, and nothing more. There is nobody to ask Him about the ideals; but having them ready-made someone can still try to get salvation.

This religion of the *Second Hé* will pass unnoticed from the Transcendental into the Transcendent. The higher possibilities once shown by Intuition, will now gradually be fossilized into ready-made casts of a metaphysical transcendent thesis. Belief in the Second Hé of the First Family easily slips down to the level of the religion of the Macroprozopos (Second Family), actually to the Point over its Yod.

D. What comes next? The Transcendent religion of the *Father* of the Second Family is summarized in the remembrance about the Sephira Chocmah, about the abidance in that Sephira of all human Souls as cells of the unique Protoplast. In it we still find a clear understanding of the brotherhood of Man with the involutionary entities (Angels). That is because, on this degree, Kether is already forgotten. Later comes forgetfulness about the fact, that Chocmah and Binah are two manifestations of Kether, having to realize the circular cycle of Life by means of the friendly and brotherly co-operation of the *Second Family*.

E. And even if the understanding of the Brotherhood disappears? Then things become bad. Sometimes wild egotism begins to rule, leading to anarchy and even to the reign of the dark forces.

It can reach to a fight against the Formula of Dynamic Evolutionary processes and even to the exchange of human individuality for the legion of passions, identical with the legion of 'devils' dwelling in the lower astral (remember the story of Dr Faust).

'Humanity as a whole, and as separate races and nations, has lived, lives, and will live through the afore-mentioned phases (A to E) and the corresponding religions and their substitutes, even the regretfully described last degree of decomposition of individualities into almost valueless personalities.' (The words of Prof. G.O.M., 1912).

Here I would like to permit myself a small digression. The basic initiatory material for these lessons dates to the last years before World War I. I intentionally did not add to them, some modern researches made since that time. Why? Just in order to show, how higher occultism is able to FORESEE, exactly and unmistakably, the future possible stages of human destiny. I am writing this work in 1958, that is after many historical, sociological and political changes have taken place in the life of humanity. I will not enumerate them, as everyone knows them too well. I would only like to ask my readers—for their own sakes—into which degree of the downfall, as described in Sections A to E, they would place the present epoch?

The solution to the great *problem of Reintegration* was most clear and feasible in the epoch, when the wise Primary Religion of the Unique Life was not yet lost or perverted. But no matter how strong were the temptations resulting from the abandonment, by the major part of humanity, of that Primary Religion, we may note that almost immediately after such a deplorable fact, there came the reaction, an effort to mend the erroneous ways through Revelation. The representatives of the fighters for the return to the initial wisdom, to the ancient clichés of contemplation, were with good reason called 'INITIATES', while those who had forgotten the cult of the ONE LIFE, were termed ignorant or laymen. The first were also not absolutely perfect beings, because they too were fallen cells of the Protoplast. But, at least they did not lose their original ties with the High, the Holy, and preserved the reflection of the LIGHT. Their attempts directed to the conversion of humanity to the right ways were vested in different forms, more or less complicated, according to the degree of the downfall of their human environment, and to the conditions of life in which lived the affected nations and races.

Hermetic Tradition used to call such attempts 'Imposed Religion'. Great Teachers, creating such religions, often had to deal with surroundings, the major part of which had already forgotten even imagination about human brotherhood (remembrance about the Sephira Chocmah).

Because of this, the Teachers had to act as follows:

(1) To remind men about the brotherhood of Souls.

(2) To resuscitate the idea of the double, involutionary, and evolutionary Current, like the Great Ladder of Jacob, on which, from the *left* descend the Angels (Binah) and from the *right* ascend the Souls (Chocmah), while at the top the Radiant Macroprozopos (Sephira Kether) sits on his throne.

(3) To establish the authority of Teachers, as an analogy of the remembrance about the *Second Hé* of the *First Family*, which mysteriously transmits the Higher Influx in the form of Emanation.

(4) To dissuade men from their proud striving to rebuild the world for their own comfort, and instead, to underline the necessity of something just the opposite: of the Hermetic rebuilding of one's own personality, so as to create, albeit, a dim and faded picture of the androgynously harmonious Logos.

(5) To purify the morale of men, in the name of the First Hé of the FIRST FAMILY, which means to compel them to understand the practice of the Commandments of the *Unique Life*.

(6) To concern themselves with the full Reintegration of humanity, purified by the True Religion, in order to let it know the reflection of the Influx of the First Yod, to subtilize its astral and mental, to realize the Sephiroth of the Spouse and the Microprozopos, and to come, ultimately, to the Unity of the *Adam-Protoplast* in the Sephira Chocmah.

To reach these aims, Initiates realized the *Arcanum of Force*, uniting themselves into CHAINS, directed by the Egregoric Principles. The mental cores of these Egregors actually were always, and still are the principles of the *Unique Primary Religion*, realized as a whole or separate groups. The astral part of the Egregor is born as the wholeness of forms, in which are vested the above-mentioned mental principles. The material (physical) counterpart of the cult is created as the physical body of the same Egregor. Its constitution depends upon its astrosome and the surroundings, into which the religion is projected; but the Egregor can generate different cults in different countries. Adaptation is necessary everywhere.

From all this it is easy to understand, that the bestowing, or even imposition of a religion can be compared to the formation of a *collective tourbillon*. The vital activity of such a tourbillon in its dynamic part must be symbolized by the sequence of the cycles ה ו ה י (Yod-Hé-Vau-Hé).

In these cycles, the most important one for us is the first, beginning with the POINT OVER THE י (Yod). We should not forget, that religion incarnates itself in order to create its adepts. Therefore, apart from the Dynamic Cycle (Tetragrammaton) in it, there must still be visible 'some kind of a battering-ram', which may in one way or another, facilitate the penetration of the religion into the physical plane, which means the attraction of new adepts and the retention of those already existing. It is symbolized by ש (Shin). This Shin is like a decoy for those who are ready to fuse themselves with the Egregor, but who have not yet done so.

From this we see, that ultimately, the first cycle of any religious current represents the formula ה ו ש ה י (Yod-Hé-Shin-Vau-Hé) and is a materialization (full or partial) of the Unique True Teaching directed to spiritualization (also full or partial) of certain environments.

The proper meaning of the terms belonging to the Primary Religious Current will give the following list, which you may call a '*plan of religion*':

(1) · THE POINT OVER THE YOD, or reason for the creation of the Egregor. It must be unselfish invariably and fully in the broadest meaning of that word.

(2) י (Yod), the METAPHYSICAL ESSENCE OF THE UNITARIAN PHILOSOPHY, taken as a whole or in part.

(3) ה (First Hé), preparation of those surroundings.

(4) שׁ (Shin), a reserve (or store) of factual knowledge or attractive astral clichés, assuring the acquisition of proselytes and guarding against heresies and secessions.

(5) ו (Vau), a good body of disciples grouped around the Master.

(6) ה (Second Hé), a sound society of the followers. More will be said about the astral birth of an Egregor in the Fifteenth Arcanum, while the conditions of life and death of Egregors has already been discussed in former lessons. I would only like to add, that into the Egregor—apart from the pentagrammatical beings of evolutionary type (living men and elementars)—the energy of the elementals, Spirituum Directorum (leading spirits) and even Angels should also be attracted. This is because the Egregor brings the teachings firstly through the *involutionary* way (current), and only later realizes the evolution of its adepts and followers. In colloquial language it can be said, that the magic Chain is composed of both living and dead men, as well as of elementals of different types.

There is no necessity to speak much about what the person of the Teacher should be like, for history gives us enough examples in this matter. Moses, Christ, Buddha are too well known to every occultist. You may find more about the *Teacher of the present epoch*—the Great Rishi Ramana, also called the Maharshi, in another of my books which is dedicated to him and entitled *In Days of Great Peace*, so there is no purpose to repeat what has already been extensively explained before.

The preparation of the 'screen' (the environment) usually finds its solution in the ethical (and sometimes also in the material) difficulties of a race or nation, which lead to the realization of the necessity to improve the shape of its life. Nations have some periods in their history, when their own conservatism or ignorance became intolerable. Then is just the appropriate time for religious regeneration and then the Teacher will be met with joy and love.

The attractive element of Shin often means the fulfilling of prophecies or miracles, performed by the Master himself or by his disciples. Sometimes this is substituted by happily chosen forms which, under certain conditions, exactly reflect the Unitarian Philosophy, extending themselves into the very essence of it. This may happen in a very cultured society, and then the Egregor has its life assured for a long time.

Disciples can be divided into two categories:

(1) The *main disciples*, or apostles of a doctrine, should be representatives of all the four Hermetic types; that of the *Eagle* (courageous thinkers);

Lion (fiery knights of Kadosh); *Man* (logical deliberations, sensitiveness, circumspection), and *Bull* (which means zealous workers).

(2) *Secondary disciples*, these should be altogether representatives of the *active element* (Yod), and extreme love of metaphysics, sometimes even to the point of being paradoxical.

The *passive elements* (First Hé) possess intuition, as well as susceptibility to hysteria in the extreme.

The *androgynous elements* (Vau) have skilful ability for the transmission of teachings and their adaptation, often with a tendency towards imposition when applying personal methods.

The *realizable elements* (Second Hé) have discipline and sacrifice in the practice of the ethical rules of the doctrine.

In the matter of *believers*, the opportunity to form a true judgement about their abilities and psyche should be given. This will ensure the selection of eminent persons, who would be ready to become disciples and to serve the Egregor actively. It is even dangerous to fail to raise the status of the able elements to the level of Initiation, if they are working devotedly and with a conscious display of energy. Just as it would be dangerous for a body artificially to tie off the blood-stream to its most important organs, which would then suffer starvation and so decay.

To finish this lesson, I will add something about the enemies of new religions, and the methods of combating them.

Any existing, or newly formed religion, or spiritual current can be undermined on all of the three planes.

(1) On the *mental plane* the religion can be harmed and even destroyed by the mixing of reasoning and argumentation into its theology. This is involution in the idealistic realm of religion.

(2) On the *astral plane*, religion can be harmed by the introduction of aesthetic principles into its formal ritual. A search after the 'beauty of symbols' destroys their purity. This is involution into the forms of ritual order.

(3) On the *physical plane*, religion is undermined by the addition of emotional principles into its code and commandments. Look into history and see, how short-lived were cults, which were spoiled by emotional manifestations in religious celebrations.

LESSON 45

Now we come to an explanation of some important Teachings, in their chronological order as given to humanity. My aim will be foremostly the aetiological point of view, as it has more relation with this arcanum than a purely historical account.

Krishna (c. 3150 B.C.)

Analysing the Egregor of Krishna's religion, according to the accepted Hermetic pattern in Lesson 44, we find that:

(1) **י** (Yod) is the metaphysical unfoldment of the Unit into the Ternary, and construction of the descending triangle, analogically to the ascending one of the same Ternary, similar to Solomon's Star.

(2) **ה** (First Hé) is a people tired by the highly emotional and sinister cult of the goddess Kali, and striving for the regeneration of morals; a people praying to ideals.

(3) **ש** (Shin) giving assurance of permanency of the acquired human degree (non-return to animal reincarnations) and also the great solace which, until not so long ago, was so dear to all Hindus: '*Matter is an illusion; suffering and disasters on the physical plane are also illusory and temporary; pleasures are still less real like a mirage. Seek reality in the astral and mental planes.*'

(4) **ו** (Vau): the whole cult leads to the adoration of Krishna, to the perpetuation of his memory, and to most devoted gratitude to him.

(5) **ה** (Second Hé) is the policy of centralization, a strong hierarchy and system of castes.

Here the strong element is *Shin*, and partially the *Second Hé*. The *First Hé* is a weak point because, when people separated themselves from the hopeless cult of Kali, their gratitude to Krishna became less intensive. The *Second Hé* also showed some weak points, for the caste segregation was followed by misuses, which tired the nation, and finally led to reaction in the form of the newly-born Buddhism.

Pho-Hi (China, 1950 B.C.)

(1) Its **י** (Yod) *is similar to that of Krishna*, but with Chinese names for the triangle's points.

(2) **ה** (First Hé) stands for the Chinese people, accustomed to suffering and misery, and surrendering themselves with full humility to destiny, but fond of work.

(3) **ש** (Shin) is the majesty of the mystery, surrounding the past and the present of the Masters of that School, their ways of life and the cult itself.

(4) **ו** (Vau) is the cult of ancestors and of the past, strongly underlined by the axiom: '*Grandfather was more initiated than Father; Father more than son. The earlier age was wiser than the one just passed, and the latter was wiser than the present epoch.*'

(5) **ה** (Second Hé) is the hierarchy constructed like a pyramid. It was a complicated system of wise men and initiatory degrees, representatives of which could always and everywhere take advantage of their prerogatives.

The positive element of the Egregor was *Vau*. Danger lay in both Hés because of their mutual interdependence. Of course, most of these statements now belong to history rather than to the actual present of the Twentieth Century. The elements of *Shin* and *Second Hé* first underwent strong attack in 1911 (the Chinese revolution against the Emperor's rule). Later, together with *Vau* they were almost utterly destroyed (at least officially) by the newly-born Egregor of materialism in the form of Communism. The element of the *First Hé* being deeper rooted, still exists, especially in the masses, who are devoid of self-rule. Their fondness for work is now the basis of the material power of the new Egregor.

As you can see, Hermetic philosophy is able to analyse everything in the clear, cold light of reality, no matter what kind of problem we would like to consider in that light.

Hermes Trismegistus (Egypt)

The name means: thrice great Hermes on all three planes of existence (mental, astral and physical).

Under this name lies hidden the *magnificent, three-plane, synthetic metaphysical system* created by the Egyptian adepts in the Initiatory Temples of Memphis and Thebes.

It will be only natural, for this Egregor to be more extensively analysed in this course, because our Tarot is indebted in its entirety to the Hermetic system, for both its existence and tradition.

The other mystical names of Hermes are: Thoth and Henoch. We will mainly use the first, classical title.

(1) The Hermetic system is *the* ‫י‬ (*Yod*) of the religion, whose Egregor was able to extend its influence and power on the physical plane for about thirty uninterrupted centuries.

(2) ‫ה‬ (First Hé) which the Egregor had to fecundate, that is the nation in which he had to manifest himself, was composed of cowardly slaves, who inhabited the Nile Valley. Their chief duty was care of the crops, upon which depended the whole life of the nation. Such a constitution of believers compelled the priests to support the authority of religion by showing their powers of realization, called 'miracles' by laymen.

This was also considered as evidence of their alliance with the gods, but for the more enlightened section of ancient Egyptian society, which believed in finer mental conceptions, it was only evidence of deep knowledge, on the part of the priestly class, of Nature's laws and the ability to apply them intelligently.

In both cases, obedience to the priests was necessary and belief in the Egregor (presented, of course, as a deity by the religious canons) was well grounded. We have to remember, that at that time the only scientists, able to regulate the economy of the country, were all priests. Science was made a servant of religion. Engineers and tradesmen, were only executors of the plans made in the temples.

The 'miracles' of the priests, according to our tradition which is a continuation of the ancient Hermetic wisdom, when adapted to the modern forms of twentieth century mentality, can be divided into two categories:

(a) The showing of things, based on a certain knowledge of physics, chemistry, personal and ceremonial magic, and psychurgy.

(b) The manipulation of atmospheric electricity, from simple exhibition of some isolated effects, to the direction of that force over quite a considerable area and distance.

Although we have no proofs, that in purely scientific knowledge of *static*

electricity the Egyptians were much more advanced in relation to our contemporary specialists, operating with their complicated machines (electro-
phores, and so on), we do know that the high Initiates of the land of the
Pharoahs were fairly well ahead of us in the *personal use* of *static electricity*.
Here I mean the ability to create phenomena based on electricity, by the
use of *psychical powers, human will*, or *prana (vital energy)*. Remnants of
the last-mentioned means still exist in some Eastern countries, such as
among the dying class of fakirs, and so on.

By this knowledge, Initiates could actively interfere with meteorological
phenomena, creating rain and thunderstorms when needed, thereby
affecting the quantity of vital Nile water, which simply controlled the crops.
What could be more impressive for a nation of agriculturalists?

In our own day we are already hearing about artificially produced rain,
made by the application of certain chemicals from aeroplanes, and so on;
but this is done by means of very complicated machinery, including air-
craft, which certainly were not at the disposal of the ancient scientists.

(3) So the strong element ♈ *Shin* was included in just these 'miracles'.

(4) ו (Vau) of the Egregoric pattern, that is the cult proper was gradually
changing itself in some periods and countries. But generally speaking, it
always consisted of showing to laymen some fragments of Teachings,
while carefully concealing their Wholeness. Not only laymen were limited
in knowledge of this or another myth, as even Initiates of different degrees
received exactly measured portions of the Doctrine and were strongly
bound to the sub-planes in their interpretations of them.

Nowadays we would call such an organization a theocratic and absolute
system of rule. But it worked for thousands of years.

In the far distant pre-history epoch of Egyptian life, the formula of the
One God was more clearly expressed than in the following periods. It was a
unitarian cult of the god 'Ptah' and the memory of the King *Menes*
(probably mythical). Later he was transformed into OSIRIS-HAMMON.
In that period the initiatory centre was in *Memphis*. But, officially we
know very little about those times.

The foundation of the *Mysteries of Isis* (2703 B.C.) connected with the
transfer of the religious centre to *Thebes*, appears more typical and picturesque to us.

Isis appears instead of *Osiris;* the *female pole* instead of the *male*, or
more exactly, instead of the *Great Androgyne* (Ptah). This fact shows us
the fear of the priests before the invasion of neighbouring cults, and in
particular, that of the grossly sensual one of *Ashtoreth*. So the cult of Isis,
exoterically similar to other female cults, had to preserve the nation from
the unwanted spreading of foreign practices of the same character.

On the other hand, the mythological part of the cult of Isis, keenly and
carefully symbolized the Ternary of Unitarianism in the form of the descending triangle.

The evil genius Typhon (otherwise also called SET) kills Osiris, cuts his
body into twelve parts and throws them into the four corners of the world.
This symbolizes the birth of the Duodenary from the Quaternary: the Sun,

because of our sins, and our merging into matter, can no longer accept us into his bosom in a fatherly fashion. It can only pour its vital fluids on us from far off through the twelve signs of the Zodiac.

The faithful Isis tries her best to collect together her husband's remains so as to restore their unity; but she can succeed only in the creation of the *astral* cliché of that unity, which means: a plan of the possible Reintegration with the *Sun's Centre*. To realize this plan was not her lot, but that of her son—*Horus*, who, of course, is the ו (Vau) of the marriage of *Isis and Osiris*.

The old order of things cannot be restored in its fullness. It is necessary for its idea to become incarnate in the form of a new life, and reshaped in an evolutionary sense.

So HORUS, wiping away his mother's tears, tells her: 'FATHER OSIRIS IS THE SUN OF THE DEAD, I AM BUT THE NEW RISING SUN OF LIVING BEINGS.'

The Hermetic explanation of this is: The High Influx (OSIRIS) reaching the PERFECT PROTOPLAST without any obstacles, was transformed—in the moment of the latter's downfall—*into the illusory, evil interests of the* MATERIAL PLANE (12). Then *Intuition* (ISIS) incites us to collect together the thrown and dispersed, and thereby lost pieces of OSIRIS. We have to seek them from all the four sides, the four Hermetic Virtues (to dare, be silent, know and will); but we will collect them *only astrally*. In order to introduce real evolution on this Earth, we will have to incarnate the collected remains into HORUS (of the Masonic Chain), who will actually lead humanity along the way of REINTEGRATION.

ISIS was not expounded in such a clear form as you have here; no, before her was a veil, impenetrable for laymen, concealing her evolutionary meaning from evil people. *Isis-Moon* at first glance appeared as an *ordinary mother*, a grossly materialistic sub-lunar deity. Only those who had passed through many occult experiences could enjoy the benefactory influences of the *Mysteries of Isis*.

(5) ה (Second Hé) of the Hermetic Egregor means the *policy of religion*, which in this case was the creation of a strong theocratic government. Subsequently, this led the priests to the exploitation of the people for the benefit of a small circle of Initiates. The discipline for guaranteeing the permanency of such an authority was so categorical and pitiless in its rules, that even in the depths of Egyptian temples there arose mutinies not only of neophytes, but also of the initiates of the *middle degrees*.

The most stubborn natures became martyrs of their own unbending liberalism. The more elastically-minded ones accepted the rules and became meek in the face of the superior power. Later, in their old age, wearing the highest degrees of initiation, they supported the theocratic rule with their full conviction, and they damned its foes.

The strong elements of the Egregor of Hermes-Thoth were those of י (Yod) and ו (Vau). The powerful synthesis of Unitarianism, and the dignity of the higher initiatory degrees, astonished and attracted by their harmony and mystery. The cautious concealing of certain mysteries of the teachings from the younger candidates removed the danger of misuse of the knowledge and the powers of realization. The weak sides of the Egyptian Theocracy were:

(a) A certain *duality in the ruling of the temples*: the chief priest was an *administrative ruler*, while the great Hierophant possessed the *Mystical Powers*. By skilful balancing, these two poles ensured stability; but if one of the poles began to overwhelm the other, the whole machine ceased to work properly, resulting in much friction and useless loss of energy.

(b) The *lack of the element of self-sacrifice* among members of the initiatory brotherhood, coupled with a tendency to exploit the laymen, the crawling after the powers of realization, and the promising of earthly boons.

These negative sides, plus the changed composition of the *Second Hé* (which awoke in the nation some desires higher than the mere securing of physical food), led the Egregor to its death.

But, we should be just towards the *great Egyptian Initiatory School*. It stubbornly supported the Egregor, and Egyptian theocracy was artificially able to hold its existence in the face of the most unfavourable conditions. And finally, when dying, it took the trouble to save its element ו (Vau). For Egypt transmitted to posterity, that which we call the *Tarot*, or Book of *Henoch*, or Book of *Thoth*.

Therefore, let us be grateful to the great Egregor of the far off land of the pyramids and the Sphinx.

LESSON 46

Zoroaster (Iran, 2450 B.C.)

(1) Zoroaster's י (Yod) was the *cognition of the Solar System's astral* in its active manifestations.

(2) The ה (First Hé) were men, favourably placed by the nature and climatic conditions of their land, but tortured by their passions, and therefore deeply unhappy. There was much of egotism and what may be termed 'spiritlessness'.

(3) ש (Shin), the lure of the passive side of the Solar astral, the divinatory element penetrating everything, and apparently making it easier to walk through the maze of earthly troubles while giving inspiration in the choice of ways.

(4) ו (Vau), the cult of Mithra, with its central part the COMMANDMENTS OF ALTRUISM, visible even in traditional relations between the Master and disciple who passes through the initiations of the Great Mysteries. The teacher-magicians (as they were called in this cult) gave the neophyte bread and told him to: '*Take it, break it, eat yourself and feed the hungry.*' The candidate was then given a chalice of wine and the Master said: '*Drink yourself and help to quench the thirst of those who are thirsty!*'

(5) The ה (Second Hé) was a liberal, but rather masonic policy of ethical regeneration of the crowd, because of the magnificent initiative and example of the more initiated leaders.

The strong side of the Egregor was its *First Hé* and *Shin*. The weak, the insufficient enlightenment of the middle term (Mithra) of the Great Ternary of Light: ORMUZD-MITHRA-ARIMAN. From this came the binary current in religion. Only the priests possessed the Ternary of the School, while simple people were bewitched by the antagonism of the poles: that of GOOD (Ormuzd) and EVIL (Ariman). Later this allowed some unscrupulous priests to terrorize the nation in the name of the '*dark pole*' and to permit themselves abuses, which finally undermined the life of the Egregor on the physical plane.

Orpheus (1580 B.C.)

(1) The principal basis of the revelation of Orpheus the Thracian, was the news of the birth of Dionysus—god of the Unique Life, by Zeus the androgynous Father. This was the י (Yod) of the Egregor. The development of this thesis led to the conception:
ART IS CREATED BY LOVE (Father) and INTELLIGENCE (Mother).
That is why the term Yod of the Orphic religion can be used for the 'ideal life in the realm of Tiphereth' aimed at the acceptance of that beauty. This striving must be considered as passive.

(2) The ה (First Hé) was the environment of people who loved their bodies. Therefore they transmitted to that body the forms known in the astral (from the passive side). Beauty was the result.

(3) The element ש (Shin) was recognition of all that is strongly aesthetical in the visible world.
(4) The cult of ו (Vau) expressed itself in feasts and holidays of a religious character, full of joy and aesthetical things.

(5) The ה (Second Hé), that is the well-planned religious policy was lacking. The garden perished simply because someone had forgotten to fence it! The cult became materialistic, so that sensuality became mixed with the aesthetic side. Symbolism degenerated into androlatry. The mental core of the Egregor showed itself to be inaccessible to the later followers and adepts.

LESSON 47

Moses (c. 1560 B.C.)

His proper name was Hosarsiph and he was born to the sister of the Pharoah Rameses II. The initiatory title 'Moses' means: 'taken from the water', symbolically equal to 'receiving astral baptism'.
Educated in the Egyptian Royal Court, Moses evidently had every opportunity to be initiated into the Mysteries of Isis; but a fateful and tragic event—the killing of a man in a state of extreme anger—put Moses

I

into a very awkward position. For an Initiate, the blood of the victim meant a spot on his astrosome, which could not be easily eradicated. Only severe repentance accompanied by an ascetic life for long years could perhaps regenerate the fallen man. He did not wish to accept suicide, which—as was believed at that time—could repay his karmic debt. So he chose exile in the desert of Sinai, where there still remained one last centre of initiation of the Black Race.

The chief priest of the temple of Ammon-Ra, the cruel Jethar, was famous for his recklessness in the tests which he imposed on those who wanted to receive initiation under his rules. It was well known in Egypt that so far no one had been able to stand up to the tests and so receive initiation from Jethar. And those who failed invariably died.

So, the intention of Moses, to go to the desert temple of Ammon-Ra was considered as another form of honourable suicide.

But Moses had luck: a prophecy given in a dream strengthened his decision to take the lesser evil.

So Hosarsiph went and was accepted by Jethar. The young daughter of the fearsome ruler of the temple, the virgin Sephora, liked the iron-willed youth and decided to choose him as her husband. Therefore she helped him at the very moment of a most dangerous experience, the choice between two identical cups of wine, one of which was poisoned. Hiding herself behind a curtain, she was able to show him which cup held the pure wine. Thus saved, Moses, in due time, passed through all the tests and occult experiences of the Black Race, reaching high initiation. He married Sephora and became the collaborator of her father. When he legally returned to Egypt, he felt himself to possess enough knowledge, self-confidence, as well as astral and mystical power, in order to fulfil the mission, years ago revealed to him in a dream. This was not to give a religion to a nation, but rather, to create a nation for a new religion. At that time the Jews living in Egypt were only a nomadic tribe, loosely bound together, without any defined religion or creed; but in them, Moses saw strong, healthy, audacious material for his great task.

About 1560 B.C. he set to work all his theurgic and magical powers, so as to influence the Pharoah from one side, while on the other to unite the Jews through their confidence in himself. And he succeeded. The Egregor of Moses had the following pattern:

(1) The · *Point over the Yod* being the idea of the transmission, in their metaphysical part, of both traditions—the Egyptian and that of the Black Race.

(2) ' (Yod), the true Unitarian Religion, courageously revealed in the full patterns of the metaphysical teaching of Hermes Trismegistus. This means, that Moses through his initiatory books and his oral commentaries revealed to the priests and Levites the full possibility of broad Initiation in that realm.

This not being enough, he was not afraid to preach monotheism even to laymen; everything that he said to his people was true and inspired from above. The very dogma of the teaching was not given to everyone, but the part which was revealed by Moses, was absolutely true and exact. All this refers purely to the metaphysical side of Egyptian Hermetism. The magic realizations, mysteries and secrets quite naturally had to be concealed by the wide use of symbolism, and were even partially covered by silence.

The main aim of Moses was the *transmission of Tradition* in possibly an unadulterated form.

(3) The ה (First Hé) of the Egregor, that is the soil into which the new religion had to be sown appeared as a people with a typical inclination towards materialistic mentality; to the exploitation of their neighbours both near and far; with a certain degree of cowardness as a natural result of materialism, and extreme changeability of moods depending upon happy or unhappy events on the physical plane.

The task of the Great Initiate Moses was almost superhuman; but the proud son of the Pharaohs performed his lifelong aim to perfection.

(4) The element שׁ (Shin) appeared as a free use of the all-powerful realizable effects of theurgic and magic origin, which were the basis of Moses' glory and fame. Because of the necessity of these demonstrations, many elements and elementars of all sub-planes entered the Chain. These components sometimes strongly affected the leadership of the Chain, making it very difficult. But they were also helpful, guaranteeing on one side, fear and respect of the Egregor's power, and on the other, gratitude and delight arising from the Egregor's visible help.

Not only the Teacher himself possessed the powers and technique of ruling over the elements and astral dwellers, but also his closest assistants were initiated into these secrets.

We know little of the amount of electrical knowledge possessed by Moses and his disciples, apart from the terrible examples of its practical use (described in the Bible as the burning alive of thousands of rebels, and so on), but Hermetic Tradition mentions about electric cables in a concealed form. In my youth I read an article by a once well-known scientist and occultist, Dr Stadelmann entitled *Die Electrotechnik in der Bibel* (*The Electrotechniques in the Bible*) who supported the view that Moses actually knew not only elementary static electricity, but also much more advanced forms of it.

(5) The element ו (Vau) was of course the cult of the ONE GOD. This was because of the necessity to create the moral bases for the principle of the *Unique Life*. We can see it best in the Ten Commandments.

Because of the typical characteristics of the Hebrew people, it was necessary to introduce more elements of the Sephira *Geburah* into the moral code, besides those of Love and Charity (Chesed). For such a nation as that which Moses created from the Jews, it was too early for the practising of Universal Love, the magnificence of Charity and of forgiveness.

It was more important to build the FRAMEWORK limiting, for the sake of the common good, the freedom of manifestation of the pentagrammatic liberty for particular individuals, or groups. As we know, the limiting activity belongs to the row of the 'left' Sephiroth. And in them flowed foremostly the lives of the adepts of Moses' teachings.

(6) The ה (Second Hé) of the Egregor was the policy of separation of the Jewish Race from all others, in order to secure the bearing and transmitting of Tradition. This policy of exclusiveness had to be carried out by some Jewish leaders even in spite of its contrariness to the nation's interests. Moses, that great Initiate of Egypt, was concerned with the preservation of that Tradition, but not of the nation.

It seems to be convenient at this stage, to say a few words about the *Five Books of Moses*, and their role as the basis of his teachings. There is no purpose to expound here all the phases of his teaching through the last few thousand years (it is almost 3,500 years old). For those who are anxious to know more about the matter, the hint is given to seek in the First Part of the Rosicrucian Initiation. So I am now passing directly to the First Century before Christ.

At that time, the books of Moses and nearly the whole of the Old Testament were not accessible to understanding even by the Levites, because of the loss of the elements of oral initiation. In that epoch the understanding of the Biblical texts was the object of a bitter fight between two Jewish sects. The literal interpretation of the holy texts was supported by the majority of Jews, with the sect of the Sadducees as their spearhead. The opposite pole was represented by another sect, that of the Pharisees, which supported an exclusively allegorical understanding of the Testament, and in that conception almost reaching a personal fantasy on the part of the interpreters.

These two contrary currents were harmoniously neutralized by the existence of the Essenian sect, which recognized the literal meaning of the Bible only as a veil, concealing from the sight of laymen, the true esoteric meaning of the texts, which were only open to persons initiated into the Tarot's arcana, that is into the same initiatory language which Moses had transferred from the Egyptian sanctuaries to the Initiatory School created by himself. The allegorical interpretation of the Essenes was recognized as a natural passage from the literal to the initiatory, hieroglyphic meaning. You can see, that the Essenes, by neutralizing a certain Binary, came closer to the true Initiation. I might even say, that according to the opinion of some very eminent Hermetists, whose works have served as a skeleton for this book, that the *Essenes were true Initiates*, in the full meaning of that word, not only feeling the true sense of the Bible, but also possessing its knowledge in the Tarot's symbolism.

Therefore, when *Demetrius Phalereus*, acting on the order of King Ptolemy I, had to translate the Bible into Greek, he turned just to the Essenes, as recognized authorities on the Scriptures.

The latter, without betraying the initiatory mysteries of the Bible performed quite an adequate and literal translation.

When the Christian Apostles began their preaching, they found the three above-mentioned currents in action, and were compelled to take them into consideration.

Buddhism (Gautama Buddha-Siddartha, 700 B.C.)

(1) The element ' (Yod), in classical Buddhism, appears as the essence of the mechanism of the *Ascending Triangle*, running through the whole chain of all the incarnations of a human individuality. Its motto is: 'MAKE REASONABLE USE OF YOUR INCARNATIONS, FOR THEY ARE GIVEN TO YOU FOR YOUR PERFECTION-ING, AND NOT FOR NOTHING.'

(2) ה (First Hé) appeared primarily as the environment of the Hindu race, tired and tortured by the oppression of caste privileges, which had become a source of abuses and misdeeds.

(3) The powerful solacing element ש (Shin) in Buddhism was the thesis of the illusory character of all matter: 'Is it hard for you to live on this material plane? Then know, that matter is a mirage-like illusion; that it is easy to save yourself from bitterness and disasters. You should not only cease to appreciate matter, but to become indifferent to the sufferings of the physical plane, liberating yourself gradually, but irresistibly, by the POWER OF MEDITATION.

Arrange similarly with the astral plane: liberate yourself from the astral personality, as you did from the physical shell. Then, enter into the *universal mental current*, which finally will bring you into Nirvana. This is the true problem of your incarnations.'

(4) The corresponding cult of ו (Vau) manifested itself in gratitude (also expressed in the ritual, invented after Buddha's death) to the Teacher, as for a Saviour, and the broadest practising of brotherhood, as a natural result of the desire to be liberated from egotism.

(5) The ה (Second Hé) of the Egregor is, of course, the policy of universal brotherhood, excluding every possibility of wars on religious grounds. This is a very positive side of the Buddhist Egregor, which makes it so different from many religious creations in Asia, which preach of the so-called 'holy wars'. Someone can reply, that a certain branch of Buddhism, that is the so-called *Lamaism*, accepts the propaganda of religious self-defence, which contradicts the true Buddhist Teachings and ideas. But, Lamaism is a perverted sect of Buddhism, and does not come under the above-mentioned Egregoric patterns.

The purest Buddhism still remains in some southern Asiatic countries like Ceylon and Burma, but there is evidence of a weakening of the Egregoric influence, because of the political currents, so feverishly flowing through the newly-created independent nations, who apparently have ever less time for spiritual things, being absorbed in materialistic troubles and economic difficulties.

Knights Templar (1118–1312 A.D.)

(1) · The Point over the ' (Yod) in the Templar's Egregor, was the ideal of the perfect world state, balanced on all planes, everywhere establishing

the penetration of gross matter by the subtle principles. The higher influx in such a state should emerge from the sphere of Mystical Authority, vivifying the Astral Power and enlightening and directing the Powers of Realization, thereby creating bliss, happiness, and an opportunity for evolutionary work, with salvation extending to all classes of human society, independent of the nationality of individuals, but with consideration for the laws of every country and its needs.

Everything was included in this theoretically magnificent conception; the dreams of destruction of all the abuses and dishonesty which, at that time, were created by the papal authority; the straightening of morals among the higher and lower classes; the increasing of trade and commerce in the whole world; removal of loss of energy resulting from fights between nations, castes or separate individuals, which were all considered to arise from ignorance and mutual lack of understanding among the fighters. Briefly, these were dreams about the Kingdom of God on Earth. Dreams of the conscious mind-brains of souls hardened in knighthood, hoping to find good points of support in their healthy bodies and in wealth realized by honest work.

(2) The element י (Yod) of their teachings was the *Code of Hermes Trismegistus*, dissolved in the healthy source of the Gnostic Philosophy.

(3) The ה (First Hé) of the Knights Templar was the environment of the Crusaders. In the beginning of the Crusades, the Gnostic Current, strongly influencing the Eastern Schools in Arabia and Palestine, swallowed part of the Knights and helped in the creation of one of the most powerful Egregors, that of the Knights Templar. The Crusaders provided the new Egregor with their most able, pure and strong elements, which at that time, were also more spiritual in their views.

(4) The element ש (Shin) of the new current was the beauty, the striving to Power and authority of the future adepts on all planes, with the tempting prospect of using that power for the realization of their ideals, dear to every individual member of that Egregoric Chain.

(5) The element ו (Vau) of the Knights Templar was that which today we call the 'Cult of Baphomet'. This word needs a clear explanation, because of its steady misunderstanding and misuse. Read kabbalistically, from right to left, using the method of notarikon (see the Tenth Arcanum), the sentence reads: TEMPLI OMNIUM HOMINUM PACIS ABBAS (the high priest of the temple of peace for all men).

Under this term the Knights Templar understood the Universal Instrument of their strivings. This instrument appeared to them as the astral vortexes (tourbillons) generated by the will-impulses of their Egregoric Chain. That is why the symbolical statue of *Baphomet*, representing the pentacle of the astral 'serpent' Nahash (actually, the astral tourbillon), played so important a role in their secret ceremonies. More will be said about this in the corresponding parts of the Fifteenth Arcanum.

(6) The ה (Second Hé) of the Knights Templar's Egregor was the theocratic policy based on hierarchic laws and principles of centralization.

The *Commanderies* were grouped into *Priorates*, then these into the *Great Priorates*, while groups of Great Priorates were united in the so-called 'Languages' (nations speaking the same language). Over all these Languages stood the *Grand Master*, who, in his pentagrammatic authority and actions, was obedient only to one general motto of the Knights Templar: CHARITY AND WISDOM.

These were the general lines along which the Order was created in about 1118 A.D.

Its destruction by the Papal Bull in 1312 is known to you from previous lessons, as well as the tragic end, at the stake, of the last Grand Master of the Knights Templar—Jacobus Molay and his closest collaborators.

History tells us, that the powerful elements of *Yod* and *First Hé* of the Templar's Egregor, together with its attractive *Shin* led the Order to flourish magnificently on all planes. When its enemies wished to destroy it, they were frightened by its magic power (strong Egregoric Chain) and were jealous of its riches on the material plane (large territories). So they cleverly chose the weapon of gossip and black invective and attacked the *Vau* of the Egregor. They charged the Knights with indulging in orgies, black magic, and indecency and immorality in ceremonies held before Baphomet. Finally, with the help of this net of lies they reached their aims on the physical plane.

But where did the remaining Knights disappear to? Certainly not all were slaughtered. In answering such a question I have to remember, that at the same time when the Knights Templar arose in France, there were two other currents growing in strength in Europe. One of them was Hermetic and strove for realization of the *Great Action*; the other was called a 'gothic building' or Freemasonry, occupied with the cult of work for and preservation of traditional symbolism in architecture. These two currents, coming together, naturally gave birth to societies composed of *both elements*, which worked on both the mental and physical planes alike. The connecting link was, of course, the astral plane or the *world of traditional initiatory symbols* vitalized by the work of the Hermetists and clad in the physical form of stone-masons.

It was just these Freemasons who were officially recognized by Rome in 1277, who decided to recognize the refugee Knights as brothers after the rout of the Knights Templar Order. The latter thereupon saw themselves in a new shell, that of the '*Accepted Masons*'.

So, now you know about the Knights, the physical body of the Egregor. But what happened to the astrosome of the Chain, to its powerful Egregor? A learned occultist would simply say: 'Just the same as would happen to your astrosome or mine, after we have discarded our physical bodies (in other words, have died).' Here we will develop such a brief answer for the sake of students and readers.

The property of powerful Egregors allows them self-purification and self-perfectioning in the astral plane, when their physical counterparts have ceased to exist, that is, when they have no point of support in the visible world.

Prof. G. O. Mebes, a recognized authority on Hermetic occultism says that: '*The shells of these Egregors, covered with the errors committed by their adepts on the physical plane, are gradually dissolved in that period of purification, thus allowing more light to emerge from the luminous core of the Egregor.*'

But this possibility of self-regeneration belongs only to those Egregors which possess a very definite 'Point over the Yod' as well as a clearly drawn finished system, again provided with the powerful Yod.

The Egregor of the Knights Templar purified itself on the astral plane in about 70 to 80 years, and then gave birth to the Brotherhood, which we may conditionally call 'Rosicrucianism of the Primary Type'.

I would like to underline here as strongly as possible, that this product of regeneration had and has nothing in common with any organization, which later assumed (even in our own day), for their own, not always clear aims, the ancient name of the 'Rosicrucians'.

We may not even be bound to believe in the existence of another brotherhood, allegedly founded by *Christian Rosenkreutz* (1378–1484) and composed of a very small number of mystics who were virgin men.

All I want to state here is that, *on the astral plane there were very distinctly created the forms of these ideals and the way leading to perfection*, about which the excellent 'FAMA FRATERNITATIS ROSAE + CRUCIS' speaks.

These ideals are registered in the form of a code, but tradition affirms that this happened much later than the awakening of the Egregor.

Now, in which form, according to the aforementioned work, as well as to the 'CONFESSIO FIDEI R + C' should the Egregor of the original Rosicrucians be presented?

It is evident, that this powerful Egregor attracted to itself, three large currents which flowed into the ocean of Truth: *Gnosticism, the Kabbalah and Hermetic Alchemy.*

LESSON 49

(1) The 'Point' of the Knights Templar's Egregor appeared here as an *ideal of theurgic action, belonging to the Kingdom* of Elijah the Artist, together with an ineffable faith in the coming of that Kingdom in the future. But what does it mean, Elijah the Artist? What is the role of Elijah in the realm of Art? The secret sources about the constitution of the original Rosicrucian Egregor tell us, that according to the Bible, Elijah and Enoch are symbols of the elements which were '*taken alive to Heaven*'. But in metaphysical empiricism only the Absolute Truth flows in a NATURAL bed. The Minor Arcana of the Book of Enoch enter into just such a *natural current*, as we can see from the lessons about them in the Tenth Arcanum.

Therefore, Elijah is like a more concrete, gross reflection of Enoch. Elijah is closer to us and more understandable than Enoch. Just as the Major Arcana are more understandable for fallen humanity than are the Minor ones, which treat of perfect, ideal conceptions, which are beyond our materialistic and not completely developed, *non-integrated minds*. Bitter as it is, this fact cannot be changed in any short period of time.

But which way will show this Elijah to us, leading us to the Minor Arcana, to the Rosicrucian Reintegration? Perhaps along the paths of those blessed, simple hearts, not learned but powerful and full of the faith 'which can move mountains'? Believers in Christ, only because they know about Him from Scriptures?

No! Our Egregor did not occupy itself with these fortunate, but very seldom encountered category of men. '*They that are well have no need of a physician, but they that are sick.*'

The newly born Rosicrucian Egregor wanted to give salvation to those who had already tasted the Knowledge and could not renounce the boons which it brings. The Rosicrucian Elijah leads his adepts to the Minor Arcana by way of artificial, searching analysis of the Major ones. He turns them round, makes new combinations and therefore deserves the name of Artist.

(2) The powerful י (Yod) by which he fecundates his adepts was reflected as an immortal symbol of the Rose + Cross. No matter in which frame you may put it, or which variations you would insert into its basic melody, IT WAS, IS and WILL BE the same in its central point.

The CROSS, a symbol of the path of self-denial, that is illimitable altruism, and infinite humility *before the Law of the Highest*, is the first pole of the Binary. The *Rose of Hermes*, the attractively perfumed symbol of Wisdom, proud of its three-plane perfection, enwraps that Cross. Whoever recognizes the CROSS may bear IT; but he will never have the power to tear the ROSE away from It. May its thorns prick the savants, never will they cease to be delighted by its perfume. Here the ROSE represents the other pole of the Binary.

The problem of Rosicrucianism is the neutralization of that Binary. The true adept of the *Rose + Cross* must neutralize, with his own person, Self-Sacrifice and Knowledge. He must add them to himself, force them to serve the unique IDEAL, and to assimilate them as the *third* symbol, placed in this pentacle at the foot of the Rose + Cross.

A *Pelican* sits there with wings wide spread, feeding her young with her own flesh and blood in an ecstasy of parental SELF-SACRIFICE. But these chicks are of different colours.

In the primary pentacle there are THREE of them; in the last one seven. They symbolize the three *Primary Causalities* and the *seven Secondary* ones. In the latter case, planetary colours are usually added. The mother-bird's elation is balanced by the *Knowledge of Colours*. The mother knows that she has to treat her chicks differently because she has tasted Wisdom and is able to adapt herself to it. This is the meditation of a true Rosicrucian his י (Yod).

(3) The ה (First Hé) of this kind of Rosicrucianism was the society (the environment) of the few chosen individuals who were able to join, within themselves, *mysticism* with subtle *intellectual strivings*.

I *

(4) The element ‫ש‬ (Shin) of the original Rosicrucianism should be considered as a certain kind of self-deification coming naturally from the habit of seeing oneself as a 'chosen container'. The number of Adepts of Wisdom and candidates for them was so limited, that the element of Shin took its peculiar form of itself. As a support, were the hard conditions of life, dictated by the morale of Rosicrucianism.

(5) In place of the element ‫ו‬ (Vau) we find *meditation about the symbols*, and foremost among them, the great pentacle of ROSE + CROSS, plus some mystical ceremonies performed during the periodical meetings of the Rosicrucians.

(6) The ‫ה‬ (Second Hé) of the School appeared as the policy of secrecy about the personalities of the Rosicrucians, wishing to anonymously realize everything that their consciences considered as helping the evolution of humanity, in *both ethical and intellectual realms*. On this Second Hé we may still see the veil of the Knights Templar, which did not have enough time to be dissolved *in the pure astral*.

The evident hatred directed against the Catholic Church went into the formal creation of Protestant elements (in 'FAMA FRATERNITATIS' and 'CONFESSIO' the Pope is compared to the Antichrist and only two sacraments are recognized, and so on). Speaking in occult language, we may, with reason, say that these sharp edges directed against Rome must be recognized as the reflection of the astral vengeance against Pope Clement the Vth.

The original Rosicrucians could not have had many adepts among them. Perhaps this was because too many different characters and types could not find a place in an organization strictly attached to a definite ideal. But in the sixteenth century, the *Primary Rosicrucianism* gave birth to the *Secondary Order*.

If the first form can be considered as Rosicrucianism for only a few chosen people, then the *second* was intended FOR ALL CONSCIOUS MEN of good will.

If the *first* almost tyrannically imposed a definite form of path for self-perfectioning on its adepts, then the *second* showed exceptional tolerance and lack of despotism in all the realms accessible to the human heart and mind.

The Point over the ‫י‬ (Yod) remained as before. But a visible change appeared in the ‫ה‬ (First Hé). The environment which was fecundated by the Rosicrucian ideas in the sixteenth, seventeenth and partially in the eighteenth centuries were mostly aggregates of Encyclopaedists in the broadest and best meaning of the word. This necessitated manysidedness in intellectual strivings, ability for scientific speculation, broadness of viewpoint, and faithful *surrender to the idea of Good*. Many deeply mystical natures, determined pantheists, and men of eminent practical abilities joined the movement. But the *militant* elements were composed only of men superior to the average from the point of view of intelligence, education, force of will, and a crystallized understanding of humanity's evolutionary paths.

Unfortunately, it is impossible for me to give here information about the element ש (Shin) of the *Secondary Rosicrucianism* as I have not been able to get the necessary permission for this from the *Initiatory Circle* which is the guardian of the Rosicrucian Testament since the Order ceased to exist on the physical plane more than 150 years ago.

In general the element ו (Vau) was represented in the formal ritual of Initiation of members of the Chain into the Rosicrucian degrees. There were also ritual meetings of the Central Councils of Adepts, connected with a definite branch of the Egregor. Special methods of astral exercises and transformations of personality were widely used, together with meditations mostly borrowed from the Eastern Schools. That which you will find in the Thirteenth Arcanum (descriptions of death's processes, its phases, and so on) has mostly been taken from the material left or willed to us by the eminent Adepts, who were in spiritual contact with the Rosicrucian Egregor on the astral and mental planes.

The ה (Second Hé) was the policy used by the Rosicrucians in order to influence society. Firstly it was purely ethical but later, strongly realizable. Branches and sub-branches of Rosicrucians in the seventeenth and beginning of the eighteenth centuries had different political and religious reforms. But the former Knights Templar's Egregor—still conscious of the tragic cliché of the downfall of *Jacobus Molay* and his Chain on the physical plane—was very cautious. Especially when the Rosicrucians were prepared to undertake an important step. The Egregor advised them of the most sure and secure ways of influencing human society, and as a result, came the foundation of the *Masonic Order*.

The subtle astral of Rosicrucianism, while useful for Teachers, was not very suitable for the solution of practical problems, and was not sufficiently tactful in the realm of handling material things, which contacted the small but burning questions of everyday life.

So was created the physical shell, the soul of which had to be Rosicrucianism, but this shell must be hardened and experienced in worldly things, having no fear of hard work. This shell is Masonry, the orthodox Freemasonry of the Scotch Ritual, with the ethical and Hermetic interpretation of the Traditional Symbolism. This organization had to preserve the symbols and to sustain respect for these symbols in its surroundings, and among the lay public.

It can be suggested, that the purity of masonic morals has as its source, just the Initiatory teachings, which have their origin in former Rosicrucianism.

Since then, Masons have had to realize in practice the Rosicrucian mottoes and problems, which act as a shield for them before the dangers of the outer world.

The founders of Masonry, among whom Elias Ashmole (1617–1692) undoubtedly holds the most important position, quickly extended their organization. From the beginning in 1646 to 1717, Masonry developed a fully organized system of Scotch Chapters. Masonry became a necessity for Rosicrucian Illuminism, and even its own policy (Second Hé) gained the name of 'Masonic', which is retained to this day.

The effects of the realization of masonic mottoes and aims were often called 'masonic coups de canon' (gun-shots). The religious reforms of Martin Luther and John Calvin are considered as such and also the political reform of liberation of the North American States from British rule (Lafayette and his Mason officers) (every coin has its other side).

But every coin has its other side. So long as Masonry was really obedient to the Rosicrucian organization, so long as it recognized the principle of the 'TRANSMISSION OF HIERARCHY', everything went well and the Masons fulfilled their mission; but when some separate branches of Masonry (unfortunately, often strong ones) began to yield to the principles of elections, with detriment to the traditional hierarchic rule, then the formerly EVOLUTIONARY masonic realizations began to change their character to REVOLUTIONARY. The turning point was the masonic revolution of *Lacorne* and his followers (1773), which separated from the orthodox masonic organization which we know as the 'Grand Orient de France'.

There is no room here for any history of Masonry, and in these lessons I want to explain only the life, work and death of Egregors, by giving examples, which are always more illuminating than mere statements.

Some currents of Christian Illuminism were alive until World War I, and I will give another series of examples about them.

LESSON 50

Martinism

About 1760 the well-known *Martines de Pasqualis* founded a brotherhood of '*Selected Initiated Servants*' with a nine-degree hierarchy. The three higher degrees were Rosicrucian. The school of Martines is a magic-theurgic one, with a preponderance of magic methods.

After his death, the beloved disciples of Martines introduced some changes into the work of his Chain. Willermooz brought rather a masonic colouring, while the famous writer Claude de St Martin remodelled the School in a mystic-theurgic way, believing that (contrary to Willermooz) 'Free Initiation' is better than organization in masonic lodges. His influence won and gave birth to the current called 'Martinism'. The Egregor of the original Martinism was strongly incarnate in many European states, especially in Russia at the beginning of the nineteenth century.

In about 1930 I encountered the wandering masters who possessed some higher degrees of modern Martinism. They had the same methods as a hundred years ago, to select among able and idealistic intellectuals in different countries, men who could realize the aims and methods of Martinism. Initiations were purely individual, and no outer obligations were placed upon the new initiates.

Of course, I cannot say anything more about the contents of these simple but impressive ceremonies, which lasted several hours. But I am entitled to remark, that, actually, the information given and some of the axioms of a philosophical and mystical character could assist the neophyte to SHAPE HIS INNER IDEALISTIC STRIVINGS BETTER, than he would be able to do when left alone.

In some West European countries we can still encounter some Martinist initiates. But only if we ourselves are also members of that mysterious Order. For otherwise, we cannot see their signs of recognition, nor understand the words they speak in order to find brother initiates. As before World War II, most of the members were of French origin, the formulas of recognition were also given and received in the French language.

The construction of the Martinist Egregor is accepted as follows:

(1) The Point over the י (Yod) being the alliance of a man with himself in the ethical sphere.

(2) י (Yod) which is the spiritual philosophy of the works of Saint Martin, which underwent some variations in his lifetime.

(3) ה (First Hé) being the surroundings of very pure and unselfish men, mystically minded in most cases, and inclined towards any philanthropic activity.

(4) The element ש (Shin) which was probably absent because of the character of the First Hé. Pure idealists do not need any baits.

(5) The element ו (Vau) was limited to a very simple ritual prayer in the ceremony of initiation, which also was simplicity itself. But for Masons who came from the ranks of the Martinists, ritual had more importance and sometimes was even rich in formality.

However, everything in Martinism was based on meditation, on the creation of the 'Man of Desire' (Homme de Désir) and not on any magic environment, as was the case in 'Willermoozism'.

(6) The ה (Second Hé) of the old Martinism was represented by the philanthropic actions of its members; anonymous assistance for the poor and the oppressed; lack of a tendency to forcible 'conversion', and allowing everyone to follow his or her own path. The sublime humility of the Martinists was very impressive for the society which was able to see it.

Martinist Initiation in the time of the First Empire (in France) up to the Eighties of the nineteenth century flowed as a fairly thin brooklet, but counted among its members such brilliant personages as Chaptal, Delaage and Constant ('Eliphas Lévi')

The present state of this very pure and most idealistic spiritual organization, as was and is Martinism, is little known. True Martinists do not advertise their activities and always prefer to remain in secrecy. I have every reason to believe that this Egregor is still alive, and acting in a particular way in different countries. The fact, that some eminent idealists and occultists of pure heart were found and subsequently initiated into Martinism speak for themselves.

But all of this is veiled in deep mystery, as one of the few obligations of an accepted Martinist is a solemn oath—'NEVER TO BETRAY THE NAME OF THE MASTER WHO PERFORMED THE INITIATION'.

Stanislas de Guaita

This famous occultist wanted to regenerate the esoteric current which began to vanish after the death of Eliphas Lévi. The new creation had to be called: 'the Kabbalistic Order of Rose + Cross'.

Its pattern was:

(1) The Point over the י (Yod) being an alliance of official science with the whole of esoteric knowledge, accessible at the time, so that fruitful cooperation would be possible.

(2) י (Yod): a synthesis of all Traditions which are accessible to our investigation using modern, experimental methods, which make many ways of analysis much easier.

(3) The ה (First Hé) in the de Guaita School again appeared as a circle of Encyclopaedists, but unfortunately, hopeless ones. For in this epoch able men rise high and quickly in their speciality, but have no time to develop along more versatile and universal lines. On the other hand, some people, disappointed in their chosen speciality, try to turn to something similar to the true Encyclopaedists. Usually they are only superficially successful, appearing to be multi-sided intellectuals, similar to the former Rosicrucians. Anyway, this *point appeared as a weak one in de Guaita's construction.* Nevertheless, we should not blame this eminent occultist, who doubtless had the best of intentions. But he could use only the material at his disposal, and this was his tragedy.

(4) The element ש (Shin) of the new Egregor was inviting and attractive for men from the *First Hé* (3) giving them the idea *to become equal* with the recognized luminaries of science, only by virtue of their Rosicrucian privileges. But academic circles which gained access to the new order founded by de Guaita were not too happy at such an *artificial equality*. Troubles were to be foreseen ahead.

(5) The element ו (Vau) appeared as a broadly planned publishing of works of classical occultism with comments and translations of the same. Because many occult treatises had become bibliographical rarities inaccessible to the wider public, this publishing brought to light many good and useful books, so that Parisian Rosicrucians of the end of the nineteenth century deserve deep gratitude from those of us who admire the great monuments to the Western Occult Tradition. This point (5) was perhaps the strongest in the whole Egregor of the Kabbalistic Order of the Rose + Cross, created by de Guaita and his closest collaborators.

(6) The ה (Second Hé) was another weak element, resulting in an opportunist policy on the side of members against the academic world, which is always jealous of its privileges and aloofness.

Some Rosicrucians were seeking recognition from official science, which of course did not raise their dignity.

Efforts and experiments on the part of a section of the School to soften some Rosicrucian theses in order to avoid too strong a clash with the

Roman Catholic Church, only led to a rift within the Order itself (the secession of Peladan).

Briefly, while de Guaita was still alive, the whole thing seemed to be doomed. The next desperate approach to Masonry again brought about the warping of the School's aims, which resulted in its decadence.

Prof. G. O. M. in his *Occult Commentaries* dated about 1912, stated that the Kabbalistic Order of Rosicrucianism was then in a vanishing state. Personally, I have no further knowledge in the matter, especially after World War II.

Energetic Stanislas de Guaita tried to form another organization and realized the resurrection of the once powerful current of *Martinism*. You already know about its original form as created by Louis Claude de Saint Martin.

The Neo-Martinism of de Guaita is not identical with that of the original pattern. From it he borrowed the ritual side of initiation into S ∴ I ∴ and rebuilt his symbolism by developing that ritual. The rather abstruse ideas of the creation of the '*Man of Desire*' (see former lessons) were not too pleasing for de Guaita's dynamic nature. He disliked the idea of *voluntarily holding someone in the cycle of magnetized surroundings*, as had happened in Saint Martin's organization. De Guaita was longing for *realizations*. In his books we often see that he mocks somewhat at such limitation of the human will, no matter for which elated purpose it had to be done.

Finally, this 'quasi-regenerated' Egregor of Saint Martin was made up according to a pattern, which could provide new adepts for the *Order of the Rose + Cross* through the selection of the most able SS ∴ II ∴ (Superior Inconnus in French). Because of similar aims of the *Kabbalistic Order of the Rose + Cross* IT WAS NECESSARY to introduce more elements of tolerance into the realm of dogmas.

(1) The Point over the ׳ (Yod) in this new pattern remained as before, the motto of the ethical alliance of man with himself. You can translate it in simpler words as—'inner harmony'.

(2) The choice of the element ׳ (Yod) was left to the free will of every member of this Neo-Martinist current. Nevertheless, the works of *Louis Claude de Saint Martin* naturally remained as formal guides for all members.

(3) The element ה (First Hé), because of the freedom given to everyone in his choice of *Yod*, was represented in different circles by larger or smaller lodges, if we prefer this term. To them came people tired by their long religious search; those disappointed in academic knowledge; those desiring something similar to Masonry, but, as they hoped, in a nobler form; ordinary, curious people of all calibres, and those who were unacceptable to other occult organizations. Finally, there were the really honest men and women (the Order also accepted women) who were striving after mystical powers, lovers of talks on occult themes in full salons, and hysterically-minded ladies, who are always keen for membership of societies, where there is a taste of mystery.

Others were strongly convinced, *that even a not too well balanced circle of neophytes and disciples is still better than a complete lack of any Egregoric assistance.*

This last reason I would like to recommend to every occultist (beginners included) for careful and sincere deliberation.

Because the Rosicrucian Order as regenerated by Stanislas de Guaita, placed as a condition of acceptance into its Chain, the obligatory passing by candidates of three degrees of Neo-Martinism, so there were always a few men, able to be teachers in the environment of Martinist 'Hommes de Désir'. They could duly direct the transformation of individualities, developing in them new occult abilities. This was the cause of the vitality of the Order, which after the death of de Guaita grew further, and before World War I had quite a considerable number of members. At that time, Dr Gérard Encausse, able propagator of occultism through the press, stood at the top of the Neo-Martinist Order (writing under his pen-name of 'Papus').

Shortly before World War II, I lost my personal contact with this organization and therefore cannot say much about its most recent fate. One thing is certain, the years after 1939 were, for many occult lodges, a period of recession and weakening of activity and influence, but as yet this period does not belong to history. Therefore I will refrain from taking any position in the matter.

(4) As the element ש (Shin) of the Neo-Martinist Order appeared, there were many different attractions, because of differences in tendencies and degrees of ethical development of its members. One was attracted by the ritual, another by the solidarity between the links of the Chain (that is friendliness amongst members), another by the possibility of esoteric development, and yet another by the purity of the inheritance of authority in the Egregor created by Martines de Pasqualis, and so on.

(5) The element ו (Vau), apart from uniting all Martinists in mystical ceremonies, represented the *obligatory meditations* on themes provided by the superiors of the Order and assisted through lectures on the initiatory matter, given by the teachers in the various Lodges.

(6) The ה (Second Hé) was a rather passive policy of waiting for advanced phases of ethical perfectioning of human society, and of influencing the same by examples of good living. Of course, I cannot state that no Martinist lodge attaches some active philanthropy to this policy. There have been many cases where this activity has manifested itself in the outer world. But always, these are individual actions, which cannot be included among the Egregoric principles.

The power and vitality of a religious Egregor can be measured by the saints who appear under that Egregor's influence.

A few great religions, founded thousands of years ago, still produce the highly-evolved men, whom we call saints. Others are like dry river-beds, no longer containing water.

With these few examples of the Egregoric manifestations we will conclude this part of the Eleventh Arcanum. I think the attentive reader has been able to see for himself how the ideas incorporated in Hermetism manifest themselves in the so-called 'real' life of humanity. An occultist is one who KNOWS things and principles unknown to the majority of men. The realm of his knowledge extends mainly to BASIC matters, to CAUSES and not only to their results. Therefore, a keen application of an occult law would be much more important for an Initiate than all the past history of a nation or tribe. There is no greater REALIST than a true occultist, for he knows what is essential and what is not.

Perhaps someone will ask me, why I have not analysed here, such a powerful Egregor as Christianity, or rather, its most developed religions. There is more than one cause for this, and not all reasons can be spoken about publicly. Hence they must be covered by silence. However, I can mention here, that the Christian Egregor is a living and ACTING power. It does not belong wholly to the past, for it concerns the lives of a great percentage of present-day humanity. As humanity is only a collection of individuals, each of which has his own 'separate' (at least so he believes) life, I leave the judgement to everyone, on their own responsibility.

To more mystically-minded students, I will only quote *once more* an esoteric interpretation of INRI, given in previous lessons. It is: IN NOBIS REGNAT IESUS (In us reigns Jesus). *Now, not before, not after! If it exists in us*, this state cannot be analysed by the mind. *If not*, then we are not entitled to make even an attempt to limit what cannot be limited.

As an enumeration of contemporary occult currents, I would still like to give the names of some secret organizations which the student might encounter at some time.

From Masonic Rituals may be mentioned:
The *Orthodox Scotch Ritual* (33 degrees)
The *Ritual of Memphis* (97 degrees)
The *Ritual of Misraim* (96 degrees)
The *French Ritual* (7 degrees)
The *Order of German Illuminates* (Philanthropy and National policy), which is closely affiliated with the masonic pattern. The *Asian Rosicrucians* (an extensive knowledge of esoterism and courageous international policy).
The English '*Rosa + Crux Esoterica*' (esoteric teachings and quite solidly conducted Rosicrucian ritual).

Finally, there exist many other circles and organizations, some of which are too unimportant to be mentioned, while others do not allow themselves to be mentioned in print, preferring to remain under a veil of complete mystery. In their communiqués, such brotherhoods use *only some initials* and never divulge the names of their leaders.

LESSON 51

The most important factor of force for an occultist and an average man alike is their WILL-POWER. If it is advisable for the latter to develop it, then it is a *condition of success* for the former (among the exercises connected with the experience of exteriorization, there are some which also imply the development of will-power). Here I want to include in a suitable form, means which have been tested and are otherwise well known to religious and occult ascetics, and which can be followed without any change in the outer life of the student.

WILL-POWER is like an electric battery. If adequately charged and not exhausted, it retains its usefulness; but if too often used for non-essential purposes, the battery will give little service in a moment of need.

The generator of *will-power* in us is just the amount of inner impulses and desires, which we consciously conquer and refuse to satisfy in order to charge our *will-power's battery*. You should know, that if you obey the slightest emotions or thoughts arising in your consciousness, *your will* shall always be close to zero.

But *every dominated desire*, unexpressed thought, unpronounced word, or unperformed deed, if they are a result of your definite WILL and DECISION, are the CURRENTS which charge your battery. Examples will be more illuminating. Suppose that you have a desire to tell your acquaintance something, which in itself has no great meaning, or importance, and you have that desire simply because you want to speak, having nothing better to do. *Suppress this desire and remain silent*. You want to buy a newspaper, in order to read about some sensational, but insignificant happening, which is announced in it. *Refuse to obey this desire*.

In both cases you may observe some greater *self-assertion* in you, something like a certain inner fullness, or feeling of strength, probably in the head (in the beginning).

Going further, sacrifice some dish, which you especially like, or a visit to the theatre; take longer to walk to your home despite your subconscious desire to be there as soon as possible. *All these movements in your consciousness will considerably fortify your will-power*. But do not attempt (especially in the beginning) to interfere in the way just shown with your vital functions or activities!

DO NOTHING SENSELESS OR UNREASONABLE! For occultism does not tolerate either unwise actions or unwise men. If your duties or other circumstances compel you to speak or act in a certain way, you should not cancel these activities, which belong to your karmic conditions. KNOW, that in your everyday life you will find innumerable opportunities to develop your will-power in the way just indicated, and if you will make use of even 10 per cent. of all these opportunities, which appear in your normal life, you will soon become a being, endowed with a will-power far superior to that of your environment.

The more you follow this simple advice, the better you will feel the increase of your realizable will-power, giving you much greater satisfaction and happiness, than you have ever experienced before. Then you will probably try to perform some more exercises, in order to grow steadily in power and inner peace, which invariably is connected with any inner strength.

What have I to tell you in such a case? *For great results greater efforts are necessary*, which means greater inner efforts and 'sacrifice', self-restraint, or *renunciations, which will charge your inner 'battery'*. I will limit myself to giving only a few hints, as the earnest and ardent student can complete the list for himself. Take the examples of *eminent occultists, saints and yogis:* all of them did and do try CERTAIN asceticism, that is limitation of their desires and needs to the possible minimum. So there lies the SECRET OF INNER STRENGTH! Every time renounce something 'dear' to you, and so *collect the power. Gradual and reasonable action* is what is foremostly needed. Do not, for example, fast yourself half to death! This would be stupid! Your unnecessary indulgences, when cut off will provide you with a never-ending amount of the 'CURRENT'.

This will-power is useful not only in occult study, but also in one's everyday life. Properly used, it brings happiness.

And this Power is the very idea of the Eleventh Arcanum.

Arcanum XII
SACRIFICIUM
THE SACRIFICE

Libra

Messia
Caritas
Zodiacus

CHAPTER XII

ARCANUM XII (ל LAMED)

THE sign of the Twelfth Arcanum is the Hebrew letter ל (Lamed) and its numerical value is 30. The corresponding astrological sign is that of balance (weight) in the Zodiac. The hieroglyph is an ARM performing a broad movement, which involves all of its joints. It is the powerful action of a man who, of his own accord has acquired certain rights and now wants to use them. It is like a new א (Aleph), not only balanced in all three planes, but also wise through the experience of life. Another aspect of the hieroglyph is an open hand.

There is also the idea of sacrifice: for the outstretched hand suggests an act of giving, even at the price of one's own detriment. It is something like the surrendering of one's own vital force.

So far Tradition teaches us. We will now pass on to the card of the Twelfth Arcanum. We see a man hanged by his *left foot*. His right leg is bent at the knee behind the left one, so that the picture suggests the figure of a cross. The man's arms are folded behind his back, so that the lower part of the figure is like a descending triangle.

The construction on which the man hangs is composed of two beams. In my card I have used them in the form of the letter 'T', but there are also variations of this picture, on which the figure hangs down between two vertical poles.

In any case, there must be twelve short branches or knots, six to each side of the pole. These, of course, symbolize the twelve signs of the Zodiac, the material world. The man is depicted as crucified on the symbol of matter.

Who is the hanged Man? What did he do? His feet are uppermost and his head is directed earthwards. This means, that his best elements serve the Earth, his attention is paid to the Earth. At the top there is only the fulcrum.

He is the messenger, from above to below, of the higher MENTAL to the LOWER physical plane. He bears in himself the end of the process connected with the *involutionary triangle*, as he sends a *higher principle into Matter* for the regeneration and subtilizing of that same matter. But his involutionary triangle is crowned with the cross of the Hermetic virtues, which showed him the way to that evolution, to that SACRIFICE. The number of twelve knots, being the symbol of the *finite*, again suggests the idea of the *finite character* of the involutionary process: this means that the Absolute, Unmanifested, is beyond forms and manifestations.

To conclude, we may say, that in the Twelfth Arcanum everything breathes the idea of service: the *High* to the *Low*.

There is still one more symbol: the head of the Man is surrounded by a bright halo. We will see the reason for this in the further analysis.

This analysis will be performed on our usual, traditional basis, which is the arithmological unfolding of the arcanum's components.

Equation No. 59: $12 = 1 + 11$

He who commands the XIIth Arcanum places his balanced essential being (1) before the arcanum of the Chain (11). In other words, it is the HEAD of a School, plus that School itself. The three-plane Aleph honoured the world by the process of giving birth to the Egregoric Chain. He descended from the higher sub-planes and did not scorn the *realization*, incarnating himself *in both meanings of that word: direct and symbolical.*

Of course, this three-plane Aleph belongs to the sphere of the *Theosophical Ternary*. Accordingly, there may be three different cases.

(1) If it was the ARCHETYPE incarnate, then the first title of the arcanum would be the *Messiah*.

(2) If our Aleph is not so high and represents a man of balanced individuality who possesses inner harmony and voluntarily brings into his astrosome the *desire to help* his neighbours, the action would be termed *Charity* (Caritas) on the plane of matter. Just the love of one's fellow-creatures, as is taught and understood in Christianity. It is also an incarnation of a harmonious man, merged in serious problems, and voluntarily accepting the duty of occupying himself, *for the sake of others*, with things which he would normally never consider, being devoid of all interest for him.

(3) Now we have to seek for a suitable corresponding example in the plane of Nature, and it is not so far away. Take the old myth, which comes from the most ancient epoch of the human race: the *feeding* of all the planets through their central radiant Sun. The visible movement of that CENTRE suggests to us the idea of the Zodiac, divided into twelve signs, which you already know.

Therefore the third and last title of the Twelfth Arcanum is 'ZODIACUS'. For us, living in this modern age of discoveries and progress in the physical and astronomical sciences, the 'old myth' is fully supported by modern knowledge. There is no room here to quote the proofs extensively, so I will mention only a few of the most illuminating examples.

Everything which lives, and everything which we need for our own lives have their origin in the Sun's activity and energy. Without the Sun there could be no flora or fauna on the Earth. Our coal, oil, atmospheric conditions, the circulation of water, warmth necessary for organic life (including our own), all and much more come from the Sun. How long could we exist on our Earth, if for one day the Sun ceased to send us its enormous quantities of life-giving energy?

The idea of the mysterious emanations of the Sun, and their transformation into plants and animals are sufficient justification for the third title of the arcanum—the *Zodiac*.

Equation No. 60: $12 = 11 + 1$

Eleven before one. Eleven has embraced the One, assimilated it, and here lies the mystery of the number 12, clear to an occultist who meditates keenly about it.

But the ONE has also given birth to ELEVEN. The result being that ONE has sacrificed itself for the Chain (11). If this Chain is the creation of the Testament, then the appearance of the Messiah has the definite character of the sacrifice of the *Archetype*, realized for the salvation (regeneration in other words) of humanity. If it was the Man who actively manifested charity towards his neighbour, then in this we may see the Law of deliberate sacrifice of the doer's own interest for the benefit of others.

If the Sun bestows its life-giving emanations on us, we should realize in this the element of sacrifice on the side of the Sun for the good of the Earth and its dwellers.

From the first lessons, we know that occultism, and Hermetism in particular, considers all things as LIVING THINGS, and NOTHING AS DEAD. I am only repeating what has already been said when I state now that: THE UNITY OF LIFE IS THE BASIC TRUTH OF EVERY EXISTENCE. Without realizing this, one cannot even approach the mysteries, enclosed in the Tarot's system of Hermetism.

LESSON 53

Further analysis brings us to the following formulas:

Equation No. 61: $12 = 2 + 10$

The efforts of knowledge (2) dominate the *World's Mill* (10). Where is the sacrifice here? It is the plan of action by those few courageous individuals who, in one or more incarnations, have consciously sacrificed their joys of life, delights of the physical plane, and sometimes even a part of their mystical strivings, for work in laboratories and scientific premises, for the dry researches of the imperfect, illusory worldly science. They know that in the last act of their incarnations they will appear like Faust in Goethe's famous poem. Nevertheless, they consciously go towards all the ordeals, in order to bring to the evolving society of their brethren, some useful discoveries, no matter how imperfect these must appear to their own inner sight.

They believe that the binaries of earthly impressions and experiences, wisely directed by the firm hand of a man of knowledge, may even partially conquer the involutionary sphere of our planet's astral. Therefore, all their lives consist of sacrifice like: $2 + 10$.

Equation No. 62: $12 = 10 + 2$

Here others may differ in their conceptions of actions. They may say: our plan of a sacrifice is better. Science is an enemy of society; the World's Mill is a better friend. Consider as a true science (2) only one, whose conclusions are in accordance with the process of the Sphinx's Wheel. Let that Wheel teach us; do not let our insignificant planetary cells (human beings) fight the powerful astral current of the whole earthly organism. Let them surrender to its feverish manifestations during the time of its inner changes; let them take rest in the moments of static self-content-ment. Down with civilization and its delusion enforced by the pentagram-matic tactics of humanity towards natural needs. To live according to Nature is the only key to salvation. Sacrifice your dear traditions of generations, which try to prolong the fight for culture, for half-victories over the slavery of the elements. Sacrifice the conclusions, and you will become rulers of Lamed's open hand. Not that you will lift it, but you will be raised together with it!

You see, Tradition gives us both forms of interpretation of the Tarot's mysteries. It is up to you which you will accept.

Equation No. 63: $12 = 3 + 9$

Develop yourself metaphysically (3) and let this progress be the degree of your ability to use the lamp of Hermes Trismegistus (9), the coat of Apollonius of Tyana, and the sceptre of human cautiousness.

Let metaphysics signify Initiation, and realization of that Initiation in practical life. Do not be afraid to recast or transform your former initiatory systems. Sacrifice the old, dear methods, if you are suddenly able to see your triangle ש מ א (Aleph-Mem-Shin) in a new light, born from your perfected absolute logic.

Equation No. 64: $12 = 9 + 3$

Is it not better to hold firmly to the tradition of the transmisison within the Chain, and quietly to apply the injunctions of the wise past, waiting for new phases of our progressive metaphysical development, based on the creative number 'THREE'?

The ancient system of initiatory centres was perhaps sometimes a little clumsy, but it was certain. Let the same School (9) lead the generations to creative activities (3), growing with the flow of the necessary period of time.

Equation No. 65: $12 = 4 + 8$

Authority should be secured. Let it give us the laws (8). The great idea of hierarchy (4) may be sacrificed for Justice of manifestations.

Equation No. 66: $12 = 8 + 4$

Here is another conception. Let Justice (Law) (8) rule everything, if that Law is derived from the natural conditions of life in the given epoch. Let the beneficial authority of Law be supreme over established individual authorities.

Equation No. 67: $12 = 5 + 7$

This is the quintessential (5) transformation of individual means, as a result of that activity, that is the victory of the *subtle* over the *dense* (7). The great task called the formation of the *pentagrammatic will* may some-times require even the sacrifice of the great Law, claiming the necessity of the triumph of THREE over FOUR.

Equation No. 68: $12 = 7 + 5$

No! It may be the opposite. Let the starting point of the pentagram's formation in man, be the motto of creation in man of the knowledge of *forms ruled by the Spirit.* Let the individuality of such a creation be sacrificed for the sake of the *Sephira Netzah.*

Equation No. 69: $12 = 6 + 6$

Here we have a concentrated summary of the polemics seen in the preceding unfoldings of the Twelfth Arcanum.

Stanislas de Guaita very talentedly described the negative sides of certain quarrels in Chapter V of his famous book: *La Clef de la Magie Noire* (*A Key of Black Magic*). 6 against 6 is the fight in the realm of the understanding of the same arcanum through two separate individuals. The fight of two consciences not enlightened by the rays of the Unitarian Philosophy, and therefore not fully incarnate in their masters. The fight of two minds, filled with different relative 'truths'. The struggle of two intelligences, operating in different spheres of life. The fight of two intuitions, differently breaking up the same clichés.

Here we have rich material for deliberation and meditation. It is pretty tangled, and it is not at all easy to find an explanation of the sacrifices, which you can and should offer. But every occultist must seek them intently if he wants to make real and not imaginary progress, which he can take with him on the other side of the grave.

In Hermetic Tradition, related to the Twelfth Arcanum there are given other types of unfolding, that is multilateral ones such as $12 = 4 + 4 + 4$; $12 = 3 + 4 + 5$, or $12 = 2 + 3 + 7$, and so on. Even the type: $12 = 2 + 2 + 2 + 2 + 2 + 2$ is used.

It would take us too long if, in this book, we try to give all the possible combinations. The student who attentively followed the basic ones, as given in these lessons, will also be in a position to deal with all the others, if he may need to find some solution to his problems in this way.

I would again like to underline, that the task of operating the arcana, developing them into their components and interpreting them correctly is by no means an easy mental exercise. I shall probably be closer to the truth, if I simply say: the task needs great effort, if the results are to be as hoped for. Anyway, most eminent Hermetists and occultists have worked assiduously with these operations, and to them have ascribed much enlightenment and the solution of many difficult problems, which otherwise could not be resolved at all. Such results do not come easily nor to every one.

LESSON 54

There is another very important kind of meditation about the symbol of the Twelfth Arcanum, the sign of the *Duodenary.* Here I will give its most useful form used by advanced occultists. It is the MYSTICAL CROSS so famous among Hermetists (see Fig. 36).

In the Western Tradition (here I mean the remnants of the occult

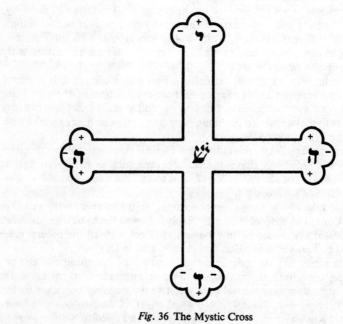

Fig. 36 The Mystic Cross

organizations mentioned in the lessons of Chapter XI, as well as some
secret circles of special study, which never act in public, and select their
members only after very intensive tests and experiences), meditations on the
theme of the Mystical Cross, as one of the most powerful of pentacles, are
an obligatory part of the work for all self-initiating, incarnate pentagrams.

The TEACHER draws this Cross on the forehead of a disciple when the
initiate goes to work independently in the world, and also as a sign of his
blessing for the pupil, on the latter's twelve thorny steps of earthly incarnations. It is taught in some secret Western Initiatory Centres, that usually
the accepted disciple still needs twelve more incarnations after his Initiation
by the Master, in order to attain LIBERATION or MASTERSHIP
for himself. Sometimes, when he so prefers it, the Master makes the sign
of this Cross with his hands raised above the head of the kneeling neophyte. To those who have read another of my books, *In Days of Great
Peace*, I would like to add, that in it, I mentioned the use of this kind of
blessing by a saintly Bishop for a young man, some forty years ago.
Neither that man nor another witness who was present, could then realize
why this apparently simple ceremony took longer time than seemed
necessary, and why the left hand of the Bishop performed some strange
movements under the broad Sign of the Cross, made by his right hand.
Now he knows.

The twelve convexities (three on each end of the Cross) symbolize these
stages. Now look attentively at Fig. 36. The vertical part of the Cross has,
in its upper extremity, the active ׳ (Yod), while in the lower, the less active
ן (Vau). Both are androgynous, possessing elements of activity as their
innate property.

The ends of the horizontal arm are marked by the passive signs of ה
(Hé); but the *right* end is more active than the left, because it is the *Second
Hé*, which is transformed into the Yod of the next cycle. Therefore, it bears
in itself the seed of the future activity, when the *First Hé*, as mother, can
give birth only to the androgynous child—Vau.

This Mystical Cross is a purely Kabbalistic pentacle. It gives priority
to the upper and right ends over the lower and left. To the vertical over
the horizontal. It establishes the superiority of the active principle over the
passive; of the subtle over the gross; all this happens, of course, through
the use of the elements of ה ו ה י (Yod-Hé-Vau-Hé, the Tetragrammaton).

But this was only the astral plane. We still have to analyse the twelve
convexities, transferring us into the realm of the Duodenary of the physical
plane. That is why in the centre of the Cross there is the sign of ש (Shin).
Now you will understand the enigma of that pentacle. It is now transformed into the REDEEMED CLICHÉ, ה ו ש ה י (Yod-Hé-Shin-
Vau-Hé), into the picture of Hermetic mastership over the world (ה ו ה י)
aiming at realization (ש), which means the UNAVOIDABLE LAW
OF SACRIFICE. No matter what the calibre is of that sacrifice: that
of the Messiah (as in the Scriptures), or human charity, or finally, of the
Sun for its planetary system.

The Twelfth Arcanum of the Tarot is the most beautiful and spiritual of
all. I would even say, the only PURELY SPIRITUAL ONE. It is

because the highest spiritual law is just that of SACRIFICE. There is nothing beyond it. True mystics know about this. For them the last chapters of St John's Gospel are an open book. They can experience the incomparable and inexpressible bliss when they understand, with all their being, the beauty and power of the Sacrifice performed by the SON OF MAN twenty centuries ago. Those who have experienced it are not afraid of anything that can happen to them in this world or another.

For the idea of sacrifice is a highly contagious one, although only more elevated souls are able to merge in it. All the disciples of Christ, except St John followed in His steps, leading to martyrdom. Moreover, they followed the Master's way with joy, according to His words: 'You will drink of My chalice and be baptized with My baptism.' Legion is the name of those who have been baptized by that severe, but most effective baptism of blood, as the Church tells us.

An occultist speaking to occultists would not try to conceal that hard, but most beautiful (at least for ripe souls) ultimate TRUTH OF SAC-RIFICE. The more you are advanced, the harder will be the Cross which you have to take on your shoulders, deliberately, and with that spiritual JOY, which dwarfs the most intensive suffering. It was probably so with the disciples of the Master Jesus. Some of us had the opportunity to see another Cross, taken by another Master, just a few years ago. I am speaking of the Great Indian Rishi Ramana. His sacrifice for us took the form of an excruciatingly painful sarcoma, which slowly killed his physical body for more than one year. Although the Rishi bore his cross without the slightest complaint or fear, some devotees were so moved by his example, that they wanted to take part in their Master's sacrifice, forgetting all fear and physical cowardice in the face of suffering, which is so common amongst contemporary average people.

I cannot speak here of the degree to which their prayers were fulfilled; it is purely the personal business of those affected.

The power of SACRIFICE is *supreme*. It is among those men, who sacrificed the MOST for their minor brethren, that arise the real rulers and transformers of our planetary lives. The greater the sacrifice, the greater is the authority and influence of the being, who has mastered the real form of spiritual realization and illumination. There was a MAN, who wanted only good and only light. And He was subjected to every form of human suffering.

His closest friends and disciples left Him alone in His most difficult and tragic hours, when He was anticipating His torture and death. One of them even betrayed Him into the hands of His reckless executioners.

He told us: 'I am the good shepherd. The good shepherd giveth his life for his sheep. But the hireling, and he that is not the shepherd, whose own the sheep are not seeth the wolf coming, and leaveth the sheep, and flieth, and the wolf catcheth, and scattereth the sheep.'

He was cruelly humiliated and ridiculed, beyond any measure. He was accused and condemned for crimes He never committed. Finally, when His last hour came, it was among miserable thieves, in agony on a devilish device, which was then the most shameful and contemptible form of capital punishment, inflicted only on the worst and most incorrigible of criminals.

He accepted all in the *spirit of sacrifice* which lived in Him. And the result? This MAN now rules over the most essential elements of life on this planet, the same which so cruelly repudiated Him almost two thousand years ago.

Sacrifice is the most guarded mystery of every *living* heart, no matter in which form or part of the universe. It was the doctrine of the true original, but few Rosicrucians whose very names are hardly known even to the most keen occult investigators and seekers. They preferred to remain unknown.

It was stated in that doctrine that: only a few chosen ones have been and are able to accept the supreme spiritual LAW of absolute sacrifice. Nevertheless, in every epoch there have been those luminous souls.

Sometimes a man, listening to the words which come from the realm of the ACTIVE SPIRIT, as is the case with the *fulfilment of sacrifice*, feels his heart caught in an inner movement, as if in an earthquake. From that moment onwards he is lost to the *relative and temporal*, but gains the eternal and absolute.

Through the supreme initiation of the LAW OF SACRIFICE all Wisdom is also attained. Who has sacrificed everything knows everything without effort and toil. Who has sacrificed everything has conquered LIFE, unlimited in time and space because he has sacrified all that is relative, over which rules the phantom of death.

'*He has trodden on Death by Death*' as is said in the Gospels. Now you may understand the mystery of these great words. The *Mystical Cross* of the Twelfth Arcanum solves all the questions of life, if you take this *Cross* on your shoulders as the Master taught us to do.

This symbol of sacrifice has a unique power of realization when applied with faith and a pure heart. You may get proof of this in your everyday life. When you think deeply about the *sublimeness of sacrifice*, that is, when you meditate about it in your heart's sanctuary, the world and men around you become changed and then you are able to SEE this fact, not only imagine it.

The reality of these words is supreme. A question might arise for an attentive student: 'Then is meditation about SACRIFICE the most fruitful and effective for us?'

It IS so, if you actually realize, feel, and understand all that has been quoted here from the inner teachings of the Knights Templar and their later successors—the first reintegrated Rosicrucians of the end of the fourteenth century.

Instead of ש (Shin) it is possible to put א (Aleph) in the middle of the Mystical Cross of the Twelfth Arcanum. Then the meaning of that pentacle becomes different. It would be transformed into the synthetic picture of the three planes of the universe. It can be said even further: into the picture of full understanding of these three planes. Do not let us listen to such a sentence without deeper deliberation about its meaning. Have we, normally speaking, any understanding of say even TWO planes (perhaps only physical and astral)? Does not our life usually pass only in the visible and tangible, lowest realm of physical matter? But there is so much for cognition apart from that unique low level, in which average human consciousnesses spend their incarnations.

The full UNDERSTANDING as mentioned above, is related to the eternal laws of Hermes Trismegistus, no matter which name or form they might take in our own time.

So, in the middle we have א (Aleph), the balanced mental monad. On the arms of the Cross (see Fig. 36) we have the great Law of the Tetragrammaton of astral creations (י ה ו ה). Further, in the protruding of the twelve convexities we see the reflection of the twelve signs of the Zodiac, that is a materialized, condensed manifestation of the same astral, as the physical plane. The last analysis of the Cross gives us the sum of the Kabbalistic elements of the Tetrade plus the sign of Aleph, that is: $10 + 5 + 6 + 5 + 1 = 27 = 9$. In other words, we obtain the arcanum of Initiation (9).

Meditations about every Kabbalistic interpretation of the Mystical Cross of the Twelfth Arcanum always lead us to useful and fruitful ideas on all corresponding sub-planes. Try it and see for yourself. It may be repeated again, that true understanding of this most mystical and spiritual arcanum of the whole construction of the Tarot requires a firm inner realization of:

(1) The *necessity of sacrifice* on the physical plane. Another conception is that:

(2) By progressive diving into the realm of continuous creation we must come to a final wall beyond which no materialistic illusion is possible any more. This means, that there *is a limit to materialistic condensation*. If we reach it, then we have to rebound from that last 'wall', so as to begin passing the sub-planes in the reversed direction.

He who will attentively read the Gospels of Christ will be able to assimilate the *first point of view*. The *second one* has been well elaborated by Buddhists.

In one way or another, we see that the complex called by us the 'human personality' appears in the Twelfth Arcanum only as a temporary guest. And a guest should behave himself well. He should not criticize the reception or the environment in which he finds himself; but remember that he also has his own home which he has to look after. He must know, that every unworthy deed outside his own home will be painfully reflected within it. In other words—which will help you to understand these similies—in our perishable physical shell we are clothed as in evening-dress; like jugglers we play with the gifts we get from our Malkuth, with these complexes of physical and physiological laws. But, if we are sufficiently evolved we will not lose sight of the blessed hour of our return to our own true home, the hour of our 'death', a picturesque symbolism of which we find in the Master's initiation in the Masonic Tradition.

About that great hour of the personality's entrance *into its rights of the purely astral life*, about the temporary stages between incarnations and about the closing period of that incarnation, we will learn from the next the Thirteenth Arcanum.

מ

Arcanum XIII
MORS
DEATH

נ

Mem –

Letter-
Mother

Permanentia in Essentia
Mors et Reincarnatio
Transmutatio Virium

CHAPTER XIII

ARCANUM XIII (מ MEM)

THE letter of the Thirteenth Arcanum is מ (Mem) and its numerical value is 40. This arcanum does not possess any corresponding astrological sign. The hieroglyph is a WOMAN, an intermediary in the process of the transformation of life. This is because it is just the woman who realizes for her child the transfer from the embryonic existence to life in the earthly atmosphere. A *woman* suggests the idea of birth and death, because she is the medium, conditioning the *birth* (1) and subsequently the *death* (2) of every incarnate being.

Both of these conceptions (1 and 2) when related to the Archetype give the arcanum its *first title*: IMMORTALITAS and PERMANENTIA in ESSENTIA (Immortality and permanency in the Essence).

The *second title*, on the plane of MAN, is quite logically: MORS et REINCARNATIO (Death and Reincarnation).

The *third*, in Nature, eternally regenerating itself and producing energy in manifold variations, will be: TRANSMUTATIO VIRIUM (Transmutation of Forces), as rightly used by the famous Helmholtz.

The card of the Thirteenth Arcanum shows us a traditional skeleton with a scythe. The meaning and significance of *Death*, being the transformer of the UNIQUE LIFE, refers to its multitude of forms.

The symbolical skeleton cuts off crowned and uncrowned heads alike, but immediately after these strokes, new hands and feet sprout from the soil like plants.

Death only apparently extinguishes something in the given plane, but actually Death transforms the values of that plane. It cannot be compared with the process of burning, say, banknotes without issuing new ones. Therefore, it can be rather compared to the process of recasting some coins to make others.

The scientific name of the Thirteenth Arcanum is 'MORS' (Death) and the vulgar one 'the Scythe'. In relation to the Archetype the arcanum gives us the image of the eternal PRESENT TIME, because the Archetype never dies. This was explained in the triangles of Fabre d'Olivet. Here the idea is a very dynamic one, as is the whole of the Thirteenth Arcanum, because all its attributes are *always present*: *birth* or *creation*, *decline* and *transformation*, *death* and *regeneration*, a new life in new forms. You may add, that there are 'Days and Nights of Brahma' as well as Pralaya.

I would answer, that the *cyclic rhythm* of life does not contradict these Eastern conceptions, which in another form is accepted by the High Hermetic Initiatory Tradition. A *large tree* once existed as a tiny seed, as seen by the consciousness of Man, who has been able to rise beyond the artificial conception of time.

And contradictions do not belong to the *nature of things*, but only to the shallowness of the mind, which perceives them from its limited point of view.

Meditation on the Thirteenth Arcanum *is a means* to make us grow above and beyond that shallowness.

Now I would like to extend my friendly advice to all who will study (and not merely read) this great arcanum of the Tarot. ITS IMPORTANCE CANNOT BE OVER-ESTIMATED. Everyone of you will have to face the mysteries connected with the knowledge of this arcanum, and likewise everyone must experience the *transformation* of his own forms.

What reasonable man would like to go deep into an unknown jungle, or travel through unknown territory without even a primitive map and compass? Certainly, if he cannot get these necessary things he may delay or even cancel the journey.

And what about the UNAVOIDABLE JOURNEY OF DEATH? Are you really prepared? Do you realize that KNOWLEDGE of death and its states is just as necessary and useful as the ability to read maps and use a compass? And that no misty theories, ideas or beliefs can replace acquaintance with the real processes connected with that of death and the ensuing states of consciousness and conditions? True occultists know about the terrible tragedies which happen 'on the other side' (that is after physical death) to those who depart from here without adequate knowledge or without any real protection from the side of a potent Egregor, to say nothing of assistance from a Perfect Being, a spiritual Master.

The fear of death is not so unreasonable as it seems to many shallow thinkers. Everything has its causes, and this applies to the shunning and fear of leaving this world, so deeply rooted in the present human race. Exceptions, of course, do not contradict this statement, but rather support it. There must be something which remains deep in the subconsciousness (or an aspect of consciousness beyond our everyday control) and which transmits the remnants of memories about a man's previous experiences of death. From the traditional Hermetic knowledge about death we may see that there is some reason in the ordinary man's attitude towards, what for him is a compulsory change of plane (death).

Look attentively at two particulars on the card of the Thirteenth Arcanum. Death is presented as an acting skeleton. But what actually is that skeleton from the symbolical point of view? Just what we consider as the most dense and least changeable part of our physical body. That, on which grow the remaining elements of the body.

The principle of death is closely connected with the beginning of the so-called 'permanent creation', and is bound by the chain of causality. We must die just because once we wanted to exist (as separate beings, of course), and this creates a truth of an almost mathematical character. This truth, logical and unchangeable, is under the care of *Saturn*, as are all implacable results of a chosen precursor. That is why there is a skeleton with a scythe on the talismans of Saturn; that is why in our everyday life we often use a skull and two crossed bones as the symbol for the motto '*Memento mori*' (remember about death . We are reminded in a ridiculous way about the necessity for the decomposition of our bodies by just *that, which has not yet had time to be utterly decomposed in other bodies,* but which is also certainly condemned to decay and fade away with time.

The completed card for death would be transformed into the picture of a new life, but the incomplete one, underlines that event which we call *death*. The crossed bones, this dimmed quaternary, *is the last call* of the creative *gnomes* directed to the subtle *salamanders;* the last threat of hampering the astrosome by the physical body because of the compulsory activity of NEPHESH, the *phantom*, whose purpose is the destruction of that body. It seems, as Tradition says, that the *bone* shouts to the personality-ego: 'You had a fulcrum on the Earth, in the form of your body, and therefore you were able to act magically. So now, as a retaliation, be bound with that fulcrum-body until you give back to Nature all the elements which you borrowed from it! You will have no fully free astral life. There will remain for you, just that little earthly anxiety, in the form of your physical remnants, not yet dissolved in the ocean of matter. You will not be able to pass immediately from the three-plane life to the two-plane one: for you must experience the transitional stage, calling it—DEATH!' That is what we see on the ominous card of the Thirteenth Arcanum, and some *deep thought* about it would not be without benefit for the student of Hermetism, who desires to introduce more awareness into not only his present temporary life, but also into the next stage of—death.

Now we may better see why humans so shun the thought of death. Perhaps they remember SOMETHING which makes them anxious before a repetition of the same troubles.

All this refers only to average, unawakened people, who are in no way connected with super-physical knowledge and interests. But they are in an overwhelming majority on this planet and in this epoch of Kali-Yuga.

For more advanced species of HOMO SAPIENS things are different, and Hermetism knows a lot about this. We are told, that the whole of the trouble lies in our attachment to earthly things, over which death reigns supreme. The transferring of our consciousness and strivings beyond material worlds cuts the strings with which births and deaths bind us so painfully.

I do not need to give many examples of this. You may find them in the lives of saints, advanced yogis, and occultists of spiritual pattern. All of them tried to make themselves as independent as they could of the physical bonds. You may find more examples about this in my former books, (*In Days of Great Peace, Concentration* and *Occultism and Spiritual Paths*).

The supreme victory over death (dissolution of the Thirteenth Arcanum of the Tarot, as learned Hermetists would say) comes together with the spiritualization of man, that is, with his ceasing to run after the material manifestations of life and with his efforts to reach the absolute existence independent of any form. Such existence is the opposite pole of the separate personal existence. Death has no power over the non-separated, eternally free consciousness, as the Scriptures so beautifully express it: '*O Death, where is thy sting?*' For a man, who is able to stop all his outer manifestations, such as thinking, feeling and interest in transient things, there is no death or birth any more.

The *Jivanmuktas* of Hindus, the *Liberated Ones* of Buddhism, the *Perfect Saints* of Christianity, are those who have raised themselves beyond the realm of all the arcana, REINTEGRATING themselves with the Primordial, unfallen Adam Kadmon-Protoplast.

In the following lessons I will explain more phenomena arising from the spiritual development of man, and his relation to the phenomenon of death and the ensuing states, but now we have to return to the further analysis of death's cliché, as given by the Hermetic Tradition.

Remember what we were told about the role of the *phantom* of the dead human being, and pass to a simple description of death's process, as it is conceived in one's former life. This means, of course, that I will try to speak in human language about things and events which do not belong any more to human life proper.

So, the body of a man became unable to fulfil its functions of life on the physical plane. This could happen as a result of different causes, such as:

(1) Man's pentagrammatic will (suicide).

(2) The will of another pentagram (death as a result of murder).

(3) Mixed causes, such as Nature's laws; conflict with the will-impulses of other men; man's own passions and other misbehaviour bringing about the exhausting of the vital force.

(4) Finally, death from old age, a slow or rapid extinguishing of life's flame in the body.

In all cases the astrosome tries to fight the dangerous factors, as his purpose is to retain the physical body for as long as possible. He sticks to it to the last in order to repair the leaks through which the prana (vital force) is escaping. This has its expression in a more or less painful agony, preceding death. Finally, the astrosome is compelled to leave and to begin a new, two-plane life also called the pause between two incarnations.

The passing away is now briefly described, but there are several phases of it. The theoretical and practical meaning of ALL these phases for an *initiate*, who desires to prepare himself and to help others to pass through these stages, are beyond the purpose of this work, so much so, that knowledge of most of these cannot be given to everyone in any book. The knowledge belongs to a special kind of transcendental magic, taught *only in higher initiatory circles, under the seal of complete silence.*

Anyway, this sort of knowledge is unnecessary for the average man, for there are assured—in the form of many Churches' practices—simple means, which greatly help the dying and the dead in their early astral experiences, in which lie the foremost difficulties and sufferings. I will speak about these in the next paragraphs. Now three questions have to be answered:

(1) Which methods do we have in order to know the process of death?

(2) What is the general character of an intelligent preparation for the passing to the other plane?

(3) What is the general system of assistance for a dying person, realized as recommended by the initiatory Teachings?

In answer to the FIRST question we can say that: we have the observations and experiences of sensitive persons, or those artificially induced to astral sensitivity (clairvoyance by suggestion or auto-suggestion) and can so investigate through the so-called SIXTH SENSE, the 'card of death' (or arcanum of death).

To the SECOND question: we have, for every true occultist, the most illuminating *Law of Analogy*, which allows us to learn of the transition from the embryonic life of the *foetus* to that in the earthly atmosphere, which is more material and accessible to the physical senses. Consequently, we have to seek and find the analogy of that process in the process of death. It is essential not only to investigate the picture of death, but also to KNOW on what *to concentrate the attention*, WHAT TO FORGET and what to separate one from another. Such instructions are given *exclusively by oral teaching*.

To the THIRD question: we have the Kabbalistic methods of learning the matter *a priori* with the help of the initiatory alphabet. These methods will lead to a number of subsequent questions, and so to a division of the phases belonging to the separate case under investigation. Naturally, to read the exposition of methods is only one small, first step into the realm of practical experience. Nevertheless, it has to be done in order that the next ones can follow.

To this classical and traditional Hermetic teaching I would like to add the idea of the Eastern methods related to Yoga. Our Eastern brethren try to develop individually the abilities of supersensory perception, and so *to see the whole thing personally*. The results of their investigations are usually in accordance with Western Tradition, only they may be expressed in different terminology. They do not like to speak much about the conditions after death, apart from what has already been said in their Holy Scriptures. The contemporary Spiritual Master, Sri Ramana Maharshi, refused even to speak about these things. He simply said, that ALL QUESTIONS WILL BE ANSWERED WHEN A MAN RAISES HIS CONSCIOUSNESS BEYOND THE LOWER LEVELS IN WHICH IT REMAINS FOR AVERAGE PEOPLE IN THIS EPOCH. He meant the Realization of the true *Self* or Atman, which in other words was defined as the 'Kingdom of God', the spiritual life beyond all veils of matter.

The way of Hermetism is different in its methods, as we can see from the previous lessons.

When, a quarter of a century ago, the matters of which you are now reading in this book were expounded as lectures, some people expressed their doubts about the processes which man undergoes after his physical death. Some simply said, that they did not believe in anything after death. The answer from the lecturer was, that the facts cannot be affected by anyone believing or disbelieving them. 'You cannot justify your wrong-doing by ignorance of the penal code. So you cannot escape anything after death by declaring yourself to be an agnostic when still physically alive.' I have mentioned this so as to underline the importance of preparation for the future events, as a logical necessity for every clearly thinking individual.

Of course, there are many kinds of this preparation. All religions give them to their faithful. A scientific, experimentai Hermetic way is only one of the many paths, discovered by seeking humanity. It has its attraction for many *strong minds* and *inflexible wills*, which want to know first rather than just to believe. They are perfectly justified in doing so.

LESSON 56

Persons investigating the process of death by means of their ability to use the 'sixth sense' (clairvoyance controllable by two other means of cognition as mentioned in Lesson 55) tell us, that the process, speaking exactly and from the occult point of view, BEGINS JUST AT THE MOMENT AT WHICH DOCTORS SAY THE PATIENT DIED. The stopping of the heart's functions and the initial cooling of the body are connected with the FIRST PHASE of the final exteriorization of the astrosome in man. Firstly is visible the separation of the astral from the legs. Then comes the exit of elements which once directed the functions of the torso. After that, the astral counterpart of the head begins to separate from the brain.

This is the usual picture as seen outwardly. But what happens to the man himself, to his consciousness in this early phase of death? Almost all occultists (Western and Eastern alike) agree, that in this period (in an average man) unconsciousness envelopes him, like a complete veil of blankness, thus hiding from him many unpleasant apparitions which otherwise could torture him even in those first hours spent in the new surroundings and conditions. This beneficial event is ascribed to highly evolved astral beings, who assist departing humans.

I have an idea, that in the case of the *two extremes*, that of a very good man (that is, a saint) and a very evil one, the initial unconsciousness does not appear: the *first* (the saint) is spiritually aware even before his death, and the loss of the body cannot dim anything for him. The *other* unfortunate one, in his desperate fight to retain the corpse as his vehicle, may not get any benefit from the assistance of good spirits, because of his refusal to yield to their efforts.

When separation of the astrosome is advanced to the point where the *whole* is apart from the corpse, and only a thread remains, issuing from the 'hole of Brahma' at the back of the skull, the *astral 'placenta'* (envelope of the newly-born child on the physical plane) leaves the body, together with the astral 'umbilical cord'. In this case the analogy with physical birth is quite striking. For an adult man this process of the 'astral birth' takes on the average about 48 hours. For children up to 7 years of age this takes only a few hours. But during that time, as well as in the following 7 to 40 days, the dying one must learn a lot, become acquainted with many things, and live through numerous phases of the conditions of the dawn of his new existence.

These conditions vary with every individual, so that it is impossible, without departing from truth, to give more exact explanations than will be found below. As were our lives, so will be our deaths: similar in one degree and different in another. Life and death are interdependent. This is the truth which every advanced occultist knows, and which is useful to assimilate, as an acceptable theory for every layman who is anxious about his supreme good, that is his EXISTENCE in all the conditions he may encounter in his wandering along the thorny path as a *separate* being. He chose this path himself, so only by his own effort can he return to the PARADISE of the WHOLE. I hope the meaning of all this is clear to the reader.

Anyway, from the beginning, the dying one, in the period immediately following the *physical agony* (there will be other ones later), has to live through the difficulties of the actual separation of his astral; these difficulties (you can also call them sufferings) are dependent upon his ability—when still incarnate—to separate, by means of meditation, his individuality from the perishable shell, which now lies immovable and lifeless. Here lies the cause why all occult teachings include MEDITATION as a condition for any progress for their followers. For this reason and for those who would be really interested and able to study deeper, I can recommend a book giving all the technicalities which may be of inestimable usefulness in the matter of developing true meditation. I am speaking about *Concentration* (published in London by G. Allen & Unwin Ltd, in New York by Harper Bros, and in West Germany by the 'Lebensweiser Verlag' in Budingen).

The sufferings of the dying one in that first phase of separation from his physical shell usually have the character of a painful PARTING from all that he considered to be his most essential reality of being. At this time are also destroyed all his complicated *illusions* so dear to him during his lifetime. Think deeper about this so as to realize its meaning: your home, surroundings, loved ones, possessions, attachments, desires, plans, and so on, all become non-existent and cannot be reached any more in any way. Only a dim but painful memory remains.

All this refers only to the *average man*, who during his lifetime did not prepare himself for the transition of death. There are no difficulties at all for real saints or spiritually advanced people, as well as learned occultists of the RIGHT (or *white*) Path, who practically anticipated their conditions after being disincarnated.

Now, when a man has been acquainted, at least to a certain degree, with the destruction of all his earthly illusions, and apparently agreed inwardly with the compulsory necessity of travelling into a world of new and entirely different impressions and conditions, he begins to feel *new difficulties*. He must now stand face to face with the astral world of the elementals. For the longer he lives in the astral, the more he is able 'to see' in it.

This means that his personality must now take account of (become conscious of) the *cliché*, related to the separation of the functions belonging to his *astrosome proper*, from the functions of his *phantom* (element NEPH-ESH), whose purpose is to destroy his former physical body and to give back to Nature all the elements which a man has 'vampirized' from the surrounding world from his embryonic life to the grave. This separation of the element RUAH (astrosome) from NEPHESH is the foremost problem of the physically dead person. The normal way for both elements is: Nephesh should occupy itself with the decomposition of the body, while Ruah analyses the forms in which were enclosed his impressions from the former incarnation as well as his voluntary actions during that period. What does it mean in simple language? Just that a man must render account to himself of all that he performed and learned in his last incarnation. In some religions it is emphatically called 'Individual Judgement', to distinguish it from the 'Last Judgement'.

Now you can see what is the true meaning of those 'hells and paradises' spoken of in some religions. The idea is a true one, for a man then *sees* in a true light, *what he did with his incarnation*. If he used it well, then he feels satisfaction and bliss. If he frustrated it, then he feels suffering or grief, painful regrets, and has a foretaste of the new and hard life. He does not know that his conditions are only temporary, and his 'hell' (if he belonged to less advanced and therefore rather evil human beings) is actually only a sort of *'purgatory'*.

Our *Hermetic Tradition* does not recognize any 'eternal hell', even for those who performed the apparent maximum of evil in their innumerable incarnations. For they 'will pay to the uttermost farthing' their karmic debts, as said the Great Teacher of humanity. But repayment in itself includes the idea and certainty of a debt-free state once they are paid in full, by suffering and experience.

When this analysis, compulsorily performed by the disincarnate *Ruah*, is finished (this may take—in our earthly time—from a few minutes, for saints, to hundreds of years for 'sinners'), then the man's consciousness —now more balanced and peaceful, after having passed through that astral 'purgatory'—must merge into contemplation of the planetary currents. These can repair his mistakes of the past and give him more opportunity to progress in the future incarnation, bringing him, in the proper time, that which is the aim of his descent into matter—THE WISDOM.

We may see, that the problems of *Nephesh* (the phantom) and *Ruah* present a kind of *Binary*, which must now be neutralized in the realm of the two-plane life, *by means of proper meditation*.

Tradition teaches us, that, unfortunately at the beginning, in the majority of cases, this meditation is immensely obstructed by the very astral environment. Imagine that our elementar has already fought his way through the layer of the ghastly, repulsive elementals, reminding him of the construction of his former physical body, even, as sometimes happens, showing him the actual loathsome state of his decomposing corpse. In other words, that he has already defined his phantom and from that ghost, has separated his problem proper as an individual.

But then the elementar enters the sphere of the elementals belonging to the lower organisms (animals, plants, minerals) which then begin to surround his cliché now dealing with the problem of perfecting the physical organs for his future incarnations.

These things are very vital for these lower elementals which are in a hurry to incarnate again. These little astral creatures and plants join themselves into CHAINS, in order to satisfy their problems in an Egregoric way. So the human elementar MUST become acquainted with how to pass quickly through these realms, which can teach him only some methods on how to make his senses and their organs in his future physical life more perfect.

So the elementar is now enriched with some knowledge about his new organs of cognition in the third plane (physical) and the fight for existence that awaits him. But this is not so important, the most essential thing is the elementar's *Hermetic perfectioning*, which alone can exercise a definite influence on his incarnations. Finally, *Ruah* feels itself separated from the old Nephesh, and is able to criticize itself. A temptation of the dark part of the universe is awaiting it, for now it has to face the *involutionary current* of the *Earth's astral*. Unhappy Ruah, having just consciously said 'Forgive me!' to its former pentagrammatic fulcrum now seems to find that the Earth is trying to invultuate it. This is because that astral current possesses the body of the planet as its point of support.

Some would say, that *Ruah can be pentagrammatically stronger than the planet*, and then its point of support would not frighten Ruah. It may be so truly, but only if the pentagram belongs to the Master, that is a fully developed human being. But if, in due time, the man did not purify his desires and attachments, and if his astral power is equal to that of the planet, then the latter will take a severe revenge on him, because of his participation in the activities of incarnate humanity on its surface. For you should know, that in Hermetic Tradition it is accepted that the being called Earth is not necessarily friendly to the tiny specks which inhabit its surface, and try to change it according to their own (that is, humanity's) aims and purposes.

So, the Earth may say to Ruah: 'You fought against me as a member of the great Chain of earthly humans who apparently chose pure aims and mottoes; but personally, you have not always been faithful to those aims. Sometimes you wanted evil things, and followed egoistic purposes. Now, when you are living on only two planes, my influence will attract you into the dark current of evil passions, according to the law of attraction between parallel currents. Therefore you will possibly establish yourself in them. Dense and dark clichés will compel you to forget your desire to separate Nephesh from Ruah, and you will create another phantom, still worse than was the old one. You will not reach the High School by contemplating clichés in the *middle astral*, in which exist opportunities for ascending to the יהשוה (Yod-Hé-Shin-Vau-Hé) and thereby saving the next incarnation. I hope that my school of egotism will tempt you, for I will teach you to taste

к*

the dark current of new combinations, which will bring you many egoistic delights. I will make peace with you, and instead of, for some time, going with face turned upwards, you will consciously fall down below.

So remain with me, do not pierce my current with your strivings and do not try to go into a far off region, where all planetary influences are completed.'

Woe to him who was not able to defeat the Great Serpent of the Planet, and to reach the Brass Serpent of the Redeemed Cliché! For he will reincarnate earlier, it is true, but for what purpose? *He will become a slave of incarnations as so often happens.*

But if you have been able to defeat the involutionary current, then you still have to sharpen your abilities of contemplation in the astral plane, in order to become a worthy student of that World's University, in which one receives plans for one's future redemptory deeds and pure intentions in the spirit of Absolute Truth.

So it happens to the dying and the dead. The question then arises: are all these particulars received exclusively through the use of the sixth sense (clairvoyance) by some persons who are able to use this sense? Of course, this method would be quite insufficient to give all information and theses about death, its phases and further fate of an elementar. Great assistance comes from a strong Kabbalah, which allows, through skilful application of its methods, penetration into the so-called mysteries of the life on the other side of the grave. For those who might be interested, I will only mention that intelligent and scientific kabbalization of the book of *Sepher Jezirah* and direct study of the vast commentaries on the book of *Zohar* give much explanation about death. Now, what actually do I mean by kabbalization of certain mystical books? JUST THE DISCOVERY OF THEIR HIDDEN CONTENTS. The authors knew a great deal and they wanted to transmit their wisdom to those, who might be able to appreciate and duly use the knowledge, deciphered from their treatises, Prophets and other advanced people put their revelations into kabbalistic form, and I believe, with very good reason. The naked truth when given to ignorant laymen, would make them mentally 'dizzy' and produce a lot of unwanted results, not to speak of the profanation of the initiatory books. No good would come from such an unwise revelation. ' . . . Neither cast ye your pearls before swine, lest perhaps they trample on them under their feet, and turning upon you, they tear you.' These words are the best explanation of the necessity to put mystical truths into some kind of a hard shell so that only the strong and wise can break through and so reach the kernel.

If he really wants to, every serious student is perfectly entitled to find for himself what I have just said; but he will have to sacrifice time and effort, in order to obtain the desired results, and so become an expert himself. However, if someone dares to criticize or deny the things *which he himself could never know, even approximately because of his own incompetence,* then such an attitude would be despised by every reasonable and honest man.

There was a time, when I had to learn Hebrew so as to be in a position to perform such studies as these, and I have never regretted the time and toil put into that endeavour. For one cannot properly understand even the visual meaning of the Tarot's cards, if he is not acquainted—at least to a certain degree—with the mysticism of the 22 letters of the alphabet, which we now call Hebrew.

But to return to our questions, the *third* practical means of studying the *arcanum of Death* is a personal exteriorization of one's astrosome. This exit in one's astral body must be made into the 'MIDDLE ASTRAL', that is into the sphere where there are more subtle currents and no obstacles from the side of the lower astral creatures, to impede the investigations. Such an endeavour in the middle astral *differs from the process of dying only in a few small particulars*.

Of course, only fairly advanced adepts of Hermetism are in a position to check and actively control all the three bases, which have been mentioned here, as being the foundation of the Hermetic knowledge about death and the subsequent states of man.

But the usefulness of this exposition is not limited to the compulsory personal experiencing of everything that has been said here. No, a certain amount of theoretical knowledge—especially if in us we find an inner conviction of its truthfulness—can be very helpful indeed on the other side of this physical life. There is a conclusive analogy: a traveller who has obtained maps and information about the character of the country he intends visiting will be in a much better position than one, who is compelled to make the same journey, but without any previous instruction.

LESSON 57

From the aforesaid there logically arise the questions:

(a) Technically, what should an average man do in order to avoid as many sufferings and mistakes as possible after his physical death?

(b) How can others help the dying and recently dead persons?

(c) What are the preparations for an adept of esoterism?

The best preparation for death is a WELL-SPENT LIFE. Good generates good, evil, evil. If you create good in your short period of a physical incarnation, then this good will go with you to the '*other side*', and you will be spared many of the unpleasant and terrifying experiences and visions of evil elementals and other inimical beings of the astral world. But there are also some direct technical means, which help those who are about to leave this world.

As I have already mentioned in another of my writings (*Occultism and Spiritual Paths*), the last thought which appears in the mind of a dying person is of overwhelming importance. If it is only a collection of confused and weak thoughts, they will be of little use. Unfortunately, this happens to the majority of people. They pass into the new and unknown life in a state of inner confusion and fear; but if a single thought dominates the mind, then it can act as a powerful magnet, attracting the man in a certain direction according to the qualities of that last thought.

Therefore, one should prepare such a last thought for oneself in advance, which will carry one through the whirlwinds and by-paths of the initial astral life.

What should such a thought be? Anything of an inspiring or sublime nature, which a man is able to create in his mind. But there are 'ready made' themes, which will serve best. It all depends upon the particular character of the person concerned. A religious will perhaps take the name of his spiritual ideal, like Christ, Buddha, a Saint, and so on, while a philosophically minded person may choose a wise sentence, a verse from his beloved spiritual or intellectual Master, or a maxim, and so on.

The lot will be best of those who were attached to a real Master, who loved him, revered, admired, and placed their whole hope in him. Such a Master, called on by his devotee in the last moment, will come to the dying one, and such a spiritual visit will have incalculable boons for the man. The Master will lead his devotee through all the treacherous regions in the astral world, shielding him from all attacks and malicious appearances, which provide so much suffering for not-so-saintly people after their deaths.

In our occult experiences many such cases are known, and there is no doubt of their authenticity.

On the other hand, for those who feel no special devotion, but who have reached a considerable degree of mind control in their earthly life, the Western Initiatory Tradition (Hermetism) recommends as the LAST THOUGHT, the intense MUTE meditation (or contemplation, if you prefer) of—I AM. Under the term 'MUTE' is understood the very idea, the core of the mental conception 'I AM', already being beyond these words in the consciousness of the occultist.

By adequate training and preparation in this kind of contemplation a *favourable cliché* will be created in the adept, which will take over the work of the mental and subconscious parts of 'I AM', beyond the sphere of the adept's mind, and will carry it securely through the usual period of unconsciousness which follows directly after the cessation of the blood's circulation in the vessels of the dead person, after his heart has ceased to supply fresh blood to the brain.

But, in this case, the man will be almost immediately 'resurrected' into the glorified, eternal 'I AM', into his new life, as a TWO-PLANE EVOLUTIONARY ELEMENTAR. This sublime method of discarding the physical body is also well known to the top representatives of the Hindu Advaita. When dying, the last Great Rishi of India (Sri Ramana Maharshi) was so absorbed into the illimitable SELF, which is the same eternal 'I AM', that he repeatedly affirmed, in a form understandable to those around him, the *absence of death for him*: '*I am not going away, I will remain here!*' To those who knew his teachings, it was clear that the Master spoke about the FINAL ABSORPTION OF THE MAN INTO THE SELF, which he also always identified with the 'I AM'.

At death, such a man, who, while still alive in his body was steadily absorbed into the SELF (Atman, Archetype), goes into the state of existence so well known to him. But even for men less advanced than the

Master, *the passing away under the right flag* of the Self is an inestimable advantage, as every true occultist will readily realize and accept.

For reference to the methods of inner development see my other books: *In Days of Great Peace, Concentration* and *Occultism and Spiritual Paths*.

From the other side, a religious act performed by a pious minister by the death-bed of a man also gives great relief to the departing human being. Especially Christian rites for the dying, which are based on deep knowledge and experience, being given to us by the saints of the early days after Christ, who were inspired by the potent influence of this Great Teacher of humanity. To those seriously interested in such an important question, as their departure—which is unavoidable—I recommend the reading of the corresponding breviaries for priests of the Catholic and Orthodox Churches containing the rituals and special prayers to prepare the dying person for his hard task after he leaves. There is neither room nor purpose to quote them here.

It is extremely important that the man departs with as much inner peace as possible. Therefore he should forgive all his imaginary and real enemies, and ask forgiveness (even mentally, if there is no other opportunity than that) from all whom he may have offended or harmed during his life. Apart from that, he must firmly realize, that for him, the material world is now becoming non-existent, like a dream which has passed away, and therefore is not worthy any more attachment. No thought about material business should dare to enter his consciousness, for such exercise an extremely morbid influence, and unnecessarily burden the departing man. That is why most religions, based on authority of a genuine Spiritual Master, always consider a sudden, unexpected death as a disaster for a human being. This is because there is then no time to make any preparation for departure, and no opportunity to reconcile man's moral and physical debts before entering the new life.

Christian tradition teaches that death without any repentance or receiving of the last sacraments is an *unholy one*, and it is a most ominous sign for the future.

From the foregoing explanations we can see that on this point—that is the necessity for reasonable preparation for death—the occult and religious traditions are in full agreement. Of course, methods and particulars of that preparation may be, and often are, apparently different, but the aim is always the same (see the foregoing paragraphs).

The SECOND question, *how can we help the dying and dead*?:

Occultism offers many magic practices which directly influence the astrosomes of the dying and the recently dead. I do not consider them very suitable for publication, because we have some which are much better and less dangerous (in the case of an inexperienced operator). By this I wish to say, that *theurgic* operations are the only recommendable ones, as they are much more useful and effective.

It is recommended to play some soft music repeatedly in the room where the body is lying. Especially, those melodies or songs which the dead person liked best. It has a very positive and soothing influence on him. Occultists usually leave instructions of this nature to their relations or other survivors.

Nowadays, it is easy to fulfil such a request because of the availability of recorded music. You know that sound is a powerful stimulant even in its reflection on the astral plane, so, the meaning of this passage should be clear to you, as a harmonizing agent for the astrosome of a newly departed brother.

The main weapon of theurgy is PRAYER. Not a blind and egoistic prayer, but an enlightened and elated effort of human consciousness, directed to a man's neighbour, and not for himself, and therefore extremely effective. Every occultist knows, that we pray our best when we pray for others. I will give some formulas, used in certain initiatory centres of Europe, together with some short rituals, which may be performed if there are appropriate conditions for them: otherwise, all that you will read now may be performed in the assisting person's mind, without pronunciation, if this is not suitable.

But if circumstances permit, proceed as follows:

(1) Burn some good incense in the room where there is the dying or already dead person. Bow to the four sides of the world. Then with utter concentration orally or mentally pronounce three times, 'Lifted be my prayer before Thee, O Lord, like this incense rising to the sky'. This will purify your mind. Do not forget to wear clean, fresh clothes and you should not have any money or pieces of metal in your pockets or on you.

(2) Now comes the actual action for the dying. Say this prayer seven times: 'And may it be forgiven to him (or her, *give the name*) all transgressions, sins and misdeeds, committed in word, thought or deed; with knowledge or without; of free will or under compulsion.' Tradition recommends that you bow to the east each time.

(3) The next prayer is: 'And may it be given to him to find that supreme rest in the Lord's blessed abode, where there are no maladies, no grief, no suffering or complaints; but only infinite life.' This is also said seven times.

(4) Then comes the final absolution: 'Grant him Eternal Peace O Lord, and may Thy perpetual Light enlighten him forever.' Also said seven times.

If properly performed, this short *theurgic* act will be of great benefit to the dead person. Pure and strong currents are created by it, and the elementar feels them like a soothing and reassuring factor, which is something which he so badly needs.

The third, and last point is: how should an adept of esoterism prepare *himself* for death? Because there are different requirements for an advanced person to those for laymen, as has already been mentioned in the two foregoing answers.

FIRSTLY, he must *never forget that death will come*. This memory is a part of his conscious life. He must always remember that this physical life is very short and impermanent, just as a Masonic master, in the midst of his initiation ceremony is reminded about the necessity of dying. If we will consider the whole of our incarnation as a sort of preparation for death, then the latter will be something with which we will become acquainted and not scared of. The student should here clearly realize, that on *this point*, my advice (according to Hermetic Tradition, which follows a strict pattern when speaking about occult practices) is directed to OCCULTISTS, and that nobody will give such advice to all and sundry. For that would only mislead people who are not prepared in order to understand esoteric doctrines, and they will think that occultism simply means just A LACK OF EVERY JOY IN LIFE something like a morbid and pessimistic, passive attitude, when the truth is just the OPPOSITE. With this warning, we may proceed further.

So an adept has to practise—by means of special meditations—the separation of his individuality (or astrosome) from its temporary material sheaths. He must realize that the life of the human 'I' is only clad in the physical plane's 'garments', but in reality it originates on and belongs to the astral plane. This is the alphabet of the preparation for an occultist, as was mentioned before. Under the term *'man's consciousness'* I do not mean a *theoretical acceptance* of the possibility of living on the astral plane, nor any *logical conviction* of independence of 'I' from the physical body. It would be insufficient, and give no realization.

But the conscious element (not always present in all men!) is something much more real. It is the ABILITY TO FEEL the separateness of the selfhood (entity) from the body; the realization that 'I' can very strongly manifest itself and perform self-analysis even in a very weak or sick body; that physical weakness can even be helpful in the development of that *consciousness*, no matter that it actually binds man in the realm of physical realization, but not in the realm of self-assertion and ethical understanding; that the fatherland of the 'I' (Self) is close to the planetary currents, but not to the physical conditions in which the body is created; that for our 'I' (some say 'soul') abidance in the body is rather a discomfort, for its organs are distasteful to a man, because they so imperfectly reflect the forms of the astrosome more permanent and uninterrupted in their creation.

The adept must gradually learn to prefer subtle things to gross ones; for example, the fluid state of matter more than the solid, gaseous more than the fluid, and radiant more than the gaseous.

One must feel, that *geometric form* is more alive and more co-related to our 'I' than the physical body. This is one of the secrets of the ability to separate the astrosome from the physical shell, and without the development of that 'feeling' no *deliberate exteriorization* IS possible.

By acquiring the habit of meditation in these directions, and supporting it through the steady studying of the classical books about the Kabbalah and High Magic, as well as closely co-operating with people working along the same lines, we can begin our systematic preparation for the process of exteriorization of our astrosome. In Hermetism the CONSCIOUS EXTERIORIZATION INTO THE ASTRAL is considered as the *first deciding step* to Reintegration.

From the aforesaid as well as from the following lessons the student will be able to realize, that this way *is not identical with the spiritual paths of attainment*, which operate on quite different principles, although they have an important common point. It is the negation of the importance of the body, and consequently, of the whole world of matter.

But the SPIRITUAL CONCEPTION rejects the astrosome as well as the gross *material body*, because of its impermanence, in spite of its comparatively much longer period of life than the *latter*. Hermetism knows about this, but being thoroughly realistic and logical, it says, that in the present epoch, purely spiritual conceptions are as good as inaccessible to the great majority of human beings, and therefore, impracticable. 'Those who are able to raise themselves into the realm where the Spirit reigns supreme, that is to reach REINTEGRATION as taught by the original Rosicrucians, do not need any more occult tricks or exercises.'

Here is the important point of the topmost teachings of Hermetism, which is common to the highest conceptions of Eastern Revelations, like pure Buddhism and Advaita-Vedanta. The same refers to the true Christian idea, as given particularly in St John's Gospel and Revelation.

But Christ said: 'IN MY FATHER'S HOUSE THERE ARE MANY MANSIONS.' And it can be added that as many ways lead to them.

Nevertheless, as exteriorization gives a man his first unshakable proofs about his true nature, so different from the physical body, it is a step which cannot be neglected.

LESSON 58

To resume about the preparation which may be made by an intelligent human being for death, we can say:

(1) A religious will expect assistance from the benefactory powers which act, according to his beliefs, in the world beyond our Earth (the astral plane of Hermetists). And this assistance will be given to him, according to the degree and sincerity of his faith. He may even see saints, angels, Christ, Buddha, Shiva and other deities, coming to him to *comfort and protect* him. We know from previous lessons that the dying and the dead actually need every assistance. There is nothing wrong in such an attitude, no matter how relative and even unreal, that is imaginary it may appear in the eyes of a learned occultist. But for a relative being, as are all average people, only the *relative* has any appeal and 'reality' for him.

(2) The attitude of an evolutionary occultist has already been sufficiently explained in these lessons of the Thirteenth Arcanum.

(3) For a true saint, a very advanced adept of Hermetism, or a yogi, all of whom have transcended the relative in themselves, death has quite a different meaning, corresponding to the FIRST title of the Thirteenth Arcanum. Now, *if you are one of these men*, the writer has nothing to teach you, for you KNOW, If you are NOT, the attitude of the above-mentioned highly evolved category of men would be of little meaning for you, being simply incomprehensible to a lower degree of consciousness in Man. So, in any case, it is useless to speak about this group of men. Anyway, the metaphysical parts of this arcanum tell about it symbolically.

(4) But what reasonable attitude towards the change of plane (the so-called death) can be expected from, and be recommended for an intellectual, non-believer in particular religious creeds, who is unacquainted with any occult tradition, and is not materialistically minded? To start with a wise saying of the famous French scientist, philosopher and saintly man (whom P. Sédir included among his 'Few Friends of God') may be useful.

Pascal says, that there is infinity before a man's birth, then a short flash of the physical, earthly life, and then death again opens the gate of Eternity. So he considers a human being as belonging rather to Eternity and Infinity, than to the limited short period of an incarnation. This idea is very comforting for a progressive intellectualist, although it seems to be too abstract for the practical Hermetic occult tradition. No matter, because anyway it gives a broad outlook on death, and creates a good basis for meditation for men of this category (4), who want to prepare themselves for death. So, their true hope and life is in Eternity, far beyond any planetary life and its attachments which, for common people, play just the major part in the fears and sufferings connected with the process of death. In such a meditation a man will consider death as a RETURN, not as a DEPARTURE, therein finding new inspiration and solace.

The next step for meditation would be to establish the conception of the FORMLESS life in us, at the same time also making us formless and unattached to any sense objects. This has been shown in Part III of my *Concentration*.

Forget the body, you are NOT it, and do not let its corpse affect you any more, neither now, theoretically, nor later, practically when the hour comes.

These two meditations, when duly mastered, will help to overcome the imaginary 'horror' of the destruction of our sick physical body, gradually (or suddenly) deformed by death and turning into a decomposing corpse. In our Hermetic language, we would say, that such an attitude will bring about the separation of our RUAH from that ominous shadow called NEPHESH, a separation so eagerly sought after by Kabbalists and other *white* occultists. You know what I mean, as it has been explained previously in this present course.

The ARCHETYPE (Ishvara and sometimes Atman in the Eastern Tradition) is far and above all exoteric creeds. Therefore, theoretically, the final RETURN (in Hermetic language—REINTEGRATION) can also be performed by men of type (4) as indicated in this lesson, although the occult tradition seems to consider such a path as exceptionally rare. But, how many true JNANI-Yogis were and are known in India?

(5) The last category is that of the involutionary 'black' occultists, also called 'brothers of the left path, or of the shadow', and their conscious or unconscious followers, the materialists, the almost soulless believers only in matter and the life in it. It is with a definite disgust that I have to mention this kind of Creation's 'refuse'.

They think that they 'know' something more than average humanity, but actually, their 'knowledge' has been anticipated in the Bible as 'stupidity in the eyes of God'. And their future? The fearsome, symbolical fiery sword (St John's *Revelation*) issuing from the mouth of the LAMB, who may return to the Earth to judge it, is prepared for just such debased beings.

Now we can pass on to practical occult exercises, leading to the exteriorization of the astrosome, performed deliberately and with full consciousness in the astral plane, as taught to us by Hermetism.

However, we should know that even the best of methods are meaningless if there is no one to perform them. This simply means that neither successful training for exteriorization of the astrosome, nor preparation for the final abandonment of the physical body (at death) can take place if we do not possess a certain degree of the ability to concentrate, which corresponds to the first three series of exercises as given in *Concentration*. This is the normal way open to everyone.

Of course, we know about cases where exteriorizations were performed by people who did not possess any considerable degree of concentration or will-power, but these are *exceptions*, due to other factors, which cannot easily be foreseen or explained, and which therefore are unpredictable. But scientific occultism does not occupy itself with them. If some Egregor or other astral powers sometimes choose to help certain individuals, that is their concern. Also, some advanced beings like Teachers, Saints or eminent white occultists are able to help dying persons, who have strong devotion to them even though they do not possess the qualities mentioned above as conditions for easy change of planes (death).

There is a question which is dear to many students who want to know what remains of the former earthly relationships after death, in other words, have we any hope of encountering our 'loved ones' on the other side of death?

Tradition teaches, that if men who were related in some ways during their earthly life die fairly close together in time, they have every opportunity of meeting and continuing, to a certain degree, their former relations on the astral plane, as elementars. Especially if they were strongly attracted to one another by love; nevertheless, even negative feelings may produce an encountering of elementars and therefore those who were filled with hatred instead of love, also have a chance of meeting their adversaries, in the life on the other side of the grave. Such meetings bring little of good for either elementar, for hatred may easily bring them to very unpleasant and harmful events, like 'fights', fear, jealousy, and so on.

The greater the difference in time between the deaths, the less likely is the chance of the elementars meeting.

The absolute limit is the *second death* of one of them. Then the new arrival will not find any astrosome of the other because the latter is already beyond the reach of all personal attractions, being unconscious in the lower sub-planes of the astral, in which the newcomer is abiding. We can paint for ourselves a true picture of the character of these relationships after physical death if we accept the traditional occult teaching, that *man is basically not changed by death*, which thereby transforms him into an elementar. His qualities remain, as well as his interests, attachments and aims. Only now they are manifested in a rather dimmed way, as we know that for ordinary people, the astral life is very much like a dream, lacking many elements of earthly reality for them.

So, happiness and suffering, cheerfulness and hostility, and so on are as common after death as they were before on the Earth. Therefore for an occultist, it is perfectly possible to foresee his future experiences after separating from the physical body, if not in 100 per cent. of course, then at least with great probability. Think for yourself: analyse your actual aims and strivings now, your relations with your fellow men, your attachments and dislikes, and you may know much of what is awaiting you after passing through that 'temporary judgement', which in this chapter about the Thirteenth Arcanum is described as the encountering with the astral serpent Nahash and all the consequences deriving from it.

Such an analysis is not easy, for one must take into consideration EVERYTHING, past and present alike, because we have to accept responsibility for everything, for all good and evil forces and currents which we have created. And human memory is often so defective from the occult point of view! We often like to 'forget' many things, while unduly emphasizing what we especially prefer. But, in the astral light there is *no loss of memory* and everything is inscribed into the clichés of our lives. We cannot escape this law.

All this refers to average, ordinary humans, that is those who are not too bad, but by no means saints, and who have mixed both noble and mean currents in their consciousness. But those who are more advanced, to say nothing of the *Reintegrated Ones*, pass through different experiences.

They do not contact any *Dark Cone* after death, nor are they affected by Nahash and its temptations, being directed into the higher regions of the astral world, similar to those of the Biblical paradise. Some of them, accepting the supreme sacrifice, return to the Earth, there to help their delayed brethren, to teach them, and to redeem their heavy karmas. Such are the *Masters*, who bring new light into the darkness of our Kali-Yuga epoch.

Incidentally, from the foregoing we may see the nonsense of the claims by some 'spiritualists', that they are able to communicate with men, who died hundreds of years ago. Such persons are beyond the reach of anyone on the Earth.

LESSON 59

The first steps to exteriorization are connected with physical training.

The main idea is: ALL EXERCISES WHICH RESULT IN THE SUBSIDING OF ANXIETY ABOUT THE NORMAL FUNC-TIONING OF SOME ORGAN OR OF A GROUP OF OR-GANS, OR ABOUT THE NORMAL EXCHANGE OF ELE-MENTS OF THE BODY WITH OUTER NATURE, GREATLY ASSIST THE FUTURE DIRECT EXERCISES, AIMED AT THE EXTERIORIZATION OF THE ASTROSOME. This is an axiom. See for yourself: what holds you in slavery to your body. Only your attachment to it, the fear of losing it, your desire 'to live in it' rather than in another, more ethereal form, say, on the astral plane. This *desire for the material separate existence* is the main obstacle for higher life. All the religions (true ones, of course, that is those founded by true Initiates), occult systems of philosophy, yogas, mystical revelations, briefly, everything which attempts to raise the present status of materialistic humanity and extract it from the Kali-Yuga, speak about one and the same thing, as expressed above in capital letters.

How can you perform exteriorization, if even in these comparatively short lapses of time you are unable to cease to prefer the material bodily existence above all else?

I hope these sentences will help you to realize the lines along which are made the preparation for the first conscious travel into a higher world. So we can proceed.

Among the exercises (physical ones) recommended as preparation are:

(1) Exercises for holding the breath (Hatha and Raja Yoga exercises).

(2) Deliberately changing the rate of the pulse of heart beats (this is closely connected with (1)).

(3) Making some parts of the body insensible to outer influences by the effort of your will (Prana exercises of Indian occultists).

(4) The ability to abstain from sleep, and the ability to sleep according to one's own will.

(5) The ability only to hear without touching or seeing, the ability to receive only visual impressions ignoring acoustic ones.

(6) To receive through the organs of sense only a definite series of impressions, for example: to hear the voice of *only one man*; to see objects of a previously *chosen colour or form*, and so on.

Here, quoting these traditional principles, I would like to add, that all these 'wonderful' abilities and exercises which are apparently too difficult for many of us, have ONLY ONE SOURCE: the ability of CON-CENTRATION, which is parallel to WILL-POWER in man. Without it no one can perform an exteriorization into the astral which will be normal and harmless for the physical body. I am not speaking here about artificial exteriorizations by use of drugs or fumes which are not recommended by classical occultism.

Exteriorizations, deliberate or spontaneous, can be realized *only in the lethargic or cataleptic* state of the physical body. I hope that I do not need to explain, that the ability to leave the body and to travel in the higher vehicle—as is the case in astral exteriorization—is not any *peak* or *aim* in itself for a serious and intelligent occultist. It is only a means to prove something which otherwise cannot be proved.

Nevertheless, no deliberate or involuntary exteriorization is sufficient. What is deciding and really helpful to a man is HIS ABILITY TO PERFORM THE OPERATION. AND TO BE CONSCIOUS

OF HIMSELF DURING IT, WITHOUT MIXING ANY
ELEMENTS IN IT, WHICH MAY BE DIFFICULT TO SEP-
ARATE FROM THE WORLD OF PHYSICAL REALIZA-
TIONS. This is the main idea and *it alone can justify* the whole endeavour.

I am obliged to add here, that the spiritual state of human consciousness
—now called in Eastern style—*Samadhi*—gives infinitely more than the
transfer of the consciousness into the next-door world (the astral), for
Samadhi takes a man beyond the reach of material planes and their conditions. But, in spite of so many books (good and bad ones) written and
published during the last 50 years, about that mysterious and so coveted
Samadhi, the numbers of those chosen ones who really attained this lofty
state is infinitesimal. Nevertheless, if we attentively study the literature
concerned, we will see that for these spiritual flights the pre-conditions are
just the same as for exteriorization, at least, in the first stages of preparation.
That is why, before writing this book, I preceded it by two others, in which
I spoke much about that immortal consciousness in man (Samadhi), and
about the *cardinal means for reaching it.*

Coming back to the exercises leading to exteriorization, I am quoting
the traditional ones most widely experimented with, which are recognized
as giving insight into the realm of death and its phases, thereby giving the
possibility of cognition of that realm as well as realization of the necessity
and normality of death.

These exercises can be grouped differently, and I would not like anyone to
follow their sequence, as given here, without some forethought. For different
individuals the sequences may be different. You may be compelled to
extend some of the exercises, and cut others to the minimum, in the event,
for example, that you have already successfully studied concentration, as
well as Hatha Yoga. Apart from that, we all have different physical bodies
and astrosomes, requiring various treatment.

There is one very important pre-condition for the exercises. It is a
'MUST' for everyone seriously engaged in the process of voluntary
exteriorization, and it is also a very welcome and useful practice for every
occultist and even layman, willing to live his life better and more reasonably.

It is, that a certain *disengagement* between the physical body and the
astrosome is required for the successful performance of exteriorization
exercises. What does this mean? Only practical examples will serve best as
an explanation. When you are performing some strenuous task, you are
also usually putting into it a certain amount of nerve-force or effort. We
then say, that 'parts of your astrosome are participating in your physical
action'. This is *undesirable* from many points of view, and should gradually
be stopped. How can this be done? By the effort of a well-directed will,
assisted by trained (to a certain degree) imaginative power, which is, as you
know from previous lessons, a constructive power in the astral and mental
planes. Man has no means for exercising his influence on these planes,
other than by *will and imagination.* All other means, about which occult
manuals speak, are only supplementary, and points of support for the same

two cardinal factors. They are NOT essential and can be omitted, so I will not mention them here.

So, begin with the simplest things. For example, try to dig hard soil in your garden. While performing the movements and feeling the strain on your hands and body, imagine yourself *as if looking from aside* at your working limbs and torso. In imagination stand *behind*, approximately one to three feet away, and SEE how your physical 'I' is toiling, watch it with an indulgent, even slightly INDIFFERENT smile. Of course, the same feelings must accompany this; but if you produce such a smile, the *feelings of indulgence and indifference will come easily*. A short meditation may be used as a mental support for this operation by thinking about the relative unimportance of that physical work, and that the performer *is only your animal counterpart*, your fleshy case, which is your LOWER and not higher part, and so on. Gradually you will reach the secret of that '*smile*', which *actually creates the necessary astral currents diverting the astrosome from participation in the work*, which can and should be done better without that participation. But, in the beginning, do not attempt to perform that exercise with any COMPLICATED work, or you may spoil the whole endeavour. Only the simplest things for a start. Next, try to separate *yourself* (of course, it will be your astrosome) when walking on a hill, or running for a short distance. In both cases you will see that the work of your physical machine goes better, your breath is not so laboured by the effort, and your heart (especially after running) works more quietly and is not so overburdened as before.

I knew some runners, who had been instructed by an occultist friend, about the techniques (as given here) of '*separation*' in imagination from the running body, and who achieved very good results in their training and races alike. The body worked longer with much less fatigue and strain, and their nerves were less affected by comparison with those who were 'not separated' from their bodily mechanism. Naturally, no occult reasons were given to them, and no 'astrosome' was mentioned.

An intelligent student will gradually extend the 'separation' to more and more kinds of work, thereby prolonging his life and efficiency on the physical plane, quite apart from the valuable occult ability, which he will most appreciate when performing the exercises of exteriorization, and finally, leaving his body according to the law of the Thirteenth Arcanum.

It is the peculiar 'feeling' created when you do 'separate' from your working body which counts. It cannot be explained more exactly, for there are no words for it in human language, which operates only for certain categories of experiences and ideas. How can that which has not yet been experienced by the creators of language be defined, like say, the activity of smoking, or the feeling of thirst, fatigue, well-being, and so on?

I have personal appreciation of the value of this exercise, otherwise I would not recommend it to my readers.

I am no longer a young man, but when sometimes I need to walk very quickly or perform a speedy movement, which can easily produce fatigue, I always use that little (but extremely useful) occult trick, and can perform twice as well and without involving the heart and nerves very much.

FIRST GROUP OF EXERCISES

To develop the abilities of:

(a) Tiring the physical organs *without yielding to their reaction*.

(b) Resisting one's physical desires and even natural needs.

(c) Creating disappointment in physical delights—by one's own effort of will—*just at the moment* of experiencing those delights.

(d) Evoking of those delights without experiencing them through the physical organs.

(e) Separating of attributes which belong to physical bodies, from their astral counterparts. Example: look at a cube and be conscious only of its geometrical form, ignoring all other impressions, such as colour, type of material, and so on.

I hardly need to mention, that this *Group of Exercises* strives directly for the creation of a CONSCIOUS PENTAGRAM in Man, that is to the definite formation of the quality which has to be created.

SECOND GROUP OF EXERCISES

(a) Meditate on happenings which we suppose will take place *far away in time and space*.

(b) Meditate on the details of actions, about which we are able to form only a general idea, created by the incomplete data given by one of our organs of sense. For example: From afar I see men chopping wood, and then proceed to meditate about, what for me are, the invisible movements of their hands and their axes, and so on.

(c) Meditate about imaginary things and events. The best will be to exercise with imaginary journeys. They must be visualized with all particulars, especially as regards our movements (including hands, legs, seeing of objects, and so on).

(d) Meditate with some grief about the other, lost, but more free life, in which we were not hampered by time or space.

These exercises are best performed in the following manner: sitting by a window, or better still, lying on grass on a warm, quiet summer evening, looking attentively at the sky, and thinking about time and space, filling ourselves with contempt for them, as well as for our own body, whose comfortable position prevents it from yielding to impressions (from outside), which could distract our meditation.

You see that exercises of the *second* group are directed to the creation in man, of contempt for the third (physical) plane. In the *first* two exercises of this group we were concentrated on contempt for the habit (also method) of experimentation with our organs of sense. In the *third* exercise we try to reject space, and in the *fourth*, we discard time itself.

THIRD GROUP OF EXERCISES

(a) Exercises in telepathy, that is transmission to a distant person of geometrical figures, emotional moods, even ideas. More will be heard of telepathy in the Fifteenth Arcanum. Here we have to be satisfied to know that telepathy is just an astral communion with another man, and therefore scientifically speaking, it is a particular case of exteriorization of some single astral ganglions.

(b) Monoideism, concentration on the desire to see in dream certain definite forms. This method is simply a frequent remembering of a thing in its selected form, in the time of our daily and evening meditations. We then give priority to that thing or idea, placing it before all other themes that interest us.

If, for example, by day, you tell yourself many times: 'I am concentrating myself in order to see this thing in dream; to obtain an answer to a given question; to realize the mechanism of a certain process; to exteriorize myself in order to enter into communication with some person or entity; AND I CONSIDER THIS AS THE MOST IMPORTANT THING UNTIL MY DESIRE IS FULFILLED.' This is the usual and practical pattern.

(c) Auto-suggestion about the ability to exteriorize as performed in one of the ways indicated in the chapter of this book dealing with the Fifth Arcanum.

(d) An elementary theurgic operation, in the form of a simple, conscious and ardent prayer to be granted the ability of exteriorization.

(e) Asking assistance of a powerful Egregor.

(f) By an effort of will to create in our bodies a state of progressive catalepsy, starting from the legs. When we come to the heart, exteriorization becomes possible, if it was seriously prepared by the meditation given above. Many have tried and successfully performed the exteriorization by auto-suggestion, which first exteriorizes the astral of feet, legs, and later of the abdomen, until the solar plexus is reached, which results in the astral exit.

Here I again wish to add some experienced practical hints. It is desirable, before the beginning of the actual exercises, which may end in real exteriorization, to perform the breathing exercises, as given in Lesson 20, for a long time. It is now well known, that prolonged breathing exercises may produce partial or full stiffness or catalepsy of the body. And this is one of the means for exteriorization. Massaging the solar plexus by means of these exercises the final exteriorization may be obtained, as was the case with me, when I was still interested in these things. Rhythmical breathing brought results after being performed for an hour or more. Of course, the concentrated imagination and effort to separate from the body, lying immobilized in a horizontal position on a couch were also factors which should not be forgotten. The meditation on the Pentagram of realization

ה ו ש ה י (Yod-Hé-Shin-Vau-Hé) which was all the time before my eyes formed—according to the teachings received at that time—an introductory principle for the new, astral surroundings. So far, in Hermetic circles, it is considered to be one of the best.

(g) Attempts to use narcotic drugs in order to evoke half lethargic states cannot be recommended, as they do not appear in the means indicated by the Great Arcanum of Magic. Sulphuric ether in the form of an inhalation, or taken in water or spirits has been used by some occultists, as it does not create a habit and leaves less after-effects; but like all drugs, it cannot bring about the full and conscious exteriorization.

(h) Meditation about a picture or form, which once produced exteriorization in a person. This is simply calculation on the force of habit to exteriorize in some definite astral conditions. It does not give much chance in general.

(i) A repetition of exteriorization on the physical plane in conditions, which once resulted in a spontaneous or even deliberate exteriorization, which means a habit of the physical body to set the astrosome free under some circumstances. For example, if some day you were exteriorized in your dreams after being very tired by a long walk, then again try to become tired, this time as an exercise and concentrate on the desire to perform the astral exit before falling asleep.

(j) Asking another person to suggest hypnotically or magnetically to you the ability to exteriorize.

(k) Presence in the chain of persons who arranged a magic seance. This method is suitable for mediumistic individuals, who have already experienced the influence of the chain on themselves in the form of exteriorization of their astrosomes.

These exercises and tests of the *third* group are dependent upon the results of the exercises given in the two former groups. I am not speaking here about the traditional use of definite *setrams* or *mantrams*, because the use of setrams corresponds to the points (d) or (h) and mantrams to those of (d) or (e). By intelligently and persistently combining exercises like those given in these three groups, one will finally come to deliberate exteriorization at the moment chosen, or a spontaneous one, when he does not expect it. By this process, if the person exteriorized acquires the ability of concentrated and active observation of what happens to him, he will clearly feel the following:

Firstly, knowledge that the process is being performed in which the individuality is separated from the body.

Secondly, that man sees (or, at least, feels by his 'sixth sense') his body (like a corpse) as something separate and not included in his 'I'.

Thirdly, the person exteriorized is able to be conscious of the *astral umbilical thread*, that is something which binds the individuality, then separated from its body, with the element still active in the vital functions of that body. Then the *second* element is called the 'astral placenta'.

LESSON 60

When we return to the physical plane and the body, we begin to analyse, in a visual form, the impressions received in the astral; therefore we can confirm that we saw the *umbilical thread* in the astral, connecting us with the body in the vicinity of the solar plexus and not with the 'Hole of Brahma' as in the case of physical death.

An attentive adept, performing exteriorization, first becomes aware of the position of his physical body and the umbilical tie. Then he perceives the astrosomes of the objects surrounding his body. Later, he sees the realm of elementals, which have been described as being pretty cumbersome and even revolting creatures.

Next comes the cognition of the *animal elementars*, working on the perfectioning of their organs in their incarnations that are to follow. This sphere is apparently not as repulsive, but it still has very little of aesthetic appeal, because the improvement of organs does not reflect any astral harmony, but only the future forms in the physical world. Thus it cannot interest and satisfy the individual who has tuned himself rather contemptuously towards the physical plane, as is the case with our adept.

Now comes the encounter with the powerful involutionary current of the Earth's astrosome. Properly speaking, if the preparation for exteriorization was correct and the experimenting person wise enough, the fight with this current should not be too difficult. But, as so often happens, the disciple slights the details of egoistic strivings, even before he is able to slight and despise the whole of their synthesis. How often the child of the planet realizes and understands its individuality, yet cannot apply the means offered by the knowledge gained, in order to renounce the desire to be occupied with the lower forms and currents of life of that individuality.

Therefore it may be quite hard to dispose of all temptations, even when theoretically knowing of what imperfect and illusory materials they are made.

Nevertheless, if a man cannot withstand the fight with the involutionary temptations and currents of the planet (in the physical world this is equal to a lack of ability to withstand material temptations and passions), the currents pull him into the *Dark Cone of the Earth* (physically corresponding to the Earth's shadow), where he must now analyse and criticize his own imperfections *separately*, one by one, because he sees his impotency to conquer and reject their synthesis.

These impressions are extremely unpleasant and morbid, resulting as a consequence—after the exteriorization—in a long period in which he lacks faith in himself (a very negative thing for an occultist), misanthropy, and melancholy moods, often transformed into anger, akin to the most unfortunate and unwise decision to turn his personality to the service of INVOLUTIONARY aims.

In such a case, we can say, that the personality has made peace with the *Dark Cone*, which actually is similar to a dunghill or dust-bin for the planetary astral. Religion sometimes calls this temporary hell 'purgatory'.

Actually, the idea of purgatory is, in the eyes of a learned occultist, much more reasonable than the unreal conception of the 'eternal' hell, which means nothing less than eternal torments, which of course do not and cannot exist.

Here we may see, how the churches which have not completely lost the *very important element of hierarchy and apostolic succession* are much closer to the truth, known to all Hermetic occult investigators. That is why some parts of the Catholic or Orthodox Masses are included in the theurgic operations of the highest degree, and recognized as very effective kinds of prayers and invocations; *but none* of the rituals or worship derived from the more 'man-made' and lay sectarian organizations are used.

However, let us abandon the unpleasant case of *falling into the Dark Cone* and suppose that we were able to withstand the temptations and lies of the ASTRAL SERPENT (Nahash) and conquer it with our purified and thereby irresistible will-power. Then we are allowed to enter into the FREE MIDDLE ASTRAL of our solar system. There we will see all the planetary currents in their various combinations. Here one may realize the principle of HARMONY, for which our personality should strive. Here it will see what is lacking in it in order to realize that principle of harmony in itself. It will see what is still one-sided in us, and what is completely absent. It is the *beginning of the planning* for those future constructions (forms of incarnation) which will serve as the fulcrums for improvement of our disharmonies, through the Hermetic Action. All that has been said in this lesson about the consequences of the successful ability to exteriorize into the astral plane should be thought over, understood and memorized, if the student is to derive some help from it, no matter whether in his voluntary exteriorization, or in the compulsory one, which we call— *death*. There is a means to control the progress made by the newly-initiated occultist. It is his dreams. If they become more reasonable, reflecting his *controlled* activities of the waking state more perfectly, then we can say, that his study has started to yield fruit. If we continue our studies in 'dreams', which are actually the astral life of a man living on the physical plane, we will do the same after our death, instead of committing different stupid (but unfortunately, so common) activities, like those of falling into the *Dark Cone*, and so on.

How far can one go in the astral plane, in order to satisfy one's curiosity of after-death travels and happenings? I can only quote here, the saying of some schools close to the *true Rosicrucian Initiation*: 'The adept, fervently and sincerely trying to know these mysteries, may be able—by way of his astral initiation—to reach the THRESHOLD OF THE SECOND DEATH.'

What is that SECOND death? In order to give you a useful answer, I would like to recommend you to a careful analysis of the ninefold construction of man. We are, as normal men (I am not referring here to the Masters, Great Teachers and Messiahs), three-plane beings as you surely know. Now, according to the *Law of Reflections*, each plane also has its representatives on all the other planes. Therefore, the human Self (or consciousness) will take the following shape:

(1) Mental in the Mental
(2) Astral in the Mental
(3) Reflection of the Physical in the Mental
(4) Mental in the Astral
(5) Astral in the Astral
(6) Reflection of the Physical in the Astral
(7) Reflection of the Mental in the Physical
(8) Reflection of the Astral in the Physical
(9) Physical in itself

This is what *a priori*, a logically constructed analysis of the question gives us. But practically, we are not in a position to discriminate—through our 'sixth sense'—between all of the nine elements. For example, the reflection of the physical in the astral may be hard to differentiate from the reflection of the astral in the physical. This is because of the imperfections connected with that superphysical, but by no means highest sense.

Similarly, it is difficult to differentiate the reflection of the physical in the mental, from that of the mental in the physical. This happens, as *Tradition says*, because of the unsatisfactory means of expression of our normal functions of logic.

As a consequence, the trained adept-investigator will distinguish practically only seven elements in man's constitution:

(1) Mental in the Mental
(2) Astral in the Mental
(3) Combination of the Physical with the Mental
(4) Mental in the Astral
(5) Astral in the Astral
(6) Combination of the Physical with the Astral
(7) Physical in itself

In the incarnate man, these seven elements should be understood as being bound together between themselves. When the SEVENTH element is used and cannot any longer serve as a fulcrum for the six higher elements, we call it the FIRST DEATH. It is the breaking of the chain at its sixth element or link. The *seventh element* (that is the body) is transformed into the corpse, and the *sixth* into its (the corpse's) phantom or 'double'. The five higher elements learn many things in the astral (like those described in former lessons). They work again, with the help of the funnelled vortexes (currents) belonging to the seeds of the sixth and seventh elements, that is they are pulled in once more, to again die their FIRST death, and so on, until *their fifth element becomes so harmonious* that they are no longer subject to these unpleasant activities (return to the vortexes, and so on). In these words have been expressed the secrets of the FIRST death, as they are for an average man.

Because the HARMONIZED Whole (the remnants of the five elements) is able to rule over itself, as is every androgynous principle, this Whole is in a position not to yield to the downward attraction.

Therefore, the life of the elementar is now reduced not only to the planning of the future incarnation, but to the subtilizing of the *fifth* element through the influence of the *fourth*. But in creating the forms (fifth element), making them every time more ideal (fourth element), we will reach the state where the possibility of passing separately into the physical becomes impossible. The *third* element cannot live in the society of the subtle *fourth* and *fifth* any more. Therefore, when the elementar has ceased to prepare itself for the new physical life, the *third* element begins to grow vapid and to fade away. And this natural fading of the *third* element (which is, of course, a 'combination of the physical with the mental') leads to the SECOND DEATH of the elementar. We can see the Law of Analogy at work here as, in this new process, the corpse will be the *fifth* element with the *fourth* as its phantom.

Those who want to clearly understand this strange process of the *second death*, may use an example from the history of the arts, where in some cases the role of the corpse is presented as being in quite a harmonious style, and its phantom, the chief idea behind that style.

This new, almost one-plane entity composed of element 1 (Mental in the Mental) plus element 2 (Astral in the Mental) will be a pole of the future androgynous cell of the reintegrated *Adam-Protoplast*. I speak about the 'pole' of the cell and not the CELL itself, for in order to create an androgynous cell, our entity must wait for the *second death* of its *sister-soul*, if the union of both has not already occurred in the astral world, which is often the fact. Indeed, some Hermetists do not accept any possibility of the separate *second death* of a male or female soul.

So far, the imagination of the harmonious state of the fifth element can hardly be considered as a mono-sexual one.

LESSON 61

We should not believe, that the essence of self-preparation for death is inseparable from the ability to use the mechanism of exteriorization. The importance lies, not in the fact of perceiving everything through the 'sixth sense', but in *knowing* (*or believing*) that beyond the grave we have to expect certain stages of transition into the new life.

You must know, that an ardent FAITH is easily transformed into KNOWLEDGE. This is one of the most mystical axioms of Hermetism, but it CAN be realized, provided enough effort is put into the search and analysis.

For the knowledge of the sphere of astrosomes, which belong to elementals leads to full recognition of our former slavery in the realm of the *four elements*. Acquaintance with the sub-plane of the organic improvement of animal and plant elementars brings the clear awareness of the future imprisonment of the same elements in the course of the next incarnation.

The FIGHT WITH THE ASTRAL SERPENT is none other than development of knowledge, that one must sooner or later separate himself from egotism, dictated to us by the conditions of life on the planets. Contemplation of the clichés in the MIDDLE ASTRAL is actually recognition of the necessity of one's harmonious self-improvement. WHOEVER BELIEVES IN THE ABOVE—NOT MERELY IN WORDS, BUT IN THE DEPTHS OF HIS HEART— WILL ALWAYS BE ABLE, DURING HIS LIFETIME, TO ESTABLISH A PERMANENT CONNECTION WITH ONE OF THE POWERFUL EVOLUTIONARY EGREGORS, who will direct him through all stages and changes, and will set him free from the strangling rings of NAHASH, the Astral Serpent.

So we may say: to BELIEVE and to PRAY, is a great help in self-preparation for dying.

I have already spoken briefly in Lesson 57 about the help which can be granted to a dying or dead person, and gave some theurgic means for that purpose. Now come more extensive explanations and advice on how a knowing and believing man can make the complicated process of dying easier for his neighbour. The assistance can be triple: we can TEACH, EDUCATE or SUPPORT.

If you have to deal with a person who has full confidence in you, then simply repeat to him or her, what has been told to you in the foregoing lessons. It is quite possible that through the process of long meditations about such matters the person will make the orientation in experiences at the hour of death much easier for him or herself. The same applies to everyone who will sacrifice the time and effort as told above. *Remember, that most sufferings which come to human beings in their last hours, are due to just ignorance and fear* of what may happen and what actually does happen with the change of planes, as we call the passing away from this Earth. So why not help our fellow-men, if they ask for help? But if a person refuses to listen to you, never try to enforce anything of that kind, as good results come about only by the listening in confidence and with good will.

If there is still time for a systematic development of your neighbour's intuition, his sensitiveness and ability of self-assertion, then you are in the position to do much more for such a brother than in the first case. You may then lead him to an acceptance and understanding of the clichés, which I revealed to your inner eyes in the Thirteenth Arcanum.

Take another case. Suppose that you gave good advice to someone in another world, but at the time it was impossible to establish any closer relations in order to better prepare the dying one for his journey. Two things remain to you according to the law (and duty also) of brotherly solidarity which unites all cells of *Adam-Protoplast*. To go to your brother's aid with magic operations, which can support his astrosome, or through *theurgic operations* (as given in Lesson 57), which are directed to the kindling of the Light of Truth before him, so as to enlighten his difficult way. Details of the purely magic operations belong to special courses of Ceremonial Magic which cannot be openly given to the public. But much more effective and powerful *theurgic activity* is at the disposal of every man of good will. These methods do not need any special ceremony, as the inner effort and love radiating from the operator do all that is necessary. THERE IS NOTHING EVEN APPROXIMATELY SO EF-FECTIVE AS A PURE PRAYER.

Nevertheless, much general advice can be given apart from magic and theurgy, which will be of great assistance to the dead and dying.

A cynic, ignorant of occult matters would perhaps laugh at many of the statements about death and its conditions which have been made in this chapter; but such an attitude cannot change the state of things, and the ignorant will be sorry in their own hour of death, when left without help because of their negative attitude towards experiences, which no human being can possibly avoid, unless he is a saint or advanced occultist.

The fear of death as manifested in average human beings does so for three reasons, although these do not affect more advanced people:

(1) Ignorance of that which actually awaits a man after death, which creates feelings similar to those arising in us if we are compelled to perform a desperate leap into darkness, where there may be a bottomless pit or abyss. This is understandable in the case of an average man, but it does not happen to advanced or reintegrated ones, for they know what to expect after leaving the physical body, as is shown in the lessons of this Thirteenth Arcanum.

(2) The mute, subconscious remembrance about former deaths and the rather morbid experiences connected with them, which has already been extensively explained in this course. Nothing similar happens to the superior type of men, whose post-mortem experiences are closer to bliss rather than to suffering. Therefore, they have no fear whatsoever.

(3) The instinctive urge to cling to and preserve the body, as the only well known form of manifestation for inferior types of men, which is based on the *natural law* imbibed in every living being, from plant to man. This permits the specimen that is stronger and better prepared to endure the fight for life and to procreate the following generations. In man there is a peculiar manifestation of that law; it is an *elemental* existing on the astral plane, but which is in touch with the physical one. It makes us identify ourselves with the body.

It is none other than, the now well-known to us, Nephesh. Clearly, one who has been subdued by that elemental will have a strong fear and disgust for shedding his body or to having it damaged, and especially to seeing it mutilated, decayed or dying.

For the more evolved type of man all this is unreal, without meaning, for he knows that he IS NOT HIS BODY, and that his life goes far beyond and above it. So then, even this last reason for fear is destroyed by the inner evolution and development of the consciousness and wisdom in us.

Again, do not forget that from the occult point of view, death begins just when medical science declares the man as dead. In order not to hold or disturb the very process of the astral birth, do not touch or move the body for at least some six hours. During that time, do not interfere with the corpse, and what is especially important, do not allow any persons to be present whose fluids (prana) were unsympathetic for the dead one. This is because the otherwise hard work of the astrosome might be hindered. Do not talk about any business of a material character, for your words may be understood and received not only through the 'sixth sense' of the dead, but even through the replicas of the physical organs, created at that time by the phantom of the man. In this period—as well as in the next few days—prayers are extremely useful, even if the dead person was an unbeliever. For the next six hours (the longer the better) imagine yourself as if accompanying your brother, who is passing into the other plane firmly decided to perform that journey, but who still needs a soft *'forgive me!'* from the side of those who still have the physical point of support on the Earth. Let him, who is now compelled to contemplate his own former slavery to the elements, which was the source of his weakness, *know and feel*, that on the same plane of elements now stands his brother, performing magic operations aimed at quicker liberation of the dying person from the elemental's clichés.

For the next period, up to 40 days, the following may be advisable. To pray for the dead, and to create in us moods full of solidarity for his interests, but carefully avoid all clichés of despair and meditation about the irreplaceable loss, and all feelings of sorrow in all its forms. It would be almost criminal to allow in us, thoughts about the material losses brought to us by the death of our fellow man. This is because, such vibrations emanating from us, will seriously harm the dead in the period of his *fight with the Astral Serpent*.

In all prayers and magic operations (if you are acquainted with the latter) carefully retain the tone of the Egregors of evolutionary type, with which the dead person was in contact when alive.

The destructive activities (in relation to the physical corpse of the dead) of the phantom, separated from the proper astrosome for that sinister purpose, do explain some 'after-death' phenomena, which otherwise would remain incomprehensible.

(1) The bodies of some great saints and yogis have remained untouched by decay after death, because such men, were spiritualized to a degree of being completely UNINTERESTED in their future incarnations, perhaps even to the extent of having a negative attitude towards them.

Therefore they do not occupy their astrosomes with any destructive activities against their former physical shell, already purified through a saintly life. As a result, if no phantom is created, there may be a lack of decay for a very long period.

(2) The desire to live on the Earth, so strong in the majority of people, has as a result, the destructive work of the phantom, aiming at the decomposition of the corpse and the return of all its elements to Nature. This is because of the law, according to which no reincarnation can take place until *all the organic matter* of the body has been *completely dissolved*. This does not affect the skeleton which may be preserved for thousands of years without affecting the destiny of its former owner. Theoretically, you can some day find one of your former skulls and hold it in your hands, if you are able to see the fact and to make such a find.

At the end of the nineteenth and beginning of the twentieth centuries, when occultism was flourishing in France, certain persons belonging to some esoteric circles, claimed that, by means of clairvoyance, their former skeletons (especially well preserved skulls) were visible to them among millions of others, collected and deposited in the great Parisian catacombs. Naturally, I am not taking any side in these statements, as they are beyond any control.

(3) In the same law related to the connection between corpses and future incarnations we may find explanation of the apparently strange desire of the ancient Egyptians, to have their bodies preserved, to a certain extent, by embalmment as mummies. Pharaohs and other important persons in ancient Egypt insisted that their bodies be mummified so as to prevent themselves being incarnated again on this Earth. By this they hoped to remain indefinitely in the astral plane, become perfectly acquainted with it, and assume some regal positions in it. Such was their faith.

The longer one remains in the astral plane, the more power one can collect in it, and so use this power in front of newcomers. Therefore, the disturbing of the eternal peace of mummies was recognized as a heavy offence. Most mummies and even the surrounding objects in the death-chamber were magnetized with a negative (and destructive) variety of Od, which discharged on those who entered the tombs and touched the sarcophagi. There are well-known stories about disastrous happenings affecting some scientists and Egyptologists who entered the crypts first. There is no need to quote them here.

(4) There is another question: what happens to the phantom and its astrosome when the body is not allowed to rot in the normal way in the earth, but is immediately cremated after death; or if it was destroyed by the blast of an explosion, or eaten by wild beasts, and so on?

Unfortunately, in some special circles of occult studies known to me, as well as in the available Hermetic literature it was impossible to find anything exact worth mentioning in this matter; but from other sources, which have little in common with occultism, it may be concluded, that a quick annihilation of the corpse, apart from the *initial shock for the astrosome*, is generally beneficial for the elementar, because it definitely breaks its ties with the physical world and thereby prevents all abnormal experiences mentioned in the following lines (see 5 and 6).

(5) After death, in some exceptional cases, the astrosome shows a strange and strong desire to be connected in some way with the body in the grave. If such a desire is even partially fulfilled (which is possible *under certain conditions*), the elementar may have some insight into the physical world, the only one dear and understandable to him. If the elementar's *last thought* was directed to such a purpose, strange and ominous things may happen.

Instead of using its energy for the decomposition of the corpse, the *phantom*, under the elementar's compulsion, begins to make efforts to hold the cells together, rather than break their ties. The body then begins to lead

L

a kind of vegetable life, if we like so to term that morbid state. It does not decompose, for all the cells are held intact by the energy of the phantom, supported by the astrosome, and often, by some sinister forms from the astral plane; but it is not enough. Actually, so as to prevent every process of decay among the cells, some amount of subtle energy from the physical plane is necessary. And then begins the worst offence. The phantom, directed by the erring astrosome, tries to vampirize the vital fluids and energy from living human beings or animals. If there is an abattoir in the vicinity the vampire does not need to attack living beings, as he is able to collect enough energy from the masses of still warm, fresh blood of slaughtered animals. Then the phantom returns to the grave and charges the body with his plunder, sufficient to stop decay for a few more days.

In other cases, the phantom may visit sleeping humans (mostly female) and try to rob them of their vital energy by, what for laymen, is a mysterious but repulsive process, about which we are not allowed to tell more.

Anyway, it is not true that such a vampire actually sucks the physical blood of its victims, as old tales tell us in a pretty naïve way. But in all respects, such visits mean much danger for the victims, whose karma allows them to be subjected to such depravity.

Tradition tells us that the destruction of the physical body in the grave is the best counter-measure against a vampire.

(6) The strange relations that exist between some corpses and their erring phantoms provide many reports, and I will quote only one case, of which I have personal knowledge. Early in the winter of 1932 I was in a large cemetery, supervising, at the request of my relatives, the erection of a monument on the tomb of my recently dead niece. I happened to see, a few yards away, a group of workers opening another fresh grave. An expensively dressed man and woman were at the grave-side, apparently in great grief. I was told that they were the father and mother of a young man, whose body was in the grave below. The lady told me, that every night in dreams, she saw her dead son, in water-soaked clothes and with a sad face, complaining that he was lying in cold water and suffering much because of the fact. At her request, her husband obtained a permit to open the grave. The metal coffin was raised while I was present, and deep in the grave I saw plenty of yellow liquid, which filled the excavation because of faulty cementing of the walls. The coffin was also full of dirty liquid.

The dead man was right in his communication to his mother. But, why should the state of the body have affected the elementar? Probably because the connection between the corpse and consciousness of the dead man was still too close, and he imagined that the condition of his body had a direct effect on him. This suggestion (or rather auto-suggestion) was as good as any objective truth for an ignorant person, as was this young man who, in his short life had had no time to think deeply about the things connected with death. The result of ignorance was grim enough, but this may happen to many other people, even without our knowledge.

There is a very important truth covering both the physical and non-physical forms of life, as they are for an average man. It is closely connected with the general unwillingness to die of less spiritually developed human beings.

Their normal consciousness, self-assertion, feeling of life, all these are most clear and 'real' for them, just when they can perceive the physical world and bodies, in their waking state.

The astro-mental life for these people is something like an unreal dream, more or less unpleasant. That is why the astrosome—after the death of its physical body—seeks so intensely for the possibility of a new incarnation, as soon as possible.

If this cannot be obtained at the time, because of different patterns of a man's karma and the unripeness of the astrosome for the next incarnation, attempts can be made from the side of the elementar to indulge in certain illegal practices, in order to enter, at any price, into the so much desired contact with the physical world of matter.

Then we may have examples of vampirism, necromancy, poltergeists and other kinds of unnatural manifestations, some of which have been explained in this course.

Men of higher evolutionary advancement prefer *just the opposite*. The less material and gross existence on the more subtle planes (like the astral and mental ones) responds better to the will's direct efforts than the clumsy (from their point of view) physical world of the senses. And they live much longer in the astro-mental regions than they did previously on the Earth. But, of course, in the case of ordinary men, things are reversed. Their intervals between their incarnations are much shorter, for they have little to do in any other world except the physical one. All occult schools teach this.

Spiritual men even deny and refuse the astro-mental life, preferring existence in the *eternal light* of pure, non-materialized conditions, which Christ called '*His Father's Mansions*'. The Maharshi called it the '*Fourth State*', beyond all thoughts and feelings, the perennial spiritual ecstasy (Sahaja Nirvikalpa Samadhi in Vedantic terminology).

The most unpleasant factor in death for a man is his struggle to prolong the physical life. This is the result of the astrosome's fulfilling of its duty: to occupy the body for as long as it is possible, as well as the dying person's attachments to this material world.

The agony of the physical sufferings are already somewhat dimmed by the gradual retiring of the higher principles of man, but the astro-mental troubles are only just beginning.

This foremostly affects all 'unprepared' people, whose ignorance and lack of interest in higher things once more brings them sufferings.

Those who appreciated the physical life just as should have been done have few troubles when dying. I am speaking here about difficulties of astro-mental origin.

The complete detachment from the body, which can be realized at death, is the most powerful factor to reduce agony and its misery. So it is in our power to get rid of those unnecessary and nonsensical troubles, created by man's ignorance and unpreparedness. We should courageously and honestly face things as they are.

All great souls in human history have warned us about it. Christ told us bluntly: 'Be ready, for you know not neither the hour nor the day.' As regards sufferings of a mental origin, the foremost is that of the desperate hope and desire to escape death. I know about an actual experience of a young man, who took part in the civil wars which raged in East Europe after World War I.

He was cornered and was to have been shot by an improvised execution squad in a cellar, from which there was no possible escape. Before him stood a row of men with ready loaded rifles, only waiting for the order to fire. The short but extremely painful agony of condemned youth was perhaps the worst experience of his life, until approaching resignation quickly cooled down the hellish fire in his brain. This resignation made him almost indifferent when the commanding officer suddenly postponed the execution. Having been with one foot already 'on the other side', he passed through the most acute part of that experience, and therefore was less sensitive to all subsequent happenings, not to be compared as before, with the suffering like that of a cornered animal, awaiting the fatal volley that would destroy his vital organs, killing the body, that is himself.

So it is usually, even on the death-bed, when people still clutch at the last strands, binding them to the dying form. Men add many unnecessary sufferings to themselves, when actually death is much more merciful in itself, than we may believe. If only we are reasonable and possess the power of decision to be such ones.

LESSON 62

Having talked about death as seen from different points of view, we may now be entitled to hear something about the reverse transformation of man. So far, we have had the change of the three planes for two, as is in death, but finally the two-plane life in the astral comes to an end and the human being has to incarnate again, changing the two-plane life for the three-plane one. This is the incarnation of the elementar.

Suppose that the elementar has fulfilled its period of being in the middle astral of the solar system, or even in the 'Dark Cone' of the planet. Let us suppose that the individualized Chains of two-plane entities, which we know under the name of 'Spiritus Directores' (or astral leaders and policemen), have decided about the next incarnation of our elementar. The *vortex* in the astral (its lower sub-plane) created by the magic operation of the sexual act of his future parents, pulls the elementar down. Then there will be chosen, among thousands (or even millions) of prospective parents, who are creating the tourbillons by their passion and lust, a pair which correspond best to the karmic qualities of the human being about to return to the physical plane. This vortex must be of the same type as that of the elementar, and the zodiacal conditions of the bodies of the parents must also be suitable for the future baby. Definite physical conditions which the parents are able to offer it, are also taken into consideration by the newcomer's karma. Being sucked into the vortex, the elementar again creates its *Nephesh*, already designed for him in the astral light. The ease of the formation of that *Nephesh* can be explained by the co-operation of the astral and physical bodies of the parents, a thing about which ordinary parents know nothing. The fact that the suitable types of parents provide all necessary material, is of great assistance to Nephesh in its work. The embryonic period is the starting point for the final work of Nephesh in the production of the body for its elementar.

The astrosome of the mother protects the astrosome of the child as it becomes involved in matter just as her physical body guards the developing embryo in her womb. The moment of birth, that is the time of the open fight of the child with the so far unknown, new conditions in the physical world is very important. Lack of experience on the side of the baby makes the planetary influences, at that moment, very ponderous ones. Zodiacal currents determine the fate of the newly born man, according to his karma. And that is why astrologers place so much importance on the exact date and hour of birth.

So far we have spoken about the influence of a three-plane human being (that is still incarnate) on elementars and dying persons. Now let us briefly examine the reverse of this, that is how those who have left their physical bodies can influence us while we still wear our fleshly shells.

This can be regarded as occurring in three different ways, dependent upon the kind of elementar which comes into play and his aims and means. We will begin *from below*.

During the first period after he has been deprived of his body, an elementar can still have certain contact with the earthly world through his still vigorous phantom—Nephesh. Naturally, it is an 'illegal' way, for the very destiny of an elementar is rather de-materialization and spiritualization, instead of unnecessary and harmful 'peeping' into the physical world (which actually is without any true meaning for the dead being), through the key-hole of his phantom's limited possibilities.

Therefore, no fairly advanced soul would do it. But how big is the percentage of these advanced humans in comparison with the mass of spiritually-blind men and women, attached only to their temporary material life? So it is with all average people. Therefore undue things may happen more often than we suspect.

If an elementar pays too much attention to this Nephesh, the latter can be considerably strengthened and its ghastly 'life' prolonged, for in such a case the ignorant one tries to use the phantom almost like a true vehicle of consciousness, similar to his former physical body.

We should remember, that immediately after death, Nephesh creates (as happens with the average man) some imperfect replicas of the former physical organs of sense. So such an artificially strengthened phantom under the influence of the elementar's astral consciousness can manifest itself in a way perceptible to the genuine physical senses of living men.

Then we have all kinds of haunted places, poltergeists, and other 'inexplicable' phenomena. If there were no 'astral police' (Spiritus Directores of the astral), about which you already know from foregoing lessons, there would be many, many more harmful apparitions to annoy earthly people.

These authorities prevent irresponsible interference from the side of silly elementars and forbid them their worst exhibitions. There is no question of any good coming through unnatural channels, by use of the temporary and involutionary Nephesh as a vehicle of consciousness on the part of our lower class brethren on the 'other side'.

Now, what can come from the *true astral plane* (apart from the phantom)? Experience and tradition show, that the foremost motives of astral intervention from the elementars' side have the same factors, which played the overwhelming role in the earthly life. They are the feelings of love and hatred.

There is no need to explain which of them will be positive (helpful) and which negative (harmful) to us.

Love from the side of an elementar of an advanced type (like a white occultist, or saint) is a boon, and brings blessings to the earthly life of the object of such a love. One then feels *inspiration;* noble emotions and thoughts come into one's consciousness, and man usually does not even suspect where flows the soothing current. Good emotions and thoughts directed from a strong two-plane pentagram are undoubtedly a very lucky event for us. Sometimes these 'good wishes' from the astral take a particular form.

I know of an example, where a loving mother always wanted her only child to become a writer, as were some of her ancestors; but karma allowed this desire to be realized only in the second half of the man's life, long after his mother had departed. But a strong and unselfish desire of the loving elementar was nevertheless fulfilled to her satisfaction.

Love 'from the other side' can even prevent a disaster or an imminent, dangerous accident for the incarnate object of love. Here is the origin of the belief in 'guardian angels'.

Occultists know a lot about the so-called 'miraculous' escapes from death or injuries in accidents, in war, and so on; but there is no purpose to speak much about these personal things to 'unbelievers', whose only god is a dim feeling of '*fate*'. Very advanced elementars connected with powerful Egregors (usually religious ones) sometimes leave certain *centres* on the planet, through which the Egregoric forces may act. Such are the graves of some saints, or genuine, advanced yogis, or other spots like Lourdes, the Holy Sepulchre, and some less known places, often accessible only to initiates.

Love is the power beyond all limitations, and it exists on every plane of the universe. Even such a giant of Light as is the Christ, had His beloved disciple (in other words, the most advanced and initiated spiritually), whom we know as St John. There is an old dogma from the early days of Christianity, that its Egregor had its ineffable *source* of life just in Christ's love for His faithful.

Lower and more egoistic forms of love from the astral plane, as that of a husband, child, parent and so on, might also have its limited influence in the general sense, as spoken of above.

On the next, that is the *mental* plane no such *ordinary* love has any access. Practically, average people are unable to form in themselves or even perceive *love* on the non-personal, *pure* and rather abstract, universal basis.

So, this field of activity directed towards the Earth is almost closed to ordinary types of men, and the influence from that source is insignificant. The *Great Ones* do the whole task.

The *second* factor coming from the astral plane is *hatred* and connected with it, jealousy, greed, fear, suspicion, ill will and similar vices. The student may realize even without consulting these pages, that in *this case* Nephesh may play a very nasty role and this is actually the case.

All primitive, evil witchcraft with its different 'zombies' and voodoos, cannot dispense with the necessary participation of the phantom. The whole of necromancy is based on its use or of its organs connected with the corpse. That is why the lowest sorts of black magic use the dead bodies of men or animals to serve as temporary support for the phantoms, and these phantoms can be influenced and used for certain phenomena just because of their magnetic links with those corpses or carcasses.

We want to limit these revolting things to these few statements.

Ill wishes and suggestions from the side of an unfriendly elementar may have just the opposite result to good ones, which come from love. Many otherwise inexplicable accidents may be referred to this kind of attack from the invisible. A perfectly experienced driver, swimmer, or flyer can sometimes commit a deadly and quite unreasonable error, and from a few survivors, some occult investigators (always remaining *incognito as such*) have heard about a sudden, irresistible, nonsensical but overwhelming suggestion, felt from an unknown source, which compels the person to perform a fatal movement or to feel a momentary crippling fear, resulting in an accident, inability to swim, and so on. A hostile elementar can suggest to those around us that they harbour unfriendly feelings towards us. Those who are able to perform conscious exteriorization of their astrosomes, know all this from their own experience, and do not need any explanation. Some occult organizations study the realm of astral influences on living men very extensively, but this does not belong to the main line of this present work, dedicated as it is to Hermetism and the Tarot.

The occult realm is so extensive that even dozens of books of this size would not cope with all the particulars and varieties of experiences, which are possible in it.

But he who knows the Hermetic Tradition in its broad lines, as given here, will also be able to solve all questions for himself, because his mental abilities developed by the 'equations' will open all doors for him.

So we come to the last lesson related to the Thirteenth Arcanum, to the analysis of its equations.

LESSON 63

The arithmological analysis of the Thirteenth Arcanum is very significant. From it we will see how the apparently 'dead' numbers can speak to the trained Hermetist.

Equation No. 70: $13 = 1 + 12$

A three-plane being (1) and the necessity of sacrifice on the physical plane

(12) leads to death. This analysis suggests the possibility of death deliberately accepted as a form of sacrifice.

Equation No. 71: $13 = 12 + 1$

Here a three-plane entity does not deliberately give up its life; on the contrary, the Zodiacal life (12) gives birth to death (13), depriving the entity of its third plane (1).

Equation No. 72: $13 = 2 + 11$

The polarity of *good* and *evil* (2) using force (11) may produce death (13). This is the formula of *compulsory death.*

Equation No. 73: $13 = 11 + 2$

Force, fully realized (11), is compelled to choose one of the poles for its application (2). It is the formula of the Knight Kadosh: *be hot or be cold* if you have power in you. But Kadosh knows, that the formula of his existence is enclosed as the embryo of that existence, that is in the degree of the Masonic Master, who has been told: 'Remember to die!'

Equation No. 74: $13 = 3 + 10$

Realization of the creative metaphysics of Hermes (3) plus knowledge of the harmony in the functions of the World's Mill (10) agree well with the idea of death (13). Therefore, $3 + 10$ is the formula of natural death, of the element generated by the normal evolutionary contemplation of the world.

Equation No. 75: $13 = 10 + 3$

This is also a natural death, but taken from the opposite point of view, a purely empirical one. The *Wheel of the Sphinx* (10) made a revolution, and this gave birth (3) to something new.

Equation No. 76: $13 = 4 + 9$

Authority (4) of Initiation (9) is based on the discovery by that Initiation of the mystery of death (13).

Equation No. 77: $13 = 9 + 4$

Initiation (9) through its degrees overcomes every authority (4) of an earthly character once we begin to realize the impermanency and mortality of everything earthly (13).

Equation No. 78: $13 = 5 + 8$

The Pentagram (5) dominating all temporary laws (8) and thereby conquering a major space of activity for itself, is compelled to change its plane (13). You may understand it as: Religion (5) placed before the laws of society (8) makes us guess that there was a thought about death (13).

Equation No. 79: $13 = 8 + 5$

Justice, understood in the broad sense of that word, oppresses the Pentagram (5), depriving it of its fulcrum (13) on the physical plane. This can be death because of the court's sentence.

Equation No. 80: $13 = 6 + 7$

The problem of good and evil (6) compelling a victory (7) of the subtle over the gross has in it a seed of knowledge of the necessity to provide oneself with PERMANENT goods for the future life (13).

Equation No. 81: $13 = 7 + 6$

A perfect Victor (7) always puts the question of good and evil (6) to himself, in order to catch the analogy of the subtle with the ASTRAL life, and of the gross with the physical. By doing this, does he not simply remember about death?

Now we have performed the analysis of the Thirteenth Arcanum in the realm of its SECOND title, and it would be extremely useful for you to make a similar analysis with the two remaining titles of the arcanum, as shown on its card. You will need to know some principles of physics and chemistry for this exercise when made in the sphere of the third (physical) title.

I feel obliged to mention, that many occultists consider the arithmological unfolding of the Thirteenth Arcanum simply as an enumeration of various kinds of deaths, which can be judged according to the Law of Karma. I will now give the full set of equations related to that idea, with their fulcrum in the SECOND component (the third or last figure). It is recommended to go through all of them, seeking the way in which the solution has been found, as was done with the series of unfoldings in the realm of the SECOND title of the arcanum.

This book is not merely for reading. Its meaning can be unveiled only to the co-operative student, who, together with the writer, works on its problems.

Equation No. 82: $13 = 1 + 12$

Deliberate sacrifice of life for an idea.

Equation No. 83: $13 = 2 + 11$

A compulsory death.

Equation No. 84: $13 = 3 + 10$

A natural death (according to karma).

Equation No. 85: $13 = 4 + 9$

Death of an adept caused by the breaking of his astral umbilical thread by exteriorization. Otherwise, astral disaster.

Equation No. 86: $13 = 5 + 8$

Death according to the requirements of law (for example, a death sentence in court).

Equation No. 87: $13 = 6 + 7$

Death in a fight, bringing victory for the idea.

Equation No. 88: $13 = 7 + 6$

Death in an unequal fight.

L*

Equation No. 89: $13 = 8 + 5$

Death as an expression of the pentagrammatic will of man (that is, suicide).

Equation No. 90: $13 = 9 + 4$

Premature death as a result of bad conditions in life.

Equation No. 91: $13 = 10 + 3$

Death in childbirth.

Equation No. 92: $13 = 11 + 2$

Death because of conscious inner disharmony of the tragedy of earthly existence.

Equation No. 93: $13 = 12 + 1$

The passing of an adept to another plane, because of having finished his task on Earth.

In other words, the Master goes to support his Egregor on the astral plane. For such a case, there is a beautiful expression in French: IL SE LAISSE MOURIR (he consents to die, or he allows himself to die).

This will conclude the Thirteenth Arcanum. If the Twelfth Arcanum is the most spiritual of the whole Tarot, the Thirteenth is the most practical and useful for everyone.

Each of us must die. *In this we are all equal.* But in the matter of the *nature of our deaths*, there are infinite differences, just as there are in our lives. Therefore, a reasonable pentagram will take every care about his passing into another form of existence, which extends in time for much more than even the longest physical life. The KNOWLEDGE given in the Thirteenth Arcanum opens new vistas and conditions in the other plane. As a last word for the 'sceptics' and 'cynics' I would like to say: if, to a certain extent, it is still possible to cheat on the physical plane, then it will be found that this far from laudable conduct is IMPOSSIBLE AFTER DEATH, in which everything becomes open and visible, that is man's feelings, thoughts and whole moral structure. That is why there are so many beliefs, that after his death, an 'evil one lives among devils, and a saint among angels'. For everyone enters the 'society' most suited to him, and sees beings having the same appearance as himself.

J

Arcanum XIV
INGENIUM SOLARE
TEMPERANCE

$M_{\nearrow}$
Scorpio

Deductio
Harmonia Mixtorum
Reversibilitas

CHAPTER XIV

ARCANUM XIV (נ NUN)

The sign of the Hebrew alphabet corresponding to the Fourteenth Arcanum is נ (Nun); the numerical value is 50, while astrologically it belongs to the Scorpion. The hieroglyph is a *foetus* (that is, that which is borne by the hieroglyph of the previous, Thirteenth Arcanum, which is a *woman*). As a fruit of the work of imagination related to death and reincarnation, there appears the realization of the necessity to harmonize hermetically one's active and passive elements, which are filtered by the human personality. From this comes the *first title* of the Fourteenth Arcanum (in the realm of the Archetype)—DEDUCTIO. As a result of learning about the energetic processes and transformations in both the Macrocosm and Microcosm, there comes the *second title* (in the world of Man)—HARMONIA MIXTORUM (harmony of mixed elements). On the plane of Nature, the *third title* will be simply REVERSIBILITAS, or reversibility of processes.

The card of the Fourteeth Arcanum presents a Solar Genius, in the form of an angel in a gleaming robe, crowned with a golden halo, and having a golden belt with a white kerchief, or more symbolically exact (as on our card), the *pentacles of the Tarot*, that is the triangle in a square with a point in its centre. The angel pours a radiant liquid from a golden vessel into a silver one, without the loss of a drop. Under the feet of the Genius we see a stream of crystal clear water, and on the horizon, the rising disc of the sun. The stream has its source in that horizon, just under the sun.

The scientific name of the arcanum is INGENIUM SOLARE, and the vulgar one—Temperance. What is the idea incorporated in this card?

It is the synthetically understood influence of the Sun, personified as the Solar Genius. The hieroglyph, a *foetus* must finally lead us to *synthesis*. It is because deduction, which in the beginning, often has an analytical character when we try to learn something, has only one aim in the end, the great synthesis. This is the pattern of all learning.

Pursuit of harmony of the astral constitution in individuality—which in its separate stages between incarnations may be satisfied by the balance of planetary influences—will choose the Solar Synthesis of these influences as the final aim. The science of energy, teaching us about the reversibility of separate processes in the transformations of energy, at the end aims at a synthetic examination of the development of definite systems.

The golden halo and girdle of the figure presented in the Fourteenth Arcanum, together with the gleaming gold (or white) robe, are unmistakable attributes of the Solar Genius, they do not need any special explanation.

The uninterrupted stream between the golden and silver vessels induces the thought about the levelling of the liquid in both. The *aim of deduction* is to level, *a priori*, the basis of existence of all objects affected by our judgement, and to establish a full system of association.

The aim of harmonizing the astrosome is to level all manifestations of our ability to accept, and to create the impulses of our will, and by that, to create the perfect inner world in the heart of the androgynous individuality.

The aim of the modern science of evolutionary development presents a general plan for the balancing of the total sum of energy in the whole complex of non-reversible phases of action.

Resuming about the idea behind the Fourteenth Arcanum, we see that it is: the law of universal equilibrium; the balance of forces in the manifestation of the universe; a similar balance in pentagrammatical beings (humans), and, as a result of the realization of both, the idea of the final, perennial PEACE, being the substratum of all movements and changes. It seems that many advanced sons of humanity had this peace as their most precious possession.

Christ spoke about HIS PEACE, which he gave to His disciples; Buddha gave the unruffled peace of his Nirvana as the element שׁ (Shin) of his whole philosophy, and the contemporary Spiritual Teacher—the Great Rishi Ramana, was himself the personification of that PEACE.

In Hermetism the Fourteenth Arcanum often assumes the meaning of 'moderation'.

This arcanum may give us rich material for arithmological analysis.

Equation No. 94: $14 = 1 + 13$

Hermes Trismegistus (1) being the lord of immortality (13) gives us the image of powerful, all embracing deduction. (I am giving here the unfolding of all three titles of the arcanum). A three-plane man (1) intelligently using his incarnations (13) must finally come to the Hermetic equilibrium (14).

An analysis of all planes of Nature, taken as NATURA NATURANS (1), plus the synthesis of the physical knowledge about the transformation of energy (13) creates the formula of the true teachings concerning evolution (14).

Equation No. 95: $14 = 13 + 1$

This reversed order of the arcana if used in an analysis of the Fourteenth, will not change the final synthesis, but will give only a variation of the story of its origin. Therefore, our further unfolding will be limited to the direct order of the components.

Equation No. 96: $14 = 2 + 12$

The Divine Substance (2) with the conception of the Incarnate Word (Logos) (12) gives the key of faith in 'a priori' judgements. If the SUBTLE CAN INCARNATE INTO THE DENSE, then why not operate mentally in order to anticipate and guess the physical facts?

Polarity in Man (2) and Laws of Charity towards our neighbour (12) equally give the key of Hermetic Harmony (14). Do not forget that *Sephira*

Geburah, although based on polarity, together with *Chesed,* gives birth to *Tiphereth.*

The image of NATURA NATURATA (2) basically static, joined with that of the dynamic Zodiac, will positively solve the question of evolution (14).

Equation No. 97: $14 = 3 + 11$

Natura Divina (3) plus Vis Divina (11) means the realm of deduction in philosophical creativeness (14).

The possibility of fecundation (3) plus the power of the Egregoric Chains (11) offers *harmony* to single organs of the Protoplast (14).

The great Gnostic Principle of creativeness (3) (in Nature) together with the forces of Nature, as we call them (11), again leads to the Egregoric Chains and explains the general character of the extinguishing of energetic transformations (14).

Equation No. 98: $14 = 4 + 10$

The understanding of forms (4) and knowledge of ways in which the Higher Influxes (10) come gives the key for deduction (14).

Intuition of authority (4) and Initiation into the Kabbalah (10) reveal the path to Hermetic Harmony (14).

The adaptation of the conditions of the environment (4) and the Wheel of Probability (10) fully explain the picture of the extinguishing of the energetic processes in Nature. Here we may remember Darwin's theory, not forgetting that occultists do not recognize any unlimited life (14).

Equation No. 99: $14 = 5 + 9$

The science of Good and Evil (5) plus High Protection (9) guarantee the infallibility of deduction (14).

The creation of the Pentagram (5) and its traditional Initiation (9) leads the individual to the Hermetic Harmony (14).

The great Natural Religion (5) realized in its contemplation, together with ideal cautiousness, dictated by the full use of the theory of probability (9), must in a mysterious way, lead us to the solution of the question about its final Peace. Such a contemplation should be conceived of as an understanding of personal qualities, in which lies the seed of that future and final Peace (14).

Equation No. 100: $14 = 6 + 8$

The Law of Analogy (6) together with the great Law of Libration of the World's Scale (8) gives birth to deduction (14). I have to apologize, by giving the results of this analysis, to those official savants who do not recognize the Law of Analogy as an instrument of deduction.

Personal freedom of will (6) combined with recognition of the Laws (8) may result in Hermetic Harmony (14).

The constitution of the environment (6) and its Karma (8) is the key to physics (14).

Equation No. 101: $14 = 7 + 7$

Deduction (14) may be presented as a fight between two ideas, having

suitable forms and dominating these forms (7). In other words, every solution made *a priori*, is also a choice made *a priori*.

Hermetic Harmony (14) is realized as opposition to the victory of
activity, to the victory of *intuition*. If you try some new ventures, you
simultaneously have to broaden the circle of your strivings.

Reversibility (14) in physics can be considered as mutually appertaining
to two phases of different energetic manifestations (7).

A keen thinker will see in meditations on the Fourteenth Arcanum, similarity to the activity of the Solar Genius. It is comparatively easy to acknow-
ledge its necessity and fruitfulness, but it is extremely difficult to convey the
mechanics of it in detail. Only one who is like that Solar Genius may be
able to perform this hard action, and he must possess the full wisdom of
metaphysics, ethics and all related physical facts.

In Eastern occultism, *Karma Yoga* corresponds to the Fourteenth Arcanum
of the Tarot. Properly speaking not even the *whole of that Yoga*, but only
its idea, which tells of the reversibility of actions and their results. No drop
falls from those mysterious gold and silver vessels, held in the hands of the
Logos (or Solar Genius). Accordingly, nothing in karma can be lost or
forgotten: repayments or rewards follow in due time and in due form.
Those who studied *Concentration* may object, that 'there is still the burning
of karma'. Yes! But is not that 'burning' a form of repayment?

□

Arcanum XV
TYPHON
THE DEVIL

Sagittaris

Logica
Serpens Nahash
Fatum

CHAPTER XV

ARCANUM XV (ם SAMECH)

The letter of the alphabet corresponding to the Fifteenth Arcanum is that of ם (Samech) and the numerical value is 60. The astrological sign is the Archer (Sagittarius). The hieroglyph of the arcanum is an A R R O W, this time flying round the circumference of a circle. It is not the target-hitting arrow of the Seventh Arcanum, but is a weapon which you will inevitably encounter when passing from the points inside the circle to those on the periphery.

And this encounter can be double-sided.

This arrow will paralyse when it strikes you, or it will compel you—as your fate—to use the weapon against others. It is like a *continuous tourbillon*, outside of which there is no life and no movement on any plane.

The Archetype speaks to us about this *tourbillon*, which being immutable LOGIC, rules over metaphysical judgements belonging to the trans-cendental sphere of the SECOND FAMILY. But the *Transcendental realm* itself, does not underlie that vortex (tourbillon).

Therefore, the *first title* of the arcanum, in the realm of the Archetype is just—LOGIC.

For humanity, this current appears as a powerful attraction, according to the immutable laws which rule over our astral world. These laws suggest different desires and passions to us, which belong to and come from our collective NEPHESH, which we have created in the process of our downfall (Lessons 43 and 44). This current which pulls us so intensely at the same time serves as an instrument for our influencing of others. It makes us—without our knowledge—unsuspecting *slaves of other penta-grams*, which have been able to stay in the higher regions of that current and therefore better able to see the realms of its activity. This current operates in all humanities that exist in the whole universe. On each planet, the Genius for each particular humanity takes his position in the higher regions of that *Universal Current* so as to perform evolutionary work for that humanity; but in the lower parts of the current, the SERPENT of planetary evolution acts, trying to pull as many souls as possible into the 'DARK CONE'. For our Earth, this lower manifestation takes the form of the *circular vortex* (whirlwind) about which I spoke in the lessons belonging to the Thirteenth Arcanum.

The general title of this universal factor—NAHASH will serve as the *second title* of the Fifteenth Arcanum. You may accept it as the biblical Ser-pent, which tempted Eve.

But even Nature itself is saturated with the currents which steadily rule over its manifestations, over every phenomenon of its life. In the realm of Nature, the union of these currents, which do not differ from *Nahash* is called 'FATUM' (Fate). This is the *third title* of the Fifteenth Arcanum.

As you may see, all manifestations of this arcanum are involutionary, that is they are directed by the currents, descending from the higher to the lower sub-planes. That is why the Fifteenth Arcanum was given negatively polarized names: the *scientific* one being *Typhon*, and the vulgar—*the Devil*.

But now, it is time to look at the complicated and ominous (at first glance) card of the arcanum.

The upper part of the picture is occupied by the traditional figure of BAPHOMET (from the Knights Templar tradition). He is seated on a cube, which stands on the surface of a great globe. From the right side (as in a mirror) we see a man, and on the left a woman. Both are naked, with small horns on their heads. They are bound together by a heavy chain, one end fastened around the neck of the man and the other around the waist of the woman. The chain is bound to *Baphomet's cube*.

And so, the tragic Baphomet, through the CUBE of his realizations in matter, divided the polarities of the human Androgyne. A simple, but from the empirical point of view, appalling true picture of the downfall of Adam and Eve.

The contemplation of the involutionary character (Eve) was the beginning of the *downfall*; striving for involutionary realization (Adam) accomplished it. Intuition and activity then appeared as finally divided in life through the very fact of materialization of that life (the cube on the globe). But, although divided, Adam and Eve are still bound together through the common chain of *Baphomet's* slavery. This slavery weighs heavily on Adam's *active neck*, binding his movements and impulses (by the elements of TIME and SPACE). This chain also binds the organs of sensitiveness in Eve, which allow her to fortify intuitional impressions and to create magnificent images. Resuming, we may state that: IF ADAM IS LIMITED AND BOUND IN HIS FREEDOM OF MOVEMENT, THEN EVE IS HINDERED IN FREEDOM OF IMAGINATION.

An ominous reversed pentagram shines with a red light above the head of the Astral God—Baphomet, just between his horns. You already know the meaning of that symbol.

However, for us at this moment a problem comes foremost: how can both of them set themselves free from their tragic slavery at the feet of Baphomet? How to re-join themselves into the primary, powerful ANDROGYNE? To those who are acquainted with our Hermetic philosophy and symbols, the card of the Fifteenth Arcanum itself gives the answer.

Firstly, the *matter* of the globe must be subtilized; then it will cease to divide both parts of the Androgyne, now separated into MAN and WOMAN. Together as a unit, Adam and Eve will dominate Baphomet, pull him to them, courageously enter into his organic life, raise themselves reaching his horns, dematerialize them and go above, burning their separate personalities in the fire of rising Unitarianism, visible above the head of the Astral God.

That is the way of Reintegration for those who despise the heavy chains of the lower part of the picture, and who are not afraid to accept upon themselves, the cumbersome image of that winged, androgynous monster. This was the path of the Knights Templar, storming Heaven in order to escape the narrow abyss of the Earth. It is necessary to study diligently the constitution and structure of Baphomet himself.

We already know, that those desiring to dominate him must first subtilize the matter of the globe, which interposes itself between man's acitvity and his sensitiveness: in other words, they must become conscious of the illusory character of the material world, and learn to despise the obstacles encountered on the path to perfection.

Let this globe be subtilized, let it become so transparent that your activity can see intuition and vice versa. What then? Further, there is the *Cube of Adaptation*, which is the ability to adapt oneself to the environment in which one is operating. We should never forget, that the 'Cube of Adaptation' is at the same time, the 'Cube of Authority' (see Fourth Arcanum).

Now we can proceed. On the cube sits the Androgyne himself, the representative of the signs of the FOUR ELEMENTS, and subsequently the ruler of the *four Hermetic virtues*, now well known to you. The globe of the Earth is under the feet of the Androgyne; fish scales, symbolizing water, cover his abdomen; wings representing air, are behind his shoulders, and fire rises to Heaven from the fiery pentagram above his head. Above are the four Hermetic virtues, while the sphere of FIRE belongs to the Great Metaphysical Ternary.

So, in Baphomet we find a higher (3) and a lower (4) sphere of the picture of the Great Arcanum. But special emphasis is placed on the figure in the middle sphere (2) of that image.

The right arm and hand of the Androgyne are MALE and bear the inscription 'SOLVE' (meaning to decide, cut off, dissolve). The hand points to the bright crescent of the new moon on the right side of the figure (not as in a mirror). The left arm and hand of Baphomet are FEMALE, and on them we see 'COAGULA' (to solidify, condense). They point towards the dark crescent of the waning moon, on the left side of the figure, or on the CUBE itself, as is shown on our card. The waning moon is placed below and the female hand points downwards to it. The new moon is above, and the male hand points upwards to it.

Baphomet has female breasts. On some cards there is a double caduceus growing from the figure's groin, and its serpent-like heads reach to Baphomet's solar plexus.

It is hard to find elsewhere more indications about the arcanum of the double astral vortex (tourbillon) and its applications, than is on the card of the Fifteenth Arcanum of the Tarot.

But $15 = 60 = 6$. Therefore the Fifteenth Arcanum must be connected with the understanding of the *problem of good and evil*, with the problem of TWO ways. If the head of the caduceus opposite the solar plexus suggests to us the thought about ascension of the Tree of Life (Sephira Tiphereth), then in the whole figure there must be a hint on the fateful *Tree of Knowledge of Good and Evil.* Look attentively on the Astral God. He has a goat's head, whose horns, ears and beard fit perfectly into the reversed pentagram. Therefore it is the ASPECT OF EVIL, which might be connected with the figure. But turn your attention to other particulars: the Ternary of the torch dominates the binary of the horns. It is the normal evolutionary pentagram which should appear in the mind of a keen occultist, initiated into the Tarot's philosophy. But for those who are not, there is the reversed fiery pentagram between the goat's horns.

Why does Baphomet have goat's legs? Because they stay on the cube, placed on the globe. The creators of the Tarot wanted to remind us, that the globe is necessary for us as a point of support, only because of our (humanity's) downfall, as symbolized by the perverted (goat's) interpretation of the pentagram.

Why are the legs crossed, so that the *right hoof* is on the left side of the globe, and the left hoof on the right side? It is a simple hint on the mirror-like transmission of the astral visions into the language of physical sight. People not well-trained in the quick transmission of *astral clichés*, obtained by them through the *sixth sense*, often describe their impressions as if seen in a mirror. Clairvoyants and somnambulists in their visions of far off things always speak about the objects which are actually on the right, as being placed on the left, and vice versa. Exteriorization of the Prophet Ezekiel which gave him the cliché of one of the Hermetic Quaternaries, made him interpret this pentacle as seen in the mirror-like reflection, and not in the direct vision. The same can be said about the Quaternary of St John the Apostle. Only those who give themselves long training in contemplation of the astral clichés get the habit of interpreting them in their normal positions in relation to the physical world.

All of the aforesaid shows us that the figure of Baphomet in the Fifteenth Arcanum is the picture of the full constitution of the ASTRAL TOUR-BILLON, with explanations of the upper metaphysical Ternary, as well as of the character of the transmission of astral clichés downwards (the crossed goat's legs). The arcanum has the misty name of Typhon only because in the normal Tarotic image of the three great septenaries, the arcana are arranged in order of their density, that is the triangles of the Archetype, Man and Nature.

As I have used (in accordance with the contemporary Tradition of Hermetism) the name of Baphomet, I should give more explanation about this fact. The word BAPHOMET read by the method of notarikon is: TEMOHPAB, that is Templi Omnium Hominum Pacis Abbas which means '*the Priest of the Temple of Peace for all Men*', if read as in Hebrew, from right to left. The Knights Templar used this term for the individualized astral tourbillon, which actually, if skilfully directed, could lead men to the way of inner peace and self-perfectioning. We should not forget, that the Knights Templar dreamed about the creation on Earth of a kingdom of Peace and Union of all nations, and for that aim they directed all the means and powerful currents of their Astral Chain (Egregor).

The description of Baphomet's figure has not been taken from the Knights Templar's tradition, for agents of the Inquisition in the time of

Pope Clement Vth destroyed every picture of it, so that nothing remained. Instead, the basis for the Fifteenth card of the Tarot has been the Great Androgyne from the picture by Kunrath, as its symbolism is almost identical with Baphomet.

In order to reflect in your mental conception the image of the Astral God as exactly as possible, I believe it is necessary to quote here more of the text of the Emerald Tablets, following that used in the Sixth Arcanum.

PATER EIUS EST SOL, MATER EIUS LUNA; PORTAVIT ILLUD VENTUS IN VENTRE SUO; UNTRIX EIUS TERRA EST.

PATER OMNIS TELESMI TOTIUS MUNDI EST HIC.

VIS EIUS INTEGRA EST, SI VERSA FUERIT IN TERRAM.

SEPARABIS TERRAM AB IGNE, SUBTILE A SPISSO, SUAVITER, CUM MAGNO INGENIO.

ASCENDIT A TERRA IN COELUM, ITERUMQUE DESCENDIT IN TERRAM.

ET RECIPIT VIM SUPERIORUM ET INFERIORUM.

The translation is:

His father is the Sun, his mother the Moon, the wind bore him in its womb and the Earth was his nourisher. In him is the source of every form in the whole universe. His power is complete if it is turned to the Earth. Thou wilt separate Earth from Fire, the subtle from the dense, quickly and with great ability. He goes from Earth to Heaven and returns again to the Earth, and receives force from higher and lower sources.

The traditional commentary will be, according to Prof. G. O. M.: 'He (Baphomet) is born according to the great Gnostic Law, from the union of a certain active *Yod* and certain passive *Hé*, exactly corresponding to that *Yod*. He vampirizes the world's environment and takes as his point of support the most dense creatures.

'He forms a double current, the *ascending part* of which has its point of support in the power of creation, and the *descending* one, in the point of gravitation to the higher metaphysical principles.'

This may be considered as one of the matters for meditation belonging to the Fifteenth Arcanum. From the first superficial look it does not seem to bring any new elements into your former store of knowledge. But, think deeper about it, about the combination of symbols of the great Androgyne and you will find the solution to many enigmatic problems of the mystery of realization. Tradition does not permit of more explanations in the matter, as they have no value except for the one who has discovered them personally by his own effort. Medicine will not work unless you swallow it yourself, instead of listening to how another did it.

LESSON 66

The time has now arrived for the beginning of the arithmological analysis of this arcanum.

Equation No. 102: $15 = 1 + 14$

The Divine Essence (1) directs deduction (14); three-plane Man (1) who undertakes the problem of harmonizing his *astrosome* (14).

Active Nature (1) leads its development (14) to the exact numerical meaning.

All these three interpretations of Equation No. 102 give us an excellent image for directing the arcanum Samech (XVth) *from above*, acting on the most refined organs of its ganglionic system. To competent occultists this picture has appeared so full and charming, through its universality, that it has tempted different kinds of initiates in the past, and probably does the same in our own epoch, in the most secret circles of initiatory societies.

(1) Some have found in it the perspective of bliss through the contemplation of that image *alone*, and so have arisen the schools of the 'CONTEM-PLATIVE UNION WITH NATURE'.

(2) Others have liked the idea of *self-perfectioning* through penetration into its currents as a PASSIVE ORGAN OF IT, and this has affected a part of the Indian schools (I am leaving the student to find out, which of the Hindu occult schools belong to this type of contemplation).

(3) Still others have discovered the perspective of improving the social and political systems of nations through the creation of a new system of ruling those nations, based on the same pattern $(1 + 14)$. To them belonged the synarchists of *China* (until 1912), of *India* and of *Western Europe*. I am making a distinction between these three representatives because of the historical changes which occurred in the meantime. The Chinese, as a mass, after their revolution, abolition of Empire and establishment of a republic, recently transformed into totalitarian rule, can hardly still be considered as 'seekers' of better forms of self-rule. They think that they have already found it.

On the other hand, India and the West were, and still are, in the camp of 'seekers', that is they are still evolving in the framework of their present political organizations, that is states.

A brief evaluation of these three currents may be advisable. If a separate human self will tune itself to passive contemplation of the powerful picture of Baphomet's currents, then—without being noticed—because of its stay in the magnetic field of that current, it will be harmoniously magnetized, concluding peace with itself, and realizing the domination of the subtle over the gross. In other words, such a contemplative mood in an occultist will initiate him into the Seventh Arcanum without those hard efforts, which usually occur when the initiate seeks the victory of the THREE over the FOUR in himself.

But the Seventh Arcanum concludes only the *Discipleship* of the Masonic education. It is evidently not sufficient to tune properly just the separate CELL OF THE GREAT PROTOPLAST (as every human being is, consciously or unconsciously). There must also be exact knowledge of the problems of *other cells*, if one has to associate with them in a right and due way. An attempt is made to solve this second important problem by those

Initiatory Schools, which teach their adepts thus: '*Let your meditation, in the realm of metaphysics, your astral exercises, and your behaviour on the physical plane*, EVERY HOUR, EVERY MINUTE and EVERY SECOND, *reflect the idea*: I AM AT PEACE WITH EVERYONE AND WITH EVERYTHING; I TRY TO WANT ONLY THAT WHICH IS WANTED BY THE EVOLUTIONARY-TUNED CURRENT OF HUMANITY. I WISH TO CONVEY ONLY THAT WHICH DICTATES THE METAPHYSICS OF THE ASCENDING TRIANGLE. I WANT TO DO ONLY THAT WHICH COLLABORATES WITH THE ACCELERATION OF MANIFESTATIONS BELONGING TO THE KARMA OF NATURE.

'Briefly, I know firmly, that my task is to be a cog-wheel which transmits exactly and truly the movements of the world's mechanism, and which does not create friction in that mechanism because of its own personal fantasies and desires.'

Such are the Schools of EVOLUTIONARY NATURALISM.

But, apart from that Masonic Hé, representing the aims of that organization, there is still the MASTER'S INITIATION, striving for the creation of VAU, born from the duly magnetized Father and fed by the duly naturalized Mother. Realization of such a VAU in the realm of the *world's policy* creates the ideas and dreams of the so-called synarchists. They have the vision of the 'united states' of all cultured nations, directed inside by the three great institutions: *Spiritual*, *Juridical* and *Economic*. The *Spiritual Department* would, say, generate the logic of the collective deduction of united conceptions in the religious, philosophical, scientific and orthodox masonic realms.

The *Juridical Department* would rule over the NAHASH of national and personal strivings and desires, creating laws, whose aims would be the harmonizing of those desires, so ensuring permanent peace on the planet and the outstripping of all breaking of laws.

The *Economic Department* should rule over the possessions of separate persons and whole nations, in order to hold humanity's prosperity at the best level, allowed by the *Fatum* (Fate) of the given epoch. This institution would operate through the full understanding of the *principle of the reversibility of values*.

Some might object: in logic there is often the choice of the *first precursor*. In the problem of adjustment of requests there is also the choice of different legal principles. The application of the *theory of probability* to the question of rotation of values allows us the choice between several different combinations.

The synarchists would answer: Yes! Every organism needs its monad, endowed with will-power, in order to make a decision in dubious cases. For this, as the Head of the Spiritual Institution there should be a Patriarch; for the Juridical a Monarch, and for the Economic a leading or senior Economist.

I have spoken here about *synarchy* only to give you a general view of the influence of the Contemplative Natural School on minds, occupied with politics. Those who are interested in the role of occult conceptions in the matter of politics are recommended to study the works of St Ives d'Alveydre, still available from some Parisian bookshops.

Equation No. 103: $15 = 14 + 1$

A ready deduction (14) of the teachings of the given epoch may strangle the intuition of the Divine Essence (1) in Man.

It is the formula of the sad atheism, which was active in the eighteenth century, on the grounds of pseudo-scientific research. There is no need to speak much about this current of the past, although it still counts a number of representatives in our own time. Fortunately, the majority of leading thinkers have ceased to support this negative current.

A ready-made, standardized, but false harmony of an undeveloped society (14) may limit and suppress the reasonable, highly directed and practical strivings of a separate self (1) which willingly agrees to the slavery of the morale of that epoch. It is also a not too bright picture of freshly appearing impulses in humanity, which give birth to chaotic currents even in contemporary literature. Because of this we find the book markets flooded by so many unaesthetical and openly pornograhpic creations, by men who are even talented, but who have weak will-power.

The general impetus of the processes of transformation in Nature (14) is the measure of its creative means (1). It is the formula of dry determinism in the realm of physical phenomena, which, with a little extension, might lead men to pure fatalism. This may allow us to live another dozen or so of unnecessary years, on account of economized fluids, resulting in security and lack of energetic manifestations of our will; but history clearly shows, that such fatalism, deprived many nations of individual life, to say nothing about the forlorn talents of separate selves.

Equation No. 104: $15 = 2 + 13$

To know the mysteries of the Divine Substance (2), to accept it as a basis for meditation, adding to it the mystery of Immortality (13) of metaphysical principles, means to dominate fully the logic of the world OLAM HA AZILUTH (15).

To know the mysteries of human sensitiveness (2) and the mystery of the reincarnation of souls (13) means to dominate the powerful serpent *Nahash* in its realm of activity against humans (15).

To rule over the synthesis of the arcana of already created Nature (2), that is over all the phenomena present in the epoch and to add to this knowledge the ability of possible transformations of energy (13) would mean full acquaintance with the *working mechanism of Fate in Nature* (15).

Equation No. 105: $15 = 13 + 2$

To seek after the permanent metaphysical principle (13) and to come to the *feeling* of the *Substance* (2) is proof of the possession of logic in the SECOND FAMILY (15).

By way of incarnation (13) to come to the subtle feeling (2), which is the characteristic of the astrosome incarnate so many times, means to become initiated into the mystery of NAHASH (15) concerning its function in the astral world.

To seek the understanding of Nature through the way of transformation of energy (13) and to be convinced, at the end, about the necessity for concentration on previously realized creations (2) as points of support for these transformations, again means the realization of Fate's action in Nature (15).

Equation No. 106: $15 = 3 + 12$
Equation No. 107: $15 = 12 + 3$

The great words of the *Emerald Tablets* tell us, that Baphomet (15) comes from the metaphysically creative Heaven (3) to the zodiacially materialized Earth (12); from recognition of the Gnostic Law of Creation (3) to understanding of the Principle of Sacrifice (12), and from Divine Nature (3) to the mystery of the Logos's Incarnation (12). Realize these words in one's heart, not forgetting that the same powerful CURRENT also goes the reverse way, that is from Earth to Heaven, and you will understand the true face of the Fifteenth Arcanum, one of the most controversial in the whole pack of the Tarot. I believe that the student, who, in his Hermetic endeavour, has come to this arcanum, long ago realized that the 'unfolding' of the arcana in the arithmological way is a matter for occultists who have attained considerable experience and degree of development. To such our equations will bring valuable material for their own meditations; but for those who are not yet sufficiently prepared, the unfolding process will seem like cumbersome mental operations, often without apparent sense. It cannot be helped. The most advanced equations of Albert Einstein speak little to insufficiently gifted mathematicians.

LESSON 67

In this lesson we have to continue the analysis of the Fifteenth Arcanum of the Tarot. If we understand its meaning, then we may say that, for example, the Old Testament was given to the Patriarch Abraham by God; but from the other side, it was magnetically attracted by the conscious search of Abraham himself. God does not speak to those who are not ready to listen to Him. This is one of the axioms of Hermetism.

If the laws which govern the multiplying of human bodies on this Earth, because of the necessity for many selves to be incarnate, invokes our charity, then, in reverse, *practical charity* will stimulate our ability to understand the brotherhood of all souls.

If the prolific emanations of Venus-Urania were coagulated on the physical plane into the densely material phenomena of the Zodiacal Cycle, then simple knowledge' of the visible yearly movement of the Sun would induce human nations to follow the great principle of the Hierarchic Law and for the unitarian formulation of all patterns belonging to the normal creation.

Equation No. 108: $15 = 4 + 11$
Equation No. 109: $15 = 11 + 4$

The form (4) and the invincible force (11) of the Metaphysical Triangle create our logic (15).

Authority (4) joining itself to the Chain (11), contains all the impulses which we can produce in the realm of form (15) (in the astral plane).

Preparation of the surroundings (4) according to the mysterious principles, which we call the 'Forces of Nature' (11) unveil to us the manifestations of Fate (15).

Equation No. 110: $15 = 5 + 10$
Equation No. 111: $15 = 10 + 5$

Knowledge of Good and Evil (5) and an understanding of the Testament (10) gives the full image of Logic (15).

Elaboration of the Pentagram (5) and the learning of the Kabbalah (10) may be summed up into the initiation of great Baphomet (15).

Religion (5) as a souvenir of Nature's past, and the ruthless World's Mill (10) in the present time, will form the proverbial FATUM (Fate) in the world of phenomena (15).

We will pay special attention to this equation, in its second (plane of Man) and third (plane of Nature) applications.

Now you will see the series of instructions, which have a purely occult character. They are valuable for those who well know psychology and its Hermetic interpretation.

If you want to produce in some system the state of equilibrium, using the mantram ש מ א (Emesh), then you must first live through your own stage of metaphysical libration; then the stage of Hermetic balance, and finally the stage of karmic reaction. If you experienced all this incompletely, or only on one side, then the effects of your operation will also be incomplete and imperfect.

If you chose the *Great Name* י ה ו ה (Yod-Hé-Vau-Hé) as a dynamic manifestation of your will, then the effect itself will show clearly, just how much and how you really did consolidate and strengthen in your own life, that great principle of the *Gnostic Formula*.

Suppose that in your lifetime you are a plagiarist, then your mantram may not give the effect which you tried to think through, but other effects imposed by the pentagrammatic elements (that is other men) of the environment in which you live.

Suppose that you carelessly accept and wrongly attend to or nurse some borrowed ideas, then the picture of manifestation will be incomplete or unfinished.

If, for example, your VAU is weak (that is the ability to realize in practice what you accept in theory), then the current you try to create will be formed, but it will be *powerless*.

If your SECOND Hé is weak, then the operation performed can apparently be a very showy one, but it cannot be a basis for any serious realization. This will be only a '*straw fire*' or a flash of will-power, a fire which is quickly extinguished and leaves no trace.

Do not try to exteriorize yourself into the astral if as yet you have not experienced any individual form of consciousness, INDEPENDENT OF ITS PHYSICAL SHELL. For that process (described in former lessons) must be YOUR EXTERIORIZATION, but NOT AN

EXTERIORIZATION IN GENERAL! This warning has an un-compromising character, and you ought to understand why.

The factor which carries your consciousness into the utterly new and usually dangerous environment, as happens in exteriorization, must first be well defined, MUST REALLY EXIST. You cannot enter into a new world without having formed a good vehicle for that purpose. Every reasonable mind will agree with this.

Do not try to invultuate anybody, if you are still powerless in the *clear imagination and understanding of the influence of that operation,* and if your ability is limited only to the imagination of the theoretical possibility of influencing magically. Otherwise the result will be deplorable for such an unripe magician.

Do not try to build any *theurgic operation,* if all you know and see, are only the ready-made patterns of the prayers of other men, and if you can only repeat such prayers with your lips, without praying with your HEART and without condensing its mysterious sounds. Briefly, do not perform such an operation if you have never heard the roar of your own Hermetic Lion. You have to realize, that the responsibility always rests with the operator, who was warned about the dangers.

Do not draw foreign pentacles, if you do not feel that they are pictures on your OWN contemplation; if the Kabbalistic signs of these pentacles do not symbolize the organs of your own astral body to you clearly, and if you do not feel their limits, like fences, built from your own active fluids. If you are an occultist, then you will know what I mean. True, scientifically performed magic operations need no less efforts and ability than is required from a famous surgeon, when performing the most delicate and skilful of operations on a human body, to save, but not to destroy its life.

I repeat, your own weak Kabbalah is still better than the best possible one which belongs to another person, and not yet experienced, studied and lived through.

Better a senseless sentence, considered by you, in ignorance as a man-tram, than the most learned counting of Kabbalistic elements, which were neither understood nor meditated upon by yourself.

This is the knowledge enclosed in the unfolding of the Fifteenth Arcanum into 5 and 10.

LESSON 68

Equation No. 112: $15 = 6 + 9$
Equation No. 113: $15 = 9 + 6$

The Law of Analogy (6) and Higher Protection (9) ensure pure and efficient Logic (15) by the choice of starting points, when applying that law.

Freedom of Will (6) and traditional Initiation (9) ensure domination over one's own passions and the making use of similar passions in others (15).

Knowledge of environment (6) and circumspection (9) ensure the right choice of the moment, favourable from the point of view of Fate (15). These are simple but deep truths which do not need any special commentary.

Equation No. 114: $15 = 7 + 8$
Equation No. 115: $15 = 8 + 7$

Victory (7) of ideas over form, and cognition of the Law of Libration (8) related to the World's Scale, make the logical thinking of the adept (15) secure.

Victory (7) over oneself and knowledge of relative laws (8) allow of the exploitation of the passions of others (15).

Knowledge of the Law of Property (7) and the Law of Revenge (8) are synonymous with an understanding of Fate's role in life (15).

These unfoldings end the theoretical analysis of the Fifteenth Arcanum. We will now pass to the practical application of its principles, which is divided into two parts—passive and active.

A. *Passive States*

Passive states realized because of an understanding of the Fifteenth Arcanum mean: the adjustment and tuning-up of currents in our astrosome, which direct the functions of its ganglionic system. In this tuning process, a Hermetist tries to harmonize these currents with the vibrations of currents from outside, which have a larger amplitude, that is are more energetic and subtle.

Imagine the whole astral plane as a living being, and observe all transformations which take place in it, as manifestations of the ONE LARGE ONE-PLANE ORGANISM. This is a practical instruction which gives you the starting point.

Now, this *living entity* will be in our case, just Baphomet, as taken from the Knights Templar's teachings. It is the *astrosome* of the MACROCOSM, with added astrosomes belonging to pentagrammatic beings of evolutionary, involutionary and neutral types, which do not enter into *Malkuth* (that is, are apart from the physical world at the time).

On the other hand, clearly imagine your own astrosome, as an astral MICROCOSM, ruled by your *mental* consciousness and operating the arcanum of adaptation. Now it depends on you, to tune your astrosome on a given amplitude of vibrations. The size of the human astral scale is unlimited in the evolutionary direction; but of course, long exercising is needed, in order to tune it to a very high tone. Such exercises may extend over many incarnations.

On lower tones your instrument may be tuned more easily; but this direction has its limits and cannot be continued to infinity, as the limits, in this case, are tones which belong to the maximum possible condensation of fluids.

Our dense state of physical matter is not the most dense, for there are still further sub-planes of it, which cannot even affect our senses, because of their extreme condensation. Through these grossly materialistic realms evolutions are passing with which we will normally never come into contact.

To those of my readers, who are especially interested in such things, I can recommend the famous book by Paul Sédir, *Initiations*, in which is given much amazing information about the non-human dwellers of the universe.

To enter into contact with some organ of Baphomet means to tune one's astral resonator, or better, the whole system of such resonators, to the scale of that organ. This can be a *very fine one* (as, for example, the Egregor of the Reintegrated Brethren of the Rose + Cross in its subtle astral constitution). It can also be of a *middle type* (for example, a synthetic cliché of a definite current in the arts). The lower type may be conceived of as a deceitful cliché of the Egregor belonging, say, to a *Chain of Satanists*.

I would like to mention here, that Hermetism agrees with the classical biblical definition of 'Father of Lies' given to the *personification of evil*, that is Satan or the Devil, for the ultimate evil is none other than the ultimate lie, negation, unreality.

Here a question usually arises: How can it be that something which is a lie, negation, non-existence can influence even pentagrammatic beings so strongly and deceive them, bringing to them, as a consequence, errings and suffering?

The true answer would be purely individual: ask yourself WHY in this life do you like (sometimes, at least) to pursue aims which you know to be only temporary, mirage-like things?

Hermetism, as well as the peak of Eastern occult philosophy, *Advaita Vedanta* with its contemporary exponent, the late Great Rishi Ramana (1879-1950), both agree that the very cause of all evil is the desire for a SEPARATE EXISTENCE, or simply *egotism*. On this being removed, a man becomes a *Reintegrated One* (in the Western Hermetic Tradition), or a *Liberated One* (Jivanmukta in Vedanta).

If we go still further we will see, that both branches of High Occult Science recognize the cause of such a *downfall* of Man as being his IGNORANCE (Avidya in the Eastern Tradition). Christ said the same: '... know the Truth, and the Truth shall make you free.'

Naturally, such a tuning of our astral resonators for a desired tone usually appears as a result of long and tedious work, affecting all the additional separate problems, which must be solved in that way. The testaments of Saints, genuine systems of Eastern and Western Yogas, and other initiatory sources give enough instructions in that matter. Meditation, and purification of consciousness leading to its separation from the material shells are the cardinal means. I gave a complete system of such exercises and theoretical exposition in *Concentration*.

Anyway, if the problem has been solved in this or another way, then our astrosome appears as an element, stimulating the vibrations of the corresponding Egregor's organ, in this case, of Baphomet himself. In other words, our astrosome has become joined to a certain Egregor. In reverse, it can also be said that the Egregor is vampirizing our astrosome.

But, which means do we possess to perform the above-mentioned operations with our astrosome, its tuning, attachment to an Egregor, and so on? Speaking exactly, there is only one proven means, that is the so-called *monoideism*. What is it?

If a certain idea is considered by us to be much more important than another, then the creation of FORMS corresponding to the FIRST idea is much easier than for forms belonging to the second less important one. If a certain idea is put into FIRST place in the realm of our mental activity, then the creation of the realizable *tourbillons*, according to the above-mentioned law, becomes very easy and effective. We can say further that: those of you *who are initiated*, or will attain *Initiation corresponding in this our epoch to that of the Knights Templar*, will recognize to what an amazing degree we are (and may be) all mighty in giving birth to those chosen FORMS.

The famous Indian occultist and mystic Swami Vivekananda was right when he stated: 'A strong thought created by someone meditating far off in a cave in India, or in a quiet room in a Western city can have repercussions anywhere on the planet.' This statement is only natural if we know and accept that no energy is ever lost in Nature.

The contemporary Spiritual Giant, Sri Ramana Maharshi, who spent all of a long life as a centre of spiritual radiations, inciting human beings to seek after their own inner, true Self (Atman), has been responsible for many of the currents arising among sincere seekers, although they might never even have heard of the Master's name.

Anticipating what properly belongs to the Twenty-first Arcanum, I would like to mention, that everything referring to *ideas and forms*, as stated before, is equally valid for the next grade, that is to FORMS and PHYSICAL REALIZATIONS, but with certain limitations in power. A key to these limitations may be found in the Initiatory Degrees of Orthodox Masonry.

Anyway, our theme does not belong to physical things, but to the astral forms which are not outside us, but just inside the astral counterpart of our own Microcosm.

So the method of application of monoideism leads to the establishment of a certain aim or aims, putting them in FIRST place until the attainment is achieved on this or another plane. This is the *essence* of MONO-DEISM. About its *substance* we know only what has been said in the First Arcanum, referring to the creation of collective units or beings.

It is hard to avoid the remark, that monoideism is a close relative (nay a brother!) of concentration, of that all-powerful art in every form of occultism and even spiritual paths. By concentrating ourselves on anything, we simply give absolute preference to some thought or feeling (even a physical act) before any other. Concentration, being the ROOT, is perhaps the most exigent in its applications, more scientific than any other occult practice, as you may see for yourself from any reliable course on concentration.

Hermetism anticipates in its adepts a certain degree of the ability to concentrate, and *this refers to all the arcana in this book*. The student will do well if he always remembers this when trying to decipher some not-so-easy part of the present exposition.

The next step of monoideism will be the preparation of the astral monoform, belonging to the monoidea given. This means that this astro-form must be built from the cells of *our own astrosome* with the addition of those astral organisms from outside, which we were able to vampirize (or to use, which is the same). As cells, we will understand here the astral currents or tourbillons. In some cases this addition may not be necessary.

Again, about the *nature of monoideism* in relation to the Tarotic philosophy, it may be said, that IT IS SIMILAR TO THE NATURE OF BAPHOMET (see the last quotation from the Emerald Tablets, Lesson 65). It means, that the current (whirlwind) of the monoform descends *from the monoidea* to its physical point of support, and being reflected from it, ascends to the idea again, thereby supporting and fortifying that monoidea, and directing its vibrations.

Now we may be able to realize the deep and practical meaning of the *breathing exercises* so closely connected with the mental and astral formulas for the desire to acquire certain abilities and moods (see lessons of the Fifth Arcanum). The same has been told there about the methods of creation (or generation) of the *'idea-forces'*.

One of the tests most common and easily performed, which would show one's real occult (not spiritual) development, is one's ability of conscious actions in the astrosome while the physical body is asleep. When your meditations—as recommended in this course—are beginning to advance, your dreams gradually start to take a different shape. Instead of misty events, apparently devoid of all sense and causality, we begin *to remember* our activities on the astral plane. Firstly, they will be connected with our earthly life and environment. We may *'see'* or *'visit'* our acquaintances or distant places, known or even unknown to us from our experiences in the waking state. All of them progressively became more clear and concise. We may even remember the smallest particulars, such as clothes of persons 'seen', the time on clocks, our own attitudes, and so on, also words spoken and heard in the astral world.

But the moment of passing through the threshold between the waking and dream states will still be enveloped in the veil of the *unconscious pause*, or lack of any awareness at the time.

However, if we continue our exercises in concentration and meditation we may find some day (better to say some night), that we were able to recognize our status while travelling in the astral *space*. It is a *magic formula* like: '*I am now in my astral vehicle independent of my body, which lies somewhere down there on the Earth.*' For an average, untrained man the first dawn of such consciousness, in so far unusual conditions, *will invariably bring* an awakening from sleep, and so a compulsory interruption to our astral experience; but if we are sufficiently trained, especially in the solution of and meditation about the 'equations' appended to every arcanum, then things may be different. Then we shall be able to PREVENT any compulsory awakening, as was before, and we may continue, with utmost clarity, to remain consciously in our astrosome and its surroundings. We then become a being endowed with a DOUBLE life: One by day, ANOTHER by night, both fully LIVED, and based on the continuous awareness—I AM! The ancient Graeco-Roman initiates knew well about this mystery, and expressed it symbolically in the *two-faced* enigmatic figure of the god JANUS. In recent times some modern occult schools taught, and still teach, the techniques of that kind of *astral awakening*, while still alive in the physical body.

M

We may see that it is something different to *astral exteriorization*, as mentioned in the Thirteenth Arcanum; it is not complicated and seemingly more accessible.

The German occultist and writer, Gustav Meyrink, referred to such a 'second life' of man in his books (see: *The Green Face, Golem* and *The White Dominican*).

Hermetic Tradition gives more attention to the problem of a CONSCIOUS passing from the waking to the dream state, and vice versa.

The best means which can be recommended, is the EFFORT OF HOLDING CONTINUOUSLY — BEFORE FALLING ASLEEP—TO THE FORMULA 'I AM' trying to retain it until we are in the astral plane, which here in plain language means bodily sleep, but with full consciousness.

This effort requires, as does all occult activity, a certain power of concentration, roughly corresponding to the *first three series* of Part III of *Concentration*. It is a very favourable condition for an occultist, who becomes acquainted to pass from one plane to another, *always being conscious of his eternal* 'I AM'. There is nothing better and at the same time more harmless, than that magic formula, when it is fully understood by the adept. *It will guard him from all dangers and unexpected conditions*.

More effort is needed in order to RETURN consciously from the dreaming state to one's physical body, than from the waking state to the astral plane. But both phases are feasible for those who KNOW what they want, and who have a sufficiently firm power of decision.

I do not need to repeat, that this operation with the formula of ABSOLUTE CONSCIOUSNESS—'I AM' is another form of mono-ideism.

LESSON 69

The Sephirothic development of the picture of auto-suggestion (as given in the Fifth Arcanum) is only a more particular method for the transfer of monoideas through their sub-planes of existence. The analogy of the *nature of the monoform* with that of Baphomet shows their common, natural desire to FILL THE VACUUM OF THE MONOFORM. This is the secret and possibility of the creation of auto-suggestion, even though not very concisely formed. The seeking after success again requires attention being subsequently paid many times over so as to support its vitality. This usually happens when the operator is not very experienced in magic activities, for a regularly created monoform lives and develops in itself, independently. Example: you may not even firmly believe that the operation of auto-suggestion will be successful, and still the thing will be done, provided that you do not consciously create any *counter forms*.

Everything said here about the application of the passive phases connected with the Fifteenth Arcanum is very important for elementary exercises in the passive form of telepathy, as well as in psychometric activity, and still more important, when we allow ourselves to be magnetized by an operator for curative or other purposes.

The passive form of telepathy is limited to the reception of outer impressions, such as light (figures), sound (sentences), smell (aromas), taste, and touch; briefly all that our five senses in one or another way bring to our consciousness. Apart from this, there are still many other telepathic impressions, moods and imagination, grief, joy, astonishment, fear, desire to perform some movement, to make a certain decision, all due to the astral contact with the operator, who is far away from the person experiencing these things.

The most valuable form of telepathic message is the seeking for a visual image when contacting the operator, as well as an attempt to be exempt from moral or physical suffering through the operator's influence. Here come the transmission of ideas, of psychical force, of nervous force, and so on.

In all this process of wireless telepathy the whole problem is to tune the astrosome of the passive person to the right reception of vibrations from the active apparatus, which in this case is the operator's astrosome. This problem is usually solved through the *monoideism* of the astral intercourse at the time previously arranged. Often the contact may be made easier through the imaginative work of the passive person's mind, who tries to build an imaginary channel between the two, or a wire, or vision of the operator as if 'visiting', and so on. Concentration in the form of monoideas in order to receive a telepathic cliché may often be substituted by the simple phase of *passive concentration*, transmitting to the operator the inner tuning through the astral channel. Of course, that reception becomes easier as more experiences occur between the two people. If the form of normal relations between the experimenters was, for example, that of disciple and teacher, then the passive part will be greatly stimulated by this, and the reception in the telepathic way will be much better and easier.

Psychometric exercises, as known to occultists, use the contact of the astrosome with certain objects, so as to catch from the aura of such objects, some clichés of astral influences, connected with them. The results of the psychometric experiences are dependent upon the presence in the astrosome of the operator of vibrations similar to these clichés.

That is why psychometry comes easier to persons with widely dispersed interests, than to those who are working with considerable concentration over some definite matters. But among advanced occultists and yogis there are those who, despite their extremely concentrated lives, possess the ability of quite a deliberate and *controlled passive receptivity*, which they use when they want to practise some kinds of telepathy.

The student will find more practical material about the methods for such development in *Concentration*.

The most important factor in the astral sensitiveness of a given astrosome for receiving impressions from outside, is knowledge of the laws governing the submission of a human will to that of another and vice versa.

The French psychologist Dr Charcot completed a series of experiments, very conscientiously, but too superficially. He recognized only *three phases* as follows:

(1) *Lethargy*, the outer signs of which are: elasticity of the patient's limbs;

lack of control over them, and rhythmical deep breathing. Briefly, very similar to deep sleep.

(2) *Catalepsy* with its outer signs of extreme strain on muscles; stiffness of limbs, neck and torso. All parts of the body tend to preserve positions artificially imposed on them. The sight is directed to one point, which can be imposed by the operator, and there is inability to hear even very loud talking. To sum up, a picture of complete separation of the patient from the outer physical world.

(3) *Somnambulism with clairvoyance:* the outer signs are: the patient replies to questions, talks with himself, but cannot realize where he is. Sometimes he feels himself to be in quite a distant place, and sees what happens there; often, according to the operator's will he transfers his consciousness elsewhere. He submits himself to the will of the operator, fulfilling his orders not only in the limits of his somnambulistic state, but also afterwards, at a time as indicated by the magnetist. In such cases the patient is not conscious of what he is doing, acting impulsively and losing sensitiveness and any criterion about real impressions. Not only will he perform everything ordered, but he will see non-existent things and hear words never spoken. He may also consider himself to be another person, and then will act according to the change of personality.

You should also know, that in a case where activities ordered by the hypnotist are very nonsensical or of a criminal nature, we may then observe a fight of the patient's pentagram with the controversial suggestion, which may end in its non-performance. Actions performed under such hypnotic suggestion may or may not be remembered according to the will of the operator.

The experiments of *De Rochas* were more exact, who, through his clinical experiences, multiplied the number of passive phases to thirteen. I will give them briefly in this lesson as they may be of interest to the student.

(1) *A State of Confidence* on the side of the patient towards the operator, who may be able, by a simple talk, to convince the patient of things, of which otherwise he would never be convinced of by another person.

Disciples of a good master-teacher are usually in this state.

(2) *Lethargy*, same as described by Charcot.

(3) *Catalepsy*, about which information has already been given. De Rochas especially points out the inclination of the patient to repeat automatically the operator's movements.

(4) *Lethargy*, similar to (2) but less deep.

(5) *Somnambulism*, as given by Charcot with its characteristic manifestations.

(6) *Lethargy*, still weaker than in (4), extremely similar to normal sleep (but produced according to the will of the operator).

(7) *The so-called State of Harmony* (French: 'Etat de Rapport') is a case of typical tuning of the patient's astrosome to that of the operator. There

are two phases in this state. The first one is when the patient receives impressions from sources different to that of the operator's person. He describes these as being rather unpleasant. For example, when touching another person, the patient says that he or she is built differently from himself and is therefore unpleasant to him.

In the second phase, the patient is simply unable to perceive anything not connected with the will of the magnetist-operator. He does not hear a piano on which a foreign person is playing; but if the operator presses his hand to the ear of the magnetized person, the latter is immediately able to hear the music. In general in this state, the patient needs the help of the operator in order even to see the objects in the room. Light irritation of his skin, if inflicted by the operator is pleasant, but similar actions by other persons cannot be felt or are disturbing. In both phases the patient is quite happy in his new state and does not wish to abandon it. Under such conditions patients are generally able to judge about the intensiveness of the magnetist's fluids, their polarization, and the colours of the positive and negative currents of these fluids.

(8) *Lethargy*, not very deep, pulse weakened, as well as muscular reactions.

(9) *State of Sympathy by contact* in which as before, the patient feels himself to be only in contact with the operator and persons touched by him. But, if one of these persons feels pain or weakness, the magnetized one immediately begins to feel the same, being unable to discover the cause of these feelings, or their relationship to the physical organs.

(10) *Lethargy*, again not very profound.

(11) *The State of Lucidity*: apart from the abilities already described, the patient, in this state, becomes clairvoyant, so that he can see the inner conditions of persons who remain in contact with the operator. He may give quite a right diagnosis of sickness or faults in the internal organs, using a comparison with his own as a starting point. Moreover, in this state he also has psychometric abilities, accurately describing who among the persons in contact with him, had touched a certain object.

(12) *Lethargy*.

(13) *The State of Sympathy at a distance*: the same phenomena as in the State of Lucidity, but without the necessity of the operator touching the patient.

The ability to accept suggestion appears in phase No. 1. It increases, reaching its peak in No. 3, then gradually declines and finally disappears in phase No. 7. That is what clinical experience tells us about the tuning of a patient's astrosome to that of the operator.

One point needs to be stressed. The *tuning of the patient's* astrosome to that of the operator is usually a result of his effort of will. On one hand this weakens the astrosome's ties with its physical body, and on the other with his mental consciousness. The first result appears as a progressive loss of memory about the patient's normal conditions of life already in the *State of Sympathy by contact*, progressing into the *State of Harmony*. The point of support in this incarnation becomes as if lost, the patient even forgetting his name and profession. Further results manifest themselves in a limitation of the activity of the spirit (monad) in the realm of contacts. The weakening of ties between the spirit and the astrosome is not so evident as between the astrosome and the physical body, because logic is still active in the patient, when other means of empirical cognition and life are disappearing. The patient can hardly add two and three together, but he still intelligently compares his organs with those of people placed in contact with him.

From this brief description of the passive astral assimilation of the Microcosm, directed to a particular organ of Baphomet, we will now pass to the processes of active applications belonging to the mysteries of the Fifteenth Arcanum.

LESSON 70

B. *Active States*

Before I pass to the active ones of occult tuning, a few particulars relating to both states might be of interest to students. The abilities of psychometry, telepathy and the sending of mental images and astral moods, are hidden in the recesses of every human being. In some, these abilities are already manifest, in others they are very close to that point, but imperfect development of corresponding cells in their brains prevents the immediate manifestation. In such cases—and they are much more numerous than people usually believe—certain intervention accelerating the adaptation of the brain's cells to the new faculties should be theoretically possible.

And it is also possible practically. In one of the occult circles, with which I co-operated for several years, some experiments were made in the direction of the quick adjustment of the physical body to astral influences. Accidentally I observed, that by massaging certain parts of the skull with an electric vibrator, telepathy and the sending of astral clichés became much easier and steadier.

Then I checked this discovery with several members, without telling them the true aim of the new treatment. The results were rather astonishing, for reports showed that many successful 'astral wireless experiments' were performed by those treated with vibratory massaging of the skull. However, we decided to retain the secret just among our members, as none of us wished to take the responsibility for the unavoidable misuse and wrong application of these abilities, if they were divulged to a wider public without discrimination. And so to this day, all the essential information regarding the place on the skull (which is small and must be located exactly), length of treatment, and the particular movements of the vibrator as well as its power, is and will be accessible only through oral initiation, to those who give the full guarantee of its right use.

The active influencing of Baphomet's organs, as mentioned in Lesson 68, is based on the production of vibrations in consciousness, reflected in the astral of the Microcosm. This Microcosm has the possibility to augment the amplitude of his own vibrations, making them, say, more durable.

Moreover, he can, under certain conditions (the well developed ability of concentration, being the first and most deciding quality), through the steadiness of his scale of vibrations, accordingly tune even other astrosomes, closely related to him in the matter of their nature and constitution. He can also attract into his Chain (Egregoric), astrosomes from his environment, which are similarly tuned, although on a less frequent amplitude of vibrations. The larger the scale of the operating astrosome, the more numerous will be the organs of Baphomet which are influenced and involved, that is vampirized.

On the other hand, the wider the amplitude of vibrations in the astrosome of the operator, the further the influence of his vibrations may be transmitted. In both cases, the astrosome is in a position to augment his store of energy and consequently his realizable means. Here the parable about the 'talents'—given to us by Christ—again finds confirmation.

So, in the work we have termed passive, we were joining the Egregors, while in the active work it is as if we are 'creating' those Egregors.

Now we will analyse the active part of the application of the Fifteenth Arcanum in operations, about which we have already spoken of as being passive.

In TELEPATHIC suggestion the active partner (we often call him the 'operator') intensifies his vibrations in the related sphere, clearly imagining the desired mood, picture, thought, and so on. Apart from that, he catches and selects from the astral plane some beings of types akin to himself, remagnetizes them harmoniously, and forms a Chain from them, directed by his Egregoric monoform of instruction.

Then he uses his own and his Chain's energy, and accordingly tunes the astrosome of the patient (or subject of suggestion) ready for service, in order to play his own melody on it. Baphomet then goes from above to below, and from below to above, as was explained in the *Sephirothic patterns* of the double diabatic process of suggestion.

Support for such an operation may come from images or geometrical figures, contemplated by the operator; his gestures, corresponding to the moods transmitted; intense gazing at a photograph of the subject (patient), and so on.

For psychometric experiences it is important to tune ourselves to a possibly larger scale or *amplitude of the resonance* belonging to that of the clichés, which are likely to be encountered in the aura of the object. Because of the accidental character of these clichés, the operator must develop sensitiveness to any impressions in himself. In other words, one should provide his telephone with a good microphone.

And this is the aim of the active concentration which precedes any psychometric intercourse with the objects.

In operations of *active magnetism* (odic forces, odic radiations) the problem is not limited to the general desire for the success of the operation, but a most perfect application of the descending and ascending astral currents is also required. This means the using of Baphomet's nature for the filling of the vacuum which might occur during the uninterrupted *building of tourbillons*. The operator must also refrain from engaging in any over adventurous actions. The more powerful the operator's astrosome is, and the more it is exercised, the less details he needs to picture in the manifestations of his suggestions. From all of the aforesaid it is clear, that it is an advantage *to learn exactly about all the elements connected with the Sephirothic creation of the entity endowed with the operator's will.* And apart from that, *to learn attentively the astral functions* directed by his own emanations, the mental consciousness of whom works according to the laws of deductive logic.

The student has certainly realized from this lesson, that its contents are principally suited to experienced, practical occultists, and so will also be the case with the next lesson, which is dedicated to the Hermetic cognition of the astrosome of the person, who is trying to perform an active operation according to the patterns of Baphomet. Exact understanding of the Sephiroth is essential.

LESSON 71

A pentagrammatic division of the fluids in man was given in the Fifth Arcanum, and in the Tenth Arcanum it was developed into the decimal Sephirothic System. Now the full picture takes the following form:—

Sephira *Kether* corresponds to the part of the face over the base of the nose. Its fluids are of the type 'N' (neutral).

Sephira *Chocmah* corresponds to the right eye being subtle emanations of a positive character (+).

Sephira *Binah* corresponds to the left eye being emanations of a negative character (−).

Sephira *Chesed or Gedulah* corresponds to the most condensed fluids on the *male* right hand (+).

Sephira *Pechad or Geburah* corresponds to similar fluids of the left hand (−).

Sephira *Tiphereth* corresponds to neutralized fluids of the solar plexus (N).

Sephira *Netzah* corresponds to the store of negative fluids in the right foot (−). I have used the word 'store' because we are seldom consciously able to emanate from our feet, but in them we usually retain emanations for use in other centres through the androgynous knots of the middle part of the Sephirothic pattern.

Sephira *Hod* corresponds to the positive store in the left foot (in the male astrosome (+)).

Sephira *Yesod* corresponds to emanations of the sexual organs, generally speaking accepted as androgynous (N) in theory; but in practice they always show a preponderance of *plus* (+) or *minus* (−).

Sephira *Malkuth* being physical in its essence, represents the whole separate world of dense matter; therefore it cannot be stabilized or defined as actually '+' or '−'. Sometimes it is positive (in certain rare periods of life) but often it is negative, and even androgynous in the periods of transition between the epochs in evolution.

Here is an example, which although brief, seems to be useful, but requires study over each statement, if it is to be truly understood by the student.

ARCANUM XV   361

It is a method, *used in magic as self-defence*, in the event of a sudden attack by a man, or wild beast, and when physical means would be inadequate or untimely.

It is called the 'throwing of astral balls', resulting in the paralysing of the enemy, the damaging of his health or simply preventing him from acting. The classical Kabbalah tells us what to do:

(a) Spare as much as possible of the NEGATIVE fluids in the astral of the right foot.

(b) To them add those negative fluids which the androgynous solar plexus and secondary ganglions of the left side of the body can supply.

(c) In that way try to concentrate as much as possible of the normally polarized fluids in both hands.

(d) Add the store of the negative fluids belonging to the left hand to that already concentrated in (a) and (c).

(e) Then throw all of this against the enemy through the finger-tips and palm of the left hand.

As you may see, the fluids will be of condensed types and their attack will derange and hold the foe. The ancients used this method in order to stop an attacking animal (like a bull or a lion) or a man who had raised his hand against them. In modern magic the proceeding is usually further fortified by the negative fluids of *Binah*. The left eye and left eyelid are chosen as the point of launching. These 'modern' astral bullets are very durable in action and may give the enemy a headache, temporary physical collapse, or a nervous disorder.

Having spoken about the astral side of the operation, I will now explain the physical conditions, which would ensure the operator a better and more efficient basis for processes for the use of emanations, as given above.

So, for a magnetist, moderation in food and in the use of all exciting or intoxicating matters is recommended, and in the measure of possibility, to limit sexual life. Also to exercise, often and systematically in the od's radiation, even on 'dead' objects, if there are no patients at the time. The operator should get sufficient sleep and be in conditions which prevent nervous excitement and feelings of dissatisfaction or pessimism.

The next kind of active influence by the environment is given to us by Hermetic Tradition in the form of the vampirizing of that environment through the introduction of more numerous elements for the disposal of the operator himself. Here the current is tuned by the operator, but is formed according to the image of Baphomet. Otherwise, this current would have no vitality, and would not penetrate into the whole astral organism as one of its component organs. As we will see in the Seventeenth Arcanum, each organ of a living unit is a certain reflection of the *whole*. Without this thesis comparative anatomy would be impossible. Without it there would be no analogy as exists between the Macrocosm and Microcosm. For here our foremost problem is: TO MAKE OUR CURRENT IMITATE THAT OF THE WHOLE OF BAPHOMET.

We cannot suspect the *mental principles* of egoistic motives, which by

M*

condensation on their peripheries, give birth to the world's astral tourbillon —Baphomet. This means that the small tourbillon of your being must also have possibly unselfish and idealistic motives. Some may say that this is very difficult, because for every influence exercised by the separate individuality there is attached a certain amount of interest, as a result of the will-current used for the creation of the tourbillon. This is so! Nevertheless, if the condition of the unselfish YOD, being the root of the operation, is not fulfilled, your tourbillons will have only very short-lived vitality. On the other hand, their lifetime will be prolonged to the measure that your unselfishness grows. This is the LAW, and nothing can change it, whether we like it or not.

Put the astral experiences on a purely mystical basis and their results will be very durable ones; but take some scientific intentions as a basis, and then the results will be less long-lived. If philanthropic altruism comes into play, the tourbillons are again less vital. The astral egotism in relation to one's family will be very short-lived and the tourbillon cannot always be created. The personal materialistic egotism will definitely bring unsuccessful results, and exceptions to this rules are extremely rare.

That is why persons, who try to apply their magic abilities in order to gain material profit from them, not only get nothing, but compromise their reputation as experienced occultists very heavily.

In Hermetic language I would like to stress, that the *Olam ha Aziluth* was reflected as *Olam ha Briah* not because it was necessary for it, but only in order to establish the *diabatic process* (see Lessons 33 to 36).

So you have to act and perform the operation without thinking about any profit from it for you or your family, being directed solely by the idea of the permissibility of that operation from the point of view of your CONS-CIENCE. Consequently, it can confer innumerable benefits on you or your relatives and friends, but that is another business which you dare not ANTICIPATE when acting. It is important that the FIRST impulse was a selfless one. In other words the YOD must be pure. Naturally, the more materialistic your operation, the less this warning will be valid, but then the vitality of your activity will be progressively diminished.

Hence many are able to tell fortunes for money with fairly good results; but magnetic cures need more selflessness, and the more serious the sickness, the more important it is for there to be a lack of any payment to the magnetizer who tries to cure it. But to teach for money in the realm of practical magic is a very problematic business.

With this we can conclude our mental construction of the CURRENT, called its 'Heaven' by Hermetists. It is time to pass on to the *middle* branch. The operative methods used here are very difficult to express in words; but mostly they must be dictated by the *intuition* of the operator. His main instrument is imaginative power. The elasticity and concentration of imagination gives him the same qualities in the forms created by the effort of that imagination. Stability of thinking guarantees durability of results. Imaginative power and the ability to use it are, for a well-trained occultist, the same as is the ability to form plastic matter (clay, wax, and so on) into the products of a sculptor's genius. Realize, that astro-mental matter which is infinitely more plastic than all physical materials, responds to the creative, imaginative effort of trained will-power just as clay responds to the hands of a sculptor.

A certain occult school, which has borrowed its ideas from the East, has an axiom, that the 'creation of the universe is just an effort of imagination of the *Supreme Unique Being*: its thought-form. And that the universe exists only so long, as this effort lasts'. This is a *relative truth*, because only relative concepts can be expressed in the language of the mind.

For a Hermetist, apart from all the aforesaid, the rightly developed power of creative imagination is also the formal recognition of his own individuality, being the basis of the Unitarian philosophy, which comes to us from thousands of years ago, through the Tarot's system of thinking and initiation.

Briefly, the Unitarian conception is the condition of the creating of the UNITARIAN BAPHOMET. Of course, there are a few secrets related to the construction and use of the middle part of the astral currents in ourselves, as well as in Nature outside us. I have no right to speak about them here, because they are a part of the second degree in the Knights Templar's initiation. The same refers to the mystery of the physical elements, serving as a starting point and support for these currents.

Surely every reasonable man will agree with such an attitude, for which excuse would justify the placing of lethal weapons in the hands of irresponsible individuals or those of crowds? So long as the mass of humanity in this present epoch of its evolution continues to lead egoistic and selfish lives, and even with its present limited means of doing evil, still does far too much, so long would the revealing of methods by which vastly superior forces can be subdued, be the most repulsive and harmful of crimes.

Some occult secrets are similar to weapons, which even an illiterate man can wield. Examples are not difficult to find: give a New Guinea head-hunter a good firearm, and he will immediately try to satisfy his thirst for killing, as soon as he understands the simple secret of loading, aiming and pulling the trigger. He does not need any theoretical knowledge for that.

However, every true seeker, treading the path of traditional occultism, supported by the authority of great Teachers of humanity, will develop in himself, through self-initiation, the so-called '*sixth sense*'. This, together with the power of human deductive logic, will lead him to the discovery of those secrets, which properly speaking, are not 'secrets', but just THE ARCANA (see Lesson 1).

Now it is time for an explanation of those points of support on the physical plane, which serve for astral operations and which are permitted to be openly spoken of in print.

You already know about the *thirteen consecutive phases* of DE ROCHAS'S system, so we may now speak about their realization.

These *thirteen phases* are the results and the products of the transmission of *positive fluids* from the operator to the patient (the subject of the operation). And what of the *negative fluids*, a curious student will ask? He will be reminded here to refer to Lesson 70 for the answer.

In the clinical practice of de Rochas the consecutive phases from 1 to 13 were obtained by the placing of the operator's RIGHT hand on the patient's face or top of his skull. In the reversed proceedings, that is from phases 13 to 1, the same was done, but with the LEFT hand. This was done with the co-operating people offering none or very little natural resistance. With stubborn ones de Rochas acted firstly with his *left* hand, so as to produce three negative phases:

(1) Excitability

(2) Faintness of limbs

(3) General paralysis.

The last phase impressed the operator so strongly, that he did not continue any further, and was satisfied with this conquest of the resistance.

It is important to observe the following: the placing of the right hand on the patient's face is not the only means supplying him with positive fluids. The same results will be produced:

(1) By putting the patient into a chain of men in contact with one another.

(2) By the patient's submission to the operator's circulating fluids. There are many methods for this among which I will mention only: the operation with the CENTRAL LOOK; a special attack on the Chocmah of the patient (fixation of his right eyelid, especially the extreme end of the eyelashes at the far corner of the right eyelid); holding the patient's left hand in the operator's right, and his right in the operator's left; good results are obtained by the holding of the patient's right thumb in the operator's left hand and vice versa; the usual passes (magnetic strokes) from the head to the lower part of the abdomen; also standing behind him with crossed hands which are moved from the top of the skull down the neck and lower still to the waist; the holding of both of the patient's thumbs in one's left palm, and simultaneously making quick passes from above to below (head to abdomen), and finally a combination of all of the foregoing methods.

(3) A direct suggestion to the patient (in his presence or at a distance) ordering him to accept the positive fluids.

(4) By putting the patient into more direct contact with the fluids of the World's Baphomet through a partial weakening of the ties between his (the patient's) mental element and the astral one, or of the astral with the physical. The *first* can be reached by ordering the patient to meditate intently on mystical or very abstract philosophical themes; the *second* through the usual hypnotic practices.

Summarizing what has just been said, we come to the following conclusions, that one can be put into:

(A) The sphere of circulation of the world's general tourbillon.

(B) The sphere of circulation of the current generated by a particular Chain, as happens at spiritualistic seances, where a sensitive medium passes through the phases 1 to 6 inclusive, as given by de Rochas.

(C) The sphere of circulation of the fluids belonging to a particular man (in this case, the operator), as was shown above.

In all cases the passive person, or the patient as we have called him, has a clear inclination to imbibe the *positive* fluids, which give us a hint about the astral instinct of self-preservation, which prevents Man from introducing anarchy into his astrosome, by the acceptance of *negative* fluids.

LESSON 72

I have mentioned above about the purely hypnotic methods of weakening the tie between Man's astral and physical bodies. Now comes an enumeration of these methods.

(1) SHINING POINT: for intensive fixation with his eyes, the patient is given a shining jewel fixed to a black background, or a small mirror placed opposite his face.

(2) WHIRLING MIRROR (special mirrors of Dr Luys were famous): a round, well-polished mirror connected with revolving apparatus is placed about two feet from the patient's face, while he sits in a comfortable chair with his head supported.

(3) GONG: after allowing the patient to sit quietly for some ten minutes in a half-darkened room, a strong sound of a gong is suddenly produced, which can easily put him into one of *Charcot's* phases.

These methods function on the grounds of an unusual irritation of one's nervous system, which makes the work of the astrosome difficult in the physical body, thereby reducing their natural relationship. Also, all *gestures and looks* serving as a basis for magnetic operations may be included among the hypnotic methods providing they are used only mechanically by the hypnotist, and without any special concentration, in order to fulfil the outer part of a traditionally prescribed operation. In this case the astrosome of the operator plays the role of a healthy organ of Nature, allowing and making easier for the patient to contact Nature in a particular way. Then the eyes, hands and words of the hypnotist play the role of the *mirror* or *gong*.

If the sudden sound of a gong can merge the patient into a hypnotic phase immediately, the slow repetition of some sounds can also do the same over a period of from 5 to 15 minutes. Recall the usual incantation practices of Hindu fakirs, who want to produce mass-hypnosis and so perform one of their 'miracles', which cannot be explained other than by such hypnosis. They sing or whisper a monotonous melody, absorbing the attention of the onlookers and so making them easily open to suggestion. Those who know the art of resisting the hypnotic suggestion will see no 'miracle' and only the fakir, sitting quietly in the midst of the crowd, and watching the people with extreme concentration.

However, Western occultists and Indian fakirs (I would not like to call them 'yogis') know another means for subduing the resistance of individuals to their hypnosis. They try to rob them temporarily of a certain amount of their *positive* astral fluids, replacing them by their own (the fakir's) *negative* ones. Then, theoretically, the awareness of a man becomes dim, and he may abandon his active concentration, which he used against the hypnotist, merging in a sort of half-conscious dream. This is all that the fakir wants. If he succeeds, the resistance is broken, and you will then see the same impossible things which the hypnotist suggests to you.

But the influencing of one's vital fluids requires some special activities from the side of the operator, and these are usually visible. He will look at you intensely, or even make some movements in your direction with his hands, often disguising the true character of such movements as in a polite invitation to be seated or to come closer. I experienced this when in India, in a suburb of Vellore, a town once famous for its fakirs and snake-charmers. A quite decent and tidy looking fakir showing his wooden dolls dancing on a triangular table in the middle of a circle formed by the curious people around, only smiled when I told him, that I could not see any doll dancing or his snake rising into the air, as others did. For this time I used a setram, which absorbed me into active concentration and thereby made me immune to the suggestion.

He bowed, looked into my eyes and invited me to come closer to his table. I used a kind of '*odic armour*' (see *Concentration*, the chapters about self-defence) against his gestures, not going closer than to within three to four feet of him. He felt the resistance, and gave up his trick. 'Sahib knows these things' he whispered to me with a smile when I gave him a rupee, although he could show me nothing.

From the optical means of hypnosis as used in the West the best results are obtained with the shining point (3 to 10 minutes), while a whirling mirror puts one to sleep in about half an hour. Magnetic methods connected with the fluidic operations—called 'pranic' in the East—mentioned by me in the description of de Rochas's experiments, are quicker than purely hypnotic ones. About 40 per cent of average men and 65 per cent of average women are susceptible to traditional means of hypnosis, as described in this lesson. Do not confuse them with the actions of a trained occultist in the West or a lower kind of yogi in the East; for any resistance *to these men* necessarily implies a special knowledge of defence and other things on the part of the person concerned. As an illustration of this I have just quoted one of my own experiences in India.

There are also methods of education leading to special sensitiveness to hypnosis and magnetism; but they are not the subject of this lesson. Instead, it is desirable to know something more about the passage from one phase to another in catalepsy and somnambulism. First remember the 13 phases of de Rochas.

The patient, being in lethargy No. 2 may be transferred into catalepsy No. 3 simply by opening his eyes with your fingers. The transfer from catalepsy No. 3 to somnambulism No. 5 may be performed by a slight rubbing of his face, or by blowing into his eyes. These methods are less sensitive than the using of passes along the patient's body or an imposition of hands, and from there comes the leap over the phase of lethargy No. 4.

Precaution compels me to say a few words about the effective methods for AWAKENING a patient from any one of the above-mentioned states.

(1) METHOD OF AWAKENING ON ORDER: a person in the somnambulistic phase, can be awakened by the order to sleep for a certain time, or after fulfilling some activities as prescribed by the hypnotist, such as counting to a certain number, and so on. A recognition of the order received and a promise of its fulfilment is required from the patient. Otherwise the result may be nil. This is also valid for the phase of the *first lethargy*, but does not work very fast.

(2) AWAKENING BY BLOWING INTO THE EYES. This may be used in all phases.

(3) AWAKENING BY PASSES: used in cases of deep lethargy. This is effected by stroking along the body of the patient, with only the *right* hand. First over the torso, and later over the face. A slow, but very reliable method. Both hands may also be used, but then the strokes should be performed from the middle of the torso or face towards the sides.

(4) AWAKENING BY LOOK: magnetically fix the Kether of the sleeping person with your central look, suggesting an immediate awakening to him, but do not pronounce any word. It is used in cases of stubborn resistance to awakening.

(5) COMBINATION OF THE FOREGOING METHODS: used in clinics. When a person is in a somnambulistic state, suggest awakening by blowing into the eyes. Then, when needed to awake, perform the blowing while making a few passes over the face with both hands from the centre to the eyelashes. When the person is already awakening again blow strongly into his face.

In practice difficulties may sometimes be encountered in awakening a person who is in a deep phase of lethargy. These cases usually resist all hypnosis. Then it is recommended first to transfer the patient from his lethargy into a phase of catalepsy or somnambulism, and finally to act as was advised in 1 to 5.

The particulars as given in this lesson are not aimed at making you into a hypnotist. My advice is just the opposite. Those who undergo hypnosis would do better if they directed their efforts to suggesting IMMUNITY from hypnosis to themselves, thereby guaranteeing that nobody will meddle in their lives.

In enumeration of the active applications of the Fifteenth Arcanum I spoke about the influence of man on man, based on the dominance of one's amplitude of vibrations over those of another. It still remains to say something about the influence of a human being on Chains of men as well as on Nature.

In both cases the energy manifested in the object of the operation might be stronger than that in the operator. Even the amplitudes of these vibrations may be superior to those of the operator.

The Western Schools do not teach much about the influence of the individual on the environment. In the realm of psychology, just the least is known about the psychology of the crowd, and we have only fragmentary knowledge in that matter. Nevertheless, we know that even in an ordinary *spiritualistic circle*, the most active member can use the fluids of all members present, and even use these against one of them. A speaker, who addresses a crowd and who creates a circle of listeners round him is quickly able to form an atmosphere of confidence in himself in that crowd. But all these things are rather fragmentary and not united into a well-built system.

On the other hand, the PSYCHURGY of the crowd was well taught by the Indian Initiatory Centres. There is no doubt that some Western politicians have possessed a considerable ability to manage large crowds and assemblies with their speeches and personalities; but from the Hermetic point of view, they do not possess any real wisdom in that matter worthy of mention. Rather they act subconsciously, FEELING the results that come from their activities, without possesssing any theoretical knowledge. I would like to use the expression *tradesmen* not *architects*.

But the Great Teachers knew the secret of mass-psychology. Only recall the fantastic powers of Moses over the rebellious Jews, when—coming alone from Mount Sinai— he was able, by the power of his sole appearance among the rioting crowds, to divide the guilty from the not-so-guilty and to exercise a terrible punishment on the former.

The prophets also sometimes showed a large degree of knowledge of the laws, ruling over collective psychology.

Napoleon I, in his best years, exercised enormous influence on his soldiers, who became as if intoxicated by the presence of the 'Little Corporal' among them and cried for battle.

The *second problem* that of the influence of Man on Nature has been somewhat better handled in Western occultism. I will touch briefly on some of its most important aspects, as presented by the Hermetic Tradition. Theoretical knowledge of the matter is divided into two parts.

(1) The School of Art and its—'How can Man need as little as possible of the illusory means supplied by the Macrocosm?' aims at making men independent and even equal to that Macrocosm. The meaning is, that Man should limit his dependence on outer conditions to the extreme, as these only entangle his dense counterparts (bodies) and involve them in suffering as a result.

In previous lessons we said enough about the particulars of such contemplative clichés. To resume, I will only mention the bare examples of those, who actively make themselves independent and free. You may guess rightly, that in the first place there should be placed the ascetics and contemplative philosophers of all time and nations. Saints and genuine yogis always fought for man's independence from material conditions, they wanted no possessions, teaching us, that Man is Spirit, and not the fragile shell which appears for some few dozens of years on this planet.

Theoretically, the victory of such a kind of attitude and philosophy has been achieved: all the leading religions of the Earth recognize this truth. But, their formal followers do not LIVE this truth, being content merely to talk about it, as of something far off, unreal, and still to come in the immeasurably distant 'future'. Karma is still the supreme Lord and Ruler of men.

(2) Another School, the *second one*, tries to attain the ability of *catching some particular organs* of the Macrocosm, that is in such positions where these are fulfilling some special activities, and are temporarily weakened because of the particular dislocation of their ganglions, then being in uncomfortable positions where they can be compelled by us to perform our will (Ceremonial Magic).

The analysis of this second School belongs to the Sixteenth Arcanum, and it will be explained there.

The exposition of the Fifteenth Arcanum can give you some realization of the fact, that SOMETIMES WE ARE TUNING THE OUTER WORLD TO OURSELVES (or, in accordance with our will): BUT SOMETIMES THE OUTER CONDITIONS, OR THE SAME WORLD, TUNE US ACCORDING TO THEIR PATTERNS. Now you can probably notice how artificial the division of the astral work into two poles seems to be: IMMO (that is the creating of YOD in us) and OBITO (that is the creating of the First Hé of our arcanum in us) (see Lesson 8).

We have to realize that neither the KING nor even the QUEEN are visibly manifesting themselves for us; but just their androgynous Knight through his Knave. The most interesting and real of the operations connected with the Fifteenth Arcanum is the *manifestation of energy at a distance*, and it is born only through the full synthesis of both systems of manifestation, that is the ACTIVE and PASSIVE ones. The last advice in this matter is: IN ORDER TO EXTERIORIZE OUR ASTROSOME WITH SOME ADVANTAGE FOR OURSELVES, WE SHOULD SIMULTANEOUSLY BE IN A POSITION TO ORIENTATE OURSELVES IN THE ASTRAL PLANE, AND TO LET OUR INFLUENCE BE FELT THERE.

To orientate ourselves in the astral is nothing less than knowledge of what we are seeking in it; but in the world of forms and energetic manifestations, in the world where the clichés are living beings, knowledge is invariably bound together with authority. In the astral plane there are no dwellers who are perfectly acquainted with, say, the activities of some ministry, and who at the same time are not endowed with authority in that ministry. Such facts are only possible in the three-plane life, where the lowest manifestation is dense matter. Only on the physical plane are such anomalies possible, where wise and good men have no authority or physical boons, while less valuable individuals have power and wealth.

Do not forget, that the PHYSICAL plane is the realm of FACTS, and the ASTRAL world is the realm of LAWS, while the MENTAL plane is the world of PRINCIPLES. Therefore, do not be puzzled to find that formalism reigns supreme in the world of forms.

And every time that we have anything to do with the two-plane, astral life, we are compelled to be lawyers and formalists.

It is very simple to become interested or involved in some particular cliché, but it is not easy to find that cliché in the astral, where all that is in our three-dimensional world, and many, many other things are placed in enormous space.

If we actually have to exteriorize, then it is best for us to choose for the purpose, a definite sub-plane with which we can be more acquainted on the ground of our earthly experiences.

Our *monoideism* must be trained to direct itself according to our actual choice, no matter whether it is a lower or higher sub-plane; but at the same time, the consciousness in other sub-planes of existence should not be lost. For, if we lose the consciousness of our manifestations in lower sub-planes, we will lose our points of support in them. With this will be connected loss of our authority from the active point of view, while from the passive side loss of memory about things seen.

To lose the higher sub-planes, means to lose the understanding of the seen, and then neither our pentagrammatic authority nor our memory will be of any help to us.

Now, what about the use of drugs, well known since time immemorial, for obtaining some superphysical states of consciousness?

They are definitely harmful and useless in the true sense of these words. They can neither perform nor help any real expansion of consciousness, because they are only a combination of physical matter, which acts on another kind of that matter—the brain.

Apart from the fact, that the Hermetic Doctrine, Christian Saints and true representatives of Hindu Yoga definitely forbid the use of drugs, the action of these chemicals is similar to that of someone who would like to enforce the opening of the eyelids of puppies or kittens long before due time. What can such an undeveloped eye see? Of course, only a distorted image of the world, with harm to any true perception. That is why all those descriptions of the state of consciousness and the visions obtained with drugs are so nonsensical, illogical and vary so much among different people.

For a keen investigator-psychologist all these visions can be found hidden deep in the subject's mind, beneath his normal waking state, being rather similar to dreams.

The true occult method is not any temporary and premature removal of material veils, but the development of inner powers in Man, which by far transcend the limitations imposed by the brain. This method is a fully scientific one.

No saint, true yogi, or occultist ever try to get something which they do not yet possess, by the use of drugs or anaesthetics.

This should be enough for us, if we are seeking after light and not for doubtful pleasures and curiosities of unrealistic visions, excitement or dreams, which at the end inevitably leave a man weakened and disappointed, especially in the moment of his physical death, when drugs are no longer valid.

A conscious exteriorization as spoken about in this course, is probably

the best practice for those Hermetists, who have an innate and unquenchable thirst to see things beyond and above the three dimensions of the
physical world.

Our idea is to visit other worlds as masters and not as timid and ignorant
pentagrams at the mercy of almost every deception and every entity in the
astral plane.

Such illegal 'visitors', that is those who try to use artificial means
(drugs, anaesthetics and hypnosis) can see *only what is 'shown'* to them, and
entities which appear far from being angel-like, if the visitor himself is not a
saintly person.

But such people would certainly not smoke opium, eat hashish or use
mescaline or other chemicals!

Common sense must be one of the main virtues of a student of Hermetism. We know well how deceptive and false are most of the clichés of
the lower astral. It is only to these which an average man has access who
is not developed by any special occult training and spiritual practices, and
who does not possess any powers, which can be listed as theurgic, or at
least magic ones.

Incidentally, apart from our Hermetic teachings about the conditions
on the astral plane, some eminent Theosophists from the former generation
(A. Besant, G. Arundale, Col. Olcott) honestly warned their members,
trying to reach the astral plane about the difficulties which might be
encountered by them, especially in evaluation of 'visions' and their meanings.
Time, space and all other perceptions are so different in the astral that
without previous training and study under a competent and practically
experienced teacher, much deception and evil will be brought back by the
unwary beginner.

Here are a few examples: without possessing some degree of the power of
concentration and the ability to direct one's thoughts and feelings, a man
would simply be deprived of freedom of movement in the astral, and
subdued by different astral currents, just like a weak swimmer in a choppy
sea. He would accept as real all thought-forms, phantoms of dead and
artificial elementals created by human and non-human dwellers of the
astral plane. Without developed will-power, one would be subjected to
incessant fears and puzzles. It is sufficient to read about the naïve visions
described by some premature adventurers in the astral, when they even speak
about seeing God, talking with Him, and in one case, even dancing because
of an excess of 'happiness'! There are plenty of books available, filled with
such 'visions', but we cannot advertise any of them here.

To conclude the exposition of the Fifteenth Arcanum, and return to the
symbolical language of the Tarot, we are entitled to ask: which *Knave*
belongs to your *Knight* (see Lesson 37)? He should be (and he IS) an
exact and systematic one, in all the endeavours which you may undertake.
This may be best appreciated in those moments of battle against outer
principles, which will be the subject of the next, the Sixteenth Arcanum.

y

Arcanum XVI
TURRIS DESTRUCTA
THE TOWER

Ծ
Capricorn

Eliminatio Logica
Constrictio Astralis
Destructio Phisica

CHAPTER XVI

ARCANUM XVI (ע AYIN)

THE alphabetic sign corresponding to the Sixteenth Arcanum is ע (AYIN) and its numerical value is 70. As the hieroglyph there is a 'material tie' or bond, or in other words 'a connection in a state of tension', similar to a stretched spring in mechanics, which will convey the idea better. The purpose of the preceding arcanum was the generation of such bonds; but, in its methods, logic excludes this or another postulate. This idea is expressed in the *first title* of the Sixteenth Arcanum (in the plane of the Archetype)—ELIMINATIO LOGICA. So, mother *deduction*, recognizing the necessity of *logic*, uses it for the building of theses. But confirmation of one thesis can be (and is) the result of the logical exclusion of all others. This exclusion creates metaphysical reactions in the basic laws of thinking, which here play the role of the 'stressed bonds'.

The necessity of harmonious existence for a separate pentagram compels that pentagram to generate an astral current of the *Nahash* type. This current uses astral reactions and *confirms* the life of one form, while it destroys another. From this comes the *second title* of the Sixteenth Arcanum—CONSTRICTIO ASTRALIS (astral constraint). It is also the basic principle of the whole of Ceremonial Magic.

The complicated way of bringing about transformations in the development of the universe sets in motion an instrument called *Fatum* (Fate) which, with the help of the physical reactions belonging to the 'bonds in a state of tension', preserves some forms, and at the same time destroys others. So we have the *third title* of the arcanum—DESTRUCTIO PHISICA (physical destruction).

The scientific name of the arcanum is TURRIS DESTRUCTA or TURRIS FULGURATA (destroyed or fulminated tower), the vulgar one is the 'House of God'. The corresponding sign is *Capricorn*.

The card of the Sixteenth Arcanum shows us a tower, shattered by a thunderbolt from the dark night sky. Struck by the lightning, two men fall from the top of the tower. One has a crown on his head, while the other has only dishevelled hair. The limbs of one of them form a figure similar to the letter ע (Ayin). Here is the justification for the third title of the arcanum, which leads, according to the Law of Analogy, to two other titles.

The *physical destruction* is clearly visible, it is the shattered tower. But there were still the two men, who evidently wanted to remain on the top, but because of energetic counteraction in the form of the electric discharge (lightning) they were thrown down, despite the authority possessed by one of them (symbolized by the crown). This is just the *astral compulsion*, which is the second title of the arcanum. The first one, *logical exclusion*, is a consequence of the second, and does not need any more explanation. The higher power does not recognize any rank and directs the principle of compulsion.

Arithmological analysis will give us more exact and practical applications of this arcanum.

Equation No. 116: $16 = 1 + 15$

The individual (1) applies the Fifteenth Arcanum (15) and as a result there appears the logical exclusion of his action (16).

Equation No 117: $16 = 15 + 1$

The arcanum acts upon the individual causing his elimination.

Equation No. 118: $16 = 2 + 14$

The metaphysical substance (2) and presence of deduction (14) lead to logical exclusion (16). Without the necessary material (2) nothing can be built.

Equation No. 119: $16 = 14 + 2$

The polar construction of human nature (2) and striving for its harmony (14) leads to *astral compulsion* (16). Without ready material objects (Natura Naturata) (2), and without the calculation of development (14) it is doubtful whether someone would like to play with physical destruction (16).

Equation No. 120: $16 = 3 + 13$

The powerful creativeness (3) of the metaphysical world and the constant presence (13) of the joint elements of that world justify the thesis of exclusion (16).

Equation No. 121: $16 = 13 + 3$

The process of birth (3) and unavoidable death (13) incite us to use the point of physical support (bodily life) in order to realize astral compulsions (16). Creativeness of Nature (3) and the possibility of the transformation of energy (13) joined together, lead to the necessity of destruction of the temporary form (16).

Equation No. 122: $16 = 4 + 12$
Equation No. 123: $16 = 12 + 4$

The unavoidable existence of the forms (4) of thinking and belief in the possibility of the incarnation of *Higher Principles* (12) result in accuracy of logical deduction (16) in the realm of philosophy.

Authority (4) together with Charity (12) will result in a change of astral compulsion (16).

Preparation (4) in connection with different forms of the Zodiacal Life (12) necessitate the destruction of realizations (16).

Equation No. 124: $16 = 5 + 11$
Equation No. 125: $16 = 11 + 5$

Universal Magnetism (5) plus the force of metaphysical principles (11) will create the thesis by themselves (16).

A pentagram (5) resting upon the Egregors of the Chains (11) may create astral compulsion (16).

Religion (5) and recognition of Nature's forces (11) reconcile us to the necessity of physical destruction (16).

Equation No. 126: $16 = 6 + 10$

Equation No. 127: $16 = 10 + 6$

The Law of Analogy (6) and the Divine Testament (10) are sufficient explanation for a normal philosophical thesis (16).

Recognition of free will (6) and knowledge of the Kabbalah (10) provide the force for astral compulsion (16).

The laws of life's surroundings (6) and of the World's Mill (10) may lead to physical ruin (16).

Equation No. 128: $16 = 7 + 9$

Equation No. 129: $16 = 9 + 7$

If the spirit in you dominates the form (7) and you are not devoid of the High Protection (9), then you may discover a complex of philosophical theses (16).

If you went as a conqueror (7) from your experiences on the two paths (and became initiated) (9), the power of astral compulsion (16) will be given to you.

Recognition of the Law of Property (7) together with probability's theory and calculations (9) may provide the explanation, why many physical objects are often destroyed (16).

Equation No. 130: $16 = 8 + 8$

The meanings are: (a) the libration of one thesis (8) fighting with the libration of another (8); (b) the conditional domination of a certain conception (8) in the fight against another man's conceptions (8); (c) the karma of one object (8) in comparison with the karma of another (8): all these three must lead to the process of the application of the Sixteenth Arcanum in the realm of the *Theosophical Ternary.*

From these unfoldments we can see the presence in the Sixteenth Arcanum of fighting elements, and the fights are of a scientific character.

LESSON 74

Among the three titles of the Sixteenth Arcanum only the SECOND (Constrictio Astralis) actually has a practical use for us within the framework of this course.

There was little said in the Fifteenth Arcanum about the fight against Nature, and reference was made to the present arcanum.

The contents of the Sixteenth Arcanum may be best explained in connection with the means offered to us by *Ceremonial Magic.*

In it the operator alone, or with the help of a Chain, chooses the favourable moment and conditions for his operation, and compels some organs of Baphomet to produce certain manifestations.

I would like to compare all the activities of a ceremonial magician to that of applying a kind of Judo against an astral being, which otherwise would probably defeat the operator and not yield to his will.

The constitution of every ceremonial magic operation has three factors: the operator himself, the magic instruments (and books) and the Pentacle of operation. The magician uses his store of mediumistic energy, and formulas of mantramic and setramic character as a help in invocations; he must carefully choose, with full knowledge in the matter, the TIME and PLACE for the operation. These main, and also many secondary means are carefully included in what we have just called the 'Pentacle' of operation. That is why I have to explain everything mentioned above, starting from an analysis of the Pentacle's parts.

Generally speaking, the pentacles of astral operation have the form of a circle. The area of these circles is traced with a *magic sword* (in this case one with an insulated hilt); also with consecrated charcoal or chalk. A very experienced operator can also do it with only the *astral hand*, that is by his imagination (remember the definitions of imagination given in the lessons of the Fifteenth Arcanum, No. 67 and the following ones?). He must possess a very technically plastic power of imagination, which will create all that he needs in the astral plane. Connected with this he must KNOW about the *starting point* for the effort of will which gives birth to the emanation of fluids. All this is based on one and the same inner power in Man: its name is CONCENTRATION. I have spoken about this corner-stone of all attainment, and particularly occult attainment, many times in my books and lectures. And I again find it useful to remind the serious student about this POWER OF CONCENTRATION. It is the *only universal power, which creates, destroys and perpetuates*.

The emanation of fluids needs a good conductor, just as electricity does. Therefore metals, charcoal or chalk are used in the tracing of the magic circles. But what is the CIRCLE itself? It is that *symbolic sphere* in which the operator feels himself to be completely *authorized* for his action, and thereby *fully protected*. No foe can penetrate into that sphere which is especially destined for the operator. Inside it there is only the influence and dynamic radiation of the operator himself. Inside it there are also entities which help him, for ever subdued by him, and finally, the influences of the Chains and Protectors, who authorized him to perform the operation through *adequate initiation, blessings, teachings and permission*. The area of the magic circle is like a fluidic fence, which separates the operator from all outer accidents and attacks. A sensitive person can see the perfectly formed circle in the shape of a FIERY FENCE.

Now, in which spheres should the operator feel himself to be a RULER? Firstly in the realm of his own metaphysical contemplation. His MONAD must clearly realize what is the SOURCE of its existence ('ALPHA') and about its AIMS ('OMEGA'). This is none other than the firm memory about the DOWNFALL and REINTEGRATION of humanity. Those acquainted with the deepest teachings of Eastern occultism will, of course, think about the ATMAN, or if they have been initiated into *Advaita-Vedanta* (by the contemporary SPIRITUAL TEACHER

—Sri Ramana Maharshi, for example), they will know that it is equal to the temporary merging into the FOURTH STATE, which is the ultimate source of all power and wisdom. It does not matter in which way this *Central Meditating Point* precedes further steps of the operation.

The INNER circle of the magic Pentacle will be filled with the figure of the rectangular Cross of the Hermetic Quaternary. The CENTRAL point of that Cross being made by the operator himself. At its eastern end is placed the letter ALPHA, while at the western—OMEGA. These must be traced in original Greek.

Apart from the aforementioned inner contemplation, the operator must concentrate on certain decisions and aims, which may create the *mental centre* and *starting point* of the operation. A powerful and inflexible will, fully conscious of its *pentagrammatic freedom*, which directs the whole endeavour, is the first factor for success. I am speaking of course, about a genuine operation, as performed by a true occultist, and *not any bungling by a layman.*

There will also be another circle, concentric with the first one, at a certain distance (between 1 to 3 feet) which symbolically limits the mental plan of the operation as conceived by the magician.

Now, how have we to characterize kabbalistically the mental plan of the action? Clearly, by the Names of God, which are the Sephirothic manifestations of activity of the Pentagram in the realm of the previously established phases of the Diabatic Process.

Tradition gives us the choice of eleven Names: EHIEH, JAH, JAVE, EL, ELOHIM, ELOHA, SABBAOTH, SHADAI, ADONAI, AB, AGLA, and the twelfth—ELHAI, if you dare use it.

From these, four Names are chosen and placed in the quadrants of the magic circle, obtained from the extension of the arms of the Hermetic Cross inside the first circle. Usually the Names are separated one from another by small crosses placed between them.

The choice of Names, and especially the addition of the fourth Name to the three already chosen, depends upon two laws used in Ceremonial Magic. I will mention only the principles concerned as particulars belong to a special knowledge of magic. If you are really interested in this branch of occultism, everything needed for a magic operation can be found in the books of Eliphas Lévi and Papus.

So, the FIRST law tells us, that the choice of Names used in the circle depends upon the aims of the operation. In the books just mentioned you can easily find an explanation of each Name, describing one of God's virtues, as expressed by those Names. Then, carefully analysing the aim of your operation, you will know which PROTECTION you will need, that is which Name you have to use.

The SECOND law directs you in the choice of the *fourth* Name which you should add to the other three, so that the circle will kabbalistically and additionally formulate also the principle of the Pentagrammatic Freedom of the operator. See also Fig. 30A of this course.

Now comes the turn of the ASTRAL part of the operation. For this the magician should know which of the most important Egregors of the

Macrocosm will be affected by his operation. For that purpose a third (astral) circle should be traced round the second (mental) one.

It will play the role of defence against harmful *astral* influences. If in the tracing of the first two circles we were directed by a *mental* definition of ourselves and of the whole operation, so now we will have exactly to calculate the role of the *Secondary Causalities*, both in ourselves and in the operation. Kabbalistically, this may be performed through the use of the names belonging to the Angels of the planets connected with the operation. In Lessons Nos. 23 and 24 and Figs. Nos. 26 and 27, tables of Secondary Causalities were given. It only remains to add the names of the planetary Angels which refer to them, in connection with the days of the week.

SATURN	= SATURDAY	= Cassiel or Shebtaiel
JUPITER	= THURSDAY	= Sachiel or Zadkiel
MARS	= TUESDAY	= Kamael
SUN	= SUNDAY	= Michael
VENUS	= FRIDAY	= Haniel
MERCURY	= WEDNESDAY	= Raphael
MOON	= MONDAY	= Gabriel

The remark about the Secondary Causalities suggests to us the idea about the necessity for the right choice of the moment of operation, that is in the right choice of the planetary day and hour. The student may have observed, that all the names of the Angels have a similar ending—'EL'.

In old Hebrew, this word is close to the meaning of 'Lord', showing the high authority of a being who possesses such a name.

It is accepted that, apart from the names, the Latin words for time 'HORA', 'DIE', and 'ANNO' must also be put inside the circle. Many also use the phases of the Moon.

Through the operations of Ceremonial Magic there is not only required communication with the entities invoked through the 'sixth sense', but also their physical manifestations, which are accessible to our five normal senses. In other words, *materialization is sought*. And this depends upon the complicated process of lower vampirizing as performed with the participation of elementals.

Under ordinary conditions evocations foremostly concern the *sylphs*, or the chains of elementals co-related to that group.

That is why a FOURTH circle is traced by the operator to counter harmful influences of the half-materialized elements of the outer sphere. In this last circle it is accepted to place the names of representatives of the sylphs in the four corners of the horizon, the eldest of them being placed between the south and the east. To each name is added the Latin 'REX' (king). All other inscriptions are in Hebrew. Knowing theoretically about the outer side of the operation, we will still need particulars touching on the preparation and activities of the operator. Tradition allows ONE, THREE or NINE men inside the circle. In the two latter cases, the speaker is the same person as the operator, but the remaining secondary operators can also use the magic instruments.

If the chief operator is a virgin or hermaphrodite, then there can be only TWO persons instead of three in the circle. One or more persons can be substituted by animals, bound inside the circle, or so trained that they will not leave the circle under any circumstances. This is almost impossible to achieve practically, so animals must be securely chained inside the inner circle.

All this refers to the so-called 'Great Operation'. According to Tradition, there is also a 'minor' operation, in which only the chief operator must remain inside the circle all the time, but his assistant has the right to leave and re-enter.

There is still the 'androgynous' operation, in which the magician can be a hermaphorodite (only one), or a man and a woman, who before the operation, spent a considerable time in mental, astral and physical relations, that is a married couple.

Operators are considered to be initiates of the Hermetic Quaternary (Cross of the Pentacle) and of the story of the Downfall and Reintegration of Man (therefore ALPHA and OMEGA are used in the circle). All this makes a *mystical preparation* (3 to 40 days, depending upon the seriousness of the operation) compulsory for them. For animals, a mystical purification ceremony is prescribed, with purifying prayers and sprinkling with consecrated water.

The FIRST circle of the Pentacle of operation reminds us about the monoideic preparation for the operation, through long meditations and consciousness of one's *pentagrammatic freedom*. Then comes the astral circle, showing the necessity for astral preparation. This takes the form of silence or half-silence for a period of time; efforts to eliminate all impurities and unbalanced vibrations from feelings and thoughts, and the defeating in us of evil or unsuitable planetary influences. In the astral circle we see the extension of the four ends of the inner Cross which should remind us about the four principal magic instruments of the magician:

The *Sceptre* for condensation of the dispersed fluids;

The *Chalice* serving as a fulcrum of imagination concerning the pure images which we had elaborated before the operation;

The *Sword* for dispersing the improperly condensed elements;

The *Pentagram* to remind us about our freedom.

The sword is *absolutely necessary* and the Pentagram is very useful, while the chalice and sceptre are not used so often.

The outer circle of elementals will remind the operator about the necessity of planned self-preparation through some restrictive rules on the physical plane, such as fasting, introductory baths, incensation of the body, looking after good health on the day of the operation, and so on.

This is the general picture of preparation for the magician. Additionally, as regards the outer form of the operation, he must be secured against any intervention from people or other beings who are inimical to him. Therefore, in the corners of the Pentacle, that is opposite the middles of the quadrants of the outer circle, will be drawn four pentagrams (with three points outwards, two inwards). This is for the repulsing of sudden attacks, the pentagrams then being the advance guards outside his fortress.

It is also important to know in advance, from which side the condensed, materialized astral beings may appear, impressions of which might be received by physical sight. So, in advance, the operator establishes a place for the apparitions, tracing in the east outside the circle, a regular triangle with its apex outermost and inscribing in it the Great Name י ה ו ה (Yod-Hé-Vau-Hé) belonging to the senior sphere of the involutionary Sephiroth which later condense themselves.

Up to now we have been occupied with the operators and their needs in magic ceremonial operations. Now it is time to see what are the interests of the entities evoked by the activities of the magician.

We have stressed the choice of time and astrological conditions, and now we should turn our attention to other corresponding factors of the Secondary Causalities. The colour of the clothes worn by the operator, the metals and stones at his disposal, the setrams and mantrams used by him, the aromas of herbs and extracts which will be burnt or evaporated in the censer, which is placed in a special, small pentacle on the southern side of the circle, just outside it, and finally, the colour of the ray which will be directed from the magic lantern into the space over the triangle י ה ו ה (Yod-Hé-Vau-Hé). This lantern should be placed outside the circle to the south-west.

All this has induced some adepts of occultism to create a number of manuscripts and printed 'Grimoires', giving particulars of the ritual belonging to different operations. It would be advisable for a scrupulous student of Ceremonial Magic to read and investigate these Grimoires, in order to realize the aims and construction of the operations. But these books cannot be considered as law-like instructions, because there is no magic operation which could be identically understood even by two operators, unless they prepared themselves together.

The operations of Ceremonial Magic do not extend only to two-plane entities, but also to incarnate ones. It is possible, under favourable conditions of course, to evoke and to compel the astrosome of a living man or Egregor of a Chain, having incarnate representatives, and so on to perform anything.

There are also magic operations, which are not called 'ceremonial' ones, but which contain in themselves the undeveloped principles of ceremonies or their equivalents. Everywhere there is a point of support on the physical plane, everywhere there are special formulas for influencing, methods of supplying the mediumistic elements, concentration on mental and astral details of the operation, and finally methods of defence, safeguarding the operator against accidents and returning blows.

Spiritualistic seances are involutionary forms of Ceremonial Magic operations. There is also a circle, traced through the circulation of fluids in a chain of men whose hands are touching. The evident danger of breaking the circle at such a seance is sufficient explanation to show that the role of the spiritualistic circle is that of a fence, defending the participants. The role of the magic sceptre, which condenses the fluids is paralleled by the table inside the circle. Experienced spiritualists often use the magic sword. A censer is usually in readiness; musical instruments replace the invocations, usually sung, which facilitate the formation of energy and its transfer.

Some conjurations are often used, and then the operator who speaks must be alone. Participants in a spiritualistic or mediumistic seance do not need any *special preparation*. This fact and the resulting lack of concentration of will-power in the circle, generates a certain amount of chaos among the phenomena at such proceedings.

LESSON 75

The beginning of Ceremonial and other forms of magic belongs to the very distant past. Perhaps, to the first conscious steps of young humanity, many thousands of years ago. Anyway, we find this magic element in every primitive tribe, when first discovered by white explorers. This does not need any special proofs or discussion. In this course, we have been occupied with the magic matters of our own race, which at the present time undoubtedly dominates the planet and is the most advanced mentally, culturally and economically. How are we to consider the old magic tradition of Hermetism (Tarot), we who are men of the atomic age, possessing enormous powers of Nature at our service, we who are preparing ourselves for interplanetary travel and exploration of the immense universe? Can magic principles stand the stream of Man's expanding knowledge in the realm of ruling over Nature's forces?

The answer will be double-edged. The fields of interests and strivings differ in different people. Some would 'deify' an atomic reactor, while others the hidden powers undoubtedly standing behind all inventions and progress (evolution) of Man. There is not one absolute standard for everyone. The standard is within each man himself. The contemporary magician is as much a scientist as is a nuclear physicist: you can see for yourself how many things he has to know and to realize. Official science is helpless against death, accidents, natural phenomena and many sicknesses. It cannot actually foresee happenings beyond a narrow physical limit. It knows nothing about the past and the future of the individual human life (before and after incarnation). This science likes to operate more with results than with causes, which it is even able to deny. It casts doubt on everything which cannot be tested every day by anyone who wants to do so.

A scientist considers himself as acting in the period between his birth and death. Occultism says that this is a somewhat one-sided attitude.

I think, that in this world there should be a place for everyone, no matter how he styles his particular interests and beliefs. The creation appears to be based on multifariousness, and not on uniformity, as manifoldness undoubtedly rules over every manifestation.

Ceremonial Magic generally requires plenty of preparation, both in time and calculations. In contemporary occult literature, this kind of magic, which perhaps is the least dangerous, is expounded in full in a few books, among which I would like to mention only the works of Papus, in which one can find *everything* necessary for the performance of a *ceremonial operation* with all its rituals. And there is reasonable certainty of success, if all the prescriptions are duly observed. But the operator must personally prepare the magic book for his endeavour. In it must be written everything which he has to enact, or pronounce and how to conjure the incoming invited 'visitors' from the other world.

I wrote such a book (based on the instructions of Eliphas Lévi and Papus) before I started to operate. It must be written on parchment paper in coloured inks (Indian or Chinese) in astrologically chosen hours of the day and night, and bound in white sheep-skin. No one can see the book, except those co-operating in the circle. Some formulas are considered as NOT TRANSLATABLE from the old Latin or French, so the operator must study the material in these languages. The pentacles and writing cannot contain even the smallest error, otherwise the whole page has to be rewritten. The material must support the operator's memory when in the circle, but at the same time, the sequence of formulas should be arranged so that any layman, accidentally getting possession of the book could not perform any evocation, for any evil proceeding from such bungling would burden the karma of the not sufficiently careful magician.

New linen clothes are essential when operating, and no metals (except a gold Pentagram, if the magician possesses one) dare be worn on the operator's body, or the bodies of his assistants.

All paraphernalia must be bought for the first price asked for by the seller, as no bargaining is allowed. These things must pass through the ritual of consecration and purification, exactly as prescribed in the above-mentioned books on magic by Papus and Eliphas Lévi.

No ailing person can perform any operation, until he is completely cured. Some *Grimoires* prescribe different proceedings before the operation, such as: a *full confession* before a priest, the partaking of the Holy Sacrament and special fasting.

D

Arcanum XVII
STELLA MAGORUM
THE STAR

Mercurius

Spes
Intuitio
Divinatio Naturalis

CHAPTER XVII

ARCANUM XVII (פ PHE)

THE letter corresponding to the Seventeenth Arcanum is פ (Phe). Its numerical value is 80 and the astrological sign is that of Mercury. As the hieroglyph we have a THROAT with a TONGUE, that is, it is a throat from which comes *speech*.

We will analyse the three titles of the arcanum as usually in the planes of the Archetype, Man and Nature.

What actually is the SPEECH of the Archetype? It is the language of eternal HOPE, understandable for those who listen to it. Even then, when apparently everything around us is silent, and when everything forecasts only peril for us, HOPE acts, and radiates its rays throughout the darkest corners of our consciousness. So the *first title* is SPES (Hope in Latin).

In our own world (that of Man) the reflection of the Archetype's language appears as human INTUITION, which warns, protects and saves us. Therefore, the *second title* is 'INTUITIO'. Human intuition is a great ability and advantage.

In the realm of NATURE the ancient nations lived in simplicity and closeness to it. Therefore they were able to listen to and understand the living language of Nature, which now is as good as dead for the present generation of men.

So the *third title* of this arcanum will be DIVINATIO NATURALIS (Natural Divination). To it belong all the varieties of *astrology*, *chiromancy*, *physiognomy*, *phrenology* and everything of that kind. Ancient people did not need so many artificial branches of fortune-telling and divinatory arts as we do at the present time.

The scientific name of the XVIIth Arcanum is STELLA MAGORUM while the vulgar one is satisfied with the simple 'STAR'.

This arcanum is like a natural, *passive* addition to the *active* Sixteenth. It is not sufficient to be logically convinced UNDER ALL CIRCUMSTANCES, often HOPE is necessary. It is not enough to enforce our will astrally, we should also have tact and intuition. It is not enough to know that Fate (FATUM) is pitiless on the *physical* plane, but it may be useful to know how to foresee its forms by the use of divinatory methods.

The card for this arcanum is rather simple in its meaning and design. High in the sky there hangs a large eight-pointed star, surrounded by seven similar, but smaller ones. Beneath them on the earth there is a naked girl, watering the dry soil and the adjacent pond from two vessels, a *gold* and a *silver* one. Behind her we see a coloured butterfly sitting on a rose.

Her right foot is half submerged in the small pond. Perhaps its water is being used for moistening the infertile, dry ground beside her.

Where there is no rain, a comforter will be found, eternally young, eternally virgin, in order to pour on the thirsty Earth the fluid of both Gnostic polarities. In a metaphysical drought of contemplation of men growing indifferent, we may be regenerated through the new freshness of expectancy of the High Influx (*silver vessel*, passive pole) and through faith in ourselves (*gold vessel*, active pole). This is the deep symbolism of the Seventeenth Arcanum's card.

HOPE belongs to the same SOURCE as CONSCIENCE, but the latter reveals itself even without *outer protection*.

If we want to develop our own INTUITION, that ability which belonged to our distant forbears, then we will, like a butterfly easily distinguish a ROSE from weeds, and so come to rest on it.

If we will not close our eyes to the sight of Nature, but if we will gain an insight into her, we will see the LIGHTS in the sky, which astrologically show us the Laws of *Libration*. These laws are dictated by *Karma*, and its conditions. They are inscribed not only in the starry sky, but in any organism which has even a very low amplitude of vibrations in its manifestation, and also in every cell.

The card of the Seventeenth Arcanum tells us, that HOPE, suspended from the apex of *Fabre d'Olivet's Triangle*, will never leave us, and that we do not need to take farewell of Intuition, which belongs to the *right-hand* point of the same mystical triangle. And also, that Karma, being the left-hand point reveals its mysteries and secrets to us every hour, every minute and every second. For everyone of us these mysteries are written in the starry sky (astrology), on our skulls (phrenology), on our faces (physiognomy), and on our hands (chiromancy). Karma unveils itself in every one of our movements, in the smallest of realizations (graphology, cartomancy), in crystal-gazing, and so on. Briefly, in everything on which we are able to concentrate and SEE.

For an occultist, these things are beyond any doubt. This does not mean that he would use all of these systems or even a particular one for divinatory purposes. Some will do so, but others will not. The Seventeenth Arcanum offers its knowledge to everyone, but only willing persons will use it.

The picture of the arcanum should be meditated upon according to the lines given in its explanation. The mystical meaning of the *Great Star* will be revealed to those who studied the Triangle of Fabre d'Olivet in the first lessons of this course. Conceptions like HOPE, INTUITION, KARMA are not dead things. They are living truths in the heart of an enlightened occultist. Moreover, they are PRACTICAL TRUTHS, that is, such which can be applied in an hour of need or trouble.

From my own personal study I can state, that Hope and Intuition are very close neighbours. They usually manifest themselves together in the consciousness of the student. Hope gives us the wings on which we can fly through all worlds, and the motive power comes just from Intuition.

In the East, occultists and Rishis use the powerful AUM, called the 'Great Bird of the Yogis'. It is supposed to 'take' the successful one on a transcendental FLIGHT, that is to perform that which is the aim of the Mystical Triangle.

Meditation on both symbols is a powerful factor for our inner development. Do not miss using it, if your heart tells you to do so.

LESSON 77

The arithmological unfolding of the Seventeenth Arcanum is especially interesting for those who like to see how apparently abstruse ideas are turned into practical hints.

Equation No. 131: $17 = 1 + 16$

The Divine Essence (1) and logical exclusion of Evil (16) for the glory of Good in the metaphysical realm, give birth to HOPE (17).

The three-plane Man (1) and his ability to exclude unnecessary astral forms (16) creates Intuition (17).

Active Nature (1) and the destruction of forms (16) give us the path which leads to the understanding (17) of the mystery of Fatalism.

Equation No. 132: $17 = 16 + 1$

A prayer for Good, metaphysically excluding (16) Evil, puts us in closer touch with the blessing of the Supreme Unique (1), and creates Hope (17).

Equation No. 133: $17 = 2 + 15$

Equation No. 134: $17 = 15 + 2$

The metaphysical Substance (2) and pure logic (15) consist in Hope (17) for the glory of the *Subtle*, manifesting itself to us as the all-penetrating Deduction.

The mystery of sexual relations (2) connected with the realization of the Tourbillon (15) gives Higher Intuition (17) of the Universal Love, to which we have to come to through many steps. One of them is the feeling of *unity* in marriage.

The ready-made world of material objects (2) and their Fate (15) shows us the signs which we may read (17).

Equation No. 135: $17 = 3 + 14$

Equation No. 136: $17 = 14 + 3$

Realization of the Gnostic nature of the Archetype (3) and ability of applying Deduction (14) establish in Man Hope (17) of favourable manifestations of the lower forms of the Archetype.

The principle of multiplication of human selves on the physical plane (3) and the striving of reincarnating souls for their inner harmony (14) create in those consciousnesses Intuition (17), which is equal to activity.

The principle of creativeness (3) and the character of the transformation of development (14) are sufficient in order to read (17) the Karma of Nature.

Equation No. 137: 17 = 4 + 13
Equation No. 138: 17 = 13 + 4

The presence of forms (4) in the Archetype's manifestations and its continuity (13) compel us to have Hope (17).

The striving for the acquisition of authority (4) and the knowledge of Man's mortality (13) incite him to elaborate Intuition (17) in himself.

The Law of Creation and Preparation (4) plus the principle of the transformation of energy (13) give birth to the visible clichés of Nature (17).

Equation No. 139: 17 = 5 + 12
Equation No. 140: 17 = 12 + 5

Knowledge of Good and Evil (5) connected with the expectance of the Messiah (12) is synonymous with the acquiring of Hope (17).

The Pentagram (5) fully realizing the duty of sacrifice (12) then possesses Intuition (17).

Natural Religion (5) applied to the Zodiacal Cycle (12) reveals the mystery of astrology (17).

Equation No. 141: 17 = 6 + 11
Equation No. 142: 17 = 11 + 6

The Law of Analogy (6) together with recognition of the existence of the High Power (11) give Hope (17).

Free will (6) and force of the Egregoric Chains (11) when united, lead to Intuition (17).

The environment (6) and the Forces (11) operating in it, paint the picture of Nature's Karma (17).

Equation No. 143: 17 = 7 + 10
Equation No. 144: 17 = 10 + 7

The victory of Spirit over form (7) and recognition of the Testament (10) give Hope (17).

Victory (7) in experiences on two paths and the understanding of the Kabbalah (10) give evidence of full Intuition (17) in the adept.

The realization of the Law of Property (7) and the mysteries of the World's Mill (10) give ability for the reading of Nature (17).

Equation No. 145: 17 = 8 + 9
Equation No. 146: 17 = 9 + 8

He who knows the Great Metaphysical Scale (8) can move to the right and the left, and who believes in the High Protectorate (9) will have hope (17) that the movement will be to the RIGHT.

Whoever knows the conditioned law (8) and is initiated (9) into the unconditioned law, possesses Intuition (17).

The cognition of Nature's Karma (8) and circumspection (9) in the choice of facts are equal to the ability to read Nature (17).

We will now pass on to the actual contents of the Seventeenth Arcanum in the matter of the scientific complex belonging to it. But first, a summarizing of all that we have learned about this arcanum:

(1) Our own *conscience* teaches us about HOPE.

(2) INTUITION can be developed by your own efforts (by way of sub-duing the mind through the study of concentration).

(3) Empiric facts and traditional knowledge of the Great Code of Initiatory Revelation (through Initiatory Circles or organizations) teach us TO LEARN ABOUT NATURE.

Therefore we will now study the divinatory science belonging to this arcanum in the order as given in these Circles.

LESSON 78

Astrology

Astrology, as well as other divinatory methods, will be given here rather from the philosophical, than the technical point of view. Simply because there are plenty of quite satisfactory books from which anyone can learn the techniques of horoscopes, calculation of houses, and so on; but only through theory, explaining the origin of astrology and its methods, can we gain a real knowledge and understanding of the subject.

All the activities and interests of the three-plane universe, taken as a united organism, are the sum total or synthesis of the activities and interests of all its organs. In the karma of Nature there are visible, schemes of the manifestations of the Archetype, as well as traces of the application of *human will.* And vice versa, in the destiny of the human *consciousness-self,* taken in the whole of its existence, or even only in the limits of the one incarnation, there is participation of the Testament's and Archetype's influence, plus the karmic phenomena of Nature.

That which has been said about Man, could also be said about the Chain of an incarnate Egregor, and about the artificially created organisms (larvas, artificial elementals and other entities) and even about the picture of the way in which flow phenomena in a given epoch. Hermetic Tradition is firm in the statement, that EVERYTHING IN THE UNIVERSE IS MUTUALLY CONNECTED AND BOUND TOGETHER OR INTERWOVEN. This is important! If you realize this, many of your troubles, fears and uncertainties will cease to exist. Let us try some examples.

If everything belongs to the essential UNITY, a LIVING UNITY, where then is there a place for 'death'? You cannot cease to exist in one form or another. If you are part of an immortal, infinite MANIFESTA-TION, what matters it then, whether you are in three planes or only two, or one? The destruction of your body (inevitable, anyway) cannot affect *you,* for there will always be a 'place' for you in the infinite creation-universe.

Everything that happens to you, happens to and affects the WHOLE. Who lives this truth, will not and cannot ever be lonely, even if he is en-closed in the cabin of a space-ship, and already sees his end fast approach-ing. The infinities through which he is flying in his last minutes—far away from his dear mother Earth, which he will never see again—do not oppress him any more: for the vibration in his consciousness, much higher than fear or grief, then takes over his being. The blackness of outer space then recedes before the *inner sight* of the departing Son of Man. His destiny then extends into another direction, or in our Hermetic terminology, on to another plane of existence. Meditate about this scene, imagining yourself in the position of that space-traveller, on his 'no-return' voyage. Live it! And then you will find what I am trying to convey with the inadequacy of words. Then perhaps you will know, *what occultists and spiritually-minded people are seeking throughout their whole lives*, often renouncing things, which average people consider add a true savour to life.

Astrology is one of the human attempts to harmonize one's PRESENT with one's IMMINENT FUTURE. It is not a spiritual effort and therefore cannot bring any spiritual achievement. But how many men are able to strive for and live a spiritual life? The majority needs something more tangible.

If we want to tell the fortune (or foresee events) of a certain group of manifestations, we have to catch the foremost strings which bind these manifestations in the complex of the analysed phenomena. The more important the strings which are accessible to the operator, the more exact and truthful will be the prediction. But *this sort* of search presupposes the inquirer to have a synthetic mind, always ready to merge completely into the essence of the problem given, and create particular methods for its examination. In other words, to tune his mechanism of thinking according to the character of that problem.

But, generally speaking our minds are lazy. They prefer what mathematicians call the 'analytical solution of the problem', that is to create once and for all an alphabet, which will reflect their researches. Men would rather agree to delete a considerable part of the question, if, for its solution, this will help them to use methods which are well known and well arranged in advance. They say: let the answer be incomplete, but in a language well known to us: do not let us touch on ALL the most important strings, if the remaining ones belong to an instrument with which we are acquainted.

It is with these instruments that we will occupy ourselves in this lesson.

The great organs of the universe, often called 'the Chandeliers' affect a lot of things in the world with their activities. Under these 'Chandeliers' we understand here the complex of the SECONDARY CAUSALITIES well known to you from previous lessons, which choose, as their point of support, the bodies in the space round our Earth, with the grouping of which our astronomy is occupied, while astrophysics concerns their constitution. We try to reduce these *Secondary Causalities*, at least in the sphere of their influence on earthly life, to the scale of the *seven planetary Egregors*, and to the so-called 'immovable' stars, which give the tune to the Zodiacal realm. The great Law of Analogy may justify such an attitude. If the degree of illumination of a surface depends directly on the angular co-ordinates of light in relation to the horizon, then why could we not accept that purely astral influences, generally and to a certain extent, are functions of these angular elements?

If the bodies of those things which we conditionally call the 'seven planets' possess large diameters in comparison to the size of earthly observers, then why should we not admit the overhwelming activities of the astral Egregors which have their points of support in those planets?

If the orbits of these celestial bodies are actually little different from the ecliptic's surface, then why should we not direct our attention to the influences, which the Egregors—supported by these bodies—must exercise round themselves?

Every new element entering the astral sphere of influence should be taken into account, especially if this concerns the changes in the already calculated influences.

So astrology is interested just in the celestial realm of the Zodiacal belt. On which sphere does astrology want to extend its investigations? Certainly not on the Archetype, about which any judgement, made on the ground of illusory physical facts, is still harder to make than about a photograph taken many times from the same film.

The general unitarian character of the Archetype's manifestations and their harmoniousness is evidently reflected in every little plant; but Sephirothic particulars of the Archetype's mental emanative activity are too general and abstruse to be measured with compasses on an imperfect photograph. I hope the meaning of this will be clear to the reader.

Human WILL often does not see its own FREEDOM. Then it becomes a slave of the *Secondary Causalities*, and then we can—to a certain degree—guess about its tendencies. This means that the activities of Man are often in accordance with astrological calculations, coupled with a slight use of the theory of probability. Here lies the field of astrology and its predictions.

We call FATE 'blind' because its manifestations can be well calculated in advance and apparently do not underlie any change in itself, that is without participation of the two remaining points of the Triangle of Fabre d'Olivet. Astrology catches just the *sphere of Destiny* and then courageously starts to predict it. If these forecasts refer to the weather or to manifestations of volcanic forces, or other cosmic phenomena, then astrology may puzzle us because of the truthfulness of its forecasts, and then we might bend our heads before the 'omniscience' of the astrologer.

If these predictions belong to human actions, then in countries where fatalism prevails, they will also be very exact, and people will say: 'Let whatever is written in the stars happen!'

But if you enter into a circle of men occupied with the development of will-power, all your praises of astrology will meet with a pretty cold reception. They will immediately tell you that: ASTRA INCLINANT, NON NECESSITANT! (the stars incline, but do not compel). *This is the central truth of astrology* which *exists* for an average man, and its predictions might be very exact, just because an average man has no developed will-power consciously leading him to a certain aim. In our lessons of the First Arcanum we spoke more explicitly about this. It is easy for an occultist to 'calculate' the average undeveloped person; but if a human being takes its fate into its own hands, then things become quite different. Spiritually advanced people do not think about any divinatory practices.

If you meet an anchorite who is not seeking any devotees or disciples, if you are lucky enough to encounter a true yogi, no matter whether of Eastern or Western origin, or a saint, then their sermons will be different. If you may see a sincere spiritual seeker, who is not going along the way of Rosicrucianism or other occult initiatory organizations, and follows the thorny, but sublime path of those 'POOR IN SPIRIT', as a Great Master said in his unsurpassed *Sermon on the Mount*, then you may hear something like this: 'What is your misty fatalism for me? What meaning does your planetary colouring of your will's manifestations have for me? I am continuously looking only on the APEX OF THE TRIANGLE, for there radiates the ETERNAL CHANDELIER OF THE CONSCIENCE, giving enough *Light* to discriminate the RIGHT Path from the LEFT one. My will incessantly leads me on the right way: no matter how your planets are placed. I always know, that all the SEVEN SECONDARY CAUSALITIES bless me on my evolutionary Path.

'Your *Saturn* will always give me the opportunity to surrender to the blows of Destiny.

'Your *Jupiter* will always support my voice by the authority of Good and Right.

'Your *Mars* will present me with virility and the power to bear suffering and martyrdom patiently.

'Your *Sun* always gives me energy and light, and so I shall renounce them for the benefit of my neighbour.

'Your *Venus* will always direct me into the place where there is need for a man to receive help and solace which comes from communion with a *healing heart*.

'Your *Mercury* will bestow on me the gifts of the Holy Spirit, allowing me to speak in a language understandable for disciples.

'Your *Moon* will give me the power of *non-resistance*, which compels the Highest Himself to stand by His devotee.

'My friend, leave all your predictions and guessing! How insignificant they are in comparison with Truth, which reveals to me my HOPE and your STARS! And know that: WE ALL REINTEGRATE!'

This was the language of Initiation into the Ultimate Truth. Not all are able to understand it, and therefore astrology still has and will have many adepts and enthusiasts. I could not hope to please them in this work by exposing the techniques of astrology. Instead I have preferred to give you some informative and philosophical lessons about this part of occultism, so that you may the easier form your own opinion about it. Moreover, there are numerous books about astrology, which explain the practice and theory of horoscopes, planetary influences, planetary 'houses', and so on, allowing the student to experience and to test what is the most interesting for him. I do not need to emphasize that all divinatory processes contain some truth in them, but this truth is a RELATIVE one, and cannot lead us to the final goal, the ABSOLUTE, UNCONDITIONED TRUTH-LIGHT.

It is interesting to note, that the fulcrum of our relation with the whole outer world—in time and space—is subconsciously based on *natural* astrology. Take our measurement of time: as the basic element we have rightly taken the way and time of the Earth's passage round the Sun. This is our *year* by which we determine everything in our lives. There is our first year on this planet, and there is the last one, when we leave the Zodiacal conditions on Earth.

But there are also purely occult reasons for giving importance to the revolutions of our mother-planet. It passes through different clichés in time and space, and these are related to one another. In its passage through the space around the Sun, the Earth each time encounters the same positions as it did exactly one year ago. The clichés of happenings are closest to us on their anniversaries. That is why we celebrate our birthdays, and other events of our temporal life.

Religious rules often recommend prayers and masses for the dead on just the anniversaries of their passing away.

Occult Tradition teaches, that the elementars of the majority of men are, for a long time after their disincarnation, 'magnetized' by the anniversaries of the important dates in their former material lives. Magicians, who want to implore or evoke the elementar of a prominent man, usually observe the anniversary of his birth, or (preferably) his death. Then the contact is easier and the two-plane being (elementar) is more inclined to communicate with the living on the Earth.

In the astral world, the subtle influences of the Planetary Spirits, as we described them in previous lessons, are much stronger and more clearly felt than in the dense matter of the physical plane. We know that for the *not-so-developed human beings* (and the majority are just this kind), the conditions and influences can easily be deciding factors in their behaviour and other manifestations. Only exceptionally advanced men can be said to be above and beyond the astro-physical surroundings.

We can test this on ourselves very easily: which do you like better, sunny or cloudy days? Spacious, airy rooms or dark basements? Nice melodies or gloomy sounds? If so, then you must recognize that surroundings and conditions play a great role in your life.

LESSON 79

Physiognomy

Physiognomical study is occupied with definitions related to the *outer* (physical) form of Man, allowing those acquainted with this branch of occult knowledge, to build a reasonably exact picture of a man's characteristics, according to his *type*, *race* and *visible qualities*. The influences of these three factors are very mixed, and we encounter practically no single type of average man who could represent a pure incarnation of one of the seven planetary entities. Therefore, Tradition teaches us about these planetary types separately, theoretically presenting them as unmixed and independent. But students must always remember, that practice is often very far from any idealistic imagination.

N*

So here, I am giving a traditional description of the planetary types, as they are accepted in Hermetism and the Tarot.

1. *The Saturn Type.* To this class of men belong slim persons, with dry and earth-coloured complexions, whose skin wrinkles easily. When young, they have strong hair, which thins gradually with age. They walk slowly with bent knees and lowered eyes. Their heads are oblong, cheeks hollow, ears long, nose thin and sharp-tipped, and the mouth large with thin lips, the lower one being rather prominent. They have very white teeth which decay easily and white gums. Often they have small black side whiskers, broad, heavy lower jaw and prominent Adam's apple. Men of this type have very hairy chests, high shoulders, slender, bony arms and distended tendons on their legs. They tire quickly, and in old age are often debilitated by breaking their legs. They do not believe anyone and are usually independent, but superstitious. They are good mathematicians and lawyers, but have limited mental horizons. They like agriculture and mining. They love black clothes, are parsimonious, prefer loneliness and often become a prey to melancholy. From this type of men are born revolutionaries and mutineers.

Their *sicknesses* are: nerves, piles, ailments of the limbs, weak teeth and ears, suffer from rheumatism, damage to limbs, self-abuse and bleeding.

Countries where this type can often be found are: Bavaria, Saxonia, North Russia, Siberia.

2. *The Jupiter Type.* To this type belong people of middle height, with pinkish-white skin and fresh faces. They have melodious voices, large, smiling eyes, brown hair, broadly arched eyebrows, medium-sized straight noses, mouths which are slightly too large, with thick lips, the upper somewhat covering the lower, and large teeth of which the two front ones are the longest. They have rounded cheeks, long chin with a groove, ears placed close to the head, handsome neck and well-developed nape. They perspire easily and abundantly, especially on the forehead. They become bald early and in later years are usually sluggish. They have great faith in themselves, enjoy feasts, amusements, ovations, eat well and drink much, briefly, they like elegance and luxury.

Although proud, they are still willing to help their neighbours. They are industrious, and strive after honours. They have expansive natures, are generally impetuous, but are good-hearted. They are attached to their families, are religious and being easy of access are always among friends.

Sicknesses: strokes, rush of blood to the head, and circulatory troubles.

Countries: Hungary, South Russia, Persia, Far East, Southern France and partially in Italy.

3. *The Mars Type.* Such people are strongly built, tall of stature, small but broad head, broad forehead, round cheeks, dark complexion, red, stiff hair, large, sparkling eyes often bloodshot, brownish eyebrows, large mouth with thin lips, heavily built lower jaw, broad sharp teeth yellowish in colour, and prominent chin with short, hard hairs on it. The nose is hook-ended, ears small and protruding, and chest broad. They always speak in a

decisive fashion and tone as if giving orders. Their movements are quick, steps full of dignity. They spend lavishly and have a cold attitude towards any danger. They like red colours, shouting and noise, spend much time in cafeterias, and prefer strong beverages and half-cooked beefsteaks. They are easily offended and have a passion to occupy themselves with surgery or butchery.

We have a parody of pure Mars type in the traditional figure of the 'gendarme'.

Sicknesses affecting Mars people are: ailments of the neck, pneumonia, and blood disorders.

Countries: Poland, Central Russia, Lombardy, Prussia.

4. *The Sun (Apollo) Type*. People of this type distinguish themselves by their beauty. They have medium stature, yellowish (or suntanned) colour of skin, strong beard, thin, blonde hair, low, arched forehead, and beautiful, large, 'smoky' eyes having a kind and strong expression. They have fleshy cheeks, thin, straight nose, long eyebrows which surround the eyes, medium sized mouth and lips, and teeth which are not too white. The chin is round, ears medium sized and protruding, neck long and muscular, shoulders broad, limbs nicely shaped, and legs beautifully slender. These people are brilliant inventors, industrialists and art lovers. They enjoy respect from their society, easily become excited, but are quickly quietened. They are sympathetic and accessible, but they lack steady friends. Their wives often betray them and children and friends leave them. They can become affectionately occupied with the 'secret science' and make excellent occultists. They are also persevering, attentively read many books, are religious and moderate, but credulous, and are proud and self-confident. They dress themselves with much taste and originality and like objects of luxury and jewels. Briefly, they always draw attention to themselves wherever they appear.

Their foremost *sicknesses* are: heart troubles and those of the eyes and throat.

Countries: Italy, Sicily, Czechoslovakia, and partially the Latin republics of South America.

5. *The Venus Type*. People of this category have many features in common with the Jupiter type, but differ in their good looks, especially the feminine beauty. Their skin is a delicate white fading into pink. They are small of height, and have a round face, small, fine, thick cheeks, small round forehead, beautiful full eyebrows, long and luxuriant hair black or dark brown, fine rounded nose with wide nostrils, and eyes large, dark and cheerful. They have florid faces with full lips, the upper seeming to be slightly swollen over the lower, and teeth white and regular with crimson gums. The chin is round and fat and often grooved, the ears are small and fleshy and the neck strong and snow-white. Their shoulders are muscular and sloping, the chest narrow and fleshy and the women's breasts are especially full. The feminine model is the ancient form of Venus. The feet are small and fine as with good dancers.

These people like white, they practise sensible love-affairs which often look naïve and their first thought is their best. They like feasts and receptions, and eat little but nutritious food. Life is of no value to them without flowers and perfumes. In music they prefer melody before harmony. They are credulous and therefore easily cheated. They charm almost everyone and avoid troubles and struggles. Men of the Venus type are rather feminine. These people have much compassion for their neighbours.

Their *ailments* include venereal diseases.

Countries: Austria, Switzerland, Caucasus, Arabia, partially Indo-China.

6. *The Mercury Type.* These are well-built people of rather small physique. They have a pleasant expression of the face, with sometimes an almost childish look. The face is pale with a honey-like complexion and a tendency to blush readily. The hair is luxuriant, blonde and curly, the skin soft, forehead high and chin short with a few hairs, mostly black. They have long, narrow eyebrows, a piercing look, a long, straight nose rounded at the tip, thin lips the upper being more developed and protruding, small teeth, well-developed chest and slender bones. They are excellent speakers, professors, doctors, metaphysicians, magicians and astrologers. They are charming because of their good character, able in business, but they are jealous and greedy, so that they should not be given full freedom in arranging commercial affairs. They like to joke, are cheerful, attached to their families, and like to play with children.

Women of this type should rather be avoided as they develop early, are deceptive and gain much experience.

Sicknesses: biliousness, liver complaints and nervous disorders.

Countries: England, France (Paris and environs), Greece, Egypt, Southern Spain.

7. *The Moon Type.* Such people are tall of stature and the skull is round with broad temples. They have a dull, pale complexion and seldom redden in the face. The muscles are white and only slightly developed. Body hair is sparse, while the hair of the head is thin and blonde. The teeth are irregular and yellowish with whitish gums; the eyes, which are round, slightly protuberant and moist are large and clear. The eyebrows are pale, almost imperceptible, the chin fat and broad, and the ears are close to the head. They have a long, slender neck and broad shoulders. The men have muscular chests while the women have undeveloped breasts. The abdomen is large and legs thin with swollen looking joints. People of this sort are changeable, freakish, capricious, cold, lazy, melancholy and egoistic. Family life has no attraction for them. They are very fond of sea-travel. From their ranks come many mystics. They possess great magnetic power. Among them we find dreamers, prophets, poets, and so on. They occupy themselves with all kinds of arts, fantastic painting and romantic lectures. They are very concerned about their health, like narcotics and always try to be in exclusive society.

Sicknesses: weakening of the sight, even blindness; self-abuse, gout, feminine complaints, kidney troubles, hydropsy.

Countries: Flanders, Transcaspian region, Africa.

It would be interesting to find a man belonging exclusively to one of the foregoing human types; but it would be too hard a task. Life teaches us, that we encounter only mixed ones, having a preponderence of a definite type. This must be carefully taken into consideration when we have to form a judgement about a man, to decide which profession or speciality would be most suitable for him, and so on. In such a case, a consulting occultist must know foremostly how to separate qualities, how to combine them, and how to find the esoteric abilities and their practical application.

For the high degrees of an Adept, a synthetic type is required, who has absorbed in himself all the seven influxes belonging to the seven Secondary Causalities, and fused them together in himself in full harmony. According to our Hermetic Tradition, I may be able to quote some particulars about this.

So, for the *Teachers of Esoterism* is indicated a blending of Saturn, Mercury and Venus, while the presence of the Sun would be appreciated, and sometimes Mars also would be good.

For the higher degrees of *Freemasonry*, Jupiter, Venus and Mars would be required; for a *magician:* Saturn, Mercury and Mars; for a *theurgist:* the Sun and Venus. A theoretical *Kabbalist* would do well with Saturn and Mercury, and this also refers to a theoretical *astrologer*.

Clairvoyants, psychometrists, fortune-tellers, and so on are always obedient to the Moon.

For one who wishes to have experiences with mediums, hysterical people, sensitive persons, and so on, the most desirable type would be one having a mixture of Venus with Moon, but when no such type is available, a Venus type will do. This last one is very open to all kinds of suggestions.

In Initiatory Chains, among the representatives of the lower degrees of initiations, young men of the Moon type can be found. At first they obey the Masters (Esoteric Teachers), they even make good progress, but later, almost inevitably, they separate themselves from the Initiatory Chains because of their susceptibility to outer and not so pure influences, which is a characteristic of people of the Moon type.

In reference to the pure or almost pure *Solar type* we may say, that for him important sacerdotal activities are proper, even without any of the complications of leadership as is the case with a Master. The pure *Jupiter type* would be most successful in the task of a *historian of esoterism*.

Popular kinds of divination are connected with a direct contacting of the astro-mental clichés, involving the use of crystal balls, shining surfaces, ink or black coffee, and so on. Here the mental contact with the clichés of past, present and future events may be obtained through an artificial, passive concentration. When our sight is fascinated and bound by gazing into one of these devices, the mind is likely to follow our sight and so stop its usual feverish vibrations (thinking), becoming immobilized and even introverted.

This is just the condition which leads to the termporary and artificially induced 'clairvoyance', allowing us to foresee and see through the shrouds of time and space, which are normally veiled to us. This sort of occult practice is comparatively easy to perform, and a relatively large percentage of people might be able to work with crystals, mirrors, and so on, in order to get some divinatory results.

The main difficulty is not the obtaining of some visions, but *in the art of interpreting them* into earthly language and conditions.

Often they are too symbolical and not coherent enough to our way of mental conceiving. Again, it is not easy to discriminate between these visions in time and space, as we know them, coming as they do from worlds where the limitations imposed by our three-dimensions and subdivisions of time (past, present, future) *are by far transcended*. Hence these impressions have to be rightly classified, by the skilled work of our mind-brain, which at the same time, *should not be allowed to engage in its normal activities*, that is to contact the usual currents of thoughts and feelings, which is its normal occupation during the periods of our physical life on this planet.

That is why there are so few good divinators and true clairvoyants. Also, the main quality which permits us to become intelligent and reliable interpreters of the astro-mental clichés as visualized through one of the aforementioned ways, is FULL DOMINATION OF THE MIND, that is possession of undisturbed *passive* and *active* powers of concentration. The *first* type will open for us the usually invisible realm, the second will enable us to control the flow of visions, to segregate them wisely and to rightly interpret their relationship with the surrounding events of life, in which we may be interested. In both cases training is essential. For one who is trained, the best thing to do would be to find the time and place where any disturbance is unlikely; next, to place the physical fulcrum of concentration (crystal ball, mirror, or liquid) on a table, some ten to fifteen inches from his eyes. A subdued light should come from a lamp placed behind the operator. The room itself should remain dark or very slightly lit. Good results are obtained with coloured lights, such as violet or blue. When gazing into the centre of our device on the table, we should first concentrate passively, that is expel all thoughts from the mind and not allow any outer impressions to disturb us.

In order to enter into contact with some definite type of clichés, all passive concentration must be preceded by a short but intense flash of imagination on the subject which now interests us. For example: a person about whom we wish to know something; the place which we want to investigate; the problem which we have to solve, and so on. Immediately after this, we should concentrate while staring into our device.

When visions begin to appear, one usually loses one's normal awareness of our actual, physical surroundings, as if forgetting all about them. But the operator should remain calm, cool and master of his nerves. No physical movement should be allowed. The position of the body should be rather relaxed and comfortable. A good alarm-clock with a soft sound may be used in order to finish the session, which should not last longer than thirty minutes in the beginning.

Little can be said about the actual art of true interpretation of the visions obtained in this way. It is too individual and difficult to convey in words.

But possession of a fair ability to concentrate will undoubtedly show the right way to the experimenting divinator. Persons with unbalanced mentality or over-sensitive nerves should not attempt to gaze into crystals or mirrors, because they might suffer severe shocks coming from the astral, which is generally inimical to any human efforts to penetrate into it. Therefore full inner balance is an essential condition for any successful divination through the physical fulcrums.

Actually, there is nothing to fear at all, for visions cannot make any direct and real damage to our body or senses. It is our own responsibility *not to allow fear to harm us*, for in it lies the only real danger. We know, that emotions and inner mental shocks can well kill a physical man; but not any 'blow' or 'sting' which comes from the astral.

The ability to obtain and interpret the astro-mental visions through crystals, and so on can be harmed or even lost in a large part, if repeatedly used for purely egotistic aims, like money, or power over others. Usually, such debased 'clairvoyants' do not want to resign their former authority and fame, and so they begin to fake the whole of their sessions by making haphazard fantasies and guesses. Then we have a case of deception and exploitation.

Unfortunately, the large majority of 'divinatory masters', who practise for money, are just such doubtful individuals. However, some modest persons, who possess a limited ability to read only certain kinds of clichés are honest, even if they do take some reward for their services to those who ask for them.

An experienced occultist will immediately discover, with whom he has to deal if he contacts such 'clairvoyants' and fortune-tellers.

LESSON 80

Chiromancy

The art of *chiromancy* was born in Ancient Egypt, and from there Moses brought it, together with all the Hermetic teachings which he included in his books, to the Bible. There is irrefutable proof that chiromancy was well known to the Patriarchs, for in the Book of Job, XXXVII, 7 we read: 'DEUS IN MANU OMNIUM SIGNA POSUIT, UT NOVERINT SINGULI OPERA SUA' (God put signs on the hands of everyone so that all people can know their things). This sentence would be better understandable in a free translation, in which the words 'their things' are substituted by the more reasonable: 'their fate'. Some Hermetists, and especially Prof. G. O. M. give still another meaning to these words 'their own abilities and qualities'. All these versions are synonymous.

Chiromancy possesses the same right of existence as all other methods of divination. Its beginnings are of a purely astrological character, and from there comes its terminology, the names of the lines on the human palm. In the mediaeval period, chiromancy passed into the possession of crude fortune-tellers, who were unacquainted with astrology. Many practical observations were added to the traditional texts, and in the fifteenth, sixteenth and seventeenth centuries *Initiatory Centres* recognized and

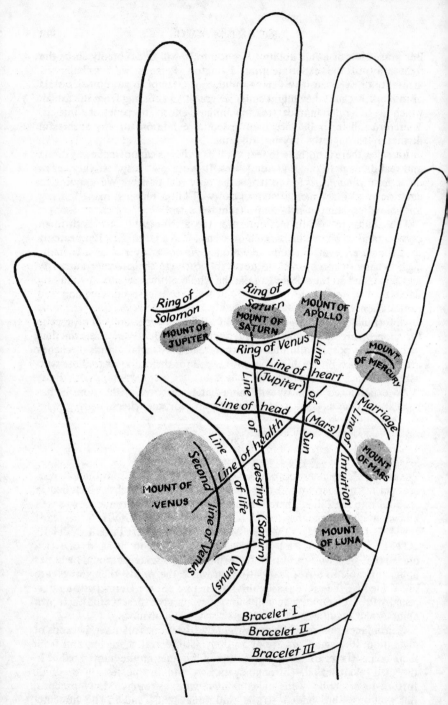

Fig. 37 Schematic Plan of the Hand

purified chiromancy, removing the superstitious additions made by the ignorant fortune-tellers.

Metaphysics of the eighteenth century did not think much about it, but the nineteenth century brought a new, flourishing epoch to chiromancy. The famous DESBAROLLE and PAPUS (of France) as well as Dr CZES- LAW CZYNSKI (of Poland) put new life into the art of reading the human hand. About 1860 another Frenchman, Capt. D'Arpentigny, added a lot of valuable researches and conclusions, and in the beginning of the twentieth century, Cheiro (Count Louis Hamon) published a few excellent books, in which he tried to give to everyone, the possibility of reading his own hand and those of other people.

Today true chiromancy is a legitimate child of Hermetism, being a definite and scientifically working system. As with every type of knowledge, so it is with chiromancy, it gives astonishing results when interpreted by a master, and it might be very discouraging, when bungled by a layman.

Now, what may chiromancy mean for a man of the present atomic age? In spite of the many centuries which have passed since the arts of divination took their place in the Tarot's system, and since they were taught in sub- terranean crypts and temples, human life has remained essentially the same, at least, in its broad outline. Happiness and misery, health and sickness, love and hatred, wealth and poverty, power and weakness, all these principles which operate in our lives, have not changed during the course of thousands of years. And it is with just these principles that chiromancy deals. So we may rightly accept that it has not lost its meaning for those, who like to look ahead in time, calculate their possibilities and so prepare themselves for the events, unveiled to them by the divinatory arts.

That is the reason why this lesson has been included in this exposition of Hermetic philosophy, reflected in the Tarot.

From the historical point of view, we are compelled to distinguish between some separate parts of chiromancy: Firstly, CHIROSOPHY, or the deductive part of chiromancy, which is connected with astrological and Kabbalistic contemplation, also often called '*analytical chiromancy*'.

Secondly, TRADITIONAL PARTICULARS being a collection of separate theses, from which Desbarolle's School tried to form a definite CODE, known as '*synthetic chiromancy*'.

Thirdly, a collection of new empiric particulars and facts, received in a clinical way, referring to the exact age of the subject, to which age different events of his life should be connected.

Fourthly, the above-mentioned chiromancy of d'Arpentigny. In this lesson dedicated to general knowledge about chiromancy and not to its depths, which need volumes for their exposition, I will explain the methods according to which chiromancy works.

CHIROSOPHY teaches us that the horoscope of each person is written and is being written on his or her hands, and that clichés of the present and the future should be read on both hands, while the past belongs principally to the left hand. In order to make an analysis of one's character, both palms must be studied.

We will now chirosophically explain only the planetary influences, leaving the Zodiacal ones alone. The influences of the planets, *as given in the previous lesson about physiognomy* (No. 79) may be termed '*static*' in relation to chirosophy. On the other hand, all the *remaining* planetary influences on the fate of Man we will call '*dynamic*'. The '*static*' elements in chirosophy are '*planetary mountains*' (sometimes also called 'hills'), while the *planetary lines* of our palms are just the '*dynamic*' elements. I believe this has been accepted in Tradition because generally the 'mounts' on our palms do not change much in our lifetime, but the lines very often do, and every attentive student can observe this fact on his own hands.

The large fleshy protuberance situated below the two lower phalanges of the thumb is the *Mount of Venus*. Under the forefinger we find the *Mount of Jupiter;* under the middle finger is a small hill called that of *Saturn;* under the ring finger the *Mount of Apollo;* while a hill under the little finger is the *Mount of Mercury*. Just below Mercury there is a large oblong protuberance called the *Mount of Mars* and still further below, that of the *Mount of the Moon*.

If a 'mount' is very pronounced, then the good influence of that planet on the horoscope is assured and will be free from unwanted additions. If the size of the mount is considerably smaller than normal, it is evident that the corresponding planetary influence is lacking. If the mount is covered with small lines going in one direction, this signifies that there is a tendency for the dispersal of the planetary force, and some authorities in the matter consider this as an evil influence. If the mount is covered with grid-like lines, then the planetary influence is hampered by a hostile factor in the horoscope. One must then perform an effort in order to restore the positive influence one needs.

If a mount seems to be inclined in the direction of a neighbouring finger, it means that this mount is subordinate to the other, which is also 'coloured' (influenced) by the particular position of the first mount.

Examples will explain best. If the Mount of Mercury leans towards the Mount of Apollo, we would say that it means 'science in the service of art', as well as 'art tinged by scientific methods'.

The melting together of mounts means the unification of the static planetary influences. For example, the Mount of Jupiter joined together with that of Saturn would tell us, that for the person concerned, the idea of destiny is closely connected with his imagination of a favourable career in his life.

To each planetary mount there runs a certain planetary line. The line of Jupiter (also called the line of heart) usually begins under the Mount of Mercury, runs horizontally across the palm and very often reaches the Mount of Jupiter.

The line of Saturn (or Destiny) most often starts from the valley between the Mounts of the Moon and Venus, ascending vertically to the Mount of Saturn. The line of Apollo (or Sun), generally speaking, begins in the same region as the line of Saturn (Destiny) and runs vertically to the Mount of Apollo. The line of Mercury (or of intuition) goes to its mount parallel to the line of the Sun (Apollo). The line of Venus (or of life) has its beginning at the foot of Jupiter's mount, forming an arc round the Mount of Venus. The line of Mars (or of the head) starts on that mount and cuts across the palm to run to the beginning of the line of Venus. The line (or rather lines) of the Moon appear as short dashes on the Moon's mount.

The line of Venus is also called the LINE OF LIFE (Vitalis)
The line of Jupiter the LINE OF HEART (Mentalis)
The line of Mars the LINE OF THE HEAD (Naturalis)
The line of Sun the LINE OF APOLLO (Solaris)
The line of Saturn the LINE OF DESTINY (Fatalis)
The line of Mercury the LINE OF LIVER (Hepatica)

It has already been said, that these lines define the role of the *Secondary Causalities* in the whole horoscope. With the line of Venus is connected the sphere of health and vital forces; with the line of Saturn things belonging to the destiny of Man; with the line of Jupiter, the sphere of feelings, emotions and attachments; with the line of Mars is connected the sphere of thinking and the central nervous system. The line of Apollo refers to material riches, prolific artistic abilities and high ideals. The line of Mercury rules over Man's speculative abilities, and his organs of digestion. The lines of the Moon tell of that which we call the 'Moon's influence', that is mystical moods, and mediumistic and magnetic abilities.

There is no need to say much about the *lack* of one or more lines on the hand, for the significance is all too plain; simply there is a lack of the influence of some corresponding planetary Causality. Details may be found in the special manuals on chiromancy, such as those of Desbarolle, Papus or Cheiro. Here I am giving general ideas on the different arts of divination, so that the student can orientate himself when he obtains a suitable manual.

In the case of *duplication* of a line it is usually a sign of the permanency of the influence connected with that line. *Interruptions* to a line mean a violent change in the character of its influence or its conditions. Islands on a line mean bifurcation of the influences and events; such an island on the line of heart tells of the division of attachment or love; on the line of Mars, hysterical manifestations or physical paralysis; on the line of Venus, it usually means headaches and neurosis, and sometimes anaemia, while an island on Saturn's line means a false position, full of duplicity.

Spots on the lines forecast a sudden attack in the realm of the corresponding influence; for example, a spot on the line of heart signifies a sudden and violent grief; on the line of Saturn, an event, a manifestation of the development of Fate, crushing because of its unexpectedness.

As a further addition to the general picture of chirosophical knowledge it can be said, that, apart from her mount, the *static* influence of Venus also includes the 'ring of Venus', in the form of an arc round the upper parts of the Mounts of Saturn and Apollo. People possessing such a ring have the ability of mental concentration in all realms which are the object of their investigations, even if these are not their main occupation, but come into existence only by accident, and so on. On the astral plane, these people refer affectionately to every form seen or imagined, in which their ideas manifest themselves. On the physical plane possessors of the ring of Venus show considerable refinement in sensual passions and pleasures.

To the *static* influence of Mars—apart from his mount, which by its convexity suggests the idea of great patience and endurance in a man, the so-called 'passive Mars'—we will add his plain. The degree of convexity of the plain characterizes the 'active Mars', that is courage, vehemence and passion. The 'Plain of Mars' is situated in the middle part of the palm, on which also occur the middle sections of the lines of head, Apollo and Saturn.

Other signs are also encountered on human palms and belong to the general traditional knowledge of chiromancy. Of these we would like to say, that a *cross* at the beginning of a line limits its manifestations; briefly, a *cross* is an unfavourable sign on a GOOD line, and a good sign on a BADLY FORMED line. A *cross* at the end of a line suggests an idea of mystical influence; a *cross* in the middle of a line, a temporary obstacle; a *cross* on a *mount* signifies *protection* in the realm of the influence of that mount. For example: found on the Mount of Jupiter, the cross forecasts a happy marriage.

In general, a *star* has the same meaning as the cross, but in many cases much more intensive and violent. So, a *star* on the Mount of Apollo means that the man will suddenly become rich. A *square* is usually a sign of protection, of support, or defence. Not necessarily in a positive meaning: for, if it is close, say, to the line of Saturn on the *Plain of Mars*, this may well mean being deprived of personal freedom.

The line of Mars, separated from the line of life and attached to it with small crosses (like a net) means, according to our tradition, a sickness of the eyes and extreme rashness in the actions of a man.

Our empiric facts, obtained in *clinical* practice, mainly refer to the so-called *age of the line*. This means that on each line, dependent upon the character and construction of the hand, which influence the mutual points of intersection of these lines, we can note some positions, which correspond to actual years in the life of the person in question.

This will permit us to connect in horoscopes and chiromantic forecasts, the right interpretation of planetary influences according to certain years in a man's life.

So we could say, that on the line of Saturn the twentieth year of life corresponds to the point of intersection of that line with the line of Mars; the fortieth year, to the point of intersection with the line of Jupiter. Again, we may see a break in the line of Saturn, and a shifting to the left in the direction of the Mount of Jupiter, of two-thirds of the part of that line between the two above-mentioned points. Then we may be able to say to the person: 'a favourable change in your career can be expected about your thirty-fourth year.'

In the case of another person a spot is visible on the Mount of Jupiter, while with others we may see a spot on the line of Jupiter, in that place where it intersects the line of Apollo. Then it would be reasonable to forecast some love-troubles at the age of twenty-five.

Fig. 37 representing the general plan of the human hand has been added to this lesson.

The Parisian School of chiromancy (whose leader for many years was

Papus) calculates the probable length of a human life by means of averaging taken from the indications of THREE lines: Saturn, Jupiter and Mars, taking from each of them the age, corresponding to its length. The ancient Hermetists, as well as some contemporary chiromantists work differently. They read the years ONLY from the line of life (Venus) and ascribe the deciding meaning to that line. The difficulty is that the line of Venus differs immensely in different individuals, and any establishment of firm points on it, is far from being easy.

But the most important thing is, that the old method is very incorrect in practice, while the Parisian system gives over seventy per cent. of exact forecasts.

D'Arpentigny in his chiromancy also refers to three basic types of finger-tips which have much in common with the type of men, who possess these fingers:

(1) Sharp-pointed fingers
(2) Square-pointed
(3) Spade-shaped

The joints of the fingers also possess similar meanings, that is the two principal ones, being those of upper and lower.

All the particulars, as I have mentioned before, may be found in the special works treating of chirosophy. Apart from the knowledge of lines, mounts and other signs of the palm, a good chirosophist will never overlook knowledge about the general circumstances of his client, because the same signs would have a different interpretation for different types of men. This is very similar to the three titles belonging to each arcanum of the Tarot: each one belongs to a different world, and therefore the same arcanum has its separate formula in every plane.

With this kind of divinatory art (that is chiromancy) we will almost end our lessons about the Seventeenth Arcanum. I am omitting phrenology and graphology, because these systems are too specialized and need long study and similar exposition.

My aim has not been to teach you about all the different kinds of divination, but just to give you a firm basic knowledge of the ideas and methods, from which professional practitioners form their own systems and ability to interpret the occult language, which speaks from the Seventeenth Arcanum.

As a historical curiosity I would like to mention a strange remark of one of the foremost 'realists' of the nineteenth century—Napoleon I, who once said:

'The human face may deceive, but the hand never.'

Personally I do not attach much importance to any divinatory art or fortune-telling. The most truthful forecast or prophecy can remain useless. In my twenties I visited a very famous Belgian chiromantist, a lady, who foretold the tragic fate of the unlucky Czar Nicholas II. She told me, among other things, which have long since been fulfilled, that I 'should be careful with ocean travel'. When I asked her if this meant death at sea, the old lady avoided a direct answer, saying that I 'should not travel far on the ocean'. But this did not prevent me from undertaking numerous and very long voyages, as I never cancelled them because of the sinister augury. And so I will do the same in the future when the need arises. Where is there any usefulness in divination for a man, who does not wish to subdue his will to any outer influences or forecasts?

LESSON 81

Dreams

The question of dreams is connected with the divinatory processes described in the Seventeenth Arcanum. I shall limit myself to a rather brief exposition of Tradition's teachings.

When dreaming, the consciousness of an *average* man is centred foremostly on the astral plane, while the body, having only a loose link with the astrosome, remains at rest and regains the energy, spent during its waking hours.

(1) The human astrosome may then enter into contact with the astral plane and its inhabitants, where a man is attracted according to his own inner attitude and interests, which prevail in the waking state. He may see and talk to his friends, relatives or other people who left the physical plane before him. Usually, no valuable information is brought back, especially as the major part of such activities does not reach the brain's consciousness after the man's awakening.

(2) However, we can encounter some valuable CLICHÉS connected with the past, present or future. Sometimes the latter are able to be revealed through the brain's consciousness and then we might get a 'prophetic dream' forecasting the events to come. These are often veiled in some symbolical outer form. This was well known to Egyptian Initiates and their successors, the ancient Greeks and Romans. Attempts have often been made to establish a definite symbolism for dreams, in order to enable men to understand them, and so there have appeared the so-called 'dream books', which try to comment on and explain the most commonly encountered forms of dream experiences and visions.

Of course, most of these publications are valueless, being compiled haphazardly by ignorant people, lacking any initiatory meaning and calculated to serve only naïve and superstitious readers. We cannot delve further into them.

But, as regards forecasting future events, some common dreams seem to have a meaning which has been established by experience.

I know, for example, from my own experience and that of others, that to ascend, in dream, to the top of a high tower or mountain and then look down from it may often be connected with the death of someone close to you. If it happens, that we see some person (especially in white clothes) on those heights, it is almost certain he or she will soon pass away. To see or to swim in a very dirty and dark stream or lake, and so on, could well mean a sickness for the dreamer himself.

Sometimes there have been cases where some sensitive person has been able to see less personal *clichés*, related to definite happenings in the political, social or national life of a country. Then we speak about 'prophetic dreams'. Only a well-trained occultist is able to extract the exact meaning from such *clichés*, without mixing them with his own personal views or convictions, and just giving a clear picture of things to come.

(3) A less interesting category of dreams would be a mental recapitulation of the day's experiences, reflected in a man's consciousness of the dream state. Some dreams can well be created when the body of the dreamer is subjected to certain influences as was explained in Chapter XIII of *Concentration*.

To such a category belong most of the dream-visions of men who have only lower mental development.

(4) Rare kinds of astral experiences, which have great importance and meaning, are the so-called astral clichés, or communications received with the utmost clarity and intensity, which compel us to accept them as unmistakable missions directed to us. This usually happens when some higher Powers find it advisable to warn us or to give us an order to do, or not to do certain definite things.

Those who have followed the mystical message know how true this can be. Sometimes, in similar cases, lives have been saved, or a major disaster avoided.

In Eastern occult schools attempts have been made to produce prophetic messages artificially. Persons who had problems to solve were left to sleep for a night in a temple or crypt. Then dreamy impressions were recorded and served as a basis of the forecast for the solution of the problem. Old Egyptian temples and Greek crypts were famous for this.

Now, what attitude would be suitable for us, who are living in this 'enlightened' Twentieth Century? Discrimination is the quality most needed, when we ask about the behaviour of a reasonable occultist towards his astral experiences. This means that we have to be able to classify the points 1 to 4 clearly, and to draw the consequences from them when we are confronted with our actual dreams. It requires a fair degree of initiation into the astral life, and a considerable ability to be conscious while in our astrosomes. Roughly speaking, at least the first thirteen arcana should be worked through, and the first group of exercises leading to exteriorization must be performed satisfactorily.

As in every occult tradition, the ability of concentrated thinking should reach a reasonable degree, in this case, corresponding to the *first three series* of *Concentration*. Then we may be pretty sure that we will not be led astray by the passive experiences in our dreams.

But, frankly, a good Hermetist would not be very much occupied with any divinatory activities and the resulting impressions. Rather he will try to do what the *active arcana* advise. And this is none other than *self-perfectioning*, which clears our way to the unique aim of Hermetism, which was, is and will be—Reintegration.

ℨ
Arcanum XVIII
CREPUSCULUM
THE MOON

Aquarius

Hierarchia Occulta
Hostes Occulti
Pericula Occulta

CHAPTER XVIII

ARCANUM XVIII (צ TZADDI)

THE sign of the Hebrew alphabet corresponding to the Eighteenth Arcanum is
צ (Tzaddi) and its numerical value is 90. The astrological symbol belonging
to this arcanum is Aquarius.

As the hieroglyph there is a ROOF, not that protective construction
which shields us against the vagaries of the weather, but a ROOF which
stifles and oppresses, limiting our freedom and bringing disaster.

Of all the arcana, this Eighteenth is the most ominous and unfavourable.
It describes the most dangerous conditions in which Man can place himself
because of his own stupidity and lack of inner sight. So let us look at the
very mysterious card of this arcanum.

Its scientific name is CREPUSCULUM (twilight, dusk), and the vulgar
one is LUNA (the Moon).

At the top of the picture the Moon sheds its light quietly, hopelessly
say, mathematically exact in accordance with the laws of the physical world
(its Fate). The Moon directs its rays down to the Earth but this light is only
REFLECTED. It cannot warm us, it cannot even give us proper light.

Where then is the Primary Source of Light? you will ask in despair.
We want to receive the LIGHT directly from that Source!

And the ominous card answers: you are subdued by the *Hierarchic
Law* (Law of Gradation), because of your downfall. You have no right to
the *True Primary Light*, you have lost that right because of your merging
into treacherous Matter. The closest hierarchic authority gives you your
due portion of light. Be satisfied with it, you, who because of your downfall,
have deliberately merged yourselves in the illusory world of BINARIES.

Such is the hard language of the Eighteenth Arcanum.

But look again, and in the background see just the BINARY of two
TOWERS (sometimes two pyramids in old Tarot cards). Between these
towers twists the serpent-like *path of your existence*, strewn with clean
sand, in order to show any visible traces of blood on it. And there is plenty
of blood in your past, present and perhaps future incarnations. You know
the meaning of blood in occultism. It is your vital force-energy, which
you dissipate because of your ignorance. Such is the sermon which comes
from between the two mysterious towers.

Now I would like to remind you to look attentively at Figs. No. 1 and
Nos. 22 to 23B where you may see the whole scheme of the Tarot, conceived
in its triangles and septenaries.

In their progressive materialization, the arcana have reached the peak of
their density. Nobody can forbid us, even now, to listen to the voice of the

Theosophical Ternary, so many times mentioned in these lessons; but with the background of the Eighteenth Arcanum even our eternal HOPE may have some uncertainty in it. That is why it now forms the gradual, measured hierarchically limited *first title* of the Eighteenth Arcanum (in the realm of the Archetype)—HIERARCHIA OCCULTA (occult hierarchy).

Having just realized this first title, we may think about the strange impression of blood on the path. Someone is losing his vital force, and this oppresses us, because it suggests an idea of our weakness. Yes, in these final arcana we are not so potent and pure as we were in the higher triangles (Figs. Nos. 1 and 22 to 23B).

From occult laws we know, that we can easily be invultuated through our blood. It is terrible. But who can invultuate us?

The answer is in the foreground of the card. There on the left sits a wolf, which has always been our enemy, openly and unmistakably. To the right of the tragic path there is a dog, which not long ago was rubbing itself against our feet calling itself our friend. So that is the picture: these are our enemies and false friends, who will try to invultuate us.

Are they *absolutely free* in their evil intentions? Not so! There is something which they do not like, they are sadly howling at the Moon: they are embarrassed and bound by the hierarchic authority closest to us, which sends us some of its light.

If our enemies are not allowed to harm us without any limitations, why then have we to be afraid of them? Only because we are often like that symbolical lobster of the Eighteenth Arcanum's card, which is crawling in the puddle that shines in the Moon's light. We can be invultuated *because we often retreat*. So, in the plane of Man, the *second title* of the Eighteenth Arcanum is HOSTES OCCULTI (hidden enemies). The *third title* in the plane of Natura is PERICULA OCCULTA (hidden dangers in general).

The student who will conscientiously co-operate with the lecturer-writer by exactly following all the mental constructions and deductions encountered in this work will gain the most benefit from a study of this book on the Tarot. However, this is *not enough*, for the student must still develop the skeleton-like theorems and analyses given here, and then he will begin to tread the true *path of self-initiation*, which is the aim of Hermetic studies. It is easy to see, that Hermetic philosophy and its application by Man is no finite quantity, but rather, something which is always extending ahead and ever ahead, without a visible end. That is why so many books have been written about the Tarot, and there is unlimited material for writers to use. Each work, no matter how eminent the adept-writer, will leave enough room for those who will come to perpetuate the magnificent task of human genius, which in spite of Man's downfall and consequently arduous labour of Reintegration, is able to create new points of light beside the thorny path.

Now we come to an analysis of this arcanum's numbers.

Equation No. 147: $18 = 1 + 17$
Equation No. 148: $18 = 17 + 1$

The Divine Essence (1) and Hope (17), which is formed in the metaphysical (also mental) plane, are sufficient to unveil to us the Hierarchic Law (18).

The three-plane Man (1) possessing Intuition (17) looks without fear on the picture of the astral dangers (18) which hang over him like clouds.

Active Nature (1) when its revelations are properly read (17) will unveil to us, the whole complex of dangers (18) which for ever remain hidden for the layman.

Equation No. 149: $18 = 2 + 16$
Equation No. 150: $18 = 16 + 2$

The Metaphysical Substance (2) and the method of logical exclusion (16) determine the constitution of the Hierarchy (18) of the World of Ideas.

The principle of polarization (2) and the possibility of astral compulsion (16) discover the mystery of invultuation (18). Note that this is possible only because of the activity of the invultuating person and the passivity of the subject of the operation.

The possibility of destruction (16) of things created by Nature (2) is just that which we call 'danger on the physical plane' (18).

Equation No. 151: $18 = 3 + 15$
Equation No. 152: $18 = 15 + 3$

The nature of the Unique Principle (3) and the logic of the metaphysical constitution (15) of the *Second Family* exactly determine the Hierarchic Law (18) for our world. This is because the formulas of that Law are closely connected with the *Mystery of the Trinity* and its logical application.

The mystery of birth (3) and the means of the element Nahash (15) constitute the process of invultuation (18).

The creativeness of Nature (3) and the application of the Law of Fate to its creatures (15) explain the essence of physical dangers (18).

Equation No. 153: $18 = 4 + 14$
Equation No. 154: $18 = 14 + 4$

The existence of forms (4) together with deduction (14) determine the Hierarchy (18).

The principle of authority (4) and the ability to balance one's activity and passivity (14) are the cause of hostility of one man against another (18).

The principle of preparation (4) and of the change of development (14) in a mysterious way result in the necessity of even physical danger (18).

Equation No. 155: $18 = 5 + 13$
Equation No. 156: $18 = 13 + 5$

The knowledge of Good and Evil (5) together with the permanency of the Higher Principles (13) are sufficient for the foundation of the Hierarchy (18).

The pentagrammatical nature of Man (5) and his submission to the laws of death (13) remind us of the idea of the possibility of invultuation (18).

The great Natural Religion (5) and the principle of the transformation of energy (13) justify physical danger (18).

Equation No. 157: $18 = 6 + 12$
Equation No. 158: $18 = 12 + 6$

Recognition of the Law of Analogy (6) and the awaiting of the Messiah (12) compel even the most indifferent man to realize the Law of Hierarchy (18).

The domination of Freedom (6) over Charity (12) can induce us to pre-form invultuation (18). But the domination of Charity (12) over Freedom of Will (6) in the form of prayers for our enemies may destroy all stratagems (18).

The features of the environment (6) in the lower sub-planes of the Zodiacal Life (12) create physical dangers (18).

Equation No. 159: $18 = 7 + 11$
Equation No. 160: $18 = 11 + 7$

The essence of Hierarchy (18) is that the Subtle dominates the Gross (7) and possesses the power (11) to penetrate into it.

The essence of invultuation (18) and in general of enmity in the astral realm (18), is based on the fact, that a man, who has learned to dominate (7) himself, is able to use both forces: his own, and those of the Chain (11).

The essence of the dangers on the physical plane (18) is hidden in the fact that we often claim the property (7) of the objects, which can be destroyed by the Forces of Nature (11).

Equation No. 161: $18 = 8 + 10$
Equation No. 162: $18 = 10 + 8$

The libration of swinging of the World's Scale (8) joined with the Great Testament (10) of the Kabbalah, give the key to the Law of Hierarchy (18).

The conditions of the ethical life of Man (8) and knowledge of the Kabbalah (10) give the key to invultuation (18).

Dangers on the physical plane (18) are determined by Karma (8) and are set in motion by the World's Mill (10).

Equation No. 163: $18 = 9 + 9$

Hierarchic conditions (18) have the character of opposition of the TWO Protectorates (9). A junior executive makes reports being mindful of the interests of a certain department, like a single organ of an organism. The senior executive, responding to the report, gives orders concerning more the organism as a whole, sometimes to the detriment of a particular part of it. The Law of Hierarchy gives priority to the interests of the WHOLE over the interests of private persons. This is the meaning of the triumph of one '9' over another '9'.

One may be initiated (9) into the business of self-preservation, another into the mystery of Baphomet; the COMMUNITY conquers the individual, the second '9' invultuates the first '9'.

A separate organism preserves its physical means when operating with the theory of probability (9). The whole of Nature possessing the knowledge of all elements directing its construction, also has another calculus, related to the degree of possiblity of happenings. For Nature this becomes not a theory of probability, but a 'theory of credibility '(9). Here the second '9' conquers the first, and we call this 'danger' on the physical plane (18) for the first '9'

This brief and schematic arithmological analysis of the Eighteenth Arcanum cannot touch on the particulars of the PHYSICAL DANGERS, encountered on the path of human life, as their name is more than legion. Actually, there is not even the need for that, because every student can imagine for himself all the possibilities that interest him. But the theory of the *Hierarchic Law* and of the *process of invultuation* will be spoken of in the following lessons.

LESSON 83

The Law of Hierarchy

The *Unitary Contemplation* of the Spiritual Schools of which the Hermetic one is the foremost, possesses as its basic thesis the following axiom: THE PRINCIPLES CLOTHE THEMSELVES WITH THE LAWS; THE LAWS CLOTHE THEMSELVES WITH FACTS.

Cloth or clothes without one who uses them are incapable of life: they can only serve as scarecrows for a time, until their nothingness is recognized. Our Western pattern of spiritual philosophy has allies in the best Eastern Schools, such as esoteric Buddhism, Sufism and foremostly Advaita Vedanta. It is difficult to find historical proofs that Western and Eastern occultists had any contacts bewteen themselves about 2,000 or 3,000 years before Christ. Nevertheless, the similarity of the Unitary Doctrine is astonishing, if we take the trouble to study it deeply enough. The Parabrahm, Nirvana, Ain-Soph, Unknown Father (as Christ told us), all these conceptions have a synonymous meaning: they all speak about the ONE WITHOUT A SECOND, Unmanifested, Absolute, Perfection without qualities.

But materialistic schools tell us something different. Their *credo* is: the complex of facts generates the law. In other words, they believe that the Monad (Self) and the will of the Chain are illusion, created by the very fact of their grouping into that Chain. For them *the cell is more real than the organ*, and *the organ more real than the whole ORGANISM*!

The contemplation of the Unitary Spiritual Schools recognizes Life OUTSIDE ITS MATERIAL REALIZATIONS AND EVEN AS INDEPENDENT OF THEM. But materialists try to deduce Life from Death.

I AM THE GOD OF ABRAHAM, ISAAC AND JACOB; NOT A GOD OF THE DEAD BUT A GOD OF THE LIVING. This text is the basis of living Unitarianism. Followers of this conception will naturally recognize the Hierarchy, starting from the *a priori* recognition of its points of support.

THERE IS AN ARCHETYPE, THEREFORE MAN AND NATURE EXIST. There is a ruler who chose his subordinates for himself. There is a leader who performs certain impulses of will, and around him gather the people, ready to defend formally and really the fulfilment of those impulses. Then the Teacher appears, then the School, and then there is the mental Monad, which forms an astrosome for itself and the latter which moulds its physical body for itself.

If we would like to imagine everything which exists FOR ONLY A SINGLE MOMENT, then we might perhaps recognize both (the materialistic and spiritual) systems of thought as acceptable.

A materialist may say to you: 'Show me the man who is not a synthesis of his cells.' You may reply, that the astrosome of a foetus, while still in its mother's womb, vampirizes (or uses) the elements of the physical subplanes of its environment. Then you can recognize for yourselves, that without the existence of that appropriate environment, no incarnation can be realized. So who can prevent me from believing, that *in every crowd there must necessarily appear a leader*, as a function of the collective existence of that crowd?

But this conception is too short-lived, if we consider not only a single MOMENT in time, but the whole CURRENT OF THE FINAL EPOCH. Write down the history of a crowd and that of a hierarchic society, and you will see, that the CROWD inevitably goes to discord, to decomposition, to death: that the *collective society* strives for common life, for unitary aims, for a definite target. In the *crowd* there are waves, but in the community circulates *Telesma* (that is the steady current). In a parliament—members of which are elected by means of the general voting system—the parties are visible from the very beginning of that institution. No parliament in the world provides its President (or speaker in some systems) with factual authority, but only expects him to be a guard for the preservation of the accepted forms of government. Compare these almost anarchical systems with the work of families and other communities, built in a patriarchal way, that is according to Hierarchic Law.

This last paragraph is actually a quotation from the words of Prof. G. O. M. made in 1912. But have these words lost their actuality now, almost fifty years later? In the time of that eminent thinker and occultist there were far fewer democratic republics (in fact, monarchies were in the majority), than can be seen today, when almost every half-wild and uncivilized tribe —when given independence—tries to form something like a 'democratic parliamentary system' among its primitive people, of course, unsuccessfully.

When looking back at historical records describing the not-so-far distant past, you will undoubtedly see, that there were far less international and social troubles than today, to say nothing of the *Sword of Damocles* so pitilessly hanging over the neck of humanity, in the form of total nuclear annihilation. In those days, a nation might suffer a revolt, a social disaster or loss of that which we like to call 'independence', but humanity as a WHOLE was never threatened with extinction. Then for example, France might fight Germany (1870-71), or Japan, Russia (1904-5), and so on, but the *total world-wide wars are an invention of recent times.*

An independent and unprejudiced mind will come to a right conclusion, no matter if such might be 'unpopular' today.

Anyway, consider a fox which falls into a trap: it systematically bites through its paw or tail, in as little as say fifteen minutes, all in order to be freed from the limitation of its will's manifestations (which in Man we may term his pentagrammatic will); to save the WHOLE of its being, and to avoid unwanted experience on the physical plane, so imminent in the event of that fox's inactivity.

It can be said, that spiritual and materialistic philosophies may be presented in the form of an immense *binary*. Yes, there have been attempts to neutralize this binary!

A *spiritualist* says: 'All comes from ABOVE, from the *Ascending Triangle*, which gave birth to everything. The Sun is the father of all.'

A *materialist* may reply: 'All comes from below, all was created by adaptation, you can see how the *Descending Triangle* gives birth to everything. The Moon is the mother of all.'

A *pantheist* now comes forward to tell us: 'There is no substance in either of your opinions. Look at the *central part* of Solomon's Star. There is the STAUROS, which symbolizes the Gnostic Law of fecundation: the *passive* through the *active*. I found that both your triangles already existed, and I am using them as ready tools. The key to my conception lies just in the *Stauros*, in the transformation of the Telesma's body, that is in the environment producing the complex of the positive ACTIVITY and the negative PASSIVITY. You may be right, that the *father* of my *Baphomet* is the SUN, that his *mother* is the MOON. In this both of you (materialists and spiritualists) are right. But the wind bore Baphomet in its bosom, this wind which I am breathing, because of which I am living together with all that exists with me and with you. I am not seeking the beginning of all beginnings, and I do not want to turn any *end* into the beginning. I have no reproaches against the PARENTS of all that IS! I am living in the realm of their androgynous CHILD, the VAU of Hermetists.'

To which school have we to join ourselves? Have we to be spiritualists, materialists or pantheists? Enlightened occultists would tell you: 'Go and follow the example of the Egyptian Schools! Bow before *Hermes Trismegistus*, the personification of the magnificent synthesis of all the three philosophical currents. Be a materialist when you yourself are rebounding from the *solid bottom* called the physical plane; it is a sure basis for one who is operating magically, when there is a need to compel facts to create facts. Use pantheism when you want forms to create forms, when your individuality speaks in you as the Pentagram, being conscious of itself, not as a slave of Nature, but as a free god.

Then, as soon as you feel that personality and individuality are losing their hold on you in the PRESENCE OF SOMETHING MUCH MORE UNIVERSAL which proclaims ITSELF to be UNITY, as soon as you notice in yourself a growing *contempt for forms* and *love of ideas*, then openly and courageously recognize yourself as a SPIRITUALIST: for then you are in the kingdom of the FATHER, of the YOD.

But which of the three systems actually belong to Man, to his essence and nature? What actually creates Man? Body, personality, or that lofty striving ABOVE, where the personality and individuality melt into something UNIVERSAL, where they dissolve alive into the broad stream of the IDEA, which carries us into INFINITY?

Friends, to such questions there are no definite answers, which can be given by one man to another. We can only exchange words, but they cannot substitute the individual Truth which must be born in each of us. Everyone must seek it through the right meditation, that is, a deep merging in his spirit. What is evident to me, is that the BODY seems to be less lasting and strong than the individuality: that INDIVIDUALITIES draw close together on the ground of their common interests, and often because of these interests they agree to play the role of the tail or paw in my recently quoted example of the fox.

Finally, I have to remind my readers to look again at the lessons of the Eleventh Arcanum about the 'downfall of souls', which may give the right hint to a deep-thinking student of Hermetism. Apart from Hermetism, an inspiring answer may be received from the study of Eastern philosophy in its form of Advaita Vedanta.

A *pure spiritualist*, of course, will be an absolutist in the realm of his views on Hierarchy; a *materialist* is logically compelled to defend the collective voting, as a privilege of the cells of the universe's organism, referring to all phenomena appearing in time and space, while a *pantheist* will fight for the kingdom of the Spiritual Monad, limited (I beg your pardon for this expression) by the passive constitution of matter.

The principles relating to the realization of Spiritual Hierarchy in life have already been given in the lessons of the Third Arcanum.

LESSON 84

Invultuation

If someone raises the question of the characteristic of initiation in the three Masonic Symbolical Degrees, exclusively from the point of view of teaching a man to influence others, the answer should be as follows:

(1) The *Degree of Disciple* teaches us to be strong in ourselves, and therefore, to combat our own weaknesses, annihilating them gradually. This degree is dedicated to the elaboration of activity in the operator.

(2) The *Degree of Companion* reveals weaknesses of others to us and teaches us to make use of those weaknesses at the time when we become freed from our own faults. This is the school of the calculus of the stupidity and passivity of others.

(3) The *Degree of Master* turns our attention to the art of planning operations in which our force of activity exactly corresponds to the passivity and weakness of others. If we are intellectually strong and possess enough knowledge, we can then lead fools where we want, because of the right use of our means. But we will certainly abstain from competing with them, say, in the field of boxing, or other physical fighting as in a circus, simply because their muscles might be stronger than ours. If we are strong in some definite techniques, we will naturally accept the fight just in that realm, leaving aside all other kinds of competition.

In general, these theses are related to the details of the process of invultuation, which may be defined as a *violent use of astral and physical resources of one incarnate man by another, equally incarnate one.*

Imagine, on one hand, a man who dissipates his fortune, or a state sense-lessly colonizing all parts of the world, without having safeguarded its colonies by necessary strategic preparations. On the other hand, consider a man who keeps all his possessions under lock and key having duly regis-tered, and then secured them by fences and watch dogs, or a state which has good connections with all its colonies, and possesses operational bases in all parts of the world, and a ready navy on all seas to defend them. Then if the *second man* or *second state* acts against the first, it is clear that success will be assured and the aim reached, no matter if this will be against the interests of the first type of man or state.

Further, if both of the men are similar to the unwise, *first* type, but one of them, forgetting for a time, his passivity and foolishness, takes the initiative in the planned attack, he will have some advantage, even if both forces are equal. Of course, the second can also awaken and try to repel the aggression, but then he must be prepared for many losses in the meantime.

In these few similes we have the whole secret of invultuation. The magic influences are always connected with some manifestations on the physical or lower astral planes. The invultuation can have numerous aims: invultua-tion for love, sickness or death, material disaster, bankruptcy, the cutting up or diminishing of some profitable activities, and so on. Just because the results of invultuation belong to the lower sub-planes of the universe, the very term is used in the sense of something evil, and *not without good reason*. It is always a very gross operation, requiring a solid basis in matter.

This is achieved as follows: an *involutionary entity* is created according to the Sephirothic plan. The world—*Olam ha Aziluth* of that created being belongs entirely to the operator. This world of Aziluth should penetrate, by its influence, the worlds—*Olam ha Briah, Jezirah* and *Aziah* of the subject of the operation. But the Aziluth of the operator is alive because of its influence in all the three worlds of the operator himself. This means that he must bind together his own *Briah, Jezirah* and *Aziah* with the same elements of the subject, acting, by the momentary lulling of the suspicions of his Olam ha Aziluth. Then the three lower worlds of the subject will enter as tem-porary participants into the common organism of both men. The next problem for the operator will be the realization of a particular suggestion, like *ethical sickness* for that part of the artificial and newly constructed Olam ha Briah, which corresponds to the former *free* Briah of the victim. He will then suggest the 'formal' sickness into that part of the common Olam ha Jezirah, which corresponds to the former separate *Jezirah* of the subject, and finally, a *physical sickness* related to the part of the common Aziah. This is the general pattern.

Some would say, that it is hard to possess completely all the three worlds of the subject of the operation. *But there is no need to take the whole of them: only a tiny part will suffice.*

This part is then contaminated with a sickness, which is left to spread to as many of the victim's organs as possible, while carefully protecting the operator's own organs, which entered the artificially fashioned common organism, as previously stated. Nobody would contest, that *ethical dissatis-faction*, because of some accident may sometimes destroy the spiritual

O

harmony of a weak man; that *erroneously built forms* around him may undermine his own formal world, and that the *contagious bacillus* inoculated into one cell of his physical body may easily contaminate his whole organism.

From the aforesaid it follows, that elements deliberately infected should belong as close as possible to those which represent the character, construction or physiological secretions of the organs, which are to be affected.

For an ethical invultuation of an ambitious man it is important to inoculate him with elements connected with his own selfishness. For a 'formal' man (one liking outer forms such as the arts, and so on), who has to be invultuated, it is essential *to introduce the element of disgrace and ugliness* into his Olam ha Jezirah.

For invultuation for death, love, sickness or hatred, and so on, it is essential to affect his Olam ha Aziah by taking his blood-cells, rather than say, part of his epidermis.

It is important to give to the so obtained unessential parts of the Olam ha Aziah of the victim, some forms which suggest a kind of reality in the visible world. If the operator can only get some hairs, he will make a wax figure and fix the hairs to its head. There was a lack of material in the world *Aziah*, but it was replenished through the world of *Jezirah* (by the making of a form and the baptizing of it with the name of the subject of the operation).

Someone wishes to suggest fear to the subject, without knowing exactly what really *scares* the man, but knowing what puzzles him. That someone would then tune the whole artificial organism (as spoken of before) firstly to puzzlement, and then add fear as only he can imagine it. When fear has been inoculated, the operator tries to subdue all feelings of fear in himself. This will work, providing he himself is not too open to being puzzled.

Otherwise the operator himself will be affected by the fear. The so-called well known *'returning blow'* or repercussion in occultism, is the result of an attempt to infect another person with a sickness, to which the operator is more sensitive than the subject. Of course, in such a case everything returns to himself. A cowardly man who cares for his well-being on the physical plane will get the returning blow if he tries to invultuate another man, in order to produce a disaster for him in the physical world. An amorous man invultuating another for love, will become stupidly and desperately enamoured himself.

Self insurance in invultuation by the introduction of a THIRD subject may be achieved by placing that subject in the background of the mental part of the operation, and also through the skilful choice of its astral and physical properties. According to this, the *third* element of the subject of the operation (physical Aziah) must be more sensitive than the operator for the acceptance of invultuation.

If one is invultuating for grief and the progressive development of that feeling, it would be wise to substitute a dog against the returning blow, which would eventually be tortured by the grief; but it would be very wrong to try to protect oneself by the transfer of the evil influence to a crow living in one's garden.

Now it may be clear to you, why invultuating magicians try to get blood, teeth, finger-nails, sweat, sperm, and so on, and why they introduce these elements into the physical basis of the whole operation, often mixing secretions from the victim's body with their own. In some cases they are satisfied with a doll, photograph or other formal image, introducing into these things actual parts of the subject's body, and also, why in some other cases, operators prefer a living organism (such as a frog), which they make similar to the victim by giving to it his or her name (the so-called black magic 'baptism').

In a purely energetic influence, like trying to make a man fall over on the street, the magician follows behind his victim, trying to imitate his steps, and infecting him with the *idea of stumbling*, but at the last moment holding himself back from a fall similar to that which has befallen his enemy.

All the wild rituals of witch-doctors, black magicians, quacks, and so on find their explanation in the foregoing. All of this is just as simple as it appears to be mysterious, and the key to it lies in one's activity when attacking another person's passivity. Of course, the element of 'know how' is as important as will-power's tension in all magic acts.

The classical Hermetic Tradition recommends one universal defence against invultuation: 'DO NOT SLEEP' in the sense of not being passive or distracted. The reason for this is that no astral arrow can stick to an *active* man (in all the three planes, of course), just as an ordinary arrow cannot pierce a rapidly rotating wheel. A man watching his garden or field will see every poacher or thief because of his watchfulness.

(1) *On the mental plane 'do not sleep' means: pray*, especially for your enemies. Who prays for his foes does not make any plans for vengeance. Who does not create such plans, will not ascribe such plans to others, and this lack of suspicion makes a man immune against any fear. Whoever is fearless, is hard to invultuate for any danger.

(2) *On the astral plane 'do not sleep' means: be occupied* with the defined forms in your consciousness, chosen by and generated by yourself, in order that *something* will not be attached to you from outside. Know what you want so that some chaotic desires from your enemies will not be suggested to you. Love your chosen companion of life so as not to be involved in false loves and passions.

Join a certain good Egregor, which corresponds to your contemplation, so that you will not be entangled with the Chain of a foreign, evil Egregor.

(3) *On the physical plane 'do not sleep' means: exercise your body* reasonably, so that its vital force will respond quantitatively and qualitatively to your occupations; so that your organs may perform their functions well, then they will offer resistance to every attempt at invultuation. Remember that people who are dissatisfied with life, and who throw away their lives on all the planes, are susceptible to that sort of evil influence. An idealistic, serious and ardent worker in any branch of human activity is protected from all outer temptations and attacks by a strong wall. His *Olam ha Aziluth* duly penetrates the other worlds. For the outer world such a man is always the active YOD, and he plays the role of the HÉ only when he is willing to accept a Higher Influx.

Therefore do not be that crayfish, retreating to the puddle, do not let the wolf and the dog frighten you, and then drops of your blood will not be strewn along the paths of service to each and everyone. You should be satiated with the slavery symbolized by the ominous binary of the TWO TOWERS, and of the conscious surrender to the dark Hierarchy of the cone of the Moon's rays.

You know their origin, and therefore in the reflected light you will learn to admire and to honour the TRUTH of the light's PRIMORDIAL SOURCE.

This is what the Hermetic Tradition and occult experience tell us.

LESSON 85

Before I speak about that which official science tells us of the elements of the Eighteenth Arcanum, I would like to explain something else, the last point concerning invultuation and its results.

We already know how to prevent being invultuated. Very well, but what if it has already happened, and you are suffering the results of the infamous and treacherous attack. Is there a means of salvation?

A practical example will probably be most enlightening. In an overwhelming number of cases, the attack culminates on the physical plane, and the black magician tries to harm his victim at just that point. How does the evil power act, which destroys one's health and affects one's psychology? If the poisoned arrow of invultuation has reached you, and you are feeling its influence, it means that the evil-doing missile has lodged in your aura, if we may use this modern expression.

Recently (I am writing this at the beginning of 1959), a person known to me was an object of attempted invultuation by some false 'masters' and 'yogis' in the East, because he had unveiled their true role in his journalistic work and in some books. These people, who are living off the naïvety and credulity of their deceived 'disciples' and devotees, call themselves by many 'impressive' names, like 'perfect masters', 'kings of yogis', 'leaders of saints', and so on. For any experienced occultist, in fact for every intelligent and reasonable man, who is even slightly acquainted with the ridiculous character of such *self-styling* on the part of these occult rogues, as he called them in his works, this is proof about the *falsity of their pretences*. But naïve and mainly HYSTERICAL people of both sexes cannot penetrate into the dark minds of their deceivers, and having an inner need for devotional surrender, are often caught and exploited by the unscrupulous rogues, who like an easy life and undeserved homage and devotion.

He was warned from a friendly and quite reliable source that an effort would be made to eliminate his *activities* in the unveiling of the evil men, thereby *depriving* them of their 'devotees'.

In his very active life he had no time to sacrifice to any occult activities in order to *prevent the attack*, otherwise he was not afraid of it.

And then it happened. First, an incurable eye-ailment appeared without any apparent reason, as he had always had very good eyesight and no adverse hereditary influences were present. No physical methods of cure were very successful, apart from possibly an operation as a last resort, which he disliked because of its uncertainty. There were some hints that the ailment had a definite occult character, because of the periodical and measured attacks. It but remained to surrender the sight, and so stop the activities which he considered useful, or to fight. He chose the latter course.

From Lesson 8 you know about the excellent magic sword of Paracelsus, used for dispersing evil concentrations of astral matter (larvas) which are one of the causes of physical suffering. So it will be small wonder to you when I tell you that he decided to use this means. The dispersing of the harmful missiles took quite a while, as the foremost difficulty lay in finding the TIME, at which they were sent into the aura. Finally, two or three daily operations (see Lesson 5) began to show results, until the whole affair was eventually cleared up. He also used some medicinal palliatives for some time, until finally he forgot the whole thing. At a special hospital, the doctors recognized that the ailment no longer existed, despite the numerous diagnoses which had been confirmed by tests and examinations made according to the latest methods. In order to solve a difficult position for themselves (the sickness is considered as incurable until an operation has been made, which is often unsuccessful and sometimes leads to loss of sight), he was told that 'probably the ailment had not existed at all'. That was sufficient for him.

Next came an attack on the *solar plexus*, a usual place for some Eastern black magic practitioners. Depending upon the ability of the operator and his powers, as well as the resistance of the victim, it can result in intestinal disorders, ulcers, and also cancer.

As usual, no medicines or normal treatment were effective, although once again no reasons for such an ailment were present. The victim was a strict vegetarian, never troubled by any abdominal complaints, and living on a most reasonable diet.

Again, the same practice as for the eyes gave the best results. You know how the *Trident* should be used (see Lesson 5), so there is no need to repeat the details. Nevertheless, I would only like to mention, that the strokes of the Trident had to be made very close to the affected region of the body (solar plexus, abdomen and chest) and then they gave the best results, which were felt in a few days. The special exorcisms, as given in *Concentration* were used in conjunction with the magic sword.

Now the question may arise: how can we know that we might be under invultuation, or that someone is trying to harm us in that way? It is not at all easy to answer. The majority of symptoms of inimical occult activity against a man can also often be diagnosed as some common physical sickness, or something very close to that. Of course, one of the means of recognition will be the absolute indifference of the stricken body to all normal medicines prescribed by a physician. Further, lack of reason for the appearance of the sickness, as, for example, a teetotaller beginning to suffer the symptoms which usually only appear in habitual alcoholics, and so on.

But even in these cases one cannot have one-hundred per cent. certainty, because the human body is a very complicated, and not yet thoroughly explored field. There are many ailments for which doctors can never give any reasonable causes. Think just about some kinds of malignant tumours, eye-diseases, digestive disorders and other similar troubles. Some get them, while others in much worse conditions of life do not get them.

Anyway, there must be a definite reason for any occult (black magic) attack against us. Invultuation is not an easily or safely performed operation, and it always involves some element of uncertainty and danger for the malicious operator, who is never in a position to foresee WITH FULL CONFIDENCE, EVERYTHING AFFECTING HIS ACTIVITIES, like complications, unexpectedly interfering with his operations and therefore with himself.

Even if he tries to invultuate an apparently utterly defenceless being, which evidently cannot possibly act against the evil forces sent against it, there are still *Higher Powers* on the astral and mental planes, who can, according to the karmic innocence of the attacked person, interfere with and destroy all the machinery arranged by the sorcerer.

We know about such cases, just as well as the black magicians do. So, there should be quite definite reasons if we are assaulted in this occult way. I will give only one or two typical examples:

(1) If one is actively engaged in combating—the so numerous in our own day—occult frauds and false 'masters', who might know some scraps of practical means and starting points stolen from certain sections of occult wisdom. They usually like to be honoured as 'great prophets', spiritual 'masters', magicians, and so on, duping and pitilessly exploiting their naïve, unfortunate followers.

Such rogues always try 'to silence' you with all the means at their disposal if your activities cross their dark paths. By obtaining objects connected with your personal magnetism, such as parts of your body (hairs, nails, blood), or clothes and other personal belongings and finally, your photographs or signature, they may be able to act against you. The proceeding has already been mentioned in this chapter.

(2) If you are standing in the way of an unscrupulous person, who knows about invultuation as a means for damaging others, without entering into conflict with the official penal code, then such a person can try to find a black occultist, and hire his services to your detriment or doom.

There are of course, many motives, but who would like to enumerate all the viciousness of our fellow men?

Nevertheless, you are studying this book, which is a proof that you are interested, more or less, in occult problems, which are the hidden side of the visible manifestations of life.

And some day this can lead you from lay-studies to real and practical work. Then, entering a particular path or current, you will have more chances to meet *those who are working in just the opposite direction*. In occultism, unlike in politics, there is no compromise. You are the 'upper hand' or you submerge. Therefore, be watchful in such cases as was recommended in Lesson 84.

There are some distinctive symptoms of imminent invultuation, which can be mentioned. If you are wearing some objects (jewellery, and so on), say, of gold or silver on your body, the former can suddenly become dull and dead looking (this also applies to pearls), while the latter can simply turn black or green, and so on. This discolouration may not be easy to remove. Anyway, water and soap are usually ineffective. Then there may be a strong suspicion that invultuation is being practised, although even such a strange phenomenon may have a certain physical origin, such as changes in the acidity of your perspiration and skin. Only then, the stain is much more easily removed.

If you suddenly become unusually and easily excited, nervous, malicious, full of fear or contempt for your environment; if some physical suffering not belonging to any known disease begins to affect you; if your acquaintances suddenly begin to shun you, without any apparent cause from your side, and so on, then all these cases might well be suspect.

If you think that someone wishes to harm you in a hidden way, the best means to get a right diagnosis would be, of course, to turn to an experienced *white occultist*, who is able to trace the evil to its source and so discover the imminent danger, while exploring the methods and forces used against you. Then he will probably be able to help by repulsing the dark arrows directed against you.

If you cannot do this then operate with a magic sword (see Lesson 8) which, if duly used with faith, will produce results which will puzzle you by their effectiveness.

Theurgic means are also highly recommendable, that is: intensive praying (several times daily) connected with some *fasting* (this is a special source of inner force in us) and the refusal of all our beloved titbits, delicious dishes, and so on. You will readily understand that all this fortifies your will-power and facilitates concentration.

Which prayers should be used? Those of course, which are strongest, and known to be of high origin. This means, that the 'Lord's Prayer' (used in FULL) or the 'Sermon on the Mount' would be supreme. Advanced occultists are able to create powerful currents of prayer and use them freely.

Another fact may be quoted as a final defence against invultuation. Some Catholic and Orthodox priests and monks are initiated into the system of exorcisms of their Churches, as well as the ritual against evil spirits, as they call the dark forces and their ominous practices. Perhaps, by asking advice and help from a bishop, the victim might be directed to such a man, who will then stand up for you with all the weapons at his disposal. Although I know about these weapons, it is not my business to publish things, which belong to certain powerful Egregors, entitled to dispense them, and which usually do not like to be interfered with in any way.

When we are extremely thirsty we will accept a glass of water from anyone, without asking his name or other details. When our lives are in danger, we will accept help from anyone, independent of his nationality, outer looks, and so on.

If we are really curious, we can satisfy this feeling later, when need or danger have been removed. It is a reasonable way. Hermetism is foremostly a practical philosophy, in which 'why' is less important than 'how'. Therefore, I cannot see any reason to delve any more into the theory of things, which have been explained in the foregoing lines of this Lesson.

LESSON 86

An often encountered, unconscious sort of black magic is vampirism, usually unknown as such, which arises when old and decaying people mix closely with younger, healthier ones. It may occur by day, or by night when sleeping in adjoining rooms, or, still worse, in the same bedroom. The older ones, through their astral bodies, which during sleep wander apart from the physical shells, then absorb the vital energy of their victims, unduly prolonging their own physical lives by such robbery.

From the point of view of the White Occult Tradition (Hermetism included) such proceedings are improper and forbidden. Although, in olden times, King David, who otherwise was considered to be a saintly and inspired person, in his old age practised vampirism, by ordering many teenage boys and girls to be close in his presence. These youths were even called 'rejuvenators' of the old king.

From our point of view, it is inadvisable for younger people to sleep closely near old and decaying folk, for they might lose their vital energy (prana) for the sake of the unconscious vampires in their families. Similarly, they should not allow their food to be prepared by old or sick people, no matter whether the sickness is absolutely not physically contagious, such as rheumatism, heart disease, and so on. Where there is sickness, there is astral disbalance, which tries to vampirize everything that comes within its reach.

All this does not affect a trained and experienced occultist, who knows about the 'odic armour' and other means of insulation (see *Concentration*).

If complete separation of sleeping arrangements is impossible from some points of view, or because of adverse conditions, then simply the placing of a large basin of fresh water beside the bed of the person defending him or herself against the vampirism (as just described), will, to a certain extent, prevent the wandering old astrosome of robbing the sleeping younger person. But in the morning, immediately after awakening, the basin must be removed, the water emptied out, and the vessel washed so that nothing from the now impure night-water remains in any contact with men.

Early in 1959, I noticed a striking example. Two very old people (a married couple) had their bedroom beside that of a younger person, who continually felt herself 'tired' and not refreshed after sleep, while the old ones, despite their numerous physical ailments, still retained their vital forces at an utterly incomprehensible level.

Noting all the well-known symptoms of unconscious vampirism in that family, I advised the affected member to use the basin of water (as just mentioned). The results were not too satisfactory and some radical measures appeared to me to be more desirable, in the form of abandonment of the bedroom, which was too close to the 'vampires'.

This worked immediately. At first, the old people became very impatient and unfriendly, and then grew weaker as they were deprived of the robbed vital energy which they used to get before.

It may be weird for men of the atomic age and space travel to hear of such things, and I thought more than once before I mentioned them here; but I believe that one must be sufficiently strong and independent in order to recognize facts, no matter how strange, they may appear to the majority of men in our 'enlightened' twentieth century. In spite of everything, the evil occult practices still exist, although their applications do not produce even the smallest percentage of casualties equivalent to those caused by one atomic or hydrogen bomb.

Fortunately, these practices seem to be on the decline, or simply are not reported any more, as people are thinking less and less about the possible causes of their illnesses and troubles. May the reader not be misguided by my report about the instances of occult attacks which had to be repelled. I do not advise anyone to swing a magic sword when his eyesight begins to weaken, or when his digestive system becomes defective. For medical science does not lose any of its value just because a few ailments of non-physical origin cannot be cured by it. Such cases are so rare and the conditions in which we may be endangered in that way are so unusual, that there is little probability of us meeting them.

Occult attacks, especially in our own time, must have—from the point of view of the aggressors—valid and urgent reasons, for the very task of invultuation is by no means easy or free from danger.

In the two instances which I have described, the person attacked could also use the tactics of the 'returning blow', thus repelling the harmful energy sent against him and sending it back to the evil-doer. It would be uncertain whether the latter could resist the impact of his own malice, reversed against him.

However, such *occult crimes* are just those which are the '*dearest paid*' for by the karma of a fool, who uses superphysical powers for evil purposes. No other kind of offence brings such extended sufferings in all three worlds, as *black magic*, especially so as even such a means as prayer, which gives relief to so many erring souls (after their disincarnation) *is denied to the black ones*.

This is because they cannot raise their consciousness, so dimmed and full of hatred, to the forgiveness and peaceful recognition of their errors, which alone can alleviate the suffering elementar, surrounded by the horrible visions of his victims, tormenting him on the astral plane.

Official science has made some interesting findings about the occult facts of invultuation, as has been proved by the extensive experiments of de Rochas in the Parisian Hospital of Charité.

Remember Lesson 69 with the list of different states which occur in the various phases of hypnotism?

After 1891, de Rochas was occupied with the experiments of the exteriorization of patients, merged in deep hypnotic sleep. You may turn your attention to the statement made by myself in explanation of the theory of invultuation, that the first step in such methods is the establishment

O*

between the operator and subject of *something*, very strongly reminiscent of the *'etat de rapport'* (state of relationship). This state also belongs to de Rochas' list. By acting magnetically on the visual realm of the patient in the form of short direct or circular *passes* of the hands on the skull or around the eyes, he reached the following results:

The surface of the skin became absolutely insensient to all irritation. The sensibility was gradually transferred, according to the passes made by de Rochas, to different surfaces *away from the body* of the patient, distant by two to six inches from the skin; but no sensibility was betrayed in the space between the surfaces. The number of these sensitive (but foreign to the body of the patient) surfaces became greater as the hypnotist worked longer. Some of them were as far away as a couple of yards from the body.

A prick with a needle made on one of these sensitive surfaces was painful for the patient. A glass of water, placed between these surfaces produced the so-called 'odic shadow', that is behind the glass a few of the surfaces lost their sensitiveness, as if it had been absorbed by the water in the glass.

However, by pricking the water it was possible to provoke a feeling of pain in the patient, and by cooling it, to cause him to shiver. The same results were obtained when a wax figure was placed on the sensitive surfaces. The pricking of the water was transferred to that part of the body which was closest to the sensitive surface. Pricks on the upper part of the wax doll were transferred to the upper part of the patient's body, and pricks on the lower parts of the doll, to the corresponding lower parts of the person.

Apart from all this, some pictures were made. In the first case parts of the skin of a non-hypnotized person were photographed, and in the second, exteriorized parts of the body (surfaces) of the patient under hypnosis. In the *first* case all attempts to invultuate were unsuccessful (because of the active state of a non-hypnotized individual). In the *second* one, every touch on the photograph was felt by the patient. A slight scratching of the photograph produced redness of the patient's skin in exactly corresponding places (stigmata).

These were the findings of the experiments performed many times in the presence of several doctors and one mathematician.

Since de Rochas' time, these experiments have been repeated in many countries and on many different occasions. Every hypnotist desiring to experience these strange things for himself is perfectly free to try them.

All this explains very clearly and beyond all doubt the methods which rule over the processes of invultuation, and no further comments seem to be necessary.

So far, we cannot determine WHY there exist such and such states of relationship (*etat de rapport*), leading to the possibility of invultuation, but we know HOW these relationships can be established. Also, we know that we *cannot deny this possibility*, if we are to retain our position as logical and scientifically thinking people.

There is no doubt, that in occult matters there has been (and still is) plenty of bungling and fraud, but this has also applied to many other branches of human knowledge, and nowhere is there any absolute defence against humbugs and their masters.

LESSON 87

It can be said that the 'famous' mediaeval (and later) travels of witches through the air, to the *Bald Mountain*, where the diabolic *Sabbath* was supposed to have been celebrated, were none other than artificial exteriorizations of astrosomes, obtained by the use of some special combinations of drugs, among which opium and perhaps hashish were the principle ingredients. Exact *quantitative* and very complicated prescriptions for means of producing exteriorization have been given in the books by the once famous occultist Stanislas de Guaita.

The unfortunates who obtained and were anxious to use these ungents and mixtures could necessarily exteriorize themselves only into the lowest regions of the astral world. On these dark sub-planes they could find every kind of astral refuse, among which were devil-like beings, and the *mental personification of darkness and evil* itself, the so-called *Monsieur Leonard* (or Mephistopheles), together with his goat's paraphernalia of hoofs and horns, and so on.

Infinitely plastic by comparison with physical matter, the astral substancè can easily (of course, only for a limited time) be moulded into any desired form, under the stress of a strong will and creative imagination, which are, as we already know from former lessons, the motive power in the astron.ental realms.

So every sort of devilish or angelic clichés can be created. Moreover, according to Baphomet's constitution and laws, these creations can be *materialized* by the use of special magic operations, and hence condensed and made visible or even tangible for the physical eye and senses.

This thesis should help put the attentive student of Hermetism in a position to explain to himself many related occult and magic phenomena about which he may hear.

Assemblies of large quantities of astro-mental images and vibrations saturated with definite feelings and thoughts attract and revive corresponding clichés around them. Therefore, if a mass is said by a saintly minister of religion it would attract POSITIVE (good) forces and clichés, and therefore bring benefits from these angelic influences to the faithful present.

A NEGATIVE (evil) ceremony, often called the '*black mass*' must logically and practically augment and intensify bad vibrations (feelings and thoughts) attracting corresponding evil clichés from the *Dark Cone* of the planet, which are images of every kind of vice and crime.

When such a '*black priest*' (who *must* traditionally be a renegade Catholic clergyman), knows some elementary practical magic, he might be able *to materialize*, for a very limited time, the terrible image of Monsieur Leonard, and to considerably increase the 'faith' of the assembled members of his satanic cult.

In the books (*En Route* and *La Bas*), famous fifty years ago, by the former satanist J. Huysmans (who subsequently repented and converted back to Catholicism), there can be found almost exact descriptions of authentic black masses, in which the author took part several times, according to his own confession.

This is no place to quote extensively details of that debased and neurotic cult. Only on broad lines it may be said that:

'The '*black mass*' is essentially a parody, caricature and blasphemy of the authentic (principally Catholic) mass. Where the Cross is venerated in the latter, in the former it is the object of hideous offences. Some black priests wore the picture of the Cross on the skin of their soles in order always to trample on this sacred sign of Christ.

When in the true mass, God is glorified and worshipped, in the black folly He is insulted to limits beyond quotation. The Holy Sacrament, instead of being adored, is blasphemously mixed with untold impurities and cursed.

Instead of the consecrated altar as in Church, the naked abdomen of a prostitute serves for this purpose in the black mass. Instead of prayers, the most evil sermons are directed against the 'enemies of the cult', and the church, imploring the *Great Goat* (Leonard) to send on them, all disasters, ailments and sudden death. A general sexual orgy usually concludes such a meeting, connected with free use of stupefying and exciting drugs, apart from alcohol.

It was mentioned that at some black masses, when there was an opportunity and the means, the 'ministering' black priest, at the culminating moment, used to perform defloration of a girl under age, who was often drugged.

These revolting ceremonies were performed in secluded places or on properties, where the members were sure that nobody could see or hear them, and that the police would not be on their trail. Most of our information about the black masses and co-related activities dates from the end of the nineteenth and beginning of the twentieth centuries, and France was the country most mentioned, especially the lonely castles whose owners belonged to the devilish cult.

Now, from our cold and clear Hermetic point of view, all this filth and debauchery are only one more manifestation of the low moral and spiritual development in men. They are involutionary currents which create unhealthy and perverted passions in the consciousness of that kind of people.

But, human nature is so arranged, that until a certain degree of inner progress is reached, men like to 'justify' their vices and passions. Satanism and other bypaths are only one of the more striking examples.

Such men speak about the 'inverted god' (usually the Devil), whom they allegedly serve. In reality, of course, they serve only their passions and perversion. Their 'god' must be worshipped just the opposite to the real Deity, hence evil, crime, debauchery and vices are the foremost pleasing factors for such a 'god'. There are reasons to believe that the 'black cults' among white men and in cultured countries are now almost extinct, but there may be a lot of occult bungling and imitation (usually for material purposes) of all that has been described about these cults. Apart from that, in an age of fast means of communication, radio and radar, authorities are in a much better position to discover and eliminate organizations, which choose to ignore the accepted code of decency. I know that between 1930 and 1933 in some European countries, there were proceedings against 'satanists', for being grossly immoral and criminal.

Still another human perversion based on black magic is NECRO-MANCY and its variation of 'necrofilia'. The main proceeding in this abhorrent depravity is that of sexual relations with corpses, usually freshly buried and then exhumed by the necromancer.

Such offences, of course, are committed on female corpses, but profanation may also occur with dead male bodies, only then the aim is different. It is the attracting of the phantom belonging to the elementar (necessarily of a lower type) and involving it in repulsive operations, which bring to the necromancer, certain gains and power over those who are his enemies, by adversely affecting their astrosomes and thereby bringing sickness or even death to them. Tradition tells us, that necrofilia occurred mostly among peoples of the Near and Middle Eastern countries.

This process, about which we cannot speak openly, is analogous to physical infection. We know that sometimes a small wound or a cut finger may result in deadly blood-poisoning. And so it may be with a wound maliciously inflicted on the astrosome of the victim, by the black magician who knows enough to be able to use the mysterious relationship between human phantoms and the astrosomes of living men. These relations are unnatural and against the Law of Life, and can be started only through perverted occult operations.

The 'zombies' of Haiti and other countries, populated by negroes, or people of mixed blood, should not be included here. The zombie-magician operates not on corpses, but on the bodies of men whom he has partially poisoned and put into a state of temporary catalepsy, thereby acquiring unlimited power over their wills. The unlucky ones remain helpless slaves of the zombie-magician, who then uses them for all kinds of work.

The bodies of the men who are stricken by the artificial catalepsy of a zombie, are secretly exhumed by the magician, usually at night, but always before the expiration of three days after 'death', otherwise true death invariably occurs.

Recent reports indicate that death-like catalepsy is usually brought about by the administration of special poisons, probably unknown to official science. We have good reasons to doubt hypnotic action by the black magicians.

To conclude, I will mention another kind of magic, which is often used both consciously and subconsciously. It is cursing in which the blasphemous use of God's name is included. It brings disastrous results, especially visible when the transgressor is in his middle or old age, for then Karma acts almost immediately, as there is no time for it to be distributed over the whole life span.

A striking example of this was recently observed in Melbourne, where a malicious old man cursed an occultist 'in the name of God' simply because he hated him. The latter did not react at all, apart from mentioning about the danger and foolishness of such cursing. The result came like lightning: the man received a stroke and was completely paralysed, while another person, who passively associated herself with the misdeed, was punished by an incurable and disabling sickness.

P

Arcanum XIX
LUX RESPLENDENS
THE SUN

♓

Pisces

Veritas Fecunda
Virtus Humana
Aurum Philosophale

CHAPTER XIX

ARCANUM XIX (ק QUOPH)

THE letter of the alphabet which corresponds to the Nineteenth Arcanum is ק (Quoph) and its numerical meaning is 100. Astrologically the arcanum belongs to the sign of the Fishes (Pisces). Its hieroglyph is an *Axe*. It is the AXE OF LIBERATION, which hews through the oppressing ROOF of the former, Eighteenth Arcanum.

This Nineteenth Arcanum is the first of the *transitional* triangles of the Tarot's system. The first eighteen are the *trumps proper*, belonging—as we already know from previous lessons—to the world of fallen humanity. But the Nineteenth, Twentieth, Twenty-first (0) and Twenty-second are the steps to the Minor Arcana, which are the scheme of the PRIMORDIAL world, as unspoilt by the downfall. These last four mysteries of the Tarot are less extensive in their meaning, but they are also less nebulous, and more exact, speaking about very definite periods in human evolution and its conditions.

We will see this in the course of the following lessons.

The Nineteenth Arcanum, cutting through the ominous darkness of that sun-hiding roof of the Eighteenth, allows us to see the Light, to get hope of progress, of future perfection and Reintegration in the world of the Minor Arcana. Tradition tells us that the Law of Hierarchy will lead us through the 'roof of dialectic' to the contemplation of the fruitful and fertile Light of the ULTIMATE TRUTH OF BEING.

Therefore, the *first title* of the Nineteenth Arcanum (plane of the Archetype) will be VERITAS FECUNDA (Fruitful Truth).

In the world of Man, the *second title* comes from the corresponding idea of the arcanum: a desire not to have any foes, creating in us all aspects of altruism, so essential in all steps of evolution, from the first crude altruism of primitive man (towards his family) to the sublime sacrifice of a Messiah, or a Spiritual Master of an epoch. Therefore Tradition gives the *second title* as VIRTUS HUMANA (human virtue).

Now, the danger of premature dissolution of matter, of the premature destruction of the body, before the highest aim of an incarnation is reached, compels us to think about the problem of the *Philosophers' Stone* (Petra Philosophorum) and the *Elixir of Life*. So this is the *third title* of the Nineteenth Arcanum—AURUM PHILOSOPHALE (gold of the philosophers).

The student will proceed wisely, when he will not take the symbolical statements, like those just given, too literally. There is mystery in their true understanding, as you will see from the present 'transitional' arcanum, that of the Nineteenth, which speaks principally about alchemy. The *unique value* of the Tarot for a thinking and progressive type of man is just its wonderful adaptability to the most practical and concrete of problems, as to the highest spiritual attempts. True, we will not find much about the pure Himalayan heights of the Absolute in this course; but it is because the writer was obliged to follow the general pattern of the Hermetic Tradition, and not allow himself to change the age-old line of initiatory thought. Nevertheless, within its framework and in conformity with it, I have tried to give as much as possible of that, which goes beyond the *Second* and *First* Families, reaching into the realm of the AIN-SOPH. In mediaeval times this was forbidden because at that period, masters of Hermetism believed that humanity was still too unripe to transcend the realm of the *Families*; but since then we have become acquainted (about seventy-five years ago) with the *spiritual* philosophies of the East, whose mysteries were revealed to the Western world in our own epoch. So there is not much reason to try to conceal what already cannot be concealed, as it has been divulged from '*another side*'. Therefore our present Tarot is much more 'modern' and also probably wider in its conceptions, than some classical works of the past, which have been restricted by many limitations. Proofs? Of course there are! In order not to quote too much, I would like to turn your attention to the tragedy of the Knights Templar (described in former lessons), whose best and most progressive (for their own period) intentions were brutally deformed, maliciously warped and cruelly condemned.

And what of our own time? Has it not been the sublime idea of some scientists to give to humanity an inexhaustible source of energy in the form of the discovery of nuclear energy and its use, now turned to the devilish atomic and hydrogen bombs, which threaten the very existence of the human species on this erring planet? Was it not the idea to transform the deserts into new kinds of Eden through the application of the all-powerful, newly discovered energy, instead of being debased into the horrible grimace of Hiroshima and Nagasaki?

You are now studying the Tarot, the system of exact and honest thinking. Let it be helpful to you in order to understand the meaning of these paragraphs.

Albert Einstein, in his saying that '*knowledge is a real power*' was not inventing anything new for a Hermetist. The old myth about destroyed Atlantis, because of the misuse of the secret laws of Nature by the inhabitants of that great continent, may not be so far from the real truth.

If this is not enough, then listen to other words: 'Neither cast ye your pearls before swine, lest perhaps they trample them under their feet, and turning upon you, they tear you.'

And so the veil of secrecy is still necessary when speaking about things which can be misused. Fortunately, human nature itself has given a good safety valve in this matter: unripe people simply DO NOT SEE THE KNOWLEDGE HIDDEN behind the symbols, thinking it to be a nebulous theory, which is for the best.

The scientific name of the Nineteenth Arcanum is LUX RESPLEN-DENS (resplendent light) and the vulgar one—the SUN.

On its card we see two children, it may be two boys or a girl and a boy. They are wilfully playing in a stone-walled enclosure, lit by the rays of the Sun high above their heads, which *is transformed into a kind of golden rain over them.* The children have almost modern clothes: I did this deliberately, for this arcanum, perhaps more so than the others, belongs to you, as it symbolizes your own enlightenment. And you belong to this twentieth century. We are all like those children, or *we WILL be like them.*

The symbolism of this arcanum is simple. The light of the Higher Influxes enlightens human beings who become sincere and good like children who have lost the maliciousness of the 'average', that is spiritually undeveloped men. Therefore we can see that this Light is *conditioned,* and very reasonably conditioned: ' ... Unless you be converted, and become as little children, you shall not enter into the kingdom of heaven.' as was truly said by a Great Teacher.

The stony fence surrounding the children of the Nineteenth Arcanum symbolizes the *complex of laws* according to which the evolution of human beings must go. This fence *not only limits*—to a certain degree—the movements of the playing children; but also *protects* them from outer dangers. It even *determines the place* over which the rays of the Sun are shed, and the *area in which these rays become the golden drops.*

The picture of the Nineteenth Arcanum may have another, still deeper meaning, if we remember a famous mystical saying of the well-known modern Indian philosopher—Sri Aurobindo Ghose: *'What is God after all? An eternal child, playing an eternal game in an eternal garden.'*

All this is a very fruitful theme for meditation about the Nineteenth Arcanum of the Tarot.

LESSON 89

The arithmological analysis of the arcanum is:

Equation No. 164: $19 = 1 + 18$
Equation No. 165: $19 = 18 + 1$

The Unitary Essence (1) and the mystery of the Hierarchy (18) joined together represent a ladder leading to the kingdom of fruitful Truth (19).

Three-plane Man (1) acquainted with the secrets of invultuation (18) will be able to defend himself against his enemies, providing he creates real Virtue (19) in himself.

Active Nature (1) producing dangers (18) through the objects created by it will lead us to recognition of the necessity of the Great Action (19) on the physical plane.

Equation No. 166: $19 = 2 + 17$
Equation No. 167: $19 = 17 + 2$

The Divine Substance (2) and Hope (17) lead to Truth (19).

The mystery of the polarity (2) in human nature together with Intuition (17) will create Virtue (19). For, if you will understand (which is — = negative, passive) the *Good* and if you know that apart from impressions, there is also an *active manifestation* (+ = active, positive), then you will necessarily do only good.

Ready-made objects in Nature (2) and the understanding of the *Secondary*, Zodiacal Causalities (17) give the key of Alchemy (19). This is because even non-noble elements (such as ordinary metals) may serve as starting points in alchemical actions, providing the operators *can read* the language of Nature.

Equation No. 168: $19 = 3 + 16$
Equation No. 169: $19 = 16 + 3$

The threefoldness of Metaphysical Nature (3) together with the methods of logical exclusion (16) will produce fruitful Truth (19).

The realization of the mystery of birth (3) and of astral compulsion (16) will lead to virtuousness (19).

The Gnostic realization of the Principle of Creativeness (3) and the necessity of physical destruction (16) determine one of the basic phases of the alchemical process (19), which is that of the 'crow's head'. First comes decomposition, then regeneration.

Equation No. 170: $19 = 4 + 15$
Equation No. 171: $19 = 15 + 4$

The Form (4) and Logic (15) will create the fruitful Truth (19).

Authority (4) and knowledge of Baphomet (15) will compulsorily produce Virtue (19), even if Clement V and Philip IV may have thought differently.

The ready laws in Nature (4) and the destiny of Matter (15) justify the Alchemical Action (19).

Equation No. 172: $19 = 5 + 14$
Equation No. 173: $19 = 14 + 5$

The knowledge of Good and Evil (5) through deduction (14) will lead the student to the fruitful Truth (19).

A Pentagram (5) establishing Harmony (14) in itself is virtuous (19).

One who has a sense of the Great Natural Religion (5) and who understands the reversibility of processes (14) will become an Alchemist (19).

Equation No. 174: $19 = 6 + 13$
Equation No. 175: $19 = 13 + 6$

The consciousness of the eternity of High Principles (13) through the application of the Law of Analogy (6) leads to the Creative Truth (19).

When the virtue of a Masonic master is established (19) he is told: 'You are free (6), but remember about your death' (13).

Acquaintance with the environment (6) and its energetic transformations (13) give a key to Alchemy (19).

Equation No. 176: $19 = 7 + 12$
Equation No. 177: $19 = 12 + 7$

If you believe in the Messiah (12), and Spirit is more important to you than form (7), you are lord of the Creative Truths (19).

If you conquered yourself (7) through severity and asceticism, but for others you are full of Charity (12), you are full of Virtue (19).

If you know that all of the matter of the Zodiacal plane (12) is at your disposal according to the Law of Possession (7), then in your soul you are an Alchemist (19).

Equation No. 178: $19 = 8 + 11$
Equation No. 179: $19 = 11 + 8$

If you can see the Metaphysical Libration (8) of the Great Scale and know the power (11) of the Higher Influxes, you are lord of the Creative Truths (19).

If you direct the moral force (11) of humanity to the fulfilment of the Laws (8), you are virtuous (19).

The Karma of Nature (8) and its forces (11) should be known to a real Alchemist (19).

Equation No. 180: $19 = 9 + 10$
Equation No. 181: $19 = 10 + 9$

The Testament (10) and Protectors (9) will guard you against erring and will lead you to Truth (19).

An Initiate (9) of the School of the Kabbalah (10) is doubtless a virtuous man (19).

Cautiousness (9) in using the World's Mill (10) is a characteristic of an Alchemist (19).

After this brief unfoldment of the Nineteenth Arcanum, we have to pass on to the three mystical processes belonging to this arcanum. They are: *acquisition of Creative Truths* (the Great Action in the realm of Ideas); *generation of Hermetic Virtue* (the Great Action of Ethical Hermetism), and the *acquisition of the Philosophers' Stone* (the Great Action in Alchemy).

LESSON 90

Hermetic Philosophy

We have already learned a lot from the *Emerald Tablets*. The following verses, not yet quoted, belong to the Nineteenth Arcanum:

1. SIC HABEBIS GLORIAM TOTIUS MUNDI.
2. IDEO FUGIET A TE OMNIA OBSCURITAS.
3. HIC EST TOTIUS FORTITUDINIS FORTITUDO FORTIS.
4. QUIA VINCET OMNEM REM SUBTILEM, OMNEMQUE SOLIDAM PENETRABIT.
5. SIC MUNDUS CREATUS EST.

6. HINC ERUNT ADAPTATIONES MIRABILES, QUA-RUM MODUS EST HIC.

7. ITAQUE VOCATUS SUM HERMES TRISMEGISTUS, HABENS TRES PARTES PHILOSOPHIAE TOTIUS MUNDI.

8. COMPLETUM EST QUOD DIXI DE OPERATIONE SOLIS.

Translation:

1. In this way you shall possess the glory of the whole world.
2. And all darkness will fly from you.
3. In this lies the potent power of all strength.
4. It will conquer everything subtle, and it will penetrate everything dense.
5. So is the whole universe created.
6. From it come all miraculous adaptations, based on the same ground (see 4).
7. That is why I am called *Hermes, thrice Great* (or: having triple great-ness), because I have all three parts of the philosophy of the whole universe.
8. What I told about the Sun's Action is realized.

Let us analyse these verses from the point of view of the first title of the Nineteenth Arcanum, that is the seeking of the Creative Truths. Before the actual text of the Emerald Tablets the characteristics of Baphomet were given. In these characteristics we should seek the elements of the *World's glory* as well as of all enlightenment. In other words, the mystery of Solomon's Star and the Gnostic contemplation are the keys to metaphysical omniscience.

How are we to understand this? In the nineteenth chapter of his *Trans-cendental Magic* Eliphas Lévi says wisely, that on the metaphysical plane the Philosophers' Stone has the form of a cube. In this cube he analyses three pairs of mutually opposed faces. On the first pair there is written: שלמה (Shlomoh = Solomon) and יהוה (God's Name Yod-Hé-Vau-Hé). On the second pair are the names: אדם (Adam) and חוה (Eve). On the third pair are the names of: AZOTH and INRI. In this way it may be said that the key to cognition of the *Creative Truths* is given by the three degrees of the Initiation of the Knights Templar. The FIRST degree, that of the *Kabbalistic Cycle*, unveils the mystery of relations between the Archetype and initiated Man, in this case—*Shlomoh*. God's Name is deliberately inserted, and the cause is known only to the initiates. The SECOND degree, that of the *Magic Cycle*, unveils the mystery of the influence of the Active on the Passive. The THIRD degree, that of the *Hermetic Cycle*, unveils the mystery of the *Universal Solvent* (AZOTH) and *Universal Reviver*—INRI.

This is what I am entitled to tell about this part of the arcanum. Without breaking the obligatory duty not to divulge the principles of REALIZA-TION, I would like to mention, how approximately and analogously (NOT EXACTLY), the principles work, acting from the subtle on the dense, and from the astral on the physical. The thing is simple from the outer point of view. When a magnetist or hypnotist makes his passes over the body of a patient, he does not touch it at all. When he orders that apparently insensient body to perform one thing or another, without the participation of the person's consciousness, it is analogous to the mystery of the passing from one plane to another.

The order—an immaterial impulse—is transformed into the visible action of the physical elements. Do not mix this with the conversation of people, who are in their normal waking state of consciousness (Jagrat in yogic initiation), for then quite different relations and forces are acting. Such a person is trained all his or her life to hear words and to understand them in a definite way, so there is no wonder in a normal human conversation. Tourbillons (vortexes) being the corner-stones of all astral operations, are created in just the same way as magnetic passes. Will is working through the 'plastic' environment, that is, that which has the property of being moulded under the impact of will-power, operating the pranic currents.

As everywhere, concentration is the secret and the motive-power. The laws ruling electric phenomena are closely connected in their principles, with the use of will-power: the invisible force of a current can move great masses of matter, in the form of the armature, rotors and other parts of electric machines.

In executions in the electric chair in the U.S.A. it has been observed, that some criminals are much more difficult to kill than others. Some try to resist the passage of the deadly current through their vital organs (heart and brain), by a sheer effort of will, as if making their bodies less conductive and offering high electrical resistance. Of course, they cannot do it indefinitely, and finally they must give up their desperate fight; but the fact of the possibility of such a fight, even for a short time, is significant.

As an old Sing Sing warder, who was present at more than 300 electrocutions, said: 'some prisoners forecast the resistance, stating that a lot of current would be needed to kill them'. And often this strange event was fully proved.

The mystery of the mechanism, range and field of activity belonging to that 'something' which we call 'human will-power' is still to be solved by official science.

LESSON 91

Ethical Hermetism

The purpose of Ethical Hermetism is already known to you from the previous arcana. In every human being there is material, whose proper grouping and consolidation allow a man to become virtuous. Individuality progresses in that way. The *Father* of virtuousness will be the ACTIVITY of the individual (the Sun); his *Mother*, PASSIVITY (the Moon), while the born virtuousness will be the WIND of the astral environment. He will be fed by mother EARTH, because he can manifest himself only in the world of Sacrifice, the Zodiacal one. But only *Telesma* itself can start the process of bearing, of birth and adaptation, which here appears as the veil of the WILL. The Pentagram itself creates its own virtuousness.

In the realm of Hermetic philosophy Man must first separate faith from science (knowledge), in order to synthetize them later into a magnificent WHOLE. So in Ethical Hermetism one cannot at first realize which impulses belong to the *Upper*, and which to the *Lower* triangles. We should advance to the point of ability to accept consciously the basic advice from ABOVE; also, we should be able to value the gross facts from BELOW.

We are told from ABOVE: 'LOVE THY NEIGHBOUR'. But how have we to love? In what way to love and what to do about it? 'AS YOURSELF' is the answer. But to know love for oneself can only be done in its full extent on the *plane of involution*, that is in the LOWER triangle. So we have to know separately the high ideals of *Reintegration*, and in a parallel way to examine our own gross egotism, and then bind both elements with the great Laws of Ethics. We must by turns raise ourselves to the sky and again to return from the sky to Earth. We must draw theses from HIGH and from BELOW.

Then virtue will get the full systematic expression and in your heart there will no longer remain any darkness.

Then virtue will appropriate everything *subtle*, and it will also penetrate everything *gross*, in other words, it will create new Chains of Egregoric character, conquering the gross egotism of the masses and inoculating them (even apart from their will) with ethical principles.

In pure Hermetic philosophy the mind also wanders from Heaven (principles) to Earth (facts), and again, from Earth to Heaven. It is occupied with both: *induction* and *deduction*. In Ethical Hermetism the *same process is performed by the human heart*. There the reward is full cognition of causes through the mind, and here the reward brings perfect PEACE in the heart, and *full harmony of the astrosome*, which then manifests itself actively through charity and justice, because then it SEES the needs and desires of everyone around it.

There the *mind* will solve every abstruse problem (the subtle will be victorious) and it will also penetrate into an explanation of the world of facts. And here the *heart* will form a brotherhood of virtuous ones and therefore will influence the moral level of society. Here and there are the miracles related to the cosmogonic things (so was the world created). Here and there are three great principles: active SULPHUR, striving to reach ABOVE; passive MERCURY, knowledge of the valleys, and balanced SALT, harmonizing these two principles. In both of them there are also FOUR elements: in *metaphysics*, the desire to know the Truth and to transmit it duly. Desire to accept and to put the material accepted into a system. The first two are *Yod* and *Vau;* the second are both Hé.

In Ethical Hermetism YOD belongs to evolutionary deeds, and VAU to involutionary. The *right* Hé represents positive feelings, and the *left* negative ones. There is still a FIFTH element present: the *operator standing in the centre of the Quaternary*.

In *metaphysics* there is the mind of fallen Adam, who cognized GOOD and EVIL of the great Libration. In *Ethical Hermetism* there is the quintessence of the WILL, operating the Hermetic Cross. Everywhere there is the MONAD, which can obtain the glory of the universe (sic habebis gloriam totius mundi).

LESSON 92

Alchemy

The principal sentences of the *Emerald Tablets* quoted previously, state that:

(1) The power of Hermes extends to all three planes.

(2) That solar action is performed, that is, that it has been realized not only in the two higher, but also on the physical plane.

This means that the great Table of the Egyptian Tradition recognizes alchemy. Whoever would like to continue this study on historical grounds, should read the fundamental work of *Papus—The Philosophers' Stone* (*La Pierre Philosophiale*).

I want to give you a brief schematic picture of alchemical action, analogous to those of the two higher planes, as we saw before. Here the Emerald Tablets will be of great importance.

Verse No. [1] tells us about the Law of Analogy, and therefore it allows us to pass from the Hermetism of the higher planes to physical alchemy.

Verse No. 2 announced the UNITY of the substance, and consequently the unity of matter.

Verse No. 3 clearly indicates the participation of gold (Sun) and of Silver (Moon) in the process of the action. It underlines the importance of support—the Earth.

Verse No. 4 suggests the participation of the personal magnetism of the operator in the process of the action.

Verse No. 5 gives a hint on the solid state of the Philosophers' Stone or powder.

Verse No. 6 explains the peculiar view of alchemists on metals, according to which the whole combination of matter in these metals can be unfolded into two polar scales: one pole of perfection corresponds to *silver* (can also be platinum), the second to *gold*. In these two metals, two principles are perfectly bound together, those of mercury and sulphur.

In silver this combination is present in order to manifest the mercurial properties perfectly, and in gold the properties of sulphur. The remaining metals are considered as combinations which have not attained the perfection of silver (in a negative direction), or that of gold (in a positive direction).

From this we can conclude, that Tradition recognizes, that in every metal (or element) there is a combination of sulphur and mercury, but only in silver and gold is this combination perfect. In order to transform another metal into silver or gold, we must first destroy the imperfect combination of its components, that is to separate the subtle

(SULPHUR—FIRE) from the gross (MERCURY—WATER) in that metal, and then to establish a new, perfect combination, passive or active according to the sort of precious metal we want to get.

The Emerald Tablets speak about this separation of the subtle from the gross. The base sulphur and the base mercury are neutralized by the base-salt, joining all together into the so-called AZOTH of the Sages. In practice we always have to deal with SALT, as a basis for the manifestation of the elements, and with the AZOTH of the Sages, as a basis for the possible liberation of captured bases, which are bound by the salt.

Verse No. 7 emphasizes the importance of action for matter, from the most subtle element (fire) to the most gross (earth). This verse directs the distillation of the alloys.

Verse No. 8 only encourages the alchemist to action.

The Emerald Tablets insist on the UNITY of material, created through alchemical action. The same result of the operation possesses different power in different stages of distillation. There are ways for obtaining the powder, which will transform non-precious metals into precious, having the proportions of 1:10, 1:100, 1:1,000 and 1:10,000 in strength, that is, for example, a certain distillation may give us a powder which will transform, say, lead into gold, using an ounce of that powder for a thousand ounces of the metal to be transformed.

Now, when we already know, that in alchemical action there are also three BASES (sulphur, mercury and salt), and also *four states* (radiant, gaseous, liquid and solid), we can speak about the Dynamic Cycle of the Great Operation, divided into four phases.

The *first phase* is preparation for the operation. This is preparation of the Universal Solvent, or Mercury of the Sages (AZOTH), or in other words, *astral light* in the form of doubly condensed and polarized currents. To obtain this solvent a mineral called 'Magnesia of the Sages' is used. The Azoth can be obtained from it through a mysterious operation involving the use of electricity or personal magnetism. From that comes the terms such as 'Steel of the Philosophers' or 'Magnesia of the Philosophers'.

The *second phase* consists of the actual operation. Normal metallic gold or silver are subjected to the action of the Azoth of the Sages, in order to free the living Sun (metal generating sulphur), and living Moon (metal generating mercury) from them in maximum amounts. It would also be possible to operate with non-precious metals, but then the whole thing would be much slower.

The two BASES in the form of two 'ferments' are then enclosed in a glass tower, called the '*egg*' and are submitted to slow heating by an oil-lamp, in the so-called ATANOR. Time and heat determine a number of chemical and physical processes in the 'egg'. In the first weeks of carbonization the material inside turns indefinite colours. This period is called the 'epoch of mercury' or 'kingdom of mercury'. Later the mass becomes greenish and then black. Firstly, blackness on the surface ('crow's-head') is observed, and later the whole of it turns black. The kingdom of Saturn is coming. The mass dies in order to be regenerated and the blackness changes into brown tones. The separation of vapours is visible, falling like rain. This is the kingdom of Jupiter. The kingdom of Diana appears when the mass in the 'egg' turns to a dazzling white colour.

If the powder is to be used for the 'white' transmutation (into silver or platinum), then the second phase of the operation is finished; but if we want the 'red' transmutation, the heating must be prolonged, without paying attention to the passing of the mass into the liquid and subsequently the solid states.

At last the material becomes green, blue then dark red, all of which belong to the kingdom of Venus. Later comes an orange colour, then all the colours of the spectrum (kingdom of Mars). Reddish vapours now appear over the mass. They become dense, the mass dries out, glows red, and when the 'egg' is slowly cooled, small grains like poppy seeds remain. This is the last stage called the kingdom of Apollo.

Some crystalline, light red, very heavy powder, with the smell of burned sea-salt is recovered from the broken 'egg'. After two hours of boiling, this powder possesses the power to transmute a ten times larger amount of lead into pure gold.

The *third phase* is the increasing of the quantity of the powder. It may again be submitted to the action of the Azoth of the Sages, or, what is simpler, the powder is again enclosed in an 'egg', with an amount of gold a hundred times its own weight. The 'egg' is put on the fire and then comes the change of colours as before, but much faster. Further increasing gives to the powder the proportion of 1:100, and after more repetitions of the process, 1:10,000, which usually suffices. Ten thousand ounces of melted lead will be transformed into gold by ONE ounce of the so obtained Philosophers' Stone.

The *fourth phase* is the actual use of the Stone. Melted lead, or liquid mercury is placed in a vessel, together with the pulverized Stone, mixed with wax and made into small pills. Two and a half hours are required for gold, but only a quarter of an hour for silver. The mass evolving in the 'egg' is called the 'rebis'. The immortal furnace or Atanor has three parts. In the lower is an oil-lamp where a four thread wick is used at first, until the 'crow's head' stage. Later, fourteen threads (Diana's kingdom), and finally twenty-four threads are used in the wick.

The middle part of the Atanor has some projections, on which to hold a pan-like vessel filled with sand. The 'egg' is placed in this sand until one-third of it is covered. The 'rebis' fills only one-fourth of the height of the 'egg'. In the upper part of the Atanor there is a glass dome, which reflects heat into the vessel inside.

In the second phase of the transmutation there is no necessity to use both gold and silver together. Many have worked only with gold and still obtained an excellent rebis.

To those who would like to read more about old alchemy, I would like to add, that in our terminology *sulphur* appears as father, *mercury* as mother, and *salt* as their androgynous child. This will mean, that under the term 'mercury' is understood not the base mercury, but the mercury-solvent (Azoth of the Sages), extracted from the Magnesia of the Sages. This is a ready-made substance, that is, something in which both *bases* are equally balanced. Only *salt* can perform this. It means that in the Magnesia of the Sages there is a *living salt*, just as a child comes from a living mother.

Alchemy, apart from the traditional particulars as given in this lesson, *has the deepest of symbolical meanings*, as does everything in the great philosophy of Hermes. *Some authors knew about this.* One of the most concise conceptions is: that the average layman—who from the occult point of view, is just that lead which has to be transformed into a precious metal —gold—needs *spiritual, moral and physical 'alchemy' until he is reintegrated.* The next, the Twentieth Arcanum of the Tarot, tells us about this.

Spiritual conversions, entering on the Path, following a true Spiritual Master, inner reformation, all these belong to the Nineteenth Arcanum, that first step (as has already been mentioned) to the ideal world of the pre-downfall symbols, which are the MINOR ARCANA.

ר

Arcanum XX

RESURRECTIO MORTUUM

THE JUDGEMENT

♄

Saturnus

Attractio Divina
Transformatio Astralis
Mutationes in Tempore

CHAPTER XX

ARCANUM XX (ר RESH)

THE letter of the Hebrew alphabet belonging to the Twentieth Arcanum is ר (Resh) and its numerical value is 200. The corresponding astrological symbol is SATURN. The hieroglyph of the arcanum is the human head, that head which realizes the usefulness of the axe, given to it in the foregoing Nineteenth Arcanum, that head, which looks through the 'window' cut through the oppressing 'roof' of darkness by the axe, or letter 'ק' (Quoph).

The only power which pulls us ahead on the path of Evolution is the ARCHETYPE, as you had the opportunity to learn in former lessons. Practically, it is all that we can conceive about the living and acting Deity. I am not speaking about the Unmanifested, Unattainable, Unconscious (in our limited sense of the word), and devoid of all qualities—ABSO-LUTE, which is the *Beginning and the End*, the Alpha and Omega, Eternity beyond all *time* and *space*, for it seems useless to speak about something, which is beyond all speech.

So, the ARCHETYPE is the ATMAN, SPIRIT and GOD for *Manifestation*, in which we, human, beings, are playing our modest role on this planet.

All the philosophy of the Tarot is under the spell of the Archetype. And this is rightly so. The influence of the Archetype pushes us along the Path, and attracts us to our SOURCE, which is—HIMSELF. That is why the *first title* of the Twentieth Arcanum is given as ATTRACTIO DIVINA (Divine Attraction).

The YOD of Divine Love attracts Man, that Hé, which needs the impulse to be showed the WAY OF RETURN, THE WAY OF REINTEGRATION.

However, for that sublime attainment an important factor is necessary, it is our *astral* regeneration, allowing us to develop our powers and use them according to intuitional knowledge, which is none other than the VOICE OF THE ARCHETYPE. That is why the *second title* of the Twentieth Arcanum is—TRANSFORMATIO ASTRALIS (astral transformation).

Living in Nature, we cannot avoid its collaboration, if the second title of the arcanum is to be realized. Great Hermes tells us, that, provided our efforts are rightly directed, Nature will invariably co-operate with us, and in parallel with our steps ahead, it will help us by the creation of the necessary CONDITIONS in time and space. Therefore, the *third title* of the Twentieth Arcanum is MUTATIONES IN TEMPORE (changes in time), for we certainly need that TIME in order to pass along our Path.

The scientific name of this arcanum is RESURRECTIO MOR-
TUUM (resurrection of the dead) and the vulgar one is—the *Judgement*.
On the card we see an angel in the sky, blowing a horn. The sound
symbolizes the 'Call of the Archetype' in us. In the foreground we see the
naked ('Naked must man stand before God') figures of a man, woman and
child, arising from graves. In the background, numerous other figures are
seen doing the same. The scene is as the Christian Scriptures conceive the
Day of Judgement and general Resurrection. The idea comes of course,
from much earlier times than Christian tradition.

Both poles of humanity are represented (man and woman) and the
neutralizing element of *Vau* is present as the *child* with its *parents*. All return
to LIFE from the realm of DEATH. A good theme for your meditation,
after having studied this lesson.

Astral self-perfectioning involves, as we know, *activity* as well as *intuition*.
The androgynous results of both are reflected in our environment. This
statement is interesting for those occupied with Karma and its work. That
is why all the three forms of human beings, man, woman, and child are
represented on the card. All three arose from their graves, which indicates
a change of surroundings, which is only logical. Every effort to get free
from the ominous ROOF of צ (Tzaddi) will lead, in the beginning, to a
change of place, of environment, instead of immediate liberation. This is
obvious, not only from our Hermetic point of view, but also from that of
Eastern Wisdom, which in its sacred books speaks widely about the
'numbers of incarnations needed for attainment of the state of *Jivanmukta*'.

A caged bird, after throwing itself in all directions against the walls of
its cage, is finally convinced about the impossibility of any immediate
escape, and merely waits. And this is what we ourselves are doing. Firstly,
we try in every way to 'tune' our earthly 'ensemble' to our wishes. We
wait in the astral (as two-plane *elementars*) for the renovation of the cells
of our bodies, only to get the conviction, that the *new* body is just the same
prison as was the former one. We try all kinds of inventions and im-
provements on the physical plane, travel through many countries, and all
the time we still remain slaves of the *Zodiacal* plane. Think about this simile,
it is very close to the actual truth of you and me.

Only after many experiences do we begin to think, that it is the BIRD
in the cage itself, which is in need of self-transformation, in order to have
a chance of liberation. Then we start to reform ourselves astrally, and at
the same time, try to subtilize Nature. We begin to hear better the sound
of the Archetype's horn, which at first is like a faint signal for us, perceptible only in moments of the full calm of our passions and the terrific
noise of the World's Mill (Wheel of Fortune, Tenth Arcanum). With a little
attention and effort each of us can test this statement personally.

And so to change, to transform ourselves, without end, but to change in
an evolutionary way is our aim and motto. Then the end will come if only
we can call the 'end' that Reintegration, which means nothing less than our
dissolution into the eternal Nirvana of the Unmanifested Perfection.

When we cannot see any direct ladder leading us above, we have to look
at the horizontal branches of the *Tree of Life* hoping that there, at their

tips, we will find what we seek. Sometimes we might even have to climb the branches, which apparently stretch down, if we are firmly convinced that this will eventually bring us to a powerful upward climb in the future. This is the fate of all seekers. Know it and be at peace with yourself.

Now it may be asked, what kind of elementary theurgic acts, that is, prayers can be recommended to an evolutionary and enlightened Hermetist? In order to give a right and reasonable answer we must know something more about prayer. For not all prayers are 'accepted' and therefore fulfilled; not all of them are a blessing, and some may even turn against an unwise person, as a condemnation for him. Therefore an occultist is always careful in his relations with the Supreme, the main means for which is prayer.

(1) We dare not pray and ask about anything harmful for our neighbours, as a revenge, punishment, and so on, directed against enemies. Christ said simply when teaching about the art of prayer, that Man must first be reconciled to his enemies before he can lift his worship towards the Father in Heaven. Wrong prayer does not rise, but rather falls on the head of the unwise author, in the form of a disaster or other karmic punishment.

(2) It is not recommended to pray for anything very definite, such as a boon, profit and foremostly material things. It is much wiser just to ask the Almighty about that '*which is best for us in our environment*'. For H E KNOWS BEST. Enlightened Buddhist priests (especially in Ceylon and Japan) used this form of prayer for their parishioners and themselves. Otherwise, some Christian Saints also used to worship the Lord in the same way. I will only mention a few of them: St Francis of Assisi, St Jean de Vianney, St Vincent de Paul, St Seraphim of Sarov, Sri Ramakrishna and others.

(3) Prayer, which as has been stated, being a kind of relation with the *Whole* or the *Supreme* (God), is an expression of the being (human) which is a RAY or PART of that WHOLE. The interests of the Whole should be beyond those of the *part*. Therefore a theurgist always follows the luminous example of the Christ Himself, when He prayed in the Garden of Gethsemane. We do not know and will never know what mystery lies behind the first part of the Redeemer's prayer about the *chalice* of His suffering and death, which He apparently asked to be removed from Him, but then immediately added: ' . . . but yet not my will, but thine be done.'

The unimaginable burden of the evil karma of this erring planet, which Christ took on His shoulders, may partly explain the phenomenon of the bloody sweat which appeared on His face during that prayer. We dare not comment on this.

But the example of a true prayer, as given by Christ, that is the LEAV-ING OF THE DECISION ABOUT THE FULFILMENT OF THE REQUEST TO THE SUPREME should be and is an immutable pattern for all true theurgic acts. Such a right and sublime form of theurgic magic does not burden our karma, nor involve any other complications, which come from subconscious egotism in us. But it adds wings to our prayers, which then rise of themselves to the utmost peaks of Attainment.

Finally, initiates try to convert their theurgy to IMPERSONAL (that is, spiritual) prayers when they forget their whole of their personalities, including names, appearance, attachments, and so on. In such a mystic process of spiritual distillation of human consciousness, only the highest and eternal principle in Man is acting (his *Yechidah* element). This brings him to the vision of the FINAL aim of all life, the ultimate REINTEGRATION.

And, by so acting, we become *one* with the irresistible Will of the WHOLE. Here lies the secret of the omnipotency of Perfect Men.

From the foregoing analysis, the student will easily understand why *prayer for others* is always more sublime and effective than that about one's own interests. This will also throw more light on the central idea of this Twentieth Arcanum, which is Resurrection from the deadly sleep in matter.

LESSON 94

The arithmological unfoldment of this inspiring Twentieth Arcanum brings us to a series of new conceptions, which we may use according to the degree of our Hermetic development in the course of our present studies. If you have only superficially 'read' this book, the 'equations' may well appear to you as not too understandable, or leading to only a few real issues. Others will judge differently, of course.

Equation No. 182: $20 = 1 + 19$

Equation No. 183: $20 = 19 + 1$

The Metaphysical Essence (1) and the creativeness of the truths offered by it (19) pull us up powerfully (20).

A three-plane Man (1) who realizes the problem of Ethical Hermetism (19) becomes regenerated in the astral plane (20).

Active Nature (1) transforming minerals (19) by its own efforts, produces changes in the Earth's crust (20).

Equation No. 184: $20 = 2 + 18$

Equation No. 185: $20 = 18 + 2$

The Unique Hierarchy (18) in the Unique Substance (2) pulls us powerfully towards our Primordial Source (20).

The mystery of Polarity (2) and the presence of foes in the astral (18) compel us to defend ourselves through our regeneration (20).

Dangers (18) to which all of Nature's creations (2) are subject, explain these 'changes in time' (20).

Equation No. 186: $20 = 3 + 17$

Equation No. 187: $20 = 17 + 3$

Realization of the Great Ternary of the Divine Nature (3) joined with Hope (17) determines the attraction towards the Above (20).

An understanding of the complexity of the multiplication of incarnate 'selves' (3) and human intuition (17) create sufficient impulses for our astral regeneration (20).

An understanding of the Gnostic Principle of Creativeness (3) in connection with the ability to read Nature (17) gives the full picture of the transformations in time (20).

Equation No. 188: $20 = 4 + 16$
Equation No. 189: $20 = 16 + 4$

The putting of ideas into forms (4) with the logical exclusion of some of them (16) will determine the metaphysical attraction of those not so excluded (20).

Our own authority (4) and the mechanism of self-suggestion (16) condition astral regeneration (20).

Preparation (4) and destruction (16) are the elements of the transformations in Nature (20).

Equation No. 190: $20 = 5 + 15$
Equation No. 191: $20 = 15 + 5$

The logical application (15) of the knowledge of Good and Evil (5) will result in attraction to the Above (20).

The Pentagram (5) possessing the secrets of Baphomet (15) rules over its renovated astrosome (20).

Natural Religion (5) and recognition of Fate (15) reconcile us to the picture of Nature's changes (20).

Equation No. 192: $20 = 6 + 14$
Equation No. 193: $20 = 14 + 6$

The use of the Law of Analogy (6) and of Deduction (14) give evidence of attraction to the Above (20).

Consciousness of the Freedom of Will (6) and inner harmony (14) give evidence of astral regeneration (20).

The environment (6) and its changes of development (14) decide about the picture of transformation of Nature in time (20).

Equation No. 194: $20 = 7 + 13$
Equation No. 195: $20 = 13 + 7$

Recognition of eternity in the Archetype (13) and priority given to the Spirit over Form (7) produce a definite attraction to the Highest (20).

Victory (7) over ourselves before the end of our incarnations (13) is the guarantee of improvement of the astrosome (20).

Recognition of the Laws of Property (7) together with that of the transformation of energy (13) compel us to feel the plan of transformations in Nature (20).

Equation No. 196: $20 = 8 + 12$
Equation No. 197: $20 = 12 + 8$

An understanding of the Libration of the Universal Scale (8) and faith in the Messiah (Redeemer) (12) are sufficient factors to pull one to the Highest (20).

P

Observation of the Law (8) and the simultaneous manifestation of Charity (12) prove the astral transformation in Man (20).

The Karma (8) of the Zodiacal Plane (12) sentenced it to eternal transformations (20).

Equation No. 198: $20 = 9 + 11$

Equation No. 199: $20 = 11 + 9$

Recognition of the High Protectorate (9) and its power (11) create attraction to the Highest (20).

Elaboration of the Moral Force (11) and Initiation (9) regenerate the astrosome (20).

In the chaos of transformation on the physical plane (20) we are led by cautiousness (9) and knowledge of Nature's forces (11).

Equation No. 200: $20 = 10 + 10$

Righteousness of the vow to the Archetype given by humanity (10) combined with the perfection of the High Testament (10) create the power of attraction to the Highest (20).

Establishment of a strong Kabbalah (10) inside of us as an answer to the outer Kabbalah (10) equals the regeneration of our astrosomes (20).

The Fortune (or Fate) of the new life (10) combined with the Fortune of the old (10) makes it possible to calculate the transformations (20) which have occurred.

As a résumé of the unfoldments and the ideas enclosed in them, we may rightly consider that Saturn plays the role of the astrological patron of this arcanum: for we judge about the development of time according to the transformations in a given group of phenomena; but formally we are again placing this group *in time*.

ש

Arcanum XXI (O)
FURCA
THE FOOL

ש

Shin –

Letter=
Mother

Radiatio
Signum
Materia

CHAPTER XXI

ARCANUM XXI (or 'O' (ZERO)) (ש SHIN)

LESSON 95

THE letter corresponding to this most mysterious of all the arcana is ש (Shin), and the numerical value is 300. The Twenty-first Arcanum does not possess any astrological relationships. The first controversy over this arcanum arises from its number. Traditionally, there is no doubt that its place is just between the Twentieth and Twenty-second Arcana, so logically the number should be Twenty-one, and so it is accepted in all the most authoritative Tarots, which comply exactly with Tradition. But, these same Tarots, apart from the number twenty-one, also use the sign of 'O' (Zero), and this is done in order to emphasize the fact, that this arcanum does not arise from any other. Its position is unique in the whole system of the Tarot, as we will see in the following lessons.

The hieroglyph of the Twenty-first Arcanum is an arrow, but unlike two of the other arcana (the Seventh and Fifteenth), which also have an arrow as their hieroglyphs, this one is in a direct but wavering flight. The idea is that of something hardly tangible, or imperceptible, unless the movements of the arrows belonging to the Seventh and Fifteenth Arcana have been previously studied. In the Seventh Arcanum the arrow is flying in a straight line, metaphysically correct and scientifically understandable. In the Fifteenth there is a circle or rather a spiral, corresponding to the astral ganglions in the current of Nahash. Here this movement is indefinite.

It can hit or miss you, depending upon what your own position is in evolution, and what your fate is in this incarnation. From further explanations you may deduce for yourself, what you have to accept in this matter.

The scientific name of the Twenty-first Arcanum is FURCA (the fork) which merely explains the strange shape of its letter ש (Shin), while the vulgar one is the FOOL, which evidently refers only to the picture. The analysis of the latter will perhaps provide us with more light on the enigma of the arcanum 'without a number', as it was often called in occult treatises.

On a rock leading to a precipice a Man is hastily walking. On his head we see a ridiculous cap, something like that of a circus clown. The fool's cap is of three colours, white, red and black. Who knows why he has put such a strange thing on himself? His clothes are good for many things except to be worn, and still less for travelling; for the Man is evidently a traveller. On his shoulders there is a bag full of many useless things, and in his right hand he holds a stick.

He does not look at what is awaiting him at the bottom of the precipice, a crocodile, with wide open jaws full of enormous teeth in readiness for the prospective fat meal. The Man turns his head away and looks somewhere into the sky. The left leg of his ridiculous and indecent attire has been torn by a vicious dog, which follows him from behind. Blood is flowing from the wound on to the stony ground.

He does not use his sceptre-stick properly, he neither leans on it nor repels the animal biting him. The left hand of the fool holds a stick which supports the heavy bag on his shoulders; but even here the arrangement is wrong: the stick is thrown over the *right* shoulder, which makes the bearing of the bag extremely uncomfortable.

Who is this traveller? The human figure shows that the forces touched on in this arcanum are individualized ones. But, how are they used here? Incarnate Man is evidently created to live on the *physical plane*, according to the laws of that world; but the fool is heading towards the abyss, where in addition a crocodile awaits him. The aim of clothes is to cover the body; but here they do not fulfil this aim, just like the sceptre-stick. The Man is in a hurry, but he fails to reject the heavy bag with its unnecessary contents. In short, a sorry and unexpected picture.

The Man has used the means at his disposal in a reversed sense. He gets no help from them. Perhaps inner contradictions are torturing him, preventing him from a reasonable use of his incarnation. If so, is he not some kind of a reflection of ourselves? Yes, he is! In him is depicted the tragedy of the family of beings called 'human', which inhabit this planet.

One will need much courage, impartiality and a clear, all-embracing insight in order to accept this fact as it is. The fool does not represent solely our own epoch, that of powerful development of applied science with its multitude of techniques, and means of luxury: for you may ask me if I have forgotten about the ultimate 'comfort' of the ominous nuclear extinction menacing us, as the crocodile menaces our close relative, the MAN OF THE Twenty-first Arcanum. No, I have not forgotten, but I preferred that this thought would be born first in the mind of the student.

If we will think in the categories of today and apply the figure of the 'ZERO' arcanum to our own period, we may find a lot of new and striking things. For example, what have we in the bag which hangs from the shoulders of the fool? Are there not the things, which we (or, at least, many of us) believe bring us necessary comfort or even happiness, that is all our modern physical gadgets, from the plastic coat to interplanetary missiles, or even 'ballistic' ones? I leave the answer to my readers, for I am more happy when able to show the other side of the picture, as offered to us by the immortal Tarot.

Now take a look at the old acquaintances from former chapters, like those of the First, Seventh, Eleventh and Seventeenth. In each picture we also see human figures, but they are far from being the degrading caricature of the Twenty-first Trump. The Magician of the First Arcanum is a link between Earth and Heaven (that is, between Spirit and Matter). The Conqueror of the Seventh Trump is a *Victor*, not the self-destroying fool of 'O'. The beauty of the Seventeenth Arcanum shows us the unmistakable HOPE, which WILL be realized by humans when the time is ripe.

It is amazing how the creators of Hermetic philosophy knew human nature and destiny so well and exactly when, more than forty centuries ago, they were in the position to show the image of Man in pictures, which could not be obliterated even by the enormous amount of time which has passed since the extinction of the earthly source of Hermetic occultism as it existed in Ancient Egypt.

And so it is, despite all of our foolishness as revealed in some periods of human history. Apart from the tragic FOOL of the Twenty-first Arcanum, there are still other types which I mentioned above. And it is in their *positive* qualities, eternally present in all men, that *Reintegration* is made a glorious *certainty* for those who have eyes and *can see*.

LESSON 96

Equation No. 201: $21 = 1 + 20$

An element (1) which is balanced and able to manifest itself (21), produces conditions of existence in a new world, that is a change in the order of things (20).

For example, the *Archetype* emanates the *mental sphere*, that is the idea clothes itself in a form, or a form of manifestation WILL itself mysteriously produce the activity of *facts* on the physical plane. According to this, we will combine the titles of the Twenty-first Arcanum in the realm of the Theosophical Ternary, as usual.

In manifestations of the *Archetype*, arcanum ש (Shin) emphasizes the highly mysterious process of Emanation of the world *Olam ha Aziluth*. The purely spiritual principle suddenly manifested itself in the form of some radiant, but still mental (that is very dense in comparison with the essence of the Archetype) emanations of the ten primordial Sephiroth. This process and the *first title* of the arcanum therefore will be RADIA-TIO (radiation).

On the plane of Man, the arcanum ש (Shin) is reflected not less mysteriously in the process of the passing from the generally human mental manifestations to that which we call '*the sign*'. Under this term we understand an element of the astral signalizing, that is that which one individuality can formally know in others through the '*sixth sense*' (sense of astral cognition). Impressions, brought through these means of perception are expressed in the language of the physical plane as *coloured*, *geometrical*, *acoustical*, *sensory*, and *olfactory*. But the thing is not how that 'sign' manifests itself, but in the mystery of its appearance, as a 'cloud-idea' (an idea symbolized as a subtle cloud).

So the *second title* of the Twenty-first Arcanum is SIGNUM (sign). Of interest on the plane of matter is the passage from the definition of ENERGY (as an astral manifestation) to the massing of that energy, and its perception by our organs of sense as MATTER. The mystery of the transformation of kinetic energy into the *attribute of hardness* (as in solid bodies), and the mystery of the mechanism for evoking movement in a patient, following the loss of some energy of imagination on the part of the operator (ordering the movement) are our ש (Shin) on the plane of Nature. This great illusion which we call the 'material world' poses many enigmas for us, just because of its existence. And here its Shin will take the form of the *third title* of the arcanum—MATERIA (matter).

Equation No. 202: 21 = 20 + 1

This reversed unfoldment will give the image of a balanced individuality (1), able to manifest itself in the moment when it is oppressed by the elements of the Twentieth Arcanum (regeneration), which are beyond its capacity to bear; when the individuality cannot manage the things encountered on its way; when it goes quickly, but not there where it should go; when it does not help itself with the sceptre of accessible initiatory elements; when it is even prepared to screen itself with false defences, like torn clothing, which neither warms nor provides decency in the sight of others; when it carefully holds on its shoulders the heavy bag filled with superstitions, prejudices and conditions, unsuitable conditions, unsuitable for the arcanum of regeneration (20).

As we may see, the card of the Twenty-first Arcanum illustrates for us the negative phase of its first arithmological unfoldment. The arcanum itself belongs to the greatest and most dangerous of initiatory mysteries.

Which way of meditation should the student choose for a positive initiation? If he is a Kabbalist, he will begin by learning the remaining unfoldments of the number 21 in the positive phases of the manifestation of *Shin*.

Equation No. 203: 21 = 2 + 19

The mystery of 𝖂 (Shin) (21) is based on the knowledge of the great Law of Analogy and Opposites (2) and on the mystery of the Great Operation (19).

Equation No. 204: 21 = 3 + 18

The mystery of *Shin* (21) presupposes full metaphysical culture in the operator (3) and full calculation of the Absolute Hierarchy of the occult powers and possible counter-action on the physical plane (18).

Equation No. 205: 21 = 4 + 17

If you want to command 𝖂 (Shin) (21), you must learn the arcana of the physical and chemical manifestations (4) well, together with the arcana of the astral influences in Nature and their mental principles (17).

Equation No. 206: 21 = 5 + 16

If you want to apply the Twenty-first Arcanum, think about the illimitable human Freedom in you and power of human Will (5), but remember that the same Freedom can be a source of the downfall and differentiations, connected with materialization (16).

Equation No. 207: 21 = 6 + 15

Know that everywhere there are TWO paths (6), and that everywhere you can become a commander, or a slave of the great Baphomet (15).

Equation No. 208: 21 = 7 + 14

When you will feel yourself a Victor (7), then die and harmonize (14) the manifestations of your force.

Equation No. 209: $21 = 8 + 13$

If you are working in the realm of established Justice (8) know and remember that the ultimate aim of your work is just preparation for the change of plane (13). If you can live justly, make a suitable and dignified preparation for death, which is B I R T H in the astral, as an aim of your life. If you are caring for a pregnant woman, you have to choose the food and regulations for the *foetus*, imagining the necessity for it to end its embryonic life and to start in the normal earthly atmosphere.

If you have to arrange a physical education for a little child do not forget that it must duly pass on to intellectual education. Also, that the pupil, with time, may be transformed into an active member of society.

Equation No. 210: $21 = 9 + 12$

Whoever wants to apply the great mystery of *Shin* (21) must become initiated (9) in the suitable planes and be ready for Sacrifice (12).

Equation No. 211: $21 = 10 + 11$

He who possesses the mystery of *Shin* (21) rests against the automatically working World's Mill (10) from one side, and from the other against the means of the powerful *Chains* (11) of the corresponding planes.

These are a few examples of meditation for those who try to penetrate into the realm of applications of the Twenty-first Arcanum.

LESSON 97

The letter ש is $300 = 3$. It is like an enlarged 3, which penetrated into the world of complications belonging to the *tenth* Sephira in its tenth manifestation. It only remains to say something about the mysterious arcanum of the mechanism of evolution and involution. It is most important for oneself N O T T O G O to the precipice, in which a crocodile's open jaws await you. It is important for one to throw away the heavy bag just in time, to repel the dog, to rest upon the sceptre, to get decent clothing, to throw away the silly clown's cap, and to look straight ahead.

Then you will no longer be a passive object for the foreign operations of *involutionary Shin*. On the contrary, when you would like to combine some realizations in the sub-planes lower than that in which your F R E E S E L F lives, then you will be able to put the fool's cap on these entities and so enjoy the sight of them being unable to throw away their bags. Then you will avoid the stages, in which they can use their sceptres, you will know how to use their entanglement in wrong clothes, to set a suitable number of dogs on them in order to put them off the path in their wrongly-planned reactions, which they may try to use against you. Finally, to look calmly at how they might come to the abyss of your realization, into the jaws of the astral scheme of your will's manifestation.

Of course, this is the realm of purely practical occultism, and no more detailed explanation can be given apart from the present one.

The arcanum Shin is presented in such a negative light in its card not only in order that an occultist will not permit others to put a fool's cap on his head, but that he himself will not deck with it, those on whom he would like to operate.

The thing is, that even the well-developed *Self*, which is aware of the illusory character of the physical plane, sometimes gravitates to its bodily shell and the false pleasures supplied by that plane. The *Self* has no right to throw away this shell before its normal term: Karma determines one's full life-programme composed of experiences and sacrifices, and the course of life should include all of these. In such moments one (if sufficiently advanced) should close one's eyes to the imperfections of the physical world, and be able to play with the toys which life here may offer to us. One should sometimes inoculate oneself with the mirage of happiness, which, seriously speaking, does not exist at all on that level.

But such an inoculation would be like jokingly using the Twenty-first Arcanum, a short rest on the hard path of life: for the '*traveller*' should not only be able to step and walk, but he should also be able to rest when needed and coldly calculate the time for refreshing his forces, the time for sleep, and so on. Further, we may say: who never rests because of his wisdom, may forget about the conditions of personal egotism, and then he may not appreciate the sacrifices which his neighbour makes for him. And we are told: 'Thou shalt love thy neighbour as thyself.' This means: give to your neighbour the same which you yourself received in your moments of taking rest from Wisdom.

At the same time, the mystery of involution is the mystery of the reversed, evolutionary process. The whole difference being, that the downfall is metaphysically and quickly performed, and the regeneration (also Re-integration) is metaphysically made slowly. That is why attempts at the Kabbalistic analysis of the process of Man's downfall appears to us to be something complicated and artificial, when we easily and patiently assimilate the images of the regeneration of humanity with the help of Ethical Hermetism. A layman may willingly and quietly learn the Gospel of Christ, but he may be astonished by the efforts of others to decipher the '*Sepher Bereshith*'.

We may see that ש (Shin) is a dreadful arcanum. Wrong, unskilled, or ill-timed use of it might endanger the development of the planetary evolution. Unfortunately, this has already been done, and probably more than once in the history of earthly humanity. Of course, we do not know much about other worlds, and it is not permitted to pin-point these tragic errors; but it is quite possible to discover them in the past (even in the very recent past) by right meditation along the lines given in the Tarot.

However, a spiritually-minded initiate would not be interested in such activity, as he does not believe in anything apart from the Supreme Reality or Spirit.

On the other hand, the most synthetic Pentagram of the whole Astral— י ה ש ו ה (Yod-Hé-Shin-Vau-Hé) through just this sign of ש (Shin), secures for itself the possibility of incarnation, of that *redeeming fulcrum* of humanity, the guarantee of the Reintegration of the Primordial, Perfect, Cosmic Man.

Do not let us be scared of realization, but let us include in our prayer of

Initiation on the first plane, the desire to know the Twenty-first Arcanum. Not as a bait, not in a thief's way, not for the price of a pact with the lower astral (as did Faust), but honestly, Hermetically and systematically penetrating into the previous twenty arcana.

And then it will not lead us to disastrous errors, nor to dark stains on our karma, but to the conscious triumph of the true Rosicrucian Reintegration, because of the full triple process of application of the Great Arcanum of Magic.

Few are and will be going along that strenuous way on which no Master appears and helps, until the disciple has passed the most perilous and difficult tests and temptations, and until he has secured the Path for himself, without any possibility of a reversal.

There are easier and better assisted Paths, like large highways on the plains. Does this mean that there are no more, or will be no more hardened mountaineers, dedicated to climbing on the most dangerous and solitary PEAKS?

ת

Arcanum XXII
CORONA MAGICA
THE WORLD

Sol

Absolutum
Adaptatio Operis Magni
Omnipotentia Naturalis

CHAPTER XXII

ARCANUM XXII (ת THAN)

OUR long course is coming to its end, and I hope, to a *happy end* for the earnest student. We have reached the last great arcanum, the *crown and peak of the whole system of the Tarot*. It is a résumé of all the experiences and teachings enclosed in the previous twenty-one arcana. But first, let us establish the usual particulars.

The Hebrew letter of the arcanum is the last of the alphabet—ת (Than). The corresponding astrological symbol is the Sun, the centre and synthesis of all astral manifestations in our planetary system. The hieroglyph is the *breast*, in the meaning of an *all-accepting* bosom.

Here everything indicates the necessity of the collection into one integrated UNIT, just as a world contains in it, everything belonging to its system. The Twenty-second Arcanum is that of the *Great Operation*, allowing the passage to the *Minor Arcana* through their *Wands* suit. From the Major to the Minor Arcana the passage is through the *Pentacles*, but as we already know, the intermediaries are the *last four arcana*, forming the transitional triangle. At the apex of this triangle there is the Nineteenth Arcanum (Yod), the passive Twentieth (First Hé) occupies the left-hand point, the neutral Twenty-first (O) (Vau) is in the right-hand point, and in the centre there is the active Second Hé, the Twenty-second Arcanum. The passage to the Minor Arcana is safeguarded by the suit of *Pentacles*.

The titles of the Twenty-second Arcanum are: the *first*, which is the sum of the upper triangle of the Great Arcanum of Magic, is ABSOLUTUM (Metaphysical Absolute), the highest manifestation of the *Archetype* accessible to our mentality. The *second title* in the world of Man is ADAPTATIO OPERIS MAGNI (adaptation of the Great Operation), and the *third*, in the world of Nature is OMNIPOTENTIA NATURALIS (omnipotence of Nature). The best explanation will be provided by an analysis of the *arcanum's card*. Additionally, it may be said, that the scientific name of the arcanum is CORONA MAGICA, or CORONA MAGORUM (the magic crown) and the vulgar, the *World*.

In the centre of the card triumphantly dances a naked woman, slightly touching the serpent with one foot. It is the metaphysical synthesis of the Absolute Truths, which do not need any protection, and which put the one, who so far has arrived at these truths, beyond all deceit. This is the highest manifestation of the Archetype accessible to our mentality's perception. That is why the first title of the arcanum is ABSOLUTUM. I repeat, this is not a hook on which we can temporarily support ourselves on the steep path to the mystery of the Great Metaphysical Arcanum. THIS IS THE ARCANUM ITSELF, a synthesis of the metaphysical bases of the world's life. Briefly, it is the UPPER triangle of the marriage of ה י (Yod-Hé) in the picture appearing in the lessons of the Fourth Arcanum.

But this synthesis does not remain dead, nor even the final one reached in the higher planes: for the *figure* of the Twenty-second Arcanum is that of a woman, and woman can bear and give birth.

Look at the figure: she has little rods in her hands, she holds them parallel to one another. This is because she possesses the mystery of the *binary* and operates freely in the astral realm, which is represented here in the form of the great *serpent* (Nahash, of course) surrounding the figure and biting its own tail. So its circle is a closed one, and it is no longer dangerous for the victorious dancer in the centre.

This serpent forms a regular oval, harmoniously obedient to the will of the woman inside, who functions because of her ability to compensate (in other words, to neutralize) the binaries; but our powerful figure, ruling over the formidable, energetic environment of the astral, which produces the forms for all the physical world, rests with only one foot on the physical plane.

This is the way of her mysterious tactics: the action comes from the mental plane as from a centre, then spreads to the whole astral, but takes its point of support in the ready-made realizations of the physical plane. This is the image of the acting figure. For humanity, the astral manifestations of the figure, this *hexagon* ו (VAU) of the middle part of the Great Arcanum's symbol, is the complex of the application of the performed *Great Operation*. This is the ability to use one's *Hermetic Victory*. Therefore the second title of the Twenty-second Arcanum is ADAPTATIO OPERIS MAGNI.

But look again at the frame of the picture: there are four *mystical animals*, well known to us from previous lessons. This is the *quaternary of the Sphinx* (to dare, to know, to be silent, to will). These are the elements differently described in different degrees of the Hermetic School, and their most used names are: AIR, WATER, EARTH and FIRE.

These elements in their different combinations are the forms of that which we call the *kingdom of Nature*. Surely there is nothing new for you in this statement. Whoever has power over these elements acts through the power of the laws of that Nature, as instruments for the fulfilment of his will. Such a man cannot be defeated simply because he CANNOT want anything which is in opposition to these eternal laws, or anything which is beyond or apart from the metaphysical, astral or absolute physical integrity. His *self* (consciousness) sounds in concert with the evolutionary tune of Nature. He is omnipotent *because he desires everything, which is enclosed in the evolutionary current of the universe.* Briefly, he wants only *that which will and must be.*

I would like to recommend very strongly to every student to meditate thoroughly about these statements, which come to us from the ancient sages of Hermetism, as in them lies concealed the foremost secret of the word '*omnipotence*', so often misunderstood and misused. Deep meditation about this will unveil to you a truth, tremendous in its consequences about which nothing more can be said.

Therefore the third title of the Twenty-second Arcanum is OMNI-POTENTIA NATURALIS as well as the name of the *ascending* (evolutionary) current, which was mentioned previously.

The numerical value of the arcanum is 400, and this further completes the explanation of the arcanum's frame (4 elements, $400 = 4 + 0 + 0 = 4$).

LESSON 99

Now, let us take a look at what a brief arithmological analysis of the Twenty-second Arcanum can bring to us, and with it *the final summary which will conclude the cycle of the 22 phases of the understanding of the universe by fallen humanity*, which now lives in that universe. The Tarot tells us the whole truth in that sentence. As members of that humanity, WE CANNOT HAVE ANY OTHER CONCEPTIONS OR UNDERSTANDING, and the student must make the problem clear to himself. There is nothing wrong in this, as we cannot be something other than we are.

Realize, that REINTEGRATED or LIBERATED (Eastern term) monads do not need any Tarot or other crutches, just as a *healthy person does not need a doctor*, who is needed only by the sick. But, some unreasonable people are apt to conclude, that because of this, no initiatory systems or practices are needed any more, since the great Sons of humanity do not use them at all. To such people the answer would be: 'First *become* like those advanced Brothers, and then act as they are acting. But before then, it would be as useless and impossible to ape those who are infinitely higher than us, as it would be for a three-years old child to behave like, and pretend to know as much as a university professor.'

Equation No. 212: $22 = 1 + 21$

The harmoniously perfect Aleph (1) is lord of the realization (22) of Shin (21).

Equation No. 213: $22 = 21 + 1$

It is the same Aleph (1), but who willingly gives himself for the service of the arcanum Shin (21). How important it is, not to be a tool in the hands of others, as is known well by all who have had to suffer in their lives because of their own superstitions, carelessness, dazzle or infatuation.

It is highly recommended to meditate on the themes concerning in which condition it would be proper for an occultist to burden himself with the *bag of superstitions, not to use the sceptre of precaution,* and *to close his eyes in senseless oblivion,* as is presented on the card of the Twenty-first Arcanum. While not thinking deeply about these things an adept of esoterism can advance very far in his spiritual development. This cannot be denied; but he will never be happy here in his earthly life. It is good to see, but sometimes it is better not to look. It is good to be careful, but sometimes how charming imprudence can be.

A good Master cannot have any superstitions, prejudices, or attachments to conditions, it is true; but for lesser men, like most of us, how empty and even sad life can appear without these pleasant tinkles. And an occultist must know all this.

Equation No. 214: $22 = 2 + 20$

Knowledge (2) together with a clear perception of the principle of regeneration (20) undoubtedly makes an adept, who has the wisdom of the Major Arcana, a true Rosicrucian, like those original brothers hundreds of years ago. But how hard it is to conquer in full the FIRST element (2), and how difficult it is to believe, with a pure heart, as does a child (*a necessary condition*), in the SECOND (20), and apparently how torturing and strenuous is the task of neutralizing BOTH in one's true life.

Equation No. 215: $22 = 20 + 2$

It is the reverse of the process of acquisition of scientific knowledge (2) by an individual, in whose heart rules the innate awareness of the principle of regeneration (20). Is it not even harder than the solution of Equation No. 214? And the Path obliges us, in due time, to perform it.

Equation No. 216: $22 = 3 + 19$

Creativeness (3) directs the Great Operation (19).

Equation No. 217: $22 = 19 + 3$

Hermetic regeneration (19) pushes us towards creativeness (3). We know of two persons who can serve as examples for these two equations. If Pythagoras may be referred to as the first (No. 216), then Orpheus must be connected with the second (No. 217).

Equation No. 218: $22 = 4 + 18$

Authority (4) in connection with occult power (18) is in general an example of a WHITE MAGICIAN.

Equation No. 219: $22 = 18 + 4$

Occult power (18) creating authority (4) and inseparably connected with it, is the pattern of a realizer-Mason of the esoteric type, of course. We cannot disregard this type of worker, knowing as we do, about some great leaders of the Reformation, or the liberation of the United States of America, as well as other idealistic doers.

Equation No. 220: $22 = 5 + 17$

Self-knowledge and elaboration in us of the Quintessence (5) and initiation into Nature's Laws (17) create harmony in relationships between the Microcosm and Macrocosm.

Equation No. 221: $22 = 17 + 5$

This reversed unfoldment suggests naturalism in theory (17), but meditated on in full (5) will lead to the same results as Equation No. 220.

Equation No. 222:   22 = 6 + 16

To know of the existence of the two paths (6) and to choose the RIGHT one because of the awareness of the Laws of the Downfall (16) is a more suitable and comfortable form of the Adept's state than:

Equation No. 223:   22 = 16 + 6

which is an example of a choice of the Path (6) based on the experience of downfalls (16) in this and former incarnations.

Equation No. 224:   22 = 7 + 15

The domination of Spirit over forms in the static sphere (7) plus knowledge of the Dynamic Processes (15), when the first (7) has the preponderance, is the way of the Adept of Illuminism.

Equation No. 225:   22 = 15 + 7

This reversed form of Equation No. 224 represents the path of the occultist, who started his career from technical knowledge of the astral (15), and perhaps has fallen many times in moments of hard experience, but through self-analysis and High Protection finally came to the Victory (7). It can be said, that this man came from *black* magic to *white*.

Equation No. 226:   22 = 8 + 14

Righteousness (8) plus the prevailing temperance in Man (14), or, as the Romans used to say: FIAT JUSTITIA, PEREAT MUNDUS (Let justice be done even if the world might perish), is the way of a strong Sephira Geburah in relation to oneself and others: the way of Moses.

Equation No. 227:   22 = 14 + 8

Temperance (14) in manifestations together with prevailing Justice (8) is the path of the Master-Teachers, gradually and carefully smoothing out the roughness in themselves and others. This refers to the good Christian-Masons; the paths of Ashmole, Willermooz, and our good theurgist, Claude de St Martin.

Equation No. 228:   22 = 9 + 13

Be initiated (9) and then change the plane (13).

Equation No. 229:   22 = 13 + 9

Change the plane (13) and at the same time be initiated (9): a formula understandable for everyone; but the choice of one of them does not always depend upon our own will.

Equation No. 230:   22 = 10 + 12

The World's Mill (10), because of its irresistible, pitiless regularity pushes us towards the idea of the necessity of Sacrifice (12).

Equation No. 231:   22 = 12 + 10

The desire for Sacrifice in a soul, seeking after God the Holy Spirit, will reveal to the magnanimous one the mystery of the finished systems

(10). In the end, the result is the same: whether the Kabbalah (10) will lead us to the Sacrifice (12), or the Sacrifice to the Kabbalah. The degree of the Adept is ensured in both cases.

Equation No. 232: $22 = 11 + 11$

Oppose the Force (11) against the Force (11) in yourself and in others. Against the Chain oppose a Chain; against certainty another certainty. Always do this in everything, and finally you will find yourself in the position of that FIGURE with the two sceptres (22); but do not forget in your dance, the necessity to seek a point of support on the Earth, even with only one foot. Then you will see the Astral Serpent, now harmless for you, although encircling you with its regular oval. Going deeper into yourself, analyse the participation of the four Initiatory Animals in the process of your evolution.

LESSON 100

The Twenty-second Arcanum with its dancing figure in the middle rightly suggests to us the idea of another initiatory 'dance' in occultism, this time from India. The well-known figure of *Shiva-Nataraja* (Shiva—King of the Dancers) in Vedantic mythology does not require much explanation for those of us, who have successfully studied the *Crown of the Arcana,* our Twenty-second. The triumphant dance of the God of the Yogis and all advanced occultists and spiritual teachers in the East, and that of the Woman in the oval of Nahash are penetrated by the same idea. The eternal dance (movement) of the worlds reflecting the idea of MANIFESTA-TION of the SUPREME exists in every form of Initiation. Here the Archetype was careful not to allow this *essential wisdom* to be forgotten, and his irresistible Will is and will be realized for ever, that is until we—his still imperfect and fallen reflections—will transcend all forms and return to the *Father of everything,* which was, is, and will still be in the aeons to come.

And then, dancing joyfully in the GREAT ULTIMATE CENTRE, we will no more be ashamed of our nakedness, in thought, word or deed, because there will be nothing to conceal: PERFECTION does not need to conceal anything.

In studying this course, some may only READ through the numerous pages of the work, yet a few others will follow the lessons with open minds, discovering in them what could not be, and cannot be expressed in words. Such people attain the path of *Self-Initiation,* which was always the aim of the original and true Rosicrucians, great occultists, and many saints of all religions. In such cases, humanity again wins some of its sons for its eternal aim, attainment of perfection for all the separate cells of *Adam-Kadmon.*

There is no need to say anything more about this. On this level of wisdom it is transmitted rather by initiatory SILENCE than by imperfect human speech. I spoke more explicitly about it in my former books, but the theme does not belong directly to the philosophy of the Tarot.

It remains for us to bow for the last time before the great, ancient

TRADITION, and to quote what it can tell us about the ultimate achievement of those, who surmounted the 22 Major Arcana and so came to the realm of the Minor ones.

If someone likes to ask, what are the privileges or rewards of Masters of the Arcana, we can say in the *Hermetic Tradition*—SEVEN GREAT PRIVILEGES:

Privilege א (*Aleph*): *the Magician possessing this privilege of the FIRST Arcanum, sees God personally without dying, and he speaks freely with the Seven Planetary Spirits* (*Geniuses*). How have we to understand the traditional text? In the mental plane, in spite of his full knowledge of the *Unitary Current*, the Initiate still fully retains his type of soul, for as long as possible. Under the word 'type' is meant the mental character of the monad, which will be *Aleph* (soul-seeker in the metaphysical realm), or *Ghimel* (soul-nurse, soul-gatherer), or *Lamed* (soul-servant, a soul seeking a sacrifice). In the astral plane the same Initiate seeing over him the all-pervading cliché ה ו ה י (Yod-Hé-Vau-Hé) and its mechanism, reaching down to the lowest plane, does not scorn to retain his own *Selfhood* and directs its planetary properties. On the physical plane, he who knows the illusion of the images belonging to earthly life, does NOT deliberately destroy either his body, or the conditions in which that body has to act.

Privilege ב (*Beth*): *the Magician stands beyond the reach of all griefs and fears.* The ruler of the Second Arcanum is unmoved by any logical brakes in the *metaphysical plane*, such as: the separation or withdrawal of his sister-soul, or the slowness of the progress of his disciples in the *astral plane*. He does not have any fear of suffering or death, neither for himself nor for his neighbours on the *physical plane*. Briefly, it is a three-plane immunity. Meditate about this!

Privilege ג (*Ghimel*): *the Third Arcanum ensures that the Magician is co-ruler in heaven and has hell at his service.* The meaning being, that in the *mental plane*, the Magician takes part in the work of Evolutionary Currents, in his character as a theurgist. In the *astral plane* he transfers (in the literal sense of the word) the currents of Baphomet from their mental source in the mental plane (heaven) into the 'hell' of their astral condensations in the lower realms. On the *physical plane* he is like an initiated Mason playing on human blindness, weakness, and other ש (Shins), which at the same time direct human virtues.

Privilege ד (*Daleth*): *the Magician disposes of his health and life as well as the health and lives of others.* This means, that he directs the currents of his epoch's philosophy in the *mental plane*. In the *astral plane* he polishes his own and his Chain's planetary properties, acting upon the will and striving of his epoch, the arts included. He can use his animal magnetism in order to heal himself and others on the *physical plane*.

Privilege ה (*Hé*): *the Adept cannot be surprised by Destiny. He is not tortured by misfortune, and enemies cannot defeat him.* This means that he understands the reactions of the basic laws of logic (metaphysical destiny), human paralogisms (metaphysical misfortune) and human sophisticalness (metaphysical foes).

This means that he knows the karma of his incarnation, knows the laws of evolution of his own astral life and the secrets of counter-action equal to action (reaction—action).

This means that in the literal sense of the work, he cannot be disturbed by the changes of the physical life's phases, and he is not afraid of the destruction of what he, in advance, considers to be illusion.

Privilege ו *(Vau): the Adept knows the reason of PAST, PRESENT and FUTURE*. The meaning: his three-plane intuition knows the world of *Causality* (in metaphysics), *Gnostic Law* (astral), and the *Theory of Probability* (physical plane).

Privilege ז *(Zain): the Magician knows the mystery of the resuscitation of the dead, and he has the key to immortality*. This means that in the *metaphysical plane*, he can live the life of unfallen humanity (mystery of resuscitation) without looking into theories, arranged by himself (key to immortality); that he himself is creating new astral formulas and clichés in the elementary forms of the old formulas and clichés, resuscitating the latter and welding together the astral forms, born from his own Chain; that he, supported by Tradition, uninterruptedly resuscitates elements of traditional symbolism realized in the physical world, and puts out strong realizable points of support, like those of the type of the immortal Phoenix.

Kabbalists call these SEVEN privileges 'GREAT'. Then follow the seven 'MIDDLE' privileges.

Privilege ח *(Heth): the Adept possesses the secret of the Philosophers' Stone*, that is the Nineteenth Arcanum in three spheres of the Theosophical Ternary.

Privilege ט *(Teth): the Adept is in command of the universal therapeutics*. This means, that he possesses the art of the absolute criticism (in the *mental plane*), the art of disinvultuation in the *astral*, and the use of medical magnetism on the *physical plane*.

Privilege י *(Yod): the Adept realizes the perpetuum mobile and quadrature of the circle*, that is he can give birth to the DOUBLE CURRENTS (see Fifteenth Arcanum), and realize the revolving of the Elementary Rota.

Privilege כ *(Caph): the Adept can turn not only other metals, BUT ALSO ALL refuse into gold*. The meaning: in metaphysics he gets direction leading to the Absolute Truths not only from relative truths, but also from foreign, accidental truths. In the astral he not only perfects the unfinished forms, but he can also use the false and broken ones. In his masonic activity he not only uses the well begun principles, but also entangled ones. This thesis can be used literally in alchemy.

Privilege ל *(Lamed): the Magician dominates all animals*. Apart from the literal meaning, this statement includes ruling over elementals, dispelling of larvas, and so on.

Privilege מ *(Mem): the Adept possesses the art of notarikon which reveals all mysteries to him*, that is he simply knows the Kabbalah.

Privilege נ *(Nun): the Adept can speak scientifically and convincingly on all themes without previous preparation*, in other words this is ARS MAGNA (see Tenth Arcanum, the 'multiplication of the arcana').

The last privileges, the *seven* 'minor' of the finished Adept-Magician are:

Privilege ס (*Samech*): *the Magician can judge a man from the first look,* that is, he is free to use intuition and divination.

Privilege ע (*Ayin*): *the Magician possesses the arcanum of compulsion in relation to Nature,* that is, Ceremonial Magic and natural science.

Privilege פ (*Phe*): *the Magician can foresee happenings dependent upon Fate.*

Privilege צ (*Tzaddi*): *the Magician can bring solace to everyone in everything and give advice in all events in life.*

Privilege ק (*Quoph*): *the Magician will overcome all obstacles.*

Privilege ר (*Resh*): *the Magician can dominate love and anger in himself.*

Privilege ש (*Shin*): *the Magician knows the secret of riches, and can be their possessor, but never their slave.* He is able to find delight even in poverty, but never sinks into nothingness.

As a conclusion, it is accepted in Tradition to add the *Privilege of the Twenty-second Arcanum* ת (*Than*): *the Adept astonishes all laymen by his ability to direct the elements, to cure the sick and to resuscitate the dead.*

LESSON 101

This brief synthesis of ancient and present-day occult wisdom is now completed. The Path of Self-Initiation lies open to the earnest student. He cannot hope to perform everything alone, that is while separated from the Initiatory Circle, proper for him and his endeavour, for he will be attracted to such a circle after strenuous and ardent work in the solitude of his own Selfhood.

In occultism, it is the Teacher who finds the pupil, and not the pupil who condescends to accept the Master. Inner achievement cannot be overlooked, and so the aspirant does not need to be afraid of it.

In concluding the Twenty-second Arcanum and with it the whole study of the Tarot, we should, for a while, return to the beginning of this magnificent memorial to human genius, that is to the First Arcanum, and especially, *to the first sentence in it* (see Lesson 1). Now, have you found an adequate answer to that question? If your study has been performed as intended and suggested, you will undoubtedly have perceived the fulfilled UNITY in the whole system of the 22 arcana, the first of them linking up with the last, just as the *serpent* in the picture of the latter, represents the closed circle of creation (Nature) and attainment (Man), by swallowing its own tail. In other words, THE ETERNAL END POINTS TO ITS ETERNAL BEGINNING.

From Alpha to Omega, from Aleph to Than!

Instead of the lone MAN of the First Arcanum, the Twenty-second presents to us the whole development of creation-manifestation. The triumphant Magician (Microcosm) of the second title of the First Arcanum is here transformed into the perfectly finished and also triumphant Universe-Macrocosm. That is why the God-Transformer of the world in Eastern philosophy—*Shiva*, dances his eternal dance of life, just like the woman on the card of the Twenty-second Arcanum. It is not any coincidence!

Here is a full analogy, and deep meditation about it will open the new, imperishable world of eternal BEING for you.

You already know about the privileges which belong to the one who masters all the 22 arcana of the Tarot, as well as the abilities he develops in the course of that strenuous work, usually covering many incarnations.

But there is something common to all humans, no matter whether or not they succeed in their occult or spiritual search for Truth. And it is: the TRUTH ITSELF EXISTS INDEPENDENTLY OF OUR KNOWLEDGE OR IGNORANCE OF IT. This is because Truth is always in us, and our true CORE is nothing other than pure TRUTH.

Now, before you close these pages, try a last experience, which is already beyond the level of mind. For those who have—to a certain degree—dominated their thinking principle (mind) there should not be much difficulty in performing that last step which leads to the inner REIN-TEGRATION, or rather, the first look into the state of a *reintegrated consciousness*.

Of course, only the mental counterpart of the spiritual consciousness obtained as a result of the full *Attainment* can be spoken of in human language. The actual *transcendental state* has no analogies with the mental experiences of everyday.

It is *Man's true place in Manifestation*, or *realization* (not just a theory or verbalization) *of how the Microcosm is reunited with the Macrocosm*. But you will never see the WHOLE apart from you, as something separate, outside: for, WHO are you and HOW could you exist apart from the WHOLE in order *to observe* IT, which cannot be observed or seen but only LIVED in perfect *silence*, which is the final *Wisdom of Being*? In IT all problems are solved for ever.

You are the WHOLE, and the ALLNESS is now your essential privilege. The consciousness, translucent and expanded into infinity, has no limits and does not perform anything like movement: for the WHOLE, which we call TRUTH, is immovable in its perfection. Do not read any further now, but try to convey to yourself the mental conception of the INCONCEIVABLE (for the mind's powers, of course) ONE.

Then, what do you 'know' or 'see' after that contemplation? Tradition as left to us by our *Older Brethren*, who, in the course of their evolution, reached the ULTIMATE TRUTH says: one contemplates all the material universe as a drop of water, in which there are suspended galaxies with their worlds and celestial bodies. One's own body is then as if dissolved in the *mirage of the outer side of the Whole*. One then feels the life of that *Whole* as being one's own life. There is nothing *inside* or *outside*, no *past* or *future*, no space as we are accustomed to imagine it. So then this '*humanity*' of ours is transformed into and united with the *Archetype;* no conception of a separate being (human) is possible any more for the *Reintegrated Consciousness*. All that one has considered in his innumerable incarnations as his attributes, are simply NO MORE. The bliss of pure, Infinite Being is all that can be expressed in our language today, for our still limited consciousness, enclosed in the perishable frame of 'Homo Sapiens'; as then there is no more separation, and the whole wealth of experience of everything that has lived, lives and will live belongs to the Reintegrated one. This might seem to be a paradox, an incomprehensible conception, but it IS the ultimate Truth.

If you learn to meditate without participation of the mind and its tools— words, then test this truth, but not earlier (see Chapter XX of *Concentration*).

Several ways lead to Truth, and one of them, perhaps the most logical and scientific is that of Hermetism, the Tarot, the last page of which now lies before you. As with every attainment, Reintegration is always the result of a definite effort. No matter that the *thirst for eternity* might be almost unconscious at the beginning of the Path, and only later might take the form of purposeful study through many incarnations and different worlds (planes).

Our older Brethren have passed along the whole Path, showing us the way by their example.

One of the milestones on that PATH for us, as we are now on this planet, is the traditional TAROT, presented in this book for those who are able:

TO WILL, TO DARE, TO KNOW and TO KEEP SILENT.

BIBLIOGRAPHY

ABANO, PETER OF, *The Heptameron or Magical Elements*

AGRIPPA (H. C.), *La Philosophie Occulte*, 1727, 2 vol.

ALBERT LE GRAND, *Les Admirables Secrets*, Lyon, 1799, 1 vol.

BARLET, F. CH., *Tarot Initiatique*

BROMAGE, B., *The Occult Arts of Ancient Egypt*, 1953

CHRISTIAN, P., *The History of Magic*, 1876

DU POTET, LE BARON, *La Magie Devoilée ou Principes de la Science Occulte*, Paris, 1875

ETTEILLA, *The Book of Thoth*

GUAITA, STANISLAS DE, MARQUISE., *Au Seuil du Mystere*, 2nd ed., Paris, Edit.: Livres du Merveilleux, 1891; *La Clef de la Magie Noire*, Paris, Edit.: Livres du Merveilleux; *Le Temple de Satan*, Paris, Edit.: Livres du Merveilleux, 1891

HASBROUCK, MURIEL BRUCE, *Pursuit of Destiny*, 1941

HOHENHEIM, BOMBAST VON, P.A.T., *Hermetic and Alchemical Writings*, 1894. Trans. by A. E. Waite.

HUYSMANS, J. K., *En Route*, Paris, 1891; *Là Bas*, Paris, 1894

KUNRATH, HENRI, *Amphitheatrum Sapientiae Aeternae*, 1609

LÉVI, ÉLIPHAS (ABBÉ CONSTANT), *Dogme & Rituel de la Haute Magie*, Paris, 1861; *Histoire de la Magie*, Paris, 1860; *La Clef de Grands Mystères*, 1861; *La Grande Arcane; La Science des Esprits*, 1865; *Transcendental Magic*, Trans. by A. E. Waite.

LULLY, RAYMOND, *Ars Magna* (Latin)

MATHERS, S. L. McGREGOR, *The Kabbala Unveiled*

MEAD, G. R. S., *Echoes from the Gnosis*

MEBES, G. O. Prof., *Encyclopaedic Course of the Tarot* (Russian)

OLIVET, FABRE D', *Histoire Philosophique du Genre Humain*, 1824, *Histoire Philosophique et Politique de l'Occultism*, Paris, 1813; *La Langue Hebraique Restituée*, Paris, 1815

PAPUS (DR. GÉRARD ENCAUSSE), *Le Tarot Divinatoire; The Tarot of the Bohemians*

Paracelsi Opera Omnia Medico-Chemico-Chirurgica, Genève, 1658

PARACELSUS, *Gesammte Werke*

REGNARD (DR PAUL), *Sorcellerie, Magnetisme, Morphinisme, Delire des Grandeurs*, Paris, 1887

REGARDIE, ISRAEL, *The Golden Dawn*

ROSENROTH (KNORR AB), *Kabbala Denudata*, Frankfurt, 1677-1684

Pack of 78 Cards with the Key to the Tarot of the Bohemians, designed by Pamela Coleman-Smith under the direction of A. E. Waite

SADHU, MOUNI, *Concentration*, London, 1959; *In Days of Great Peace*, London, 1957; *Samadhi*, London, 1962

ST MARTIN, LOUIS CLAUDE DE, *Tableau Naturel des Rapports qui existent entre Dieu, l'Homme et l'Univers*

THIERENS, A. E. *The General Book of the Tarot, Containing the Astrological Key to the Tarot System*, 1928

WAITE, A. E. *The Pictorial Key to the Tarot*

WIRTH, OSWALD, *Les XXII Clefs du Tarot Kabbalistique*, Paris, 1889; *Le Symbolisme Hermetique*

INDEX

Abdomen, 60, 113, 124, 312
Ability(ies), 21, 22, 25, 107, 151, 303, 308, 399
Abognazar, Rabbi, 236
Aboriginals, 67
Abraham, 347
Abraxas, 155
Absolute, 11, 16, 28, 74, 90, 188, 205, 213, 214, 277, 285, 298, 354, 392, 413, 445, 461
Absolution, 302
Abstention, 188
Abstract, 16
Abyss, 319, 341
Accomplishment, 134
Accumulation, 38
Ace, 217, 219
Aconitum, 138
Action(s), 16, 21, 25, 29, 36, 92, 137, 242, 263, 272, 279, 302, 311, 324, 334
Active, 16, 18, 21, 36, 56, 70, 75, 76, 104, 107, 123, 213, 283, 285, 333, 369
Active state(s), 358
Activity(ies), 18, 27, 28, 38, 40, 45, 56, 77, 117, 122, 135, 136, 137, 210, 219, 242, 280, 283, 291, 297, 320, 336, 415, 437, 446
Adam, 40, 136, 180, 242, 245, 246, 292, 317, 318, 340, 438, 466
Adaptation, 136, 156, 249, 335, 350
Adaptation, cube of, 341
Adept(s), 26, 59, 218, 249, 253, 264, 266, 267, 299, 300, 302, 303, 314, 316, 329, 345, 397, 465, 466
Advaita-Vedanta, 85, 300, 304, 351, 376, 413, 416
Aeroplanes, 254
Africa, 23, 396
Age, 252, 292
Aggression, 165, 425
Aggressiveness, 24, 116
Agnostic(s), 181, 182
Agony, 284, 292, 295, 323, 324
Agriculturalist(s), 254
Ahimsa, 187
Ailment(s), 24, 110, 138, 421, 422
Ain-Soph, 13, 90, 154, 195, 197, 205, 237, 413, 432
Air, 11, 19, 21, 65, 78, 91, 96, 223, 462
Akasha, 65
Alcaic World, 170
Alchemy, 13, 19, 78, 79, 219, 221, 264, 434, 435, 439
Alcohol, 116, 121, 122, 152

Alexander the Great, 148
Alexandrian School, 184
Algebra, 12, 14
Allen, George & Unwin Ltd., 104, 169
Allergy(ies), 125
Alliette, 21
Allopathy, 137, 138, 139
Almighty, 63, 72
Alpha, 61, 74, 84, 154
Alphabet, 11, 16, 30, 34, 55, 192, 201, 212, 221, 293, 299
Altruism, 219, 256, 265, 362
Ammon-Ra, 258
Analogous, 125
Analogy, 11, 59, 104, 134, 135, 293, 294, 299, 317, 329, 335, 349, 373, 388, 390, 412, 439
Analysis, 14, 15, 21, 34, 62, 91, 92, 170, 183, 193, 211, 214, 241, 279, 315, 316, 327, 328, 329, 334, 335, 343, 374
Anatomy, 361
Ancestors, 252, 326
Anchorite, 121, 184, 185
Andreas, 24, 26
Androgyne, 57, 133, 134, 137, 141, 195, 254, 340, 343
Androgynous, 56, 70, 75, 90, 133, 150, 161, 213, 216, 223, 243, 251, 257, 283, 317, 341, 379
Androgyny, 235
Androlatry, 257
Angel(s), 53, 145, 147, 151, 191, 192, 243, 244, 245, 247, 248, 304, 326, 330, 333, 378
Animal(s), 62, 79, 120, 121, 278, 297, 317, 322, 324
Animistic, 120, 122, 125
Animosity, 157
Anniversary, 393
Antagonism, 257
Antichrist, 266
Antigone, 84
Antipathy, 125
Aorta, 119
Apex, 392
Apocalypse, 55, 236
Apollo, 150, 402, 404, 441
Apollonius of Tyana, 184, 280
Apostle(s), 250, 260, 342
Apostolic Succession, 315
Apparition(s), 128, 294
Aquarius, 409
Arabia, 262, 396

A PERSONAL WORD FROM MELVIN POWERS
PUBLISHER, WILSHIRE BOOK COMPANY

Dear Friend:

My goal is to publish interesting, informative, and inspirational books. You can help me accomplish this by answering the following questions, either by phone or by mail. Or, if convenient for you, I would welcome the opportunity to visit with you in my office and hear your comments in person.

Did you enjoy reading this book? Why?

Would you enjoy reading another similar book?

What idea in the book impressed you the most?

If applicable to your situation, have you incorporated this idea in your daily life?

Is there a chapter that could serve as a theme for an entire book? Please explain.

If you have an idea for a book, I would welcome discussing it with you. If you already have one in progress, write or call me concerning possible publication. I can be reached at (213) 875-1711 or (818) 983-1105.

Sincerely yours,

MELVIN POWERS

12015 Sherman Road
North Hollywood, California 91605

MELVIN POWERS SELF-IMPROVEMENT LIBRARY

ASTROLOGY

_____ ASTROLOGY: HOW TO CHART YOUR HOROSCOPE *Max Heindel*	5.00
_____ ASTROLOGY AND SEXUAL ANALYSIS *Morris C. Goodman*	5.00
_____ ASTROLOGY MADE EASY *Astarte*	5.00
_____ ASTROLOGY, ROMANCE, YOU AND THE STARS *Anthony Norvell*	5.00
_____ MY WORLD OF ASTROLOGY *Sydney Omarr*	7.00
_____ THOUGHT DIAL *Sydney Omarr*	4.00
_____ WHAT THE STARS REVEAL ABOUT THE MEN IN YOUR LIFE *Thelma White*	3.00

BRIDGE

_____ BRIDGE BIDDING MADE EASY *Edwin B. Kantar*	10.00
_____ BRIDGE CONVENTIONS *Edwin B. Kantar*	7.00
_____ BRIDGE HUMOR *Edwin B. Kantar*	5.00
_____ COMPETITIVE BIDDING IN MODERN BRIDGE *Edgar Kaplan*	7.00
_____ DEFENSIVE BRIDGE PLAY COMPLETE *Edwin B. Kantar*	15.00
_____ GAMESMAN BRIDGE—Play Better with Kantar *Edwin B. Kantar*	5.00
_____ HOW TO IMPROVE YOUR BRIDGE *Alfred Sheinwold*	5.00
_____ IMPROVING YOUR BIDDING SKILLS *Edwin B. Kantar*	4.00
_____ INTRODUCTION TO DECLARER'S PLAY *Edwin B. Kantar*	5.00
_____ INTRODUCTION TO DEFENDER'S PLAY *Edwin B. Kantar*	5.00
_____ KANTAR FOR THE DEFENSE *Edwin B. Kantar*	7.00
_____ KANTAR FOR THE DEFENSE VOLUME 2 *Edwin B. Kantar*	7.00
_____ SHORT CUT TO WINNING BRIDGE *Alfred Sheinwold*	3.00
_____ TEST YOUR BRIDGE PLAY *Edwin B. Kantar*	5.00
_____ VOLUME 2—TEST YOUR BRIDGE PLAY *Edwin B. Kantar*	5.00
_____ WINNING DECLARER PLAY *Dorothy Hayden Truscott*	5.00

BUSINESS, STUDY & REFERENCE

_____ CONVERSATION MADE EASY *Elliot Russell*	4.00
_____ EXAM SECRET *Dennis B. Jackson*	3.00
_____ FIX-IT BOOK *Arthur Symons*	2.00
_____ HOW TO DEVELOP A BETTER SPEAKING VOICE *M. Hellier*	4.00
_____ HOW TO SELF-PUBLISH YOUR BOOK & MAKE IT A BEST SELLER *Melvin Powers*	10.00
_____ INCREASE YOUR LEARNING POWER *Geoffrey A. Dudley*	3.00
_____ PRACTICAL GUIDE TO BETTER CONCENTRATION *Melvin Powers*	3.00
_____ PRACTICAL GUIDE TO PUBLIC SPEAKING *Maurice Forley*	5.00
_____ 7 DAYS TO FASTER READING *William S. Schaill*	5.00
_____ SONGWRITERS' RHYMING DICTIONARY *Jane Shaw Whitfield*	7.00
_____ SPELLING MADE EASY *Lester D. Basch & Dr. Milton Finkelstein*	3.00
_____ STUDENT'S GUIDE TO BETTER GRADES *J. A. Rickard*	3.00
_____ TEST YOURSELF—Find Your Hidden Talent *Jack Shafer*	3.00
_____ YOUR WILL & WHAT TO DO ABOUT IT *Attorney Samuel G. Kling*	5.00

CALLIGRAPHY

_____ ADVANCED CALLIGRAPHY *Katherine Jeffares*	7.00
_____ CALLIGRAPHER'S REFERENCE BOOK *Anne Leptich & Jacque Evans*	7.00
_____ CALLIGRAPHY—The Art of Beautiful Writing *Katherine Jeffares*	7.00
_____ CALLIGRAPHY FOR FUN & PROFIT *Anne Leptich & Jacque Evans*	7.00
_____ CALLIGRAPHY MADE EASY *Tina Serafini*	7.00

CHESS & CHECKERS

_____ BEGINNER'S GUIDE TO WINNING CHESS *Fred Reinfeld*	5.00
_____ CHESS IN TEN EASY LESSONS *Larry Evans*	5.00
_____ CHESS MADE EASY *Milton L. Hanauer*	3.00
_____ CHESS PROBLEMS FOR BEGINNERS *edited by Fred Reinfeld*	5.00
_____ CHESS SECRETS REVEALED *Fred Reinfeld*	2.00
_____ CHESS TACTICS FOR BEGINNERS *edited by Fred Reinfeld*	5.00
_____ CHESS THEORY & PRACTICE *Morry & Mitchell*	2.00
_____ HOW TO WIN AT CHECKERS *Fred Reinfeld*	3.00
_____ 1001 BRILLIANT WAYS TO CHECKMATE *Fred Reinfeld*	5.00
_____ 1001 WINNING CHESS SACRIFICES & COMBINATIONS *Fred Reinfeld*	5.00

_____ SOVIET CHESS *Edited by R. G. Wade*   3.00

COOKERY & HERBS

_____ CULPEPER'S HERBAL REMEDIES *Dr. Nicholas Culpeper*   3.00
_____ FAST GOURMET COOKBOOK *Poppy Cannon*   2.50
_____ GINSENG The Myth & The Truth *Joseph P. Hou*   3.00
_____ HEALING POWER OF HERBS *May Bethel*   4.00
_____ HEALING POWER OF NATURAL FOODS *May Bethel*   5.00
_____ HERB HANDBOOK *Dawn MacLeod*   3.00
_____ HERBS FOR HEALTH—How to Grow & Use Them *Louise Evans Doole*   4.00
_____ HOME GARDEN COOKBOOK—Delicious Natural Food Recipes *Ken Kraft*   3.00
_____ MEDICAL HERBALIST *edited by Dr. J. R. Yemm*   3.00
_____ VEGETABLE GARDENING FOR BEGINNERS *Hugh Wiberg*   2.00
_____ VEGETABLES FOR TODAY'S GARDENS *R. Milton Carleton*   2.00
_____ VEGETARIAN COOKERY *Janet Walker*   4.00
_____ VEGETARIAN COOKING MADE EASY & DELECTABLE *Veronica Vezza*   3.00
_____ VEGETARIAN DELIGHTS—A Happy Cookbook for Health *K. R. Mehta*   2.00
_____ VEGETARIAN GOURMET COOKBOOK *Joyce McKinnel*   3.00

GAMBLING & POKER

_____ ADVANCED POKER STRATEGY & WINNING PLAY *A. D. Livingston*   5.00
_____ HOW TO WIN AT DICE GAMES *Skip Frey*   3.00
_____ HOW TO WIN AT POKER *Terence Reese & Anthony T. Watkins*   5.00
_____ WINNING AT CRAPS *Dr. Lloyd T. Commins*   4.00
_____ WINNING AT GIN *Chester Wander & Cy Rice*   3.00
_____ WINNING AT POKER—An Expert's Guide *John Archer*   5.00
_____ WINNING AT 21—An Expert's Guide *John Archer*   5.00
_____ WINNING POKER SYSTEMS *Norman Zadeh*   3.00

HEALTH

_____ BEE POLLEN *Lynda Lyngheim & Jack Scagnetti*   3.00
_____ DR. LINDNER'S SPECIAL WEIGHT CONTROL METHOD *P. G. Lindner, M.D.*   2.00
_____ HELP YOURSELF TO BETTER SIGHT *Margaret Darst Corbett*   3.00
_____ HOW YOU CAN STOP SMOKING PERMANENTLY *Ernest Caldwell*   3.00
_____ MIND OVER PLATTER *Peter G. Lindner, M.D.*   3.00
_____ NATURE'S WAY TO NUTRITION & VIBRANT HEALTH *Robert J. Scrutton*   3.00
_____ NEW CARBOHYDRATE DIET COUNTER *Patti Lopez-Pereira*   2.00
_____ REFLEXOLOGY *Dr. Maybelle Segal*   4.00
_____ REFLEXOLOGY FOR GOOD HEALTH *Anna Kaye & Don C. Matchan*   5.00
_____ 30 DAYS TO BEAUTIFUL LEGS *Dr. Marc Selner*   3.00
_____ YOU CAN LEARN TO RELAX *Dr. Samuel Gutwirth*   3.00
_____ YOUR ALLERGY—What To Do About It *Allan Knight, M.D.*   3.00

HOBBIES

_____ BEACHCOMBING FOR BEGINNERS *Norman Hickin*   2.00
_____ BLACKSTONE'S MODERN CARD TRICKS *Harry Blackstone*   3.00
_____ BLACKSTONE'S SECRETS OF MAGIC *Harry Blackstone*   3.00
_____ COIN COLLECTING FOR BEGINNERS *Burton Hobson & Fred Reinfeld*   5.00
_____ ENTERTAINING WITH ESP *Tony 'Doc' Shiels*   2.00
_____ 400 FASCINATING MAGIC TRICKS YOU CAN DO *Howard Thurston*   4.00
_____ HOW I TURN JUNK INTO FUN AND PROFIT *Sari*   3.00
_____ HOW TO WRITE A HIT SONG & SELL IT *Tommy Boyce*   7.00
_____ JUGGLING MADE EASY *Rudolf Dittrich*   3.00
_____ MAGIC FOR ALL AGES *Walter Gibson*   4.00
_____ MAGIC MADE EASY *Byron Wels*   2.00
_____ STAMP COLLECTING FOR BEGINNERS *Burton Hobson*   3.00

HORSE PLAYERS' WINNING GUIDES

_____ BETTING HORSES TO WIN *Les Conklin*   5.00
_____ ELIMINATE THE LOSERS *Bob McKnight*   3.00
_____ HOW TO PICK WINNING HORSES *Bob McKnight*   5.00
_____ HOW TO WIN AT THE RACES *Sam (The Genius) Lewin*   5.00
_____ HOW YOU CAN BEAT THE RACES *Jack Kavanagh*   5.00

____ MAKING MONEY AT THE RACES *David Barr*	5.00
____ PAYDAY AT THE RACES *Les Conklin*	5.00
____ SMART HANDICAPPING MADE EASY *William Bauman*	5.00
____ SUCCESS AT THE HARNESS RACES *Barry Meadow*	5.00
____ WINNING AT THE HARNESS RACES—An Expert's Guide *Nick Cammarano*	5.00

HUMOR

____ HOW TO FLATTEN YOUR TUSH *Coach Marge Reardon*	2.00
____ HOW TO MAKE LOVE TO YOURSELF *Ron Stevens & Joy Grdnic*	3.00
____ JOKE TELLER'S HANDBOOK *Bob Orben*	5.00
____ JOKES FOR ALL OCCASIONS *Al Schock*	5.00
____ 2000 NEW LAUGHS FOR SPEAKERS *Bob Orben*	5.00
____ 2,500 JOKES TO START 'EM LAUGHING *Bob Orben*	5.00

HYPNOTISM

____ ADVANCED TECHNIQUES OF HYPNOSIS *Melvin Powers*	3.00
____ BRAINWASHING AND THE CULTS *Paul A. Verdier, Ph.D.*	3.00
____ CHILDBIRTH WITH HYPNOSIS *William S. Kroger, M.D.*	5.00
____ HOW TO SOLVE Your Sex Problems with Self-Hypnosis *Frank S. Caprio, M.D.*	5.00
____ HOW TO STOP SMOKING THRU SELF-HYPNOSIS *Leslie M. LeCron*	3.00
____ HOW TO USE AUTO-SUGGESTION EFFECTIVELY *John Duckworth*	3.00
____ HOW YOU CAN BOWL BETTER USING SELF-HYPNOSIS *Jack Heise*	4.00
____ HOW YOU CAN PLAY BETTER GOLF USING SELF-HYPNOSIS *Jack Heise*	3.00
____ HYPNOSIS AND SELF-HYPNOSIS *Bernard Hollander, M.D.*	5.00
____ HYPNOTISM *(Originally published in 1893) Carl Sextus*	5.00
____ HYPNOTISM & PSYCHIC PHENOMENA *Simeon Edmunds*	4.00
____ HYPNOTISM MADE EASY *Dr. Ralph Winn*	3.00
____ HYPNOTISM MADE PRACTICAL *Louis Orton*	5.00
____ HYPNOTISM REVEALED *Melvin Powers*	3.00
____ HYPNOTISM TODAY *Leslie LeCron and Jean Bordeaux, Ph.D.*	5.00
____ MODERN HYPNOSIS *Lesley Kuhn & Salvatore Russo, Ph.D.*	5.00
____ NEW CONCEPTS OF HYPNOSIS *Bernard C. Gindes, M.D.*	7.00
____ NEW SELF-HYPNOSIS *Paul Adams*	7.00
____ POST-HYPNOTIC INSTRUCTIONS—Suggestions for Therapy *Arnold Furst*	5.00
____ PRACTICAL GUIDE TO SELF-HYPNOSIS *Melvin Powers*	3.00
____ PRACTICAL HYPNOTISM *Philip Magonet, M.D.*	3.00
____ SECRETS OF HYPNOTISM *S. J. Van Pelt, M.D.*	5.00
____ SELF-HYPNOSIS A Conditioned-Response Technique *Laurence Sparks*	7.00
____ SELF-HYPNOSIS Its Theory, Technique & Application *Melvin Powers*	3.00
____ THERAPY THROUGH HYPNOSIS *edited by Raphael H. Rhodes*	5.00

JUDAICA

____ SERVICE OF THE HEART *Evelyn Garfiel, Ph.D.*	7.00
____ STORY OF ISRAEL IN COINS *Jean & Maurice Gould*	2.00
____ STORY OF ISRAEL IN STAMPS *Maxim & Gabriel Shamir*	1.00
____ TONGUE OF THE PROPHETS *Robert St. John*	7.00

JUST FOR WOMEN

____ COSMOPOLITAN'S GUIDE TO MARVELOUS MEN Fwd. by *Helen Gurley Brown*	3.00
____ COSMOPOLITAN'S HANG-UP HANDBOOK Foreword by *Helen Gurley Brown*	4.00
____ COSMOPOLITAN'S LOVE BOOK—A Guide to Ecstasy in Bed	7.00
____ COSMOPOLITAN'S NEW ETIQUETTE GUIDE Fwd. by *Helen Gurley Brown*	4.00
____ I AM A COMPLEAT WOMAN *Doris Hagopian & Karen O'Connor Sweeney*	3.00
____ JUST FOR WOMEN—A Guide to the Female Body *Richard E. Sand, M.D.*	5.00
____ NEW APPROACHES TO SEX IN MARRIAGE *John E. Eichenlaub, M.D.*	3.00
____ SEXUALLY ADEQUATE FEMALE *Frank S. Caprio, M.D.*	3.00
____ SEXUALLY FULFILLED WOMAN *Dr. Rachel Copelan*	5.00
____ YOUR FIRST YEAR OF MARRIAGE *Dr. Tom McGinnis*	3.00

MARRIAGE, SEX & PARENTHOOD

____ ABILITY TO LOVE *Dr. Allan Fromme*	7.00
____ GUIDE TO SUCCESSFUL MARRIAGE *Drs. Albert Ellis & Robert Harper*	7.00
____ HOW TO RAISE AN EMOTIONALLY HEALTHY, HAPPY CHILD *A. Ellis*	5.00

____ SEX WITHOUT GUILT *Albert Ellis, Ph.D.*	5.00
____ SEXUALLY ADEQUATE MALE *Frank S. Caprio, M.D.*	3.00
____ SEXUALLY FULFILLED MAN *Dr. Rachel Copelan*	5.00
____ STAYING IN LOVE *Dr. Norton F. Kristy*	7.00

MELVIN POWERS' MAIL ORDER LIBRARY

____ HOW TO GET RICH IN MAIL ORDER *Melvin Powers*	20.00
____ HOW TO WRITE A GOOD ADVERTISEMENT *Victor O. Schwab*	20.00
____ MAIL ORDER MADE EASY *J. Frank Brumbaugh*	20.00

METAPHYSICS & OCCULT

____ BOOK OF TALISMANS, AMULETS & ZODIACAL GEMS *William Pavitt*	7.00
____ CONCENTRATION—A Guide to Mental Mastery *Mouni Sadhu*	5.00
____ EXTRA-TERRESTRIAL INTELLIGENCE—The First Encounter	6.00
____ FORTUNE TELLING WITH CARDS *P. Foli*	5.00
____ HOW TO INTERPRET DREAMS, OMENS & FORTUNE TELLING SIGNS *Gettings*	5.00
____ HOW TO UNDERSTAND YOUR DREAMS *Geoffrey A. Dudley*	3.00
____ ILLUSTRATED YOGA *William Zorn*	3.00
____ IN DAYS OF GREAT PEACE *Mouni Sadhu*	3.00
____ LSD—THE AGE OF MIND *Bernard Roseman*	2.00
____ MAGICIAN—His Training and Work *W. E. Butler*	3.00
____ MEDITATION *Mouni Sadhu*	7.00
____ MODERN NUMEROLOGY *Morris C. Goodman*	5.00
____ NUMEROLOGY—ITS FACTS AND SECRETS *Ariel Yvon Taylor*	3.00
____ NUMEROLOGY MADE EASY *W. Mykian*	5.00
____ PALMISTRY MADE EASY *Fred Gettings*	5.00
____ PALMISTRY MADE PRACTICAL *Elizabeth Daniels Squire*	5.00
____ PALMISTRY SECRETS REVEALED *Henry Frith*	4.00
____ PROPHECY IN OUR TIME *Martin Ebon*	2.50
____ SUPERSTITION—Are You Superstitious? *Eric Maple*	2.00
____ TAROT *Mouni Sadhu*	10.00
____ TAROT OF THE BOHEMIANS *Papus*	7.00
____ WAYS TO SELF-REALIZATION *Mouni Sadhu*	3.00
____ WITCHCRAFT, MAGIC & OCCULTISM—A Fascinating History *W. B. Crow*	7.00
____ WITCHCRAFT—THE SIXTH SENSE *Justine Glass*	7.00
____ WORLD OF PSYCHIC RESEARCH *Hereward Carrington*	2.00

SELF-HELP & INSPIRATIONAL

____ CHARISMA How To Get "That Special Magic" *Marcia Grad*	7.00
____ DAILY POWER FOR JOYFUL LIVING *Dr. Donald Curtis*	5.00
____ DYNAMIC THINKING *Melvin Powers*	5.00
____ GREATEST POWER IN THE UNIVERSE *U. S. Andersen*	7.00
____ GROW RICH WHILE YOU SLEEP *Ben Sweetland*	7.00
____ GROWTH THROUGH REASON *Albert Ellis, Ph.D.*	7.00
____ GUIDE TO PERSONAL HAPPINESS *Albert Ellis, Ph.D. & Irving Becker, Ed. D.*	7.00
____ HANDWRITING ANALYSIS MADE EASY *John Marley*	5.00
____ HANDWRITING TELLS *Nadya Olyanova*	7.00
____ HELPING YOURSELF WITH APPLIED PSYCHOLOGY *R. Henderson*	2.00
____ HOW TO ATTRACT GOOD LUCK *A. H. Z. Carr*	5.00
____ HOW TO BE GREAT *Dr. Donald Curtis*	5.00
____ HOW TO DEVELOP A WINNING PERSONALITY *Martin Panzer*	5.00
____ HOW TO DEVELOP AN EXCEPTIONAL MEMORY *Young & Gibson*	5.00
____ HOW TO LIVE WITH A NEUROTIC *Albert Ellis, Ph. D.*	5.00
____ HOW TO OVERCOME YOUR FEARS *M. P. Leahy, M.D.*	3.00
____ HOW TO SUCCEED *Brian Adams*	7.00
____ HUMAN PROBLEMS & HOW TO SOLVE THEM *Dr. Donald Curtis*	5.00
____ I CAN *Ben Sweetland*	7.00
____ I WILL *Ben Sweetland*	3.00
____ KNIGHT IN THE RUSTY ARMOR *Robert Fisher*	10.00
____ LEFT-HANDED PEOPLE *Michael Barsley*	5.00
____ MAGIC IN YOUR MIND *U. S. Andersen*	7.00

_____ MAGIC OF THINKING BIG *Dr. David J. Schwartz*	3.00
_____ MAGIC OF THINKING SUCCESS *Dr. David J. Schwartz*	7.00
_____ MAGIC POWER OF YOUR MIND *Walter M. Germain*	7.00
_____ MENTAL POWER THROUGH SLEEP SUGGESTION *Melvin Powers*	3.00
_____ NEVER UNDERESTIMATE THE SELLING POWER OF A WOMAN *Dottie Walters*	7.00
_____ NEW GUIDE TO RATIONAL LIVING *Albert Ellis, Ph.D. & R. Harper, Ph.D.*	7.00
_____ PROJECT YOU *A Manual of Rational Assertiveness Training Paris & Casey*	6.00
_____ PSYCHO-CYBERNETICS *Maxwell Maltz, M.D.*	5.00
_____ PSYCHOLOGY OF HANDWRITING *Nadya Olyanova*	7.00
_____ SALES CYBERNETICS *Brian Adams*	7.00
_____ SCIENCE OF MIND IN DAILY LIVING *Dr. Donald Curtis*	5.00
_____ SECRET OF SECRETS *U. S. Andersen*	7.00
_____ SECRET POWER OF THE PYRAMIDS *U. S. Andersen*	7.00
_____ SELF-THERAPY FOR THE STUTTERER *Malcolm Frazer*	3.00
_____ SUCCESS-CYBERNETICS *U. S. Andersen*	6.00
_____ 10 DAYS TO A GREAT NEW LIFE *William E. Edwards*	3.00
_____ THINK AND GROW RICH *Napoleon Hill*	5.00
_____ THINK YOUR WAY TO SUCCESS *Dr. Lew Losoncy*	5.00
_____ THREE MAGIC WORDS *U. S. Andersen*	7.00
_____ TREASURY OF COMFORT *edited by Rabbi Sidney Greenberg*	5.00
_____ TREASURY OF THE ART OF LIVING *Sidney S. Greenberg*	5.00
_____ WHAT YOUR HANDWRITING REVEALS *Albert E. Hughes*	3.00
_____ YOUR SUBCONSCIOUS POWER *Charles M. Simmons*	7.00
_____ YOUR THOUGHTS CAN CHANGE YOUR LIFE *Dr. Donald Curtis*	7.00

SPORTS

_____ BICYCLING FOR FUN AND GOOD HEALTH *Kenneth E. Luther*	2.00
_____ BILLIARDS—Pocket • Carom • Three Cushion *Clive Cottingham, Jr.*	5.00
_____ CAMPING-OUT 101 Ideas & Activities *Bruno Knobel*	2.00
_____ COMPLETE GUIDE TO FISHING *Vlad Evanoff*	2.00
_____ HOW TO IMPROVE YOUR RACQUETBALL *Lubarsky Kaufman & Scagnetti*	5.00
_____ HOW TO WIN AT POCKET BILLIARDS *Edward D. Knuchell*	5.00
_____ JOY OF WALKING *Jack Scagnetti*	3.00
_____ LEARNING & TEACHING SOCCER SKILLS *Eric Worthington*	3.00
_____ MOTORCYCLING FOR BEGINNERS *I. G. Edmonds*	3.00
_____ RACQUETBALL FOR WOMEN *Toni Hudson, Jack Scagnetti & Vince Rondone*	3.00
_____ RACQUETBALL MADE EASY *Steve Lubarsky, Rod Delson & Jack Scagnetti*	5.00
_____ SECRET OF BOWLING STRIKES *Dawson Taylor*	5.00
_____ SECRET OF PERFECT PUTTING *Horton Smith & Dawson Taylor*	5.00
_____ SOCCER—The Game & How to Play It *Gary Rosenthal*	5.00
_____ STARTING SOCCER *Edward F. Dolan, Jr.*	3.00

TENNIS LOVERS' LIBRARY

_____ BEGINNER'S GUIDE TO WINNING TENNIS *Helen Hull Jacobs*	2.00
_____ HOW TO IMPROVE YOUR TENNIS—Style, Strategy & Analysis *C. Wilson*	2.00
_____ PSYCH YOURSELF TO BETTER TENNIS *Dr. Walter A. Luszki*	2.00
_____ TENNIS FOR BEGINNERS, *Dr. H. A. Murray*	2.00
_____ TENNIS MADE EASY *Joel Brecheen*	4.00
_____ WEEKEND TENNIS—How to Have Fun & Win at the Same Time *Bill Talbert*	3.00
_____ WINNING WITH PERCENTAGE TENNIS—Smart Strategy *Jack Lowe*	2.00

WILSHIRE PET LIBRARY

_____ DOG OBEDIENCE TRAINING *Gust Kessopulos*	5.00
_____ DOG TRAINING MADE EASY & FUN *John W. Kellogg*	3.00
_____ HOW TO BRING UP YOUR PET DOG *Kurt Unkelbach*	2.00
_____ HOW TO RAISE & TRAIN YOUR PUPPY *Jeff Griffen*	5.00

*The books listed above can be obtained from your book dealer or directly from
Melvin Powers. When ordering, please remit $1.00 postage for the first book
and 50¢ for each additional book.*

Melvin Powers
12015 Sherman Road, No. Hollywood, California 91605